Patent Law

Cases, Problems, and Materials

2nd Edition 2022

Jonathan S. Masur

John P. Wilson Professor of Law, David and Celia Hilliard Research Scholar,
Director of the Wachtell, Lipton, Rosen & Katz Program in Behavioral Law,
Finance and Economics

University of Chicago Law School

Lisa Larrimore Ouellette

Professor of Law and Justin M. Roach, Jr. Faculty Scholar

Stanford Law School

For generous comments on earlier versions of this casebook, we are grateful to Michael Abramowicz, Bernard Chao, Thomas Cotter, Tabrez Ebrahim, Janet Freilich, Dmitry Karshtedt, Amy Landers, Mark Lemley, Doug Melamed, Amy Motomura, Jason Rantanen, Jason Reinecke, Jacob Sherkow, Marketa Trimble, Heidi Williams, Stephen Yelderman, Samantha Zyontz, and participants at the Notre Dame Patent Colloquium. Special thanks to the Honorable Timothy B. Dyk for his time and thoughtful suggestions. Thanks also to Gabrielle Dohmen, Hayk Esaghoulyan, Mila Gauvin, Trip Henningson, Yiwei Jiang, Casey Lincoln, Yiming Sun, and Elizabeth Trujillo for extraordinary research assistance.

We would like to thank Kavita, Kiran, and Alice for their inspiring and unending curiosity. We hope that your love of science never fades and your love of law never grows.

When editing cases and the MPEP, our goal has been pedagogical clarity, not *Bluebook*-compliant accuracy. We have frequently dropped citations and portions of text without the usual ellipses and brackets where they seemed more cumbersome than helpful. As James Grimmelmann explained in his own free IP casebook, "These are pedagogical materials, not a legal brief. If it matters to you what the original said, consult the original."

Contents

I. Overview

1. The Patent System and Patent Claims

A *patent* is a government-granted intellectual property right over a new invention, which can range from a new pharmaceutical to a software algorithm. Patents don't cover new works of art, music, or literature, such as the new Taylor Swift album (which is all three)—those are the subject of copyright. They don't cover brand names or symbols, like the Nike swoosh—those are the subject of trademark. Instead, patent law covers only inventions: tangible objects that have practical purposes, or methods of accomplishing some sort of useful purpose.[1]

As you may recall from 1L Property, "property" can be understood as a bundle of different rights, often referred to with the "bundle of sticks" metaphor. Intellectual property is no different. The most important right in the patent owner's bundle is the right to exclude others. A patent does not provide an affirmative right to make or use the invention it describes, and many patent owners do not in fact produce their inventions. Rather, the owner of a patent can *prevent others* from making, using, or selling the invention during the life of the patent, which typically lasts twenty years from when the patent application is filed.

This right applies not only to whatever the inventor actually made—it also covers all other uses of the invention, including future uses not contemplated by the inventor. For instance, suppose Xavier invents a new type of lawnmower that is excellent at cutting grass and obtains a patent on it. Xavier's patent only discusses the use of this lawnmower for mowing lawns and its virtues as a grass-cutting device. Ten years later, however, Jamilla figures out that Xavier's lawnmower can be used to transport humans to Mars. (Don't ask.) Xavier's patent covers the use of the lawnmower in this fashion. If Jamilla starts a company that uses the lawnmower for Mars transport, she must obtain a license from Xavier or face a lawsuit for infringement.

The basic rationale for granting inventors these exclusionary rights is to provide incentives to create new inventions in the first place. The problem for innovators is that it is frequently much more expensive to create a new invention in the first place than it is to copy one. Imagine a firm that spends a substantial amount

---

[1] In addition to patents on inventions, sometimes called *utility patents*, there are also *design patents* on new ornamental designs and *plant patents* on new plant varieties. In 2020, the U.S. Patent and Trademark Office granted 352,049 utility patents, 34,877 design patents, and 1,398 plant patents. This casebook focuses on utility patent law.

of money researching and developing a new invention, such as a prescription drug, and then begins selling it. Competitors could swoop in, copy the drug, and then sell it at a lower price. These competitors would bear only the cost of producing the drug itself. They would not have to recoup any initial expenditures in R&D. (Think about how much cheaper it usually is to buy the generic version of a drug than the brand-name version.) Accordingly, the competitors could undercut the firm that invented the drug and force it out of business (or cause it to lose money). With the looming threat of being undersold like this, what firm would want to invest in R&D in the first place, knowing that it might never recoup its investment? The result could be a reduction in innovation, to all of our detriment.

Patent law solves this problem by giving the inventor a right to exclude competitors for a limited period. This prevents it from being undersold, allows it to charge higher prices, and thereby enables it to recoup its R&D investments. Patents thus make it more profitable for a firm to invest in innovation. This economic rationale is explored in more detail later in this chapter.

Because patent law constantly must adapt to new technologies, it is one of the most dynamic areas of legal practice, and it has grown in importance as the global economy becomes increasingly reliant on technology-based industries. Patent law can be used to both enforce and subvert structural inequalities, and it is hard to understand the modern economy—including venture capital, corporate deals, and international trade—without understanding patent law and its reach. It is also a field in which any law student can excel: a technical background is *not* required for patent litigation or transactional work.

We begin this casebook with an overview of the legal institutions that compose the patent system, its underlying economic justifications, and its effects on global inequality. This overview includes examples of the basic architecture of a patent and an introduction to drafting patent *claims*, which define the boundaries of the legal rights protected by a patent. For example, a simple patent claim for a pencil might read as follows:

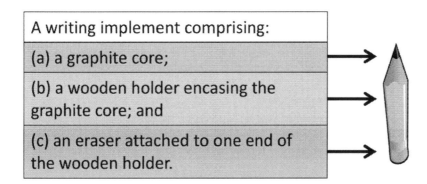

Chapters 2–7 then focus on the legal requirements for obtaining a patent. Most importantly, a claimed invention must be *novel* and *nonobvious* when compared with

everything available to the public that preceded it, including earlier publications, patents, and other inventions that have been sold or used. The collection of information available to the public before a patent application is filed is known as the *prior art*. For example, our pencil claim might be rejected as an obvious combination of prior art erasers and wooden cylinders with graphite cores. The patent document also must disclose technical details about how to make and use the claimed invention to prevent inventors from receiving legal rights broader than what they actually contributed. The inventor of a wooden pencil thus cannot receive a patent claim covering the future development of pens.

Chapters 8–12 cover patent infringement and defenses. We begin with a module on claim construction, the critical process of determining what the technical language of a patent claim actually covers. For example, does a pencil made from a wood-plastic composite infringe a claim covering pencils with a "wooden holder"? Again, the owner of a valid patent claim can prevent others from directly exploiting the invention—including by making, using, or selling it—or from indirectly inducing or contributing to infringement by others. And there are limited defenses to patent infringement; it typically doesn't matter if the infringer was unaware of the patent or was using the invention for research, and there is no patent equivalent to copyright fair use.

Chapters 13–16 examine the remedies patent owners can receive if their patents are valid and infringed. In some cases, the patent owner can obtain an injunction to block infringers from making, using, or selling the patented invention. But injunctions to stop the infringing conduct are not guaranteed, especially if the patent is on a small component of a complex product, so courts are often tasked with calculating money damages for both past and future infringement. Damages are intended to return patent holders to the position they would have been in but for the infringement, which can include lost profits that a patentee would have made or a reasonable royalty that a patentee and infringer would have agreed to. Patent owners can also receive attorneys' fees and enhanced damages in exceptional cases.

In Chapter 17, we explain additional details of U.S. patent litigation procedure. Patent practitioners should be familiar with the patent procedural rules many federal district courts have adopted, the options for challenging the validity of granted patents at the U.S. Patent and Trademark Office (USPTO), the procedures for litigating patents covering imported goods at the International Trade Commission, and alternative dispute resolution.

Chapter 18 briefly reviews the law surrounding patent licensing and transactions. Although this casebook focuses on patent litigation, most uses of patented technology involve voluntary licenses rather than formal judicial proceedings. For the most part, licenses are evaluated under standard contract principles, but there are some specialized concerns that stem from patent transactions, including in the context of standards-essential patents (SEPs) and agreements to license under fair, reasonable, and non-discriminatory (FRAND) terms.

Patents on useful inventions, the focus of this casebook, are sometimes called *utility patents*. Chapter 19 provides a brief overview of the most prominent forms of non-patent IP (trade secrets, copyright, trademark, and regulatory exclusivity), as well as the two other kinds of U.S. patents: *design patents* on new ornamental designs and *plant patents* on new plant varieties. Many of the rules of patent validity and infringement are the same for all three types of patents, but we highlight some important differences.

This casebook focuses on U.S. patent law, but in Chapter 20 we turn to the increasingly global nature of the patent system. Under international treaties—particularly the Agreement on Trade-Related Aspects of Intellectual Property Rights (TRIPS) administered by the World Trade Organization—almost every country must grant patents for new, nonobvious, and useful inventions in all fields of technology, including to foreign inventors. Since 2008, foreign inventors have filed for *more* U.S. patents each year than American inventors have. In turn, U.S. inventors file nearly as many patents in other countries as they do in the United States. The five largest patent offices—in China, the United States, Japan, Korea, and Europe—collectively employ more than 27,000 patent examiners who are tasked with evaluating over 2.7 million patent applications filed each year. U.S. patent lawyers regularly need to advise clients on acquiring, licensing, and litigating patents across the globe.

A. U.S. Patent Institutions

U.S. patent law is centered around two institutions: the U.S. Patent and Trademark Office (USPTO), an agency within the Department of Commerce, and the Court of Appeals for the Federal Circuit, which is unique among the thirteen federal circuit courts in having a jurisdiction based entirely on subject matter—including patent law—rather than geography.

The Life of a Patent

As illustrated below, the life of a patent begins when a patent application is filed by an inventor with the USPTO. Inventors often file patent applications for multiple aspects of a potential new product, with the number of patents per product scaling with complexity. A simple chemical used as a pharmaceutical might be covered by a handful of patents, while a smartphone may be covered by tens or hundreds of thousands.

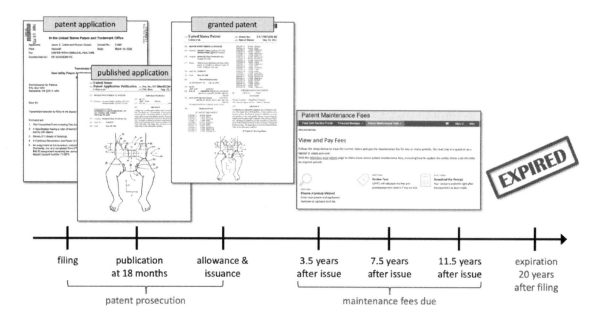

Filing a patent involves a fee, typically a few thousand dollars, depending upon the size of the party filing for the patent and the complexity of the application. The inventor is often represented by a professional known as a "patent prosecutor," who can be an attorney (also referred to as a "patent attorney") or a non-lawyer who has been licensed to practice before the USPTO (also known as a "patent agent").[2] The patent application is initially assigned to an examiner within the agency, who possesses technical expertise in the appropriate field of technology and is tasked with determining whether the application meets the necessary criteria for patentability. The period when an application is pending at the USPTO is known as "patent prosecution."

The USPTO received 597,175 utility patent applications in 2020, and examiners are often pressed for time when reviewing each one. The typical examiner spends an average of 19 hours reviewing each patent application, including the time to search for prior art and write rejections and responses to the applicant's arguments. Empirical evidence suggests that these time constraints cause examiners to erroneously grant too many invalid patents. *See* Michael D. Frakes & Melissa F. Wasserman, *Is the Time Allocated to Review Patent Applications Inducing Examiners to Grant Invalid Patents?: Evidence from Micro-Level Application Data*, 99 Rev. Econ. & Stat. 550 (2017).

---

[2] To become a patent prosecutor, one must pass the registration examination, colloquially known as the patent bar, a test administered by the USPTO that is analogous to the bar exams administered by the states. An applicant must have scientific or technical training to sit for the patent bar. But fear not, philosophy majors: this is the only job in patent law that requires a technical degree. Many of the greatest patent litigators in the country—the people who argue patent cases in federal court—have no technical background.

Errors in patent grants also stem from examiners' limited experience in the technical fields they examine and difficulty searching for non-patent prior art. Patents are not "peer reviewed," the way that scientific publications are, and there have been many suggestions for adding a peer review component to the patent system. A recent study has shown, however, that doing so would create considerable expense and yield relatively modest benefits. *See* Daniel E. Ho & Lisa Larrimore Ouellette, *Improving Scientific Experiments in Law and Government: A Field Study of Patent Peer Review*, 17 J. Emp. Leg. Stud. 190 (2020).

Perhaps even more importantly, patent prosecution is ex parte: at this stage, there is no party opposing the patent application and offering evidence and arguments as to why the patent should not be granted. The only parties involved in examination are the USPTO and the applicant.[3] That means that it is very common for patent examiners to miss key pieces of evidence when a patent is being examined, only for those pieces of evidence to come to light years later when a motivated (and well-funded) counter-party challenges a patent's validity.

Patent applications usually remain secret for 18 months after they are filed, at which point they typically are published and become part of the public record.[4] In many cases, a patent examiner does not even begin to look at the patent until the 18-month mark has passed. However, patent applicants can pay an additional fee for expedited examination,[5] which moves them to the front of the line and spurs action more quickly.

If the examiner determines that the application is legally flawed in some manner, the application is sent back to the applicant with a description of the problem (in what is known as an "office action"). The applicant can then respond to the objection, such as by amending the claims or arguing that the examiner is mistaken. The back and forth of patent examination generates a written record, which remains associated with the patent in perpetuity.[6] The written examination record is typically referred to as the patent's "prosecution history," or sometimes the "file wrapper." (The latter name comes from the fact that the documents were attached to the outside of the file that contained the patent document.) Prosecution history will be relevant to several patent infringement doctrines.

---

[3] Under a limited and little-used exception, within six months of an application's publication, a third party may submit relevant prior art along with a concise description of its relevance for consideration by the patent examiner. *See* 35 U.S.C. § 122(e).

[4] For the roughly 50% of applications without foreign counterparts, applicants can opt out of publication at 18 months, but only about 10% of applicants do so. *See* 35 U.S.C. § 122(b).

[5] Options for expediting examination include the "Accelerated Examination" introduced in 2006, which has low fees but requires high effort, and the "Track One Prioritized Examination" system introduced in 2011, which requires less effort but has high fees and an annual cap.

[6] These written records can be found here: https://portal.uspto.gov/pair/PublicPair.

Notably, even after multiple salvos back and forth with a patent applicant, U.S. patent examiners—unlike most foreign counterparts—do not have the authority to reject a patent application with finality. An examiner can issue a "final rejection," but applicants have numerous options to continue the examination process, often by paying an additional fee. In theory, an applicant could continue amending an application and re-filing it in perpetuity. The downside of this approach for applicants is that it would involve substantial costs (in filing fees and attorney payments) and delay, and the patent applicant might be forced to amend the patent in a manner she does not wish. Accordingly, a patent applicant can appeal a patent examiner's denial to a tribunal within the USPTO: the Patent Trial and Appeal Board (PTAB). (This tribunal was previously known as the Board of Patent Appeals and Interferences (BPAI), and you will see that name crop up occasionally in older cases.) The PTAB is staffed by administrative "patent judges," and they have the power to reverse an examiner's decision and send the application back to the examiner for allowance.

If the PTAB affirms the examiner's rejection, the applicant may appeal further to the Court of Appeals for the Federal Circuit, the second institution around which patent law orbits. The Federal Circuit is an Article III court of appeals that sits in Washington, D.C. (not to be confused with the D.C. Circuit) and has exclusive jurisdiction over all appeals in cases arising under the Patent Act (as well as over an assortment of other cases). Every appeal from every patent case around the country goes to the Federal Circuit, not to the regional courts of appeal (the 7th Circuit, 9th Circuit, etc.). In addition, appeals from denials by the PTAB go directly to the Federal Circuit, without passing through the lower federal courts.[7] The Federal Circuit was created in 1982; before then, appeals from the BPAI (the predecessor to the PTAB) went to the Court of Customs and Patent Appeals, and appeals from other patent cases were sent to the regional circuits. If the patent applicant loses before the Federal Circuit, she may seek certiorari from the United States Supreme Court. The Supreme Court has shown considerable interest in patent law in recent years, with an average of over three patent cases per year since 2010.[8]

The animating principle behind the creation of the Federal Circuit was the idea that patent law should be uniform throughout the country. Congress believed that it would cause too many problems for inventors and innovative firms if patent law in California differed from patent law in Illinois. As you proceed through this course, you should consider three questions: (1) Was Congress right to view patent law as more in need of national uniformity than other areas of federal law, such as employment law or securities law? (2) Has the Federal Circuit succeeded in bringing national uniformity to the law? (3) What are the costs of judicial specialization?

---

[7] Applicants may first file in the U.S. District Court for the Eastern District of Virginia if they wish to gather additional evidence before appealing to the Federal Circuit, but this is relatively uncommon. *See* 35 U.S.C. § 145.

[8] For a list, see https://writtendescription.blogspot.com/p/patents-scotus.html.

Note that the ex parte nature of patent examination means that only the applicant can appeal, and thus only patent denials are ever appealed. If the USPTO incorrectly grants a patent, there is no party on the other side to appeal the grant. This asymmetry has the potential to introduce distortions in the law, as it offers the Federal Circuit more opportunities to grant patents that were initially denied and fewer opportunities to invalidate patents that were initially granted. *See* Jonathan Masur, *Patent Inflation*, 121 Yale L.J. 470 (2011). *But see* Lisa Larrimore Ouellette, *What Are the Sources of Patent Inflation?*, 121 Yale L.J. Online 347 (2011).

The typical patent takes approximately 22 months to be granted by the USPTO. For the patent to be granted, the patent applicant must pay an issuance fee. The now-patent owner must also pay additional maintenance fees 3.5, 7.5, and 11.5 years after the patent was issued to keep the patent in force. Failure to pay any of these fees renders the patent unenforceable against infringers. These fees—which can be quite substantial, in the thousands of dollars—do not really exist to cover the cost of "maintaining" the patent (which involves trivial expense). Rather, they are used by the USPTO to cover the costs of examination and of the office more generally. Because they are administered later in a patent's life, they serve a separate function as well: they "weed the patent thicket"—that is, they help to screen out worthless patents that have no real value but can make it more difficult for innovative firms to operate. *See* Jonathan S. Masur, *Costly Screens and Patent Examination*, 2 J. Legal Analysis 687 (2010). Assuming that all the maintenance fees are paid, patents remain valid for 20 years from the date on which they are *filed, not the date they are issued*. This is part of the reason why delays in the patent examination process can be so costly to inventors: once the patent is filed, the 20-year clock is ticking, and any delay eats into the patent's useful life. Extensions to the patent term are available in some cases; in particular, patent term adjustment (PTA) compensates for delays caused by the USPTO, and patent term extension (PTE) partially compensates pharmaceutical patent owners for delays in the drug commercialization process caused by clinical trials.[9] But in general, utility patents will expire 20 years from filing.[10]

As a practical matter, however, patent applicants often receive protection lasting 21 years from their initial filing date because many applicants begin with a patent application in another country (after which they have one year to file at the

---

[9] On average, about half of patents receive additional term through PTA, with an average adjustment of over four months. *See* 35 U.S.C. § 154(b). The USPTO processes about 100 PTE applications per year, which allow up to five years of extension for patents claiming products that require approval by the Food and Drug Administration (FDA), Drug Enforcement Agency (DEA), or Department of Agriculture (USDA). *See* 35 U.S.C. § 156.

[10] For patents filed before June 8, 1995, the patent term was 17 years from issuance rather than 20 years from filing. *See* Uruguay Round Agreements Act, Pub. L. No. 103-465, § 532(a)(1), 108 Stat. 4809, 4983 (1994) (amending 35 U.S.C. § 154, and stating that patents filed before June 8, 1995 shall have a term of the greater of 17 years from issuance or 20 years from filing).

USPTO[11]) or with a U.S. *provisional* patent application filed under 35 U.S.C. § 111(b). A provisional application must describe the invention, but it need not have claims and the USPTO will not commence examination. The inventor then has one year to file a nonprovisional application, which will be evaluated based on the provisional filing date—known as "claiming priority" to that date. Provisional applications thus allow inventors to establish an early priority date—which is important for demonstrating the novelty of the invention—while delaying the expense of filing and prosecuting a full nonprovisional application. After an applicant files a first nonprovisional application, known as a "parent" application, she often files additional "child" applications that claim priority to the same earliest provisional filing date. A *divisional* application under 35 U.S.C. § 121 is a child with claims to an "independent and distinct invention" that were originally filed in the parent, which often results when an examiner issues a *restriction requirement* asking the original application to be restricted to one related set of claims. A *continuation* application may have new claims, and results when a new application is filed claiming priority to a pending application. There is little legal difference between divisionals and continuations; both have the same priority date as the parent and must be supported by the parent's disclosure. Applicants may also file a *continuation-in-part*, which may add new matter to the disclosure, with the priority date of each claim based on whether it requires the new matter for support. A patent owner may also obtain a *reissue* patent to correct substantive errors in a granted patent under 35 U.S.C. § 251; a reissue broadening claim scope must be applied for within two years of the original patent grant.

Even though third parties cannot insert themselves into the ex parte patent examination process, there are administrative avenues available to them once a patent has been granted. Three separate processes exist. Post-grant review (PGR) allows any party who pays the necessary (substantial) filing fee to challenge a patent's validity within the first nine months after it is issued. The patent can be challenged only on certain grounds, but the range of options available to the challenger is relatively wide. Second, after the first nine months have passed, any party may challenge a patent via the separate inter partes review (IPR) procedure, which allows for challenges on a more limited set of grounds than PGR. Finally, anyone—including anonymous parties—can petition for ex parte reexamination, which allows challenges on the same limited grounds as IPR, but with less expense, less risk of estoppel, and less opportunity for the third party to participate. All three of these processes exist in order to facilitate challenges to patents that should not have been granted without forcing the challenger to wait to be sued and then undergo the expense of litigation in federal court. The most popular procedure, IPR, is often initiated by a party who has been sued for infringement, which often results in a stay of the district court litigation. We discuss these procedures in more detail in Chapter 17.

---

[11] For more on the process of acquiring patent protection in multiple countries, see Chapter 20.

Once a patent has been granted, the patent's owner can bring suit against any party believed to be infringing the patent.[12] The federal district courts have exclusive jurisdiction over all lawsuits arising under the Patent Act; unlike for almost any other claim under federal law, patent cases cannot be brought in state court. 28 U.S.C. § 1338(a). Importantly, a party sued for patent infringement may defend itself by arguing not only that it does not infringe the patent, but also that the patent is invalid. That is, the USPTO's decision to grant a patent is not final, although the USPTO's decision to grant the patent does receive deference. *See* Jonathan S. Masur & Lisa Larrimore Ouellette, *Deference Mistakes*, 82 U. Chi. L. Rev. 643 (2015). The losing party in a patent litigation in district court may appeal that court's decision to the Federal Circuit, and from there again to the Supreme Court.

The Federal Circuit and Supreme Court thus consider patent validity in two types of cases: appeals from the USPTO in which the agency does not think the claims at issue are valid (with captions of the form "*In re Inventor*" at the Federal Circuit and "*Inventor v. USPTO Director*" at the Supreme Court), and appeals from patent infringement litigation in which the accused infringer challenges the patent's validity (with captions of the form "*Patent Owner v. Accused Infringer*," or reversed if the infringer filed the suit as a declaratory judgment action). The following figure represents this institutional structure in graphic form:

Administrative Structure of the Patent System

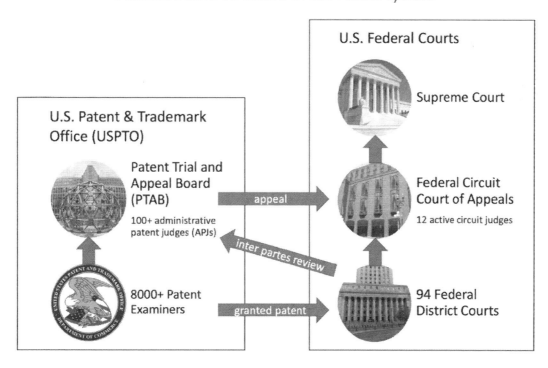

---

[12] Pre-issuance damages are also available under 35 U.S.C. § 154(d) if the infringer had knowledge of a published patent application.

To decide patent cases, the primary source of legal authority is the Patent Act, found at Title 35 of the U.S. Code, which Congress passed under the authority of the Constitution's IP Clause. As we will see, many provisions of the Patent Act are short and provide little guidance on how they should be applied, so many core patent law doctrines have been developed and elaborated by the courts through doctrinal development. The USPTO does not have rulemaking authority over substantive patent law, but it has issued regulations (at 37 C.F.R.) governing the procedural rules of practice before the agency. The USPTO also publishes a Manual of Patent Examining Procedure (MPEP), which provides guidance on patent law to patent examiners and prosecutors.[13] The federal courts have never treated the MPEP as binding authority, but it exerts significant influence over the patents that the USPTO chooses to grant, many of which are never challenged in court. The USPTO updates the MPEP regularly in accord with changes in patent law. We will refer to this document throughout the book, most prominently when discussing the law of patentable subject matter.

B. Patent Practice

Most U.S. patent law work falls into three general categories: (1) being involved in the patent examination process before the USPTO, either by helping inventors obtain patents (which, as noted above, is known as "prosecution") or by working for the USPTO to decide which patent applications to grant; (2) helping clients assert their patent rights in court or defend against patent lawsuits ("litigation"); or (3) helping arrange transfers of patent rights ("licensing" or "transactional work"). There are other options, including the growing field of patent office litigation (a hybrid of litigation and practice before the USPTO) and advocacy work at nonprofits like the Electronic Frontier Foundation that include patent policy in their portfolios. Practice environments also vary, with many patent practitioners starting at law firms and then moving "in house" to a private firm or a nonprofit such as a university technology transfer office.

Patent prosecution involves interviewing inventors, writing patents, and rebutting patent examiners' arguments about why your applications shouldn't be granted. Patent prosecution does not require a legal degree; rather, prosecutors need to have a bachelor's degree in a technical field or its equivalent, and to pass the registration examination (also known as the "patent bar exam"), a six-hour multiple-choice exam that tests knowledge of USPTO rules.[14] Passing the patent bar makes

---

[13] The MPEP is available at: https://www.uspto.gov/web/offices/pac/mpep/index.html.

[14] For information about the registration examination and its requirements, see https://www.uspto.gov/learning-and-resources/patent-and-trademark-practitioners/becoming-patent-practitioner/registration. For advice about the exam compiled by Eric E. Johnson, see https://writtendescription.blogspot.com/2021/03/advice-about-patent-bar-for-current-and.html.

you a "patent agent." If you are also admitted to a state bar, which typically requires going to law school and passing a state bar exam, you may call yourself a "patent attorney" and are allowed to provide legal advice.

Many patent prosecutors find the work gratifying because they enjoy learning and writing about different successful technologies and communicating with people from different backgrounds, and they often appreciate the relatively stable work hours compared with other areas of law. Scientists who are interested in pursuing patent prosecution careers sometimes begin by applying for a job as a patent examiner at the USPTO, which is often a transition step to other careers. If you have an advanced technical degree (usually an M.S. in engineering or a Ph.D. in science), you may also be able to start with a higher-paying job at a law firm as a "technical advisor" or "scientific advisor" who helps draft patent applications. The firm will typically pay for your patent bar exam course so that you can become a patent agent, and will sometimes also pay for you to attend law school.

Aspiring patent prosecutors might initially think they need only learn the materials in Chapters 2–7 on the requirements for obtaining a patent, but writing patents well also requires a thorough understanding of patent infringement and remedies. Many patent claims can often be obtained on the same invention, but some are more likely to be infringed—or to be infringed by more parties. And some claims are more likely to allow the patent owner to receive an injunction or a larger damages award. Your clients will be well served by a thorough knowledge of not only how claims are likely to fare at the USPTO, but also what happens to them afterwards.

Patent litigation involves duking out patent rights in court. Contrary to most court TV shows, your day-to-day life will not involve arguments in front of a jury. Rather, as with other types of commercial litigation, you will be reviewing documents, drafting questions and responses related to "discovery" (gathering information for cases), doing legal research, and writing legal arguments in memos and briefs. Patent litigators must be admitted to a state bar. A technical degree is not required, and many terrific patent litigators spin their lack of technical background as an asset that allows them to communicate more effectively with lay judges and juries. But many firms also look for new patent litigation associates who do have some technical training, so this is another common route for those transitioning from science to patent law.

Patent litigators often enjoy the opportunity to strategize on behalf of their clients, to translate technical ideas for lay audiences, and to work on high-stakes cases. Patent litigators typically earn higher salaries than patent prosecutors, although they also work longer hours. Some litigators start as prosecutors and then broaden their practice to include litigation assignments, but it is more common to begin litigation straight out of law school, and many patent litigators have not taken the patent bar exam.

In the nineteenth century, patent litigation was a staple of many large, general-practice commercial law firms. Over the course of the twentieth century, most patent litigation moved to smaller patent-centered firms, typically known as "patent boutiques." Over the past thirty years, however, patent litigation has again become a centerpiece of many large general-practice firms. Many of these firms acquired smaller patent boutiques as a means of creating patent litigation shops out of whole cloth; others built them from the ground up. It is now quite common for the largest and most profitable law firms to have substantial patent litigation departments. And there are many patent litigation jobs available to budding associates, whether or not they have technical degrees.

Patent licensing and transactional work involves arranging deals involving patents. It involves the least engagement with the technical aspects of patents and can be an attractive option for those with economics and business skills. Like litigation, transactional practice does not require the patent bar but does require admission to a state bar. Some patent-related transactional work involves individual commercial transactions where patents are important, including patent licenses and collaboration agreements, with day-to-day work focused on independently reading large documents to spot potential concerns to discuss with your client. Patent-focused transactional lawyers also help with patent issues for mergers and acquisitions ("M&A work"), where the corporate team reaches out to specialists to discuss patent-related portions of the deal. For example, deals often include representations ("reps") and warranties as to the title of patent rights, that those rights are sufficient to continue the business, that the business isn't infringing others' patent rights, etc. Salaries are similar to those for patent litigators. We discuss patent licensing in more detail in Chapter 18, but transactional lawyers will also benefit from understanding the rules of patent validity, infringement, and remedies.

Based on a recent survey by the American Intellectual Property Law Association, the median legal charge for filing a new utility patent ranged from $7,000 for an invention of minimal complexity to $10,000 for more complex biotech or electrical inventions, and the median charge for a patent license was $5,000. Of course, arranging a more complex deal that involves patent licenses is far more expensive. For litigation, the median legal costs for a full trial with less than $1 million at risk was $700,000; for a case with more than $25 million at risk, the median cost was $4 million.

C. Locating Patent Documents: An Online Exercise

We think it is important for patent law students to feel comfortable finding and interpreting patent documents. The best way to acquire this skill is through active practice. This assignment will guide you through the process of locating a U.S. patent, understanding its contents, and finding additional information about the patent on the USPTO website.

Consider the important problem of removing corks from wine bottles. The most common approach is to use a corkscrew, such as the one shown below on the left, which is screwed into the cork and then pulled out. Another cork remover, shown in the center, is known as an ah-so, butler's friend, or twin-prong cork puller. The prongs are pushed between the cork and the neck of the bottle, and then the cork is twisted out of the bottle. These two cork-removing mechanisms can also be combined, as shown at right below. This combination corkscrew and ah-so is sold as "The Durand."

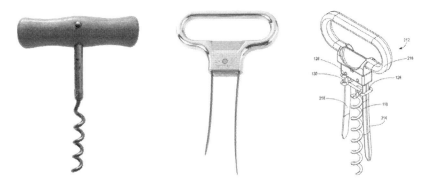

1. The Durand website includes information on patents in six countries, including U.S. Patent No. 7,237,455. Can you find a PDF of this patent? One option is to use the USPTO website (www.uspto.gov); their Patent Search page has separate options for granted patents (PatFT, which is what you want) and patent applications (AppFT). If you use the Advanced Search option for patents since 1976, you can query pn/7237455 to pull up the text of the patent in HTML form. Click "Images," and then you'll see a PDF you can save. Another option is to simply Google patent 7237455, click the first link, and then click "Download PDF." Who invented this bottle opener?

2. For utility patents filed on or after June 8, 1995, the patent term is 20 years from the filing date of the earliest non-provisional application on which the patent is based. Many patents are tied to earlier or later patents (referred to as "parents" and "children," and collectively as "families"), so in general you should *not* assume that you can just add 20 years to the filing date. Some patents also receive term adjustments or extensions for government-caused delays, or the patent applicant may disclaim a portion of the term. But for this patent, the "Related U.S. Application Data" field only contains a provisional application, and there was no term adjustment or disclaimer. If all maintenance fees are paid and it is not invalidated, what year will patent 7,237,455 expire?

3. After the cover information (including a list of prior art references cited by the applicant or the examiner), you can see the patent drawings. Then, starting on p. 13 of the PDF, is the background of the invention, which often reads like an

infomercial. (The text of patents is printed in 2 columns with line numbering every 5 lines. The line numbers are rarely aligned with the text, but they are nevertheless used for citation. E.g., U.S. Patent No. 7,237,455 col. 2 ll. 14–18.) According to this patent, what are the problems with the traditional spiral corkscrew and with the ah-so?

4. Next comes the summary of the invention, a brief description of the drawings, and a detailed description of the invention, including "preferred embodiments" (i.e., what the inventor thinks are the best ways to make the invention). Together with the drawings, this information is known as the "specification." The specification cannot be amended during prosecution because it represents the definitive statement of what the inventor has actually invented as of the date the application was filed. (This is relevant to a variety of patent law doctrines.) A specification can be painful to read, particularly due to the references to figure numbers, but it usually makes sense if you go slowly. Note that patent applicants may be their own lexicographers, meaning that they may use terms in idiosyncratic ways. What does this patent mean by "stabilizer"?

5. At the very end of the patent are the "claims," which are what the patent legally covers. The claims are the fence posts that mark out the metes and bounds of a patent owner's intellectual property. The first claim begins on column 6, line 65, and is an "independent" claim because it does not refer to other claims. The second claim, beginning with "The bottle opener of claim 1, wherein . . ." is a "dependent" claim. Technically speaking, the claims are considered part of the specification. But it's easier to think of the claims and specification as separate parts of the patent. The specification describes what the invention actually is; the claims describe its legal boundaries. How many independent claims does this patent have?

6. As we explained above, the "prosecution history" or "file wrapper" of a patent is everything that happened during patent examination. To find the file wrapper for the Durand patent, go back to the USPTO patent search page and find the link for Patent Application Information Retrieval (PAIR), and then access Public PAIR and search by patent number (7237455). The "Transaction History" tab lists the events that occurred during prosecution, and the "Image File Wrapper" tab lists these events with links to the relevant documents for patents filed after 2003. On average, it takes over a year from when a patent is filed (the first date in the transaction history) for a patent examiner to issue a "first office action" in which the claims are either allowed ("Notice of Allowance") or rejected (typically, "Non-Final Rejection"). Approximately how many months did it take in this case?

7. This application is unusual in that after the examiner allowed the claims, the applicant submitted an Information Disclosure Statement (IDS) listing

additional prior art documents on Jan. 12, 2007, along with payment for the issuance fee, which caused the examiner to issue a "Final Rejection" on Feb. 8, 2007. You can read this file on the "Image File Wrapper" tab. What statutory provision was used to reject some of the claims in light of this new prior art?

8. The "Continuity Data" tab lists any "parent" or "child" applications, including applications filed under the Patent Cooperation Treaty (PCT) to facilitate patenting in multiple countries. When a child application claims priority to a parent, it is as if claims in that application were filed at the same time as the parent. The child application relies on the same description of the invention and has the same effective filing date. Can you find the U.S. patent number (not application number) of a child of the 7,237,455 patent?

9. The "Assignee" field on the patent tells you something about patent ownership at the time the patent was issued. Typically, the assignee is the company or institution that employs the inventors (unless they are independent inventors). The "Assignments" tab in Public PAIR provides any information about transfers of interests in the patent that have been recorded with the USPTO. Assignments are not always recorded, and requiring greater transparency about patent ownership is surprisingly controversial. Who owned the 7,237,455 patent at the time of issuance, and what month was ownership transferred?

D. Patent Claims and Claim Construction

At the beginning of this chapter, we explained that claims define the legal rights protected by a patent, and we gave an example of a simple patent claim for a pencil. You have also seen patent claims for the Durand wine opener. Understanding how to read patent claims like this is an essential preliminary for applying patent law doctrines. Because they define the legal metes and bounds of a patent, the claims are key to the patent's value. The broader the claims, the broader the property right and the more inventive territory the patent holder owns; the narrower the claims, the narrower the property right. Patent applicants thus have an incentive to draft claims that are as broad as possible. For example, the Durand inventors would have loved to claim "all methods of removing corks from bottles." But there are two significant constraints on the breadth of claims an applicant can write:

1. An applicant cannot claim anything that has already been invented—that is, she cannot claim anything that is in the prior art. The Durand inventors thus could not have claimed a simple corkscrew or ah-so. This requirement is policed primarily by the law of novelty (Chapter 2) and nonobviousness (Chapter 3).

2. Second, an applicant cannot claim what she has not invented! Her claim must be limited to what she has actually invented and documented to the world. The

Durand inventors thus could not have claimed a cork remover powered by nuclear fusion. This requirement is policed primarily by the law of enablement and written description (Chapter 4).

Patent claim drafting thus representing a careful balancing act between the desire for breadth and the limitations on breadth imposed by law.

The process of interpreting what a patent claim covers—known as claim construction—is a key step in analyzing the claim's validity and whether a given product or process infringes the claim. During patent examination, claims are construed to have their "broadest reasonable interpretation." Once claims are granted, they are construed based on their "ordinary meaning" to a researcher of "ordinary skill" in the relevant field. We save a more detailed discussion of claim construction for Chapter 8; for now, it is enough to recognize that many claim terms have some ambiguity. Consider the pencil claim at the start of this chapter. Does the claim cover pencils with cores containing any percentage of graphite? Pencils with holders made from a wood-plastic composite? Wooden mechanical pencils? Broader claims are both more likely to be infringed and less likely to be valid, making claim construction a critical part of patent infringement litigation.

For another example, consider a more recent invention: the Swiffer mop, introduced by Procter & Gamble in 1997. As illustrated below on the left, the Swiffer eliminates the need to clean the mop head or to use a separate bucket by using a disposable cleaning pad and an integrated system for delivering the cleaning solution, which can be sprayed by pressing a button on the handle.

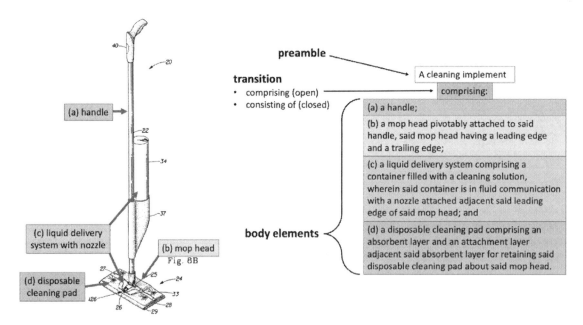

Sales of Swiffer products quickly grew to over $1 billion per year, and Procter & Gamble protected this market with numerous patents. A simplified version of claim 1

OVERVIEW   27

from one such patent, U.S. Patent No. 6,663,306, is shown above on the right. Can you spot any ambiguities in any of the claim terms? We will return to this example later.

Patent claims follow stylized drafting rules:

1. *Preamble.* Claims begin with a preamble introducing the kind of invention at issue—like "A cleaning implement"—which generally does not limit the legal scope of the claim unless necessary, such as for more detailed preambles that describe features of the invention. (The Federal Circuit's less-than-helpful test for whether a preamble is limiting considers whether it "breathes life and meaning into the claim." *See generally* Mark A. Lemley, *Without Preamble*, 100 B.U. L. Rev. 357 (2020).) What are the advantages to the patentee of writing a broad preamble?

2. *Transition.* After the preamble comes the transition, which for the *vast* majority of claims is "comprising," an "open" term signaling that the invention includes but is not limited by the body elements that follow. In contrast, the "closed" transition "consisting of" signals that the invention is limited to the following elements, and not more. A claim to "A writing implement *comprising* graphite encased by a wooden holder" covers pencils that include added elements such as an eraser, whereas a claim to "A writing implement *consisting of* graphite encased by a wooden holder" does not cover pencils with erasers. Claims can also use the middle ground of "consisting essentially of," which covers devices that include the following elements and may include others that "do not materially affect the basic and novel properties of the invention," but this transition is even rarer than "consisting of." Why do you think patentees prefer the "comprising" transition? Why would a patentee ever use "consisting of"?

3. *Body Elements.* After the transition come the claim elements, which define the scope of the invention. The Swiffer claim covers mops with four elements—a handle, a mop head, a liquid delivery system, and a disposable cleaning pad. A few important points:

- As will be discussed in detail in later chapters, understanding the body elements is essential for determining whether the claim is valid and infringed. If any earlier mop (or a description of a mop) has all four of the Swiffer claim elements, the claim would be invalid for lack of novelty. And if the claim is valid, Procter & Gamble can prevent others from making, using, or selling mops that include all four of these elements (even if the infringing mops have additional elements).

- For understanding the scope of the Swiffer claim, Procter & Gamble's actual product is completely irrelevant. In fact, many patent owners do not sell products covered by their patent claims. Rather, the legal right is defined by the words in the claim text.

- Drafting rules require the claim to explain how each element interacts with at least one other element that has already been introduced. For example, the mop head is "attached to said handle" (i.e., to the handle already introduced).

4. *The Interaction between Novelty, Infringement, and Transitions.* Imagine that Jemele obtains a patent "comprising elements A, B, C, and D." Fernando later obtains a separate patent "comprising elements A, B, C, D, and E." Suppose that Rebecca then begins producing a product that includes elements A, B, C, D, and E. Whose patent does she infringe? The answer is both Jemele's and Fernando's. The transition word "comprising" means that any product that has all four of the elements of Jemele's patent infringes her patent, even if it includes one or more additional elements.

Now, consider the question of novelty. As we just noted above, if all the elements of a claim are found in one piece of prior art, the claim is not novel. Thus, if all the elements of Fernando's patent were found in Jemele's earlier patent, then Fernando's patent would be invalid. Jemele used the transition word "comprising," which means "includes A, B, C & D but is not limited to them." Does this mean that Fernando's patent is invalid because Jemele's patent could include E as well? The answer is no. Jemele's patent doesn't actually include E. The word "comprising" ensures that any product that includes element E (or element F, or G) will infringe, so long as it includes A, B, C & D as well. But because Jemele does not mention E, her patent will not destroy the novelty of any subsequent patent that includes E as an element—which means the patent system still provides some incentive for Fernando.

Claim elements	Jemele's patent	Fernando's patent	Rebecca's product
A	✓	✓	✓
B	✓	✓	✓
C	✓	✓	✓
D	✓	✓	✓
E		✓	✓

This means that sequential inventors can (and do) obtain patents that stack on additional elements as technology progresses, known as *blocking patents*. After Jemele obtains a patent claiming an invention comprising A, B, C & D and Fernando obtains one comprising A, B, C, D & E, Rebecca could obtain a patent comprising A, B, C, D, E & F. All three of these patents can be valid. Woe unto the manufacturer who seeks to sell a product that includes A, B, C, D, E & F; this manufacturer infringes all three patents and must negotiate licenses with all three inventors. That is, each of

Jemele, Fernando, and Rebecca can independently block the manufacturer if the manufacturer does not license their patents.

5. *Single-Sentence Rule.* The USPTO requires each claim to be a single sentence (typically beginning "I claim: 1. A cleaning implement comprising . . ." or "The invention claimed is: 1. A cleaning implement comprising . . ."). Needless to say, this rule does not enhance claim clarity.

6. *Antecedent Basis.* If the Swiffer claim read: "A cleaning implement comprising a mop head pivotally attached to the handle," it would be rejected because it is unclear what handle is being referred to—i.e., "the handle" lacks "antecedent basis." The first time a limitation is introduced, it must be introduced with "a" or "an" (as in "a handle"); subsequently, that limitation can be referred to using either "said" or "the" (as in "said handle"). In the following claims, each term has proper antecedent basis:

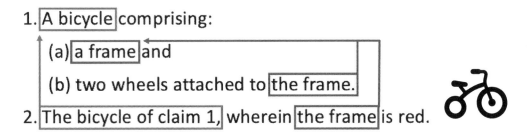

7. *Independent and Dependent Claims.* Inventions can be described at many different levels of abstraction, so inventors will often seek multiple claims in a patent. As noted in the Durand exercise above, patent claims can be "independent," meaning that they stand on their own, or "dependent," meaning that they refer to a claim previously set forth and further limit that claim. For example, a dependent claim in the Swiffer patent states: "6. The cleaning implement of claim 1, wherein said absorbent layer has a t_{1200} absorbent capacity of at least about 5 grams/gram." (The patent defines "t_{1200} absorbent capacity" as the number of grams of water per gram of cleaning pad absorbed at a pressure of 0.09 psi after 1200 seconds.) Each dependent claim is a separate legal right that is legally equivalent to writing out the full independent claim with the additional limitation. *See* 35 U.S.C. § 112(c)-(f). That is, the elements of dependent claim 6 of the Swiffer patent are (a) the handle, (b) the mop head, (c) the liquid delivery system, and (d) the disposable cleaning pad, where (e) the absorbent layer has an absorbent capacity of at least 5 grams/gram.

Because they have additional limitations, dependent claims are necessarily *narrower* than the claims from which they depend. This means that they are more likely to be valid and less likely to be infringed. A product could include all of the elements of the independent claim but not the additional element of the dependent claim and thus not infringe the dependent claim. Or, if the product existed before the patent application, it could invalidate the independent claim, but not invalidate the dependent claim because it lacks that additional element.

Importantly, for this reason, invalidation of an independent claim does *not* imply that any associated dependent claims are invalid. This is often counterintuitive—the independent claim feels like the foundation on which the dependent claims rest, and we naturally expect that when the foundation is destroyed, the rest of the building will fall. But that is not the case. However, the converse is very often true: if a dependent claim is invalid because it is not novel, any independent claim to which it refers will be invalid as well, so long as the independent claim uses the transition word "comprising." Can you see why? Why do you think patent drafters include more than one dependent claim?

8. *Product and Process Claims.* The claims you have seen so far—for a pencil, the Durand wine opener, and the Swiffer mop—are all examples of claims to a *product*, or a tangible thing. But the majority of new patents also include at least one *method* or *process* claim, which is written in the form of a series of steps. For example, Procter & Gamble has received claims along these lines:

> A method of cleaning a surface comprising the steps of:
> (a) providing a cleaning implement comprising: [the four elements above—a handle, a mop head, a liquid delivery system, and a disposable cleaning pad];
> (b) actuating said liquid delivery system; and
> (c) mopping said surface with said cleaning pad.

This claim is infringed by someone who carries out these steps of using a Swiffer-like mop to clean a surface, but not by someone who merely makes or sells a Swiffer-like mop. Similarly, inventors of software algorithms often claim both the method of the algorithm and a product—such as some electronic storage medium—containing instructions for carrying out the algorithm. What are the advantages of writing claims in both product and process formats?

Claims can also be written in *product-by-process* format, such as "A [product] prepared by a process comprising the steps of . . . ." In a product-by-process claim, the process is a claim limitation, so the product obtained by other processes would not be infringing. Why might a claim drafter use this format?

9. *Means-Plus-Function Claim Elements.* An additional option for claim drafting is provided in 35 U.S.C. § 112(f), under which a claim element may be "expressed as a means or step for performing a specified function"—known as a means-plus-function claim element—which is then interpreted "to cover the corresponding structure . . . described in the specification." For example, if one step of your software algorithm method claim involves sorting data entries based on some criterion, your claim does not need to explicitly list all the different sorting algorithms—quick sort, merge sort, bubble sort, etc. Instead, you can include a step with a "means for sorting" the data, and then this element will legally cover all the means for sorting listed in the patent specification. (If the specification doesn't list any means for sorting, the claim is invalid.) If a claim element includes the phrase "means

for," it is a strong signal that it is a means-plus-function claim element, but elements written in similar functional terms will also trigger § 112(f). We will discuss these rules in more detail in Chapter 5 on Definiteness and Functional Claiming.

10. *Other Claim Formats.* Patent claims may also be drafted in other formats. For example, a claim with a *Markush* group (named after the case that approved this format) contains an element such as "material selected from the group consisting of A, B, and C," which is frequently used for chemical structures. A *Jepson* claim explains how the invention improves on some existing product or process, with a form such as: "In an [existing product] having A, B, and C, the improvement comprising . . . ." A "kit" claim of the form "A kit for X comprising A, B, and C" is used to claim products that involve separate parts that are used together. We will not discuss these formats in more detail in this casebook, but you may encounter them in practice.

Practice Problems: Patent Claims

Consider the first three claims from U.S. Patent No. 6,635,133, titled "Method for Making a Multilayered Golf Ball":

1. A method of making a ball, comprising:
   (a) forming an inner sphere by forming an outer shell with a fluid mass center;
   (b) forming a plurality of core parts from elastomeric material;
   (c) arranging and adhesively joining the core parts around the inner sphere with a flexible adhesive and then crosslinking the core parts to each other by compressing them together at an elevated temperature to form a substantially spherical core;
   (d) molding a cover around the assembled core.

2. The method of claim 1, further comprising molding nonplanar mating surfaces on the core parts.

3. The method of claim 1, wherein forming the inner sphere comprises freezing a sphere of a fluid.

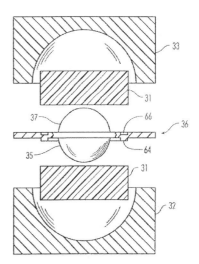

What is the preamble for all three claims? Are these claims open or closed? What are the elements of dependent claim 2? If claim 1 is invalid because an earlier publication already describes this method, what can you say about the validity of claims 2 and 3? If instead it is claim 3 that is invalid because of an earlier publication, what can you say about the validity of claims 1 and 2?

Claim Drafting Exercise: Spikeball

Spikeball, also known as roundnet, is a backyard game played with a small trampoline (typically with a three-foot diameter), called a "net," and a small bouncing ball (typically with a 3.8-inch diameter), as shown. In a standard game, two teams of two people take turns bouncing the ball on the net. After an initial serve to the net, each team has three hits to return the ball onto the net. There are no boundaries; players may run anywhere around the net. Play continues until a team fails to return the ball onto the net within three touches. For a video illustration, see https://spikeball.com/pages/how-to-play-1. There are numerous variations of the basic rules, including allowing the ball to bounce off the ground once per possession, playing with tennis rackets, requiring one touch to be with a player's foot, and two- or three-player games. The Spikeball trampoline has foldable legs to allow for easy transport and storage.

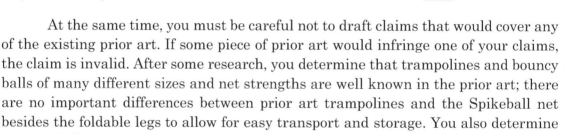

The inventor of Spikeball has asked you to draft a patent claim (or set of claims) that covers this invention and that will be as useful as possible in preventing others from entering the market with competing products that might reduce Spikeball sales.

At the same time, you must be careful not to draft claims that would cover any of the existing prior art. If some piece of prior art would infringe one of your claims, the claim is invalid. After some research, you determine that trampolines and bouncy balls of many different sizes and net strengths are well known in the prior art; there are no important differences between prior art trampolines and the Spikeball net besides the foldable legs to allow for easy transport and storage. You also determine that the following games have sometimes been played on large trampolines:

- *Volleyball.* Two teams attempt to hit a ball back and forth over a net without allowing the ball to touch the trampoline, and each team may touch the ball three times before it must be returned over the net.

- *Four Square.* Four players each have their own quadrant of the trampoline, and when a ball is bounced in a player's quadrant, it must be bounced back into another quadrant.

- *Basketball.* Players dribble a ball on the trampoline and attempt to shoot it through hoops mounted high in the air.

- *Hacky Sack.* Players stand in a circle on the trampoline and attempt to keep a ball in the air using only their feet. A player who allows the ball to hit the trampoline loses.

For purposes of this exercise, assume that this is all the relevant prior art.

E. Economics of Patent Law

The dominant framework for justifying and analyzing U.S. patent laws is *utilitarianism*—the idea that the government grants patents because the benefits they create for society are larger than their social costs. In other words, patents should be granted only when they have a positive effect on *social welfare*. This purpose is reflected in the "IP Clause" of the Constitution: Article 1, Section 8, Clause 8 grants Congress the power to enact patent laws to "promote the Progress of Science and useful Arts." Similarly, the Supreme Court explained in *Graham v. John Deere Co.*, 383 U.S. 1 (1966): "The patent monopoly was not designed to secure to the inventor his natural right in his discoveries. Rather, it was a reward, an inducement, to bring forth new knowledge."

Why should the government intervene in the market for new ideas? Consider some ideas that might be protected by a patent: the design of a new mousetrap, a cheaper method of manufacturing mousetraps, an algorithm for a faster computational search method, the formula for a new pharmaceutical compound, or the fact that a certain chemical is effective at treating cancer. Ideas like these—which we will refer to as *knowledge goods*—are fundamentally different from most tangible property in that they have the two characteristics of what economists call *public goods*:

1. *Nonrivalry*: One person's use of some piece of information does not decrease others' ability to use it. The social benefit from producing a new knowledge good is thus greater than the private benefit to its producer. Because an additional user can benefit without imposing costs on others—or in economic terms, the marginal cost of production is zero—the good should be as widely and freely available as possible.

2. *Nonexcludability*: The producer of a knowledge good often cannot prevent others from using the good. Persons other than the producer can thus free-ride off the producer's efforts. And because a self-interested firm will not consider the benefits of these free-riders when deciding how much to invest in producing knowledge goods, it will invest less than the socially optimal amount.

Can you think of other goods that are nonrivalrous and at least somewhat nonexcludable? Common examples outside the innovation context include things like national defense and clean air. Public goods such as knowledge goods will be underproduced by the market, providing a justification for government intervention.

The fundamental problem for producers of knowledge goods is that it is often far cheaper to copy the invention than it is to create the invention in the first place. Consider a new cancer drug. Once one company has undertaken the tremendous expense of developing the drug and testing whether it is safe and effective at treating cancer, it is comparatively inexpensive for a generic manufacturer to copy the drug and enter the market. Estimates vary, but R&D costs have been estimated at around $1 billion per approved drug, while generic entry costs are on the order of $10 million.

If patents did not exist, a generic manufacturer could wait until someone else has developed the drug and then enter the market and sell generic versions of the drug at a much lower price. (Many of you have probably had the experience of being offered the generic alternative to a brand-name prescription drug at a much lower price than the brand-name drug would cost.) By itself, this wouldn't necessarily constitute a *social* problem—it's not clear that society should care whether the original pharmaceutical developer (a large corporation) or the generic manufacturer (a large corporation) makes more money. The problem is that pharmaceutical firms would anticipate this problem. If they thought their drugs would be underpriced, such that they couldn't recover their R&D costs, they wouldn't invest in R&D in the first place! *This* would represent a major social problem because the public would lose the benefit of new drugs. Put another way, the high cost of pharmaceutical development relative to generic production means that even if a new drug has enormous *social* value relative to existing treatments, the *private* value often will not be enough to induce development absent government intervention.

To be sure, the economics of public goods do not mean that no innovation will occur without government intervention. For one thing, knowledge goods are often partially excludable, such as through secrecy or social norms. For another, in some cases the private value will be enough to recover the costs of R&D. But in many cases the gap between social and private value will cause society to miss out on valuable innovations.

Policymakers have numerous policy tools to address the concern that inventors will not have sufficient incentives to invest in R&D. *See generally* Daniel J. Hemel & Lisa Larrimore Ouellette, *Beyond the Patents–Prizes Debate*, 92 Tex. L. Rev. 303 (2013). They can directly fund R&D, such as through grants to universities or firms or through government-run laboratories like the National Institutes of Health. They can offer prizes for successful innovations, such as the fixed prizes offered at Challenge.gov or the market subsidies provided by government health insurance programs. They can use R&D tax incentives to reduce firms' R&D costs, such as those at I.R.C. §§ 41, 174. And they can use patents.

If the government grants the drug developer an exclusive right to sell or license the drug for a limited time, then the developer can prevent generic entrants and have a limited monopoly over that drug. In this way, patents can address the nonexcludability problem by making knowledge goods more excludable, such that others cannot benefit from the goods without the patent owner's permission. In practice, few patents confer a true monopoly, but many patents do allow their owners to charge prices above marginal cost—that is, the cost of producing one more unit of that good. In a competitive market, firms will sell goods at marginal cost, which means that they will not earn much profit for each unit of the good sold. But when a firm has market power (like in a monopoly), the firm can increase its profits by selling a smaller quantity of the goods at a higher price. In this sense, the patent system is equivalent to a sales tax on patented technologies, with revenues going to the knowledge-good producers.

Patents have the virtue of rewarding inventors based on how much consumers value the goods they are creating. If an inventor creates a very useful product, such as a treatment for a debilitating disease, it can use the power of its patent to sell that invention at a high price. This creates an incentive for inventive firms to pursue the inventions that will be most highly valued by the public, which is of course the objective. But using patents as an allocation mechanism has costs. Most importantly, if the patent owner is unable to *price discriminate* by charging different prices to different consumers, those who value the good above its competitive price—the price the good would sell for absent a patent, equal to marginal cost—but below the patent owner's price will be denied access to the good. For example, if a month's supply of a patented new cancer drug would have a competitive price of $100 but is sold by the patent owner for $10,000, then consumers who value the drug at $5,000 (more than $100 but less than $10,000) will be priced out of the market by the patent. This lack of access—and the resulting cost to human health and lives—is a real cost to society known as *deadweight loss*. Under the conventional account, patents thus create a fundamental tradeoff between *incentives* on the one hand and *access* on the other, or what economists call a tradeoff between *dynamic efficiency* (incentives to create more inventions) and *allocative efficiency* (access to existing inventions).

This incentives/access tradeoff is not inevitable, however. As one of us has explored in work with Daniel Hemel, society can have both widespread access and substantial rewards for innovation. First, the patent system itself may affect the demand for a new technology: patents incentivize manufacturers to invest in *creating* demand for their products, such as through marketing, which increases the number of patients who access them. In the pharmaceutical context, this means that patent expiration often leads to a decrease in *price* without a corresponding increase in *use*.[15] This patent-driven increase in demand and access could be either beneficial or harmful. In some cases, perhaps including mental health treatments, marketing by developers prior to a patent's expiration may have encouraged patients to seek treatment for conditions that otherwise might have been unrecognized or stigmatized in the absence of a patented treatment. In other cases, such as Purdue Pharma's misleading marketing in support of their patented and addictive opioid OxyContin,

---

[15] Patent expiration does not always lead to a decrease in price; in many cases, other features of the pharmaceutical industry such as high entry costs or natural monopolies provide market power. For example, there are over 300 off-patent drugs with no approved generic, and it typically takes multiple generic competitors to lead to a substantial price decrease. The revolutionary cancer drug Gleevec (imatinib) had a list price of over $10,000 per month when it first faced a generic competitor, but the price declined by only 10% in the first 20 months after generic entry. Ashley L. Cole & Stacie B. Dusetzina, *Generic Price Competition for Specialty Drugs: Too Little, Too Late?*, 37 Health Aff. 738 (2018).

this expansion in pharmaceutical use has been disastrous. *See* Daniel J. Hemel & Lisa Larrimore Ouellette, *Innovation Institutions and the Opioid Crisis*, 7 J.L. & Biosciences (2020).

More importantly, the choice of patents as an incentive mechanism does not mean that the patent system must be used to allocate access to the resulting technologies: financial incentives for developers could be made distinct from out-of-pocket costs for consumers. For example, if the government purchases products or patent rights from the patent owner for fair market value and then distributes the patented products at no cost, the innovator receives the same patent-based incentive while consumers get access for free. And this kind of matching of patent incentives with non-patent allocation is not merely hypothetical: other countries like the United Kingdom already purchase medicines directly from patent holders and distribute them at low or no cost to patients, and Medicare and Medicaid achieve much the same thing for many patients in the United States. *See* Daniel J. Hemel & Lisa Larrimore Ouellette, *Innovation Policy Pluralism*, 128 Yale L.J. 544 (2019). This is part of the reason why price decreases for pharmaceutical drugs don't always lead to increases in use of the drug, as we noted above. Many people who might not be able to afford the expensive, brand-name drug at retail are nonetheless able to access it through Medicare, Medicaid, or private insurance. In short, patents can create deadweight loss by limiting access, but this is not inevitable.

Patents can also create other social costs, although the extent of each cost is contested. Perhaps most importantly, patents can over-incentivize innovation. To be clear, by "over-incentivizing," we do not mean providing rewards greater than whatever is "just enough" to induce invention—such rewards are transfers from one party to another, not true social costs.[16] Rather, over-incentivizing occurs when patents spur R&D costs that are greater than the expected social value of those expenditures, where social value accounts for the risk of failure and is measured compared with the next-best alternative. For example, if multiple firms compete to solve a particular technological problem, their combined R&D expenditures might be greater than the prize for the winning firm. This problem is variously known as the "patent racing" or "common pool" problem, and numerous scholarly articles have debated how significant it is in practice and whether alternative reward systems might be preferable. *See generally* Michael Abramowicz, *The Uneasy Case for Patent Races over Auctions*, 60 Stan. L. Rev. 803 (2007).

---

[16] If the reward is in the form of monopoly power that leads to deadweight loss, then there is a social loss, but as noted above, patent rewards need not be coupled to allocation through proprietary pricing. Alternative allocation mechanisms do require taxpayer funding, but tax scholars have explained why the deadweight loss of taxation is largely irrelevant to choices about the magnitude of public spending. *See* Louis Kaplow, *On the (Ir)Relevance of Distribution and Labor Supply Distortion to Government Policy*, 18 J. Econ. Persp. 4 (2004); David A. Weisbach, Daniel J. Hemel & Jennifer Nou, *The Marginal Revenue Rule in Cost-Benefit Analysis*, 160 Tax Notes 1507 (2018).

Over-incentivizing innovation can also occur without patents. One such mechanism is "business stealing," whereby a firm expends a significant amount of resources to produce an invention that is different from—but no better than—existing inventions and then captures some of the existing market share. (Think about how many roughly identical statins are on the market.) A firm might reap a great deal of profit from this strategy without creating any social value, if its product is no better than the ones that existed. But here too, patents can exacerbate the problems.

In addition to the costs from raising prices on patented products and from patent racing, the patent system creates substantial administrative and transaction costs.[17] A rough estimate suggests the costs of obtaining and litigating patents are on the order of $10 billion per year. Hemel & Ouellette, *Beyond the Patents–Prizes Debate*, *supra* at 365. And this estimate does not include nonlitigation legal costs such as the cost to an inventor of determining whether she is at risk of infringing her competitors' patents and negotiating patent licenses. For a complex product, conducting a patent clearance search and negotiating with multiple holders of overlapping patent rights can be costly, leading to concern about "patent thickets" slowing commercialization. *See* Carl Shapiro, *Navigating the Patent Thicket: Cross Licenses, Patent Pools, and Standard Setting*, 1 Innovation Pol'y & Econ. 119 (2000). Litigation and licensing are complicated by the many patents that are erroneously granted by the USPTO and invalidated only when subjected to greater scrutiny, or that are intentionally written in vague terms that make it difficult to determine what they cover. Concern about this "patent quality" problem has driven many of the recent doctrinal changes we will discuss in subsequent chapters.

Complex patent landscapes have given rise to some firms that are solely in the business of patent litigation and licensing. These firms are known variously as "non-practicing entities," "patent assertion entities," or (least favorably) "patent trolls." The terms are not used exactly interchangeably. For instance, a major research university such as Stanford University or the University of Chicago is a non-practicing entity, in that it does not produce and sell products, but it would be odd to refer to it as a patent assertion entity. Patent assertion entities are typically for-profit firms whose business is asserting patents; any patent assertion entity is also (by definition) a non-practicing entity. And "patent troll" is the unfavorable word used to describe any non-practicing entity that is attempting to capture value from a patent in situations where it does not deserve to do so, perhaps because the patent is invalid or vaguely worded. There are ongoing policy debates about whether these types of firms increase the efficiency of technology markets or merely serve as a drag on truly innovative companies.

---

[17] The patent system can also *reduce* transaction costs for joint technology ventures by solving what is known as Arrow's information paradox. Without patents, transacting over a knowledge good is difficult because no one will want to buy an idea without knowing what it is, but once the idea is disclosed, what's to stop the prospective purchaser from walking away and pursuing the idea herself? *See* Jonathan M. Barnett, *Property as Process: How Innovation Markets Select Innovation Regimes*, 119 Yale L.J. 284 (2009).

Given the magnitude of the many social costs arising from the patent system, society should ensure it is obtaining some offsetting benefit. Unfortunately, "we lack sufficient evidence to inform this big picture question of whether strengthening the patent system—through longer or stronger patents—would increase or decrease research investments and innovation, much less whether this benefit is large enough to outweigh patents' costs." Lisa Larrimore Ouellette & Heidi Williams, *Reforming the Patent System* (Hamilton Project Policy Proposal 2020-12). We have chosen examples from the pharmaceutical industry because this is the industry in which patents appear to play the largest role. For example, pharmaceutical executives report that they regularly drop drugs that lack strong patent protection from their development pipelines. Benjamin N. Roin, *Unpatentable Drugs and the Standards of Patentability*, 87 Tex. L. Rev. 503, 545 (2009). One of the best empirical efforts to study the effect of patent protection on research investments documented less private R&D investment in cancer drugs that require longer clinical trials and thus have shorter effective patent terms. Eric Budish, Benjamin N. Roin & Heidi Williams, *Do Firms Underinvest in Long-Term Research? Evidence from Cancer Clinical Trials*, 105 Am. Econ. Rev. 2044 (2015). But even this study could not determine whether the decreased investment incentive was caused by the shorter effective patent term or from corporate short-termism.

All of this is to say that there are good justifications for having a large-scale innovation incentive system such as patent law. The social returns to *innovation*, even accounting for racing and business stealing, appear to be enormous. *See* Benjamin F. Jones & Lawrence H. Summers, *A Calculation of the Social Returns to Innovation* (Nat'l Bureau of Econ. Rsch., Working Paper No. 27863, 2020). But the details of where and when patent law provides too much, too little, or just the right amount of protection are very much up for grabs.

Patents also serve other objectives. Part of the *quid pro quo* for obtaining patent rights is disclosure: in exchange for the right to exclude, the inventor must teach the public how to make and use the invention. This disclosure enables subsequent inventors to improve upon the invention and further grow the store of public knowledge. (Subsequent research efforts might infringe the patent, however, which is a subject we take up later in the book.) Patents can also be privately valuable to market participants—as a signal to potential investors that an invention is new and nonobvious, or as a feather in the cap of an inventor. Here, we can think of patents as providing information to the market, though it may be hard to know how much that information is worth given the problem of patent quality. In any event, these considerations are undoubtedly important, and for some patentees they may be the principal reason for pursuing patents. On the whole, however, they are generally viewed as second-order to the objective of creating incentives for innovation.

As you read through this book and learn patent law, you should consider which legal changes might be warranted to enable the patent system to better achieve all of its objectives.

F. Innovation and Inequality

The focus on a utilitarian framework for patent law doesn't mean that patent law is just about money, or that patent lawyers and scholars shouldn't or don't care about issues of inequality. Throughout history, innovation has been a leading driver of economic growth and has helped lift communities out of poverty. The importance of knowledge goods to the global economy has only increased with the rise of computing and information technologies. But the benefits of innovation are not evenly distributed. Patent law and other legal institutions that incentivize innovation and allocate access to knowledge goods are used both to reinforce and subvert existing power structures and inequalities, including issues related to gender, race, geography, and income.

The connection between innovation and inequality has been the subject of scholarly interest in fields ranging from economics to critical legal studies. Here, we briefly highlight inequalities in two key aspects of innovation: Who becomes an inventor, and who benefits from innovation?

1. Inequality Among Innovators

Inequality among innovators is a pervasive social problem. As one of us has explained:

> Disparities in innovation by gender, race, and class raise concerns for both equity and economic growth. For example, Professor Raj Chetty's team of economists has estimated that if women, racial minorities, and people from low-income backgrounds invented at the same rate as white men from families in the top income quintile, these "lost Einsteins"—or perhaps "lost Maryam Mirzakhanis"—would quadruple the rate of innovation in America. But progress on increasing participation of underrepresented groups in the innovation ecosystem has been glacial. Unless something dramatic changes, gender inequality . . . will persist among American innovators in science and engineering for well over a century.

Amy C. Madl & Lisa Larrimore Ouellette, *Policy Experiments to Address Gender Inequality Among Innovators*, 57 Hous. L. Rev. 813 (2020) (citing Alex Bell et al., *Who Becomes an Inventor in America? The Importance of Exposure to Innovation*, 134 Q.J. Econ. 647 (2019)). These gaps affect not only the *rate* of innovation, but also what *kinds* of innovations are produced. For example, "patents with all-female inventor teams are 35% more likely than all-male teams to focus on women's health." Rembrand Koning, Sampsa Samila & John-Paul Ferguson, *Who Do We Invent for? Patents by Women Focus More on Women's Health, but Few Women Get to Invent*, 372

Science 1345 (2021). Unfortunately, "the evidence base for most policy interventions to reduce the innovation gender gap is depressingly shallow, and there is even less evidence for disparities by race and ethnicity." Madl & Ouellette, *supra*, at 816.

Does the choice of patent law as a key innovation policy ameliorate or exacerbate these inequalities? Some scholars have argued that because patent law places relatively little discretion in the hands of government decisionmakers—requiring the USPTO to grant patents to any inventions that meet relatively objective criteria, without regard to the race, class, or gender of the inventor—it has democratized innovation. *See, e.g.*, B. Zorina Khan, *The Democratization of Invention: Patents and Copyrights in American Economic Development, 1790–1920* (2005). Other scholars have argued, however, that patent law is far from "neutral" to societal identities in its design. *See, e.g.*, Anjali Vats & Deidré A. Keller, *Critical Race IP*, 36 Cardozo Arts & Ent. L.J. 735 (2018) (arguing that "race is an exceedingly important site for intellectual property analysis for which existing considerations of power, inequality, or distributive justice simply do not fully account"); Keith Aoki, *Distributive and Syncretic Motives in Intellectual Property Law (with Special Reference to Coercion, Agency, and Development)*, 40 U.C. Davis L. Rev. 717, 741 (2007) (arguing that the early U.S. patent system exacerbated race-based wealth disparities between inventors).

Additionally, even if patent laws are objectively applied, receiving a patent from the USPTO is worth little in isolation; financially benefiting from patents depends on institutions such as corporate rent-sharing and venture capital, which may have their own biases. *See, e.g.*, Patrick Kline et al., *Who Profits from Patents? Rent-Sharing at Innovative Firms*, 134 Q.J. Econ. 1343 (2019); Dana Kanze et al., *Male and Female Entrepreneurs Get Asked Different Questions by VCs—and It Affects How Much Funding They Get*, Harv. Bus. Rev. (June 27, 2017).

Should these considerations affect the choice of patent law versus other innovation institutions? Although direct funding of R&D through federal grants involves far more discretion for government decisionmakers, race and gender gaps among grant recipients are smaller than among patent inventors.

2. Inequality in Access to Innovation

The patent system is built around the notion that rewarding innovators based on consumers' willingness to pay is a good way to aggregate dispersed information about the social value of new knowledge goods. Policymakers do not have to make tough decisions in doling out R&D funding, such as whether Pfizer or Gilead will make better drugs or whether Apple or Samsung will make better smartphones—they can let the market decide. But this means that R&D investment decisions are often based on consumers' ability to pay, which affects both what innovations are produced and who has access to them.

Consider what innovations will emerge from a patent-based reward system. Firms focused on market returns may choose to invest in lifestyle drugs like Viagra rather than essential medicines, or in the next generation iPhone rather than more accessible internet devices. Private firms will also overinvest in products with negative externalities—ranging from addictive opioids to carbon-emitting power plants—for which the social burden often falls disproportionately on marginalized communities. A system based on disaggregated R&D decisions can also intensify social problems like technological unemployment—job loss due to innovations like automation. The net effect of private R&D investment decisions is product innovations that disproportionately benefit high-income households. *See* Xavier Jaravel, *The Unequal Gains from Product Innovations: Evidence from the U.S. Retail Sector*, 134 Q.J. Econ. 715 (2019); David Rotman, *Technology and Inequality*, MIT Tech. Rev. (Oct. 21, 2014).

One might look at these market failures and conclude that society should rely less on patents and more on non-patent incentives such as direct public funding for R&D. But failures of political markets can be devastating. Government actors are subject to corruption and capture and are limited by the constraints of the next election. And even absent explicit bias, government funding can still compound social inequalities. For example, NIH grants targeted at the most common causes of U.S. infant mortality were effective at reducing mortality, but they exacerbated racial disparities in infant outcomes. *See* David M. Cutler et al., *Induced Innovation and Social Inequality: Evidence from Infant Medical Care*, 47 J. Hum. Res. 456 (2012). More targeted legislation may be needed to shift the distributive balance of what innovations are produced. *See, e.g.*, Christopher Buccafusco, *Disability and Design*, 95 N.Y.U. L. Rev. 952 (2020) ("[T]wo of the most important drivers of innovation for accessible design have been social welfare laws and antidiscrimination laws.").

In addition to distorting what innovations are produced, the patent system can magnify inequalities in who has access to new innovations. Recall the example above of a cancer drug with a competitive price of $100 but a profit-maximizing patent-protected price of $10,000. Unless the government takes steps to increase access to the drug—such as by instituting a national healthcare system—consumers who cannot afford to pay $10,000 will be priced out of the market, resulting in a substantial social loss. For health technologies, many government programs do exist to increase access, alleviating the incentives/access tradeoff. But healthcare is an exception. For other types of technology—including technology that is nearly essential in the modern world, such as computers and smartphones—access is based on willingness to pay.

Again, these distributional concerns are not necessarily a sufficient reason to abandon the patent system, especially if we think political institutions are even less likely to make the right R&D investment decisions. First, as famously articulated in Louis Kaplow & Steven Shavell, *Why the Legal System is Less Efficient than the Income Tax in Redistributing Income*, 23 J. Legal Stud. 667 (1994), the first-best approach to distributional problems would be to make innovation institutions as efficient as possible and then use the tax system to redistribute income so as to promote greater equality. This would have the effect of promoting greater access to patented goods as well. Of course, this argument that distribution should be left to the tax-and-transfer system can be challenged on a number of grounds; for example, see the discussion of political action costs in Lee Anne Fennell & Richard H. McAdams, *The Distributive Deficit in Law and Economics*, 100 Minn. L. Rev. 1051 (2016). Second, and perhaps more compellingly, there is a distributive argument *for* patent law's user-pays allocation system in the case of nonessential goods, and especially luxury goods. The patent system allocates the costs of developing those goods to the consumers who actually use them. *See* Hemel & Ouellette, *Beyond the Patents–Prizes Debate, supra,* at 349–52.

All of this is to say that the patent system will suffer from all of the same pathologies as the markets on which it is based. Those pathologies are amplified by the fact that patent law deliberately distorts markets, creating monopolies or quasi-monopolies. This can exacerbate existing inequalities in access to patented goods. The challenge for policymakers lies in determining how to harness the advantages of patent law while simultaneously ensuring access to essential goods for everyone who needs them.

II. Patentability

The following six chapters examine the requirements for patentability:

Requirements	Overview
2. Novelty (§ 102)	A claimed invention must be *new* compared with each piece of *prior art* (e.g., an earlier publication, patent, use, or sale). The governing statute changed dramatically from a "first to invent" system for applications filed before March 16, 2013, to a "first to disclose" system for more recent applications.
3. Nonobviousness (§ 103)	A claim cannot be an obvious variation or combination of the prior art. To avoid hindsight bias, a court may look to "secondary considerations" such as near-simultaneous invention and failure of others.
4. Utility and Disclosure (§ 112(a), § 101)	An invention must be *useful* at the time of filing: the specification must demonstrate that the invention is operable and that it has a specific and substantial real-world use. The disclosure also must show that the claim satisfies *enablement* (teaching how to make and use the invention without "undue experimentation") and *written description* (showing that the inventor "possessed" the invention at the time of filing).
5. Definiteness and Functional Claiming (§ 112(b), (f))	A claim must describe the scope of the invention with "reasonable certainty" or it is invalid as indefinite. If a claim element is in "means-plus-function" form (like "a means for fastening"), its scope is limited to the corresponding structure in the specification, and the claim is indefinite if there is no corresponding structure.
6. Patentable Subject Matter (§ 101)	If the claim is directed to a patent-ineligible category (laws of nature, natural phenomena, or abstract ideas), it must add "significantly more" to be patentable. Adding conventional steps—implementing an abstract idea on a general-purpose computer or drawing blood for a diagnostic—is not enough.
7. Inventorship (§§ 116, 256) **and Double Patenting** (nonstatutory)	Omitted inventors may seek correction of inventorship and then may independently license the patent. Double patenting prevents an inventor from patenting the same invention or obvious variants thereof unless a terminal disclaimer is filed so that later patents expire at the same time as the first one.

Before turning to the first requirement of novelty, we emphasize several points that apply across the patentability requirements:

Common Law Statutory Interpretation. Most of the patentability requirements are codified in the Patent Act, but many of these statutory provisions are short and vaguely worded. A substantial portion of the law of patentability has been developed by the courts through a common-law process that is informed by the underlying social welfare goals of the patent laws. The following chapters will frequently refer to the policy considerations introduced in Chapter 1 and will include numerous problems to help students develop a lawyer's situation sense for how courts evaluate different cases.

The PHOSITA. These requirements are generally evaluated from the perspective of the Person Having Ordinary Skill in the Art (PHOSITA) as of the effective filing date for the claim at issue.[1] The PHOSITA is a hypothetical person like the "reasonable person" in tort law—you can think of her as a "reasonable researcher" in the field of the patent at issue, with a level of skill and general background knowledge that increases as the field becomes more complex. For example, the PHOSITA will have more skill for a bioinformatics invention than for a simple mechanical invention.

Claim Construction. As noted in Chapter 1, interpreting what a claim covers (i.e., "construing" the claim) is an important preliminary step for assessing its validity. We save a detailed discussion of the law of claim construction for Chapter 8 because it is difficult to understand what is at stake in claim construction without some understanding of the patentability requirements, and because the Federal Circuit has emphasized the importance of the context of a specific allegation of infringement when ruling on claim construction. *See, e.g., Jang v. Bos. Sci. Corp.*, 532 F.3d 1330, 1337 (Fed. Cir. 2008). For now, it is sufficient to know that claims in a patent application are given their "broadest reasonable interpretation," whereas claims in a granted patent are given their "ordinary meaning" to a PHOSITA at the time of filing. As you read the cases in the following chapters, look for places where the interpretation of a claim term might affect the outcome.

Questions of Law or Fact? Most of the patentability requirements are questions of law based on underlying questions of fact. The main exception is determining whether a given prior art reference renders a claim invalid for lack of novelty under § 102 because this is simply a question of whether the reference discloses every claim element, as we discuss in the following chapter. Additionally, the written description requirement of § 112(a) is a question of fact for reasons that seem "inexplicable."

---

[1] One of the hottest debates in patent law is exactly how to abbreviate and pronounce this hypothetical person. *See* Dennis Crouch, *Person (Having) Ordinary Skill in the Art*, Patently-O (Nov. 30, 2018), https://patentlyo.com/patent/2018/11/person-having-ordinary.html.

Anascape v. Nintendo of Am., 601 F.3d 1333, 1342 (Fed. Cir. 2010) (Gajarsa, J., concurring).

    Evidentiary Standards. Patentability is relevant both before and after a patent is granted: the USPTO evaluates whether a patent application satisfies these requirements when deciding whether to grant the application, and the USPTO or the courts may be asked to reevaluate these issues if an accused infringer argues that a granted patent is invalid (in the context of infringement litigation in court or a post-grant review such as IPR at the USPTO). In any of these contexts, the patentee does not have to prove that her patent is valid—the burden is on the USPTO or on the party challenging the patent to show that it is *invalid*. The substantive legal test is generally the same in each context, but the evidentiary standard is different. During examination or during post-grant review at the USPTO, a claim should be rejected if the patent examiner or third-party challenger establishes unpatentability by a *preponderance of the evidence*, meaning it is more likely than not that the claim is unpatentable. But in district court, granted patents are entitled to a presumption of validity, meaning that a challenger must establish invalidity by *clear and convincing evidence. See Microsoft Corp. v. i4i Ltd. P'ship*, 564 U.S. 91 (2011).

Patent examination at the USPTO	Post-grant review at the USPTO's PTAB	Infringement litigation in district court
Claim in patent application	Granted patent claim	Granted patent claim (presumption of validity)
↓	↓	↓
Examiner's rejection (establishing unpatentability by a *preponderance of the evidence*)	Invalidity challenge by third party (establishing invalidity by a *preponderance of the evidence*)	Invalidity challenge by accused infringer (establishing invalidity by *clear and convincing evidence*)
↓	↓	↓
Applicant's response (amend the claim or try to argue against the rejection, including by appeal to the PTAB and then to the Federal Circuit)	Patent owner's response (petition to amend the claim or rebut the argument, with appeal to the Federal Circuit)	Patent owner's response (rebut the argument, with appeal to the Federal Circuit)

It is thus important to pay attention to the context in which a case arises, as we have written previously: "Just because there is not clear and convincing evidence that a patent is invalid does not mean that it should not be held invalid under a lower standard. It is often a mistake for the PTO to rely on precedent from infringement cases when deciding to grant patents." Jonathan S. Masur & Lisa Larrimore Ouellette, *Deference Mistakes*, 82 U. Chi. L. Rev. 643 (2015). That is, it is possible that the same patent could be declared not invalid during litigation—where the "clear and convincing evidence" standard applies—but invalid in a direct appeal from the USPTO, where the "preponderance of the evidence" standard applies. Courts that reason from validity precedents should take care to consider whether the precedent arose in the context of litigation or a direct appeal from the USPTO.

Validity and Preclusion. Neither the USPTO nor the courts determine that a patent claim is legally valid; rather, examiners determine that they have not been able to establish a prima facie case of unpatentability, and the courts determine that a patent challenger has not been able to establish invalidity by clear and convincing evidence. We will thus often write that a claim was held "not invalid"—avoid the temptation to rewrite the double negative! Because courts do not hold a claim to be valid, the validity of a patent can be challenged repeatedly by different defendants. In contrast, once a claim has been held invalid, issue preclusion (also known as collateral estoppel) prevents a patentee from relitigating its validity. *Blonder–Tongue Laboratories v. University of Illinois Foundation*, 402 U.S. 313 (1971).

Additional Resources. As noted in Chapter 1, courts do not grant deference to the USPTO's interpretation of substantive patent law, but the USPTO generally updates training materials and guidance to examiners to be consistent with the most recent caselaw. The MPEP has a free and useful summary of the law of patentability in Chapter 2100.[2] The leading patent treatise is *Chisum on Patents* (available on Lexis), although it is so detailed that it can be difficult to read. Westlaw's resources include *Matthews Annotated Patent Digest*, *Moy's Walker on Patents*, and the Patents section of *Business and Commercial Litigation in Federal Courts* by the Honorable Timothy B. Dyk & Samuel F. Ernst.

---

[2] https://www.uspto.gov/web/offices/pac/mpep/mpep-2100.html.

2. Novelty

To be patentable, an invention must be new. This rule derives from the fundamental patent tradeoff between the benefits of creating incentives for research and development and the costs that arise from patents themselves. If an invention is truly new, the public gains something in exchange for the cost of granting a patent: the benefit of an invention it might otherwise not have enjoyed. If the invention already exists, however, the public can benefit from it without bearing the costs that a patent would create for consumers and subsequent innovators. The goal of patent law is to provide incentives for people to create new and useful inventions, not to claim patent rights on inventions that already exist. The novelty requirement is meant to police these incentives.

This policy justification for patent law's novelty requirement is longstanding and generally compelling. Nonetheless, as we will see, the doctrine of novelty extends well beyond these boundaries. In some cases, even inventions that enrich the store of knowledge—and that were invented by the person who is filing for the patent—may be barred from patenting. In these cases, the law rests upon different principles, which we explore below.

A claimed invention is unpatentable for lack of novelty only if a single piece of *prior art*—an earlier reference, such as a publication or item for sale—discloses every element of the claim, which is also referred to as *anticipating* the claim. For example, as illustrated in the chart below, the simplified Swiffer patent claim described in Chapter 1, which combines a handle, a mop head, a liquid delivery system for cleaning solution, and a disposable cleaning pad, is not anticipated by a sponge mop that has long been in use, by an article describing a mop with a disposable pad, or by an earlier patent on a broom with an integrated cleaning solution. Only a single prior art reference teaching all four claim elements arranged together as they are in the claim would destroy the claim's novelty. *See Net MoneyIN v. VeriSign*, 545 F.3d 1359, 1371 (Fed. Cir. 2008). As we discuss later, however, the separate article and earlier patent references might render the claim invalid as obvious. Claim charts like this are a useful tool for organizing a novelty analysis, as we discuss in more detail below.

Novelty Claim Chart

The Swiffer claim is not anticipated because no single prior art reference discloses every claim element.

Claim elements of simplified Swiffer patent	Prior art references		
	Traditional sponge mop in public use	Article describing mop with disposable pad	Earlier patent on broom with cleaning solution
handle	✓	✓	✓
mop head	✓	✓	
liquid delivery system			✓
disposable cleaning pad		✓	

Novelty doctrine often operates as rules, not as standards, and occasionally harsh rules at that. U.S. patent law takes an expansive approach to novelty: even obscure references can prevent a later inventor from receiving a patent. This rule can have substantial consequences. If an invention was described decades ago in an obscure publication but never implemented in practice, the public has received little benefit—and the resulting unpatentability might deter others from further developing that invention. Unpatentable drugs are regularly dropped from pharmaceutical development pipelines, for example, even if they have tremendous potential social value. *See* Benjamin N. Roin, *Unpatentable Drugs and the Standards of Patentability*, 87 Tex. L. Rev. 503 (2009).

The rule that an invention must be new is simple to state but is the most challenging doctrine to master for many students. When assessing the novelty of a given patent claim in practice—or on an exam—you typically will have a list of references that might invalidate the claim, like publications, other patents, or actions taken by the inventor of the claim at issue or by an independent inventor.

As a preliminary step, you will need to determine which statute applies. The law governing novelty, 35 U.S.C. § 102, was significantly changed by the 2011 America Invents Act (AIA). As discussed in more detail below, if the effective filing date of the claim at issue is before March 16, 2013, it is governed by the "pre-AIA" rules; later claims are governed by the current "post-AIA" statute.

We then recommend the following plan of attack:

A. For each reference that might invalidate the claim, does the *timing* of the reference allow it to serve as prior art under the relevant statute? For example, both the pre-AIA and post-AIA statutes give inventors a one-year grace period between disclosing or using their invention and filing a patent.

B. If yes, does the reference fall under some *statutory category* of prior art: (1) paper prior art (for a "printed publication" or "patent"), (2) real-world prior art (for a reference that is "in public use" or "on sale"), or (3) earlier invention (which is relevant only pre-AIA)?

C. If yes, does the information disclosed in the prior art reference anticipate the patent claim, meaning that it explicitly or inherently discloses every element of the invention? (If not, don't ignore the reference—it may still be relevant for assessing obviousness!)

Sometimes, the answer to each of these questions is straightforward. If you try to claim a particular chemical compound, but that exact compound was disclosed in a published scientific journal article ten years ago, then under either pre- or post-AIA law the article is a printed publication that anticipates the claim. This is true whether the article was published by someone else or by you. But each question can also present more challenging issues. How does a claim's *effective* filing date differ from its actual filing date? What if the reference is a conference poster that is no longer available, or a secret offer for sale that was declined and never made public? What if the chemical compound was frequently made by a prior art process, but no one realized it? What if someone else invented the compound first but did not disclose or use it for many years? The following sections explore these subtleties.

We will tackle the three "plan of attack" questions in order. Section A presents the two versions of § 102 and examines whether the timing of a reference allows it to serve as prior art under the relevant statute. Sections B1, B2, and B3 then discuss three categories of prior art: paper prior art (printed publications and earlier patents), real-world prior art (references that are in public use or on sale), and prior inventions (which are relevant pre-AIA). Finally, Section C explains how to determine whether a given reference anticipates a claim.

A. The America Invents Act and Prior Art Timing

When the AIA was enacted in September 2011, it became the most significant statutory revision to the Patent Act since 1952. A key change was shifting the United States from a "first-to-invent" system to a "first-to-file" system for patent applications with an effective filing date on or after March 16, 2013. Under the pre-AIA law, whether a particular invention was novel was determined primarily by whether there was some piece of prior art that predated the patent applicant's invention. This accorded with widespread intuition about what it meant for an invention to be "new"—

that it is the first time that invention has come into existence—but created administrative difficulties. To resolve a dispute between competing independent inventors under the pre-AIA first-to-invent system, the USPTO had to conduct an evidence-intensive inquiry into invention dates.[1]

Under the post-AIA first-to-file system, the USPTO now joins most other patent offices around the world in simply looking to which inventor got to the patent office first (or, as we will see, publicly disclosed and then got to the patent office within one year). Under this system, invention dates are largely irrelevant. (As we will see, invention dates are not *entirely* irrelevant; for example, the date an invention is "ready for patenting" is relevant to when it may be placed "on sale.") What matters for judging novelty is which party made the invention public first, either by filing for a patent or through some other means.

It is important for students of patent law to learn both systems because many litigated patents will be governed by pre-AIA rules for the next decade. The last pre-AIA patents will not expire until around 2033 (twenty years after filing in 2013), and over one-third of patent assertions are not resolved until within three years of expiration. Additionally, courts interpreting the post-AIA statutory language have looked to pre-AIA caselaw.

Note that the key to determining whether pre- or post-AIA law applies is the *effective filing date of the patent*. As described in Chapter 1, patent applications often "claim priority" to earlier "parent" applications, which include (1) provisional U.S. applications, (2) earlier U.S. applications, (3) applications filed under the Patent Cooperation Treaty, and (4) applications directly filed in a foreign country and then filed in the United States within one year.[2] These are listed on the cover page under "Related U.S. Application Data." If a patent application properly claims priority to an application filed before March 16, 2013, then it is governed by pre-AIA rules.[3]

Below is part of the cover page of a patent filed by the Broad Institute and MIT on CRISPR gene-editing technology, which has been the subject of a high-profile dispute with UC Berkeley. (Jennifer Doudna and Emmanuelle Charpentier won the

---

[1] If two inventors file competing patent applications, this proceeding is known as an *interference*. If one inventor wants to show that her invention predates a prior art reference, she must file an affidavit *swearing behind* the reference with facts demonstrating earlier invention.

[2] For relevant statutes, see 35 U.S.C. § 119 (provisionals and patents filed in other countries); § 120 (claiming priority to an earlier U.S. application); § 121 (divisionals); § 365 (Patent Cooperation Treaty (PCT) applications); § 386 (Hague Agreement (international design) applications).

[3] If an applicant files a first application before March 16, 2013 and a second application on or after March 16, 2013 that includes "new matter," then claims that require the new matter for support do not receive the earlier effective filing date, and the *entire* second application—including claims with a pre-AIA effective filing date—is governed by post-AIA rules. This is true even if claims based on the new matter are later amended or cancelled.

2020 Nobel Prize in Chemistry for developing CRISPR at Berkeley, which filed its own patent applications, but Feng Zhang's group at Broad was the first to use the gene-editing technique in human cells.) Before you look at the answer in the footnote, try to figure out: What is the effective filing date of this application? Which § 102 applies: pre-AIA or post-AIA?[4]

---

(12) **United States Patent**   (10) **Patent No.:**   **US 8,697,359 B1**

Zhang   (45) **Date of Patent:**   *Apr. 15, 2014

---

(54) **CRISPR-CAS SYSTEMS AND METHODS FOR ALTERING EXPRESSION OF GENE PRODUCTS**

(71) Applicants: **The Broad Institute Inc.**, Cambridge, MA (US); **Massachusetts Institute of Technology**, Cambridge, MA (US)

(72) Inventor: **Feng Zhang**, Cambridge, MA (US)

(73) Assignees: **The Broad Institute, Inc.**, Cambridge, MA (US); **Massachusetts Institute of Technology**, Cambridge, MA (US)

(*) Notice: Subject to any disclaimer, the term of this patent is extended or adjusted under 35 U.S.C. 154(b) by 0 days.

This patent is subject to a terminal disclaimer.

(21) Appl. No.: **14/054,414**

(22) Filed: **Oct. 15, 2013**

Related U.S. Application Data

(60) Provisional application No. 61/842,322, filed on Jul. 2, 2013, provisional application No. 61/736,527, filed on Dec. 12, 2012, provisional application No. 61/748,427, filed on Jan. 2, 2013, provisional application No. 61/791,409, filed on Mar. 15, 2013, provisional application No. 61/835,931, filed on Jun. 17, 2013.

(56) **References Cited**

U.S. PATENT DOCUMENTS

2010/0076057 A1	3/2010	Sontheimer et al.
2011/0189776 A1	8/2011	Terns et al.
2011/0223638 A1	9/2011	Wiedenheft et al.
2013/0130248 A1	5/2013	Haurwitz et al.

FOREIGN PATENT DOCUMENTS

WO	WO/2008/108989	9/2008
WO	WO/2010/054108	5/2010
WO	WO/2012/164565	12/2012
WO	WO/2013/098244	7/2013
WO	WO/2013/176772	11/2013

OTHER PUBLICATIONS

Makarova et al., "Evolution and classification of the CRISPR-Cas systems" 9(6) Nature Reviews Microbiology 467-477 (1-23) (Jun. 2011).*

Wiedenheft et al., "RNA-guided genetic silencing systems in bacteria and archaea" 482 Nature 331-338 (Feb. 16, 2012).*

Gasiunas et al., "Cas9-crRNA ribonucleoprotein complex mediates specific DNA cleavage for adaptive immunity in bacteria" 109(39) Proceedings of the National Academy of Sciences USA E2579-E2586 (Sep. 4, 2012).*

Jinek et al., "A Programmable Dual-RNA-Guided DNA Endonuclease in Adaptive Bacterial Immunity" 337 Science 816-821 (Aug. 17, 2012).*

Carroll, "A CRISPR Approach to Gene Targeting" 20(9) Molecular Therapy 1658-1660 (Sep. 2012).*

U.S. Appl. No. 61/652,086, filed May 25, 2012 69 pages.*

Al-Attar et al., Clustered Regularly Interspaced Short Palindromic Repeats (CRISPRs): The Hallmark of an Ingenious Antiviral Defense Mechanism in Prokaryotes, *Biol Chem.* (2011) vol. 392, Issue 4, pp. 277-289.

Hale et al., Essential Features and Rational Design of CRISPR RNAs That Function With the Cas RAMP Module Complex to Cleave RNAs, *Molecular Cell,* (2012) vol. 45, Issue 3, 292-302.

---

[4] The application was *actually* filed on Oct. 15, 2013, but the *effective* filing date is generally the earliest date in the "Related U.S. Application Data" section—in this case, December 12, 2012. Because there was not "new matter" added to the specification after March 16, 2013 (which one can confirm in Public PAIR), the application was governed by the pre-AIA first-to-invent rules. Note also that this patent issued extraordinarily fast—five months after it was actually filed—because the applicant filed an Accelerated Examination Request. See MPEP § 708.02(a).

1. Pre- and Post-AIA § 102 Statutory Text

Both versions of § 102 are complicated, and we recommend reading them multiple times and bookmarking this section for easy reference. What differences do you see between the statutes, and what statutory terms seem particularly important?

Post-AIA § 102 (for patents filed on or after March 16, 2013)

(a) Novelty; Prior Art.—A person shall be entitled to a patent unless—

(1) [**Prior Art Disclosures**] the claimed invention was patented, described in a printed publication, or in public use, on sale, or otherwise available to the public before the effective filing date of the claimed invention; or

(2) [**Prior Patent Filing Disclosures**] the claimed invention was described in a patent issued under section 151, or in an application for patent published or deemed published under section 122(b), in which the patent or application, as the case may be, names another inventor and was effectively filed before the effective filing date of the claimed invention.

(b) Exceptions.—

(1) [**Exceptions to (a)(1) Disclosures**] Disclosures made 1 year or less before the effective filing date of the claimed invention.—A disclosure made 1 year or less before the effective filing date of a claimed invention shall not be prior art to the claimed invention under subsection (a)(1) if—

(A) [**Inventor Disclosures**] the disclosure was made by the inventor or joint inventor or by another who obtained the subject matter disclosed directly or indirectly from the inventor or a joint inventor; or

(B) [**Third-Party Disclosures that Follow *Public* Inventor Disclosures**] the subject matter disclosed had, before such disclosure, been publicly disclosed by the inventor or a joint inventor or another who obtained the subject matter disclosed directly or indirectly from the inventor or a joint inventor.

(2) [**Exceptions to (a)(2)**] Disclosures appearing in applications and patents.—A disclosure shall not be prior art to a claimed invention under subsection (a)(2) if—

(A) [**Inventor Patent Disclosures**] the subject matter disclosed was obtained directly or indirectly from the inventor or a joint inventor;

(B) [**Third-Party Patent Disclosures that Follow *Public* Inventor Disclosures**] the subject matter disclosed had, before such subject matter was effectively filed under subsection (a)(2), been publicly disclosed by the inventor or a joint inventor or another who obtained the subject matter disclosed directly or indirectly from the inventor or a joint inventor; or

(C) [**Commonly Owned Patent Disclosures**] the subject matter disclosed and the claimed invention, not later than the effective filing date of the claimed invention, were owned by the same person or subject to an obligation of assignment to the same person.

(c) Common Ownership Under Joint Research Agreements.—Subject matter disclosed and a claimed invention shall be deemed to have been owned by the same person or subject to an obligation of assignment to the same person in applying the provisions of subsection (b)(2)(C) if—

(1) the subject matter disclosed was developed and the claimed invention was made by, or on behalf of, 1 or more parties to a joint research agreement that was in effect on or before the effective filing date of the claimed invention;

(2) the claimed invention was made as a result of activities undertaken within the scope of the joint research agreement; and

(3) the application for patent for the claimed invention discloses or is amended to disclose the names of the parties to the joint research agreement.

(d) Patents and Published Applications Effective as Prior Art.—For purposes of determining whether a patent or application for patent is prior art to a claimed invention under subsection (a)(2), such patent or application shall be considered to have been effectively filed, with respect to any subject matter described in the patent or application—

(1) if paragraph (2) does not apply, as of the actual filing date of the patent or the application for patent; or

(2) if the patent or application for patent is entitled to claim a right of priority under section 119, 365(a), 365(b), 386(a), or 386(b), or to claim the benefit of an earlier filing date under section 120, 121, 365(c), or 386(c), based upon 1 or more prior filed applications for patent, as of the

filing date of the earliest such application that describes the subject matter.

Pre-AIA § 102 (for patents filed before March 16, 2013)

A person shall be entitled to a patent unless —

(a) [**Novelty**] the invention was known or used by others in this country, or patented or described in a printed publication in this or a foreign country, before the invention thereof by the applicant for patent, or

(b) [**Statutory Bars**] the invention was patented or described in a printed publication in this or a foreign country or in public use or on sale in this country, more than one year prior to the date of the application for patent in the United States, or

(c) [**Abandonment**] he has abandoned the invention, or

(d) [**Late Filing in the U.S.**] the invention was first patented or caused to be patented, or was the subject of an inventor's certificate, by the applicant or his legal representatives or assigns in a foreign country prior to the date of the application for patent in this country on an application for patent or inventor's certificate filed more than twelve months before the filing of the application in the United States, or

(e) [**Earlier U.S. Patent Applications**] the invention was described in — (1) an application for patent, published under section 122(b), by another filed in the United States before the invention by the applicant for patent or (2) a patent granted on an application for patent by another filed in the United States before the invention by the applicant for patent, except that an international application filed under the treaty defined in section 351(a) [the Patent Cooperation Treaty] shall have the effects for the purposes of this subsection of an application filed in the United States only if the international application designated the United States and was published under Article 21(2) of such treaty in the English language; or

(f) [**Derivation**] he did not himself invent the subject matter sought to be patented, or

(g) [**First-to-Invent**] (1) during the course of an interference conducted under section 135 [for USPTO proceedings] or section 291 [for federal district court proceedings], another inventor involved therein establishes, to the extent permitted in section 104, that before such person's invention thereof the invention was made by such other inventor and not abandoned, suppressed, or concealed, or (2) before such person's invention thereof, the invention was made in this country by another inventor who had not abandoned, suppressed, or concealed it. In determining priority of invention under this subsection, there shall be considered not only the respective dates of conception and reduction to practice of the invention, but also the reasonable diligence of one who was first to conceive and last to reduce to practice, from a time prior to conception by the other.

2. The Structure of Pre- and Post-AIA § 102

Below is a graphical illustration of each statute mapped onto an invention timeline; can you match the statutory sections above onto these pictures?

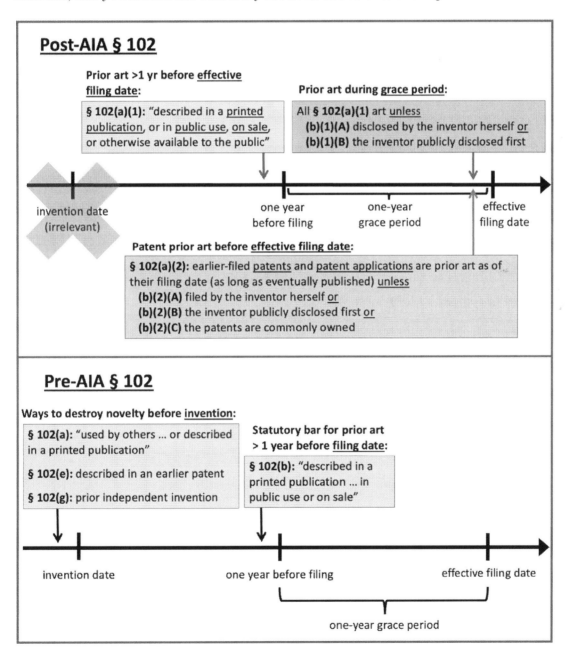

Let us look at post-AIA law first. Section 102(a) is best understood as the baseline requirement of novelty: if the invention was available to the public before the person seeking a patent filed their patent application, then it cannot be patented. That is, if patent applicant is not enriching the state of knowledge available to the public but instead merely duplicating knowledge that already exists, the applicant cannot obtain a patent. This is the meaning of the word "disclosure" in § 102(a)(1): a disclosure is a mechanism by which the invention becomes "available to the public" in some form—although as we will see, "public" in § 102 is a term of art that encompasses many things that might seem rather private!

Section 102(a)(1) lists the categories of prior art that will prohibit a subsequent filer from obtaining a patent. Much of this chapter will be devoted to figuring out what falls within those categories—what does it mean for an invention to be in public use or described in a printed publication, for instance? For the moment, the only important thing is to know that these are the statutory categories. In addition, note that a prior art reference under post-AIA § 102(a) does not have to come from someone other than the patent applicant. The *patent applicant herself* can create prior art that will block her own patent. Section 102(a)(1) does not distinguish between prior art created by the patent applicant and prior art created by someone else.

Section 102(a)(2) is why the post-AIA law is described as a "first to file" regime. That section says that an inventor cannot obtain a patent if anyone has previously filed a patent application on the same invention, even if that application has not yet been published. That is, absent § 102(a) prior art, the first party to file a patent application will be entitled to the patent. However, this section only applies if the patent is eventually granted or if the application is eventually published. (Recall that patent applications are kept secret for 18 months and then usually published.) If the applicant abandons the application before the 18-month mark and the application is never published, it does not block subsequent applications under § 102(a)(2).

Section 102(b) contains the exceptions to § 102(a): the situations in which § 102(a) prior art *will not* block an applicant from receiving a patent. Section 102(b) parallels § 102(a): § 102(b)(1) applies to § 102(a)(1), and § 102(b)(2) applies to § 102(a)(2). Section 102(b)(1)(A) states that a § 102(a) piece of prior art will not block a patent applicant from receiving a patent *if the prior art was created by the applicant herself,* **and** *if the applicant files within a year of the prior art being created.* Section 102(b)(1)(A) thus creates a one-year "grace period" for prior art that was disclosed by the patent applicant. This includes § 102(a) prior art that was disclosed by someone who obtained the relevant information from the patent applicant herself. That is, if Ava tells Boyd about an invention, and then Boyd discloses the information in a way that creates § 102(a)(1) prior art, patent law treats that disclosure as if it came from Ava. Ava can still obtain a patent if she files within a year.

Section 102(b)(1)(B) states that § 102(a)(1) prior art *that comes from someone else* won't bar an applicant so long as the applicant "publicly disclosed" the invention before the creation of the § 102(a) prior art, and so long as the applicant files within a year. (What it means to "publicly disclose," and how that might differ from merely "disclosing," is a subject we take up later in the chapter.) Put together, §§ 102(b)(1)(A) and 102(b)(1)(B) create both a safe harbor and a ticking clock for a prospective patent applicant who discloses an invention publicly. Once that applicant discloses the invention per § 102(a), (a) her clock starts ticking and she must file within a year, per § 102(b)(1)(A), and (b) if her disclosure was public, she is protected against disclosures by any other parties that occur during that time period, per § 102(b)(1)(B).

Section 102(b)(2) operates the same way as § 102(b)(1), but with respect to patent application filings. An earlier patent filing does not count as § 102(b)(1) prior art against a later applicant if the filing was based on information derived from the applicant (§ 102(b)(2)(A)) or if the applicant had previously publicly disclosed the invention (§ 102(b)(2)(B)). Section 102(b)(2)(C) also exempts patent filings with the same owner or assignee. These § 102(b)(2) exceptions do not have the same one-year limit as the § 102(b)(1) exceptions, but as we discuss below, patent filings that fall within these exceptions can still become § 102(a)(1) prior art after they are published.

Accordingly, post-AIA § 102 is best understood as a "first to publish" regime, rather than a first to file regime. The first inventor to publicly disclose an invention (by creating public § 102(a) prior art) blocks every other party from ever obtaining a patent and locks in a one-year grace period within which she can file and obtain a patent herself.

Now consider pre-AIA § 102. Pre-AIA law functions similarly in many respects, but the timing rules and trigger dates are different. Pre-AIA § 102(a) lists essentially the same categories of prior art as post-AIA § 102(a), but under pre-AIA law those categories of prior art only bar an inventor when they come into existence before the inventor's date of *invention*, not her date of *filing*. It's generally hard to disclose an invention without first having invented it, so it's nearly impossible for an inventor to create pre-AIA § 102(a) prior art that blocks herself, unlike under post-AIA law. (It's not entirely impossible, and we describe one situation in which this can occur below.) The principle behind pre-AIA § 102(a) is the same as the principle behind post-AIA § 102(a): if the public already knew about the invention, you haven't added anything to the store of public knowledge and don't deserve a patent.

Pre-AIA § 102(b), sometimes known as the "statutory bar" provision, includes very similar categories of prior art and operates even more similarly to post-AIA law. Under § 102(b), by and large, if *anyone* creates prior art, then *everyone* has a one-year grace period in which to file for a patent; after a year, *everyone* is barred. Unlike post-AIA law, by and large, § 102(b) does not distinguish based on who created the prior art. (The "by and large" is the subject of much debate within patent law and is covered in detail in the chapter below.)

Pre-AIA § 102(e) operates similarly to post-AIA § 102(a)(2) by preventing an inventor from obtaining a patent if anyone has previously filed a patent application on the same invention, as long as the patent is eventually granted or the application is eventually published. But like for pre-AIA § 102(a), these other patent applications become prior art only if they were filed before the inventor's date of invention, not her date of filing.

Finally, pre-AIA law couples these novelty provisions with § 102(g), which asks whether the party seeking a patent actually invented first, or whether some other party beat her to the invention. Section 102(g) is the provision that really makes pre-AIA law a "first to invent" regime.

One important consequence of the way these statutes are written is that many of the novelty cases that arise under both pre-AIA and post-AIA law involve prior art that was created by the inventor herself and may now bar her patent. These "first-party cases" are instances where the party seeking the patent has indeed created something new and enriched the state of knowledge, and yet nonetheless she is barred from patenting her creation. Accordingly, they require policy justifications separate from the standard policy rationale that undergirds the requirement of novelty (which is that the applicant has not enriched the store of public knowledge). We will discuss these policy justifications below in the course of discussing the various forms of prior art, as there are different justifications for various types of prior art.

Practice Problems: Pre- and Post-AIA § 102 Timing

Although some students find the bright-line rules of § 102 timing refreshing after encountering the ambiguous standards of many legal doctrines, many others find these statutes to be the most challenging aspect of a Patent Law course. To check your own understanding, we highly recommend tackling the following practice problems.

Alyssa, an entrepreneur in Palo Alto, invents a novel diaper in April 2012 and files a U.S. patent application in September 2013. Consider each of the following additional sets of facts. In each scenario, is Alyssa entitled to receive a patent based on the facts presented? In your explanation, please note the relevant statutory section (e.g., "post-AIA § 102(a)(2)").

1. In May 2013, Alyssa publishes an article describing the diaper in *Parenting* magazine.

2. In June 2013, Luis independently invents the same diaper in Mexico and immediately puts the diapers into public use in his publicly accessible childcare facility in Mexico City.

3. In June 2013, Luis independently invents the same diaper, and in July 2013, he publishes a Spanish-language article describing it in *Mi Bebé*.

4. In May 2013, Alyssa publishes an article describing the diaper in *Parenting* magazine. In June 2013, Luis independently invents the same diaper. And

then in July 2013, Luis publishes a Spanish-language article describing it in *Mi Bebé.*

5. In June 2013, Luis independently invents the same diaper, and in July 2013, he files a U.S. patent application claiming the diaper. His patent application is published 18 months after filing.

6. In May 2013, Alyssa publishes an article describing the diaper in *Parenting* magazine. In June 2013, Luis independently invents the same diaper. In July 2013, Luis files a U.S. patent application claiming the diaper.

7. In August 2012, Alyssa places her diaper on sale by offering to sell it to Strawberry Baby, a boutique in Menlo Park. The boutique declines.

8. Please re-answer questions 1–7 after shifting all dates in the scenarios above back by one year. Alyssa now invents in April 2011 and files her patent application in September 2012, her publication in question 1 is in May 2012, etc.

Discussion Questions: Distinctions Between Pre- and Post-AIA Law

Post- and Pre-AIA law differ in a variety of important ways, many of which we have already discussed or will explore further below. Here, we pause to highlight two large-scale impacts wrought by the change in law.

1. *International Prior Art.* Pre-AIA law is in many respects quite American-centric. Although printed publications count as prior art anywhere in the world, sections 102(a), 102(b), and 102(g)(2) all classify other types of activities as prior art only if they occurred in the United States. This means that inventors who, for instance, placed their inventions into public use in a foreign country before the critical date could nonetheless find themselves squeezed out of the American market if someone obtained an American patent that their prior use did not bar. The existence of this rule might have been due in part to a nationalistic desire to benefit American inventors at the expense of foreign inventors; it might also have been due to concerns regarding reliable evidence from overseas. (These provisions of the law are quite old.)

Regardless, the AIA eliminated these geographic limitations, as some of the practice problems above indicate. This is an appropriate recognition of the fact that innovation can easily cross borders, as well as the fact that the internet and related technologies have made it easier to prove that various activities took place abroad. There may well be other consequences from the change in law as well. For instance, some scholars have argued that the AIA will lead to greater legal protection for long-standing cultural knowledge. *See* Ryan Levy & Spencer Green, *Pharmaceuticals and Biopiracy: How the America Invents Act May Reduce the Misappropriation of Traditional Medicine*, 23 U. Miami Bus. L. Rev. 401 (2015). Do you think these are unequivocally positive changes, or will there be downsides for the American innovation system?

2. *First-to-File and Small Inventors.* One concern that accompanied the passage of the AIA was that it would disadvantage inventors with fewer resources—small and medium-sized business, as well as solo inventors—to the advantage of larger corporations. Larger corporations of course have many advantages in the race to invent, including economies of scale and substantial resources that can be deployed toward a particular line of R&D. But the AIA threatened to add another layer of advantage: no longer would it be enough for a smaller inventor to beat a large corporation to the invention; now the small inventor would have to beat the larger player to the Patent Office. Larger corporations typically have greater access to patent counsel—either in-house or external—to file patent applications, not to mention the resources to devote to those operations. There was thus concern that the AIA would exacerbate the trend toward large corporations dominating patent filings. *See, e.g.,* David S. Abrams & R. Polk Wagner, *Poisoning the Next Apple? How the America Invents Act Harms Inventors*, 65 Stan. L. Rev. 517 (2013).

The AIA offers a partial solution to this issue by creating what is effectively a "first-to-publish" regime, rather than strictly a first-to-file regime. If an inventor is the first to publish her invention, she will (1) bar anyone else from obtaining a patent on the invention under § 102(a), (2) disqualify any subsequently published prior art (such as prior art from a competing inventor) from serving as prior art against her, via § 102(b)(2)(B), and (3) create a year-long grace period for herself during which time she may file for a patent, under § 102(b)(1)(A). We will explore all of these provisions and rules in greater detail below, but the bottom line is that a smaller inventor who fears losing a race to the patent office has a better alternative: simply publish the details of the invention, such as on a website. It is too early to say with certainty whether these provisions of the AIA have helped level the playing field between large and small innovators. But it is fair to say that the first-to-publish rule represents at least a creative potential solution to the inequities created by a race to the patent office. Can you think of other possible solutions that Congress might have enacted to level the playing field between small and large inventors? Does this seem like the best approach, or is there another option that would have been preferable? Why do you think Congress chose this one?

B1. Paper Prior Art: Printed Publications & Patents

Both versions of § 102 describe various statutory categories of prior art. We'll begin with written disclosures in printed publications and patents—which we will collectively refer to as "paper prior art"—before turning to real-world disclosures through use or sale of the invention.

1. Printed Publications

A "printed publication" can be prior art under pre-AIA § 102(a) or (b), or under post-AIA § 102(a)(1), and (so far as we know) the term has the same meaning under either statute. The Federal Circuit has interpreted the "printed publication" category broadly, encompassing a reference that is obscure or only temporarily available as long as "persons interested and ordinarily skilled in the subject matter or art, exercising reasonable diligence, can locate it." *Samsung Elecs. v. Infobridge Pte.*, 929 F.3d 1363, 1369 (Fed. Cir. 2019). A reference can be a printed publication even if no member of the public actually accessed it. Electronic publications, including digital videos, can be printed publications, although a purely oral presentation that is not recorded cannot.

Whether a reference is sufficiently accessible to constitute a printed publication is a legal conclusion based on a case-by-case balancing of underlying factual determinations. Courts have interpreted this standard to include many references that might not seem very accessible. If even a single copy of a reference is in a public library indexed by subject matter, it is a printed publication. See *In re Hall*, 781 F.2d 897 (Fed. Cir. 1986). Other factors favoring accessibility include distribution without confidentiality restrictions, a large number of people of ordinary skill in the art having access, availability for longer periods of time (e.g., days rather than minutes), relative ease of copying, and the absence of restrictions on copying the material (or the lack of reasonable expectations that the material would not be copied). *See In re Klopfenstein*, 380 F.3d 1345 (Fed. Cir. 2004). Where the underlying facts are not in dispute, the Federal Circuit has often resolved the question of whether something is a printed publication as a matter of law.

The date a publication is available as a reference is determined by when a member of the relevant public could have accessed it. Journal articles are thus dated by when they become available to the public, not when they are submitted to the publisher or mailed. The date of accessibility can be established through routine business practices. For online materials, the Wayback Machine at archive.org can be used to establish the date of accessibility. Timestamped material from social media websites can also be used as prior art.

Again, remember that invalidating prior art can be disclosed by either a third party or the inventor herself, although both pre- and post-AIA rules generally provide the inventor a one-year grace period between disclosing the invention and filing a U.S. patent.

The following references have been held to be sufficiently accessible to constitute printed publications:

- A single cataloged doctoral thesis in a German university library that has a routine business practice of cataloging, even without specific evidence of the date the thesis was cataloged. *In re Hall*, 781 F.2d 897 (Fed. Cir. 1986).

- A poster displayed at two scientific conferences for a total of about three days, with no restriction on copying, even though the poster was not indexed in any database or distributed to the public. *In re Klopfenstein*, 380 F.3d 1345 (Fed. Cir. 2004).

- A paper distributed orally to between 50 and 500 people in the relevant art, after which copies were distributed on request, without restrictions, to as many as six people. *Massachusetts Inst. of Tech. v. AB Fortia*, 774 F.2d 1104 (Fed. Cir. 1985).

- An Australian patent application kept on microfilm at the Australian Patent Office. *In re Wyer*, 655 F.2d 221 (C.C.P.A. 1981).

- An electronic post to a newsgroup populated by people in the relevant art, even though the post was non-indexed and non-searchable. *Suffolk Techs., LLC v. AOL Inc.*, 752 F.3d 1358 (Fed. Cir. 2014).

- A sales catalog for which hundreds of copies were distributed at a trade show without restriction, even though the trade show was open exclusively to dealers and not the general public, and there was no evidence as to whether or not a person of ordinary skill in the art attended the show. *GoPro, Inc. v. Contour IP Holding LLC*, 908 F.3d 690 (Fed. Cir. 2018).

In contrast, these references were found to *not* be printed publications:

- Student theses that were not cataloged or indexed in a meaningful way. *In re Cronyn*, 890 F.2d 1158 (Fed. Cir. 1989); *In re Bayer*, 568 F.2d 1357 (C.C.P.A. 1978).

- An article uploaded in 1999 to a university library website organized by author and year but without a working keyword search option. *Acceleration Bay v. Activision Blizzard*, 908 F.3d 765 (Fed. Cir. 2018).

- A presentation of lecture slides that was of limited duration. *Univ. of California v. Howmedica, Inc.*, 530 F. Supp. 846 (D.N.J. 1981) (discussed by *Klopfenstein, supra*).

- An abstract that was brought to a technical conference to distribute upon request to the authors, where there was no evidence that it had been requested or disseminated. *Norian Corp. v. Stryker Corp.*, 363 F.3d 1321 (Fed. Cir. 2004).

- Four technical reports distributed to fifty persons or organizations involved in a military computing project that were of the class of documents typically distributed with a "not for public release" notice. *Telecom, Inc. v. Datapoint Corp.*, 908 F.2d 931 (Fed. Cir. 1990).

- Monographs distributed by an inventor to (1) university and hospital colleagues, where there was evidence in the record that academic norms gave rise to an expectation that the disclosures would remain confidential, and (2) two commercial entities, where there was an oral agreement on confidentiality. *Cordis Corp. v. Bos. Sci. Corp.*, 561 F.3d 1319 (Fed. Cir. 2009).

Discussion Questions: Printed Publications

1. *First-Party Printed Publications.* It is easy to see why a printed publication created by someone other than the patent applicant should bar the applicant from obtaining a patent. If the invention already existed, and the applicant did not enrich the store of knowledge, then there is nothing to be gained from awarding a patent. The question is, why should a printed publication *created by the applicant* bar the applicant from obtaining a patent? (Note that many of the cases mentioned above involve applicant-created prior art.) Suppose Alice invents something new and publishes a paper about her invention. Thirteen months later, Alice files for a patent on her invention. Under pre-AIA § 102(b) or post-AIA § 102(a), she cannot obtain a patent. (Her safe-harbor period under post-AIA § 102(b)(1)(A) has expired.) What do you think is the policy rationale behind this rule? From the perspective of the public, or of society as a whole, what is gained from barring patents in these situations? What, if anything, is lost?

2. *Obscure Printed Publications.* What are the advantages and disadvantages of interpreting "printed publication" so broadly that a patent can be invalidated based on an obscure or ephemeral piece of third-party prior art that most inventors are unlikely to be aware of? If the invention has already been described, even in an obscure reference, is that evidence that the patent incentive is less important for spurring that invention? Would a requirement that the publication be more easily accessible by the public be difficult to implement in practice? Would this policy change have an affect on inequalities among innovators? How does the rise of search tools like Google Scholar affect the inquiry into public accessibility of online references?

3. *Patenting Academic Research.* After the 2004 *Klopfenstein* decision held a temporary conference poster to be a prior art printed publication, commentators worried that the decision "could have a further chilling effect on conference presentations by university researchers seeking to disseminate early results." Margo A. Bagley, *Academic Discourse and Proprietary Rights: Putting Patents in Their Proper Place*, 47 B.C. L. Rev. 217, 244 (2006). The availability of state university research files under open records laws may also limit the patentability of some university research. *See* Jason Rantanen & Madison Murhammer Colon, *Can Public Universities Patent Their Research?: The Tension Between Open Records Laws and*

Patentability, 69 Drake L. Rev. (2021). Is this a policy concern, and if so, should it be addressed through patent law or through open records rules? Should academic research be treated differently from industry research?

Practice Problems: Printed Publications

Do you think the references described below are sufficiently publicly accessible to count as prior art printed publications? (Assume they qualify under the relevant timing provisions.) If you are unsure, what additional facts would you want to know to determine whether or not they qualify?

1. A medical device manufacturer has been sued for infringement of a patent claiming a method for correcting spinal column deviations such as scoliosis. In arguing that the patent is invalid, the manufacturer points to a CD containing a video demonstration and related slide presentation that it distributed to spinal surgeons at three industry meetings before the patent's effective filing date. The meetings were attended by nearly 100 surgeons. *See Medtronic v. Barry*, 891 F.3d 1368 (Fed. Cir. 2018).

2. The inventors of a cybersecurity patent on "event monitoring enabling responses to anomalous live disturbances" (EMERALD) submitted a paper on the invention for publication in conference proceedings more than one year before filing a patent. When submitting the paper, one of the inventors also placed a copy on his firm's file transfer protocol (FTP) server at ftp://ftp.csl.sri.com/pub/emerald/ndss98.ps for a week, making it publicly accessible to anyone who visited that address without restrictions on copying. In seven other instances, the inventor directed third parties to the papers in the same "emerald" FTP subdirectory to find other papers related to the EMERALD project. *See SRI Int'l v. Internet Sec. Sys.*, 511 F.3d 1186 (Fed. Cir. 2008).

3. A scientist attends a conference of experts in her field, where she presents her invention at a plenary session attended by 250 other leading scientists. During the presentation she talks for 60 minutes and takes questions for another 30 minutes but does not show slides or make copies of her paper available. *See In re Klopfenstein*, 380 F.3d 1345, 1349 n.4 (Fed. Cir. 2004).

2. Patents as Prior Art

Patents are an important category of paper prior art for subsequent inventions. Despite efforts to improve search tools for "non-patent literature," U.S. patent examiners overwhelmingly focus on patent prior art when evaluating applications.

Patent prior art is also treated differently under both pre- and post-AIA § 102. Patents can be prior art under three categories:

First, patents (including most foreign patents) are "patented" prior art under the same sections as printed publications—pre-AIA § 102(a) or (b), and post-AIA § 102(a)(1)—as of when they are issued. But the nuances of the "patented" category are generally irrelevant because almost all patents become prior art under other provisions, and usually sooner.

Second, patents and patent applications—whether U.S. or foreign—are prior art "printed publications" when published. At most patent offices, patent applications are generally published when granted or 18 months after the earliest priority date, whichever is sooner.[5] When considering a patent as a "printed publication," there is no need to distinguish between the specification and the claims—the entire patent document is prior art.

Third, under pre-AIA § 102(e) and post-AIA § 102(a)(2), any U.S. patent or patent application that is eventually published is prior art *as of its effective filing date*. This means that if Alice files a U.S. patent application that is published 18 months later, Alice's application is prior art against an application Becca files a month after Alice, even though Becca has no way of knowing about Alice's prior art for the first 17 months that her application is pending. This rule applies only to patents and patent applications filed *in the United States*, including international applications filed under the Patent Cooperation Treaty that designate the United States.[6] A patent application that is filed only in China is prior art as of when it is published, not when it is filed.

Note that Alice's application does need to be *published* (including through issuance) to trigger this pre-publication prior art rule. If Alice's application is abandoned before publication, it never becomes prior art. But if a patent application is abandoned *after* publication, it is still prior art as of its filing date. One study found that abandoned applications are actually more likely than issued patents to be used by patent examiners as prior art. Christopher A. Cotropia & David L. Schwartz, *The Hidden Value of Abandoned Applications to the Patent System*, 61 B.C. L. Rev. (2020).

Additionally, note that an inventor's *own* patent applications are prior art against her only as of the date they are published. Pre-AIA § 102(e) applies only to patents filed "by another," which means patents not filed by the same combination of inventors (known as an "inventive entity"). Similarly, post-AIA § 102(a)(2) applies

---

[5] 35 U.S.C. § 122(b)(2) contains exceptions to this rule for U.S. patents, including that an applicant who has not filed corresponding foreign patents at offices that require 18-month publication may request that an application not be published until it is granted.

[6] If a U.S. application claims priority to an earlier-filed foreign patent application not filed under the Patent Cooperation Treaty, the relevant prior art date is the U.S. filing date pre-AIA and the foreign filing date post-AIA. For more on international patent institutions, see Chapter 20.

only to a patent that "names another inventor," and post-AIA § 102(b)(2)(C) creates an even broader exception for patents "owned by the same person or subject to an obligation of assignment to the same person." Thus, § 102 does not prevent an inventor from filing a second patent application that is identical or very similar to an application she filed a year earlier. Instead, the double patenting doctrine, discussed in Chapter 7, prevents an inventor from obtaining multiple patents on the same invention.

Practice Problems: Patents as Prior Art

1. Mila invents a novel roller skate in January 2012 and files a U.S. patent application in July 2013. Hayk independently invents the same roller skate in April 2013 and files a U.S. patent application in May 2013. Both patent applications are published in due course, 18 months after filing. Who gets a patent?

2. Same facts as question 1, but Hayk decides to abandon his patent application in May 2014 because he does not think there is a large market for the roller skate.

3. Same facts as question 2, but Hayk now abandons his patent application in May 2015.

3. "Known . . . by Others" and "Otherwise Available to the Public"

For the most part, knowledge that becomes publicly available—and thus will invalidate a patent—will fall into one of the categories described here or in the next section. Either the prior art will be written down, in which case it will be a printed publication or a patent; or the prior art will relate to a real-world embodiment of the invention, in which case it will be in public use or on sale. However, it is possible to imagine cases in which knowledge of an invention becomes public without one of the denominated categories of prior art being implicated. For instance, imagine the following hypothetical scenario:

> On January 1, Alice creates an invention, which she stores in her laboratory. On January 2, she gives a public lecture about the invention to a group of 1000 leading scientists in her field in which she describes the invention in detail. Her lecture is purely audial; there are no slides displayed and no papers distributed. Many of the scientists who attend the lecture take careful notes, but their notes are never published. On January 3, Brian independently creates the same invention, and on January 4 he files for a patent.

Will Brian be able to obtain a patent in this scenario? Alice did not herself create a printed publication. The notes of the conference attendees, while printed, were never made public, so they cannot qualify. Alice also did not put the invention into public use or offer to sell it, so those types of prior art are not implicated. (More on that below.) Yet information about the invention is widely known by people in the field before Brian invents or patents it, and thus it would be hard to say that Brian meaningfully enriched the store of public knowledge. Granting him a patent in these circumstances would seem to run counter to the principles that undergird the law of novelty.

If these events took place before March 2013, it seems likely that Brian's patent would be barred by pre-AIA § 102(a) because the invention was "known . . . by others" before Brian's invention. Some litigants have gone so far as to argue that under pre-AIA § 102(a), information "known . . . by others" before the date of invention could anticipate a patent even if that information is not disclosed or used, but courts have rejected these arguments. "[T]o invalidate a patent based on prior knowledge or use, that knowledge or use must have been available to the public." *Woodland Tr. v. Flowertree Nursery, Inc.*, 148 F.3d 1368 (Fed. Cir. 1998). Here, however, the fact that the information was known to 1000 people in the field seems sufficiently public to qualify. Nonetheless, we are unaware of a single case in which a patent was invalidated by virtue of being "known . . . by others" without reference to any other category of prior art. Situations in which knowledge of an invention reaches the public without implicating any of the other categories of prior art appear to be very rare.

The "known . . . by others" language was removed by the AIA. Post-AIA law contains its own catch-all category: "otherwise available to the public." The Federal Circuit has yet to decide a case that squarely implicates this provision, but an oral presentation, unaccompanied by any printed matter, might well be an example of something that is "otherwise available to the public." Accordingly, it seems unlikely that Brian would be able to obtain a patent if these events took place after March 2013, with post-AIA law in effect.

The upshot is that these provisions in pre- and post-AIA law likely exist to capture situations, such as the hypothetical scenario above, in which information has been made public but without implicating one of the other enumerated categories of prior art. It is difficult to know for sure, however, precisely because such situations so rarely arise.

4. The Enablement Standard for Paper Prior Art

As we will explore in more detail later, a patent is only valid if it satisfies the *enablement* requirement of 35 U.S.C. § 112, meaning that it must teach a researcher in that field how to make and use the invention without "undue experimentation." Similarly, printed publications and patents are only prior art for what they enable.

After all, if a printed publication or patent does not teach a researcher in the field how to make an invention, it can hardly be said to have added that invention to the store of public knowledge. A subsequent inventor who actually figures out how to build this invention and teaches the public should not be barred from obtaining a patent by a publication that does not do the same.

For example, the fictional 1995 film *Clueless*, in which the lead character Cher uses a computer program to determine whether certain clothing combinations match, would not anticipate a real-world outfit-choosing algorithm. The program is fictitious and contains no details to help a programmer implement it in real life. The film is prior art, however, for what it does contain: the idea of using a computer to select matching outfits, which may be relevant for determining whether an outfit-choosing invention is obvious. *See Symbol Techs., Inc. v. Opticon, Inc.*, 935 F.2d 1569 (Fed. Cir. 1991) ("While a reference must enable someone to practice the invention in order to anticipate under § 102[], a non-enabling reference may qualify as prior art for the purpose of determining obviousness under § 103.").

Prior art is presumed to be enabling. The patentee thus has the burden of showing that an otherwise anticipatory prior art reference is not enabling, both during examination and in subsequent challenges to validity. *See In re Antor Media Corp.*, 689 F.3d 1282, 1289 (Fed. Cir. 2012); *Amgen Inc. v. Hoechst Marion Roussel, Inc.*, 314 F.3d 1313, 1354 (Fed. Cir. 2003). For an argument that this burden of proving non-enablement has a negative effect on innovation due to the large number of references that disclose an invention (such as a chemical structure) without actually enabling it, see Sean B. Seymore, *Rethinking Novelty in Patent Law*, 60 Duke L.J. 919 (2011).

The enablement standard for paper prior art is similar to the enablement requirement of § 112, but there is an important difference. As we will discuss later, § 112—in conjunction with the utility requirement of § 101—requires a patentee to disclose a known *use* for an invention in addition to disclosing how to make the invention. The predecessor court to the Federal Circuit explained this distinction in *In re Hafner*, 410 F.2d 1403 (C.C.P.A. 1969), in which a patent applicant's own earlier patent application—which had been rejected under § 112 for failing to disclose any use for a new chemical compound—was used as prior art under § 102 against his later patent application that included a use:

> In essence, appellant is contending that a double standard should not be applied in determining the adequacy of a disclosure to anticipate under § 102, on the one hand, and to support the patentability of a claim under § 112 on the other. He feels that a disclosure adequate for the one purpose is necessarily adequate for the other but, unhappily for him, this is not so. As we shall develop, a disclosure lacking a teaching of how to use a fully disclosed compound for a specific, substantial utility or of how to use for such purpose a compound produced by a fully disclosed process is, under the present

state of the law, entirely adequate to anticipate a claim to either the product or the process and, at the same time, entirely inadequate to support the allowance of such a claim. This is so because of the requirements of law engrafted on sections 101 and 112 by the decision of the Supreme Court in *Brenner v. Manson*, 383 U.S. 519 (1966), with respect to the meaning to be given to the words "useful" and "use" in those sections. In construing them, we must of course, give them the meaning demanded by the Supreme Court.

Standing alone, appellant's argument against a double standard is a plausible proposition. However, when considered in light of the specific provisions of § 102, and § 112 as it has been interpreted, it is seen to be untenable—§ 112 provides that the specification must enable one skilled in the art to "use" the invention whereas § 102 makes no such requirement as to an anticipatory disclosure. The disclosure of how to use must relate to a use of the kind considered by the Supreme Court in *Brenner v. Manson* to be a sufficient utility. Thus, the double standard which appellant criticizes is now, implicitly if not explicitly, required by law, at least in situations such as we have here, although the "invention" per se claimed is fully disclosed and though the manner of "making," as distinguished from "using," the invention is also fully disclosed or is obvious.

Note that to satisfy the enablement standard for prior art, a reference need not be a technical scientific publication. For example, in *Iovate Health Sciences v. Bio-Engineered Supplements & Nutrition*, 586 F.3d 1376 (Fed. Cir. 2009), the Federal Circuit affirmed the district court's grant of summary judgment of invalidity based on a prior art advertisement that listed the ingredients for a dietary supplement:

Here the parties do not dispute that the Professional Protein ad was published in Flex and that the magazine was accessible to those interested in the art of nutritional supplements prior to [the critical date of] November 13, 1996. To be anticipatory, the ad must also describe, either expressly or inherently, each and every claim limitation and enable one of skill in the art to practice an embodiment of the claimed invention without undue experimentation.

We agree with [defendant] that all one of ordinary skill in the art would need to do to practice an embodiment of the invention is to mix together the known ingredients listed in the ad and administer the composition as taught by the ad. We have already rejected [plaintiff's] argument that the claims require administering an effective amount of the claimed composition. But even if the claims did require an effective amount, one of skill in the art would have been able to determine such an amount based on the ad and the knowledge in the art at the time.

Again, the ad teaches the amount of protein an active athlete needs per day per kilogram of body weight and that Professional Protein should be taken once before and once after exercise. In addition, the '287 patent specification lists numerous pre–1996 publications that teach acceptable clinical dosages of the two claimed components. It also lists pre–1996 publications that teach the effects of the components' administration on humans .... Thus, contrary to [plaintiff's] assertions, the district court correctly concluded, as do we, that a person of skill in the art, combining his or her knowledge of the art with the advertisement's suggestions, would have considered the advertisement to be enabled.

As emphasized in *Iovate*, an anticipatory prior art publication must only enable the *claimed* limitations, not the most effective embodiment of an invention, and enablement may depend on knowledge the person of ordinary skill in the art obtains from other sources. Whether a paper prior art reference is enabled is a question of law based on underlying facts.

Discussion Questions: Enablement Standard for Paper Prior Art

1. Why should there be any enablement requirement for paper prior art? Why is it not enough that the prior art disclose every element of the invention?

2. Can you justify the distinction drawn by the *Hafner* court between enablement for § 102 and § 112, either as a matter of statutory interpretation or as a matter of policy?

B2. Real-World Prior Art: In Public Use & On Sale

The previous section involved what might be thought of as "paper" categories of prior art: patents and printed publications. In this section we consider categories that cover real-world embodiments of the invention: "in public use" and "on sale." We will refer to these as "real-world" prior art.[7] Many of the rules governing these types of prior art, including the timing rules we described above, function similarly. But as you will see, a number of doctrinal rules function very differently.

---

[7] As we will see, the "on sale" category also includes sales that were never consummated, and where the invention was never actually built, and thus in which the invention technically never entered the real world.

1. Public Use

An invention is no longer patentable if it was "in public use" more than one year before the patent was filed, under post-AIA § 102(a) and pre-AIA § 102(b), or if it was "used by others" before the invention date under pre-AIA § 102(a). (Despite the slight difference in language, these phrases are understood to mean the same thing.) As with printed publications, it is easy to see why public use initiated by one party should bar another party from obtaining a patent. That is, if Firm A develops an invention and places that invention into public use, Firm B should not be permitted to patent the invention because it has not enriched the store of public knowledge.

But, again in parallel with the printed publication rule, there are many instances—including several of the cases below—in which it is the inventor herself who has placed the invention into public use, thus barring herself from obtaining a patent if she does not file quickly enough. This is possible under pre-AIA § 102(b) and post-AIA § 102(a)(1) and (b)(1), which provide the inventor with a one-year grace period by which time she must file or lose any right to the patent. These situations, where the inventor *does* enrich the store of knowledge but is denied a patent nonetheless, call for additional justification.

One important principle behind applying the public use bar in these "first-party" situations—where the party seeking the patent is the same party who created the public use—is that inventions available to the public should not be removed from the public domain via patenting. Doing so would upset the reliance interests that members of the public might have formed regarding access to the invention. *See Continental Plastic Containers v. Owens Brockway Plastic Products, Inc.*, 141 F.3d 1073, 1079 (Fed. Cir. 1998). Another rationale is to speed up patenting: the public use bar gives parties incentives to file their patents more quickly lest they find themselves barred if they—or someone else—puts the invention into public use.

Accordingly, the canonical "public use" case would involve widespread use of an invention among members of the public for years before the inventor files for a patent on it. This would squarely implicate the policies behind imposing the bar, whether it is the inventor herself or a third party who made the invention available to the public. Of course, courts have had to adjudicate a number of cases involving much more borderline instances of public access.[8] In particular, there can be a great deal of uncertainty surrounding how "public" or widespread a use must be before it qualifies as "public use." The following two cases consider that question.

---

[8] One study of district court litigation from 2011 to 2017 estimated that prior art based on uses and sales were 52% of prior art in § 102 invalidations, of which only 14% were even *potentially* secret uses or sales (such as when proof of sale relied on a contract or use was performed by a limited group). Stephen Yelderman, *Prior Art in the District Court*, 95 Notre Dame L. Rev. 837 (2019).

Netscape Communications v. Konrad, 295 F.3d 1315 (Fed. Cir. 2002)

Haldane R. Mayer, Chief Judge.

Background

1   Allan Konrad is the owner of the '320, '901, and '444 patents, all directed to systems that allow a computer user to access and search a database residing on a remote computer. He began working as a staff scientist for the Lawrence Berkeley Laboratory in 1977, where he studied how an individual computer workstation user could obtain services from a remote computer. On September 26, 1990, while working with Cynthia Hertzer, a Lawrence Berkeley Laboratory staff assistant, Konrad successfully tested the remote database object system. The first prototype of this system was configured to access Lawrence Berkeley Laboratory's STAFF database from a remote workstation. The Lawrence Berkeley Laboratory STAFF database resided on an IBM mainframe computer on the Berkeley campus of the University of California. In 1991, Konrad and Hertzer adapted the Lawrence Berkeley Laboratory STAFF remote database object system prototype for the high energy physics database, maintained at the Stanford Linear Accelerator Center, which is a national laboratory operated by Stanford University. The high energy physics database was a compilation of abstracts and technical papers used as a research tool for physicists worldwide.

2   The '320 patent, Konrad's first issued patent, is a continuation of an application filed on January 8, 1993. The '901 patent is a continuation of the '444 patent application, which is a continuation of the '320 patent application. Thus, the earliest filing date that Konrad is entitled to is January 8, 1993, making the critical date for the public use and on-sale inquiry January 8, 1992.

3   On February 8, 2000, Konrad filed a patent infringement suit in the District Court for the Eastern District of Texas, alleging that thirty-nine commercial entities, all customers of Netscape, had infringed the '320, '901, and '444 patents. Citing threatened customer relationships, Netscape filed a declaratory judgment action against Konrad in the District Court for the Northern District of California, seeking a judgment of invalidity, noninfringement, and unenforceability. Netscape moved for partial summary judgment that prototypes of the invention were in public use or on-sale under 35 U.S.C. § 102(b) based on Konrad's activities prior to January 8, 1992. The California district court entered partial summary judgment for Netscape concluding that: (1) Konrad's demonstration of the claimed invention to Shuli Roth and Dick Peters, University of California computing personnel, without any obligation of confidentiality was a public use; [and] (2) his demonstration of the high energy physics remote database object to the Stanford Linear Accelerator Center in conjunction with the use of the remote database object by University Research Association Superconducting Super Collider Laboratory employees was a public use

. . . .

Discussion

Public use includes "any use of [the claimed] invention by a person other than the inventor who is under no limitation, restriction or obligation of secrecy to the inventor." *Petrolite Corp. v. Baker Hughes Inc.,* 96 F.3d 1423, 1425 (Fed. Cir. 1996). "The public use bar serves the policies of the patent system, for it encourages prompt filing of patent applications after inventions have been completed and publicly used, and sets an outer limit to the term of exclusivity." *Allied Colloids v. Am. Cyanamid Co.,* 64 F.3d 1570, 1574 (Fed. Cir. 1995).

The law recognizes that an inventor may test his invention in public without incurring the public use bar. "The use of an invention by the inventor himself, or of any other person under his direction, by way of experiment, and in order to bring the invention to perfection, has never been regarded as such a use." *City of Elizabeth v. Am. Nicholson Pavement Co.,* 97 U.S. 126, 134 (1877).

We look to the totality of the circumstances when evaluating whether there has been a public use within the meaning of section 102(b). The circumstances may include: the nature of the activity that occurred in public; the public access to and knowledge of the public use; whether there was any confidentiality obligation imposed on persons who observed the use; whether persons other than the inventor performed the testing; the number of tests; the length of the test period in relation to tests of similar devices; and whether the inventor received payment for the testing. There may be additional factors in a particular case relevant to the public nature of the use or any asserted experimental aspect. On summary judgment, once Netscape presented facts sufficient to establish a prima facie case of public use, it fell to Konrad to come forward with some evidence raising a genuine issue of material fact to the contrary.

A.

Konrad argues that the district court erred in determining that his 1991 demonstration of the Lawrence Berkeley Laboratory STAFF remote database object to University of California computing personnel was an invalidating public use. He maintains that the invention disclosure he submitted to the Lawrence Berkeley Laboratory patent department in October of 1990, established an expectation of confidentiality from Roth and Peters.

[We do not agree with Konrad.] Konrad did not show that Roth or Peters were ever made aware of any requirement of confidentiality or even apprised of the invention disclosure forms that he submitted to the Lawrence Berkeley Laboratory patent department. He also did not make any discernable effort to inform the 1991 demonstration attendees of the requirement of confidentiality, or otherwise indicate to them that they would owe him a duty of confidentiality. Lack of a confidentiality agreement is significant here because Roth and Peters were computer personnel who could easily demonstrate the invention to others.

9   Konrad also argues that the 1991 demonstration was an experimental use for the purpose of obtaining technical support to incorporate upgrades and make the invention run more smoothly. To establish that an otherwise public use does not run afoul of section 102(b), it must be shown that the activity was "substantially for purposes of experiment." Konrad presented no objective evidence to support experimental use. Indeed, his testimony leads to the opposite conclusion. He said that the purpose of the demonstration "was to convince the people in the Berkeley computer center VM systems group that there was a viable project." He added that he hoped showing them the remote database object would make them supportive of it. Konrad's demonstration was geared more toward making the remote database object more commercially attractive, with endorsements from outside technical people, than for experimental use purposes. The experimental use negation is unavailable to a patentee when the evidence presented does not establish that he was conducting a bona fide experiment. Furthermore, Konrad presented no objective evidence that he maintained any records of testing the remote database object. This failure weighs against him.

10   Konrad also argues that at all relevant times he took affirmative steps to maintain control of his invention and questions the substantiality of the evidence to the contrary. He asserts that *Moleculon Research Corp. v. CBS, Inc.*, 793 F.2d 1261 (Fed. Cir. 1986), applies here. That case said that the display of a device to friends and colleagues of the inventor was subject to an implied restriction of confidentiality, and thus did not constitute a public use. However, that inventor always retained control over the use of the device as well as over the distribution of information concerning it. Here, Konrad testified that during 1991 he did not monitor tests of the remote database object, but that he would simply turn on the system and let people try it out. He further testified that he was aware that a workstation was made available to use the remote database object system, but was unaware of where it was located. There was no indication that he ever monitored this workstation's use or imposed a confidentiality agreement on those persons exercising the database.

B.

11   Konrad argues that the district court erred in determining that the demonstration of the high energy physics remote database object system to Stanford Linear Accelerator Center and use by University Research Association Superconducting Super Collider Laboratory employees were invalidating public uses under section 102(b). He contends that the Department of Energy owned all of the intellectual property rights to the invention, and that all Department of Energy laboratory employees were under an obligation of confidentiality to the government during all demonstrations and testing.

12   Konrad tries to cloak his failure to protect the confidentiality of his invention and maintain control of others' use by arguing that because the Department of Energy was providing the funding for his project, it ultimately owned the invention; therefore,

anyone working on the remote database object server was subject to Department of Energy confidentiality. This argument is without merit. Konrad is the inventor of the patents; the limitation, restriction, or obligation of secrecy of others using the invention is owed to him, not the persons or entities providing the funding. *See Egbert v. Lippmann,* 104 U.S. 333, 336 (1881). The onus is on him, as the inventor, to protect the confidentiality of his invention and its use by others before the critical date. The contract between Lawrence Berkeley Laboratory and the Department of Energy provides for the protection of government property, the University of California's duty to safeguard restricted data and provide written disclosures, and the government's right to duplicate and disclose the subject invention. Moreover, Konrad has not shown that this contract applied to the University Research Association Superconducting Super Collider Laboratory or Stanford Linear Accelerator Center employees.

Motionless Keyboard v. Microsoft, 486 F.3d 1376 (Fed. Cir. 2007)

Randall R. Rader, Circuit Judge.

1   [Independent inventor Thomas L. Gambaro developed a new ergonomic keyboard for handheld devices while working part-time as a graphic artist and dishwasher. On February 22, 1987, he developed a prototype known as the Cherry Model 5. He entered a partnership with Keith Coulter to further develop and patent the keyboard. In 1987, Mr. Gambaro demonstrated the keyboard to potential investors who signed two-year non-disclosure agreements (NDAs), and to his friend Kathie Roberts who did not sign a NDA. He also disclosed the keyboard to Sheila Lanier on June 25, 1990 to conduct typing tests. On June 6, 1991, he filed an application that became Patent No. 5,178,477, and on January 11, 1993, he filed an application that became Patent No. 5,332,322. He then assigned both patents to Motionless Keyboard Co. (MKC), which sued Microsoft and other parties for patent infringement. MKC appeals the district court grant of summary judgment that both patents are invalid for public use under 35 U.S.C. § 102(b).]

2   The classical standard for assessing the public nature of a use was established in *Egbert v. Lippman,* 104 U.S. 333 (1881). In *Egbert,* the inventor of a corset spring gave two samples of the invention to a lady friend, who used them for more than two years before the inventor applied for a patent. Although the inventor in *Egbert* did not obtain any commercial advantage, the Court determined that the invention had been used for its intended purpose for over a decade without limitation or confidentiality requirements. Thus, even though not in public view, the invention was in public use. In *Electric Storage Battery Co. v. Shimadzu,* 307 U.S. 5 (1939), the Court found "the ordinary use of a machine or the practice of a process in a factory in the usual course of producing articles for commercial purposes is a public use." On the other hand, in *TP Laboratories, Inc. v. Professional Positioners, Inc.,* 724 F.2d 965 (Fed. Cir. 1984), this court found that premature installation of an inventive orthodontic appliance in several patients without a written confidentiality agreement was not a public use due

to the expectation of confidentiality inherent in the dentist-patient relationship. This case again presents the question of the meaning of public use under 35 U.S.C. § 102(b).

3   In this case, Mr. Gambaro disclosed his Cherry Model 5 to his business partner, a friend, potential investors, and a typing tester (Ms. Lanier). In all these disclosures, except in the case of Ms. Lanier, however, the Cherry Model 5 was not connected to a computer or any other device. In the case of Ms. Lanier, the Cherry Model 5 was used to conduct typing tests on July 25, 1990, and thereby connected to a computer for its intended purpose. With respect to the '477 patent, the typing test occurred after the critical date of June 6, 1990. With respect to the '322 patent, [the test was before the January 11, 1992 critical date but under a NDA]. In this case, the one time typing test coupled with a signed NDA and no record of continued use of the Cherry Model 5 by Ms. Lanier after July 25, 1990 did not elevate to the level of public use. Thus, the Cherry Model 5 was never in public use. All disclosures, except for the one-time typing test, only provided a visual view of the new keyboard design without any disclosure of the Cherry Model 5's ability to translate finger movements into actuation of keys to transmit data. In essence, these disclosures visually displayed the keyboard design without putting it into use. In short, the Cherry Model 5 was not in public use as the term is used in section 102(b) because the device, although visually disclosed and only tested one time with a NDA signed by the typing tester, was never connected to be used in the normal course of business to enter data into a system.

4   Unlike the situations in *Egbert* and *Electric Storage Battery*, where the inventions were used for their intended purpose, neither the inventor nor anyone else ever used the Cherry Model 5 to transmit data in the normal course of business. The entry of data did not ever occur outside of testing and the tester signed an NDA. The Cherry Model 5 was not used in public, for its intended purpose, nor was the Cherry Model 5 ever given to anyone for such public use. Thus, the disclosures in this record do not rise to the level of public use.

Discussion Questions: Public Use

1. *The Expansive Understanding of "Public."* The court's holding in *Netscape v. Konrad* is based on the disclosure of the invention without any obligation of confidentiality or secrecy. But it would be hard to describe it as "public" in the conventional sense. The disclosures occurred in private offices, behind closed doors, not out in the open. And the invention was shared with only a handful of people, not broadcast widely to the masses.

Netscape v. Konrad indicates that it is not necessary for "the public" to make widespread use of an invention for it to be in public use. Rather, even use by a handful of people or even a single member of the public is sufficient. This should indicate the breadth of the courts' understanding of what is "public" for purposes of the public use bar. Note the similarity to courts' broad interpretation of "printed publication," as discussed above.

What effect does the expansive understanding of "public" have on unsophisticated or less resourced inventors? Remember that innovative entrepreneurs interact with the patent system as producers, consumers, or both. In some instances they may be concerned about inadvertently creating prior art against themselves; in others they may need to determine the patentability of their inventions; and in still others they may need to assess their freedom to operate based on others' patents. Do you think those tasks will be easy or difficult for less sophisticated inventors to accomplish? Are there particular aspects of this doctrine that will pose especially greater problems?

2. *Public Use Without the Public Using?* In both *Konrad* and *Motionless Keyboard*, the potential public use at issue was thought to involve actual *use* of the patented invention. This is typically thought of as a bright-line requirement in the law of public use: there can be no public use if the invention is not actually being used by a member of the public.

However, a small but influential line of cases suggests that there is another route to public use: if the invention is being used *by its inventor*, but under non-secret conditions such that members of the public could learn how the invention works, this is a public use. You might think of this as a constructive knowledge standard: if information about how the invention operates could have reached the public through use by the inventor, then the invention is in public use, even if there is no evidence that information about the invention has actually seeped out. This line of cases begins with *Electric Storage Battery Co. v. Shimadzu*, 307 U.S. 5 (1939). There, a third-party inventor had "continuously employed the alleged infringing machine and process"—a process for producing lead oxide for use in batteries—in its own factory without protecting the process through confidentiality agreements and other measures. The court found that no "efforts were made to conceal [the inventions] from anyone who had a legitimate interest in understanding them" and held that this constituted a public use.

The Fifth Circuit reached a similar result in *Rosaire v. Nat'l Lead Co.*, 218 F.2d 72, 75 (5th Cir. 1955), where it held that any type of work "done openly and in the ordinary course of the activities of the employer" was sufficiently public. The activity in *Rosaire*—an underground oil-drilling method on private property—was not "public" in any usual sense of the word, but because it was done "without any deliberate attempt at concealment or effort to exclude the public" it was held to be a public use that anticipated a third party's patent. Here, too, the court's holding appears to rely on the idea of constructive public knowledge: someone from the public *could have* learned how the invention operated from observing its operation, and that was enough to constitute public use.

The Federal Circuit appears to have confirmed this understanding of the law as recently as 2020. In *BASF Corp. v. SNF Holding Co.*, 955 F.3d 958 (Fed. Cir. 2020), a third party had operated the claimed invention in its factory before the critical date and had given tours of its factory to the general public. Citing *Shimadzu*, the court stated that "the public-use bar applies to uses of the invention not purposely hidden and that the use of a process in the ordinary course of business—where the process was well known to the employees and no efforts were made to conceal it from anyone else—is a public use." On the factual record presented to the Federal Circuit, it was unclear whether the tours revealed enough information about the invention to enable a person of ordinary skill in the art to construct it. But the court made clear that if a person of ordinary skill in the art would have been able to glean sufficient information about the invention from these tours, the invention would have been in public use—without any member of the public ever having laid a finger on the invention, and irrespective of whether any person of ordinary skill in the art had actually ever taken a tour. Again, the court appears to be using a constructive knowledge standard.

Despite the potential reach of this doctrine, we suspect that it has been largely limited by how rarely inventors are willing to show their work to the public before it is ready for actual public use. The vast majority of inventive activity in private firms takes place behind closed *and locked* doors, both literally and metaphorically, and those firms closely guard their secrets. If a curious member of the public knocked on Apple's headquarters and asked what new inventions the firm was working on, that person would be laughed (and escorted) off the premises. Accordingly, while it is undoubtedly important to understand this separate track to finding public use, we suspect that cases invoking this line of doctrine will arise much less frequently than "standard" public use cases.

What are the policy considerations that justify the courts' holding that an invention can be in public use without any member of the public actually using the invention? Can this line of doctrine be justified by the same considerations described in *Konrad* and *Motionless Keyboard*, or are additional policy justifications necessary?

3. *Experimental Use.* In some cases, courts have held that uses that would otherwise constitute public use are exempted if they are for experimental purposes. The seminal case is *City of Elizabeth v. Am. Nicholson Pavement Co.*, 97 U.S. 126 (1877). In that case, an inventor installed a new type of wooden paving on a heavily trafficked street. Under normal circumstances, this would have obviously put the invention into public use. During the time that it was installed, hundreds or thousands of members of the public used that stretch of road. Nonetheless, the Supreme Court carved out an exception to the general public use bar for uses that take place for "experimental" purposes. The Court held that the inventor's use had been experimental, and thus he was not barred from obtaining a patent. Three factors were critical to the Court's decision:

First, while the invention was physically complete, the inventor did not yet know that it would work properly for its intended purpose. (In patent parlance, the invention had not yet been "reduced to practice," a concept we will discuss at length in the section below on § 102(g).) Here, that purpose was durability: the point of the invention was to create a type of paving that could remain intact for a period of years under heavy use. Second, the best way to test the paving was through use by the public. There was no good substitute for actually installing the paving on a segment of road and allowing people to walk and drive (their horses) over it, exposing it to use and to the elements. Third, the inventor kept the invention "under his own control." Here, that meant that he kept it under observation on a regular basis and did not distribute it more widely. It is at least plausible that members of the public did not think that they would have unfettered access to the invention.

Again, once an invention has been built and proven to work for its intended purpose—that is, once it has been reduced to practice—experimental use does not apply. *See Continental Plastic Containers v. Owens Brockway Plastic Prods.*, 141 F.3d 1073, 1079 (Fed. Cir. 1998). For instance, market testing to gauge consumer demand is not experimental use. *In re Smith*, 714 F.2d 1127, 1135 (Fed. Cir. 1983). The experimental use exception is thus narrow, but some cases still arise in which it applies. The Federal Circuit upheld jury findings that the exception applied to otherwise valid § 102(b) public use prior art in *Barry v. Medtronic*, 914 F.3d 1310 (Fed. Cir. 2019) (spinal correction device), and *Polara Engineering Inc. v. Campbell Co.*, 894 F.3d 1339 (Fed. Cir. 2018) (crosswalk control system), although it was not applied for at least a decade before *Polara*. What do you think are the policy rationales behind the experimental use exception? How effectively do you think it is serving these goals? Do you think the narrow role of the experimental use exception is salutary?

Practice Problems: Public Use

Do you think the following uses constitute "public use"? What additional facts would you want to know?

1. An inventor develops a new small, wooden toy. He brings it to his office workplace and allows his boss to play with the toy and examine how it works. Both the inventor and his boss tell their friends and acquaintances about the toy, but no one else has a chance to play with it. *See Moleculon Research v. CBS*, 793 F.2d 1261 (Fed. Cir. 1986).

2. An inventor develops a new type of toy. She holds a party, to which she invites approximately 20–30 friends, to solicit feedback about the toy. At the party, her friends play with the toy and then offer suggestions regarding how it might be improved or changed. The inventor did not impose any confidentiality obligation, and one of the guests testified that she did not think the information was confidential. None of the inventor's friends are allowed to take copies of

the toy home. *See Beachcombers v. WildeWood Creative Products, Inc.*, 31 F.3d 1154 (Fed. Cir. 1994).

If your answer to this question is different from your answer to the prior question, what do you think differentiates the situations?

3. An inventor developed a new strain of table grape. Unbeknownst to the inventor, an employee of the inventing company gave samples of the grape to another grape grower. The grape grower was instructed "not to let the material 'get away from [him]' and not to 'put them in a box,' which [he] understood to mean that he should not sell the resulting grapes until the varieties were commercially released." The grape vines "bore no usable fruit, and the [grower] sold no grapes from those plantings prior to the critical date. Although the various plantings were visible from publicly accessible roads, none of the vines were marked or labeled in any way, and the evidence showed that the particular variety of the grapes could not be readily ascertained from simply viewing the vines." *See Delano Farms v. California Table Grape Comm'n*, 778 F.3d 1243 (Fed. Cir. 2015).

2. The Enablement Standard for Real-World Prior Art

Unlike printed publications and patents, real-world prior art—including the public uses discussed above and putting the invention "on sale," discussed in the next section—generally need not be enabling. As summarized by the Federal Circuit: "Beyond [an] 'in public use or on sale' finding, there is no requirement for an enablement-type inquiry. . . . [T]he question is not whether the sale, even a third party sale, 'discloses' the invention at the time of the sale, but whether the sale relates to a device that *embodies* the invention." *In re Epstein*, 32 F.3d 1559, 1568 (Fed. Cir. 1994). That is, it only matters whether some members of the public have the opportunity to buy or use the invention, not whether a member of the public could learn how the invention functions.

The only exception is the type of public use described in Discussion Question 2 above, where the public acquires constructive knowledge of how an invention works without ever actually using it. There, enablement appears to be necessary, although the Federal Circuit has not explicitly described this as an enablement requirement. *See BASF Corp. v. SNF Holding Co.*, 955 F.3d 958, 966–67 (Fed. Cir. 2020). When an invention is placed on public display without a possibility of public use, an enablement requirement makes sense because the disclosure is more similar to a conference poster or an oral presentation—it only enriches the public to the extent that the public can learn how to make and use the invention from the display.

The rule that real-world prior art typically need not be enabled stems from the principles underlying the public use and on sale bars. Again, the public use bar operates to prevent an inventor from depriving the public of an invention to which it has had (unpatented) access, thus upsetting the public's reliance interests. Those reliance interests can form irrespective of whether members of the public are able to learn how the invention actually functions, so long as they believe they will have access to it and be able to use it. For its part, the on sale bar exists to prevent an inventor from improperly extending her monopoly, which could occur even if a sale was not enabling.

Lockwood v. American Airlines, 107 F.3d 1565 (Fed. Cir. 1997), is a prototypical example of this rule. The invention at issue was the SABRE system, which is used for searching and booking airline tickets across airlines. (If you've booked a ticket through Kayak, Expedia, or similar platforms, you've used SABRE.) SABRE was widely in use among members of the public—particularly travel agents— before the filing of a patent on the technology. But nobody who used SABRE would have been able to determine precisely how it worked, just as an individual user of Kayak today cannot see the inner workings of the program. The Federal Circuit held that this was immaterial to the question of public use:

> American submitted an affidavit averring that the SABRE system was introduced to the public in 1962, had over one thousand connected sales desks by 1965, and was connected to the reservation systems for most of the other airlines by 1970. Lockwood does not dispute these facts, but argues that because "critical aspects" of the SABRE system were not accessible to the public, it could not have been prior art. American's expert conceded that the essential algorithms of the SABRE software were proprietary and confidential and that those aspects of the system that were readily apparent to the public would not have been sufficient to enable one skilled in the art to duplicate the system. However, American responds that the public need not have access to the "inner workings" of a device for it to be considered "in public use" or "used by others" within the meaning of the statute.

> We agree with American that those aspects of the original SABRE system relied on by the district court are prior art to the '359 patent. The district court held that SABRE, which made and confirmed reservations with multiple institutions (*e.g.,* airlines, hotels, and car rental agencies), combined with the terminal of the '631 patent rendered the asserted claims of the '359 patent obvious. The terminal of the '631 patent admittedly lacked this "multiple institution" feature. It is undisputed, however, that the public was aware that SABRE possessed this capability and that the public had been using SABRE to make travel reservations from independent travel agencies prior to Lockwood's date of invention.

If a device was "known or used by others" in this country before the date of invention or if it was "in public use" in this country more than one year before the date of application, it qualifies as prior art. *See* 35 U.S.C. § 102(a) and (b). Lockwood attempts to preclude summary judgment by pointing to record testimony that one skilled in the art would not be able to build and practice the claimed invention without access to the secret aspects of SABRE. However, it is the claims that define a patented invention. As we have concluded earlier in this opinion, American's public use of the high-level aspects of the SABRE system was enough to place the *claimed* features of the '359 patent in the public's possession. *See In re Epstein,* 32 F.3d 1559, 1567–68 (Fed. Cir. 1994) ("Beyond this 'in public use or on sale' finding, there is no requirement for an enablement-type inquiry."). Lockwood cannot negate this by evidence showing that other, *unclaimed* aspects of the SABRE system were not publicly available. Moreover, the '359 patent itself does not disclose the level of detail that Lockwood would have us require of the prior art. For these reasons, Lockwood fails to show a genuine issue of material fact.

3. On Sale

Post-AIA § 102(a) and pre-AIA § 102(b) similarly bar an inventor from patenting an invention that was placed "on sale" more than one year before filing.[9] As with "printed publication" and "public use" prior art, whether an invention has been placed "on sale" is a question of law based on underlying facts.

Though it is often considered in conjunction with the "public use" bar, the principle underlying the on sale bar is actually quite different. As explained in the following case, the on sale bar is designed to prevent an inventor from using the patent system to enable exclusive commercial exploitation of an invention for longer than the twenty-year statutory patent term. Without the on sale bar, an inventor could conceivably hold an invention as a trade secret for a period of years, and then patent the invention for an additional twenty years—effectively controlling exclusive rights over an invention for much longer than the statutory twenty-year period. The on sale bar forces an inventor to choose between trade secret protection and patent protection, rather than availing herself of both. Thus, whereas the public use bar is focused on the public and the reliance interests formed around available inventions, the on sale bar is focused on the inventor and the possibility that she will attempt to exploit the

---

[9] Technically speaking, post-AIA 35 U.S.C. § 102(a) bars a patent if the invention was placed on sale before the date of filing. However, if it was the patent applicant who placed the invention on sale, post-AIA 35 U.S.C. § 102(b)(1)(A) provides the applicant with a one-year grace period. This aligns pre- and post-AIA law and means that under both versions of the law, inventors must file within a year of placing an invention on sale or risk losing the ability to obtain a patent.

invention for longer than allowed. This difference in underlying policy has ramifications for the on sale bar doctrine, as the sections below will make clear.

The on sale bar is triggered whenever "the invention" is "on sale." This raises the question of what it means for "the invention" to be on sale—for instance, must the invention physically exist? It also raises the question of what it means for the invention to be "on sale"—must the invention actually have been sold? How many units of the invention? What if the invention is available for purchase but has not been sold? And so forth. In 1998, the Supreme Court granted certiorari in the case below to answer these questions.

Pfaff v. Wells Electronics, 525 U.S. 55 (1998)

Justice John Paul Stevens delivered the opinion of the Court.

1   Section 102(b) of the Patent Act of 1952 provides that no person is entitled to patent an "invention" that has been "on sale" more than one year before filing a patent application. We granted certiorari to determine whether the commercial marketing of a newly invented product may mark the beginning of the 1–year period even though the invention has not yet been reduced to practice.

I

2   On April 19, 1982, petitioner, Wayne Pfaff, filed an application for a patent on a computer chip socket. Therefore, April 19, 1981, constitutes the critical date for purposes of the on-sale bar of 35 U.S.C. § 102(b); if the 1–year period began to run before that date, Pfaff lost his right to patent his invention.

3   Pfaff commenced work on the socket in November 1980, when representatives of Texas Instruments asked him to develop a new device for mounting and removing semiconductor chip carriers. In response to this request, he prepared detailed engineering drawings that described the design, the dimensions, and the materials to be used in making the socket. Pfaff sent those drawings to a manufacturer in February or March 1981.

4   Prior to March 17, 1981, Pfaff showed a sketch of his concept to representatives of Texas Instruments. On April 8, 1981, they provided Pfaff with a written confirmation of a previously placed oral purchase order for 30,100 of his new sockets for a total price of $91,155. In accord with his normal practice, Pfaff did not make and test a prototype of the new device before offering to sell it in commercial quantities.[10]

---

[10] [n.3 in opinion] At his deposition, respondent's counsel engaged in the following colloquy with Pfaff:

"Q. Now, at this time [late 1980 or early 1981] did we [sic] have any prototypes developed or anything of that nature, working embodiment?

5   The manufacturer took several months to develop the customized tooling necessary to produce the device, and Pfaff did not fill the order until July 1981. The evidence therefore indicates that Pfaff first reduced his invention to practice in the summer of 1981.

6   The Court of Appeals [found] all six claims invalid. Four of the claims (1, 6, 7, and 10) described the socket that Pfaff had sold to Texas Instruments prior to April 8, 1981. Because that device had been offered for sale on a commercial basis more than one year before the patent application was filed on April 19, 1982, the court concluded that those claims were invalid under § 102(b). That conclusion rested on the court's view that as long as the invention was "substantially complete at the time of sale," the 1–year period began to run, even though the invention had not yet been reduced to practice. The other two claims (11 and 19) described a feature that had not been included in Pfaff's initial design, but the Court of Appeals concluded as a matter of law that the additional feature was not itself patentable because it was an obvious addition to the prior art. Given the court's § 102(b) holding, the prior art included Pfaff's first four claims.

II

7   The primary meaning of the word "invention" in the Patent Act unquestionably refers to the inventor's conception rather than to a physical embodiment of that idea. The statute does not contain any express requirement that an invention must be reduced to practice before it can be patented. Neither the statutory definition of the term in § 100 nor the basic conditions for obtaining a patent set forth in § 101 make any mention of "reduction to practice." The statute's only specific reference to that term is found in § 102(g), which sets forth the standard for resolving priority contests between two competing claimants to a patent. That subsection provides:

> In determining priority of invention there shall be considered not only the respective dates of conception and reduction to practice of the invention, but also the reasonable diligence of one who was first to conceive and last to reduce to practice, from a time prior to conception by the other.

"A. No.

"Q. It was in a drawing. Is that correct?

"A. Strictly in a drawing. Went from the drawing to the hard tooling. That's the way I do my business.

"Q. 'Boom-boom'?

"A. You got it.

"Q. You are satisfied, obviously, when you come up with some drawings that it is going to go—'it works'?

"A. I know what I'm doing, yes, most of the time."

8   Thus, assuming diligence on the part of the applicant, it is normally the first inventor to conceive, rather than the first to reduce to practice, who establishes the right to the patent.

9   It is well settled that an invention may be patented before it is reduced to practice. In 1888, this Court upheld a patent issued to Alexander Graham Bell even though he had filed his application before constructing a working telephone. When we apply the reasoning of [the cases concerning Bell's invention] to the facts of the case before us today, it is evident that Pfaff could have obtained a patent on his novel socket when he accepted the purchase order from Texas Instruments for 30,100 units. At that time he provided the manufacturer with a description and drawings that had "sufficient clearness and precision to enable those skilled in the matter" to produce the device. The parties agree that the sockets manufactured to fill that order embody Pfaff's conception as set forth in claims 1, 6, 7, and 10 of the '377 patent. We can find no basis in the text of § 102(b) or in the facts of this case for concluding that Pfaff's invention was not "on sale" within the meaning of the statute until after it had been reduced to practice.

III

10   Pfaff nevertheless argues that longstanding precedent, buttressed by the strong interest in providing inventors with a clear standard identifying the onset of the 1–year period, justifies a special interpretation of the word "invention" as used in § 102(b). We are persuaded that this nontextual argument should be rejected.

11   As we have often explained, most recently in *Bonito Boats, Inc. v. Thunder Craft Boats, Inc.,* 489 U.S. 141 (1989), the patent system represents a carefully crafted bargain that encourages both the creation and the public disclosure of new and useful advances in technology, in return for an exclusive monopoly for a limited period of time. The balance between the interest in motivating innovation and enlightenment by rewarding invention with patent protection on the one hand, and the interest in avoiding monopolies that unnecessarily stifle competition on the other, has been a feature of the federal patent laws since their inception.

12   Consistent with these ends, § 102 of the Patent Act serves as a limiting provision, both excluding ideas that are in the public domain from patent protection and confining the duration of the monopoly to the statutory term.

13   We originally held that an inventor loses his right to a patent if he puts his invention into public use before filing a patent application. "His voluntary act or acquiescence in the public sale and use is an abandonment of his right." *Pennock v. Dialogue,* 27 U.S. (2 Pet.) 1, 24 (1829) (Story, J.). A similar reluctance to allow an inventor to remove existing knowledge from public use undergirds the on-sale bar.

14   Nevertheless, an inventor who seeks to perfect his discovery may conduct extensive testing without losing his right to obtain a patent for his invention—even if

such testing occurs in the public eye. The law has long recognized the distinction between inventions put to experimental use and products sold commercially. In 1878, we explained why patentability may turn on an inventor's use of his product.

> It is sometimes said that an inventor acquires an undue advantage over the public by delaying to take out a patent, inasmuch as he thereby preserves the monopoly to himself for a longer period than is allowed by the policy of the law; but this cannot be said with justice when the delay is occasioned by a *bona fide* effort to bring his invention to perfection, or to ascertain whether it will answer the purpose intended. His monopoly only continues for the allotted period, in any event; and it is the interest of the public, as well as himself, that the invention should be perfect and properly tested, before a patent is granted for it. *Any attempt to use it for a profit, and not by way of experiment, for a longer period than two years before the application, would deprive the inventor of his right to a patent.*

Elizabeth v. Am. Nicholson Pavement Co., 97 U.S. 126, 137 (1877) (emphasis added).

15   The patent laws therefore seek both to protect the public's right to retain knowledge already in the public domain and the inventor's right to control whether and when he may patent his invention.

16   The word "invention" must refer to a concept that is complete, rather than merely one that is "substantially complete." It is true that reduction to practice ordinarily provides the best evidence that an invention is complete. But just because reduction to practice is sufficient evidence of completion, it does not follow that proof of reduction to practice is necessary in every case. Indeed, both the facts of [the Alexander Graham Bell cases] and the facts of this case demonstrate that one can prove that an invention is complete and ready for patenting before it has actually been reduced to practice.

17   We conclude, therefore, that the on-sale bar applies when two conditions are satisfied before the critical date. First, the product must be the subject of a commercial offer for sale. An inventor can both understand and control the timing of the first commercial marketing of his invention. The experimental use doctrine, for example, has not generated concerns about indefiniteness, and we perceive no reason why unmanageable uncertainty should attend a rule that measures the application of the on-sale bar of § 102(b) against the date when an invention that is ready for patenting is first marketed commercially. In this case the acceptance of the purchase order prior to April 8, 1981, makes it clear that such an offer had been made, and there is no question that the sale was commercial rather than experimental in character.

18   Second, the invention must be ready for patenting. That condition may be satisfied in at least two ways: by proof of reduction to practice before the critical date; or by proof that prior to the critical date the inventor had prepared drawings or other

descriptions of the invention that were sufficiently specific to enable a person skilled in the art to practice the invention. In this case the second condition of the on-sale bar is satisfied because the drawings Pfaff sent to the manufacturer before the critical date fully disclosed the invention.

19   The evidence in this case thus fulfills the two essential conditions of the on-sale bar. As succinctly stated by Learned Hand:

> [I]t is a condition upon an inventor's right to a patent that he shall not exploit his discovery competitively after it is ready for patenting; he must content himself with either secrecy, or legal monopoly.

Metallizing Engineering v. Kenyon Bearing & Auto Parts, 153 F.2d 516, 520 (2d Cir. 1946).

20   The judgment of the Court of Appeals finds support not only in the text of the statute but also in the basic policies underlying the statutory scheme, including § 102(b). When Pfaff accepted the purchase order for his new sockets prior to April 8, 1981, his invention was ready for patenting. The fact that the manufacturer was able to produce the socket using his detailed drawings and specifications demonstrates this fact. Furthermore, those sockets contained all the elements of the invention claimed in the '377 patent. Therefore, Pfaff's '377 patent is invalid because the invention had been on sale for more than one year in this country before he filed his patent application.

Discussion Questions: On Sale

1. *Commercial Offer for Sale.* The first prong of the *Pfaff* test is that the product must be the subject of a "commercial offer for sale." Note that this means that the offer need not be accepted, no money need change hands, the product need not be delivered, and so forth. All that is required is that the product be offered for sale. But this is different from a mere advertisement. An advertisement that says "Coming soon: a brand new widget!" is not an offer for sale (though it may be a printed publication if it enables the widget).

Whether there is an offer for sale is a standard question of contract law and is treated as such by the Federal Circuit. However, the Federal Circuit does not look to the law of the relevant state to determine whether there has been an offer for sale. Instead, the Federal Circuit has created its own version of federal/patent contract law, which it uses to determine whether a product has been offered for sale.

What work do you think the word "commercial" is doing in the phrase "commercial offer for sale?" What would be an example of a non-commercial offer for sale? Why do you think the Supreme Court chose to trigger the on sale bar merely with an offer for sale, rather than holding that the bar is triggered when the product is actually sold?

As you consider these questions, keep in mind that the purpose of the on sale bar is to prevent the patentee from exploiting the patented invention beyond the twenty-year exclusivity period. That means that the on sale bar is typically only triggered when the patentee offers a sale to an outside party in a manner that is intended to earn profit. For instance, in *Medicines Co. v. Hospira, Inc.* (*Medicines I*), 827 F.3d 1363 (Fed. Cir. 2016) (en banc), the patentee contracted with a manufacturing company to produce the patented invention, with the intention of later selling the invention to the public. The Federal Circuit, sitting en banc, held that this did not place the invention on sale for purposes of the on sale bar. In contrast, in *Medicines Co. v. Hospira, Inc.* (*Medicines II*), 881 F.3d 1347 (Fed. Cir. 2018), an exclusive distribution agreement that required the distributor to make commercially reasonable efforts to fill purchase orders established an offer for sale. Does this seem like the right result, and if so, why?

2. *Ready for Patenting.* The second prong of the *Pfaff* test is that the invention must be ready for patenting. What, exactly, does it mean for an invention to be ready for patenting? Does it mean that the invention has to exist in finished form (such that it could be put into public use)?

Later in this chapter, you will learn about two important moments in an invention's lifespan: the moment of conception, and the moment of reduction to practice. When you do, consider whether "ready for patenting" is equivalent to either of those moments. Why do you think the Supreme Court chose to trigger the on sale bar at this point in the invention's lifespan, as opposed to earlier or later?

3. *Alternatives to Barring the Patent.* As we have explained, the purpose of the on sale bar is to prevent the patentee from exploiting the patented invention for longer than the designated twenty-year term. But barring the patentee from obtaining a patent if the invention was placed on sale is not the only way of doing this. Can you think of alternatives?

One option would be to simply run the twenty-year patent term from the date of the first offer for sale. So, for instance, if a putative patentee placed the invention on sale in 2021, and then filed for a patent in 2026, the patent would expire in 2041 (20 years from the first sale), not in 2046. What do you think would be the advantages and disadvantages of this approach? Try to think about this question from the perspectives of the patentee, the public, and potential competitors to the patentee.

4. *Timing Problems.* The timing of events in *Pfaff* was relatively conventional: the invention was ready for patenting, and the inventor then placed it on sale. The on sale bar was triggered when the offer for sale occurred. But what if these events happened in a different order, or in a more scattered fashion? For each of the following

situations, can you identify the date on which the on sale bar is triggered (if it is triggered at all)?

> (a) The prospective invention is placed on sale on March 1, before it is ready for patenting. It becomes ready for patenting on April 1.
>
> (b) The prospective invention is placed on sale on March 1. The offer for sale is then withdrawn on April 1, with no sales having been made. The invention becomes ready for patenting on May 1.
>
> (c) The same situation as (b), except now the offer for sale was accepted by one purchaser on March 15, before the offer was withdrawn (with regard to others) on April 1.

4. Trade Secrets and Third-Party Rules

The simplest types of public use and on sale bar situations involve an inventor who has put the invention on sale or in public use in a "public" fashion, observable to outsiders—say, listing an invention for sale on Amazon. But these prior art provisions can give rise to much more complicated situations as well. In some cases, the complexity is generated by secrecy: the inventor is attempting to hold the invention as a trade secret and either sell it or use it in secret. In other cases, complexity stems from the fact that someone other than the patent applicant has put the invention on sale or into public use. The question that arises is whether the activities of this third party should affect the applicant's patent rights. Though they arise from different sources, these additional complexities raise related questions.

Secret Sales and Secret Commercial Use

Pfaff implies that even entirely "secret" sales—sales in which no enabling information is made public, and the very fact of the sale itself is not made public—will nonetheless trigger the on sale bar. After all, in that case Pfaff's patent was invalidated due to a sale without the product changing hands and without enabling information about the device reaching the public. Nonetheless, the Supreme Court did not explicitly hold that secret sales would trigger the on sale bar.

This question garnered renewed attention after the passage of the AIA. Recall that § 102(a)(1) of the post-AIA law states that an inventor is entitled to a patent unless "the claimed invention was patented, described in a printed publication, or in public use, on sale, or *otherwise* available to the public" (emphasis added). The inclusion of the word "otherwise" led some commentators to argue that the phrase "available to the public" should be seen as modifying each of the other categories of prior art listed in the statute. This would not affect our understanding of "patented," "in public use," or "printed publication," all of which by their nature are publicly available. Rather, it was suggested that the on sale bar could now only be triggered by "public" sales, and a purely private or secret sale (such as the one in *Pfaff*) would not implicate the on sale bar.

The Supreme Court rejected that argument in *Helsinn Healthcare S.A. v. Teva Pharmaceuticals USA, Inc.*, 139 S. Ct. 628 (2019):

> Although this Court has never addressed the precise question presented in this case, our precedents suggest that a sale or offer of sale need not make an invention available to the public. For instance, we held in *Pfaff* that an offer for sale could cause an inventor to lose the right to patent, without regard to whether the offer discloses each detail of the invention. *E.g.*, 525 U.S. at 67. Other cases focus on whether the invention had been sold, not whether the details of the invention had been made available to the public or whether the sale itself had been publicly disclosed. *E.g.*, *Consolidated Fruit–Jar Co. v. Wright,* 94 U.S. 92, 94 (1877) ("[A] single instance of sale or of use by the patentee may, under the circumstances, be fatal to the patent . . . .").

> The Federal Circuit—which has "exclusive jurisdiction" over patent appeals, 28 U.S.C. § 1295(a)—has made explicit what was implicit in our precedents. It has long held that "secret sales" can invalidate a patent. *E.g.*, *Special Devices, Inc. v. OEA, Inc.,* 270 F.3d 1353, 1357 (Fed. Cir. 2001) (invalidating patent claims based on "sales for the purpose of the commercial stockpiling of an invention" that "took place in secret"); *Woodland Trust v. Flowertree Nursery, Inc.,* 148 F.3d 1368, 1370 (Fed. Cir. 1998) ("Thus an inventor's own prior commercial use, albeit kept secret, may constitute a public use or sale under § 102(b), barring him from obtaining a patent").

> In light of this settled pre-AIA precedent on the meaning of "on sale," we presume that when Congress reenacted the same language in the AIA, it adopted the earlier judicial construction of that phrase. The new § 102 retained the exact language used in its predecessor statute ("on sale") and, as relevant here, added only a new catchall clause ("or otherwise available to the public"). As *amicus* United States noted at oral argument, if "on sale" had a settled meaning before the AIA was adopted, then adding the phrase "or otherwise available to the public" to the statute "would be a fairly oblique way of attempting to overturn" that "settled body of law." The addition of "or otherwise available to the public" is simply not enough of a change for us to conclude that Congress intended to alter the meaning of the reenacted term "on sale."

Helsinn thus confirms what was implicit in *Pfaff*: even secret sales in which no enabling information reaches the public—and even when the fact of the offer for sale is not public—will still trigger the on sale bar under both pre- and post-AIA law. This holding also reinforces the policy justification for the on sale bar by preventing an inventor from having exclusive rights over her invention for longer than the statutory patent term.

In some cases, an inventor can earn money from an invention not by selling the invention itself, but by selling some product or service that is produced using the invention. This is particularly true when the invention is a process or method, rather than a physical product, but it can be true as well for certain types of machines that are used to produce other physical products, rather than being sold themselves. When an inventor makes commercial use of an invention in this fashion, it is not immediately obvious which provisions in pre-AIA § 102(b) or post-AIA § 102(a) are implicated by the inventor's actions. It is not obvious that this activity implicates the on sale bar because "the invention" is not exactly being placed on sale. Instead, the inventor is selling a "fruit" of the invention (a related product or service). It is also not obvious that this implicates the public use bar because "the invention" is not exactly in public use. Instead, in many cases the invention itself is being used in secret, behind closed doors, and what is made public is only the product or fruit of the invention.

These are commonly referred to as cases involving "secret commercial use." The following case illustrates the Federal Circuit's approach to these situations.

Quest Integrity USA v. Cokebusters USA, 924 F.3d 1220 (Fed. Cir. 2019)

Timothy B. Dyk, Circuit Judge.

On December 15, 2014, Quest filed suit against Cokebusters in the District of Delaware, alleging infringement of the '874 patent. Cokebusters defended on the ground that the claims were invalid under 35 U.S.C. § 102(b) because there was a commercial sale of services that used the claimed methods, computer-readable media, and system more than one year before June 1, 2004, the date the application that led to the '874 patent was filed in the United States.

The basis for the on-sale bar defense was an offer by Quest itself to provide furnace tube inspection services to a client in the petrochemical industry. In February and March 2003, Quest performed furnace tube inspection services for Orion Norco Refinery in Norco, Louisiana in exchange for $72,060 ("the Norco Sale"). Cokebusters alleged that these commercial activities rendered the claims invalid because of the on-sale bar. Cokebusters argued that during those inspections, Quest used its commercial furnace tube inspection method, computer-readable medium, and system and generated two inspection reports ("the Norco Reports"), which Quest provided to the customer. The Norco Reports contained two-dimensional, color-coded strip charts displaying the collected furnace inspection data ("the Norco Strip Charts"). Cokebusters alleged that the method, computer-readable medium, and system used to prepare the Norco Strip Charts satisfied the limitations of the asserted claims. Quest did not sell any hardware or software to the customer.

Discussion

Section 102(b) prevents a person from receiving a patent if, "more than one year prior to the date of the application for patent in the United States," "the invention was . . . on sale" in the United States. This is known as the "on-sale bar." The date exactly one year prior to the date of the patent application is known as the critical date. As noted above, since the application for the '874 patent was filed on June 1, 2004, the critical date here is June 1, 2003.

The on-sale bar seeks to prevent "[a]ny attempt to use [the claimed invention] for a profit, and not by way of experiment," for more than one year before filing for a patent application. *Pfaff v. Wells Elecs., Inc.*, 525 U.S. 55, 65 (1998). And "[i]t is a condition upon an inventor's right to a patent that he shall not exploit his discovery competitively after it is ready for patenting; he must content himself with either secrecy, or legal monopoly." *Pfaff*, 525 U.S. at 68 (quoting *Metallizing Eng'g Co. v. Kenyon Bearing & Auto Parts Co.*, 153 F.2d 516, 520 (2d Cir. 1946)).

In *Pfaff*, the Supreme Court outlined a two-part test for determining whether an invention is "on sale" within the meaning of § 102(b). The patented invention must have been (1) "the subject of a commercial offer for sale" and (2) "ready for patenting." There is no dispute here that the method, system, and computer-readable medium used by Quest during the Norco Sale were ready for patenting at the time of the Norco Sale. The question is whether the invention was the subject of a commercial offer for sale before the critical date. This inquiry requires there have been a "commercial offer," and "the invention that [wa]s the subject matter of the offer for sale must satisfy each claim limitation of the patent, though it may do so inherently." *Scaltech, Inc. v. Retec/Tetra, LLC*, 269 F.3d 1321, 1328–29 (Fed. Cir. 2001). Further, "a sale or offer of sale need not make an invention available to the public," and "'secret sales' can invalidate a patent." *Helsinn Healthcare v. Teva Pharm. USA, Inc.*, 139 S. Ct. 628, 633 (2019).

The parties agree on appeal that the Norco Sale, which includes the Norco Strip Charts, was "a commercial offer for sale" under § 102(b). The fact that Quest did not sell its furnace inspection hardware or software (i.e., its method, computer-readable medium, or system) does not take Quest's commercial activities outside the on-sale bar rule. Rather, Quest used its method, computer-readable medium, and system commercially to perform furnace inspection services and produce the Norco Reports for its customer.

Sale of a product (here, sale of the Norco Reports) produced by performing a claimed process implicates the on-sale bar. *Cf. Quanta Comput., Inc. v. LG Elecs., Inc.*, 553 U.S. 617, 629 (2008) ("[T]his Court has repeatedly held that method patents were exhausted by the sale of an item that embodied the method."). Performance of a claimed method for compensation, or a commercial offer to perform the method, can also trigger the on-sale bar, even where no product is sold or offered for sale. As we held in *Scaltech*, "[t]he on sale bar rule applies to the sale of an 'invention,' and in this case, the invention was a process." 269 F.3d at 1328.

8   The same approach necessarily applies where a service (here, furnace tube inspection) is performed for compensation using a claimed computer-readable medium or system that generates a "product" (here, the Norco Reports). The method, system, and software used during the Norco Sale to perform furnace inspection services for compensation for a customer were thus "on sale."

Note on Secret Commercial Use

In some instances, the courts have treated secret commercial use cases as implicating the public use bar, rather than the on sale bar. One important early example is *Metallizing Engineering Co. v. Kenyon Bearing & Auto Parts Co.*, 153 F.2d 516 (2d Cir. 1946). There, an inventor was using a metal reconditioning process in secret (behind the closed doors of his workshop) and selling the fruits of the process—the reconditioned metal—to the public. Judge Learned Hand held that the inventor was barred from obtaining a patent by the public use bar. Some scholars have similarly treated these types of cases as implicating the public use bar. *See, e.g.*, Mark A. Lemley, *Does "Public Use" Mean the Same Thing It Did Last Year?*, 93 Tex. L. Rev. 1119 (2015).

Notwithstanding the courts' waffling on the question, secret commercial use cases are better understood as implicating the on sale bar, not the public use bar. The most important reason is that secret commercial use more strongly implicates the central principle animating the on sale bar: concern that the inventor will exploit the invention commercially for longer than the prescribed patent term. As Judge Hand says in *Metallizing* (again, a case in which he relied upon the public use bar), "it is a condition upon an inventor's right to a patent that he shall not exploit his discovery competitively after it is ready for patenting; he must content himself with either secrecy, or legal monopoly." In addition, "public" use is an odd fit for cases of secret commercial use, which are (by definition) not public. And finally, this doctrine operates like the on sale bar and not like the public use bar in that it applies only to the inventor, as the next section will explain. Regardless, the outcome of the cases is consistent: irrespective of which particular doctrinal category is triggered, instances of secret commercial use by an inventor before the critical date will bar that inventor from later patenting the invention.

Third-Party Rules

In all the public use and on sale cases above, it is the patent applicant who has created the prior art that makes the invention unpatentable. Indeed, this is one of the salient features of those categories of prior art: a careless inventor who does not file in time can bar herself from ever obtaining a patent.[11] Nonetheless, these cases beg the question as to when public use or sale by Party A will bar Party B from obtaining a patent, even if Party B meets all of the other requirements of patentability. That is, what are the third-party effects of placing an invention in public use or on sale? The following cases address that question, first for on sale, and then for public use.

W.L. Gore & Associates v. Garlock, 721 F.2d 1540 (Fed. Cir. 1983)

Howard T. Markey, Chief Judge.

Background

1   In late October, 1969, Dr. Gore discovered that stretching [rods of polytetrafluorethylene (PTFE), also known by du Pont's trademark TEFLON] as fast as possible enabled him to stretch them to more than ten times their original length with no breakage. The rapid stretching also transformed the hard, shiny rods into rods of a soft, flexible material. On May 21, 1970, Gore filed the patent application that resulted in the patents in suit. The '566 patent has 24 claims directed to processes for stretching highly crystalline, unsintered, PTFE.

2   The district court declared all claims of the patent invalid under 102(b) because the invention had been in public use and on sale more than one year before Gore's patent application, as evidenced by Budd [Company]'s use of the Cropper machine.

Opinion

§ 102(b) and the Cropper Machine

3   In 1966 John W. Cropper of New Zealand developed and constructed a machine for producing stretched and unstretched PTFE thread seal tape. In 1967, Cropper sent a letter to a company in Massachusetts, offering to sell his machine, describing its operation, and enclosing a photo. Nothing came of that letter. There is no evidence and no finding that the present inventions thereby became known or used in this country.

---

[11] This is unlike the "known or used by others . . . before the invention thereof" provision from pre-AIA § 102(a), under which it is nearly impossible for an inventor to bar herself from obtaining a patent. After all, an inventor cannot inform "others" of an invention before she has invented it herself.

In 1968, Cropper sold his machine to Budd, which at some point thereafter used it to produce and sell PTFE thread seal tape. The sales agreement between Cropper and Budd provided:

ARTICLE "E"—PROTECTION OF TRADE SECRETS Etc.

1. BUDD agrees that while this agreement is in force it will not reproduce any copies of the said apparatus without the express written permission of Cropper nor will it divulge to any person or persons other than its own employees or employees of its affiliated corporations any of the said known-how or any details whatsoever relating to the apparatus.

2. BUDD agrees to take all proper steps to ensure that its employees observe the terms of Article "E" 1 and further agrees that whenever it is proper to do so it will take legal action in a Court of competent jurisdiction to enforce any one or more of the legal or equitable remedies available to a trade secret plaintiff.

Budd told its employees the Cropper machine was confidential and required them to sign confidentiality agreements. Budd otherwise treated the Cropper machine like its other manufacturing equipment.

A former Budd employee said Budd made no effort to keep the secret. That Budd did not keep the machine hidden from employees legally bound to keep their knowledge confidential does not evidence a failure to maintain the secret. Similarly, that du Pont employees were shown the machine to see if they could help increase its speed does not itself establish a breach of the secrecy agreement. There is no evidence of when that viewing occurred. There is no evidence that a viewer of the machine could thereby learn anything of which process, among all possible processes, the machine is being used to practice. As Cropper testified, looking at the machine in operation does not reveal whether it is stretching, and if so, at what speed. Nor does looking disclose whether the crystallinity and temperature elements of the invention set forth in the claims are involved. There is no evidence that Budd's secret use of the Cropper machine made knowledge of the claimed process accessible to the public.

The district court held all claims of the '566 patent invalid under 102(b) because "the invention" was "in public use [and] on sale" by Budd more than one year before Gore's application for patent. [I]t was error to hold that Budd's activity with the Cropper machine, as above indicated, was a "public" use of the processes claimed in the '566 patent, that activity having been secret, not public.

Assuming, arguendo, that Budd sold tape produced on the Cropper machine before October 1969, and that that tape was made by a process set forth in a claim of the '566 patent, the issue under § 102(b) is whether that sale would defeat Dr. Gore's right to a patent on the process inventions set forth in the claims.

9   If Budd offered and sold anything, it was only tape, not whatever process was used in producing it. Neither party contends, and there was no evidence, that the public could learn the claimed process by examining the tape. If Budd and Cropper commercialized the tape, that could result in a forfeiture of a patent granted them for their process on an application filed by them more than a year later. *D.L. Auld Co. v. Chroma Graphics Corp.*, 714 F.2d 1144, 1147–48 (Fed. Cir. 1983); *see Metallizing Engineering Co. v. Kenyon Bearing & Auto Parts Co.*, 153 F.2d 516 (2d Cir. 1946). There is no reason or statutory basis, however, on which Budd's and Cropper's secret commercialization of a process, if established, could be held a bar to the grant of a patent to Gore on that process.

10   Early public disclosure is a linchpin of the patent system. As between a prior inventor who benefits from a process by selling its product but suppresses, conceals, or otherwise keeps the process from the public, and a later inventor who promptly files a patent application from which the public will gain a disclosure of the process, the law favors the latter. *See Horwath v. Lee*, 564 F.2d 948 (C.C.P.A. 1977). The district court therefore erred as a matter of law in applying the statute and in its determination that Budd's secret use of the Cropper machine and sale of tape rendered all process claims of the '566 patent invalid under § 102(b).

Nat'l Rsch. Development v. Varian Assocs., 30 U.S.P.Q.2d 1537 (Fed. Cir. 1994)

Raymond C. Clevenger III, Circuit Judge.

1   U.S. Patent No. 3,999,118 ('118 patent), entitled "Spectrographic Analysis of Materials," issued on December 21, 1976, to Hoult, who assigned his rights thereunder to NRDC. The subject matter of the '118 patent's four claims concerns a method and apparatus for eliminating systemic noise produced in a Nuclear Magnetic Resonance (NMR) spectrometer during sample analysis.

2   The invention resulted from the endeavors of Dr. David Hoult, a graduate student at Oxford University, England, while under the supervision of his advisor, Dr. (Sir) Rex Richards. A patent application to Dr. Hoult's invention was filed in the United Kingdom on April 8, 1974. The patent application from which the '118 patent issued was filed on February 27, 1975, in the United States.

3   During the period of Dr. Hoult's development work, Dr. Richards attended an Experimental NMR Conference in the United States in April 1973. While travelling to the conference one morning, Dr. Richards had an informal, one-on-one conversation on a bus with Dr. Stejskal, a Monsanto Company research scientist. During that conversation, Dr. Richards disclosed the essence of Dr. Hoult's invention to Dr. Stejskal. It is undisputed, and the district court expressly found, that Dr. Richards at that time did not ask Dr. Stejskal to keep the information confidential, and did not inform him that either he or Dr. Hoult intended to file for a patent thereon.

Upon his return to Monsanto, Dr. Stejskal and his colleague, Dr. Schaefer (the Monsanto scientists), collaborated in incorporating Dr. Hoult's invention as disclosed by Dr. Richards into one of the NMR spectrometers in their Monsanto research laboratory. As the district court found, "by the summer of 1973, more than one year before the application for Hoult patent [sic] was filed in the United States," the Monsanto NMR spectrometer modified by the Monsanto scientists was using the subject matter of the '118 patent. The Monsanto scientists then used this modified spectrometer as an analytical tool to determine, *inter alia,* whether the then-experimental herbicide "Roundup" was safe for release into the environment.

In 1989, NRDC filed suit against Varian Associates, Inc. in the U.S. District Court for the District of New Jersey alleging infringement of its '118 patent. [The district court held a bench trial.] The court held "the patent" invalid under the public use bar of 35 U.S.C. § 102(b) because the Monsanto scientists were using the spectrometer in the usual course of Monsanto's business, without restriction, more than one year before the filing date of Dr. Hoult's patent application in the United States.

[Discussion]

This court in *In re Smith,* 714 F.2d 1127 (Fed. Cir. 1983), defined the public use of a claimed invention under section 102(b) as including "any use of that invention by a person other than the inventor who is under no limitation, restriction or obligation of secrecy to the inventor." *Id.* at 1134 (citing *Egbert v. Lippmann,* 104 U.S. (14 Otto) 333, 336 (1881)).

On appeal, NRDC argues that the district court erred in concluding that the facts of this case evidence a prior public use, as defined by *In re Smith,* because the totality of the circumstances indicates that there was an "understanding" between Drs. Richards and Stejskal that the information was not to be disclosed to the public, and therefore that the information was provided under enough of a restriction to preclude a public use bar. Relying on *W.L. Gore & Assocs., Inc. v. Garlock, Inc.,* 721 F.2d 1540 (Fed. Cir. 1983), NRDC reasons that the district court therefore erred as a matter of law in placing undue emphasis on the absence of a restrictive or confidentiality agreement. We disagree.

There is ample evidence in the record to support the district court's factual finding that the information was disclosed to Dr. Stejskal without any restriction on use or dissemination. The "totality of the circumstances," even including describing the conversation on the bus as "private," simply does not support NRDC's position. Moreover, the mere fact that Drs. Richards and Stejskal had known each other for many years cannot of itself create the "understanding" of confidentiality that NRDC struggles to establish, especially since the NMR Conference was specifically designed to encourage intellectual discourse through the free disclosure of information. Thus, the unrestricted disclosure of the invention, coupled with use of that information in the ordinary course of business, renders that use public.

9   Moreover, use by only one member of the public, without that use informing other members of the public as to the true nature of the invention, is sufficient under Supreme Court jurisprudence to invalidate a patent under section 102(b) for prior public use. *See, e.g., Egbert v. Lippmann,* 104 U.S. (14 Otto) at 336 ("If an inventor . . . gives or sells [the invention] to another, to be used by the donee or vendee, without limitation or restriction, or injunction of secrecy and it is so used, such use is public, even though the use and knowledge of the use may be confined to one person."). Thus, even assuming that only the Monsanto scientists had access to the modified spectrometer, and that others visiting the laboratory had no idea as to the true nature thereof, the Monsanto scientists' knowledge and use alone provide sufficient basis on which to invoke the statutory bar of section 102(b). Monsanto's internal policies concerning dissemination of information are to that extent irrelevant.

10   *W.L. Gore* is not contrary to this result. In that case, this court concluded that the facts did not support a public use bar because an entity entirely separate from the inventor, Cropper, had independently developed the subject matter of the subsequently issued patent and had kept it entirely secret from the public, even though it had been used in a commercial process. We reasoned:

> As between a prior inventor who benefits from a process by selling its product but suppresses, conceals, or otherwise keeps the process from the public, and a later inventor who promptly files a patent application from which the public will gain a disclosure of the process, the law favors the latter.

721 F.2d at 1550. The present case, however, does not involve a secret development of the patent's subject matter wholly separate from the patentee. Rather, the source of the information about the invention which led to the public use was indirectly the patentee himself. Under United States patent law, an inventor has the obligation to avoid public use of his invention more than one year before filing, in order to preserve his right to receive a patent thereon. *See Moleculon Research,* 793 F.2d at 1265. This applies as much to the inventor's confidants as it does to the inventor himself. Thus, in order to avoid application of the public use bar of section 102(b), Dr. Richards, having free access to Dr. Hoult's invention, had to refrain from freely disclosing information concerning that invention. Since Dr. Richards failed to do so, Dr. Hoult failed to meet his obligation and the resulting public use of the invention invalidates NRDC's patent on the subject matter publicly used. This result furthers the important public policy of discouraging the removal of inventions from the public domain which members of the public justifiably have come to believe are freely available.

Note on Third-Party Rules

Gore v. Garlock is really a case of third-party secret commercial use: Budd was using the process in secret and selling the (non-informing) fruits of that process publicly. The Federal Circuit held that Budd's secret commercial use did not bar Gore from later obtaining a patent. This echoed a result from 43 years earlier, when the Second Circuit (in the person of Judge Learned Hand) held in *Gillman v. Stern*, 114 F.2d 28 (2d Cir. 1940), that a third party's secret commercial use of a pneumatic machine used in quilting did not invalidate another inventor's later effort to obtain a patent. The Federal Circuit again affirmed this understanding in *BASF Corp. v. SNF Holding Co.*, 955 F.3d 958, 967 (Fed. Cir. 2020).

One would imagine that other types of secret sales similarly should not bar third parties if they do not lead to public use. For instance, suppose Alice creates an invention and offers it for sale (without disclosing any information about it), but the sale is never accepted. Alice has triggered the on sale bar, and under *Pfaff* she will be barred from obtaining a patent if she does not file within a year. But should her offer for sale bar Brian, another inventor who is unconnected with Alice? Everything we know about the on sale bar indicates that the answer should be "no." Per *Pfaff*, the on sale bar exists to prevent inventors from commercially exploiting their inventions for longer than the twenty-year statutory period. Brian is not doing that; only Alice is. And from the perspective of patent law, there is no meaningful difference between secret commercial use that does not disclose the invention and a secret sale that does not disclose the invention. Both involve commercial exploitation, neither involves any sort of public use, and neither creates enabling prior art. It would seem that they should be treated identically.

However, this is not what the Federal Circuit has said. That court has stated explicitly, on multiple occasions, that third-party sales will bar *anyone* from obtaining a patent. *See, e.g., Zacharin v. United States*, 213 F.3d 1366, 1371 (Fed. Cir. 2000) ("Finally, under this court's precedents, it is of no consequence that the sale was made by a third party, not by the inventor."); *Abbott Laboratories v. Geneva Pharmaceuticals, Inc.*, 182 F.3d 1315, 1318 (Fed. Cir. 1999) ("Furthermore, the statutory on-sale bar is not subject to exceptions for sales made by third parties either innocently or fraudulently."). At the same time, every case in which the Federal Circuit has held that a third-party sale bars another inventor has involved a sale that was not secret. In all of those cases, the sale either put the invention into public use—by making embodiments of the invention publicly available—or disclosed the invention to the public in an enabling way.

Zacharin offers a good example. In that case, the inventor, an engineer working for the Army, disclosed the invention to the Army. The Army in turn disclosed it to a third-party private company (Breed), which manufactured 6000 units and sold them back to the Army. The court held that this third-party sale (Breed to the Army) barred the inventor. There is no mention of Breed being bound by any duty of secrecy. At minimum, then, the invention appears to have been in public use by Breed itself. The argument for public use here is even stronger than it would be in a typical case because Breed was actively induced by the inventor to use the invention, without any mention of a patent. The public use bar exists to protect reliance interests on the part of members of the public who believe that they have access to an unpatented invention. Those reliance interests loom especially large in a case such as this one. And as *National Research Development Corp. v. Varian* teaches, the public use bar is not party-specific, precisely because the concern is for the public's reliance interests, which can be triggered regardless of which party puts the invention into public use.

Lower courts have gone back and forth on this question. Some lower courts have held that the on sale bar is party-specific: a sale by one party does not preclude another party from obtaining a patent, so long as the sale does not also trigger the public use bar. *See, e.g., Schlumberger Tech. Corp. v. BICO Drilling Tools*, 2019 WL 2450948 (S.D. Tex. June 12, 2019); *MDS Associates v. United States*, 37 Fed. Cl. 611 (1997). *MDS* is illustrative. That case involved a patent on technology used to prevent ship-to-ship collisions. More than a year before the patent application was filed, a third party—the United States Navy—sold the invention to the nation of West Germany. As befitting a sale from one country's military to another's, the sale was confidential and the technology was protected by various secrecy and classification rules. The court held that the secret third-party sale did not bar the patent. In other cases, however, courts have held that truly secret sales nonetheless trigger the on sale bar against third parties. *See, e.g., Piet v. United States*, 176 F. Supp. 576 (S.D. Cal. 1959).

Accordingly, there are two ways of understanding this area of law. The first accords with the language of Federal Circuit opinions: the on sale bar is not party-specific. A sale by one party will bar a patent by another party who was unconnected to the sale. However, there are two problems with this approach. The first is that it requires incorporating at least one exception for secret commercial use (as in *Gore v. Garlock*). (Again, the Federal Circuit has never decided a case involving a truly secret sale by a third party.) There is of course nothing wrong with exceptions to a doctrine when the exceptions are motivated by some compelling reason. But here, there is no reason whatsoever that secret commercial use should be treated differently than secret sales when they implicate precisely the same policy concerns. This relates to the second—and more significant—problem, which is that the policy underlying the on sale bar dictates that it should be party-specific. Again, as the Supreme Court explains in *Pfaff*, the primary focus of the on sale bar is the threat that a party will attempt to exploit a patent beyond the prescribed twenty-year term. Actions by one party simply do not implicate this concern with respect to another party; the second party has done nothing wrong.

The second way of understanding this area of law is to view the on sale bar as purely party-specific: sales by A can only bar A, not B. However, sales by A will often give rise to other types of statutory bars. If Alice sells 1000 units of her invention to the public, the invention is now in public use. The public use bar is not party-specific, so those uses will bar Brian from obtaining a patent on the same invention. But if Alice's sale had been non-public, or if her offer for sale had never been accepted, the offer itself would bar only Alice and not Brian.

There are several important virtues to this approach. First, and most importantly, it would align the on sale and public use doctrines with their underlying policies. The on sale bar would be party-specific because it exists to vindicate a party-specific policy objective; the public use bar would not be party-specific because it exists to vindicate a policy objective that concerns the public at large, rather than any specific patent applicant. Second, it would eliminate the need for a special, unprincipled exception for secret commercial use. The downside of this approach is that it would conflict with the Federal Circuit's language. But critically, it would not actually conflict with any of the Federal Circuit's results. As we explained above, every case in which the Federal Circuit has stated that the on sale bar applies to third parties has also involved some element of public use. Those cases are better understood as instances in which a sale led to public use, which in turn barred all parties from patenting. Indeed, the Federal Circuit has at least once described the two bars as operating in this manner. In a footnote to *In re Caveney*, 761 F.2d 671 (Fed. Cir. 1985), the court wrote:

> The "on sale" provision of 35 U.S.C. § 102(b) is directed at precluding an inventor from commercializing his invention for over a year before he files his application. Sales or offers made by others and disclosing the claimed invention implicate the "public use" provision of 35 U.S.C. § 102(b).

For these reasons, we think that this second route is the best way to understand the on sale and public use bars. It better aligns doctrine with policy and principle, and it rationalizes the doctrine without epicycles of caveats and exceptions.[12] From the perspective of students looking to learn and understand the law, we believe this is the cleanest and most rational approach. We hope that the Federal Circuit will soon come to see it our way and alter how it discusses these cases. But please exercise caution! If you are writing a brief to a court or a memo to a senior partner, you are well-advised not to blithely state that the on sale bar is party-specific. Less enlightened lawyers who have not learned from this book may not understand what you mean. Rather, you should explain that the Federal Circuit claims that sales bar everyone from patenting, but that in fact it has never held that a secret sale bars a third party when that secret sale did not also create public use. Lower courts tend to treat the on-sale bar as party-specific, and this is the better understanding for the reasons detailed above. Accordingly, the law is in flux, and good arguments to the Federal Circuit will be necessary to clarify it.

---

[12] There is one other potential option, which is that the court could maintain that the on sale bar is not party-specific but carve out an exception for "secret" sales, which would bar only the party making the sale, where "secret" means "does not create a public use." This would harmonize the rules for secret sales and secret commercial use, but only by creating yet another exception to the general rule. If this is how the court believes these cases should be decided (as it should), better to simplify matters by treating the on sale bar as party-specific and the public use bar as not.

Practice Problem: Third-Party Rules

In 1998, S invented a new type of motor to be used in drilling for oil and gas. Separately, K invented the same type of motor the same year. In 1999, K exhibited the motor itself, as well as drawings of the motor, at a trade show. The motor was available for viewing but could not be touched or examined. The drawings outlined the basic features of the motor but did not contain all of the technical detail that would have been necessary to build the motor. In 2000, K reached a confidential agreement to sell 1000 motors to B. B planned to resell the motors on the retail market. Those motors were eventually delivered in 2003, and B resold them on the retail market in 2004. In 2002, S filed for a patent on the invention. Is S's patent valid? Why or why not?

(a) Would your answer have been different if K had delivered the motors to B in 2000, and B had immediately resold them to retail purchasers who began using them?

(b) Would your answer be different in either scenario above if the events were shifted forward in time so they were governed by the AIA?

See Schlumberger Tech. Corp. v. BICO Drilling Tools, 2019 WL 2450948 (S.D. Tex. June 12, 2019).

5. Public Disclosure and the AIA Third-Party Grace Period

Post-AIA § 102(b)(1)(A) provides a one-year grace period for prior art disclosed by the patent filer herself. For instance, if an inventor discloses an invention via a printed publication, under § 102(b)(1)(A) that inventor has one year to file for a patent before she will have barred herself. In this respect, the post-AIA and pre-AIA law are identical. And this one-year grace period distinguishes the U.S. patent system from that in many other jurisdictions, in which any public disclosure bars a later patent.

Now consider post-AIA § 102(b)(1)(B). That section provides a one-year grace period with regard to prior art disclosed by a *third party*, but only if the invention had *previously been "publicly disclosed"* by the applicant herself or someone associated with her. So, for instance, if Alice creates a printed publication disclosing an invention on March 1, before Kavita has disclosed anything, Kavita is forever barred from filing a patent on that invention. However, if Kavita discloses the invention via a printed publication on February 1, and then Alice discloses on March 1, Kavita's earlier disclosure creates a one-year grace period with respect to her own disclosure *and* Alice's disclosure. So long as she files before February 1 of the following year, she will not be barred by these pieces of prior art. Because of this feature, the AIA is sometimes referred to as a "first-to-publish" system, rather than a first-to-file system.

Importantly, however, post-AIA § 102(b)(1)(B) states that the grace period only applies if the patent applicant *publicly* disclosed before the other party's prior art came into existence. This is in contrast to §§ 102(b)(1) and 102(b)(1)(A), which refer to the various categories of prior art merely as "disclosures," without the "public" modifier. What does it mean to publicly disclose, as opposed to merely disclosing? This statutory provision has never been adjudicated, so it is difficult to say for certain. But we can guess. Paper prior art—which must necessarily be both public and enabling— are almost surely public disclosures of the invention. Public use, by its very nature, is presumably a public disclosure as well. (After all, public use is defined by its publicness.) However, we suspect that secret commercial uses and secret sales—sales that do not create public uses—would not be considered public disclosures. These types of disclosures create no enabling information and do not make the invention available to the public. If the requirement that a disclosure be "public" is to have any meaning, it must disqualify disclosures that do neither of those things.

This understanding of the § 102(b)(1)(B) third-party grace period has the virtue of unifying that provision of law with the general third-party prior art rules described above. Paper prior art and public uses, which bar third parties from patenting, would similarly insulate the disclosing party against subsequent third-party disclosures. Secret commercial uses and secret sales, which do not bar third parties from patenting, would not insulate the "disclosing" party against subsequent third-party disclosures. Public disclosures are public for all purposes; secret "disclosures" are secret for all purposes.

Practice Problems: Third-Party AIA Grace Period

1. On January 1, 2015, A writes a blog post describing and enabling a new invention. Four days later, completely independently, B writes a blog post describing the same invention. B files for a patent on October 15, 2015, and A files for a patent on November 1, 2015. What result?

2. Same facts as question 1, but now A filed on February 1, 2016, and B filed on February 10, 2016. What result then?

3. A invents a widget on Jan. 1, 2015. On June 1, 2015, A reaches an agreement to sell the widget to B. This agreement is never made public. C invents the same widget on July 1, 2015 and files for a patent on October 1, 2015. A files for a patent on October 2, 2015. What result?

4. A invents a widget on Jan. 1, 2015. On April 1, 2015, A gives an enabling oral presentation about the widget to an audience of 50 widget purchasers. The next day, one of them writes an enabling blog post about the widget. Without reading the blog post, B files for a patent on the widget on April 3, 2015. A files for a patent on April 5, 2015. What result?

5. A invents a widget on Jan. 1, 2015. On May 1, 2015, A offers the widget for sale to some widget users. Word leaks out that a new widget is for sale, but no details about it are revealed. On June 1, 2015, A tells three friends, B, C, and D, all about the widget. On June 1, 2015, B writes a blog post about the widget but does not explain how to manufacture it. On June 2, 2015, E independently figures out how to make the widget and files for a patent on it. A files for a patent on July 1, 2015. What result?

6. A invents a widget on Jan. 1, 2015. On Feb. 1, 2015, B steals technical information that enables the widget from A and publishes it on her blog. On Jan. 15, 2015, C invents the same widget. On Jan. 16, 2015, C offers to sell 50 widgets to D. The offer is secret, and no information regarding it reaches the public. On April 2, 2015, C puts up a website describing the widget in enabling fashion. On October 1, 2015, C files for a patent on the widget. On November 1, 2015, A files for a patent on the widget. Result?

7. Same facts as question 6, but now A files Mar. 1, 2016. Result?

B3. Earlier Invention as Prior Art Under Pre-AIA § 102(g)

In some cases, the pre-AIA question of who invented first can be settled with reference to the types of § 102(a) prior art discussed above. Before the second inventor can invent, the first inventor will have already produced a printed publication, a patent application, or put the invention into public use. But in other instances, two (or more) parties might invent before either of them can publicize the invention. Section 102(g) exists to govern invention races in these sorts of cases.

Section 102(g) is complex; you should take a moment to reread that statutory section and then probably read it a third time. Importantly, § 102(g) is phrased in the negative. It states that a party *cannot* obtain a patent if there is another party who (a) invented first *and* (b) did not abandon, suppress, or conceal the invention. Thus, it is possible to obtain a patent even if one *did not* invent first, or if one abandoned, suppressed, or concealed the invention. So long as there is not *another party* with a stronger claim to having invented, § 102(g) will not bar an applicant from receiving a patent.

Also pay attention to the two key differences between § 102(g)(1) and § 102(g)(2). First, they differ in whether both independent inventors are seeking U.S. patent rights. When both are, the USPTO declares an "interference" between the parties under § 102(g)(1) and conducts a trial-like hearing to determine which party will receive the patent. When only one inventor seeks patent rights, a second inventor's earlier invention can serve as prior art under § 102(g)(2) as long as she did not abandon, suppress, or conceal the invention. That is, you can win an invention race and bar others from patenting without ever filing yourself. The second difference between § 102(g)(1) and § 102(g)(2) is that they differ in territorial scope. For interferences under § 102(g)(1), the invention locations can be almost anywhere (since 1995, any country that is a member of the World Trade Organization). For § 102(g)(2), the prior art invention must have been in the United States.

The following subsections will decompose the various component parts of § 102(g) in depth. In brief, as illustrated in the following figure, the process of *invention* starts with *conception*—having a definite and permanent idea of the complete and operative invention—and ends with *reduction to practice*.

The Process of Invention

1. Constructive reduction to practice by filing enabling patent application

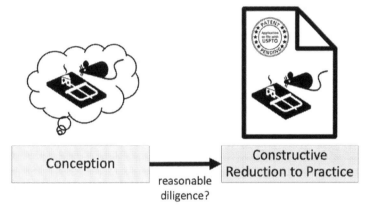

2. Actual reduction to practice through real-world embodiment

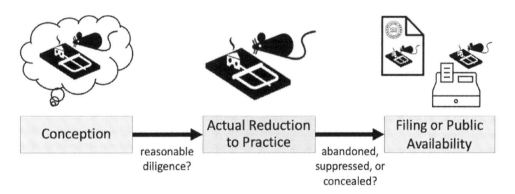

Reducing an invention to practice can be done either by constructing a product or performing a process within the scope of the claim (known as *actual* reduction to practice) or by filing an enabling patent application (*constructive* reduction to practice). If the inventor demonstrates *reasonable diligence* throughout the entire period between conception and reduction to practice, then the priority date for invention is the date of conception; otherwise, it is the date of reduction to practice. If the first inventor has engaged in actual reduction to practice, patent rights could still go to a second inventor under § 102(g) if the first inventor has *abandoned, suppressed, or concealed* the invention rather than bringing the invention to the public by either filing a patent application or commercializing it. As we will explain more below, "abandoned, suppressed or concealed" is a unified idea, not three separate concepts, and it does not require active suppression—delay due to neglect can fall under this category, although the standard is not as exacting as the diligence inquiry.

1. Conception and Reduction to Practice

Invention begins with conception. The term "conception" might bring to mind the first moment an inventor has an idea for an invention—the "aha" moment that sparks the process of inventing. In fact, however, conception is much more than a spark of an idea. Rather, conception is the "formation in the mind of the inventor, of a *definite and permanent idea of the complete and operative invention*, as it is thereafter to be applied in practice." *Coleman v. Dines,* 754 F.2d 353, 359 (Fed. Cir. 1985). Thus, to have conceived of an invention, an inventor must have a sense of how the full invention will be constructed and how it will function. This doesn't necessarily mean that the inventor needs to have built the invention or even produced detailed blueprints and schematics. But it does require much more than just an initial idea.

Invention concludes with reduction to practice, which can be established in either of two ways. First, the party can simply file a patent application. This is known as "constructive reduction to practice." Second, the party can (a) make the actual invention and (b) ascertain that it works for its intended purpose. This is known as "actual reduction to practice." These two routes to reduction to practice are treated as equivalent because either way, the inventor has concluded the inventive process: either the invention has been completed and the inventor knows it will work, or the inventor has filed a patent, which requires legal affirmation that the inventor has enabled the invention.

The text of § 102(g) does not explain the relationship between conception and reduction to practice or the conditions under which an inventor who is first to one stage or another will be declared the first inventor. However, the courts have clarified this issue. The first inventor is the party who reduced to practice first, *unless* another party can prove that it (a) conceived first and (b) was diligent during the relevant period. We will discuss the requirement of diligence at greater length in the next subsection.

Finally, note that if a party cannot prove when it conceived of an invention or when it reduced to practice, the party can always rely on its filing date. Filing the patent counts as constructive reduction to practice, and so a party that cannot prove conception or reduction to practice prior to the date of its filing will be treated as if it conceived and reduced to practice on its filing date.

Practice Problems: Conception and Reduction to Practice

1. Suppose I'm working on inventing a cancer drug. I know what the chemical compound is, but I don't know whether it should be administered in pill or liquid form. Have I conceived?

2. Suppose I want to make a new type of electric car. It needs a special battery, and I don't know yet if there's a battery that will work for it. Have I conceived?

3. Once I have conceived of my electric car, how can I reduce the invention to practice? Are there advantages to the inventor of pursuing one route over the other?

4. Recall that in *Pfaff*, the Supreme Court held that "the invention" exists once it is "ready for patenting," meaning that the inventor would be capable of constructively reducing the invention to practice at that point by filing for a patent. How does "ready for patenting" map onto the conception → reduction-to-practice timeline of an invention? Is it the same thing as reduction to practice? Is it the same thing as conception?

2. Reasonable Diligence

If an inventor is first to conceive but second to reduce to practice, she may stretch her invention date back past her reduction-to-practice date if she shows *reasonable diligence*; any periods of inactivity must be legally excused. The Federal Circuit has stated that the purpose of this inquiry is to ensure the invention was not "unreasonably delayed by the first inventor during the period after the second inventor entered the field." *Brown v. Barbacid*, 436 F.3d 1376, 1379 (Fed. Cir. 2006).

To establish reasonable diligence, the first party to conceive must demonstrate "reasonably continuing activity" directed toward actual or constructive reduction to practice during the critical period between the second party's conception and the first party's reduction to practice. *Id.* at 1380. Diligence is a strict standard. Reasonable diligence must be shown "throughout the entire critical period." *Monsanto v. Mycogen Plant Science*, 261 F.3d 1356, 1369 (Fed. Cir. 2001). Although "there need not necessarily be evidence of activity on every single day if a satisfactory explanation is evidenced," all gaps must be accounted for with either activity related to reduction to practice or a reasonable excuse. *Id.* Diligence and its corroboration may be shown by a variety of activities, including time obtaining necessary supplies, testing, and preparing a patent application. Reasonable diligence is a question of fact that is assessed on a case-by-case basis, and an inventor's testimony must be corroborated.

Efforts directed to "ongoing laboratory experimentation" are the clearest evidence of diligence, whereas "pure money-raising activity that is entirely unrelated to practice of the process" does not demonstrate diligence. *Scott v. Koyama*, 281 F.3d 1243 (Fed. Cir. 2002). Delay will be excused for "reasonable everyday problems and limitations" such as illness, short vacations, the demands of an everyday job, or delays in receiving necessary materials, but not for "efforts to refine an invention to the most marketable and profitable form." *Griffith v. Kanamaru*, 816 F.2d 624 (Fed. Cir. 1987). To provide some sense of how courts evaluate diligence, inventors were found to be reasonably diligent in the following cases:

- The inventor's laboratory notebook showed evidence of activity on all but six days of the 31-day critical period, and each of those six days was a single-day gap. *Brown v. Barbacid*, 436 F.3d 1376 (Fed. Cir. 2006).

- During an eleven-month critical period, laboratory notebooks demonstrated activity during every month, from which a jury could reasonably infer the work was ongoing without interruption, despite the lack of daily entries. *Monsanto Co. v. Mycogen Plant Science*, 261 F.3d 1356 (Fed. Cir. 2001).

- The inventor's patent attorney was working on the patent application during the three-month critical period. There was no specific evidence of activity during three portions of this period (lasting nineteen, three, and eighteen days), but there was evidence from which the court could infer what activities occurred during those gaps (such as time the inventor spent responding to the attorney's questions). *Perfect Surgical Techniques v. Olympus America*, 841 F.3d 1004 (Fed. Cir. 2016).

- Over a seventeen-day critical period, the inventor showed daily activity directed toward building a facility for large-scale commercial practice of a chemical process. Although these activities "were not of themselves an actual reduction to practice," they were "directly aimed at achieving actual practice" and are not disqualified by their commercial scale. *Scott v. Koyama*, 281 F.3d 1243 (Fed. Cir. 2002).

In contrast, the activities in these cases were found to not constitute reasonable diligence:

- A "bald assertion" of diligence during an eighteen-month critical period fails to raise a genuine issue of material fact because a party must "account for the entire period during which diligence is required." *Creative Compounds, LLC v. Starmark Labs.*, 651 F.3d 1303 (Fed. Cir. 2011).

- The inventor, a professor at Cornell University, had a three-month period of inactivity to wait for a graduate student to arrive and for grant funding to come through. Cornell's standard academic policy of waiting for outside research funding reflects a choice "to assume the risk that priority in the invention might be lost to an outside inventor." *Griffith v. Kanamaru*, 816 F.2d 624 (Fed. Cir. 1987).

- Over a five-month critical period, the inventor's patent attorney "had a few conversations with [the inventor], conducted a prior art search, billed for under 30 hours of work, and drafted the patent application." There were few records showing the exact days when activity specific to the application occurred, allowing the Federal Circuit to find that substantial evidence supported the PTAB's finding that the inventor had failed to demonstrate sufficient attorney diligence. *In re Enhanced Sec. Rsch.*, LLC, 739 F.3d 1347 (Fed. Cir. 2014).

Discussion Questions: Reasonable Diligence

1. *Why Require Diligence?* Why do you think patent law has a diligence requirement at all, and what's the best justification for such a strict standard?

2. *Why Not Require Everyone's Diligence?* Diligence is only relevant in one situation: when the party who was first to reduce to practice was not first to conceive. That is, if a given party is both first to conceive and first to reduce to practice, it is irrelevant how diligent that party was during the period between conception and reduction to practice. The inventor could have taken 10 year-long vacations to Tahiti in the intervening time, and she still would win the § 102(g) priority race. Why should this be? What policy rationale explains this rule? And what policies would be furthered by adopting a contrary rule that required diligence irrespective of who was first to conceive and reduce to practice?

Practice Problems: Reasonable Diligence

1. Suppose I conceive of an idea, but I have a full-time job teaching patent law. So I work on my new idea one or two evenings/week, though I'm mostly spending time on my full-time job. Have I been diligent?

2. Suppose I conceive of an idea, and then I take a five-year vacation. Toward the end of my vacation, I hear that you're about to start doing research on the same technologies. I rush home and get back to work on my invention immediately, two days before you begin work. Have I been diligent?

3. Consider the following timeline:

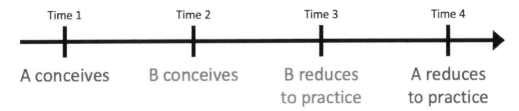

If both parties are diligent, who will win the § 102(g) priority race? Whose diligence is relevant in this scenario? During what period must that party establish diligence? Why not require that each party be diligent from the moment of her conception until the moment of her reduction to practice?

3. Abandonment, Suppression, Concealment

An earlier inventor will not win an interference under § 102(g)(1) or have her invention count as prior art under § 102(g)(2) if she "abandoned, suppressed, or concealed" the invention between actual reduction to practice and bringing the invention to the public by filing a patent application or commercializing the invention. Like the reasonable diligence inquiry, whether a first inventor abandoned, suppressed, or concealed an invention is a fact-specific equitable inquiry, but the standard is less exacting than it is for diligence—delays are typically measured in years rather than days or weeks.

Abandonment, suppression, or concealment can be shown not only through deliberate concealment but also through inactivity and neglect. For example, in *Peeler v. Miller,* 535 F.2d 647 (C.C.P.A. 1976), Miller invented in 1966, Peeler filed in 1968 (and could not establish an earlier invention), and then Miller filed in 1970. During the four years between invention and filing, Miller's invention was sitting in a backlog of invention disclosures in the legal office of his employer, Monsanto. The court held that "a four-year delay from the time an inventor is satisfied with his invention and completes his work on it and the time his assignee-employer files a patent application is, prima facie, unreasonably long" and constituted abandonment, suppression, or concealment. *Id.* at 654.

The abandonment, suppression, concealment inquiry is an equitable one. Accordingly, not all delays are treated equally. It matters what the first inventor was doing between reduction to practice and filing. The Federal Circuit has indicated that if the inventor was working to "improve or perfect the invention," a multi-year delay is excusable. *Lutzker v. Plet*, 843 F.2d 1364, 1367 (Fed. Cir. 1988). However, these improvements (or perfections) must be reflected in the final patent application: they must involve claimed elements, and they must be described in the specification. If the delay is due to efforts to commercialize the invention—prepare it for market, but not in a way that changes the actual patented invention—a court will not excuse a longer delay (although the standard is still less strict than for diligence). Lutzker's patent was on a machine for making canapes (!), but his post-reduction to practice activity involved creating different canape molds and publishing a recipe book, none of which appeared in the patent application. Accordingly, the court held that Lutzker had abandoned his invention for purposes of § 102(g) by waiting over 4 years to file.

On the other hand, as we noted at the beginning of this section, not every § 102(g) priority contest involves two parties who both filed for patents. Sometimes one party will bring the invention directly to market without attempting to patent it or disseminate it to the public through a printed publication or some other means.

That party can still bar others from patenting under § 102(g)(2) if it was the first party to invent and did not abandon, suppress, or conceal. In such cases, the relevant time period for measuring abandonment, suppression, concealment is from reduction to practice to when the invention hits the market or appears in a printed publication (at which point it is no longer concealed from the public and can serve as § 102(a) prior art). *Palmer v. Dudzik,* 481 F.2d 1377 (C.C.P.A. 1973). When the inventor takes the product to market without patenting it, the Federal Circuit has been more permissive regarding the types of activities the inventor may engage in between reduction to practice and commercialization without the court finding that the inventor has abandoned, suppressed, or concealed. In particular, the court is more inclined to excuse time spent commercializing the invention and preparing it to be marketed and sold. *See Checkpoint Sys., Inc. v. U.S. Intern. Trade Commn.,* 54 F.3d 756, 762 (Fed. Cir. 1995). It is not necessary that the inventor have spent the intervening time improving or perfecting the invention for the equities to tilt in her favor.

As some additional examples of how courts have adjudicated these cases, the following cases found that inventors had *not* abandoned, suppressed, or concealed their inventions:

- The inventor corresponded nearly monthly with his employer's patent department in the seven months before publicly disclosing the invention, and then filed a patent application one month later, satisfying "the public policy requirement of early public disclosure." Seven months has never "been seen as raising a presumption" of abandonment. *Correge v. Murphy,* 705 F.2d 1326 (Fed. Cir. 1983).

- During a three-year period from reduction to practice to filing a patent, the inventor worked on improving the invention until his firm went into bankruptcy, and after finding work at another firm he continued to communicate with the new owner of the invention rights and was eventually hired back, at which point he continued to work on the invention until he filed a patent. "The delay of active work in these circumstances was not unreasonable and was consistent with a continuing commitment to pursuing the project to the full extent conditions allowed." *Fleming v. Escort,* 774 F.3d 1371 (Fed. Cir. 2014).

- An earlier invention as reflected in a web browser that was demonstrated to industry colleagues without a confidentiality agreement could be § 102(g)(2) prior art even though the browser was then replaced with an improved version that was posted on a public website. If improvements to an invention removed it from the prior art, "the public would lose the benefit of diligent efforts to produce a more useful product." *Eolas Techs. v. Microsoft,* 399 F.3d 1325 (Fed. Cir. 2005).

- A firm that spent two and one-half years after reduction to practice engaged in "reasonable efforts towards commercialization" and never filed a patent did not abandon, suppress, or conceal, and the firm's earlier invention constituted § 102(g)(2) prior art. *Dow Chemical v. Astro-Valcour*, 267 F.3d 1334 (Fed. Cir. 2001).

In contrast, the activities in these cases were found to constitute abandonment, suppression, or concealment:

- After reducing to practice, the inventor forwarded an invention disclosure to his firm's patent department. The matter was treated under standard docketing practice, and an application was filed twenty-nine months later. The delay raised an inference of suppression that the inventor had not rebutted. *Shindelar v. Holdeman*, 628 F.3d 1337 (C.C.P.A. 1980).

- The two-year delay in patenting after reduction to practice constituted suppression because it was due to the inventor's pursuit of a cheaper manufacturing process as opposed to perfecting the invention itself. *Young v. Dworkin*, 489 F.2d 1277 (C.C.P.A. 1974).

- During the nineteen months between reduction to practice and commercial release of a software invention, the earlier inventors failed to take "affirmative steps to make the invention publicly known" and instead entered "a web of nondisclosure agreements, confidentiality agreements, and noncompete agreements." These facts supported a jury verdict of suppression. *TQP Dev. v. 1-800-Flowers.com*, 120 F. Supp. 3d 600 (E.D. Tex. 2015), *aff'd*, 677 F. App'x 683 (Fed. Cir. 2017).

Discussion Questions: Abandonment, Suppression, Concealment

1. *Charting Time for Abandonment, Suppression, and Concealment.* The relevant time period for determining whether an inventor abandoned, suppressed, or concealed, is not entirely clear. In *Peeler*, the court counted four years of delay from Monsanto's reduction to practice until its filing date, despite the fact that Peeler only took action halfway through that four-year period. On the other hand, in *Paulik v. Rizkalla*, 760 F.2d 1270 (Fed. Cir. 1985) (en banc), Paulik invented in 1970, but his employer (again Monsanto!) did not begin work on the patent application until January or February of 1975. The second inventor, Rizkalla, filed in March 1975 (and could not establish an earlier invention), and then Paulik filed in June 1975. The en banc Federal Circuit held that Paulik did not abandon, suppress, or conceal because "the first inventor will not be barred from relying on later, resumed activity antedating an opponent's entry into the field." *Id.* at 1276. The court noted the similarities with the four-year period in *Peeler v. Miller* but distinguished the cases: "Peeler had entered the field and filed his patent application while Miller remained dormant; Rizkalla entered the field, according to the record before us, after Paulik had renewed activity on the invention." Based on this discussion, what is the relevant time period for determining whether a first inventor A has abandoned, suppressed, or

concealed if A files a patent after a second inventor B, as illustrated by the following timeline?

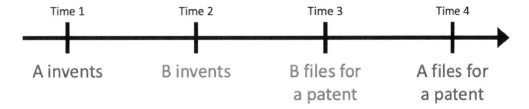

Even though *Paulik* says A can rely on resumed activity before B's entry, suggesting that the relevant period should be between Time 2 and Time 4 (as with the diligence inquiry above), *Peeler* focuses on a four-year delay, and *Paulik* claims to be consistent with *Peeler*. We think the best way to understand this is that we measure abandonment using the entire period of inactivity (Time 1 to Time 4), but that a party that abandoned can still win the priority race if it resumed activity before the other party invented (Time 2) and then did not again abandon between the resumption and filing (at Time 4). The best way to understand the law is that A "loses" the initial invention date (Time 1) upon abandonment, but can establish a new invention date upon resumption of activity.

Now consider the following timeline:

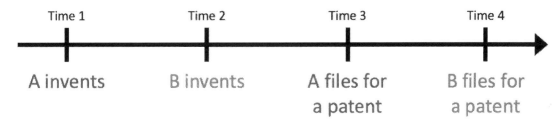

A is first to invent and first to file, so is A necessarily entitled to a patent? We think not. If A abandons immediately after invention (Time 1) and does not resume activity until A files (Time 3), then A's invention date is now Time 3, and B is the first to invent at Time 2. B will thus win the § 102(g) priority contest—unless B abandons the invention before filing. In this sense, the abandonment inquiry is not symmetric with the diligence inquiry: although we only ever care about the diligence of the first party to conceive, there may be cases in which *both* parties' abandonment becomes relevant. Do you think the Federal Circuit's approach to charting time for abandonment purposes makes sense?

2. *When Does the Second Inventor Enter the Field?* In *Paulik*, the first inventor is saved by his resumption of activity prior to the moment when the second inventor "enters the field." However, the *Paulik* court does not specify what it means to "enter the field"—is it conception, reduction to practice, or something else? As best as one can tell, the Federal Circuit dates a party's entrance into the field to its earliest invention date. So, for instance, the court will view a party as having entered the field on the date of its conception if it was diligent between conception and reduction to

practice. If the party was not diligent, or if it cannot establish an earlier conception date (like Rizkalla), it will have entered the field on the date of its reduction to practice. *Fleming v. Escort*, 774 F.3d 1371, 1378–79 (Fed. Cir. 2014). What are the pros and cons of this approach?

3. *What Time Period Should Be Relevant?* Consider again the timeline above, in which A invents first but files a patent after a second inventor B. What are the policy arguments in favor of treating the entire period of time from A's invention to A's filing as relevant to the abandonment inquiry? What are the policy arguments in favor of only considering the period from B's invention until A's filing?

4. *Why Treat Abandonment Differently from Diligence?* Recall that when evaluating diligence in a comparable situation where A is first to conceive and last to reduce to practice, the only relevant time period is between B's conception and A's reduction to practice, not the full span of time between A's conception and A's reduction to practice. Is there an argument for treating abandonment differently?

5. *Why Treat Patenting Differently from Commercialization?* What is the policy rationale for permitting different activities depending on whether the endpoint is a patent or a commercialized product?

Practice Problems: § 102(g)

Consider the following hypotheticals. What do the answers to these various hypotheticals tell you about the advantages and disadvantages of the various strategies an inventor can pursue with a new invention?

1. Suppose I reduce to practice, then let my invention sit around for 6 months, then file my patent. Have I abandoned, suppressed, or concealed?

2. Suppose I conceive, then let the invention sit around for 6 months before reducing to practice. Was I diligent? If your answer is different from question 1, why do you think that is? Why is diligence a stricter standard than abandonment, suppression, or concealment. Should it be that much stricter?

3. Suppose I reduce to practice, and then (since I'm an academic) go off and give talks for five years about how great I am and how exciting my invention is. Then I file. Have I abandoned, suppressed, or concealed?

4. Suppose in 2000 I reduce to practice, then I put the invention down to work on other things. In 2010, I pick it back up and then file. Two days later, a competitor conceives of the same invention, reduces to practice, and then files. Have I abandoned, suppressed, or concealed in the intervening decade?

5. Same question as 4, but here the other party conceives of the invention two days *before* I picked it back up? Who is going to get the patent? If your answer

is different from question 4, can you explain why they should be different? Why should a few days here or there make such a difference, as against a decade of inactivity?

6. Suppose I invent something and reduce it to practice. I then spend one year working to create a product and bring it to market. Halfway through this year-long period, you invent the same thing, reduce it to practice, and quickly bring it to market. We each file for a patent at the end of the year. Who gets the patent?

7. In January 2000, I invent a new invention. I then do nothing for five years. In January 2001, you invent the same thing. You spend a year and a half working to commercialize the invention, and in July 2002 you file for a patent on it and confidentially offer it for sale. Nobody buys the invention. In January 2005, I file for a patent on the same invention. Who is entitled to the patent?

C. The Anticipation Analysis

The rule for whether a piece of prior art anticipates a given patent claim is easy enough to state: Does the prior art reference disclose every element of the claim? (This rule is sometimes called the "identity requirement.") Recall the Swiffer patent example from the beginning of this chapter: none of the three prior art references had all four elements of the Swiffer patent claim, so it was not anticipated. But applying this rule in practice is not always straightforward. What is an "element" of a claim? Is what the reference discloses the same thing as that element?

1. Anticipation Claim Charts

As an example of how courts grapple with these kinds of questions, consider U.S. Patent No. 6,161,226, which was filed in 1999 and disclosed a baseball chest protector. Here are three of the figures from the '226 patent:

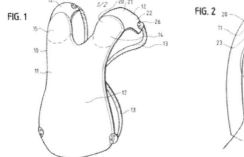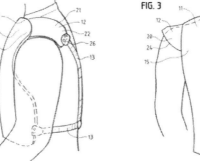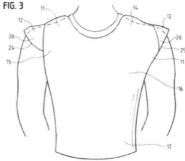

The '226 patent issued in 2000 with a single claim, to which we have added numbers corresponding to the figures above:

1. A baseball chest protector comprising:

> a flexible main pad [11] having a left shoulder portion [14], a right shoulder portion [15], a chest portion [16], and an abdomen portion [17];
>
> a flexible shoulder guard [12] extending from the left shoulder portion of the main pad over the shoulder of a wearer and having a front portion [20] adjacent the main pad, a top portion [21], and a back portion [22];
>
> and adjustable straps [13], each adjustable strap attached at one end to the abdomen portion of the main pad and at the other end to the back portion of the shoulder guard.

The assignee of the '226 patent, Everything Baseball, sued manufactures of baseball chest protectors including Wilson Sporting Goods, Rawlings Sporting Goods, and Adidas America. The defendants moved for summary judgment of invalidity, arguing that the claim was anticipated by each of three prior art references related to a chest protector invented by Major League Baseball umpire Joe West, illustrated below: (1) a chest protector manufactured and sold by Douglas Athletic Equipment beginning in 1993; (2) the paper "hang tag" for a protector sold by Wilson Sporting Goods; and (3) U.S. Patent No. 5,530,966, filed by West in 1992.

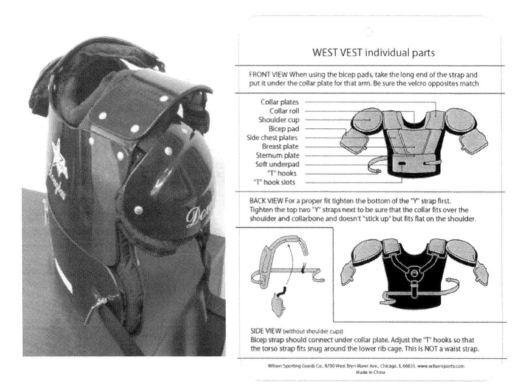

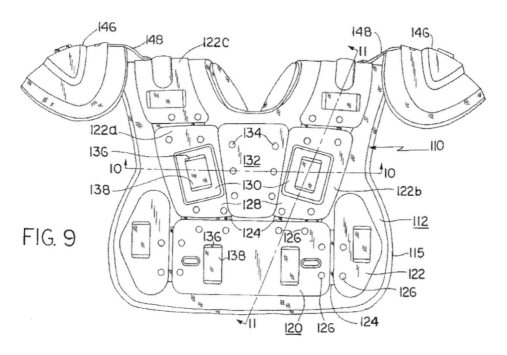

FIG. 9

In their motion for summary judgment, defendants argued:

> As each West embodiment shows, the West designed chest protector
> features both a flexible inner layer and outer shell portions. It is the
> flexible inner layer that is significant to Defendants' motion. The West
> chest protector has a flexible main pad (the inner layer) that protects
> the user's shoulders, chest, and abdomen; right and left shoulder guards
> that bend over the shoulder to protect the front, top and rear of the
> shoulder, and adjustable straps that attach and connect to the back of
> the shoulder guards and the abdomen region of the main pad.

Before you keep reading to see how the district court ruled on this motion, look
back at the claim language above and compare it with the West references. At trial,
this is typically done through what is known as a "claim chart." In a claim chart, a
party separates the claim into its component elements and attempts to identify some
feature in the prior art that matches each element—or, for the plaintiff, attempts to
show that there is no match for at least one of the claim elements.[13] We have created
a sample claim chart below. Try to identify the part of each of the three West
references that meets each claim limitation. Do you agree with the defendants that
each reference clearly anticipates the claim?

---

[13] Claim charts are also used in infringement analysis to match claim elements with
components of the product or process that is accused of infringing the patent.

Claim 1 elements	Location of element in prior art?
(1) a flexible main pad [11] having	
(a) a left shoulder portion [14],	
(b) a right shoulder portion [15],	
(c) a chest portion [16],	
(d) an abdomen portion [17];	
(2) a flexible shoulder guard [12]	
(a) extending from the left shoulder portion of the main pad over the shoulder of a wearer and having	
(b) a front portion [20] adjacent the main pad,	
(c) a top portion [21], and	
(d) a back portion [22]; and	
(3) adjustable straps [13],	
(a) each adjustable strap attached at one end to the abdomen portion of the main pad	
(b) and at the other end to the back portion of the shoulder guard.	

Everything Baseball v. Wilson Sporting Goods, 611 F. Supp. 2d 832 (N.D. Ill. 2009)

Elaine E. Bucklo, District Judge.

[1]   Although patent claims are presumed valid, that presumption can be overcome—and the claims invalidated as "anticipated"—where clear and convincing evidence shows that the claimed subject matter was previously described in a single prior art reference. To anticipate, a single reference must teach every limitation of the claimed invention. Anticipation is a question of fact.

[2]   The parties agree that to anticipate the '226 patent, at least one of the West references must demonstrate all of the following limitations: "a flexible main pad having . . . an abdomen portion"; "a flexible shoulder guard" that extends "over the shoulder of a wearer"; and "adjustable straps attached at one end to the abdomen

portion of the main pad." The parties also generally agree on the structure of the West references. Nevertheless, the parties' positions on whether these references disclose the aforementioned limitations are diametrically opposed: defendants assert that each West reference demonstrates all of the limitations, while plaintiff argues that none of the references contains any of them. I need not examine all of these disputes, however, because even a single material dispute relating to each of the references is sufficient to deny summary judgment.

1. The Douglas chest protector

3   After viewing, handling, and observing the Douglas embodiment as worn by a law clerk, I am not persuaded that this reference indisputably contains "an abdomen portion" as required by the '226 patent. When worn in what appears to be the proper position (as I assume was the case in the photographs defendants submitted in support of their motion), the Douglas chest protector comes down to just below the sternum, i.e., several inches above the navel, leaving a large portion of the abdomen exposed. I am thus baffled by defendants' contention that it is "self-evident from just looking at" this reference that it has an abdomen portion. At the very least, whether the Douglas chest protector contains an abdomen portion is a question of fact for the jury. Accordingly, the Douglas chest protector does not anticipate the patent-in-suit as a matter of law.

2. The '966 Patent

4   I am also not persuaded that the '966 patent indisputably contains "a flexible main pad." Defendants concede that the '966 patent discloses a protective garment with an outer shell layer of plastic plates (which both the specification and the claims of that patent describe as "stiff"), but they argue that the invention is nevertheless "flexible" because 1) the inner portion of the garment is flexible, which satisfies the requirement that the reference contain a "flexible main pad," and 2) the assembly taken together is flexible because the plastic plates of the outer shell are themselves flexible and, in any event, are hingedly linked so as to be capable of folding when disassembled from the inner portion.

5   To set the stage for their first argument, defendants characterize the plates as "separate components added to the flexible inner pad," then argue that the presence of "additional" features (i.e., the external plastic plates) in the '966 patent do not diminish the reference's satisfaction of the "flexible" limitation in the asserted claim. But it is not the "inner pad" that must be flexible according to the claim; it is the "main pad." I share plaintiff's skepticism that the term "main pad" can be construed as referring to the "inner pad" (rather than to the assembly of the inner and outer portions), which is how the phrase would have to be interpreted for defendants' argument to win the day. Defendants are correct that the transition "comprising" (which precedes the limitation "a flexible main pad") typically suggests an open-ended claim, and that provided all limitations of the patent-in-suit are present in a prior art reference, the presence of "additional" features in the prior art reference does not

undermine its satisfaction of the criteria for anticipation. If the claim language read, for example, "a main pad comprising a flexible inner pad," defendants might have a point, since a "main pad" having both a flexible inner pad and inflexible outer plates would presumably satisfy the limitation as written. The asserted claim, however, recites "a flexible main pad," and a reasonable interpretation of this language is that the main pad must be "flexible" when all of its components are considered together.

6   This brings me to defendants' second argument, which is that even if the inner and outer layers of the chest protector disclosed in the '966 patent are considered collectively to be the "main pad," the assembly still meets the requirement of the '226 patent that the chest protector be "flexible." I cannot decide this question as a matter of law, despite the parties' agreed-upon construction of the term "flexible" as meaning "capable of being bent or flexed." As to the first prong of defendants' argument (that the plastic plates are themselves flexible), most any material is capable of being bent or flexed if sufficient pressure is exerted (indeed, even steel structures such as buildings and bridges are engineered to be flexible enough to withstand the pressures of wind and earthquakes, for example). That some amount of pressure will cause the plastic plates to bend or flex thus does not compel the conclusion that the plates are "flexible" as that term is used in the patent-in-suit. Moreover, the '966 patent repeatedly describes the plastic plates used in the invention as "stiff." Defendants point out that the '226 patent itself also contemplates the use of plastic for the "outer casing" of the main pad. Unlike the '966 patent, however, which specifically describes the plastic plates used for the outer portion of the garment as "stiff," there is nothing in the patent-in-suit to suggest that the invention contemplates the use of "stiff" outer material in the "flexible main pad." The disclosure states only that the outer layer "may be made of any suitable material, such as fabric or plastic." In light of the overall requirement that the main pad be flexible, a reasonable interpretation of this language is that it contemplates the use of malleable, rather than "stiff" plastic for the outer casing. In sum, defendants have not demonstrated, as a matter of law, that the plastic plates of the '966 patent are "flexible" as that term is used in the patent-in-suit.

7   This leaves the second prong of defendants' second argument: that the assembly of the inner and outer portions of the invention embodied in the '966 patent is "flexible" because the "stiff" outer plates are "hingedly connected by flexible straps." This issue also cannot be resolved as a matter of law. Plaintiff and defendants point to the same portion of the '966 disclosure in support of their respective positions: a passage that discusses the relationship among the various plastic plates. The relevant text describes an embodiment of the '966 patent in which the plastic plates are connected by "flexible straps" that "afford hinge-like displacement of the associated plate elements about a hinge axis." In addition, the description specifies that "the straps are of a width and stiffness so as to resist flexing of the straps except along the hinge axis." Unsurprisingly, plaintiff focuses on the "of a width and stiffness so as to resist flexing" portion of this excerpt, while defendants emphasize the "except along

the hinge axis" portion, which they say "directly contradicts" plaintiff's argument that the invention in the '966 patent is "rigid."

8   Defendants' argument fails because even assuming the presence of flexible hinges means the exterior shell cannot accurately be characterized as "rigid," reasonable minds can differ as to whether the ability of the stiff plastic plates to be "displaced" about their axes—but not in any other direction—satisfies the requirement that the main pad be "flexible" as that term is used in the patent-in-suit. A reasonable interpretation of "flexible" as used in the '226 patent is that the main pad must be flexible in various directions, not merely among a particular axis or axes. Indeed, such an interpretation would support the patent-in-suit's stated object of protecting a catcher "without restricting the catcher's mobility," which presumably is not limited to movement along the axes formed by the interconnected plates. In other words, the hinged movement among the stiff plastic plates disclosed in the '966 patent may render the invention non-rigid without rendering it "flexible" as that term is used in the '226 patent.

9   For at least these reasons, the '966 patent does not anticipate the patent-in-suit as a matter of law.

3. The Wilson West Vest "Hang Tag"

10   First of all, other than identifying what appears to be the inner layer of the garment as the "soft underpad," there is no evidence that any or all of the portion of the West Vest corresponding to the "main pad" of the '226 patent is "flexible." The front view drawing depicts and identifies the following parts: collar plates; collar roll; shoulder cup; bicep pad; side chest plates; breast plate; sternum plate; soft underpad; "T" hooks; and "T" hook slots. (I note in passing that no "abdomen plate" is identified, and the extent to which the "sternum plate" descends below the sternum when worn is not ascertainable from the drawing.) It is not clear from the picture whether certain of these parts are overlapping or adjacent. I cannot discern, for example, whether the portion identified as the "breast plate" overlaps with the parts identified as "side chest plates," or whether one of these plate ends where the other begins. Moreover, nothing tells me the extent to which the "plate" components are themselves flexible or stiff, or how they are connected to one another, if at all. For at least these reasons, I cannot conclude as a matter of law that the Wilson "hang tag" anticipates the patent-in-suit.

11   For the foregoing reasons, defendants' motion for summary judgment is denied. [After the summary judgment motion was denied, the parties agreed to a stipulated dismissal, indicating a likely settlement.]

Practice Problem: Creating an Anticipation Claim Chart

As explained above, patent practitioners create claim charts to demonstrate which elements of a patent claim are present in another work. Invalidity claim charts show how each element is present (or not) in the prior art; infringement claim charts show how each element is present (or not) in the defendant's accused product. In this exercise,[14] you will assemble an invalidity claim chart for claim 1 of U.S. Patent No. 5,026,109 (the '109 patent), which claims a tarp system for covering a truck trailer. You represent the accused infringer, who wants to argue that the claim is anticipated by prior art U.S. Patent No. 4,189,178 (Cramaro). (Conventionally, the patent-in-suit is referred to by its last three digits, and prior art patents are referred to by the first inventor's last name.) Please download PDFs of these patents. If you forget how to do this, look back at the "Locating Patent Documents" exercise in Chapter 1.

For each limitation of claim 1 of the '109 patent, provide one or more quotes, cites, or figures from the reference demonstrating how the limitation is disclosed by that reference. If you do not believe that the reference includes one or more of the limitations, indicate that as well. We have filled in two of the rows already as models. Do you think Cramaro anticipates the '109 patent?

U.S. Patent No. 5,026,109	U.S. Patent No. 4,189,178 (Cramaro prior art)
1. A retractable segmented cover system used with a truck trailer comprising	"A tarpaulin cover system for use in trucks eliminates the need for usual side tracks for guiding the tarpaulin supporting rods." Abstract. "This invention relates to a new tarpaulin cover system for use in a truck box. More particularly, the present invention relates to a tarpauline cover system suitable for vehicles such as dump trucks or the like, frequently used in hauling sand, gravel, rocks etc." Col. 1, ll. 6–10.
(a) a plurality of flexible cover sections with	
(b) a plurality of substantially parallel supporting bows spaced therebetween and	 *Fig-6-* "Turning now to the embodiment of FIGS. 6 and 7, it will be seen that the rods 5' 6' of this embodiment are of the type of upwardly arched bows." Col. 3, ll. 45–47.

---

[14] We thank Roger Ford for creating the original version of this exercise.

(c) a drive assembly,	
(d) wherein each cover section is detachably connected between substantially parallel supporting bows,	
(e) the bows are slideably supported on the truck trailer and	
(f) at least one bow is fixedly connected to the drive assembly such that the cover system can be extended or retracted by the drive assembly and	
(g) wherein a cover section can be removed from the cover system independent of the other cover sections.	

2. Accidental and Inherent Anticipation

As we explained at the very beginning of this section on novelty, a claimed invention is unpatentable for lack of novelty only if a single piece of prior art discloses every element of the claim. Much of the time, this analysis is straightforward: a printed publication or a prior patent either does or does not describe all of the elements of the claim; an invention that is in public use or on sale either does or does not include every claim element. But in some cases, the elements of a patent claim will necessarily be present in a prior art reference without explicitly being mentioned or described in that reference. Or a reference will disclose the elements of a claim without the party who created the reference having any idea (or intention) that it does so.

These situations involve what is known as "accidental" or "inherent" anticipation, and they raise a number of related questions. Can prior art anticipate if the elements of a claim are necessarily present in the prior art reference, even if they are never explicitly mentioned? If so, under what circumstances? And must the creator of a piece of prior art realize that the claimed elements are present in the prior art in order for that prior art to anticipate a claim? If not, why not? The following two cases attempt to answer these questions.

In re Seaborg, 328 F.2d 996 (C.C.P.A. 1964)

Arthur M. Smith, Judge.

1   The application and the claims in issue relate to a new transuranic element having atomic number 95, now known as Americium (Am). Two isotopes of Americium are disclosed, Americium 241 and 242. Two general methods of synthesizing element 95 are set forth, namely (1) bombardment of plutonium with deuterons or neutrons; and (2) in a neutronic reactor operated at a relatively high power level for an extended period of time (approximately 100 days). A suitable reactor is said to be that described in Fermi et al. application Serial No. 568,904, filed December 19, 1944, which is now U.S. Patent No. 2,708,656.

The claims in issue read simply:

1. Element 95.

2. The isotope of element 95 having the mass number 241.

2   There is but a single ground of rejection involving the above claims, i.e., unpatentability over the Fermi et al. patent, for the reason that element 95 must be inherently produced in the operation of the reactor disclosed therein.

3   The Fermi et al. patent discloses several nuclear reactors. The patent does not mention elements 95 and 96. The claims in issue were first rejected on the Fermi patent in the examiner's letter of May 25, 1955.

4   Appellant, however, asserts in his brief:

The statements are exemplary only. [T]he maximum amount of americium 241 that could have been produced in the reactor operated for 100 days at 500 kilowatts power can be calculated to be 6.15×10^{-9} gram. Thus the reactor could have produced no more than one billionth [sic][15] of a gram of americium-241, and this one billionth of a gram would have been distributed throughout forty tons of intensely radioactive uranium reactor fuel. This amount of an unknown, unconcentrated isotope, if present, would have been undetectable.

---

[15] [n.3 in opinion] It would appear that appellant meant 'one one-hundred millionth' rather than 'one billionth,' since 6.15×10^{-9} gram amounts to more than six billionths of a gram.

5   The solicitor has taken no issue with appellant's assertion. In fact, the solicitor states in his brief:

> The facts are relatively simple and not actually in dispute. The rejection is not based upon a finding that the patent expressly discloses the formation of the claimed element, but rather upon the conclusion reached that that product is inherently produced in the operation of the Fermi reactor.

6   The issue here arises by application of what both the appellant and the solicitor term the "inherency doctrine," which, as we understand it, is a Patent Office doctrine which infers a lack of novelty in a product if a comparable process for making the product is found to exist in the art. When so stated and applied to the facts here this doctrine establishes a broader basis for refusing a patent than is required by the courts in finding anticipation of an issued patent. It goes beyond the rule as stated by Judge Learned Hand in *Dewey & Almy Chemical Co. v. Mimex Co.*, 124 F.2d 986, 989 (2d Cir. 1942):

> No doctrine of the patent law is better established than that a prior patent or other publication to be an anticipation must bear within its four corners adequate directions for the practice of the patent invalidated. If the earlier disclosure offers no more than a starting point for further experiments, if its teaching will sometimes succeed and sometimes fail, if it does not inform the art without more how to practice the new invention, it has not correspondingly enriched the store of common knowledge, and it is not an anticipation.

7   The record before us . . . is replete with showings that the claimed product, if it was produced in the Fermi process, was produced in such minuscule amounts and under such conditions that its presence was undetectable.

8   In the companion appeal [involving a patent application for element 96, Curium], the board stated what we consider to be the fact here, that:

> The exhibits submitted do not show that appellant could predict with any degree of definiteness the properties or characteristics of the new elements or specify with any certainty the exact procedures which could be followed, without the exercise of more than the ordinary skill of the art, to prepare these elements. Indeed, in view of the unpredictability both as to the character of the product elements and of the processes by which they might be achieved, it is particularly reasonable to hold that conception and reduction to practice are necessarily concurrent for an invention of this kind.

9   We also agree with the summary statement in appellant's brief that:

There is no positive evidence that americium was produced inherently in the natural uranium fuel by the operation of the reactor for the times and at the intensity mentioned in the exemplary statement relied upon by the Patent Office. The calculations show that the element, if produced, was produced in the most minute quantities. If the one billionth of a gram were produced, it would have been completely undetectable, since it would have been diluted with the 40 tons of intensely radioactive uranium fuel which made up the reactor.

10   Since we reject the position of the board in affirming the rejection on the Fermi patent, there is no reason to here consider the sufficiency of the Rule 131 affidavits as establishing for appellant a date of invention prior to the date of the Fermi reference.

11   For the foregoing reasons, the decision of the board is reversed.

Schering Corp. v. Geneva Pharmaceuticals, 339 F.3d 1373 (Fed. Cir. 2003)

Randall R. Rader, Circuit Judge.

1   On summary judgment, the United States District Court for the District of New Jersey determined that claims 1 and 3 of U.S. Patent No. 4,659,716 (the '716 patent) are invalid. Because the district court correctly found that U.S. Patent No. 4,282,233 (the '233 patent) inherently anticipates claims 1 and 3 of the '716 patent, this court affirms.

I.

2   Schering Corporation owns the '233 and '716 patents on antihistamines. Antihistamines inhibit the histamines that cause allergic symptoms. The prior art '233 patent covers the antihistamine loratadine, the active component of a pharmaceutical that Schering markets as CLARITIN™. Unlike conventional antihistamines when CLARITIN™ was launched, loratadine does not cause drowsiness.

3   The more recent '716 patent at issue in this case covers a metabolite of loratadine called descarboethoxyloratadine (DCL). A metabolite is the compound formed in the patient's body upon ingestion of a pharmaceutical. The ingested pharmaceutical undergoes a chemical conversion in the digestion process to form a new metabolite compound. The metabolite DCL is also a non-drowsy antihistamine. The '716 patent issued in April 1987 and will expire in April 2004 (the '233 patent issued in 1981 and has since expired).

4   The numerous defendants-appellees sought to market generic versions of loratadine once the '233 patent expired. [Under the Hatch–Waxman framework that this casebook describes in Chapter 11, defendants submitted Abbreviated New Drug Applications to the FDA along with "paragraph IV" certifications that the '716 patent

was invalid. Schering then filed this suit for infringement under 35 U.S.C. § 271(e)(2)(A).]

5   The district court construed claims 1 and 3 of the '716 patent to cover DCL in all its forms, including "metabolized within the human body" and "synthetically produced in a purified and isolated form." The parties agreed to that construction. Applying that claim construction, the district court found that the '233 patent did not expressly disclose DCL. Nonetheless, the district court also found that DCL was necessarily formed as a metabolite by carrying out the process disclosed in the '233 patent. The district court concluded that the '233 patent anticipated claims 1 and 3 of the '716 patent under 35 U.S.C. § 102(b). The district court therefore granted the appellees' motions for summary judgment of invalidity. Schering timely appealed . . . .

II.

A.

6   At the outset, this court rejects the contention that inherent anticipation requires recognition in the prior art. Precedents of this court have held that inherent anticipation does not require that a person of ordinary skill in the art at the time would have recognized the inherent disclosure. The district court therefore did not err in allowing for later recognition of the inherent characteristics of the prior art '233 patent.

7   Cases dealing with "accidental, unwitting, and unappreciated" anticipation also do not show that inherency requires recognition. *See Eibel Process Co. v. Minn. & Ontario Paper Co.*, 261 U.S. 45 (1923); *Tilghman v. Proctor*, 102 U.S. 707 (1880). The patent at issue in *Tilghman* claimed a method of forming free fatty acids and glycerine by heating fats with water at high pressure. In *Tilghman*, the record did not show conclusively that the claimed process occurred in the prior art. In reviewing the prior art, the Court referred hypothetically to possible disclosure of the claimed process. For example, the Court stated "[w]e do not regard the accidental formation of fat acid in Perkins's steam cylinder . . . (if the scum which rose on the water issuing from the ejection pipe was fat acid) as of any consequence in this inquiry." 102 U.S. at 711.

8   Applying an inherency principle in the context of an on sale bar under 35 U.S.C. § 102(b), this court has distinguished *Eibel* and *Tilghman*. *See Abbott Labs. v. Geneva Pharms., Inc.*, 182 F.3d 1315, 1319 (Fed. Cir. 1999) ("If a product that is offered for sale inherently possesses each of the limitations of the claims, then the invention is on sale, whether or not the parties to the transaction recognize that the product possesses the claimed characteristics."); *Scaltech, Inc. v. Retec/Tetra, LLC*, 269 F.3d 1321, 1330 (Fed. Cir. 2001) ("[A]ppreciation of the invention is not a requirement to trigger the statutory [on sale] bar.").

9   In the context of accidental anticipation, DCL is not formed accidentally or under unusual conditions when loratadine is ingested. The record shows that DCL necessarily and inevitably forms from loratadine under normal conditions. DCL is a necessary consequence of administering loratadine to patients. The record also shows that DCL provides a useful result, because it serves as an active non-drowsy antihistamine.

B.

10   This court recognizes that this may be a case of first impression, because the prior art supplies no express description of any part of the claimed subject matter. The prior art '233 patent does not disclose any compound that is identifiable as DCL. In this court's prior inherency cases, a single prior art reference generally contained an incomplete description of the anticipatory subject matter, i.e., a partial description missing certain aspects. Inherency supplied the missing aspect of the description. Upon proof that the missing description is inherent in the prior art, that single prior art reference placed the claimed subject matter in the public domain. This case does not present the issue of a missing feature of the claimed invention. Rather, the new structure in this case, DCL, is not described by the prior '233 patent.

11   Because inherency places subject matter in the public domain as well as an express disclosure, the inherent disclosure of the entire claimed subject matter anticipates as well as inherent disclosure of a single feature of the claimed subject matter. The extent of the inherent disclosure does not limit its anticipatory effect. In general, a limitation or the entire invention is inherent and in the public domain if it is the "natural result flowing from" the explicit disclosure of the prior art.

12   In reaching this conclusion, this court is aware of *In re Seaborg*, 328 F.2d 996 (C.C.P.A. 1964). In that case, this court's predecessor considered claims drawn to an isotope of americium made by nuclear reaction in light of a prior art patent disclosing a similar nuclear reaction process but with no disclosure of the claimed isotope. This court's predecessor found that the prior art process did not anticipate the claims because the process would have produced at most one billionth of a gram of the isotope in forty tons of radioactive material, i.e., the isotope would have been undetectable. In this case, DCL forms in readily detectable amounts as shown by the extensive record evidence of testing done on humans to verify the formation of DCL upon ingestion of loratadine.

13   This court sees no reason to modify the general rule for inherent anticipation in a case where inherency supplies the entire anticipatory subject matter. The patent law principle "that which would literally infringe if later in time anticipates if earlier," *Bristol–Myers Squibb Co. v. Ben Venue Labs., Inc.*, 246 F.3d 1368, 1378 (Fed. Cir. 2001), bolsters this conclusion. Similarly, "if granting patent protection on the disputed claim would allow the patentee to exclude the public from practicing the prior art, then that claim is anticipated." *Atlas Powder v. Ireco*, 190 F.3d 1342, 1346 (Fed. Cir. 1999). "The public remains free to make, use, or sell prior art compositions or

processes, regardless of whether or not they understand their complete makeup or the underlying scientific principles which allow them to operate. The doctrine of anticipation by inherency, among other doctrines, enforces that basic principle." *Id.* at 1348. Thus, inherency operates to anticipate entire inventions as well as single limitations within an invention.

14   Turning to this case, the use of loratadine would infringe claims 1 and 3 of the '716 patent covering the metabolite DCL. This court has recognized that a person may infringe a claim to a metabolite if the person ingests a compound that metabolizes to form the metabolite. An identical metabolite must then anticipate if earlier in time than the claimed compound.

C.

15   This court next examines whether Schering's secret tests of loratadine before the critical date placed DCL in the public domain. Before the critical date, Schering only tested loratadine in secret. Thus, according to Schering, "DCL was not publicly used, or described in any printed publication, until after February 15, 1983, the critical date for the '716 patent."

16   Anticipation does not require the actual creation or reduction to practice of the prior art subject matter; anticipation requires only an enabling disclosure. Thus, actual administration of loratadine to patients before the critical date of the '716 patent is irrelevant. The '233 patent suffices as an anticipatory prior art reference if it discloses in an enabling manner the administration of loratadine to patients.

17   To qualify as an enabled reference, the '233 patent need not describe how to make DCL in its isolated form. The '233 patent need only describe how to make DCL in any form encompassed by a compound claim covering DCL, e.g., DCL as a metabolite in a patient's body. The '233 patent discloses administering loratadine to a patient. A person of ordinary skill in the art could practice the '233 patent without undue experimentation. The inherent result of administering loratadine to a patient is the formation of DCL. The '233 patent thus provides an enabling disclosure for making DCL.

D.

18   Finally, this court's conclusion on inherent anticipation in this case does not preclude patent protection for metabolites of known drugs. With proper claiming, patent protection is available for metabolites of known drugs.

19   For example, the metabolite may be claimed in its pure and isolated form, or as a pharmaceutical composition (e.g., with a pharmaceutically acceptable carrier). The patent drafter could also claim a method of administering the metabolite or the corresponding pharmaceutical composition. The '233 patent would not provide an enabling disclosure to anticipate such claims because, for instance, the '233 patent does not disclose isolation of DCL.

20   The '716 patent contains claims 5–13 covering pharmaceutical compositions and claims 14–16 covering methods of treating allergic reactions by administering compounds that include DCL. These claims were not found anticipated by the '233 patent.

21   The district court did not err in finding that the '233 patent discloses administering loratadine to a patient, and that DCL forms as a natural result of that administration. The district court correctly concluded that DCL is inherent in the prior art. Without any genuine issues of material fact, the district court correctly granted summary judgment that claims 1 and 3 are invalid as anticipated by the '233 patent.

Discussion Questions: *Schering* and *Seaborg*

1. *Distinguishing* Seaborg. The court in *Schering* offers an argument for distinguishing the result in that case from the result in *Seaborg*. Is the distinction the *Schering* court draws persuasive? Is it compelling from a policy standpoint? Why or why not?

2. *Infringement–Anticipation Symmetry.* One of the bedrock principles of patent law is the symmetry between infringement and anticipation. Any product that would infringe a patent if it postdates the patent should anticipate the patent if it predates the patent. And vice versa. Does *Schering* preserve this symmetry? That is, the *Schering* court holds that loratadine use bars Schering from patenting DCL. If individuals had only started taking loratadine after Schering successfully patented DCL, would they infringe the DCL patent? Does *Seaborg* preserve this symmetry? That is, would use of Fermi's reactor infringe Seaborg's patent?

3. *Why Patent an Element?* When Fermi's prior art reactor patent was filed, Fermi and Seaborg were working together in Chicago on the Manhattan Project, and Seaborg's group had already synthesized americium; it was just being kept secret. Both patents were filed by the Atomic Energy Commission. Why do you think the United States patented these inventions? A front-page *New York Times* story after the C.C.P.A. decision stated: "As Dr. Seaborg explained, he was 'just a name' that the Atomic Energy Commission was using on the patents. In effect, he said, they are Government patents, taken out to protect the public against the possibility that some individual would lay a patent claim to the elements and their production methods and then attempt to force payment of royalties." Is this "defensive patenting" justification convincing?

Practice Problems: Accidental and Inherent Anticipation

1. The claims at issue involve "preparing a food product rich in glucosinolates, comprising germinated cruciferous seeds" such as broccoli and cauliflower, and

harvesting the resulting sprouts. The inventors did not create a new kind of sprout but were the first to recognize that certain kinds of sprouts are rich in glucosinolates (compounds that purportedly detoxify carcinogens). Are the claims anticipated by prior art describing preparing, harvesting, and eating sprouts including broccoli and cauliflower? *See In re Cruciferous Sprout Litig.*, 301 F.3d 1343 (Fed. Cir. 2002).

2. The claims at issue cover methods for treating hair loss by applying the chemical bimatoprost topically to the scalp. An earlier patent discloses using the same chemical to treat glaucoma by applying eyedrops to the eye. That patent's disclosure taught that the application of bimatoprost would, among other things, lead to the growth of eyelashes. However, it did not disclose any other location on the body where bimatoprost might be applied, other than the eye. Are the claims anticipated? *See Allergan v. Apotex*, 754 F.3d 952 (Fed. Cir. 2014).

3. The only claim at issue reads in its entirety: "Crystalline paroxetine hydrochloride [PHC] hemihydrate." PHC hemihydrate is a more stable version of the compound PHC, and is the active ingredient in the antidepressant drug Paxil. A prior art patent discloses a method for making PHC, and it is now recognized that practicing this method inevitably produces trace amounts of PHC hemihydrate, although the technology to detect these trace levels did not exist at the time. Is the claim anticipated by this prior art patent? *See SmithKline Beecham v. Apotex*, 403 F.3d 1331 (Fed. Cir. 2005).

4. The patent claimed methods for removing body hair using a laser. They required aligning the laser vertically over the hair follicle opening. The prior art is an instruction manual that describes how to remove tattoos using a laser. The manual did not discuss hair follicles, and it did not specify that the laser must always be aligned vertically with the skin. In some situations, however, a user who follows the manual might align the laser vertically over a hair follicle opening. Are the claims anticipated? *See MEHL/Biophile v. Milgraum*, 192 F.3d 1362 (Fed. Cir. 1999).

5. The claims recite "administering, to a patient diagnosed as in need of [stroke] treatment or prevention, an inhibitor of the renin-angiotensin system." One inhibitor of the renin-angiotensin system is the compound ramipril. Are the claims anticipated by a paper describing a protocol for a randomized trial in which ramipril would be administered to over 9000 patients at high risk for cardiovascular events such as myocardial infarction and stroke"? The study had begun before the critical date, but it was only completed (and the results were only published) after the critical date. The study ultimately found that patients who received ramipril had a statistically significant reduction in the risk of stroke, but again these results were not published until after the patent was filed and are thus irrelevant to the anticipation analysis. Are the claims anticipated? *See In re Montgomery*, 677 F.3d 1375 (Fed. Cir. 2012) (including a dissent on the inherency analysis).

3. Nonobviousness

As we've discussed, the requirement that patents be granted only on new inventions is the bedrock rule of the patent system. But the novelty doctrine is also quite limited: an invention is anticipated only if a *single* prior art reference discloses *all* elements of the claimed invention. As you might imagine, many inventions differ only slightly from the prior art. And many inventions are predictable combinations of two or more pieces of prior art.

These types of inventions would not seem to warrant patent protection for many of the same reasons that inventions that fail the test of novelty do not warrant patent protection. If an invention is so obvious that no true innovation is required to create it, then it is unlikely that a patent is necessary to incentivize its development. *See* Tun-Jen Chiang, *A Cost-Benefit Approach to Patent Obviousness*, 82 St. John's L. Rev. 39 (2008); Glynn S. Lunney, Jr., *E-Obviousness*, 7 Mich. Telecomm. & Tech. L. Rev. 363 (2001); Michael Abramowicz & John F. Duffy, *The Inducement Standard of Patentability*, 120 Yale L.J. 1590 (2011). If an invention would have been obvious to an ordinary researcher—that is, easily discovered by someone who is not relying on a patent—then awarding a patent would generate social costs (the deadweight loss from the patent) without any corresponding social benefit. In addition, the proliferation of patents on obvious inventions would create other types of costs. It is expensive and difficult for firms to comb through the stock of existing patents to determine what has and has not been patented (and thus what freedom they have to operate). And if firms were able to obtain obvious patents, they might also invest energy in acquiring those valuable property rights rather than researching new innovations.

Nonobviousness is the patent doctrine for achieving these policy goals. As the Supreme Court stated in *Graham v. John Deere*, 383 U.S. 1 (1966), the doctrine is intended to be a "means of weeding out those inventions which would not be disclosed or devised but for the inducement of a patent." But it does not do so directly. In an ideal world, judges and patent examiners evaluating obviousness would seek direct evidence regarding whether the patent was necessary to the development of the invention. They would examine the costs required to develop the invention in comparison to what the market for the invention would look like with or without a patent. If the cost of development were sufficiently low and the market sufficiently robust that the inventor could have turned a profit without a patent, the court would rule the patent obvious. If, however, the invention was expensive to develop and bring to market, and the market was such that the inventor would never have recouped these costs without a patent, then the court would consider the patent to be nonobvious.

As a doctrinal matter, however, this type of evidence is difficult to obtain and difficult for courts to work with. The costs of invention might be hard to measure, and reconstructing what a market for a given product would look like without a patent requires substantial guesswork. Whether for this reason or others, Congress and the courts have not attempted to pursue this type of inquiry directly. Instead, they have settled on a doctrine that looks primarily at one half of the equation: how costly was it to create the invention in the first place. And rather than examine costs themselves, Congress and the courts have focused on a proxy: how much technical skill was required to create the invention in the first place. (We call this a proxy because technical skill is of course one input into the overall cost, but not the only input.) As this chapter will explain, the doctrine of nonobviousness is focused on this technical question. That is, obviousness is typically framed as a cognitive inquiry, not an economic one. *But see* Abramowicz & Duffy, *supra* (arguing that courts can and should shift toward a more economic approach).

A. Applying the *Graham* Test

The relevant statutory section is § 103 of the Patent Act:

35 U.S.C. § 103

A patent for a claimed invention may not be obtained, notwithstanding that the claimed invention is not identically disclosed as set forth in section 102, if the differences between the claimed invention and the prior art are such that the claimed invention as a whole would have been obvious before the effective filing date of the claimed invention to a person having ordinary skill in the art to which the claimed invention pertains. Patentability shall not be negated by the manner in which the invention was made.

Unlike for § 102, the relevant text of § 103 was only slightly amended by the 2011 America Invents Act; the main difference is that for pre-AIA patents, obviousness is assessed "at the time the invention was made" rather than on "the effective filing date." Pre-AIA § 103(c) also excluded prior art owned by the same person from the obviousness analysis, which has been replaced to the same effect with post-AIA § 102(b)(2)(C) and § 102(c).

As you can see, the nonobviousness statute is not particularly informative; it merely states that obvious inventions cannot be patented. In *Graham v. John Deere*, 383 U.S. 1 (1966), the Supreme Court set out what remains the official four-part test for obviousness. A court attempting to determine whether an invention would have been obvious should:

1. Determine the scope and content of the prior art;
2. Determine the differences between the prior art and the claimed invention;

3. Determine the level of skill of someone skilled in the art (the PHOSITA); and then

4. Determine whether the PHOSITA would have found the invention obvious in light of the prior art.

Graham does not explain how to determine the content of the prior art, but the Federal Circuit has concluded that all § 102 prior art qualifies, including under pre-AIA § 102(e), (f), (g). *See, e.g., OddzOn Products v. Just Toys*, 122 F.3d 1396, 1403 (Fed. Cir. 1997); 2 *Chisum on Patents* § 5.03[3]. In the colorful "*Winslow* Tableau," obviousness is evaluated by "pictur[ing] the inventor as working in his shop with the prior art references—which he is presumed to know—hanging on the walls around him." *In re Winslow*, 365 F.2d 1017, 1020 (C.C.P.A. 1966). That means that just like for anticipation, a patent could be judged obvious based on prior art that was not public at the time the inventor created the invention. Imagine that Kathryn invents a widget in 2014 (that may or may not be obvious), just a week after Jamal files for a patent on a component piece of technology. Jamal's patent application remains secret for 18 months until it is published. But for obviousness purposes, Jamal's patent would be prior art to Kathryn's invention (under the AIA), even though the patent is not yet published and Kathryn has no way of knowing about it.

The one caveat to this rule on prior art is that unlike for anticipation, the scope of the prior art for an obviousness analysis is limited to "analogous" art. This means that the art must either be "from the same field of endeavor" or "reasonably pertinent to the problem with which the inventor is involved." *In re Bigio*, 381 F.3d 1320, 1325 (Fed. Cir. 2004). The "field of endeavor" is determined from the patent specification; for example, a toothbrush and a hairbrush can be in the same field of endeavor because of their structural similarities. *Id.* Similarly, an inventor considering a hinge mechanism for laptops would consider hinges from other fields—such as in "a desktop telephone directory, a piano lid, a kitchen cabinet, a washing machine cabinet, a wooden furniture cabinet, or a two-part housing for storing audio cassettes"—to be "reasonably pertinent" to the problem to be solved. *In re Paulsen*, 30 F.3d 1475, 1481 (Fed. Cir. 1994).

Graham also does not explain how to determine the level of skill of someone skilled in the art. The Federal Circuit has stated that nonexhausive factors for determining the level of skill include "(1) the educational level of the inventor; (2) type of problems encountered in the art; (3) prior art solutions to those problems; (4) rapidity with which innovations are made; (5) sophistication of the technology; and (6) educational level of active workers in the field." *Daiichi Sankyo v. Apotex*, 501 F.3d 1254, 1256 (Fed. Cir. 2007). For example, in evaluating the obviousness of a method of treating an ear infection, the district court erred in concluding that the level of skill was that of a general practitioner who might *prescribe* the invention, rather than that of an ordinary researcher in the field the invention was trying to solve; i.e., a person with expertise in both ear treatments and pharmaceutical development. *Id.* But this factor is rarely dispositive; one empirical study concludes that "despite its ostensible claim to ground these doctrinal decisions in an objective reference point, the PHOSITA plays a surprisingly minor role in judicial decisions." Laura Pedraza-Fariña & Ryan Whalen, *The Ghost in the Patent System: An Empirical Study of Patent Law's Elusive "Ordinary Artisan,"* Iowa L. Rev. (forthcoming).

Once one has determined the scope and content of the prior art and the level of skill in the art, the *Graham* test is no more helpful than the statute. Essentially all of the action occurs at step four, and *Graham* provided no guidance as to how that analysis is meant to occur. This left lower courts at sea for decades as they attempted to find ways to bring structure to the obviousness inquiry.

Perhaps the most important legal innovation in response to this uncertainty was the Federal Circuit's development of the "teaching, suggestion, or motivation" (TSM) test. The Federal Circuit understood quite correctly that many important innovations consist of combinations of prior inventions. In the world of science and technology, progress is typically incremental, and nearly everyone stands on the shoulders of giants. The Federal Circuit was concerned that in hindsight even true innovations would appear to be merely obvious combinations of multiple pre-existing inventions, a problem known as *hindsight bias*.

Accordingly, before two or more pieces of prior art could be combined to show that an invention was obvious, the Federal Circuit required that there be an explicit teaching, suggestion, or motivation to combine those references. This teaching, suggestion, or motivation had to be something specific—either another piece of prior art that specifically suggested the combination, or something particular in the PHOSITA's training that would lead the PHOSITA to combine the elements. A party could not merely wave its hands at the problem and claim that it would have been obvious for a PHOSITA to try combining the existing prior art.

Over the years, the TSM test played a larger and larger role in nonobviousness cases. In many instances, finding multiple pieces of prior art that together contained all the elements of the claimed invention was relatively easy; finding an explicit teaching, suggestion, or motivation to combine those elements was frequently much harder. A large number of cases thus turned on the presence or absence of a TSM. Although this made § 103 decisions more predictable, it also drew criticism as making weak patents too difficult to invalidate, including in academic articles and in reports from the Federal Trade Commission and the National Academies. It is against that background that the Supreme Court granted certiorari in *KSR v. Teleflex*.

KSR International v. Teleflex, 550 U.S. 398 (2007)

Justice Anthony Kennedy delivered the opinion for a unanimous Court.

Teleflex Incorporated sued KSR International Company for patent infringement. The patent at issue, United States Patent No. 6,237,565, is entitled

"Adjustable Pedal Assembly With Electronic Throttle Control," referred to as "the Engelgau patent."

2   Claim 4 of the Engelgau patent describes a mechanism for combining an electronic sensor with an adjustable automobile pedal so the pedal's position can be transmitted to a computer that controls the throttle in the vehicle's engine. When Teleflex accused KSR of infringing the Engelgau patent by adding an electronic sensor to one of KSR's previously designed pedals, KSR countered that claim 4 was invalid under the Patent Act, 35 U.S.C. § 103, because its subject matter was obvious.

3   In *Graham v. John Deere Co. of Kansas City*, 383 U.S. 1, 17–18 (1966), the Court set out a framework for applying the statutory language of § 103:

> Under § 103, the scope and content of the prior art are to be determined; differences between the prior art and the claims at issue are to be ascertained; and the level of ordinary skill in the pertinent art resolved. Against this background, the obviousness or nonobviousness of the subject matter is determined. Such secondary considerations as commercial success, long felt but unsolved needs, failure of others, etc., might be utilized to give light to the circumstances surrounding the origin of the subject matter sought to be patented.

4   Seeking to resolve the question of obviousness with more uniformity and consistency, the Court of Appeals for the Federal Circuit has employed an approach referred to by the parties as the "teaching, suggestion, or motivation" test (TSM test), under which a patent claim is only proved obvious if "some motivation or suggestion to combine the prior art teachings" can be found in the prior art, the nature of the problem, or the knowledge of a person having ordinary skill in the art. KSR challenges that test, or at least its application in this case. Because the Court of Appeals addressed the question of obviousness in a manner contrary to § 103 and our precedents, we granted certiorari. We now reverse.

I

A

5   In car engines without computer-controlled throttles, the accelerator pedal interacts with the throttle via cable or other mechanical link. The pedal arm acts as a lever rotating around a pivot point. In a cable-actuated throttle control the rotation caused by pushing down the pedal pulls a cable, which in turn pulls open valves in the carburetor or fuel injection unit. The wider the valves open, the more fuel and air are released, causing combustion to increase and the car to accelerate. When the driver takes his foot off the pedal, the opposite occurs as the cable is released and the valves slide closed.

6   In the 1990's it became more common to install computers in cars to control engine operation. Computer-controlled throttles open and close valves in response to

electronic signals, not through force transferred from the pedal by a mechanical link. Constant, delicate adjustments of air and fuel mixture are possible. The computer's rapid processing of factors beyond the pedal's position improves fuel efficiency and engine performance.

7   For a computer-controlled throttle to respond to a driver's operation of the car, the computer must know what is happening with the pedal. A cable or mechanical link does not suffice for this purpose; at some point, an electronic sensor is necessary to translate the mechanical operation into digital data the computer can understand.

8   Before discussing sensors further we turn to the mechanical design of the pedal itself. In the traditional design a pedal can be pushed down or released but cannot have its position in the footwell adjusted by sliding the pedal forward or back. As a result, a driver who wishes to be closer or farther from the pedal must either reposition himself in the driver's seat or move the seat in some way. In cars with deep footwells these are imperfect solutions for drivers of smaller stature. To solve the problem, inventors, beginning in the 1970's, designed pedals that could be adjusted to change their location in the footwell. Important for this case are two adjustable pedals disclosed in U.S. Patent Nos. 5,010,782 (filed July 28, 1989) (Asano) and 5,460,061 (filed Sept. 17, 1993) (Redding). The Asano patent reveals a support structure that houses the pedal so that even when the pedal location is adjusted relative to the driver, one of the pedal's pivot points stays fixed. The pedal is also designed so that the force necessary to push the pedal down is the same regardless of adjustments to its location. The Redding patent reveals a different, sliding mechanism where both the pedal and the pivot point are adjusted.

9   We return to sensors. Well before Engelgau applied for his challenged patent, some inventors had obtained patents involving electronic pedal sensors for computer-controlled throttles. These inventions, such as the device disclosed in U.S. Patent No. 5,241,936 (filed Sept. 9, 1991) ('936), taught that it was preferable to detect the pedal's position in the pedal assembly, not in the engine. The '936 patent disclosed a pedal with an electronic sensor on a pivot point in the pedal assembly. U.S. Patent No. 5,063,811 (filed July 9, 1990) (Smith) taught that to prevent the wires connecting the sensor to the computer from chafing and wearing out, and to avoid grime and damage from the driver's foot, the sensor should be put on a fixed part of the pedal assembly rather than in or on the pedal's footpad. [Eds: As noted in Chapter 2, the convention is to refer to a patent-in-suit by its last three digits and a prior art patent by the last name of the first inventor, but the Supreme Court often ignores patent conventions.]

10   In addition to patents for pedals with integrated sensors inventors obtained patents for self-contained modular sensors. A modular sensor is designed independently of a given pedal so that it can be taken off the shelf and attached to mechanical pedals of various sorts, enabling the pedals to be used in automobiles with computer-controlled throttles. One such sensor was disclosed in U.S. Patent No. 5,385,068 (filed Dec. 18, 1992) ('068). In 1994, Chevrolet manufactured a line of trucks

using modular sensors attached to the pedal assembly support bracket, adjacent to the pedal and engaged with the pivot shaft about which the pedal rotates in operation.

11   The prior art contained patents involving the placement of sensors on adjustable pedals as well. For example, U.S. Patent No. 5,819,593 (filed Aug. 17, 1995) (Rixon) discloses an adjustable pedal assembly with an electronic sensor for detecting the pedal's position. In the Rixon pedal the sensor is located in the pedal footpad. The Rixon pedal was known to suffer from wire chafing when the pedal was depressed and released.

B

12   Ford Motor Company hired KSR in 1998 to supply an adjustable pedal system for automobiles with cable-actuated throttle controls. KSR developed an adjustable mechanical pedal for Ford and obtained U.S. Patent No. 6,151,986 (filed July 16, 1999) ('986) for the design. In 2000, KSR was chosen by General Motors Corporation to supply adjustable pedal systems for Chevrolet and GMC light trucks that used engines with computer-controlled throttles. To make the '986 pedal compatible with the trucks, KSR merely took that design and added a modular sensor.

13   Teleflex is a rival to KSR in the design and manufacture of adjustable pedals. It is the exclusive licensee of the Engelgau patent. Engelgau filed the patent application on August 22, 2000, as a continuation of a previous application for U.S. Patent No. 6,109,241, which was filed on January 26, 1999. The Engelgau patent discloses an adjustable electronic pedal described in the specification as a "simplified vehicle control pedal assembly that is less expensive, and which uses fewer parts and is easier to package within the vehicle." Claim 4 of the patent, at issue here, describes:

> A vehicle control pedal apparatus comprising:
>
> a support adapted to be mounted to a vehicle structure;
>
> an adjustable pedal assembly having a pedal arm moveable in for[e] and aft directions with respect to said support;
>
> a pivot for pivotally supporting said adjustable pedal assembly with respect to said support and defining a pivot axis; and
>
> an electronic control attached to said support for controlling a vehicle system;
>
> said apparatus characterized by said electronic control being responsive to said pivot for providing a signal that corresponds to pedal arm position as said pedal arm pivots about said pivot axis between rest and applied positions wherein the position of said pivot remains constant while said pedal arm moves in fore and aft directions with respect to said pivot.

14   Before issuing the Engelgau patent the U.S. Patent and Trademark Office (PTO) rejected one of the patent claims that was similar to, but broader than, the present claim 4. The claim did not include the requirement that the sensor be placed on a fixed pivot point. The PTO concluded the claim was an obvious combination of the prior art disclosed in Redding and Smith. Redding provided an example of an adjustable pedal, and Smith explained how to mount a sensor on a pedal's support structure, and the rejected patent claim merely put these two teachings together.

15   Although the broader claim was rejected, claim 4 was later allowed because it included the limitation of a fixed pivot point, which distinguished the design from Redding's. Engelgau had not included Asano among the prior art references, and Asano was not mentioned in the patent's prosecution. Thus, the PTO did not have before it an adjustable pedal with a fixed pivot point.

16   KSR refused to enter a royalty arrangement with Teleflex; so Teleflex sued for infringement.

C

17   The District Court granted summary judgment in KSR's favor. By direction of 35 U.S.C. § 282, an issued patent is presumed valid. The District Court applied *Graham*'s framework to determine whether under summary-judgment standards KSR had overcome the presumption and demonstrated that claim 4 was obvious in light of the prior art in existence when the claimed subject matter was invented. The District Court determined, in light of the expert testimony and the parties' stipulations, that the level of ordinary skill in pedal design was "an undergraduate degree in mechanical engineering (or an equivalent amount of industry experience) [and] familiarity with pedal control systems for vehicles." The court then set forth the relevant prior art, including the patents and pedal designs described above.

18   Following *Graham*'s direction, the court compared the teachings of the prior art to the claims of Engelgau. It found "little difference." Asano taught everything contained in claim 4 except the use of a sensor to detect the pedal's position and transmit it to the computer controlling the throttle. That additional aspect was revealed in sources such as the '068 patent and the sensors used by Chevrolet.

19   The Court of Appeals reversed. It ruled the District Court had not been strict enough in applying the [TSM] test, having failed to make "finding[s] as to the specific understanding or principle within the knowledge of a skilled artisan that would have motivated one with no knowledge of [the] invention . . . to attach an electronic control to the support bracket of the Asano assembly." The Court of Appeals held that the District Court was incorrect that the nature of the problem to be solved satisfied this requirement because unless the "prior art references address[ed] the precise problem that the patentee was trying to solve," the problem would not motivate an inventor to look at those references.

20   Here, the Court of Appeals found, the Asano pedal was designed to solve the "constant ratio problem"—that is, to ensure that the force required to depress the pedal is the same no matter how the pedal is adjusted—whereas Engelgau sought to provide a simpler, smaller, cheaper adjustable electronic pedal. As for Rixon, the court explained, that pedal suffered from the problem of wire chafing but was not designed to solve it. When the patents were interpreted in this way, the Court of Appeals held, they would not have led a person of ordinary skill to put a sensor on the sort of pedal described in Asano.

II

A

21   We begin by rejecting the rigid approach of the Court of Appeals. Throughout this Court's engagement with the question of obviousness, our cases have set forth an expansive and flexible approach inconsistent with the way the Court of Appeals applied its TSM test here. For over a half century, the Court has held that . . . [t]he combination of familiar elements according to known methods is likely to be obvious when it does no more than yield predictable results.

22   The principles underlying [prior] cases are instructive when the question is whether a patent claiming the combination of elements of prior art is obvious. When a work is available in one field of endeavor, design incentives and other market forces can prompt variations of it, either in the same field or a different one. If a person of ordinary skill can implement a predictable variation, § 103 likely bars its patentability. For the same reason, if a technique has been used to improve one device, and a person of ordinary skill in the art would recognize that it would improve similar devices in the same way, using the technique is obvious unless its actual application is beyond his or her skill.

23   Following these principles may be more difficult in other cases than it is here because the claimed subject matter may involve more than the simple substitution of one known element for another or the mere application of a known technique to a piece of prior art ready for the improvement. Often, it will be necessary for a court to look to interrelated teachings of multiple patents; the effects of demands known to the design community or present in the marketplace; and the background knowledge possessed by a person having ordinary skill in the art, all in order to determine whether there was an apparent reason to combine the known elements in the fashion claimed by the patent at issue. To facilitate review, this analysis should be made explicit. As our precedents make clear, however, the analysis need not seek out precise teachings directed to the specific subject matter of the challenged claim, for a court can take account of the inferences and creative steps that a person of ordinary skill in the art would employ.

B

24   When it first established the requirement of demonstrating a teaching, suggestion, or motivation to combine known elements in order to show that the combination is obvious, the Court of Customs and Patent Appeals captured a helpful insight. A patent composed of several elements is not proved obvious merely by demonstrating that each of its elements was, independently, known in the prior art. Although common sense directs one to look with care at a patent application that claims as innovation the combination of two known devices according to their established functions, it can be important to identify a reason that would have prompted a person of ordinary skill in the relevant field to combine the elements in the way the claimed new invention does. This is so because inventions in most, if not all, instances rely upon building blocks long since uncovered, and claimed discoveries almost of necessity will be combinations of what, in some sense, is already known.

25   Helpful insights, however, need not become rigid and mandatory formulas; and when it is so applied, the TSM test is incompatible with our precedents. The obviousness analysis cannot be confined by a formalistic conception of the words teaching, suggestion, and motivation, or by overemphasis on the importance of published articles and the explicit content of issued patents. The diversity of inventive pursuits and of modern technology counsels against limiting the analysis in this way. In many fields it may be that there is little discussion of obvious techniques or combinations, and it often may be the case that market demand, rather than scientific literature, will drive design trends. Granting patent protection to advances that would occur in the ordinary course without real innovation retards progress and may, in the case of patents combining previously known elements, deprive prior inventions of their value or utility.

26   There is no necessary inconsistency between the idea underlying the TSM test and the *Graham* analysis. But when a court transforms the general principle into a rigid rule that limits the obviousness inquiry, as the Court of Appeals did here, it errs.

C

27   The flaws in the analysis of the Court of Appeals relate for the most part to the court's narrow conception of the obviousness inquiry reflected in its application of the TSM test. In determining whether the subject matter of a patent claim is obvious, neither the particular motivation nor the avowed purpose of the patentee controls. The Court of Appeals failed to recognize that the problem motivating the patentee may be only one of many addressed by the patent's subject matter. The question is not whether the combination was obvious to the patentee but whether the combination was obvious to a person with ordinary skill in the art. Under the correct analysis, any need or problem known in the field of endeavor at the time of invention and addressed by the patent can provide a reason for combining the elements in the manner claimed.

28   The second error of the Court of Appeals lay in its assumption that a person of ordinary skill attempting to solve a problem will be led only to those elements of prior art designed to solve the same problem. Common sense teaches, however, that familiar items may have obvious uses beyond their primary purposes, and in many cases a person of ordinary skill will be able to fit the teachings of multiple patents together like pieces of a puzzle. Regardless of Asano's primary purpose, the design provided an obvious example of an adjustable pedal with a fixed pivot point; and the prior art was replete with patents indicating that a fixed pivot point was an ideal mount for a sensor. The idea that a designer hoping to make an adjustable electronic pedal would ignore Asano because Asano was designed to solve the constant ratio problem makes little sense. A person of ordinary skill is also a person of ordinary creativity, not an automaton.

29   The same constricted analysis led the Court of Appeals to conclude, in error, that a patent claim cannot be proved obvious merely by showing that the combination of elements was "[o]bvious to try." When there is a design need or market pressure to solve a problem and there are a finite number of identified, predictable solutions, a person of ordinary skill has good reason to pursue the known options within his or her technical grasp. If this leads to the anticipated success, it is likely the product not of innovation but of ordinary skill and common sense. In that instance the fact that a combination was obvious to try might show that it was obvious under § 103.

30   The Court of Appeals, finally, drew the wrong conclusion from the risk of courts and patent examiners falling prey to hindsight bias. A factfinder should be aware, of course, of the distortion caused by hindsight bias and must be cautious of arguments reliant upon ex post reasoning. Rigid preventative rules that deny factfinders recourse to common sense, however, are neither necessary under our case law nor consistent with it.

III

31   When we apply the standards we have explained to the instant facts, claim 4 must be found obvious. We agree with and adopt the District Court's recitation of the relevant prior art and its determination of the level of ordinary skill in the field. As did the District Court, we see little difference between the teachings of Asano and Smith and the adjustable electronic pedal disclosed in claim 4 of the Engelgau patent. A person having ordinary skill in the art could have combined Asano with a pedal position sensor in a fashion encompassed by claim 4, and would have seen the benefits of doing so.

32   The District Court was correct to conclude that, as of the time Engelgau designed the subject matter in claim 4, it was obvious to a person of ordinary skill to combine Asano with a pivot-mounted pedal position sensor. There then existed a marketplace that created a strong incentive to convert mechanical pedals to electronic pedals, and the prior art taught a number of methods for achieving this advance. The proper question to have asked was whether a pedal designer of ordinary skill, facing

the wide range of needs created by developments in the field of endeavor, would have seen a benefit to upgrading Asano with a sensor.

33   In automotive design, as in many other fields, the interaction of multiple components means that changing one component often requires the others to be modified as well. Technological developments made it clear that engines using computer-controlled throttles would become standard. As a result, designers might have decided to design new pedals from scratch; but they also would have had reason to make pre-existing pedals work with the new engines. Indeed, upgrading its own pre-existing model led KSR to design the pedal now accused of infringing the Engelgau patent.

34   For a designer starting with Asano, the question was where to attach the sensor. The consequent legal question, then, is whether a pedal designer of ordinary skill starting with Asano would have found it obvious to put the sensor on a fixed pivot point. The prior art discussed above leads us to the conclusion that attaching the sensor where both KSR and Engelgau put it would have been obvious to a person of ordinary skill.

35   The '936 patent taught the utility of putting the sensor on the pedal device, not in the engine. Smith, in turn, explained to put the sensor not on the pedal's footpad but instead on its support structure. And from the known wire-chafing problems of Rixon, and Smith's teaching that "the pedal assemblies must not precipitate any motion in the connecting wires," the designer would know to place the sensor on a nonmoving part of the pedal structure. The most obvious nonmoving point on the structure from which a sensor can easily detect the pedal's position is a pivot point. The designer, accordingly, would follow Smith in mounting the sensor on a pivot, thereby designing an adjustable electronic pedal covered by claim 4.

36   Just as it was possible to begin with the objective to upgrade Asano to work with a computer-controlled throttle, so too was it possible to take an adjustable electronic pedal like Rixon and seek an improvement that would avoid the wire-chafing problem. Following similar steps to those just explained, a designer would learn from Smith to avoid sensor movement and would come, thereby, to Asano because Asano disclosed an adjustable pedal with a fixed pivot.

37   Teleflex indirectly argues that the prior art taught away from attaching a sensor to Asano because Asano in its view is bulky, complex, and expensive. The only evidence Teleflex marshals in support of this argument, however, is the Radcliffe declaration, which merely indicates that Asano would not have solved Engelgau's goal of making a small, simple, and inexpensive pedal. What the declaration does not indicate is that Asano was somehow so flawed that there was no reason to upgrade it, or pedals like it, to be compatible with modern engines. To judge Asano against Engelgau would be to engage in the very hindsight bias Teleflex rightly urges must be avoided.

38   Like the District Court, finally, we conclude Teleflex has shown no secondary factors to dislodge the determination that claim 4 is obvious. Proper application of *Graham* and our other precedents to these facts therefore leads to the conclusion that claim 4 encompassed obvious subject matter. As a result, the claim fails to meet the requirement of § 103.

39   We need not reach the question whether the failure to disclose Asano during the prosecution of Engelgau voids the presumption of validity given to issued patents, for claim 4 is obvious despite the presumption. We nevertheless think it appropriate to note that the rationale underlying the presumption—that the PTO, in its expertise, has approved the claim—seems much diminished here.

IV

40   A separate ground the Court of Appeals gave for reversing the order for summary judgment was the existence of a dispute over an issue of material fact. We disagree with the Court of Appeals on this point as well. The ultimate judgment of obviousness is a legal determination. Where, as here, the content of the prior art, the scope of the patent claim, and the level of ordinary skill in the art are not in material dispute, and the obviousness of the claim is apparent in light of these factors, summary judgment is appropriate.

41   We build and create by bringing to the tangible and palpable reality around us new works based on instinct, simple logic, ordinary inferences, extraordinary ideas, and sometimes even genius. These advances, once part of our shared knowledge, define a new threshold from which innovation starts once more. And as progress beginning from higher levels of achievement is expected in the normal course, the results of ordinary innovation are not the subject of exclusive rights under the patent laws. Were it otherwise patents might stifle, rather than promote, the progress of useful arts. *See* U.S. Const. art. I, § 8, cl. 8. These premises led to the bar on patents claiming obvious subject matter established in *Hotchkiss v. Greenwood*, 52 U.S. 248 (1850), and codified in § 103. Application of the bar must not be confined within a test or formulation too constrained to serve its purpose.

42   KSR provided convincing evidence that mounting a modular sensor on a fixed pivot point of the Asano pedal was a design step well within the grasp of a person of ordinary skill in the relevant art. Its arguments, and the record, demonstrate that claim 4 of the Engelgau patent is obvious. In rejecting the District Court's rulings, the Court of Appeals analyzed the issue in a narrow, rigid manner inconsistent with § 103 and our precedents. The judgment of the Court of Appeals is reversed, and the case is remanded for further proceedings consistent with this opinion.

KSR Claim Chart Exercise

Try putting check marks in this chart to indicate which claim elements are present in each prior art reference, as well as which elements were in Teleflex's earlier rejected claim.

Teleflex Claim 4 (Engelgau)	Prior art references					Rejected Teleflex Claim
	Asano	Redding	Smith	'068 & Chevy sensors	Rixon	
adjustable pedal						
fixed pivot point						
electronic pedal sensor						
sensor on pedal support						

Is claim 4 of Teleflex's patent invalid for lack of novelty? Why? What references did the USPTO use to reject Teleflex's earlier patent claim? Why didn't the USPTO reject claim 4 as an obvious combination of the references relied on by the Supreme Court?

Discussion Questions: KSR and Nonobviousness

1. *Combining the Prior Art*. Although the Supreme Court lowered the bar for finding a combination of prior art to be obvious, in general it must still be shown that two or more references together disclose all the limitations of the claim at issue. If a claim limitation is missing from the prior art, it may sometimes be filled in with the PHOSITA's general knowledge or common sense, but the Federal Circuit has "invoked common sense to fill in a missing limitation only when the limitation in question was unusually simple and the technology particularly straightforward." *DSS Tech. Mgmt. v. Apple*, 885 F.3d 1367, 1375 (Fed. Cir. 2018). Do you think the Supreme Court would view this stringent test for when common sense may be invoked to supply a missing limitation as consistent with *KSR*?

2. *Predictability*. The Supreme Court repeatedly references the question of whether a combination is "predictable"—as the Court says, predictable combinations and variations are obvious and not patentable. What do you think the Court means

by "predictable"? Is predictability a useful measure for the purpose of the nonobviousness requirement as described by the Supreme Court in *Graham*: a "means of weeding out those inventions which would not be disclosed or devised but for the inducement of a patent"? 383 U.S. at 11. For example, should patents be available for inventions that are scientifically predictable but that have a high ratio of development costs to imitation costs, such that they won't be developed without patent protection? Can "predictability" include the kind of market uncertainty that sometimes makes patents necessary to induce development?

3. *The Teaching, Suggestion, or Motivation Test.* What is the applicability of the TSM test after *KSR*? The Supreme Court stated that the TSM test is a "helpful insight" and that the underlying idea is consistent with *Graham* but criticized the Federal Circuit's transformation of the test into a "rigid rule." In subsequent cases, the Federal Circuit has required that a PHOSITA have both a "reasonable expectation of success" in combining pre-existing elements and *also* "a motivation to combine" the references before an invention can be judged as obvious. *Intelligent Bio-Sys., Inc. v. Illumina Cambridge Ltd.*, 821 F.3d 1359, 1367–68 (Fed. Cir. 2016). Consider the two elements of the test separately: is requiring a "reasonable expectation of success" consistent with the Supreme Court's approach in *KSR*? Is requiring a "motivation to combine" consistent? Note that some version of the TSM test was applied in nearly half of all obviousness decisions in the five years after *KSR*. *See* Ryan T. Holte & Ted Sichelman, *Cycles of Obviousness*, 105 Iowa L. Rev. 107, 158 (2019).

At the same time, a careful read of these cases suggests that the new "motivation to combine" test "is hardly a reincarnation of the TSM requirement, both in terms of vigor and analytical structure." Jason Rantanen, *The Federal Circuit's New Obviousness Jurisprudence: An Empirical Study*, 16 Stan. Tech. L. Rev. 709 (2013). Rather, post-*KSR* caselaw is less focused on explicit statements in published materials; more focused on predictability, market forces, and the fact that a PHOSITA has some degree of creativity and common sense; and more cognizant that PHOSITAs understand that the prior art can have uses beyond any explicitly stated purposes. *See, e.g., Arctic Cat v. Bombardier Recreational Products*, 876 F.3d 1350, 1359 (Fed. Cir. 2017) ("[A] motivation to combine can be found explicitly or implicitly in the prior art references themselves, in market forces, in design incentives, or in any need or problem known in the field of endeavor at the time of invention and addressed by the patent."). Does this change your assessment of the test's consistency with *KSR*?

4. *Other Factors for Assessing Obviousness.* In addition to emphasizing "predictability" and noting that the TSM test may be "helpful," what other guidance does *KSR* offer on performing an obviousness analysis?

- The Court resurrected the "obvious to try" test: When there are a finite number of predictable solutions to a known problem, "the fact that a combination was obvious to try might show that it was obvious under § 103." What if it is obvious to try something, but the result is unpredictable and unexpected? *See* Mark A. Lemley, *Expecting the Unexpected*, 92 Notre Dame L. Rev. 1369 (2017).

- Decisionmakers can consider "common sense" (a phrase *KSR* uses five times).

- The Court quotes *Graham*'s statement that "[s]uch secondary considerations as commercial success, long felt but unsolved needs, failure of others, etc., might be utilized." We discuss these factors in detail in the following section. One secondary factor that seemed important here was advances in collateral technology: *KSR* notes the relevance of "design incentives and other market forces" such as the technological developments in computing that "created a strong incentive to convert mechanical pedals to electronic pedals."

5. *Presumption of Validity.* As we noted at the beginning of the section on patentability, a granted patent carries a presumption of validity. This requirement is statutory: the first sentence of 35 U.S.C. § 282 reads, "A patent shall be presumed valid." This presumption is operationalized via the rule that a party seeking to prove that a granted patent is invalid must do so by "clear and convincing evidence." *Microsoft v. i4i*, 564 U.S. 91 (2011). The most compelling argument for this rule is that a granted patent has already undergone review by an expert patent examiner. The presumption of validity, and the clear and convincing evidence rule, represent deference to the USPTO's judgment. If we assume that is the rationale, can you think of a reason why the presumption of validity should not have attached to Teleflex's patent when evaluating its obviousness over the prior art discussed by the Court?

6. *The PHOSITA.* In *KSR*, the Supreme Court takes a more expansive view of the PHOSITA than had the Federal Circuit in prior cases. Whereas the Federal Circuit treats the PHOSITA almost as an automaton who will not try combining two prior inventions without explicitly being told to do so, the Supreme Court describes the PHOSITA as flexible and creative—someone who will use "common sense" and try any combination that is "obvious to try." One way to understand this disagreement is as simple divergence over the level of skill of someone in the art and what that person is capable of. Is there another way to understand what the Supreme Court is doing, and why it rejects the Federal Circuit's construction of the PHOSITA? Take a look at the Supreme Court's statement beginning with "These advances, once part of our shared knowledge . . . ." What is the Court saying there?

7. *An Identity-Conscious PHOSITA?* Should the nonobviousness standard be applied differently for innovators who face structural barriers to successful innovation, such as by using a "woman of ordinary skill in the art" standard for inventions by women? *See* Dan L. Burk, *Diversity Levers*, 23 Duke J. Gender L. & Pol'y 25 (2015). Are there better ways to address these concerns?

8. *Is Racial Application Nonobvious?* Should patents restricting an invention to a particular race be considered nonobvious? In 2005, the FDA approved the drug BiDil to treat heart failure in "self-identified black patients." The FDA had previously

denied approval of the drug for all patients due to inadequate statistical support, but when the sponsors re-examined the data along racial lines and then ran a new trial on patients who identified as African-American, they found a statistically significant effect. The FDA's decision was controversial for applying questionable statistical standards (i.e., re-examining data for a subgroup raises concerns about "p-hacking" or "data fishing") in ways that could reinforce the idea that race is biological rather than a social and political construct. *See* Dorothy E. Roberts, *What's Wrong with Race-Based Medicine?: Genes, Drugs, and Health Disparities*, 12 Minn. J.L. Sci. & Tech. 1 (2011). A patent on using BiDil to treat heart failure in all patients expired in 2007, but the USPTO also granted a later patent claiming the use of BiDil to treat heart failure "in a black patient," without defining "black." The race-based patent did not expire until 2020, providing thirteen additional years of protection. What does the USPTO's conclusion that this claim is nonobvious over the general claim imply about the baseline from which obviousness is judged? Does the decision seem wrong as a matter of standard patent law? *See* Jonathan Kahn, *Race-ing Patents/Patenting Race: An Emerging Political Geography of Intellectual Property in Biotechnology*, 92 Iowa L. Rev. 353 (2007).

Practice Problems: § 102 Review and § 103 Warm Up

In July 2013, Serena secretly invented a device for harvesting maple syrup.[1] Syrup producers have realized that if you stop harvesting sap from a maple tree once it gets below a certain concentration of sugar, you can sell the resulting syrup for a premium. Old-timers can taste the sap to know the concentration of sugar, but that's expensive. Serena's device automates this process using a refractometer, which measures the concentration of sugar in a liquid. Serena keeps her invention secret and files a patent on December 1, 2013, claiming:

1. A device for harvesting maple syrup comprising:
    (a) an electronically closable tap for insertion into a maple tree;
    (b) a refractometer connected to said electronically closable tap;
    (c) fastening means for attaching a container to said tap; and
    (d) a container suitable for collecting maple sap attached to said tap by said fastening means.

The first step of a § 103 analysis is determining the content of the prior art. You have determined that the prior art definitely includes these two references:

A. A refractometer, patented in 1986 and widely available.

B. A manual tap for maple trees with a hook for hanging a bucket, marketed in 1941.

---

[1] We thank Nicholson Price for creating the original version of this problem.

Do the following facts create any additional prior art under the relevant § 102?

   C. A sap-harvesting device invented by Trip in Vermont in June 2009. The sap-harvesting device includes an electronically closable tap with a bucket hanging on it by a hook; the device is operated by having a knowledgeable maple farmer taste the sap and close the tap for a group of nearby trees all at once if the sugar concentration is below the relevant threshold. Trip kept his invention secret and didn't pursue the idea further until he filed for a patent on September 1, 2013, which was published in due course.

   D. An automatic milking system for cows, designed for making all-natural sweet cream cheese: it involves an automatic milking machine with an attached bucket, and uses a refractometer to measure the sugar content of the milk, then shuts off the milking machine when the sugar concentration gets too low. Natalia invented the system in Germany at her dairy and cheese farm outside of Frankfurt, where she has proudly demonstrated it to cheese-buyers and allowed them to use it since 2011. No one has published about or patented this invention.

Is a court likely to find Serena's invention obvious under § 103? What if you subtract three years from all dates, so that Serena's patent is filed on December 1, 2010, Trip's device is invented in 2006, and so forth?

Practice Problem: Creating an Obviousness Claim Chart

   In Chapter 2, you created an anticipation claim chart to show where (if at all) each limitation of a truck-covering system (claim 1 of the '109 patent) could be found in a prior art reference (the Cramaro patent). Please add an additional column to your claim chart now for another prior art reference, U.S. Patent No. 3,415,260 (Hall). Do you think claim 1 of the '109 patent would have been obvious in light of Cramaro and Hall?

U.S. Patent No. 5,026,109	U.S. Patent No. 3,415,260 (Hall prior art)
1. A retractable segmented cover system used with a truck trailer comprising	
(a) a plurality of flexible cover sections with	
(b) a plurality of substantially parallel	"A plurality of frames or arch members are independently movable between two fixed posts or

supporting bows spaced therebetween and	support members and each is maintained in aligned parallelism by four cables, each cable being disposed in a Z-pulley arrangement." Col. 1, ll. 10–14. "Referring now to FIG. 1, it is to be noted that the structure embodies a plurality of frames, as for example, a first or forward frame and a first rightwardly adjacent frame 61. Other adjacent frames 62, 63, 64 and 65 are spaced rearwardly toward a rear frame 66, which frame may be attached to a wall indicated in phantom outline." Col. 4, ll. 8–14.
(c) a drive assembly,	
(d) wherein each cover section is detachably connected between substantially parallel supporting bows,	
(e) the bows are slideably supported on the truck trailer and	
(f) at least one bow is fixedly connected to the drive assembly such that the cover system can be extended or retracted by the drive assembly and	
(g) wherein a cover section can be removed from the cover system independent of the other cover sections.	

B. Secondary Considerations

In addition to scrutinizing the technical details of an invention, in both *Graham* and *KSR* the Supreme Court referred to "secondary considerations" that "might be utilized" to assess obviousness. The secondary considerations are external indicators that are thought to shed light on the obviousness inquiry and help guard against hindsight bias. The Federal Circuit has offered a laundry list of potential secondary considerations, *see, e.g., Ecolochem, Inc. v. S. California Edison Co.*, 227 F.3d 1361, 1379 (Fed. Cir. 2000); *Allergan, Inc. v. Sandoz Inc.*, 796 F.3d 1293, 1305 (Fed. Cir. 2015), which can be broken down into what we might call technical and economic factors. Technical factors include:

- *Teaching away.* Whether the prior art discouraged the invention, such as by suggesting that the patented combination would not work well.

- *Unexpected results.* Whether there is evidence that experts would not have expected the results of the experiment producing the invention.

- *Failure of others.* Whether other people with skill in the art have tried and failed to construct the invention or to solve the problem addressed by the invention.

- *Skepticism.* Whether experts initially expressed skepticism or surprise when they learned of the invention.

- *Professional approval.* Whether the invention received awards or praise from experts or professional organizations.

- *Near-simultaneous invention.* Whether the invention was independently created by other parties (suggesting that it may not have required great innovation), particularly if other inventors disclosed the invention without seeking a patent (suggesting obviousness).

These six considerations all relate to the technology of the invention. The first two—teaching away and unexpected results—are directly relevant to determining technologically whether the invention would have been obvious. What the prior art teaches (and whether it "teaches away" from the invention) is simply part of the inquiry as to the scope and content of the prior art. And whether the invention yielded "unexpected results" is another way of restating the question as to whether the combination yielded a "predictable" outcome, which the Supreme Court describes as a key to the obviousness inquiry in *KSR*. Accordingly, these two considerations should be thought of as part of the primary obviousness inquiry, not as secondary.

The latter four considerations are all proxies for whether the invention was obvious, rather than direct evidence of the invention's obviousness or nonobviousness. Accordingly, they are properly understood as true "secondary" considerations.

The list of "secondary considerations" also includes a set of economic factors. We describe these as economic in the sense that they offer economic proxy evidence as to whether the invention was technically challenging to create. (They are not necessarily any more probative with respect to the overarching economic question of whether the invention would have been created absent patent rights.) Those factors are:

- *Long-felt need.* Whether there is long-standing demand for the invention or one like it.

- *Copying by others.* Whether others have deliberately copied the invention from the patent holder.

- *Commercial success.* Whether the invention was commercially successful once produced (on the controversial theory that such success indicates a long-felt need for the invention, and that if it were obvious how to satisfy that need, someone would have done so earlier).

- *Licensing activity.* Whether competitors in the market have acquiesced to the validity of a patent through acceptance of a license.

- *Advances in collateral technology.* Whether there is evidence that the invention was made possible by a recent change in the cost of invention, the tools available for invention, or market demand, rather than by nonobvious innovation. This consideration can be thought of as an explanation for—or rebuttal to—some of the preceding factors.

The Federal Circuit has emphasized that secondary considerations "may often be the most probative and cogent evidence in the record" and that courts must consider any evidence of secondary considerations before reaching an obviousness conclusion. *See, e.g., In re Cyclobenzaprine Hydrochloride Extended-Release Capsule Patent Litig.*, 676 F.3d 1063, 1075 (Fed. Cir. 2012). However, these are only considerations, and secondary ones at that. Even strong evidence of secondary considerations can sometimes be overborne by a more straightforward technical analysis of the claimed invention and the prior art. The following case provides an example of how the Federal Circuit has dealt with secondary factors.

Apple v. Samsung Electronics, 839 F.3d 1034 (Fed. Cir. 2016) (en banc)

Kimberly A. Moore, Circuit Judge.

[As part of a multinational patent war, Apple sued Samsung for infringement of numerous patent claims, including claim 8 of U.S. Patent No. 8,046,721, which covered the "slide-to-unlock" iPhone feature that Samsung allegedly copied. A jury found the claim infringed and not invalid, and the district court denied Samsung's request for judgement as a matter of law (JMOL) that the claim was obvious. On appeal, a Federal Circuit panel reversed the denial of JMOL, and the court took the case en banc without further briefing.]

2   The '721 patent discloses a portable device with a touch-sensitive display that can be "unlocked via gestures" performed on the screen. The patent teaches that a "problem associated with using touch screens on portable devices is the unintentional activation or deactivation of functions due to unintentional contact with the touch screen," commonly referred to as "pocket dialing." The '721 patent also describes the importance of making phone activation as "user-friendly" and "efficient" as possible. Apple's expert, Dr. Cockburn, explained that there was a tension between preventing pocket dialing and ease of use: "[I]t has to work. It has to succeed in preventing accidental activation by mistake. But yet it needs to be something that's easy to do, but not so easy that it can occur by accident, and it succeeds in that."

3   Apple asserted claim 8, which depends from claim 7, against several Samsung devices. These claims recite:

7. A portable electronic device, comprising:

a touch-sensitive display;

memory;

one or more processors; and

one or more modules stored in the memory and configured for execution by the one or more processors, the one or more modules including instructions:

> to detect a contact with the touch-sensitive display at a first predefined location corresponding to an unlock image;

> to continuously move the unlock image on the touch-sensitive display in accordance with the movement of the detected contact while continuous contact with the touch-sensitive display is maintained, wherein the unlock image is a graphical, interactive user-interface object with which a user interacts in order to unlock the device; and

> to unlock the hand-held electronic device if the unlock image is moved from the first predefined location on the touch screen to a predefined unlock region on the touch-sensitive display.

8. The device of claim 7, further comprising instructions to display visual cues to communicate a direction of movement of the unlock image required to unlock the device.

4   Samsung argues claim 8 would have been obvious in light of the combination of Neonode and Plaisant. "Neonode" refers to the Neonode N1 Quickstart Guide. Neonode discloses a mobile device with a touch-sensitive screen. It explains that a user may unlock the device by pressing the power button. After the user presses the power button, text appears instructing the user to "Right sweep to unlock." Sweeping right then unlocks the unit.

5   "Plaisant" refers to a video and corresponding two-page paper published in 1992 titled "Touchscreen Toggle Design" by Catherine Plaisant and Daniel Wallace. The authors of the paper conducted an experiment to determine which controls ("toggles") users prefer on wall-mounted controllers for "entertainment, security, and climate control systems." These controllers were intended to be installed "flushmounted into the wall or the cabinetry." The authors presented six alternative unlocking mechanisms to a group of fifteen undergraduate students, including a "slider toggle" where a user could activate the controller by "grab[bing] the pointer and slid[ing] it to the other side." The students preferred "toggles that are pushed" over "toggles that slide," and generally ranked the slider fifth of the six alternatives.

6   On appeal, Apple does not contest that, together, Neonode and Plaisant disclose all the elements of claim 8. Rather, the parties dispute whether a person of ordinary skill in the art would have been motivated to combine one of the unlocking mechanisms disclosed in Plaisant with Neonode. Samsung argues "there was no evidence of any kind suggesting that Plaisant's application to a wall-mounted device would lead inventors not to combine Plaisant with Neonode." Its expert, Dr. Greenberg, testified that "a person looking at this would just think it natural to combine these two, as well taking the ideas in Plaisant, the slider, and putting them on the Neonode is, is just a very routine thing to think about in terms of interaction design." Samsung points to the Plaisant reference which states that sliding movement "is less likely to be done inadvertently."

7   Apple counters that a skilled artisan designing a mobile phone would not have been motivated to turn to a wall-mounted air conditioning controller to solve the pocket dialing problem. Its expert, Dr. Cockburn, testified that a person of ordinary skill would not have been naturally motivated to combine Neonode and Plaisant. He also explained to the jury that Plaisant itself discloses that sliding toggles were less preferred than the other switches disclosed. Apple points to Plaisant's teachings that "sliders were not preferred," "sliding is a more complex task," and "sliders are more difficult to implement." Apple argues there was substantial evidence for the jury to conclude that there would not have been a motivation to combine Plaisant and Neonode to arrive at the claimed invention.

8   Because the jury found the issue of validity in favor of Apple, we presume it resolved the conflicting expert testimony and found that a skilled artisan would not have been motivated to combine the slider toggle in Plaisant with the cell phone disclosed in Neonode. The question for our review is whether substantial evidence

supports this implied fact finding. We conclude that it does. Neonode discloses a mobile phone. Plaisant discloses a wall-mounted air conditioning controller. The jury had both references before it. Although Samsung presents arguments for combining the two references, these arguments were before the jury. Our job is not to review whether Samsung's losing position was also supported by substantial evidence or to weigh the relative strength of Samsung's evidence against Apple's evidence. We are limited to determining whether there was substantial evidence for the jury's findings, on the entirety of the record.

1. The Objective Indicia of Non–Obviousness

9   The Supreme Court explained that various factors "may also serve to guard against slipping into use of hindsight, and to resist the temptation to read into the prior art the teachings of the invention in issue." *Graham*, 383 U.S. at 36. These factors are commonly known as secondary considerations or objective indicia of non-obviousness. Apple introduced evidence of industry praise, copying, commercial success, and long-felt need. We presume the jury found that the evidence was sufficient to establish each by a preponderance of the evidence. We find substantial evidence in the record to support each of those findings.

a. Industry Praise

10   Evidence that the industry praised a claimed invention or a product that embodies the patent claims weighs against an assertion that the same claimed invention would have been obvious. Industry participants, especially competitors, are not likely to praise an obvious advance over the known art. Thus, if there is evidence of industry praise of the claimed invention in the record, it weighs in favor of the non-obviousness of the claimed invention.

11   The district court cited numerous internal Samsung documents that both praised Apple's slide to unlock feature and indicated that Samsung should modify its own phones to incorporate Apple's slide to unlock feature [such as presentations calling Apple's slide to unlock invention a "creative way of solving UI complexity" and recommending a "direction of improvement" to make Samsung's phone the "same as iPhone" with "unlocking standard by sliding"]. Such internal documents from the patentee's top competitor represent important admissions, acknowledging the merits of the patented advance over the then state of the art and can be used to establish industry praise. The court also explained that Apple presented a video at trial showing Steve Jobs unveiling the slide to unlock feature at an Apple event. When Mr. Jobs swiped to unlock the phone, "the audience burst into cheers."[2]

12   In light of this evidence, we find [Samsung's] argument that the district court cited only generic praise of the iPhone, and not praise tied to the claimed slide to unlock feature, is without merit. The jury was presented with substantial evidence of

---

[2] [You can see this video here: https://www.youtube.com/watch?v=kx2XpSgeAiY]

praise in the industry that specifically related to features of the claimed invention, thereby linking that industry praise with the patented invention.

b. Copying

13   Samsung does not dispute in its briefing that the jury heard substantial evidence that it copied Apple's slide to unlock feature, nor does it challenge on appeal that this evidence of copying supports a conclusion that claim 8 would not have been obvious. Apple cites the same Samsung internal documents for both industry praise and copying, as they show evidence of both. This is substantial evidence of copying by Samsung, and it supports the jury's verdict that the claimed invention would not have been obvious.

c. Commercial Success

14   In its opening appellate brief, Samsung also glosses over commercial success, giving it one sentence: "Apple made no effort to establish a nexus between commercial success and the subject matter of claim 8." Commercial success requires a nexus to the claimed invention. We look to the record to ascertain whether there is substantial evidence for the jury's fact finding that Apple established a nexus between commercial success and the invention in claim 8.

15   At trial, Apple's expert, Dr. Cockburn, testified that the iPhone practiced the asserted claim of the '721 patent, and "clearly there's been commercial success of the iPhones that use this invention." Critically, Apple presented survey evidence that customers would be less likely to purchase a portable device without the slide to unlock feature and would pay less for products without it, thus permitting the jury to conclude that this feature was a key driver in the ultimate commercial success of the products. Apple's Senior Vice President of Worldwide Marketing testified that slide to unlock was the very first feature shown in Apple's original iPhone TV commercial, and the jury saw that commercial during the trial. A reasonable jury could have found evidence that Apple's marketing experts elected to emphasize the claimed feature as evidence of its importance. It is likewise reasonable to conclude that advertising that highlights or focuses on a feature of the invention could influence customer purchasing decisions. And an inventor of the '721 patent—an Apple Vice President—confirmed that slide to unlock was important because it "would possibly be [a customer's] first experience even in a retail environment" when the customer was "deciding whether they want to buy it." Finally, the video of the crowd "burst[ing] into cheers" when Steve Jobs demonstrated the slide to unlock feature supports a conclusion that consumers valued this particular feature.

16   This record overall contains substantial evidence of a nexus between the slide to unlock feature and the iPhone's commercial success, and we are required to give this jury fact finding deference. It is not our role to reweigh the evidence or consider what the record might have supported. This commercial success evidence supports the jury's verdict that the claimed invention would not have been obvious.

d. Long–Felt Need

17   Evidence of a long-felt but unresolved need can weigh in favor of the non-obviousness of an invention because it is reasonable to infer the need would not have persisted had the solution been obvious. There is substantial evidence for the jury to have found that there was a long-felt but unresolved need for a solution to the pocket dialing problem until Apple's claimed invention, with its slide to unlock feature, solved that problem. Denying JMOL on this issue, the district court cited testimony from Apple's expert: "Dr. Cockburn's testimony that phone designers had been trying to solve the problem of accidental activation and the 'pocket dial problem' before the iPhone existed, but had only come up with 'frustrat[ing]' solutions." While the expert discusses particular examples in the first person: "I have been very frustrated with [the prior art options]," the jury could still reasonably find that this testimony was probative of a long-felt need.

18   The record [also] contained a document in which Samsung listed all the alternatives to the iPhone slide to unlock. Apple's expert went through several of the alternatives . . . and explained how each of these failed to solve the accidental activation problem. The jury could have reasonably found that this testimony established long-felt unresolved need.

19   In addition, the jury could have found that the same internal Samsung documents Apple relied upon for industry praise and copying demonstrate that Samsung compared four of its own rejected alternative unlock mechanisms to the iPhone slide to unlock mechanism, and that Samsung concluded the iPhone slide to unlock was better. The jury could have found that these Samsung documents show that Samsung, Apple's fiercest competitor, was unsuccessfully trying to solve the same problem. This evidence constitutes substantial evidence for the jury fact finding that there was a long-felt but unresolved need, which Apple's '721 patented invention solved.

2. Conclusion on Obviousness of the '721 Patent

20   With [KSR's] principles in mind, we review de novo the ultimate legal determination and conclude that it would not have been obvious to a skilled artisan to combine the prior art to arrive at the claimed invention.

21   Common sense and real world indicators indicate that to conclude otherwise would be to give in to hindsight, to allow the exact ex post reasoning against which the Supreme Court cautioned in *Graham* and *KSR*. Though the prior art references each relate to touchscreens, the totality of the evidence supports the conclusion that it would not have been obvious for a skilled artisan, seeking an unlock mechanism that would be both intuitive to use and solve the pocket dialing problem for cell phones, to look to a wall-mounted controller for an air conditioner. The two-page Plaisant paper published in 1992 reported the results of a user-preference survey of fifteen undergraduates on six different computer-based switches. That a skilled

artisan would look to the Plaisant paper directed to a wall-mounted interface screen for appliances and then choose the slider toggle, which the study found rated fifth out of six options in usability, to fulfill a need for an intuitive unlock mechanism that solves the pocket dialing problem for cell phones seems far from obvious.

22   We have considered the jury's implicit fact findings about the teachings of Plaisant and Neonode. We have also considered the objective indicia found by the jury which are particularly strong in this case and powerfully weigh in favor of validity. These real world indicators of whether the combination would have been obvious to the skilled artisan in this case "tip the scales of patentability," *Graham*, 383 U.S. at 36, or "dislodge the determination that claim [8 would have been] obvious," *KSR*, 550 U.S. at 426. Weighing all of the *Graham* factors, we agree with the district court on the ultimate legal determination that Samsung failed to establish by clear and convincing evidence that claim 8 of the '721 patent would have been obvious. We affirm the district court's denial of JMOL.

Timothy B. Dyk, Circuit Judge, dissenting.

23   [Judge Dyk criticized the procedural irregularity of taking a case en banc without further briefing before turning to "the profound changes in the law of obviousness that the majority creates."]

24   First, the majority turns the legal question of obviousness into a factual issue for a jury to resolve, both as to the sufficiency of the motivation to combine and the significance to be given to secondary considerations. *KSR* explicitly rejected the contention that obviousness is always a matter of fact requiring jury resolution. In *KSR*, the patentee argued that the question of motivation to combine was for the jury. The Supreme Court rejected this contention. Here too, "the content of the prior art, the scope of the patent claim, and the level of ordinary skill in the art are not in material dispute," *KSR*, 550 U.S. at 427, and there is no indication that the combination of the relevant prior art does more than yield a predictable result. Yet the majority holds that the question of the sufficiency of the motivation here was a jury question.

25   Second, the majority lowers the bar for nonobviousness by refusing to take account of the trivial nature of the two claimed inventions. The slide to unlock feature was known in the prior art (Neonode) and the only innovation is an image associated with the sliding gesture from fixed starting to ending points.[3] Treating such minimal advances over the prior art as nonobvious is contrary to *KSR*, where the Supreme Court confirmed that the obviousness doctrine is designed to ensure that "the results of ordinary innovation are not the subject of exclusive rights under the patent laws."

---

[3] [n.3 in opinion] Courts in other countries [including the UK, the Netherlands, and Germany] have uniformly found the '721 patent invalid.

550 U.S. at 427. On the face of these patents, only ordinary, indeed trivial, innovation is involved.

26   Third, the majority concludes that combinations of prior art used to solve a known problem are insufficient to render an invention obvious as a matter of law. According to the majority, there must be evidence of a specific motivation to combine. Both aspects of these conclusions are contrary to *KSR*. Under *KSR*, the existence of each patented feature in the prior art is alone not sufficient to establish obviousness. There must be a reason to make a combination. But *KSR* holds that the reason may be found as a matter of law in the solution to a known problem. *KSR* was quite clear that the existence of a known problem suffices: "[o]ne of the ways in which a patent's subject matter can be proved obvious is by noting that there existed at the time of invention a known problem for which there was an obvious solution." 550 U.S. at 419–20. "[W]hen a patent simply arranges old elements with each performing the same function it had been known to perform and yields no more than one would expect from such an arrangement, the combination is obvious." *Id.* at 417. *KSR* also held, contrary to the majority, that evidence of a specific motivation to combine is not required. The Court rejected our court's approach in requiring a "specific understanding or principle" that creates a specific motivation to combine. In *KSR* itself, the combination was held obvious despite no "precise teachings" to combine the previous references.

27   Here, the inventions combine features known in the prior art. Apple does not dispute that the combination of the prior art Neonode and Plaisant references produces the claimed invention. There is no claim that the combination yielded unpredictable results. The patent also addresses a known problem: ease-of-use and avoidance of inadvertent activation. Contrary to *KSR*, the majority now holds that a known problem is not sufficient and that there must be evidence of a specific motivation.

28   Fourth, the majority errs in cabining the relevant technology in the field of prior art. The majority invites the factfinder to dismiss prior art evidence on the theory that it concerns a different device than the patented invention, even if the references are directed to solving the same problem and pertain to a related device. For example, the majority holds that the jury could dismiss the Plaisant reference because it was directed to wall-mounted rather than portable devices. The Supreme Court in *KSR* rejected the theory that prior art addressing the same problem can be dismissed because it concerns a different device. "[I]f a technique has been used to improve one device, and a person of ordinary skill in the art would recognize that it would improve similar devices in the same way, using the technique is obvious unless its actual application is beyond his or her skill." *KSR*, 550 U.S. at 417.

29   The '721 patent concerns unlocking touchscreen devices. Here, the prior art dismissed by the majority concerns the general field of touchscreen devices. The majority errs in two respects. First, the '721 patent is not limited to cell phones or to the cell phone pocket-dialing problem, and indeed makes no reference to a pocket-

dialing problem. The '721 patent is directed to portable devices generally, and to ease of use and inadvertent activation with respect to all such devices. Second, the Plaisant prior art was concerned with the same problems as the '721 patent in the field of touch screen devices. Plaisant indicated that the study's "focus is on providing . . . systems that are easy for the home owner to use." Plaisant also indicated that an "advantage of the sliding movement is that it is less likely to be done inadvertently." Plaisant was thus directed to solving the same problem in the same area as the patented invention.

30   This change is evident from comparing the majority's holding here to our past jurisprudence. We have previously held that "[a] reference is reasonably pertinent if, even though it may be in a different field from that of the inventor's endeavor, [it] logically would have commended itself to an inventor's attention in considering his problem." *In re Clay*, 966 F.2d 656, 659 (Fed. Cir. 1992). "We therefore have concluded, for example, that an inventor considering a hinge and latch mechanism for portable computers would naturally look to references employing other housings, hinges, latches, springs, etc., which in that case came from areas such as a desktop telephone directory, a piano lid, a kitchen cabinet, a washing machine cabinet, a wooden furniture cabinet, or a two-part housing for storing audio cassettes." *In re ICON Health & Fitness, Inc.*, 496 F.3d 1374, 1380 (Fed. Cir. 2007). Not only does the majority alter our jurisprudence with respect to district court proceedings, its approach would affect patent examiners who are currently instructed that analogous prior art "does not require that the reference be from the same field of endeavor as the claimed invention." Manual of Patent Examining Procedure § 2141.01(a).

31   Fifth, the majority errs in elevating secondary considerations of nonobviousness beyond their role as articulated by the Supreme Court. Secondary considerations "without invention[ ] will not make patentability." *Sakraida*, 425 U.S. at 278. Thus, when, as here, a patent is plainly not inventive, that is, when the prima facie case of obviousness is strong, secondary considerations carry little weight. The majority holds that secondary considerations must "always" be considered and that even a strong case of obviousness involving small advances in the prior art can be outweighed by secondary considerations. But under Supreme Court authority, secondary considerations are insufficient to outweigh a strong case of obviousness involving small advances over the prior art.

32   *KSR* and *Graham* assigned a limited role to secondary considerations. *KSR* required inquiry into secondary considerations only *"where appropriate."* 550 U.S. at 415. In *Graham*, secondary considerations are referred to as factors that *"might* be utilized to give light to the circumstances." 383 U.S. at 17. For example, the *Graham* Court weighed (in evaluating the Scoggin insecticide sprayer patent) that despite the presence of "long-felt need in the industry" and "wide commercial success" of the patentee, "these factors do not, in the circumstances of this case, tip the scales of patentability." 383 U.S. at 35–36. This was so because in that case the invention "rest[ed] upon exceedingly small and quite non-technical mechanical differences in a device which was old in the art." *Id.* at 36. Similarly, even though the patentee in *KSR*

introduced evidence of commercial success, the Court dismissed it because it "conclude[d] Teleflex has shown no secondary factors to dislodge the determination that claim 4 is obvious." 550 U.S. at 426.

33   This case also is not a close one. The combination of references, the known problem, the predictable results, and the exceedingly small differences from the prior art make the combination evident and secondary considerations insufficient as a matter of law.

34   Finally, even if secondary considerations in this case were legally relevant, the majority fails to compare to the closest prior art to properly assess the innovation over the prior art. Secondary considerations must be directed to what is claimed to be inventive. In other words, there must be a demonstrated nexus to the claimed invention—a nexus to what is new in comparison to the prior art. Furthermore, the proponent of such evidence of secondary considerations, in this case Apple, "bears the burden of showing that a nexus exists between the claimed features of the invention and the objective evidence offered to show nonobviousness." *WMS Gaming v. Int'l Game Tech.*, 184 F.3d 1339, 1359 (Fed. Cir. 1999).

35   [Under prior Federal Circuit caselaw,] ascertaining the significance of the innovative leap over the prior art using secondary considerations requires a comparison to the closest prior art. The majority's secondary considerations analysis repeatedly compares to inferior or non-existent prior art, rather than to the relevant, closest prior art. For example, for commercial success, Apple and the majority rely on survey evidence developed for Apple's damages case that consumers are more likely to purchase (and pay more for) a phone with a slide to unlock feature. However, this is an irrelevant comparison because Neonode provides a slide-to-unlock feature. There was no showing of nexus between the inventive steps (over the closest prior art) and the surveyed consumer demand. For long-felt but unresolved need, the majority compares to an older Nokia device with a very different non-touchscreen, button-based unlocking feature, as well as to Samsung touchscreen unlocking mechanisms that do not have the slide-to-unlock feature of Neonode. The majority also cites Steve Job's unveiling of the slide to unlock feature at an Apple event and the audience's cheers as evidence of industry praise for the '721 patent. Again, however, Apple provides no evidence that this praise was specifically for the '721 patent's innovative step beyond Neonode or even that the audience was comprised of industry experts. The majority thus errs in elevating such irrelevant comparisons as providing "particularly strong" and "powerful[ ]" evidence of nonobviousness.

36   In summary, the majority decision here materially raises the bar for obviousness by disregarding Supreme Court precedent.

37   [Separate dissents by Chief Judge Prost and Judge Reyna are omitted. In 2017, the Supreme Court denied Samsung's cert petition after calling for the views of the Solicitor General, who recommended against review. In 2018, Apple and Samsung

settled all lawsuits—including a suit involving design patents that did make it to the Supreme Court.]

Discussion Questions: Secondary Considerations

1. *Advantages?* What are the advantages to courts of looking to the secondary considerations as opposed to focusing solely on the technical characteristics of the inventions? What does a court have to gain from scrutinizing, for instance, the success or failures of other inventors or the commercial success of a product instead of looking directly at the technical aspects of the invention?

2. *The Inferences and Assumptions Underlying Secondary Considerations.* The weakness of secondary considerations is that they are only proxies for nonobviousness, not the real thing. This means that each secondary consideration relies on background assumptions or requires additional information to be made useful. Consider the most frequently used secondary consideration: commercial success. This factor has been criticized as "a poor indicator of patentability because it is indirect; it depends for its effectiveness on a long chain of inferences, and the links in the chain are often subject to doubt." Robert P. Merges, *Commercial Success and Patent Standards: Economic Perspectives on Innovation*, 76 Calif. L. Rev. 803, 838 (1988). The Federal Circuit has repeatedly emphasized that evidence of secondary considerations must have a "nexus" to the claimed invention. A nexus is presumed to exist "when the patentee shows that the asserted objective evidence is tied to a specific product and that product embodies the claimed features, and is coextensive with them." *Fox Factory v. SRAM*, 944 F.3d 1366, 1373 (Fed. Cir. 2019). To have relevance for the obviousness inquiry, the commercial success of a product also must be due to the claimed invention, and that future success must have been apparent to numerous firms before the invention's development. What else is required before a court can infer nonobviousness from commercial success?

Are all secondary considerations subject to this critique to the same degree? For each of the following, what are those potential confounding variables, and what additional information is necessary to interpret the secondary consideration?

A. Failure of others, skepticism, professional approval, and near-simultaneous invention? *See* Merges, *supra*, at 862 ("Unlike commercial success, the failure of others to make an invention proves *directly* that parallel research efforts were under way at a number of firms, and that one firm (the patentee) won the race to a common goal."). Do you agree with this quote from the Merges article that the failure of others provides direct evidence of nonobviousness?

B. Long-felt need?

C. Copying by others and licensing activity?

3. *Secondary Considerations as Secondary.* One case that starkly poses the question of how much to weigh the primary and secondary considerations is *Ritchie v. Vast Resources, Inc.*, 563 F.3d 1334 (Fed. Cir. 2009). This case, decided by Judge Richard Posner sitting by designation, involved a highly commercially successful invention that seemed technically trivial, but which nobody until the plaintiffs had thought to invent despite the raw materials existing for nearly a century:

> Both [plaintiff and defendant] firms produce what the parties call "sex aids" but are colloquially referred to as "sex toys." The devices are generally in the shape of rods of various curvatures and are made out of rubber, plastic, glass, or some combination of these materials. Until the plaintiffs began manufacturing their patented sexual devices, glass sexual devices were made out of soda-lime glass, the most common form of glass. The plaintiffs' patent claims [devices made from] "borosilicate glass," [which is] "resistant to heat, chemicals, electricity and bacterial absorptions." Borosilicate glass is the glass out of which Pyrex glassware was originally made, and is sometimes still made.
>
> Given that it has commercial value, as heavily emphasized by the plaintiffs, and given that Pyrex has been sold for almost a century, to call its use in a sexual device "obvious" may seem the triumph of hindsight over insight. Commercial value is indeed one of the indicia of nonobviousness, because an invention that has commercial value is likely to come on the market very shortly after the idea constituting the invention (in this case the use of borosilicate glass in a sexual device) became obvious; if the invention did not appear so soon despite its value in the market, this is some evidence that it wasn't obvious after all. But for a variety of reasons commercial success is deemed a "secondary" indicator of nonobviousness. The commercial success of a product can have many causes unrelated to patentable inventiveness; for example, the commercial success of an "invention" might be due not to the invention itself but to skillful marketing of the product embodying the invention.
>
> Among the inventions that the law deems obvious are efforts at routine experimentation with different standard grades of a material used in a product—standard in the sense that their properties, composition, and method of creation are well known, making successful results of the experimentation predictable. This is such a case.
>
> This case thus exemplifies the Supreme Court's analysis in *KSR*. "If a person of ordinary skill can implement a predictable variation, § 103 likely bars its patentability. For the same reason, if a technique has been used to improve one device, and *a person of ordinary skill in the art would recognize that it would improve similar devices in the*

same way, using the technique is obvious unless its actual application is beyond his or her skill." (The last sentence describes our case to a tee.)

In *Ritchie,* Judge Posner makes clear that when the secondary considerations cut strongly in one direction and the technical approach to nonobviousness cuts strongly in the other, the courts will side with the technical approach. This was particularly remarkable given the identity of the opinion's author, perhaps the most famous law and economics scholar and judge in history. Do you think this is appropriate? Should the court in *Ritchie* have given greater credence to the secondary considerations, given how strongly they favored a finding of nonobviousness?

4. *Other Evidence of Obviousness?* Can you think of any evidence not captured by the Federal Circuit's list of potential secondary considerations that might be probative of obviousness or nonobviousness?

Judge Dyk's dissent notes in a footnote that other countries had uniformly found the slide-to-unlock patent invalid; should this be relevant to the assessment by a U.S. court?

Should courts consider evidence of how "distant" the invention is from the prior art as determined by algorithmic measures of technological networks? If so, should this be considered a secondary consideration or direct evidence? *See* Laura G. Pedraza-Fariña & Ryan Whalen, *A Network Theory of Patentability,* 87 U. Chi. L. Rev. 63 (2020).

Practice Problems: Post-*KSR* Federal Circuit Cases on Nonobviousness

The following problems are based on real Federal Circuit cases decided after *KSR.* Do you think the claims at issue are obvious or nonobvious?

1. Tai Hoon and Eric applied for a patent on a paper shredder with two sensors: a "presence" sensor, which will turn on the shredder when it senses the presence of one or more sheets of paper; and a "thickness" sensor, which will prevent the shredder from operating if the stack of paper inserted is too thick and risks jamming the shredder. The key claim is as follows:

A shredding machine for shredding sheet material comprising:
(a) a feed-aperture;
(b) an electric cutting mechanism, the feed-aperture being configured to receive multiple sheets and direct said sheets in a feeding direction towards the cutting mechanism for shredding;
(c) a controller coupled to the cutting mechanism;
(d) a thickness detector coupled to the controller; and

(e) a presence sensor along the feed-aperture for detecting a presence of the sheet material inserted into the feed-aperture, coupled to the controller,

(f) wherein the controller will turn the shredder on only when the presence sensor detects the presence of at least one sheet of paper inserted into the feed-aperture, and when the thickness detector detects that the paper is not too thick for the shredder.

Prior art shredders have features including (1) presence sensors that automatically turn on the shredder when paper is present; (2) the ability to sense when a paper jam has occurred (by measuring a spike in voltage from the electric motor) and switch off the shredder's motor with a controller; and (3) thickness sensors that can determine the thickness of a stack of paper. A competitor independently invented a shredder with presence and thickness sensors shortly after Tai Hoon and Eric applied for their patent. *See ACCO Brands Corp. v. Fellowes, Inc.*, 813 F.3d 1361 (Fed. Cir. 2016).

2. LeapFrog Enterprises, a manufacturer of technology-based learning products for children, sued Fisher-Price and Mattel for infringement of this patent claim on a device to help young children read phonetically:

An interactive learning device, comprising:
(a) a sound production device in communication with a plurality of switches and including a processor and a memory;
(b) at least one depiction of a sequence of letters, each letter being associable with a switch; and
(c) wherein selection of a depicted letter activates an associated switch to communicate with the processor, causing the sound production device to generate a signal corresponding to a sound associated with the selected letter, the sound being determined by a position of the letter in the sequence of letters.

The prior art includes (1) a patent describing a learning toy for which pressing any letter from a word produces the sound of that letter using a phonograph record controlled with an electric motor and (2) a Texas Instruments toy that allows a child to press the first letter of a word or the remaining letters (e.g., "c" or "at" for "cat") and hear those sounds played using a processor, memory, and a speaker. At trial, LeapFrog presented substantial evidence of commercial success, praise, and long-felt need. *See LeapFrog Enterprises v. Fisher-Price, Inc.*, 485 F.3d 1157 (Fed. Cir. 2007).

3. University scientists sought a patent on a method of disinfecting surfaces for methicillin-resistant *Staphylococcus aureus* (MRSA) and other "Gram-positive" bacteria that have developed resistance to antibiotics. It was well known that these bacteria could be inactivated with exposure to light of certain wavelengths, but most prior art methods involved the time-consuming step of applying a "photosensitizer" to the surface before the light exposure. The university scientists developed a method that did not require a photosensitizer. The key claim is as follows:

A method for disinfecting comprising:

(a) exposing one or more Gram-positive bacteria to visible light without using a photosensitizer,

(b) wherein the one or more Gram-positive bacteria are selected from the group consisting of Methicillin-resistant *Staphylococcus aureus* (MRSA), Coagulase-Negative *Staphylococcus* (CONS), *Streptococcus*, *Enterococcus*, and *Clostridium* species, and

(c) wherein a portion of the visible light consists of wavelengths in the range 400–420 nm.

One prior art article by Dr. Helena Ashkenazi noted that porphyrin—a compound that naturally occurs in Gram-positive bacteria including MRSA—damages bacteria when exposed to blue light. The article described inactivation of Gram-positive bacteria using a photosensitizer that enhances porphyrin production inside cells, followed by exposure to light with 407–420 nm wavelengths. A second prior art article by Dr. Yeshayahu Nitzan described exposure of MRSA and other Gram-positive bacteria to 407–420 nm light without a photosensitizer, which did not successfully achieve inactivation. *See Univ. of Strathclyde v. Clear-Vu Lighting*, 17 F.4th 155 (Fed. Cir. 2021).

4. The Wrigley chewing gum company sued Cadbury (the candy company) for infringing its patent on "cool flavored" gum:

A chewing gum composition comprising:

(a) about 5% to about 95% gum base;

(b) about 5% to about 95% bulking and sweetening agent; and

(c) about 0.1% to about 10% flavoring agent wherein the flavoring agent comprises WS-23 and menthol.

WS-23 is a flavoring agent that, like menthol, produces a "cool" sensation. The prior art includes (1) gum with a gum base of 45%; (2) gum with 53% bulking and sweetening agent; (3) gum using combinations of menthol and WS-3 (another flavoring agent that produces a "cooling" effect); and (4) printed publications disclosing that WS-3 and WS-23 are similar substitutes for menthol. Wigley's gum, which fell within this claim scope and contained other ingredients, was a commercial success, and Cadbury copied the Wrigley formula after conducting an internal study showing that consumers greatly preferred Wrigley's product. *See Wm. Wrigley Jr. Co. v. Cadbury Adams USA LLC*, 683 F.3d 1356 (Fed. Cir. 2012).

4. Utility and Disclosure

In the previous chapters, we addressed the question of when an inventor has created a novel and nonobvious invention that is eligible for patenting. But these are not the only requirements for patentability. An invention must also be useful at the time of filing, and it must be adequately disclosed in the patent document. Four doctrines have evolved to police these requirements: utility, enablement, written description, and best mode.

All of these doctrines stem from 35 U.S.C. § 112(a), which was previously known as § 112, ¶ 1 before the 2011 America Invents Act added letters to the paragraphs. Pre-AIA claims are governed by the old § 112, ¶ 1, but the only difference is the addition of "or joint inventor," and we will refer throughout to § 112(a) for simplicity.

35 U.S.C. § 112(a)

> The specification shall contain a written description of the invention, and of the manner and process of making and using it, in such full, clear, concise, and exact terms as to enable any person skilled in the art to which it pertains, or with which it is most nearly connected, to make and use the same, and shall set forth the best mode contemplated by the inventor or joint inventor of carrying out the invention.

In addition, utility depends on § 101's requirement that inventions be "useful." Some references suggest that utility depends *only* on § 101, but the first case below explains how the statutes are linked. As MPEP § 2107 states: "A deficiency under the utility prong of 35 U.S.C. 101 also creates a deficiency under 35 U.S.C. 112(a)."

In short, *utility* requires that the invention be operable and that it have some demonstrated real-world use at the time of filing. *Enablement* requires that the patent teach the PHOSITA how to make and use the invention without "undue experimentation." *Written description* requires the patent demonstrate that the inventor "possessed" the invention at the time of filing, meaning that the inventor understood that she had invented the invention. And under the *best mode* requirement, an inventor must disclose not just *a* way of practicing the invention, but her *preferred* way. Best mode is relevant only during prosecution: under the 2011 America Invents Act, "failure to disclose the best mode shall not be a basis on which any claim of a patent may be canceled or held invalid or otherwise unenforceable." Pub. L. No. 112-29, § 15, 125 Stat. 284 (2011). The other three doctrines—utility, enablement, and written description—will be discussed in greater detail in the following sections.

We discuss these doctrines together not only because they stem from the same statutory provision but also because each of these doctrines serves—to varying degrees—three distinct policy goals.

1. *Promoting Knowledge Dissemination.* First, these doctrines encourage dissemination of scientific knowledge. The benefit of these disclosures is contested—the Supreme Court has stated that "such additions to the general store of knowledge are of such importance" that they are worth the "high price . . . of exclusive use." *Kewanee Oil Co. v. Bicron Corp.*, 416 US. 470, 481 (1974), but numerous legal scholars have worried that scientists do not read patents, both because they are obfuscated with legal jargon and because reading patents might lead to increased liability for willful patent infringement. What percentage of scientists do you think read patents and find useful information in them? To compare your priors with a recent survey, see Lisa Larrimore Ouellette, *Who Reads Patents?*, 35 Nature Biotechnology 421 (2017).

2. *Limiting Premature Patenting.* Second, utility, enablement, and written description limit premature patenting based on predictions and speculation. We have already seen how the novelty and nonobviousness requirements encourage inventors to get to the patent office early; these are the doctrines that prevent them from going *too* early. The fundamental problem of when someone has done enough to merit a new property right "has bedeviled property theorists for centuries, as demonstrated by the enduring resonance of the 1805 property case *Pierson v. Post.* Should the fox belong to the hunter who begins the chase or the one who makes the kill? Should an invention belong to the researcher who begins work on it or the one who brings it to fruition?" Lisa Larrimore Ouellette, Pierson, *Peer Review, and Patent Law*, 69 Vand. L. Rev. 1825 (2016). What's the harm of granting patents before inventors have figured out all the details of their invention or what it is good for? When should patent law require inventors to demonstrate that their ideas work in practice?

3. *Limiting Overbroad Claims.* Third, and most importantly, these doctrines prevent overbroad patents, or patents with claims that are broader in scope than what the inventor contributed to the art. Patent claims have never been limited to exactly what the inventor has done or to the examples listed in the patent specification, but how far beyond the inventor's actual work should patent rights stretch? Consider the following hypothetical:

> [S]uppose an inventor produced a method of curing AIDS using radiation therapy, specifically using X-radiation, and then built a radiation machine that implemented the method. This would be a working embodiment. The ideas that underlie this cure can be broken into many different levels of abstraction, each progressively more specific and narrower in the resulting patent's scope:
>
> 1.   The idea of curing AIDS, covering all cures that might ever be devised.

2. The idea of curing AIDS by using radiation therapy, covering all cures using any type of radiation but not other methods.

3. The idea of curing AIDS by using radiation therapy specifically by using X-radiation, thereby excluding methods not using X-radiation.

4. The idea of curing AIDS using radiation therapy specifically by using X-radiation and more specifically by using the exact make and model of the patentee's radiation machine.

As can be seen from this example, each idea at a different level of abstraction can be accurately described as the "invention." . . . How this choice is exercised, however, has tremendous consequences for both the incentives of inventors and the rights of subsequent improvers and users.

Tun-Jen Chiang, *The Levels of Abstraction Problem in Patent Law*, 105 Nw. U. L. Rev. 1097 (2011). We will see that choosing the right level of abstraction is both a critical policy question and one that eludes easy answers.

As you read the cases that follow, consider how effectively each of the three doctrines serve the goals of promoting knowledge dissemination and limiting premature and overbroad patenting. It is also worth noting that these last two considerations are policed by the law of patentable subject matter, which we discuss in Chapter 6. As you study the doctrines described here and in Chapter 6, you should consider the extent to which they are mutually reinforcing or redundant, and whether one of these doctrines accomplishes the desired policy goals better than the other.

A. Utility

The utility requirement stems from § 101's requirement that inventions be "useful" and § 112(a)'s requirement of disclosure of "the manner and process of making and *using*" the invention. A claim that is unpatentable for lack of utility is thus deficient under both § 101 and § 112(a). *See* MPEP § 2107. Utility is a low bar that is usually easily satisfied. If an invention were not useful, who would bother patenting or infringing it?

There are three strands of utility cases, of which we will focus only on the third:

1. *Beneficial utility* is a now-defunct doctrine that previously imposed limits on illegal, immoral, or socially harmful inventions. For example, in *Lowell v. Lewis*, 15 F. Cas. 1018 (C.C.D. Mass. 1817), Justice Story said inventions "to poison people, or to promote debauchery, or to facilitate private assassination" would lack utility, and subsequent cases frequently concerned gambling devices. But in a case involving a deceptive juice dispenser—which created an illusion it was dispensing fresh juice

when the actual beverage was from concentrate, as shown at right—the Federal Circuit rejected this view: "Congress never intended that the patent laws should displace the police powers of the States, meaning by that term those powers by which the health, good order, peace and general welfare of the community are promoted." *Juicy Whip, Inc. v. Orange Bang, Inc.*, 185 F.3d 1364, 1368 (Fed. Cir. 1999) (quoting *Webber v. Virginia*, 103 U.S. 344, 347–48 (1880)). Courts no longer use utility to assess whether an invention is socially beneficial, although some moral concerns have motivated the growth of a separate doctrine, patentable subject matter, which we will consider later. And some other countries do have public policy exceptions to patentability—known as "*ordre public*" exceptions—as we discuss in Chapter 20. Do you think beneficial utility doctrine should be revived in the United States?

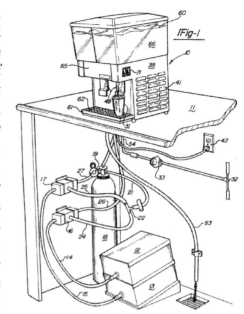

2. *Credible utility* requires an invention to be operable—one cannot patent a perpetual motion machine or an invention that simply does not work for its intended purpose. But this does not mean that patentees must demonstrate that their inventions work. A patent application's assertion of utility is presumed credible, so examiners have the burden of establishing the incredibility of the asserted utility. The USPTO notes that credible utility rejections are "rare" and limited to cases in which the asserted utility is "inconsistent with known scientific principles," "the logic underlying the assertion is seriously flawed," or "the facts upon which the assertion is based are inconsistent with the logic underlying the assertion." MPEP § 2107. Aside from these rare cases, patent law leaves the task of policing operability to the market—if an invention does not work, it should have limited commercial success. Do you think the USPTO should do more to limit these patents?

3. *Practical utility*, also known as *specific and substantial utility*, requires a disclosed use at the time of filing that is *specific* to the subject matter claimed and that has a *substantial* real-world use, meaning it is useful to the public in its current form, and not merely after further research. For example, the following inventions lack practical utility:

- A method of diagnosing or treating an unspecified disease or condition.

- A method of identifying or making a material that itself has no practical utility, such as a material that is merely an input to further research.

- A claim to a polynucleotide whose use is disclosed simply as a "gene probe" or "chromosome marker" to gain further information about underlying genes. *See In re Fisher*, 421 F.3d 1365 (Fed. Cir. 2005).

- A research intermediate that will be used to make some final product that itself has no known utility.

Note that unpatentable research intermediates should be distinguished from patentable research tools. "Many research tools such as gas chromatographs, screening assays, and nucleotide sequencing techniques have a clear, specific and unquestionable utility (e.g., they are useful in analyzing compounds). An assessment that focuses on whether an invention is useful only in a research setting thus does not address whether the invention is in fact 'useful' in a patent sense. Instead, [examiners] must distinguish between inventions that have a specifically identified substantial utility and inventions whose asserted utility requires further research to identify or reasonably confirm." MPEP § 2107. The requirement of "specific utility" also means that the invention has to have utility that is particular to itself and not the sort of use to which any object could be put. For instance, an inventor can't establish utility by pointing out that her new machine can be used as a paperweight.

What is the harm of allowing patents on inventions that do not yet have a specific or substantial use?

The following case shows how practical utility doctrine can be applied to limit premature patenting in the pharmaceutical context.

In re '318 Patent Infringement Litigation, 583 F.3d 1317 (Fed. Cir. 2009)[1]

Timothy B. Dyk, Circuit Judge.

Janssen Pharmaceutica N.V., Janssen L.P., and Synaptech, Inc. ("Janssen"), appeal from a final judgment of the United States District Court for the District of Delaware. After a bench trial, the district court determined that the claims of U.S. Patent No. 4,663,318 were invalid for lack of enablement. We affirm.

BACKGROUND

Janssen's '318 patent claims a method for treating Alzheimer's disease with galantamine. Claim 1 is representative. It claims "[a] method of treating Alzheimer's disease and related dementias which comprises administering to a patient suffering from such a disease a therapeutically effective amount of galantamine or a

---

[1] [Eds: This opinion's unusual caption indicates that multiple cases were consolidated for multi-district litigation (MDL) under 28 U.S.C. § 1407. MDLs are intended to reduce the burden on federal district courts by consolidating cases involving common questions of fact. MDLs are initiated after parties file a motion to transfer to the Judicial Panel on Multidistrict Litigation, which decides whether to transfer and which judge should oversee the consolidated proceedings. After pretrial proceedings, cases that have not been resolved, dismissed, or settled are transferred back to their original districts for trial.]

pharmaceutically-acceptable acid addition salt thereof." The application for the '318 patent was filed on January 15, 1986, by Dr. Bonnie Davis, the claimed inventor.

3   At the time of the '318 patent's application in early 1986, researchers had observed a correlation between Alzheimer's disease symptoms and a reduced level of the neurotransmitter acetylcholine in the brain. During neurotransmission, acetylcholine is released by a transmitting neuron and binds to receptors on a receiving neuron. At that time, galantamine, a small molecule compound, was known to inhibit acetylcholinesterase, an enzyme that breaks down acetylcholine. Acetylcholinesterase inhibitors like galantamine increase the amount of acetylcholine available for binding to receptors.

4   The specification for the '318 patent was only just over one page in length, and it provided almost no basis for its stated conclusion that it was possible to administer "an effective Alzheimer's disease cognitively-enhancing amount of galantamine." The specification provided short summaries of six scientific papers in which galantamine had been administered to humans or animals. The specification summarized the first paper as showing that administering galantamine with the drug atropine to humans under anesthesia raised blood levels of the hormone cortisol, and the second paper as showing that administering galantamine and atropine together during anesthesia also raised levels of adrenocorticotropic hormone ("ACTH") in humans. There was no explanation of the significance of increasing cortisol or ACTH levels, but it was known to those skilled in the art in early 1986 that the production of cortisol and ACTH was controlled by the central nervous system rather than the peripheral nervous system, and that the studies thus suggested that galantamine was able to cross the blood-brain barrier and have effects within the brain.

5   The specification then provided brief summaries of four scientific papers reporting brain effects and positive effects on memory from administering galantamine to animals. The first paper concluded that galantamine intravenously administered to rabbits affected brain wave activity. The second paper concluded that galantamine increased short-term memory in dogs. The third and fourth papers concluded that galantamine reversed amnesia in rats that had been induced by administering the drug scopolamine. The specification did not suggest that such scopolamine-induced amnesia was similar to Alzheimer's disease. The specification did not provide analysis or insight connecting the results of any of these six studies to galantamine's potential to treat Alzheimer's disease in humans.

6   The specification noted that another prior art scientific paper described an animal testing model for replicating in animals the acetylcholine deficit and other effects of Alzheimer's disease. The specification agreed that acetylcholine deficiency in animals is a "good animal model for Alzheimer's disease in humans" because the deficiency produces "[n]umerous behavioral deficits, including the inability to learn and retain new information." The specification cited the prior art for the conclusion that "[d]rugs that can normalize these abnormalities would have a reasonable

expectation of efficacy in Alzheimer's disease." However, the specification did not refer to any then-existing animal test results involving the administration of galantamine in connection with this animal model of Alzheimer's disease.

7   In April 1986 an examiner at the United States Patent and Trademark Office rejected the claims in the '318 patent's application for obviousness in light of the animal studies cited in the specification describing the use of galantamine to treat scopolamine-induced amnesia and in improving short-term memory.

8   In September 1986 the applicant, Dr. Davis, responded to the obviousness rejection by explaining that, because the brains of the animals in the studies cited in the specification were "normal" (rather than having "physiological changes" similar to Alzheimer's disease), the studies were conducted under "circumstances having no relevance to Alzheimer's disease."

9   In addition, Dr. Davis responded by stating that "experiments [are] underway using animal models which are expected to show that treatment with galantamine does result in an improvement in the condition of those suffering from Alzheimer's disease," and that it was "expected that data from this experimental work will be available in two to three months and will be submitted to the Examiner promptly thereafter." The '318 patent issued on May 5, 1987. Dr. Davis did not learn the results of the animal testing experiments—which suggested that galantamine could be a promising Alzheimer's disease treatment—until July 1987. These studies required several months and considerable effort by researchers at the Johns Hopkins University under the supervision of Dr. Joseph T. Coyle. No such testing results were ever submitted to the PTO.

10   After the '318 patent issued in May 1987, Dr. Davis licensed the patent in November 1995 to Janssen. In February 2001 Janssen received approval from the Food and Drug Administration ("FDA") for using galantamine to treat mild to moderate Alzheimer's disease.

11   In February 2005 several generic drug manufacturers filed abbreviated new drug applications ("ANDAs") and so-called "Paragraph IV" certifications with the FDA [a procedure discussed in more detail in Chapter 11], and Janssen sued each manufacturer for infringing the '318 patent. The actions were consolidated, the defendants conceded infringement of claims 1 and 4 of the '318 patent, and a bench trial was held in May 2007 on the invalidity issues of anticipation, obviousness, and enablement.

12   The district court concluded that the '318 patent was invalid for lack of enablement on two distinct grounds. The district court found that the specification did not demonstrate utility because relevant animal testing experiments were "not finished . . . by the time the '318 patent was allowed" and the specification provided only "minimal disclosure" of utility. The district court alternatively found that the specification and claims did not "teach one of skill in the art how to use the claimed

method" because the application "only surmise[d] how the claimed method could be used" without providing sufficient galantamine dosage information. The district court entered judgment in favor of the defendants that the '318 patent was invalid for lack of enablement.

DISCUSSION

13   Enablement is closely related to the requirement for utility. As we noted in *Process Control Corp. v. HydReclaim Corp.*, 190 F.3d 1350, 1358 (Fed. Cir. 1999),

> The enablement requirement of 35 U.S.C. § 112, ¶ 1 requires that the specification adequately discloses to one skilled in the relevant art how to make, or in the case of a process, how to carry out, the claimed invention without undue experimentation. The utility requirement of 35 U.S.C. § 101 mandates that any patentable invention be useful and, accordingly, the subject matter of the claim must be operable. *If a patent claim fails to meet the utility requirement because it is not useful or operative, then it also fails to meet the how-to-use aspect of the enablement requirement.*

The Supreme Court in *Brenner v. Manson,* 383 U.S. 519, 534–35 (1966), discussing the utility requirement, stated that inventions must have "substantial utility" and "specific benefit exist[ing] in currently available form."

14   The utility requirement prevents mere ideas from being patented. As we noted in *Genentech, Inc. v. Novo Nordisk A/S*, 108 F.3d 1361, 1366 (Fed. Cir. 1997), "[p]atent protection is granted in return for an enabling disclosure of an invention, not for vague intimations of general ideas that may or may not be workable. Tossing out the mere germ of an idea does not constitute enabling disclosure." *See also In re Fisher*, 421 F.3d 1365, 1373 (Fed. Cir. 2005) (inventions fail to meet the utility requirement if their "asserted uses represent merely hypothetical possibilities, objectives which the claimed [inventions] *could* possibly achieve, but none for which they have been used in the real world").

15   The utility requirement also prevents the patenting of a mere research proposal or an invention that is simply an object of research. Again as the Supreme Court stated in *Brenner*, "a patent is not a hunting license. It is not a reward for the search, but compensation for its successful conclusion." 383 U.S. at 536. A process or product "which either has no known use or is useful only in the sense that it may be an object of scientific research" is not patentable. *Id.* at 535. As we observed in *Fisher*, inventions do not meet the utility requirement if they are "objects upon which scientific research could be performed with no assurance that anything useful will be discovered in the end." 421 F.3d at 1373. Allowing ideas, research proposals, or objects only of research to be patented has the potential to give priority to the wrong party and to "confer power to block off whole areas of scientific development, without compensating benefit to the public." *Brenner*, 383 U.S. at 534.

16   Typically, patent applications claiming new methods of treatment are supported by test results. But it is clear that testing need not be conducted by the inventor. In addition, human trials are not required for a therapeutic invention to be patentable. As we observed in *In re Brana*, "[w]ere we to require Phase II testing [human trials] in order to prove utility, the associated costs would prevent many companies from obtaining patent protection on promising new inventions, thereby eliminating an incentive to pursue . . . potential cures." 51 F.3d 1560, 1568 (Fed. Cir. 1995).

17   We have held that results from animal tests or in vitro experiments[2] may be sufficient to satisfy the utility requirement. We noted in *Cross v. Iizuka* that "[w]e perceive no insurmountable difficulty, under appropriate circumstances, in finding that the first link in the screening chain, *in vitro* testing, may establish a practical utility for the [pharmaceutical] compound in question" in order for a patent to issue. 753 F.2d 1040, 1051 (Fed. Cir. 1985). We concluded that in vitro test results for a claimed pharmaceutical compound, combined with animal test results for a structurally similar compound, showed "a reasonable correlation between the disclosed *in vitro* utility and an in vivo activity, and therefore a rigorous correlation is not necessary where the disclosure of pharmacological activity is reasonable based upon the probative evidence." *Id.* at 1050.

18   In this case, however, neither in vitro test results nor animal test results involving the use of galantamine to treat Alzheimer's-like conditions were provided. The results from the '318 patent's proposed animal tests of galantamine for treating symptoms of Alzheimer's disease were not available at the time of the application, and the district court properly held that they could not be used to establish enablement.

19   Nor does Janssen contend that the prior art animal testing summarized in the '318 patent application's specification established utility. Indeed, both in responding to the examiner's obviousness rejection and in responding to the obviousness defense at trial, the inventor (Dr. Davis) and Janssen's witnesses explicitly stated that the utility of the invention could not be inferred from the prior art testing described in the application. The response of the inventor, Dr. Davis, to the examiner's obviousness rejection stated, with regard to studies cited in the specification showing galantamine's ability to reverse scopolamine-induced amnesia in normal rats, that "[n]othing in this teaching leads to an expectation of utility against Alzheimer's disease." The response of Dr. Davis also stated that "predict[ing] that galantamine would be useful in treating Alzheimer's disease just because it has been reported [in the prior art studies cited in the specification] to have an effect on memory in circumstances having no relevance to Alzheimer's disease" would be "as baseless as a prediction that impaired eyesight due to diabetes would respond to devices

---

[2] [n.7 in opinion] "In vitro" experiments are performed in artificial environments outside living organisms (such as in a test tube or culture media), while "in vivo" experiments are performed within living organisms.

(eyeglasses) or treatments (eye exercises) known to improve the vision of normal persons."

20   However, Janssen argues that in some circumstances utility may be established without testing the proposed treatment in the claimed environment or a sufficiently similar or predictive environment; that is, Janssen argues that utility may be established by analytic reasoning. Although no case has been called to our attention where utility was established simply by analytic reasoning, the PTO's Manual of Patent Examining Procedure ("MPEP") has recognized that "arguments or reasoning" may be used to establish an invention's therapeutic utility.[3]

21   Janssen goes on to argue that the specification here establishes utility by analytic reasoning. Relying on trial testimony, Janssen reasons that the selection and description of the prior art tests, while not directly pertinent, "set[ ] forth the evidence from existing studies demonstrating galantamine's effects on central nicotinic as well as muscarinic receptors and connect[ed] it to a model for Alzheimer's therapy rendering those effects therapeutically relevant." These insights, however, are nowhere described in the specification. Nor was there evidence that someone skilled in the art would infer galantamine's utility from the specification, even if such inferences could substitute for an explicit description of utility.

22   Janssen relies on the testimony of its expert Dr. Coyle, the scientist who later supervised the performance of the animal studies suggested in the specification. He testified that the specification "connected the dots" for galantamine as a potential Alzheimer's disease treatment. This testimony of Dr. Coyle on which Janssen relies, however, characterized the use of galantamine to treat Alzheimer's disease as "a *proposal* that connected the dots that raised very interesting questions and *worth the effort to check it out* in a model in which both nicotinic and muscarinic receptors would come into play." *Id.* (emphases added). Similarly, agreement by another of Janssen's expert witnesses, Dr. Raskind, that a person of ordinary skill in the art in early 1986 would have viewed the "invention as set forth in the patent as scientifically grounded" falls far short of demonstrating that a person of ordinary skill in the art would have recognized that the specification conveyed the required assertion of a credible utility. In fact, the inventor's own testimony reveals that an ordinarily skilled artisan would not have viewed the patent's disclosure as describing the utility of galantamine as a treatment for Alzheimer's disease: "[W]hen I submitted this patent, I certainly wasn't

---

[3] [n.10 in opinion] As stated in the MPEP, establishing "a reasonable correlation between" a compound's activity and its asserted therapeutic use may involve "statistically relevant data documenting the activity of a compound or composition, arguments or reasoning, documentary evidence (e.g., articles in scientific journals), or any combination thereof." MPEP § 2107.03. *See also Fisher*, 421 F.3d at 1372 ("The MPEP and [PTO Utility] Guidelines are not binding on this court, but may be given judicial notice to the extent they do not conflict with the statute.").

sure, and a lot of other people weren't sure that cholinesterase inhibitors [a category of agents that includes galantamine] would ever work."

23   Thus, at the end of the day, the specification, even read in the light of the knowledge of those skilled in the art, does no more than state a hypothesis and propose testing to determine the accuracy of that hypothesis. That is not sufficient. *See Rasmusson v. SmithKline Beecham Corp.*, 413 F.3d 1318, 1325 (Fed. Cir. 2005) ("If mere plausibility were the test for enablement under section 112, applicants could obtain patent rights to 'inventions' consisting of little more than respectable guesses as to the likelihood of their success. When one of the guesses later proved true, the 'inventor' would be rewarded the spoils instead of the party who demonstrated that the method actually worked. That scenario is not consistent with the statutory requirement that the inventor enable an invention rather than merely proposing an unproved hypothesis.").

24   The '318 patent's description of using galantamine to treat Alzheimer's disease thus does not satisfy the enablement requirement because the '318 patent's application did not establish utility.

25   [Judge Gajarsa dissented, arguing that the case should be remanded for additional factual findings.]

Discussion Questions: Utility and Patent Timing

1. *Demonstrating Utility at the Time of Filing.* The invention claimed in the '318 patent—using galantamine to treat Alzheimer's—did turn out to have a specific and substantial utility; as the opinion notes, the patent owner received FDA approval for this pharmaceutical method. And the inventor described how to administer galantamine to Alzheimer's patients so that a PHOSITA could practice the invention. What did she do wrong?

2. *Only One Disclosed Utility Is Required.* Suppose Dr. Bonnie Davis were the first researcher to discover the compound galantamine, and the first to show that galantamine improves short-term memory in dogs. Could she patent the compound, with a disclosed utility of treating short-term memory in dogs? Would such a claim cover use in humans? Should pharmaceutical compound claims be treated differently from method-of-use claims? *See generally* Rebecca S. Eisenberg, *The Problem of New Uses*, 5 Yale J. Health Pol'y L. & Ethics (2005).

3. *Effect on Pharmaceutical R&D.* Based on *In re '318 Patent Infringement Litigation*, what kind of evidence is needed to patent the use of a drug to treat some disease in humans? The court holds that a research hypothesis is not sufficient, but what would be sufficient? Does a patent applicant have to complete full-scale clinical trials showing that the drug is safe and effective? Or is something between a research hypothesis and full-scale clinical trials required?

Keep in mind that full-scale clinical trials can be immensely costly (in the tens or hundreds of millions of dollars) and take years to complete. If the applicant has filed for a patent before the clinical trial begins, the patent term will run during the clinical trial. On the other hand, there can be risk in embarking on a multimillion-dollar clinical trial without knowing whether one will obtain a patent in the end. How does the rule in this case affect the effective patent term for pharmaceutical companies? From the perspective of a pharmaceutical firm, what is the optimal rule about what sorts of tests and evidence are required before the firm can obtain a patent?

4. *Constructive Reduction to Practice.* As we previously discussed in the context of pre-AIA § 102(g), one can receive a patent without actually reducing it to practice; that is, without actually demonstrating that it works in the real world. It is enough to *constructively* reduce the invention to practice by filing a patent application that satisfies the disclosure requirements. As *'318 Patent Infringement Litigation* illustrates, an inventor needs to have more than a plausible hypothesis for a successful constructive reduction to practice; she must demonstrate utility at the time of filing. But she can patent the use of a drug in humans without ever having administered that drug to a human patient. What are the costs and benefits of permitting constructive reduction to practice?

5. *Prophetic Examples.* To assist with constructive reduction to practice, patent applicants sometimes include predicted and hypothetical experimental methods and results, known as prophetic or paper examples. MPEP § 608.01(p) specifies that prophetic examples are permitted but "should not be described using the past tense." Using this tense rule, one study estimated that 17% of examples in U.S. chemistry and biology patents are prophetic, and that almost one-quarter of these patents have at least one prophetic example. Janet Freilich, *Prophetic Patents*, 53 U.C. Davis L. Rev. 663 (2019). For example, the present tense used in the following patents for a chemical synthesis, a medical procedure, and a medical device suggests that the procedures had not been conducted at the time of filing:

- U.S. Patent No. 3,931,205: 2.5 g of 2-(5H-[1]benzopyrano[2,3-b]pyridin-7-yl)acrylic acid is dissolved in 20 ml of 0.5 N aqueous sodium hydroxide solution, and 1 g of Raney nickel is added. The solution is stirred in a hydrogen stream at ordinary pressure and temperature until absorption of 230 ml of hydrogen is attained. The Raney nickel is removed by filtration, and the filtrate is neutralized with hydrochloric acid. The resulting crystalline precipitate is filtered off, washed with water, and recrystallized from aqueous dioxane to give 1.8 g of 2-(5H-[1]benzopyrano[2,3-b]pyridin-7-yl) propionic acid melting at 183°–184°C.

- U.S. Patent No. 6,869,610: A 46-year-old woman presents with pain localized at the deltoid region due to an arthritic condition. The muscle is not in spasm, nor does it exhibit a hypertonic condition. The patient is treated by a bolus injection of between about 50 units and 200 units of intramuscular botulinum toxin type A. Within 1 to 7 days after neurotoxin administration the patient's pain is substantially alleviated. The duration of significant pain alleviation is from about 2 to about 6 months.

- U.S. Patent No. 7,291,497: Each patch [for drawing and sampling 0.1 ml of blood for vancomycin] consists of two parts. Micro-needles automatically draw small quantities of blood painlessly. A mechanical actuator inserts and withdraws the needle mak[ing] several measurements after the patch is applied. Needles are produced photolithographically in molds at [the Stanford Nanofabrication Facility]. Blood flows through the micro-needles into the blood reservoir.

The third example is drawn from one of many patents granted to the failed Silicon Valley biotech startup Theranos. Given the possibility of confusing patent readers such as scientists, investors, and foreign patent examiners, is there any good justification for not requiring prophetic examples to at least be labeled more clearly? *See* Janet Freilich & Lisa Larrimore Ouellette, *Science Fiction: Fictitious Experiments in Patents*, 364 Science 1036 (2019) (citing the above examples and arguing for clearer labeling). Do you think prophetic examples should be allowed at all, especially as constructive reduction to practice does not require specific, numerical examples that read like actual experiments?

B. Enablement

35 U.S.C. § 112(a) requires inventors to describe their inventions "in such full, clear, concise, and exact terms as to enable any person skilled in the art to which it pertains, or with which it is most nearly connected, to make and use the same." To illustrate this doctrine, we provide two cases: *Incandescent Lamp*, the canonical treatment (of the predecessor to this requirement) from 1895, and *Idenix v. Gilead*, a 2019 Federal Circuit decision that wiped out a record-breaking damages award by holding the patent invalid.

The Incandescent Lamp Patent, 159 U.S. 465 (1895)

This was a bill in equity, filed by the Consolidated Electric Light Company against the McKeesport Light Company, to recover damages for the infringement of letters patent No. 317,676, issued May 12, 1885, to the Electro-Dynamic Light Company, assignee of Sawyer and Man, for an electric light. The defendants justified [their actions] under certain patents to Thomas A. Edison, particularly No. 223,898, issued January 27, 1880; denied the novelty and utility of the complainant's patent; and averred that the same had been fraudulently and illegally procured. The real defendant was the Edison Electric Light Company, and the case involved a contest between what are known as the Sawyer and Man and the Edison systems of electric lighting.

2   In their application, Sawyer and Man stated that their invention related to "that class of electric lamps employing an incandescent conductor inclosed in a transparent, hermetically sealed vessel or chamber, from which oxygen is excluded, and more especially to the incandescing conductor, its substance, its form, and its combination with the other elements composing the lamp. Its object is to secure a cheap and effective apparatus; and our improvement consists, first, of the combination, in a lamp chamber, composed wholly of glass, of an incandescing conductor of carbon made from a vegetable fibrous material, in contradistinction to a similar conductor made from mineral or gas carbon, and also in the form of such conductor so made from such vegetable carbon, and combined in the lighting circuit with the exhausted chamber of the lamp."

3   The following drawings exhibit the substance of the invention:

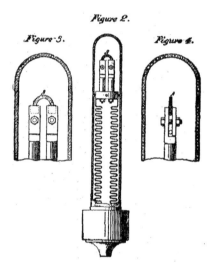

4   The specification further stated that:

> In the practice of our invention, we have made use of carbonized paper, and also wood carbon. We have also used such conductors or burners of various shapes, such as pieces with their lower ends secured to their respective supports, and having their upper ends united so as to form an inverted V-shaped burner. We have also used conductors of varying contours—that is, with rectangular bends instead of curvilinear ones—but we prefer the arch shape.

> No especial description of making the illuminating carbon conductors, described in this specification, and making the subject-matter of this improvement, is thought necessary, as any of the ordinary methods of forming the material to be carbonized to the desired shape and size, and carbonizing it according to the methods in

practice before the date of this improvement, may be adopted in the practice thereof by any one skilled in the arts appertaining to the making of carbons for electric lighting or for other use in the arts.

The advantages resulting from the manufacture of the carbon from vegetable fibrous or textile material instead of mineral or gas carbon are many. Among them may be mentioned the convenience afforded for cutting and making the conductor in the desired form and size, the purity and equality of the carbon obtained, its susceptibility to tempering, both as to hardness and resistance, and its toughness and durability.

5 The claims were as follows:

(1) An incandescing conductor for an electric lamp, of carbonized fibrous or textile material, and of an arch or horseshoe shape, substantially as hereinbefore set forth.

(2) The combination, substantially as hereinbefore set forth, of an electric circuit and an incandescing conductor of carbonized fibrous material, included in and forming part of said circuit, and a transparent, hermetically sealed chamber, in which the conductor is inclosed.

(3) The incandescing conductor for an electric lamp, formed of carbonized paper, substantially as described.

6 The commercial Edison lamp used by the appellee is composed of a burner, A, made of carbonized bamboo of a peculiar quality, discovered by Mr. Edison to be highly useful for the purpose. This filament of carbon is bent into the form of a loop, and its ends are secured by good electrical and mechanical connections to two fine platinum wires, B, B. These wires pass through a glass stem, C, the glass being melted and fused upon the platinum wires. A glass globe, D, is fused to the glass stem, C. This glass globe has originally attached to it, at the point d, a glass tube, by means of which a connection is made with highly organized and refined exhausting apparatus, which produces in the globe a high vacuum, whereupon the glass tube is melted off by a flame, and the globe is closed by the fusion of the glass at the point d.

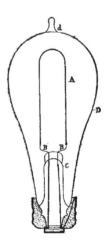

7 Upon a hearing in the circuit court, the court held the patent to be invalid, and dismissed the bill. Thereupon complainant appealed to this court.

8 Mr. Justice Brown, after stating the facts in the foregoing language, delivered the opinion of the court.

9   In order to obtain a complete understanding of the scope of the Sawyer and Man patent, it is desirable to consider briefly the state of the art at the time the application was originally made, which was in January, 1880.

10   Two general forms of electric illumination had for many years been the subject of experiments more or less successful, one of which was known as the 'arc light,' produced by the passage of a current of electricity between the points of two carbon pencils placed end to end, and slightly separated from each other. This form of light had come into general use as a means of lighting streets, halls, and other large spaces; but by reason of its intensity, the uncertain and flickering character of the light, and the rapid consumption of the carbon pencils, it was wholly unfitted for domestic use. The second form of illumination is what is known as the 'incandescent system,' and consists generally in the passage of a current of electricity through a continuous strip or piece of refractory material, which is a conductor of electricity, but a poor conductor; in other words, a conductor offering a considerable resistance to the flow of the current through it. It was discovered early in this century that various substances might be heated to a white heat by passing a sufficiently strong current of electricity through them. The production of a light in this way does not in any manner depend upon the consumption or wearing away of the conductor, as it does in the arc light.

11   For many years prior to 1880, experiments had been made by a large number of persons, in various countries, with a view to the production of an incandescent light which could be made available for domestic purposes, and could compete with gas in the matter of expense. Owing party to a failure to find a proper material, which should burn but not consume, partly to the difficulty of obtaining a perfect vacuum in the globe in which the light was suspended, and partly to a misapprehension of the true principle of incandescent lighting, these experiments had not been attended with success. The chief difficulty was that the carbon burners were subject to a rapid disintegration or evaporation, which electricians assumed was due to the disrupting action of the electric current, and hence the conclusion was reached that carbon contained in itself the elements of its own destruction, and was not a suitable material for the burner of an incandescent lamp.

12   It is admitted that the lamp described in the Sawyer and Man patent is no longer in use, and was never a commercial success; that it does not embody the principle of high resistance with a small illuminating surface; that it does not have the filament burner of the modern incandescent lamp; and that the lamp manufactured by the complainant, and put upon the market, is substantially the Edison lamp; but it is said that, in the conductor used by Edison (a particular part of the stem of the bamboo, the peculiar fitness for which purpose was undoubtedly discovered by him), he made use of a fibrous or textile material covered by the patent to Sawyer and Man, and is therefore an infringer. It was admitted, however, that the third claim—for a conductor of carbonized paper—was not infringed.

13   The two main defenses to this patent are (1) that it is defective upon its face, in attempting to monopolize the use of all fibrous and textile materials for the purpose of electric illuminations; and (2) that Sawyer and Man were not in fact the first to discover that these were better adapted than mineral carbons to such purposes.

14   Is the complainant entitled to a monopoly of all fibrous and textile materials for incandescent conductors? If the patentees had discovered in fibrous and textile substances a quality common to them all, or to them generally, as distinguishing them from other materials, such as minerals, etc., and such quality or characteristic adapted them peculiarly to incandescent conductors, such claim might not be too broad. If, for instance, minerals or porcelains had always been used for a particular purpose, and a person should take out a patent for a similar article of wood, and woods generally were adapted to that purpose, the claim might not be too broad, though defendant used wood of a different kind from that of the patentee. But if woods generally were not adapted to the purpose, and yet the patentee had discovered a wood possessing certain qualities, which gave it a peculiar fitness for such purpose, it would not constitute an infringement for another to discover and use a different kind of wood, which was found to contain similar or superior qualities. The present case is an apt illustration of this principle. Sawyer and Man supposed they had discovered in carbonized paper the best material for an incandescent conductor. Instead of confining themselves to carbonized paper, as they might properly have done, and in fact did in their third claim, they made a broad claim for every fibrous or textile material, when in fact an examination of over 6,000 vegetable growths showed that none of them possessed the peculiar qualities that fitted them for that purpose. Was everybody, then, precluded by this broad claim from making further investigation? We think not.

15   The injustice of so holding is manifest in view of the experiments made, and continued for several months, by Mr. Edison and his assistants, among the different species of vegetable growth, for the purpose of ascertaining the one best adapted to an incandescent conductor. Of these he found suitable for his purpose only about three species of bamboo, one species of cane from the valley of the Amazon (impossible to be procured in quantities on account of the climate), and one or two species of fibers from the agave family. Of the special bamboo, the walls of which have a thickness of about 3/8 of an inch, he used only about 20/1000 of an inch in thickness. In this portion of the bamboo the fibers are more nearly parallel, the cell walls are apparently smallest, and the pithy matter between the fibers is at its minimum. It seems that carbon filaments cannot be made of wood—that is, exogenous vegetable growth—because the fibers are not parallel, and the longitudinal fibers are intercepted by radial fibers. The cells composing the fibers are all so large that the resulting carbon is very porous and friable. Lamps made of this material proved of no commercial value. After trying as many as 30 or 40 different woods of exogenous growth, he gave them up as hopeless. But finally, while experimenting with a bamboo strip which formed the edge of a palm-leaf fan, cut into filaments, he obtained surprising results. After microscopic examination of the material, he dispatched a man to Japan to make arrangements for securing the bamboo in quantities.

16   It seems that the characteristic of the bamboo which makes it particularly suitable is that the fibers run more nearly parallel than in other species of wood. There is no generic quality, however, in vegetable fibers, because they are fibrous, which adapts them to the purpose. Indeed, the fibers are rather a disadvantage. If the bamboo grew solid, without fibers, but had its peculiar cellular formation, it would be a perfect material, and incandescent lamps would last at least six times as long as at present. All vegetable fibrous growths do not have a suitable cellular structure. In some the cells are so large that they are valueless for that purpose. No exogenous, and very few endogenous, growths are suitable. The messenger whom he dispatched to different parts of Japan and China sent him about 40 different kinds of bamboo, in such quantities as to enable him to make a number of lamps, and from a test of these different species he ascertained which was best for the purpose. From this it appears very clearly that there is no such quality common to fibrous and textile substances generally as makes them suitable for an incandescent conductor, and that the bamboo which was finally pitched upon, and is now generally used, was not selected because it was of vegetable growth, but because it contained certain peculiarities in its fibrous structure which distinguished it from every other fibrous substance. The question really is whether the imperfectly successful experiments of Sawyer and Man, with carbonized paper and wood carbon, conceding all that is claimed for them, authorize them to put under tribute the results of the brilliant discoveries made by others.

17   It is required by Rev. St. § 4888 [the precursor to today's 35 U.S.C. § 112], that the application shall contain "a written description of the device, and of the manner and process of making constructing, compounding, and using it in such full, clear, concise, and exact terms as to enable any person, skilled in the art or science to which it appertains or with which it is most nearly connected, to make, construct, compound, and use the same." The object of this is to apprise the public of what the patentee claims as his own, the courts of what they are called upon to construe, and competing manufacturers and dealers of exactly what they are bound to avoid. If the description be so vague and uncertain that no one can tell, except by independent experiments, how to construct the patented device, the patent is void.

18   It was said by Mr. Chief Justice Taney in *Wood v. Underhill*, 46 U.S. (5 How.) 1, 5 (1857), with respect to a patented compound for the purpose of making brick or tile, which did not give the relative proportions of the different ingredients:

> But when the specification of a new composition of matter gives only the names of the substances which are to be mixed together, without stating any relative proportion, undoubtedly it would be the duty of the court to declare the patent void. And the same rule would prevail where it was apparent that the proportions were stated ambiguously and vaguely; for in such cases it would be evident, on the face of the specification, that no one could use the invention without first ascertaining, by experiment, the exact proportion of the different ingredients required to produce the result intended to be

obtained. . . . And if, from the nature and character of the ingredients to be used, they are not susceptible of such exact description, the inventor is not entitled to a patent.

19   So in *Tyler v. Boston*, 74 U.S. (7 Wall.) 327 (1868), wherein the plaintiff professed to have discovered a combination of fusel oil with the mineral and earthy oils, constituting a burning fluid, the patentee stated that the exact quantity of fusel oil which is necessary to produce the most desirable compound must be determined by experiment. And the Court observed: "Where a patent is claimed for such a discovery, it should state the component parts of the new manufacture claimed with clearness and precision, and not leave a person attempting to use the discovery to find it out by experiment."

20   Applying this principle to the patent under consideration, how would it be possible for a person to know what fibrous or textile material was adapted to the purpose of an incandescent conductor, except by the most careful and painstaking experimentation? If, as before observed, there were some general quality, running through the whole fibrous and textile kingdom, which distinguished it from every other, and gave it a peculiar fitness for the particular purpose, the man who discovered such quality might justly be entitled to a patent; but that is not the case here. An examination of materials of this class carried on for months revealed nothing that seemed to be adapted to the purpose; and even the carbonized paper and wood carbons specified in the patent, experiments with which first suggested their incorporation therein, were found to be so inferior to the bamboo, afterwards discovered by Edison, that the complainant was forced to abandon its patent in that particular, and take up with the material discovered by its rival. Under these circumstances, to hold that one who had discovered that a certain fibrous or textile material answered the required purpose should obtain the right to exclude everybody from the whole domain of fibrous and textile materials, and thereby shut out any further efforts to discover a better specimen of that class than the patentee had employed, would be an unwarranted extension of his monopoly, and operate rather to discourage than to promote invention. If Sawyer and Man had discovered that a certain carbonized paper would answer the purpose, their claim to all carbonized paper would, perhaps, not be extravagant; but the fact that paper happens to belong to the fibrous kingdom did not invest them with sovereignty over this entire kingdom, and thereby practically limit other experimenters to the domain of minerals.

21   [W]e are all agreed that the claims of this patent, with the exception of the third, are too indefinite to be the subject of a valid monopoly.

22   For the reasons above stated, the decree of the circuit court is affirmed.

Idenix Pharmaceuticals v. Gilead Sciences, 941 F.3d 1149 (Fed. Cir. 2019)

Sharon Prost, Chief Judge.

I

1   This appeal stems from Idenix's December 2013 patent infringement suit against Gilead. At the time of the suit, both Idenix and Gilead were researching and developing drugs for treatment of the hepatitis C virus ("HCV"). HCV is a leading cause of chronic liver disease, infecting hundreds of millions of people worldwide, and accounting for tens of thousands of deaths per year in the United States alone. Idenix alleged that the imminent Food and Drug Administration approval, and launch, of Gilead's HCV treatment drug sofosbuvir [sold under the brand name Sovaldi] would infringe Idenix's U.S. Pat. No. 7,608,597.[4]

2   Following years of litigation, Chief Judge Stark held a two-week jury trial in December 2016. Gilead stipulated to infringement under the district court's claim construction but argued that the '597 patent was invalid for failure to meet the written description and enablement requirements. The jury found for Idenix, upholding the validity of the patent and awarding [a record-breaking $2.54 billion in] damages. After trial, Gilead filed a renewed motion for JMOL with respect to written description and enablement. The district court denied the motion with respect to written description but granted JMOL on enablement, holding the '597 patent invalid.

II

3   Enablement requires that "the specification teach those in the art to make and use the invention without undue experimentation." *In re Wands*, 858 F.2d 731, 737 (Fed. Cir. 1988). A claim is not enabled when, "at the effective filing date of the patent, one of ordinary skill in the art could not practice their full scope without undue experimentation." *Wyeth & Cordis Corp. v. Abbott Labs.*, 720 F.3d 1380, 1384 (Fed. Cir. 2013).

III

4   The '597 patent claims a method of treating HCV by administering nucleoside compounds having a specific chemical structure. The nucleosides claimed in the '597 patent contain a sugar ring having five carbon atoms, numbered 1' (one prime) to 5' (five prime), as well as a base. At each carbon, substituent atoms or groups of atoms can be added in either the "up" or "down" position. This structure is illustrated below, with a hydroxyl group (OH) shown attached at the 2'-down and 3'-down positions:

---

[4] [Eds: Idenix was purchased by Merck in 2014, which then dropped Idenix's HCV candidate uprifosbuvir in 2017 after poor clinical trial results.]

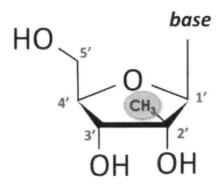

5   The parties' arguments focus on the presence of various possible substituents at the 2'-up and 2'-down positions.

6   Idenix argues that the key to its invention, and to treatment of HCV, is the use of 2'-methyl-up nucleosides: nucleosides "having a methyl substitution ('CH₃') at the 2' 'up' position of the molecule's sugar ring," illustrated below.

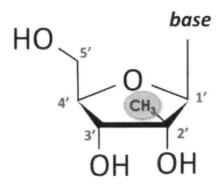

7   [It is not necessary to have a deep understanding of chemical structures to understand the legal issue in this case. In the structures above, known as "nucleosides," the five places where lines intersect with labels 1' to 5' represent carbon atoms, and they can have additional molecules attached to them (known as "substituents") pointing "up" or "down." The 2' carbon has a methyl in the up position (CH₃, or one carbon and three hydrogens) and a hydroxyl in the down position (OH, or one oxygen and one hydrogen). This case is about the many other molecules that can be attached while keeping the methyl in the 2'-up position.]

8   Gilead argues that this characterization is overly broad, as the '597 patent provides no guidance in determining which of the billions of potential 2'-methyl-up nucleosides are effective in treating HCV. According to Gilead, the '597 patent primarily describes 2'-methyl-up nucleosides that have a hydroxyl group (OH) at the 2'-down position. But Gilead's accused product has fluorine (F), not OH, at the 2'-down position. According to Gilead, the '597 patent cannot enable the full scope of effective 2'-methyl-up nucleosides at least because its accused embodiment, 2'-methyl-up 2'-fluoro-down, is not disclosed in or enabled by the specification.

9   The only independent claim of the '597 patent recites:

1. A method for the treatment of a hepatitis C virus infection, comprising administering an effective amount of a purine or pyrimidine ß-D-2'-methyl-ribofuranosyl nucleoside or a phosphate thereof, or a pharmaceutically acceptable salt or ester thereof.

10   The district court construed the structural limitation "ß-D-2'-methyl-ribofuranosyl nucleoside" to require "a methyl group in the 2' up position and non-hydrogen substituents at the 2' down and 3' down positions." Thus, while the claim requires methyl at the 2'-up position, it allows nearly any imaginable substituent at the 2'-down position.

11   At Idenix's urging, the district court also construed the preamble, "[a] method for the treatment of a hepatitis C virus infection," as a narrowing functional limitation. In combination with the requirement to administer an "effective amount," this claim language "limit[s] the scope of the claims to the use of some set of compounds that are effective for treatment of HCV."

12   Neither party challenges the district court's claim constructions in this appeal. Claim 1, therefore, encompasses any nucleoside meeting both the structural limitations (including a methyl group at 2'-up) and the functional limitations (efficacy in treating HCV). It is undisputed, however, that there are billions of potential 2'-methyl-up nucleosides. The key enablement question is whether a person of ordinary skill in the art would know, without undue experimentation, which 2'-methyl-up nucleosides would be effective for treating HCV. We conclude that they would not. Taking into account the evidence presented at trial, a reasonable jury would not have had a legally sufficient basis to find otherwise.

13   In analyzing undue experimentation, we consider the factors first enumerated in *In re Wands*:

    (1) the quantity of experimentation necessary;

    (2) how routine any necessary experimentation is in the relevant field;

    (3) whether the patent discloses specific working examples of the claimed invention;

    (4) the amount of guidance presented in the patent;

    (5) the nature and predictability of the field;

    (6) the level of ordinary skill; and

    (7) the scope of the claimed invention.

See Wands, 858 F.2d at 737. The parties agree that the level of ordinary skill in the art is high, but dispute the impact of the remaining factors. We discuss each in turn.

A

14   We agree with the district court that the quantity of experimentation required to determine which 2'-methyl-up nucleosides meet claim 1 is very high, which favors a finding of non-enablement. The evidence presented to the jury could not support any other finding. At trial, Gilead presented expert testimony that because the claim allows for nearly any substituent to be attached at any position (other than 2'-up), a person of ordinary skill in the art would understand that "billions and billions" of compounds literally meet the structural limitations of the claim.

15   Idenix did not dispute that math, but argued to the jury that this approach was merely "theoretical," because a person of ordinary skill in the art ("POSA") would not attach substituents at random. Instead, Idenix argued, a POSA would know to "take into account the patent as a whole" to focus on a "significantly smaller" set of candidate compounds. The district court accepted this argument, but concluded that even taking into account the knowledge and approach of a POSA, the candidate compounds number "likely[ ] millions or at least many, many thousands."

16   On the evidence presented, a reasonable jury could only have concluded that at least "many, many thousands" of candidate compounds exist. Idenix's evidence, which supports at best an unspecified number "significantly smaller" than "billions," could not lead a reasonable jury to any other conclusion. Idenix's counsel conceded that in its "best case," considering the knowledge of a POSA, the structural limitations still encompass "some number of thousands" of compounds.

17   This conclusion is supported by the '597 patent itself, which discloses enormous quantities of 2'-methyl-up nucleosides that would need to be tested for efficacy against HCV. The specification contains 18 Formulas, each of which is represented by a diagram with variables at multiple positions. For example, Formula XVII, described as the "eleventh principal embodiment," provides: [a complicated chemical structure with a methyl group as one of two dozen possible substituents at 2'-up].

18   Even limiting this formula only to its 2'-methyl-up variations, however, the formula provides more than a dozen options at the [5'] position, more than a dozen independent options at the 2'-down position, more than a dozen independent options at the 3'-down position, and multiple independent options for the base.

19   As the district court meticulously calculated, this formula alone discloses more than 7,000 unique configurations of 2'-methyl-up nucleosides. Other formulas in the specification provide equally large numbers of compounds. Idenix argues that a POSA would have focused on only a narrow subset of billions of possible candidates, but the jury was not free to adopt a number lower than the many, many thousands of configurations identified as "principal embodiments" in the patent itself. Testing the compounds in the specification alone for efficacy against HCV requires enough experimentation for this factor to weigh in favor of non-enablement.

20   Idenix relatedly argues that a POSA would understand the "focus" of the claim to be "the inhibition of the NS5B polymerase" to effectively cure HCV. Therefore, Idenix argues, a POSA would know which candidates were likely to inhibit NS5B, and would test only those, resulting in a "predictable and manageable" group of candidate compounds. This argument improperly attempts to narrow the claim to only those nucleosides that would inhibit the NS5B polymerase. But the district court's claim construction, not challenged in this appeal, made clear that "as a matter of law, NS5B activity is *not* a claim limitation."

21   Moreover, it would be improper to rely on a POSA's knowledge of NS5B to fill the gaps in the specification. "It is the specification, not the knowledge of one skilled in the art, that must supply the novel aspects of an invention in order to constitute adequate enablement." *Genentech, Inc. v. Novo Nordisk A/S*, 108 F.3d 1361, 1366 (Fed. Cir. 1997). Idenix's attempt to treat NS5B as a claim limitation, based on the knowledge of a POSA, would be an impermissible end-run around the requirement to enable the full scope of the claim.[5]

22   At oral argument here on appeal, Idenix presented an additional theory for why little or no experimentation was required. According to Idenix, "the jury could have concluded that *all* 2'-methyl-up ribonucleosides were active against the hepatitis C virus, so that the numbers don't matter. Screening [of each candidate for efficacy against HCV] was irrelevant." We do not agree that the evidence presented could have supported this conclusion. Indeed, Idenix's own evidence contradicts it.

23   At trial, Idenix's expert agreed that the field of modifying nucleosides for anti-HCV activity was "in its infancy" and "unpredictable." Another of Idenix's experts testified that screening was performed to "actually cut down on the number of compounds, by removing all in-active ones to a few interesting ones." A third Idenix expert testified that "you don't know whether or not a nucleoside will have activity against HCV until you make it and test it." And at oral argument on the post-trial motions, Idenix's counsel agreed that "not all 2' methyl up ribonucleosides will be effective to treat HCV," and therefore screening was necessary. In light of this evidence, and this concession, no reasonable jury could have concluded that all 2'-methyl-up nucleosides were effective against HCV or that no screening was needed.

24   Because the claims of the '597 patent encompass at least many, many thousands of 2'-methyl-up nucleosides which need to be screened for HCV efficacy, the quantity of experimentation needed is large and weighs in favor of non-enablement.

---

[5] [n.6 in opinion] Idenix does not argue that the full scope of the claim includes only compounds that inhibit NS5B polymerase. Nor could it, as the '597 patent describes treating HCV in other ways.

B

25   The district court concluded that a reasonable jury could only find that many candidate nucleosides would need to be synthesized before they could be screened, as not all candidate nucleosides were available for purchase. We agree.

26   We do agree with Idenix, however, that a jury could have found that the synthesis of an individual compound was largely routine. Gilead argued that synthesis was difficult, presenting the jury with evidence of an Idenix scientist who repeatedly tried and failed to synthesize 2'-methyl-up 2'-fluoro-down, which is the nucleoside at issue in Gilead's accused product. Idenix countered this with evidence of a scientist at a Gilead subsidiary who produced a 2'-methyl-up 2'-fluoro-down compound "in relatively short order." As a reviewing court, we are mindful that we may not weigh the evidence, determine the credibility of witnesses, or substitute our version of facts for the jury's version. In light of this conflicting testimony, a reasonable jury was entitled to conclude that a POSA could synthesize this particular compound in relatively short order.

27   Because a jury could only have found that synthesis of many 2'-methyl-up nucleosides was necessary, but could have concluded that synthesis of an individual nucleoside was largely routine, this factor weighs against a finding of non-enablement.

C

28   We analyze the presence of working examples and the amount of guidance presented in the specification together. Idenix argues that these factors weigh against non-enablement because the specification "identifies the 'key' modification (2'-methyl-up)" and contains "working examples of active 2'-methyl-up ribonucleosides that were tested." We disagree.

29   Idenix contends that the '597 patent provides meaningful guidance as to which nucleosides meet the functional limitations of the claim because it identifies the "key" modification of 2'-methyl-up. That is insufficient. An enabling disclosure must "be commensurate in scope with the claim." *In re Hyatt*, 708 F.2d 712, 714 (Fed. Cir. 1983). Claim 1 requires more than just an identification of 2'-methyl-up: it requires identification of which 2'-methyl-up nucleosides will effectively treat HCV. Without specific guidance on that point, the specification provides "only a starting point, a direction for further research." *ALZA Corp. v. Andrx Pharm., LLC*, 603 F.3d 935, 941 (Fed. Cir. 2010). That guidance is absent from the '597 specification.

30   Idenix argues that the '597 patent provides this guidance because a POSA would understand NS5B to be the "target" enzyme or would understand that the modified nucleoside must have "either the natural –OH (hydroxyl) or a mimicking substitute at 2'-down." But reliance on a POSA is insufficient to meet the enablement requirement. A patent owner is "required to provide an enabling disclosure in the

specification; it cannot simply rely on the knowledge of a person of ordinary skill to serve as a substitute for the missing information in the specification." *ALZA*, 603 F.3d at 941. Even if we credit Idenix's position that a POSA would look for compounds that would "target" NS5B, the specification fails to provide an enabling disclosure. It is not enough to identify a "target" to be the subject of future testing. A specification that requires a POSA to "engage in an iterative, trial-and-error process to practice the claimed invention" does not provide an enabling disclosure. *Id.*

31   It is true that the specification contains some data showing working examples of 2'-methyl-up nucleosides with efficacy against HCV. As discussed, however, the specification alone encompasses tens if not hundreds of thousands of "preferred" 2'-methyl-up nucleosides that would need to be tested for efficacy against HCV. In the face of that broad disclosure, four examples on a single sugar are insufficient to support enablement. Where, as here, working examples are present but are "very narrow, despite the wide breadth of the claims at issue," this factor weighs against enablement. *Enzo Biochem, Inc. v. Calgene, Inc.*, 188 F.3d 1362, 1374 (Fed. Cir. 1999).

32   Because the '597 patent fails to provide meaningful guidance as to which 2'-methyl-up nucleosides are or are not effective against HCV, and because the only working examples provided are exceedingly narrow relative to the claim scope, these two factors weigh in favor of non-enablement.

D

33   Based on the testimony presented at trial, a reasonable jury could only have concluded that the use of modified nucleosides to treat HCV was an unpredictable art. Gilead's experts testified at trial that the art was "highly unpredictable" because "in the nucleoside area . . . the smallest change can have a dramatic effect not only on the activity of that compound but on the toxicity of the compound. So nothing is predictable."

34   Idenix's experts also testified at trial that the field was new and unpredictable. On cross-examination, Idenix's expert admitted that at the time the '597 patent was invented, the field of "modified nucleosides activity for HCV" was "in its infancy." He also admitted that, even as late as 2012, it was "unpredictable to make a compound and determine whether or not it is active" against HCV. Another of Idenix's witnesses confirmed that "you don't know whether or not a nucleoside will have activity against HCV until you make it and test it."

35   In light of both parties' testimony that the art was unpredictable, this factor could only weigh in favor of non-enablement. *See In re Fisher*, 427 F.2d 833, 839 (C.C.P.A. 1970) ("In cases involving unpredictable factors, such as most chemical reactions and physiological activity, the scope of enablement obviously varies inversely with the degree of unpredictability of the factors involved.").

E

36   For largely the same reasons discussed with respect to the quantity of experimentation factor, we conclude that the scope of the claims could only support a finding of non-enablement. On appeal, Idenix makes two arguments specifically directed to this factor. Neither is persuasive.

37   First, Idenix argues that "[w]hen required to take all of the claim limitations into account, Gilead's witnesses described the claims as embracing only a 'small' number of compounds." This analysis is backwards. Gilead's expert testified that, in order for the '597 patent to teach which 2'-methyl-up nucleosides effectively treat HCV, the patent would need to detail "how to get from a large number [of candidate compounds] to a relatively speaking small number [of effective compounds]." In other words, the '597 patent leaves a POSA searching for a needle in a haystack to determine which of the "large number" of 2'-methyl-up nucleosides falls into the "small" group of candidates that effectively treats HCV. The size disparity between those two groups requires significant experimentation, which weighs against enablement, not for it.

38   Second, Idenix argues that the claim is not broad because "evidence showed that the POSA, with common sense, the claims, and the specification as guidance, would focus on a narrow set of candidates." This factor, however, considers the scope of the claim as written, not just the subset of the claim that a POSA might practice. Idenix does not, and cannot, argue that the scope of the claim is actually limited to this narrow set of candidates. "[A]s a matter of law, NS5B activity is *not* a claim limitation." We therefore conclude that the breadth of the claims weighs in favor of non-enablement.

F

39   Weighing each of these factors, we conclude as a matter of law that the '597 patent is invalid for lack of enablement. The immense breadth of screening required to determine which 2'-methyl-up nucleosides are effective against HCV can only be described as undue experimentation.

40   Our decision in *Wyeth and Cordis Corp. v. Abbott Laboratories* compels this conclusion, and as the district court correctly acknowledged, the similarities between that case and this one are striking. In *Wyeth*, as here, we considered a claim that encompassed "millions of compounds made by varying the substituent groups," while only a "significantly smaller" subset of those compounds would have the claimed "functional effects." 720 F.3d at 1384. We then credited the patent owner's argument that, based on the knowledge of a POSA, the number of candidate compounds to be tested could be as little as "tens of thousands." *Id.* at 1384–85. In both cases, scientific testimony confirmed that practicing the full scope of the claims would require synthesizing and screening tens of thousands of candidate compounds for the claimed efficacy.

41   Notwithstanding the fact that screening an individual compound for effectiveness was considered "routine," we concluded as a matter of law in *Wyeth* that the claim was not enabled because there were "at least tens of thousands of candidate compounds" and "it would be necessary to first synthesize and then screen *each* candidate compound." *Id.* at 1385–86. As we explicitly stated: "The remaining question is whether having to synthesize and screen each of at least tens of thousands of candidate compounds constitutes undue experimentation. We hold that it does." *Id.* at 1385. That principle controls here. A reasonable jury could only have concluded that there were at least many, many thousands of candidate compounds, many of which would require synthesis and each of which would require screening. That constitutes undue experimentation.

42   [The Federal Circuit also held that the '597 patent is invalid for lack of written description; this section of the opinion is excerpted below. A dissent by Judge Pauline Newman is omitted. She would have construed the claim more narrowly to require hydroxyl groups at the 2'-down position, such that Gilead's product (with fluorine rather than hydroxyl at 2'-down) would not be within the scope of the claims.]

Discussion Questions: Enablement

1. *Species and Genus Claims.* The patentees in the above cases did make inventions that worked—Sawyer and Mann made light bulbs with filaments of carbonized paper and wood carbon, and Idenix provided working examples of specific chemicals with some evidence of efficacy against HCV. In both cases, the problem was that the patentees invented a particular type of invention—a species—and then tried to patent a broader class of inventions—a genus. What could these inventors have claimed, based on the work they actually did? Can you write a claim or set of claims for them that would have been valid?

What would the inventors have to have discovered—or, for that matter, what would have to be true about the relevant technology—for them to patent the entire genus (carbonized fibrous and textile materials in *Incandescent Light Bulb* and the genus of thousands of chemicals in *Idenix*)? After all of his experiments, would it have been possible for Edison to patent all fibrous and textile materials? If Idenix's claim covered only the species made by Gilead, would the result be the same?

2. *The Differential Treatment of Uses and Products.* Recall from our discussion in Chapter 1 that a patent on a product will cover all uses of that product, whether or not they were known to the patentee. So, if Pfizer patents sildenafil citrate thinking it will function as a hypertension medication, and it turns out to treat erectile dysfunction instead (as was the case for Viagra), Pfizer's patent will cover the use of sildenafil citrate to treat erectile dysfunction just as much as it would any other use. However, the same broad rule does not apply to products themselves. If Sawyer and Mann patent the particular type of carbonized vegetable material that they have used,

that does not entitle them to a patent on all other types of carbonized vegetable materials. What is the reason for this discrepancy? It is easy to understand why Sawyer and Mann should only be allowed to patent the particular type of light bulb they have invented. But why should Pfizer be allowed to patent sildenafil citrate in such a way as to cover every conceivable use for the drug, as opposed to limiting their patent to the uses they discovered?

3. *Trade Secrets and Enablement.* It is common for patentees to patent some aspects of their inventions while keeping other aspects as trade secrets. Google patented PageRank—the method of ranking search results based on the number and quality of links each website receives—but has kept most of its search algorithm details as a trade secret; pharmaceutical manufacturers often have numerous patents on each drug but keep manufacturing details as trade secrets. Could the USPTO or the courts require greater disclosure of some trade secrets under the enablement doctrine? For an argument that many patents on complex biologic drugs fail enablement because they do not provide enough details for reproduction, see Gregory N. Mandel, *Industry's Unintended Admission that Biotech Patents Fail Enablement*, 11 Va. J.L. & Tech. 8 (2006).

4. *Deposit Requirements, Biological Materials, and Computer Code.* Sometimes, a written description alone is not enough to enable a PHOSITA to make and use the invention without undue experimentation because specialized materials are required. Since 1970, courts have found that disclosure of living materials such as microorganisms or cultured cells can be satisfied by placing samples of these materials in a public depository, and the Budapest Treaty of 1977 set out requirements for internationally recognized depositories. There are three such depositories in the United States—in Illinois, Maine, and Virginia—from which anyone may request samples for fees ranging from $40 to $330. Biological depositories are not heavily used by patentees; a GAO study found that only 0.6% of patents granted in the last three months of 1999 were supported by deposits. Similarly, inventors may submit computer code along with their applications—known as a "computer program listing appendix"—but only about 0.1% of patents include such an appendix. Should the USPTO require deposit more often? Do you think patent examiners are well equipped to determine when a deposit is needed to legally enable an invention?

Applying the Undue Experimentation Standard: Excerpts from MPEP § 2164

[As explained in Chapter 1, the Manual of Patent Examining Procedure (MPEP) provides guidance to USPTO examiners and is thus useful for understanding how the agency applies patent validity doctrines to new patent applications. It does not receive any formal deference from the courts, but footnote 10 from *In re '318 Patent Infringement Litigation* showed how it may still be influential.]

2   The fact that experimentation may be complex does not necessarily make it undue, if the art typically engages in such experimentation. The determination that "undue experimentation" would have been needed to make and use the claimed invention is not a single, simple factual determination. Rather, it is a conclusion reached by weighing all the above noted factual considerations [from *In re Wands*, as quoted in *Idenix*].

3   An applicant need not have actually reduced the invention to practice prior to filing. Lack of a working example, however, is a factor to be considered, especially in a case involving an unpredictable and undeveloped art. For a claimed genus, representative examples together with a statement applicable to the genus as a whole will ordinarily be sufficient if one skilled in the art (in view of level of skill, state of the art and the information in the specification) would expect the claimed genus could be used in that manner without undue experimentation.

4   The scope of the required enablement varies inversely with the degree of predictability involved, but even in unpredictable arts, a disclosure of every operable species is not required. A single embodiment may provide broad enablement in cases involving predictable factors, such as mechanical or electrical elements. In cases involving unpredictable factors, such as most chemical reactions and physiological activity, more may be required. This is because it is not reasonably predictable from the disclosure of one species, what other species will work.

5   *Example of Reasonable Experimentation:* In *United States v. Telectronics, Inc.*, 857 F.2d 778 (Fed. Cir. 1988), the court reversed the findings of the district court for lack of clear and convincing proof that undue experimentation was needed. The court ruled that since one embodiment (stainless steel electrodes) and the method to determine dose/response was set forth in the specification, the specification was enabling. The question of time and expense of such studies, approximately $50,000 and 6-12 months standing alone, failed to show undue experimentation.

6   *Example of Unreasonable Experimentation:* In *In re Ghiron*, 442 F.2d 985 (C.C.P.A. 1971), functional "block diagrams" were insufficient to enable a person skilled in the art to practice the claimed invention with only a reasonable degree of experimentation because the claimed invention required a "modification to prior art overlap computers," and because "many of the components which appellants illustrate as rectangles in their drawing necessarily are themselves complex assemblages. It is common knowledge that many months or years elapse from the announcement of a new computer by a manufacturer before the first prototype is available. This does not bespeak of a routine operation but of extensive experimentation and development work."

7   The presence of inoperative embodiments within the scope of a claim does not necessarily render a claim nonenabled. The standard is whether a skilled person could determine which embodiments that were conceived, but not yet made, would be inoperative or operative with expenditure of no more effort than is normally required

in the art. *Atlas Powder Co. v. E.I. du Pont de Nemours & Co.*, 750 F.2d 1569 (Fed. Cir. 1984). A disclosure of a large number of operable embodiments and the identification of a single inoperative embodiment did not render a claim broader than the enabled scope because undue experimentation was not involved in determining those embodiments that were operable. *In re Angstadt*, 537 F.2d 498 (C.C.P.A. 1976). However, claims reading on significant numbers of inoperative embodiments would render claims nonenabled when the specification does not clearly identify the operative embodiments and undue experimentation is involved in determining those that are operative.

Practice Problems: Enablement

1. The asserted claims cover methods of collecting and processing data from "disparate databases" without an intermediate step of converting the data to compatible formats and storing the converted data in a new database. The specification lacks any working examples, and it took the inventor three years from filing to build a commercial-grade embodiment of the invention, though there was evidence that a functional prototype could have been produced in far less time. Are the claims enabled? *See Vasudevan Software v. MicroStrategy*, 782 F.3d 671, 684 (Fed. Cir. 2015).

2. The claim involves a single step: "adding a chemically-stabilizing amount of polyethoxylated castor oil (PECO)" to a prostaglandin (a composition used as an eye ointment). This step was construed as requiring an increase in the prostaglandin's ability to resist chemical change. PECO is generally understood to increase stability, though the degree of increase can vary greatly. There are a range of PECOs and prostaglandins encompassed by the claims, and expert testimony indicated that "various parameters including pH, buffer, and preservatives may affect the chemical stability of prostaglandins in ophthalmic formulations," and that "when you have a lot of variables on top of one another, the experimentation needed to optimize stability gets out of control quickly." Is the claim enabled? *See Alcon Research v. Barr Laboratories*, 745 F.3d 1180 (Fed. Cir. 2014).

3. The patent discloses a "tri-layer tunnel junction," which is an electronic device used in computer memory storage systems. The asserted claims cover any tri-layer tunnel junction wherein "applying a small magnitude of electromagnetic energy to the junction . . . causes a change in the resistance by at least 10% at room temperature." The specification teaches that the inventors' best efforts achieved a change in resistance of 11.8% at room temperature. The specification also notes that the fundamental science of the tunnel junction had been known for many years, and a twenty-year-old publication predicted that an "ideal" tunnel junction could yield around a 24% change in resistance, but past efforts had not produced effective use of the phenomenon. During prosecution, the inventors achieved resistance changes of 18% and stated that there was not a clear theoretical upper limit. A tunnel junction

with a 120% resistive change was achieved over ten years later, and 604% junctions were achieved a few years after that. Are the claims enabled? What if they were amended during prosecution from "causes a change in the resistance by <u>at least 10%</u> at room temperature" to "causes a change in the resistance by <u>up to about 12%</u> at room temperature"? *See MagSil Corp. v. Hitachi Glob. Storage Techs., Inc.*, 687 F.3d 1377 (Fed. Cir. 2012).

C. Written Description

As we explained in Chapter 1, the process of patent examination can involve an extended back-and-forth between the inventor and the USPTO. During that time, the inventor cannot add "new matter" to her specification (without losing her priority date), but she can—and often must—amend her claims. While this is taking place, many savvy patent applicants keep tabs on what their competitors are doing and what new products they might be placing on the market. The applicant, whose patent is still being examined by the USPTO, can then amend her claims to explicitly cover competitors' products. In addition, because patent applications remain secret for 18 months, the very fact of the patent's existence can remain a surprise to competitors until the patent is issued (or shortly beforehand). Imagine a competitor's unpleasant surprise when the patent is published and the competitor realizes that there exists a patent that is specially designed to cover her new product.

We hope it goes without saying that this is not how the patent system is supposed to work. Applicants should be required to claim what they have actually invented, not whatever inventions of others they can retrofit into their own patents. The Federal Circuit addressed this concern by turning to written description doctrine, which had previously played only a small role in adjudicating patent validity. As we noted at the start of this chapter, the written description requirement limits patent claims to what the inventor actually invented at the time of filing, or in other words, what inventions the inventor "possessed." The Federal Circuit leveraged this requirement as a check on patents that seemed to claim territory that the inventor had not obviously invented, based on what was disclosed in the specification. In that respect, written description is a close cousin of enablement. Both doctrines govern the claim breadth that a given specification can be used to support.

As you read the following cases, one question to consider is what work the written description doctrine is doing that the enablement doctrine could not perform.

Gentry Gallery v. Berkline, 134 F.3d 1473 (Fed. Cir. 1998)

Alan D. Lourie, Circuit Judge.

The Gentry Gallery appeals from the judgment of the United States District Court for the District of Massachusetts holding that the Berkline Corporation does not infringe U.S. Patent 5,064,244. Berkline cross-appeals from the decision that the patent was not shown to be invalid. [B]ecause the court clearly erred in finding that the written description portion of the specification supported certain of the broader claims asserted by Gentry, we reverse the decision that those claims are not invalid under 35 U.S.C. § 112, ¶ 1 (1994).

BACKGROUND

Gentry owns the '244 patent, which is directed to a unit of a sectional sofa in which two independent reclining seats ("recliners") face in the same direction. Sectional sofas are typically organized in an L-shape with "arms" at the exposed ends of the linear sections. According to the patent specification, because recliners usually have had adjustment controls on their arms, sectional sofas were able to contain two recliners only if they were located at the exposed ends of the linear sections. Due to the typical L-shaped configuration of sectional sofas, the recliners therefore faced in different directions. Such an arrangement was "not usually comfortable when the occupants are watching television because one or both occupants must turn their heads to watch the same [television] set. Furthermore, the separation of the two reclining seats at opposite ends of a sectional sofa is not comfortable or conducive to intimate conversation."

The invention of the patent solved this supposed dilemma by, *inter alia*, placing a "console" between two recliners which face in the same direction. This console "accommodates the controls for both reclining seats," thus eliminating the need to position each recliner at an exposed end of a linear section. Accordingly, both recliners can then be located on the same linear section allowing two people to recline while watching television and facing in the same direction. Claim 1, which is the broadest claim of the patent, reads in relevant part:

> A sectional sofa comprising:
>
> a pair of reclining seats disposed in parallel relationship with one another in a double reclining seat sectional sofa section being without an arm at one end . . . ,
>
> each of said reclining seats having a backrest and seat cushions and movable between upright and reclined positions . . . ,
>
> a *fixed console* disposed in the double reclining seat sofa section between the pair of reclining seats and with the console and reclining seats together comprising a unitary structure,

said console including an armrest portion for each of the reclining seats;
said arm rests remaining fixed when the reclining seats move from one
to another of their positions,

and *a pair of control means,* one for each reclining seat; *mounted on the
double reclining seat sofa section* . . . .

'244 patent; col. 4, l. 66 to col. 5, ll. 1-27 (emphasis added). Claims 9, 10, 12–15, and
19–21 are directed to a sectional sofa in which the control means are specifically
located on the console. [Eds: A figure from the patent is shown below.]

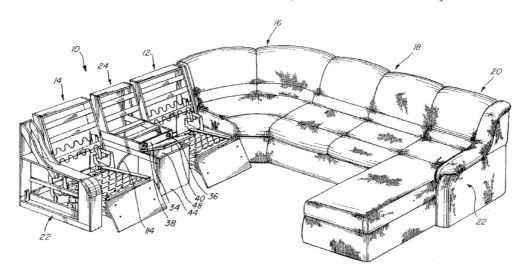

In 1991, Gentry filed suit alleging that Berkline infringed the patent by
manufacturing and selling sectional sofas having two recliners facing in the same
direction. In the allegedly infringing sofas, the recliners were separated by a seat
which has a back cushion that may be pivoted down onto the seat, so that the seat
back may serve as a tabletop between the recliners. The district court granted
Berkline's motion for summary judgment of non-infringement, but denied its motions
for summary judgment of invalidity and unenforceability.

DISCUSSION

Berkline argues that claims 1–8, 11, and 16–18 are invalid because they are
directed to sectional sofas in which the location of the recliner controls is not limited
to the console. According to Berkline, because the patent only describes sofas having
controls on the console and an object of the invention is to provide a sectional sofa
"with a console . . . that accommodates the controls for both the reclining seats," the
claimed sofas are not described within the meaning of § 112, ¶ 1. Berkline also relies
on [the inventor] Sproule's testimony that "locating the controls on the console is
definitely the way we solved [the problem of building sectional sofa with parallel
recliners] on the original group [of sofas]." Gentry responds that the disclosure
represents only Sproule's preferred embodiment, in which the controls are on the
console, and therefore supports claims directed to a sofa in which the controls may be

located elsewhere. Gentry relies on *Ethicon Endo–Surgery, Inc. v. United States Surgical Corp.*, 93 F.3d 1572, 1582 n.7 (Fed. Cir. 1996), and *In re Rasmussen*, 650 F.2d 1212, 1214 (C.C.P.A. 1981), for the proposition that an applicant need not describe more than one embodiment of a broad claim to adequately support that claim.

6   We agree with Berkline that the patent's disclosure does not support claims in which the location of the recliner controls is other than on the console. Whether a specification complies with the written description requirement of § 112, ¶ 1, is a question of fact, which we review for clear error on appeal from a bench trial. To fulfill the written description requirement, the patent specification "must clearly allow persons of ordinary skill in the art to recognize that [the inventor] invented what is claimed." *In re Gosteli*, 872 F.2d 1008, 1012 (Fed. Cir. 1989). An applicant complies with the written description requirement "by describing *the invention,* with all its claimed limitations." *Lockwood v. American Airlines, Inc.*, 107 F.3d 1565, 1572 (1997).

7   It is a truism that a claim need not be limited to a preferred embodiment. However, in a given case, the scope of the right to exclude may be limited by a narrow disclosure. For example, as we have recently held, a disclosure of a television set with a keypad, connected to a central computer with a video disk player did not support claims directed to "an individual terminal containing a video disk player." *See id.* (stating that claims directed to a "distinct invention from that disclosed in the specification" do not satisfy the written description requirement); *see also Regents of the Univ. of Cal. v. Eli Lilly & Co.*, 119 F.3d 1559, 1568 (Fed. Cir. 1997) (stating that the case law does "not compel the conclusion that a description of a species always constitutes a description of a genus of which it is a part").

8   In this case, the original disclosure clearly identifies the console as the only possible location for the controls. It provides for only the most minor variation in the location of the controls, noting that the control "may be mounted on top or side surfaces of the console rather than on the front wall . . . without departing from this invention." No similar variation beyond the console is even suggested. Additionally, the only discernible purpose for the console is to house the controls. As the disclosure states, identifying the only purpose relevant to the console, "[a]nother object of the present invention is to provide . . . a console positioned between [the reclining seats] that accommodates the controls for both of the reclining seats." Thus, locating the controls anywhere but on the console is outside the stated purpose of the invention. Moreover, consistent with this disclosure, Sproule's broadest original claim was directed to a sofa comprising, *inter alia,* "control means located upon the center console to enable each of the pair of reclining seats to move separately between the reclined and upright positions." Finally, although not dispositive, because one can add claims to a pending application directed to adequately described subject matter, Sproule admitted at trial that he did not consider placing the controls outside the console until he became aware that some of Gentry's competitors were so locating the recliner controls. Accordingly, when viewed in its entirety, the disclosure is limited to sofas in which the recliner control is located on the console.

9   Gentry's reliance on *Ethicon* is misplaced. It is true, as Gentry observes, that we noted that "an applicant is generally allowed claims, when the art permits, which cover more than the specific embodiment shown." *Ethicon*, 93 F.3d at 1582 n.7. However, we were also careful to point out in that opinion that the applicant "was free to draft claim[s] broadly (within the limits imposed by the prior art) to exclude the lockout's exact location as a limitation of the claimed invention" only because he "did not consider the precise location of the lockout to be an element of his invention." *Id.* Here, as indicated above, it is clear that Sproule considered the location of the recliner controls on the console to be an essential element of his invention. Accordingly, his original disclosure serves to limit the permissible breadth of his later-drafted claims.

10   Similarly, *In re Rasmussen* does not support Gentry's position. In that case, our predecessor court restated the uncontroversial proposition that "a claim may be broader than the specific embodiment disclosed in a specification." 650 F.2d at 1215. However, the court also made clear that "[a]n applicant is entitled to claims as broad as the prior art *and his disclosure* will allow." *Id.* at 1214 (emphasis added). The claims at issue in *Rasmussen,* which were limited to the generic step of "adheringly applying" one layer to an adjacent layer, satisfied the written description requirement only because "one skilled in the art who read [the] specification would understand that it is unimportant how the layers are adhered, so long as they are adhered." Here, on the contrary, one skilled in the art would clearly understand that it was not only important, but essential to Sproule's invention, for the controls to be on the console.

11   In sum, the cases on which Gentry relies do not stand for the proposition that an applicant can broaden his claims to the extent that they are effectively bounded only by the prior art. Rather, they make clear that claims may be no broader than the supporting disclosure, and therefore that a narrow disclosure will limit claim breadth. Here, Sproule's disclosure unambiguously limited the location of the controls to the console. Accordingly, the district court clearly erred in finding that he was entitled to claims in which the recliner controls are not located on the console. We therefore reverse the judgment that claims 1–8, 11, and 16–18, were not shown to be invalid.

Discussion Questions: *Gentry Gallery*

1. *Why Not Enablement?* Recall that enablement requires that the specification teach the PHOSITA how to make and use the invention without "undue experimentation." Why didn't the court simply invalidate Gentry's claim as not enabled? What additional information would you need to know in order to judge whether the claim is enabled?

2. *Gentry's Best Argument.* If you were Gentry's attorney, what is the best defense you could have offered to save the patent's validity? How would you have tried to describe the language in the specification describing the controls on the console?

3. *Sproule's Inspiration.* At some point, Sproule (the inventor) considered placing the controls somewhere other than the console. When was this? What gave him the idea? What is the significance of this fact for the case? If Sproule had come to the idea of placing the controls on the console after the patent was filed, but for separate reasons, do you think the case would have come out the same way?

4. *Claim Amendment.* When Sproule decided to amend his claim to permit the controls to be anywhere on the invention (not just on the console), why did he not simply amend his specification as well to match the breadth of his claims? What would have been the downside of taking that approach?

5. *The Expansion of Written Description.* As we noted at the beginning of this section, written description originally evolved to police claim amendments introduced during prosecution. Is there anything special about claim amendments that justifies limiting the doctrine to that context? Is anything in the doctrine naturally self-limiting? As the cases below indicate, over time the Federal Circuit has applied the written description doctrine even where no claim amendment is at issue.

Ariad Pharmaceuticals v. Eli Lilly, 598 F.3d 1336 (Fed. Cir. 2010) (en banc)

Alan D. Lourie, Circuit Judge.

1   Ariad Pharmaceuticals, Inc., Massachusetts Institute of Technology, the Whitehead Institute for Biomedical Research, and the President and Fellows of Harvard College (collectively, "Ariad") brought suit against Eli Lilly & Company ("Lilly") in the United States District Court for the District of Massachusetts, alleging infringement of U.S. Patent 6,410,516 ("the '516 patent"). After trial, at which a jury found infringement, but found none of the asserted claims invalid, a panel of this court reversed the district court's denial of Lilly's motion for judgment as a matter of law ("JMOL") and held the asserted claims invalid for lack of written description.

2   Ariad petitioned for rehearing en banc, challenging this court's interpretation of 35 U.S.C. § 112 as containing a separate written description requirement. Because of the importance of the issue, we granted Ariad's petition. We now reaffirm that § 112 contains a written description requirement separate from enablement, and we again reverse the district court's denial of JMOL and hold the asserted claims of the '516 patent invalid for failure to meet the statutory written description requirement.

BACKGROUND

3   The '516 patent relates to the regulation of gene expression by the transcription factor NF-κB [nuclear factor kappa B]. The inventors discovered that NF-κB normally exists in cells as an inactive complex with a protein inhibitor, named "IκB" ("Inhibitor of kappa B"), and is activated by extracellular stimuli, such as bacterial-produced lipopolysaccharides, through a series of biochemical reactions that

release it from IκB. Once free of its inhibitor, NF-κB travels into the cell nucleus where it binds to and activates the transcription of genes containing a NF-κB recognition site. The activated genes (e.g., certain cytokines), in turn help the body to counteract the extracellular assault. The production of cytokines can, however, be harmful in excess. Thus the inventors recognized that artificially interfering with NF-κB activity could reduce the harmful symptoms of certain diseases, and they filed a patent application on April 21, 1989, disclosing their discoveries and claiming methods for regulating cellular responses to external stimuli by reducing NF-κB activity in a cell.

4 Ariad brought suit against Lilly on June 25, 2002, the day the '516 patent issued. Ariad alleged infringement of claims 80, 95, 144, and 145 by Lilly's Evista and Xigris pharmaceutical products. [Representative claim 80], rewritten to include the claims from which [it] depend[s], [is] as follows:

> 80. [A method for modifying effects of external influences on a eukaryotic cell, which external influences induce NF-κB-mediated intracellular signaling, the method comprising altering NF-κB activity in the cells such that NF-κB-mediated effects of external influences are modified, wherein NF-κB activity in the cell is reduced] wherein reducing NF-κB activity comprises reducing binding of NF-κB to NF-κB recognition sites on genes which are transcriptionally regulated by NF-κB.

The claims are thus genus claims, encompassing the use of all substances that achieve the desired result of reducing the binding of NF-κB to NF-κB recognition sites. Furthermore, the claims, although amended during prosecution, use language that corresponds to language present in the priority application. The specification also hypothesizes three types of molecules with the potential to reduce NF-κB activity in cells: decoy, dominantly interfering, and specific inhibitor molecules.

DISCUSSION

I.

A.

5 As in any case involving statutory interpretation, we begin with the language of the statute itself. Section 112, first paragraph, reads as follows:

> The specification shall contain a written description of the invention, and of the manner and process of making and using it, in such full, clear, concise, and exact terms as to enable any person skilled in the art to which it pertains, or with which it is most nearly connected, to make and use the same, and shall set forth the best mode contemplated by the inventor of carrying out his invention.

6   According to Ariad, a plain reading of the statute reveals two components: a written description (i) of the invention, and (ii) of the manner and process of making and using it. Yet those two components, goes Ariad's argument, must be judged by the final prepositional phrase; both written descriptions must be "in such full, clear, concise, and exact terms as to enable any person skilled in the art . . . to make and use the same."

7   Ariad argues that its interpretation best follows the rule of English grammar that prepositional phrases (here, "of the invention," "of the manner and process of making and using it," and "in such full, clear, concise, and exact terms") modify another word in the sentence (here, "written description"), and that it does not inexplicably ignore the comma after "making and using it" or sever the "description of the invention" from the requirement that it be in "full, clear, concise, and exact terms," leaving the description without a legal standard.

8   Ariad also argues that earlier versions of the Patent Act support its interpretation. Specifically, Ariad contends that the first Patent Act, adopted in 1790, and its immediate successor, adopted in 1793, required a written description of the invention that accomplished two purposes: (i) to distinguish the invention from the prior art, and (ii) to enable a person skilled in the art to make and use the invention.[6] Ariad then asserts that when Congress assigned the function of defining the invention to the claims in 1836, Congress amended the written description requirement so that it served a single purpose: enablement.[7]

9   Lilly disagrees, arguing that § 112, first paragraph, contains three separate requirements. Specifically, Lilly parses the statute as follows:

> (1) "The specification shall contain a written description of the invention, *and*"
>
> (2) "The specification shall contain a written description . . . of the manner and process of making and using it, in such full, clear, concise, and exact terms as to enable any person skilled in the art to which it

---

[6] [n.1 in opinion] Section 3 of the 1793 Patent Act provided, in relevant part: "[E]very inventor, before he can receive a patent shall . . . deliver a written description of his invention, and of the manner of using, or process of compounding the same, in such full, clear and exact terms, as to distinguish the same from all other things before known, and to enable any person skilled in the art or science, of which it is a branch, or with which it is most nearly connected, to make, compound, and use the same."

[7] [n.2 in opinion] Section 6 of the 1836 Patent Act provided, in relevant part: "[B]efore any inventor shall receive a patent for any such new invention or discovery, he shall deliver a written description of his invention or discovery, and of the manner and process of making, constructing, using, and compounding the same, in such full, clear, and exact terms, avoiding unnecessary prolixity, as to enable any person skilled in the art or science to which it appertains, or with which it is most nearly connected, to make, construct, compound, and use the same."

pertains, or with which it is most nearly connected, to make and use the same, *and*"

(3) "The specification . . . shall set forth the best mode contemplated by the inventor of carrying out the invention."

10   Lilly argues that Ariad's construction ignores a long line of judicial precedent interpreting the statute's predecessors to contain a separate written description requirement, an interpretation Congress adopted by reenacting the current language of § 112, first paragraph, without significant amendment.

11   We agree with Lilly and read the statute to give effect to its language that the specification "shall contain a written description of the invention" and hold that § 112, first paragraph, contains two separate description requirements: a "written description [i] of the invention, *and* [ii] of the manner and process of making and using [the invention]." 35 U.S.C. § 112, ¶ 1 (emphasis added).

12   [W]e see nothing in the statute's language or grammar that unambiguously dictates that the adequacy of the "written description of the invention" must be determined solely by whether that description identifies the invention so as to enable one of skill in the art to make and use it. The prepositional phrase "in such full, clear, concise, and exact terms as to enable any person skilled in the art . . . to make and use the same" modifies only "the written description . . . of the manner and process of making and using [the invention]," as Lilly argues, without violating the rules of grammar. That the adequacy of the description of the manner and process of *making* and *using* the invention is judged by whether that description enables one skilled in the art to *make* and *use* the same follows from the parallelism of the language.

13   While Ariad agrees there is a requirement to describe the invention, a few amici appear to suggest that the only description requirement is a requirement to describe enablement. If Congress had intended enablement to be the sole description requirement of § 112, first paragraph, the statute would have been written differently. Specifically, Congress could have written the statute to read, "The specification shall contain a written description of the invention, in such full, clear, concise, and exact terms as to enable any person skilled in the art . . . to make and use the same," or "The specification shall contain a written description of the manner and process of making and using the invention, in such full, clear, concise, and exact terms as to enable any person skilled in the art . . . to make and use the same." Under the amicis' construction a portion of the statute—either "and of the manner and process of making and using it" or "[a written description] of the invention"—becomes surplusage, violating the rule of statutory construction that Congress does not use unnecessary words.

B.

14   [Discussion of Supreme Court precedent omitted.]

C.

15   In addition to the statutory language and Supreme Court precedent supporting the existence of a written description requirement separate from enablement, stare decisis impels us to uphold it now. Ariad acknowledges that this has been the law for over forty years, and to change course now would disrupt the settled expectations of the inventing community, which has relied on it in drafting and prosecuting patents, concluding licensing agreements, and rendering validity and infringement opinions. As the Supreme Court stated in admonishing this court, we "must be cautious before adopting changes that disrupt the settled expectations of the inventing community." *Festo Corp. v. Shoketsu Kinzoku Kogyo Kabushiki Co.*, 535 U.S. 772, 739 (2002). If the law of written description is to be changed, contrary to sound policy and the uniform holdings of this court, the settled expectations of the inventing and investing communities, and PTO practice, such a decision would require good reason and would rest with Congress.

D.

16   [Discussion of prior Court of Claims and Patent Appeals precedent omitted.]

E.

17   In contrast to amended claims, the parties have more divergent views on the application of a written description requirement to original claims. Ariad argues that *Regents of the University of California v. Eli Lilly & Co.*, 119 F.3d 1559 (Fed. Cir. 1997), extended the requirement beyond its proper role of policing priority as part of enablement and transformed it into a heightened and unpredictable general disclosure requirement in place of enablement. Rather, Ariad argues, the requirement to describe what the invention is does not apply to original claims because original claims, as part of the original disclosure, constitute their own written description of the invention. Thus, according to Ariad, as long as the claim language appears *in ipsis verbis* in the specification as filed, the applicant has satisfied the requirement to provide a written description of the invention.

18   Lilly responds that the written description requirement applies to all claims and requires that the specification objectively demonstrate that the applicant actually invented—was in possession of—the claimed subject matter. Lilly argues that § 112 contains no basis for applying a different standard to amended versus original claims and that applying a separate written description requirement to original claims keeps inventors from claiming beyond their inventions and thus encourages innovation in new technological areas by preserving patent protection for actual inventions.

19   Again we agree with Lilly. If it is correct to read § 112, first paragraph, as containing a requirement to provide a separate written description of the invention, as we hold here, Ariad provides no principled basis for restricting that requirement to establishing priority. Certainly nothing in the language of § 112 supports such a

restriction; the statute does not say "The specification shall contain a written description of the invention *for purposes of determining priority.*" And although the issue arises primarily in cases involving priority, Congress has not so limited the statute, and neither will we.

20   Furthermore, while it is true that original claims are part of the original specification, *In re Gardner*, 480 F.2d 879, 879 (C.C.P.A. 1973), that truism fails to address the question whether original claim language necessarily discloses the subject matter that it claims. Ariad believes so, arguing that original claims identify whatever they state, e.g., a perpetual motion machine, leaving only the question whether the applicant has enabled anyone to make and use such an invention. We disagree that this is always the case. Although many original claims will satisfy the written description requirement, certain claims may not. For example, a generic claim may define the boundaries of a vast genus of chemical compounds, and yet the question may still remain whether the specification, including original claim language, demonstrates that the applicant has invented species sufficient to support a claim to a genus. The problem is especially acute with genus claims that use functional language to define the boundaries of a claimed genus. In such a case, the functional claim may simply claim a desired result, and may do so without describing species that achieve that result. But the specification must demonstrate that the applicant has made a generic invention that achieves the claimed result and do so by showing that the applicant has invented species sufficient to support a claim to the functionally-defined genus.

21   Recognizing this, we held in *Eli Lilly* that an adequate written description of a claimed genus requires more than a generic statement of an invention's boundaries. 119 F.3d at 1568. The patent at issue in *Eli Lilly* claimed a broad genus of cDNAs purporting to encode many different insulin molecules, and we held that its generic claim language to "vertebrate insulin cDNA" or "mammalian insulin cDNA" failed to describe the claimed genus because it did not distinguish the genus from other materials in any way except by function, i.e., by what the genes do, and thus provided "only a definition of a useful result rather than a definition of what achieves that result." *Id.*

22   We held that a sufficient description of a genus instead requires the disclosure of either a representative number of species falling within the scope of the genus or structural features common to the members of the genus so that one of skill in the art can "visualize or recognize" the members of the genus. *Id.* at 1568–69. We explained that an adequate written description requires a precise definition, such as by structure, formula, chemical name, physical properties, or other properties, of species falling within the genus sufficient to distinguish the genus from other materials. *Id.* at 1568. We have also held that functional claim language can meet the written description requirement when the art has established a correlation between structure and function. *See Enzo*, 323 F.3d at 964 (quoting 66 Fed. Reg. 1099 (Jan. 5, 2001)). But merely drawing a fence around the outer limits of a purported genus is not an

adequate substitute for describing a variety of materials constituting the genus and showing that one has invented a genus and not just a species.

23   In fact, this case similarly illustrates the problem of generic claims. The claims here recite methods encompassing a genus of materials achieving a stated useful result, i.e., reducing NF-κB binding to NF-κB recognition sites in response to external influences. But the specification does not disclose a variety of species that accomplish the result. Thus, as indicated *infra,* that specification fails to meet the written description requirement by describing only a generic invention that it purports to claim.

F.

24   Since its inception, this court has consistently held that § 112, first paragraph, contains a written description requirement separate from enablement, and we have articulated a "fairly uniform standard," which we now affirm. Specifically, the description must "clearly allow persons of ordinary skill in the art to recognize that [the inventor] invented what is claimed." In other words, the test for sufficiency is whether the disclosure of the application relied upon reasonably conveys to those skilled in the art that the inventor had possession of the claimed subject matter as of the filing date.

25   The term "possession," however, has never been very enlightening. It implies that as long as one can produce records documenting a written description of a claimed invention, one can show possession. But the hallmark of written description is disclosure. Thus, "possession as shown in the disclosure" is a more complete formulation. Yet whatever the specific articulation, the test requires an objective inquiry into the four corners of the specification from the perspective of a person of ordinary skill in the art. Based on that inquiry, the specification must describe an invention understandable to that skilled artisan and show that the inventor actually invented the invention claimed.

26   This inquiry, as we have long held, is a question of fact. There are, however, a few broad principles that hold true across all cases. We have made clear that the written description requirement does not demand either examples or an actual reduction to practice; a constructive reduction to practice that in a definite way identifies the claimed invention can satisfy the written description requirement. Conversely, we have repeatedly stated that actual "possession" or reduction to practice outside of the specification is not enough. Rather, as stated above, it is the specification itself that must demonstrate possession. And while the description requirement does not demand any particular form of disclosure, a description that merely renders the invention obvious does not satisfy the requirement.

27   We also reject the characterization, cited by Ariad, of the court's written description doctrine as a "super enablement" standard for chemical and biotechnology inventions. The doctrine never created a heightened requirement to provide a

nucleotide-by-nucleotide recitation of the entire genus of claimed genetic material; it has always expressly permitted the disclosure of structural features common to the members of the genus.

28   Perhaps there is little difference in some fields between describing an invention and enabling one to make and use it, but that is not always true of certain inventions, including chemical and chemical-like inventions. Thus, although written description and enablement often rise and fall together, requiring a written description of the invention plays a vital role in curtailing claims that do not require undue experimentation to make and use, and thus satisfy enablement, but that have not been invented, and thus cannot be described. For example, a propyl or butyl compound may be made by a process analogous to a disclosed methyl compound, but, in the absence of a statement that the inventor invented propyl and butyl compounds, such compounds have not been described and are not entitled to a patent. *See In re DiLeone*, 58 C.C.P.A. 925 (1971) ("[C]onsider the case where the specification discusses only compound A and contains no broadening language of any kind. This might very well enable one skilled in the art to make and use compounds B and C; yet the class consisting of A, B and C has not been described.").

29   The written description requirement also ensures that when a patent claims a genus by its function or result, the specification recites sufficient materials to accomplish that function—a problem that is particularly acute in the biological arts.[8] *See Guidelines for Examination of Patent Applications Under the 35 U.S.C. 112, 1, "Written Description" Requirement*, 66 Fed. Reg. 1099, 1105–06 (Jan. 5, 2001). This situation arose not only in *Eli Lilly* but again in *University of Rochester v. G.D. Searle & Co., Inc.*, 358 F.3d 916 (Fed. Cir. 2004). In *Rochester*, we held invalid claims directed to a method of selectively inhibiting the COX–2 enzyme by administering a non-steroidal compound that selectively inhibits the COX–2 enzyme. *Id.* at 918. We reasoned that because the specification did not describe any specific compound capable of performing the claimed method and the skilled artisan would not be able to identify any such compound based on the specification's function description, the specification did not provide an adequate written description of the claimed invention. *Id.* at 927–28. Such claims merely recite a description of the problem to be solved while claiming all solutions to it and, as in Eli Lilly and Ariad's claims, cover any compound later actually invented and determined to fall within the claim's functional boundaries—leaving it to the pharmaceutical industry to complete an unfinished invention.

---

[8] [n.5 in opinion] The record does not reflect how often the PTO rejects claims as enabled but not described, but the government believes the number to be high. At least one example has made it to this court in recent years, *In re Alonso*, in which the PTO found claims to a method of treating a tumor by administering an effective amount of an antibody that recognizes the tumor enabled but, as we affirmed, not adequately described. 545 F.3d 1015, 1021–22, 1022 n.6. (Fed. Cir. 2008).

30   That research hypotheses do not qualify for patent protection possibly results in some loss of incentive, although Ariad presents no evidence of any discernable impact on the pace of innovation or the number of patents obtained by universities. But claims to research plans also impose costs on downstream research, discouraging later invention. The goal is to get the right balance, and the written description doctrine does so by giving the incentive to actual invention and not "attempt[s] to preempt the future before it has arrived." *Fiers v. Revel*, 984 F.2d 1164, 1171 (Fed. Cir. 1993). As this court has repeatedly stated, the purpose of the written description requirement is to "ensure that the scope of the right to exclude, as set forth in the claims, does not overreach the scope of the inventor's contribution to the field of art as described in the patent specification." *Rochester*, 358 F.3d at 920. It is part of the *quid pro quo* of the patent grant and ensures that the public receives a meaningful disclosure in exchange for being excluded from practicing an invention for a period of time.

II.

31   The '516 patent must adequately describe the claimed methods for reducing NF-κB activity, including adequate description of the molecules that Ariad admits are necessary to perform the methods. The specification of the '516 patent hypothesizes three classes of molecules potentially capable of reducing NF-κB activity: specific inhibitors, dominantly interfering molecules, and decoy molecules. We review the specification's disclosure of each in turn to determine whether there is substantial evidence to support the jury's verdict that the written description evidenced that the inventor possessed the claimed invention.

32   Specific inhibitors are molecules that are "able to block (reduce or eliminate) NF-κB binding" to DNA in the nucleus. '516 patent col.37 ll.44–45. The only example of a specific inhibitor given in the specification is I-κB, a naturally occurring molecule whose function is to hold NF-κB in an inactive state until the cell receives certain external influences. Nearly all of Ariad's evidence regarding the disclosure of I-κB relies upon figure 43. Ariad's expert, Dr. Kadesch, testified that figure 43 discloses the sequence of DNA that encodes I-κB and relied on this disclosure with regard to his opinion that the written description requirement was satisfied by disclosure of specific inhibitor molecules. But as Ariad admits, figure 43 was not disclosed until 1991. Because figure 43 was not in the 1989 application, neither it nor Dr. Kadesch's testimony regarding it can offer substantial evidence for the jury determination. The only other testimony of Dr. Kadesch with regard to I-κB was that it existed in 1989 and that one of ordinary skill could through experimentation isolate natural I-κB. In the context of this invention, a vague functional description and an invitation for further research does not constitute written disclosure of a specific inhibitor.

33   Dominantly interfering molecules are "a truncated form of the NF-κB molecule." '516 patent col.38 l.11. The specification provides no example molecules of this class. Moreover, the specification acknowledges that dominantly interfering

molecules can work only "*if* the DNA binding domain and the DNA polymerase domain of NF-κB are spatially distinct in the molecule." *Id.* at col.38 ll.9–10 (emphasis added). The jury also heard Dr. Kadesch's testimony that "it is a fair representation" that "the '516 patent itself doesn't disclose in its text that the DNA binding domain and the RNA preliminary activating domain of NF-κB are, in fact, separable or spatially distinct." Considering that the inventors of the '516 patent discovered NF-κB, if they did not know whether the two domains are distinct, one of ordinary skill in the art was at best equally ignorant. Perhaps one of ordinary skill could discover this information, but this does not alter our conclusion that the description of the dominantly interfering molecules "just represents a wish, or arguably a plan" for future research. Nor is it sufficient, as Ariad argues, that "skilled workers actually practiced this teaching soon after the 1989 application was filed."

34   Decoy molecules are "designed to mimic a region of the gene whose expression would normally be induced by NF-κB. In this case, NF-κB would bind the decoy, and thus, not be available to bind its natural target." '516 patent col.37 ll.51–54. Like the other two classes of molecules, decoy molecules are presented hypothetically, but unlike the other two classes of molecules, the specification proposes example structures for decoy molecules. As Dr. Kadesch explained, because the specification discloses specific example sequences, there is little doubt that the specification adequately described the actual molecules to one of ordinary skill in the art. Yet this does not answer the question whether the specification adequately describes using those molecules to reduce NF-κB activity. The full extent of the specification's disclosure of a method that reduces NF-κB activity using decoy molecules is that NF-κB "would bind the decoy" and thereby, "negative regulation can be effected." *Id.* at col.37 ll.50–54. Prophetic examples are routinely used in the chemical arts, and they certainly can be sufficient to satisfy the written description requirement. But this disclosure is not so much an "example" as it is a mere mention of a desired outcome. As Dr. Latchman pointed out, there is no descriptive link between the table of decoy molecules and reducing NF–κB activity.

35   Whatever thin thread of support a jury might find in the decoy-molecule hypothetical simply cannot bear the weight of the vast scope of these generic claims. Here, the specification at best describes decoy molecule structures and hypothesizes with no accompanying description that they could be used to reduce NF-κB activity. Yet the asserted claims are far broader. We therefore conclude that the jury lacked substantial evidence for its verdict that the asserted claims were supported by adequate written description, and thus hold the asserted claims invalid.

Idenix Pharmaceuticals v. Gilead Sciences, **941 F.3d 1149** (Fed. Cir. 2019)

1   [The previous casebook section on enablement contained an edited portion of this opinion in which the Federal Circuit affirmed the district court's grant of judgment as a matter of law (JMOL) that patent 7,608,597 is invalid for lack of enablement. In this portion of the opinion, the Federal Circuit reverses the district court's denial of JMOL on written description and holds that the patent is also invalid on this basis.]

2   We separately address the district court's denial of JMOL on the issue of written description. The Patent Act contains a written description requirement distinct from the enablement requirement. 35 U.S.C. § 112; *see Ariad Pharm., Inc. v. Eli Lilly & Co.*, 598 F.3d 1336, 1340 (Fed. Cir. 2010) (en banc). To fulfill the written description requirement, a patent owner "must convey with reasonable clarity to those skilled in the art that, as of the filing date sought, he or she was in possession of the invention, and demonstrate that by disclosure in the specification of the patent." *Carnegie Mellon Univ. v. Hoffmann-La Roche Inc.*, 541 F.3d 1115, 1122 (Fed. Cir. 2008). That test "requires an objective inquiry into the four corners of the specification from the perspective of a person of ordinary skill in the art." *Ariad*, 598 F.3d at 1351.

3   The question in this case is whether the '597 patent demonstrates that the inventor was in possession of those 2'-methyl-up nucleosides that fall within the boundaries of the claim (i.e., are effective against HCV), but are not encompassed by the explicit formulas or examples provided in the specification. The parties focus in particular on whether the specification demonstrates possession of the 2'-methyl-up 2'-fluoro-down nucleosides that are the basis for Gilead's accused product.

4   There is no dispute that neither the '597 patent nor any of its predecessor applications discloses a 2'-methyl-up 2'-fluoro-down nucleoside, including in any formulas or examples. Nor is there any dispute as to why. Idenix only came up with the methyl up fluoro down embodiment a year or so after the application was filed. Idenix argues instead that its claims are directed to the entire genus of 2'-methyl-up compounds for treating HCV, and are enabled by the disclosure of a number of examples, without needing to disclose each species of nucleoside.

5   Idenix is correct that generally a genus can be sufficiently disclosed by "either a representative number of species falling within the scope of the genus or structural features common to the members of the genus so that one of skill in the art can visualize or recognize the members of the genus." *Ariad*, 598 F.3d at 1350. We have alternatively described this inquiry as "looking for blaze marks which single out particular trees" in a forest, rather than simply "pointing to trees." *See Fujikawa v. Wattanasin*, 93 F.3d 1559, 1570 (Fed. Cir. 1996).

6   In this case, we hold that the '597 patent is invalid for lack of written description, as it fails to provide sufficient blaze marks to direct a POSA to the specific subset of 2'-methyl-up nucleosides that are effective in treating HCV. The patent

provides eighteen position-by-position formulas describing "principal embodiments" of compounds that may treat HCV. However, the specification provides no indication that any nucleosides outside of those disclosed in its formulas could be effective to treat HCV—much less any indication as to *which* of those undisclosed nucleosides would be effective. "A written description of an invention involving a chemical genus, like a description of a chemical species, 'requires a precise definition, such as by structure, formula, [or] chemical name' of the claimed subject matter sufficient to distinguish it from other materials." *Bos. Sci. Corp. v. Johnson & Johnson*, 647 F.3d 1353, 1363 (Fed. Cir. 2011) (quoting *Regents of the Univ. of Cal. v. Eli Lilly & Co.*, 119 F.3d 1559, 1568 (Fed. Cir. 1997)). The '597 patent provides adequate written description for the compounds within its formulas. The specification, however, provides no method of distinguishing effective from ineffective compounds for the compounds reaching beyond the formulas disclosed in the '597 patent.

7   Idenix argues that it provides "abundant traditional blazemarks for the claims—working examples, formulas, data, synthesis routes, and the target." Each of these suffer from the same flaw. They provide lists or examples of supposedly effective nucleosides, but do not explain what makes them effective, or why. As a result, a POSA is deprived of any meaningful guidance into what compounds beyond the examples and formulas, if any, would provide the same result. In the absence of that guidance, the listed examples and formulas cannot provide adequate written description support for undisclosed nucleosides that also happens to treat HCV. The written description requirement specifically defends against such attempts to "cover any compound later actually invented and determined to fall within the claim's functional boundaries." *See Ariad*, 598 F.3d at 1353.

8   We are mindful of *Ariad*'s caution that written description does not require "a nucleotide-by-nucleotide recitation of the entire genus." *Id.* at 1352. The purpose of that rule is to allow relatively few representative examples or formulas to support a claim on a structurally similar genus. It does not extend to this case, where the specification lists tens or hundreds of thousands of possible nucleosides, substituent-by-substituent, with dozens of distinct stereochemical structures, and yet the compound in question is conspicuously absent.

9   The absence of 2'-fluoro-down is indeed conspicuous. Seven of the provided formulas permit 2'-methyl-up. All seven formulas explicitly list fluorine as a possibility at other positions, including 2'-up. Yet not one of them includes fluorine at 2'-down, despite each listing more than a dozen possible substituents at that position. This is true even though the formulas include every other recited halogen at both positions.

10   Further, to the extent Idenix argues that, although not disclosed, a POSA would have known to include fluorine at 2'-down based on its similarities to other halogens, that is insufficient for written description. "[A] description that merely

renders the invention obvious does not satisfy" the written description requirement. *Ariad*, 598 F.3d at 1352.

11   We therefore disagree with Idenix's characterization that "the specification plainly embraces the use of the [2'-fluoro-down] embodiment." In light of the conspicuous absence of that compound, a POSA would not "visualize or recognize the members of the genus" as including 2'-fluoro-down, and the specification could not demonstrate to a POSA that the inventor had possession of that embodiment at the time of filing. *Ariad*, 598 F.3d at 1350.

Applying the Possession Test: Excerpts from MPEP § 2163

1   [The following excerpts from MPEP § 2163 are from guidance for applying the written description doctrine to original claims; the MPEP offers additional guidance for evaluating new or amended claims. As MPEP § 2163 emphasizes, these guidelines "do not constitute substantive rulemaking and hence do not have the force and effect of law," but they reflect the USPTO's effort to summarize relevant caselaw.]

2   Whether the specification shows that the applicant was in possession of the claimed invention is not a single, simple determination, but rather is a factual determination reached by considering a number of factors. Factors to be considered in determining whether there is sufficient evidence of possession include the level of skill and knowledge in the art, partial structure, physical and/or chemical properties, functional characteristics alone or coupled with a known or disclosed correlation between structure and function, and the method of making the claimed invention. Disclosure of any combination of such identifying characteristics that distinguish the claimed invention from other materials and would lead one of skill in the art to the conclusion that the applicant was in possession of the claimed species is sufficient.

3   In most technologies which are mature, and wherein the knowledge and level of skill in the art is high, a written description question should not be raised for claims present in the application when originally filed, even if the specification discloses only a method of making the invention and the function of the invention. In contrast, for inventions in emerging and unpredictable technologies, or for inventions characterized by factors not reasonably predictable which are known to one of ordinary skill in the art, more evidence is required to show possession.

4   The written description requirement for a claimed genus may be satisfied through sufficient description of a representative number of species by actual reduction to practice, reduction to drawings, or by disclosure of relevant, identifying characteristics, i.e., structure or other physical and/or chemical properties, by functional characteristics coupled with a known or disclosed correlation between function and structure, or by a combination of such identifying characteristics, sufficient to show the applicant was in possession of the claimed genus.

5   A "representative number of species" means that the species which are adequately described are representative of the entire genus. Thus, when there is substantial variation within the genus, one must describe a sufficient variety of species to reflect the variation within the genus. The disclosure of only one species encompassed within a genus adequately describes a claim directed to that genus only if the disclosure indicates that the patentee has invented species sufficient to constitute the genus. "A patentee will not be deemed to have invented species sufficient to constitute the genus by virtue of having disclosed a single species when . . . the evidence indicates ordinary artisans could not predict the operability in the invention of any species other than the one disclosed." *In re Curtis*, 354 F.3d 1347 (Fed. Cir. 2004).

6   The Federal Circuit has explained that a specification cannot always support expansive claim language and satisfy the requirements of 35 U.S.C. § 112 "merely by clearly describing one embodiment of the thing claimed." *LizardTech v. Earth Resource Mapping, Inc.*, 424 F.3d 1336 (Fed. Cir. 2005). The issue is whether a person skilled in the art would understand the applicant to have invented, and been in possession of, the invention as broadly claimed. In *LizardTech*, claims to a generic method of making a seamless discrete wavelet transformation (DWT) were held invalid because the specification taught only one particular method for making a seamless DWT and there was no evidence that the specification contemplated a more generic method.

7   For inventions in an unpredictable art, adequate written description of a genus which embraces widely variant species cannot be achieved by disclosing only one species within the genus. Instead, the disclosure must adequately reflect the structural diversity of the claimed genus, either through the disclosure of sufficient species that are "representative of the full variety or scope of the genus," or by the establishment of "a reasonable structure-function correlation." Such correlations may be established "by the inventor as described in the specification," or they may be "known in the art at the time of the filing date." *AbbVie Deutschland GmbH v. Janssen Biotech, Inc.*, 759 F.3d 1285 (Fed. Cir. 2014).

Discussion Questions: Written Description

1. *More on the Expansion of Written Description.* As we discussed above, the written description doctrine originally evolved to focus on opportunistic claim amendments, but it has expanded in cases like *Ariad* and *Idenix* to include situations where applicants claimed too broadly in their original applications. Are you convinced by the argument in *Ariad* that it is necessary to apply a robust written description requirement that is distinct from enablement in cases where the claims were not amended? In both *Gentry*-type cases and *Ariad*-type cases, the doctrinal test is the same: Does the specification convey to the PHOSITA that the inventor possessed the full scope of the claim as of the filing date? In cases like *Gentry*, lack of possession is

demonstrated by amendment of the claim to cover inventions the inventor did not seem to have in mind at the time of filing. How does the "possession" test work in *Ariad* and *Idenix*? How would a challenger to the patent demonstrate that the inventor lacked possession?

Note that the MPEP states that "a written description question should not be raised for claims present in the application when originally filed" with respect to "technologies which are mature," whereas it is appropriate to apply the written description requirement to claims present in the original application in the context of new and emerging technologies. Why do you think that is? Does it shed light on the more general question of whether the written description requirement should remain applicable to claims present in the original application, and why the courts believe that it does?

2. *Early-Stage Biomedical Inventions.* Many of the important *Ariad*-type written description cases—including *Ariad, Idenix*, and *Regents of the University of California v. Eli Lilly & Co.*, 119 F.3d 1559 (Fed. Cir. 1997)—have involved early-stage biomedical inventions. Is there something special about chemistry and biotechnology that makes it more difficult for inventors in these fields to demonstrate possession of broad claims at the time of filing? Is it relevant that the inventions at issue in these cases often involve research conducted at universities? Unlike typical pharmaceutical patent infringement cases, in which a brand-name manufacturer of a biomedical product asserts patents to prevent generic competitors from entering the market, these cases all involve patent assertion *against* brand-name manufacturers. (Remember that brand-name manufacturers are firms that are typically in the business of researching and developing new drugs and then patenting them; generic firms do not conduct independent research and typically enter the market after the patent on a brand-name drug has expired or is invalid.) Can you think of reasons why so many of these cases involve the assertion of patents based on university research against brand-name pharmaceutical manufacturers? Do you think that affects how courts view these cases?

3. *Enough Species to Support a Genus.* The MPEP notes repeatedly that the description of a single species is not enough to support a claim to a genus unless the single species is representative of the full genus. Instead, the specification must "adequately reflect the structural diversity of the claimed genus" through "the disclosure of sufficient species that are 'representative of the full variety or scope of the genus.'" What does this mean with respect to a claim for a very large genus? Or how about a genus in which not all of the species are operative?

For instance, imagine a claim that would cover any operable member of a genus of thousands of structurally similar chemical compounds. Suppose that only approximately 10% of the species of that genus are operable. Someone skilled in the art could quickly and easily identify a handful of operable species, and any given species could be tested to determine whether it is operable relatively quickly.

However, testing the entire genus to determine which of the many species are operable and which are not would be tremendously time-consuming and expensive. Should this claim be patentable? In other words, is it enough if someone skilled in the art could determine a substantial number of operative species, more than enough to make the invention work for its intended purpose? Or is it necessary for patentability that someone skilled in the art be able to determine the precise boundaries of the genus, including which species are included and not included? For an argument that claims of this sort should be patentable, see Dmitry Karshtedt, Mark A. Lemley & Sean B. Seymore, *The Death of the Genus Claim*, 35 Harv. J.L. & Tech. 1 (2021).

Practice Problems: Written Description

Do you think any of the claims below are invalid for lack of written description? What about lack of enablement or utility? These are *not* simplified cases—the facts and claims are drawn from recent Federal Circuit cases, some of which involve complex technologies—but you now have the doctrinal tools to tackle them.

1. The claims are directed to a method for processing debit purchase transactions, with numerous steps that include "entering a general authorization code," "entering a customer authorization code," and "entering a clerk authorization code." The specification provides numerous examples of the invention that involve entering authorization codes, but no example includes all three authorization codes. *See Stored Value Solutions v. Card Activation Techs.*, 499 F. App'x 5 (Fed. Cir. 2012).

2. The claims at issue recite a method of treating restenosis, the renarrowing of an artery. For example:

> A method of treating restenosis in a mammal . . . which comprises administering an antirestenosis effective amount of rapamycin . . . .

"Rapamycin" is a genus that, in this case, includes tens of thousands of chemical compounds, most of which have not been synthesized. Synthesizing a species and testing it for efficacy against restenosis each require lengthy experiments. The specification discloses a rapamycin species called sirolimus, which is naturally produced by a bacterium, and it discloses in vitro and in vivo test data showing that sirolimus has the desired antirestenosis effect. The defendants sell a different species of rapamycin that also has an antirestenosis effect. *See Wyeth & Cordis Corp. v. Abbott Laboratories*, 720 F.3d 1380 (Fed. Cir. 2013).

3. The claims are directed to the chemical compound dutasteride, which has medical uses such as treating enlarged prostate glands. For example:

> [Dutasteride] or a pharmaceutically acceptable solvate thereof.

The specification defines a "solvate" by its structure—a complex of dutasteride molecules and molecules from a liquid "solvent"—as well as by the process of creating that structure—dissolving dutasteride in the solvent. The universe of solvents thought to be pharmaceutically acceptable (i.e., suitable for administering to patients) was well known and relatively small, though testing whether each solvate will allow the dutasteride to be effectively received by patients takes about a week. The patent provides one example of forming a solvate by dissolving dutasteride in liquid propylene glycol. *See GlaxoSmithKline LLC v. Banner Pharmacaps, Inc.*, 744 F.3d 725 (Fed. Cir. 2014).

4. The patented technology is a "handguard" system for attaching ancillary devices like laser systems to a rifle barrel without damaging the barrel. The specification discloses that the handguard system, surrounding the barrel, is supported by two points: the "receiver sleeve" and the "barrel nut." The specification also discloses an invention where the receiver sleeve provides complete support for the handguard. The patentee obtained a reissue patent claiming a handguard system supported only at the barrel nut. *See Atlantic Research Marketing Systems, Inc. v. Troy*, 659 F.3d 1345 (Fed. Cir. 2011).

Note on Distinguishing Utility, Enablement, and Written Description

By now, you may be wondering about how best to understand the distinction between enablement, written description, and utility. If the relationship (and distinctions) between these doctrines seem confusing or unclear, do not despair! You are not alone. The Federal Circuit devoted a substantial portion of its *Ariad* opinion to explaining the difference, and that is hardly the last word on the subject. Note the MPEP's discussion above, with respect to written description, of the relationship between a claim to a genus and a specification that discloses one or more species. That analysis is not much different than the analysis one would use for enablement. If you had read those MPEP paragraphs without knowing whether the MPEP was discussing enablement or written description, it may have been difficult or impossible to guess which doctrine it was referring to.

Here is a very simple formulation for understanding the difference between these doctrines: Written description requires that you describe *the thing* you are trying to claim with specificity, such that you can prove that you actually knew what you were inventing and are now patenting. Enablement requires that you teach someone how to make and use the thing. Utility requires that you show that the thing is useful. In this respect, the best way to understand *Gentry* is that the inventor never described the thing he was trying to patent—namely, dual recliners with the controls somewhere other than the console—in the specification. This is why that claim fails for lack of written description. But it could very well be that a PHOSITA would know how to construct dual recliners with controls somewhere other than the console— maybe the art of recliner construction is well understood?—even if the specification does not describe that embodiment. That is why the claim was not invalid for lack of enablement.

Let's explore this point further with some hypothetical claims. Suppose an inventor claims "treating cancer with a compound selected from set X" where X is a list of 10,000 compounds. The specification explicitly lists all 10,000 compounds, but it is not necessarily the case that any given compound in the set will actually treat cancer. This area of technology is unpredictable, and a PHOSITA cannot know whether a particular compound from the list will treat cancer without first testing it in a process that involves undue experimentation. It might be that a few thousand of the compounds will treat cancer, or a few dozen of them, or none. Is this claim invalid, and if so, under what doctrine?

For starters, the claim is invalid for lack of utility under the logic of *In re '318*, because the inventor has not demonstrated that the claim is useful the time it was filed. Without knowing for certain whether even a single compound will treat cancer, there is no demonstrated utility. If there were evidence that most of the compounds would be effective at treating cancer due to some common structural feature, then the patent would have demonstrated utility. But as described, it falls short on this dimension.

The claim is also invalid for lack of enablement because (by hypothesis) it would require undue experimentation on the part of a PHOSITA to determine which embodiments work and don't work. This is a canonical example of having invented a species and trying to claim the genus, as in the *Incandescent Lamp* case. If, however, a machine existed that could manufacture and screen all 10,000 compounds for efficacy against cancer in a single day, then it would no longer require undue experimentation to determine which do and do not work. Accordingly, the claim would be enabled.

Finally, the claim would also be invalid for lack of written description. The invention is claimed in functional terms: the claim is for treating cancer with any compounds from set X that can be used to treat cancer. This leaves open the question of which compounds actually treat cancer and which do not. Recall that written description requires the inventor to describe the thing that she is attempting to claim. In order to successfully describe the thing, you have to describe the boundary between what is the thing and what is not the thing. The problem for this inventor is that the claim might actually include only a few species in the 10,000-species genus (set X), and if the inventor hasn't explained which species are actually included in the claim and which are not, then she has not successfully identified the thing she is trying to claim. By way of even more extreme illustration, imagine claiming "treating cancer with any chemical known to humans that effectively treats cancer," and then listing all chemicals known to humans in the specification. It would be implausible to argue that the patent describes the thing it is claiming with specificity, as required by written description doctrine.

With this in mind, consider the three types of molecules at issue in *Ariad*: specific inhibitors, dominantly interfering molecules, and decoy molecules. Suppose that instead of claiming all methods for reducing NF-κB activity, the *Ariad* patent had separately claimed the use of each of these types of molecules. Could written description still be used to reject each of those hypothetical claims? What about enablement and utility?

There is an argument that a claim using the decoy molecules would have satisfied the written description requirement. As *Ariad* explains, the patent specification did describe the decoy molecules by structure, formula, or physical properties. By disclosing the decoy molecules, the specification necessarily disclosed reducing NF-κB activity with the decoy molecules, because the means of that reduction is simply to administer the decoy molecules to a person. Where the specification failed is that it did not provide any evidence that administering decoy molecules would actually reduce NF-κB activity. That constitutes a failure to satisfy the utility requirement. It might also constitute a lack of enablement, depending on whether the specification adequately disclosed how to produce the decoy molecules.

Now consider how enablement and written description interact with "comprising" claims. Imagine a claim for a chair, as follows:

> 1. An object for supporting a human body, comprising a substantially flat surface sized to accommodate a human posterior, and three legs supporting said surface.

(This example is borrowed from Jeffrey A. Lefstin, *The Formal Structure of Patent Law and the Limits of Enablement*, 23 Berkeley Tech. L.J. 1141, 1169 (2008).) Imagine that the specification describes how to make a three-legged wooden stool, 1 foot in diameter and 1 foot tall.

This claim is drafted broadly enough to cover stools with more than three legs, chairs with backs, and non-wooden stools/chairs. For that matter, if someone constructed a chair with three legs that had a seat-warmer powered by a cold fusion reactor, it would still infringe this claim. Can a claim that is broad enough to cover a chair with a cold fusion reactor possibly be enabled by a specification that only mentions wooden stools?

The answer is yes, and the reason is that the law of enablement does not require the inventor to enable "unclaimed elements"—namely, those elements that are not mentioned in the claim (but could be part of an infringing device via the "comprising" term). *See* Matthew's Annotated Patent Digest § 20:48 ("While the disclosure must enable the practice of the claimed invention, disclosure of unclaimed aspects of the invention is generally not required."); *id.* § 22:34 ("The written-description requirement generally does not require a description of unclaimed aspects of the invention, unless those aspects are critical to the claimed invention.").

This may seem like an odd rule, but it is inherent to the idea of allowing the "comprising" transition word to capture future inventions that have additional elements. If an inventor had to enable every conceivable permutation of an invention every time she used the word "comprising," that word would simply no longer be useable. Some challenger would always be able to imagine a variant on the patented invention that includes an element the inventor did not enable ("It's a Swiffer with a nuclear reactor!") and thereby invalidate the claim. Perhaps, then, the issue is that the word "comprising" is too powerful. Maybe this claim for a three-legged stool shouldn't cover a much more advanced invention that uses cold fusion. That argument has force, but it would represent a sea change from a doctrine that has always permitted broad, pioneering patents that cover both early embodiments of an invention and more advanced later ones that depend on the pioneering work. And without the word "comprising," a subsequent inventor could always add an irrelevant additional feature and evade the patent.[9] In any event, the law on this point is relatively clear.

So now suppose these are the claims:

1. An object for supporting a human body, comprising a substantially flat surface sized to accommodate a human posterior, and three legs supporting said surface.

2. The object of claim 1, further comprising a seat warmer powered by nuclear fusion.

Imagine that the specification still includes just the single embodiment, a three-legged wooden stool.

Are there § 112 problems with any of these claims? Claim 2 is surely invalid for lack of enablement, and it might also be invalid for lack of written description unless the claim was part of the original application (in which case the claim language itself might demonstrate possession at the time of filing).

How about claim 1? Claim 2 is necessarily narrower than claim 1, because it is a dependent claim. If the patent does not enable claim 2, the narrower claim, then how could it possibly enable claim 1? Or, put in reverse, if claim 1 (the broader claim) is enabled, then must it not be the case that claim 2 (the narrower claim) is also enabled? Indeed, the USPTO has taken exactly this position and treated as axiomatic the idea that if a broader claim is enabled, the narrower claim must be as well. *Ex parte Forstova*, No. 1998-0667, 2002 WL 32349992 3 (B.P.A.I. Apr. 11, 2002).

As you have probably realized, this rule of enablement runs headlong into the rule (described above) that an inventor need not enable unclaimed elements. *See* Matthew's Annotated Patent Digest § 20:45.75 ("This proposition—if the dependent claim is not enabled, the independent claim must also not be enabled—

---

[9] Enterprising students who have read ahead may realize that the doctrine of equivalents would be an alternative means of capturing subsequent inventions that differ only trivially, but that doctrine would then raise the same sorts of enablement questions.

may, in some instances, be in tension with another aspect of enablement law, namely, that only one mode of an invention needs to be enabled in a manner that permits one of skill in the art to practice the full scope of the claimed invention without undue experimentation."). One of these two rules has to give.

The rule that should give is the one that if the dependent claim is not enabled, the independent claim is not enabled either. As we explained above, there is a strong reason, grounded in patent policy, for the rule that unclaimed elements need not be enabled: the alternative would be to eliminate the word "comprising" from the lexicon and render patent claims much weaker. The enablement rule about dependent claims, by contrast, is a pure formalism that makes logical sense given the structure of claims but leads to absurd results. It is clear that claim 1 would be valid without claim 2; why should the addition of claim 2 all of a sudden render claim 1 invalid? It's not as if claim 2 has changed either the meaning of claim 1 or the content of the specification. For this reason, we believe that the USPTO should simply let go of the rule that invalidating a dependent claim for lack of enablement necessarily means invalidating its independent claim. Each claim should be judged on its own merit, and the patentee need not enable unclaimed elements.

5. Definiteness and Functional Claiming

The previous chapter described the patentability requirements of § 112(a), which ensure that the claims are commensurate in scope with the specification. In this chapter, we turn to § 112(b), which requires patent claims to be sufficiently definite that a PHOSITA can understand what they cover:

35 U.S.C. § 112(b)

The specification shall conclude with one or more claims particularly pointing out and distinctly claiming the subject matter which the inventor or a joint inventor regards as the invention.

Any claim that fails to satisfy this requirement is invalid as indefinite. As with § 112(a), pre-AIA claims are governed by the old § 112, ¶ 2 rather than § 112(b), but there are no substantive differences, so we focus on § 112(b) for simplicity.

The policy tradeoff embedded in § 112(b) is straightforward: Clearer claims provide better *notice* to others of what they cover, allowing competitors to more easily determine whether they are infringing and preventing patent applicants from engaging in creative reinterpretation of vague claim language in later litigation. But language is inherently imprecise, and too strict a demand of clarity raises drafting costs for patentees and risks invalidating claims for technicalities, lowering incentives for innovation. Have any of the claims we have encountered so far seemed insufficiently definite to you?

Although many claims could be written more clearly, claim definiteness has been a relatively toothless requirement for much of its history. The first section of this chapter examines the legal standard for definiteness, which was revised by the Supreme Court in *Nautilus v. Biosig Instruments*, 572 U.S. 898 (2014). We then turn to the area in which the claim definiteness requirement has had the most bite: claims with means-plus-function claim elements under § 112(f) (or § 112, ¶ 6 for pre-AIA claims).

A. The Standard for Definiteness

Nautilus v. Biosig Instruments, 572 U.S. 898 (2014)

Justice Ruth Bader Ginsburg delivered the opinion of the Court.

The Patent Act requires that a patent specification "conclude with one or more claims *particularly pointing out and distinctly claiming* the subject matter which the applicant regards as [the] invention." 35 U.S.C. § 112, ¶ 2. This case, involving a heart-rate monitor used with exercise equipment, concerns the proper reading of the statute's clarity and precision demand. According to the Federal Circuit, a patent claim passes the § 112, ¶ 2 threshold so long as the claim is "amenable to construction," and the claim, as construed, is not "insolubly ambiguous." We conclude that the Federal Circuit's formulation, which tolerates some ambiguous claims but not others, does not satisfy the statute's definiteness requirement. In place of the "insolubly ambiguous" standard, we hold that a patent is invalid for indefiniteness if its claims, read in light of the specification delineating the patent, and the prosecution history, fail to inform, with reasonable certainty, those skilled in the art about the scope of the invention. Expressing no opinion on the validity of the patent-in-suit, we remand, instructing the Federal Circuit to decide the case employing the standard we have prescribed.

I

Authorized by the Constitution "[t]o promote the Progress of Science and useful Arts, by securing for limited Times to . . . Inventors the exclusive Right to their . . . Discoveries," Art. I, § 8, cl. 8, Congress has enacted patent laws rewarding inventors with a limited monopoly. "Th[at] monopoly is a property right," and "like any property right, its boundaries should be clear." *Festo Corp. v. Shoketsu Kinzoku Kogyo Kabushiki Co.*, 535 U.S. 722, 730 (2002). Thus, when Congress enacted the first Patent Act in 1790, it directed that patent grantees file a written specification "containing a description . . . of the thing or things . . . invented or discovered," which "shall be so particular" as to "distinguish the invention or discovery from other things before known and used." Act of Apr. 10, 1790, § 2, 1 Stat. 110.

The patent laws have retained this requirement of definiteness even as the focus of patent construction has shifted. Under early patent practice in the United States, we have recounted, it was the written specification that "represented the key to the patent." *Markman v. Westview Instruments*, 517 U.S. 370, 379 (1996). Eventually, however, patent applicants began to set out the invention's scope in a separate section known as the "claim." The Patent Act of 1870 expressly conditioned the receipt of a patent on the inventor's inclusion of one or more such claims, described with particularity and distinctness. *See* Act of July 8, 1870, § 26, 16 Stat. 201 (to obtain a patent, the inventor must "particularly point out and distinctly claim the part, improvement, or combination which [the inventor] claims as his invention or discovery").

The 1870 Act's definiteness requirement survives today, largely unaltered. Section 112 of the Patent Act of 1952, applicable to this case, requires the patent applicant to conclude the specification with "one or more claims particularly pointing out and distinctly claiming the subject matter which the applicant regards as his invention." 35 U.S.C. § 112, ¶ 2. A lack of definiteness renders invalid "the patent or any claim in suit." § 282, ¶ 2(3).[47]

II

A

The patent in dispute, U.S. Patent No. 5,337,753, issued to Dr. Gregory Lekhtman in 1994 and assigned to respondent Biosig Instruments, Inc., concerns a heart-rate monitor for use during exercise. Previous heart-rate monitors, the patent asserts, were often inaccurate in measuring the electrical signals accompanying each heartbeat (electrocardiograph or ECG signals). The inaccuracy was caused by electrical signals of a different sort, known as electromyogram or EMG signals, generated by an exerciser's skeletal muscles when, for example, she moves her arm, or grips an exercise monitor with her hand. These EMG signals can "mask" ECG signals and thereby impede their detection.

Dr. Lekhtman's invention claims to improve on prior art by eliminating that impediment. The invention focuses on a key difference between EMG and ECG waveforms: while ECG signals detected from a user's left hand have a polarity opposite to that of the signals detected from her right hand, EMG signals from each hand have the same polarity. The patented device works by measuring equalized EMG signals detected at each hand and then using circuitry to subtract the identical EMG signals from each other, thus filtering out the EMG interference.

As relevant here, the '753 patent describes a heart-rate monitor contained in a hollow cylindrical bar that a user grips with both hands, such that each hand comes into contact with two electrodes, one "live" and one "common." The device is illustrated in figure 1 of the patent, reproduced [below].

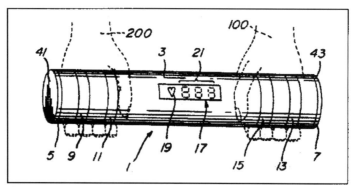

Patent No. 5,337,753, Figure 1

---

[47] [n.1 in opinion] In the Leahy–Smith America Invents Act, Pub. L. 112–29, 125 Stat. 284, enacted in 2011, Congress amended several parts of the Patent Act. Those amendments modified §§ 112 and 282 in minor respects not pertinent here. In any event, the amended versions of those provisions are inapplicable to patent applications filed before September 16, 2012.

8   Claim 1 of the '753 patent, which contains the limitations critical to this dispute, refers to a "heart rate monitor for use by a user in association with exercise apparatus and/or exercise procedures." The claim "comprise[s]," among other elements, an "elongate member" (cylindrical bar) with a display device; "electronic circuitry including a difference amplifier"; and, on each half of the cylindrical bar, a live electrode [9 and 13 in fig. 1] and a common electrode [11 and 15] "mounted . . . in spaced relationship with each other." The claim sets forth additional elements, including that the cylindrical bar is to be held in such a way that each of the user's hands "contact[s]" both electrodes on each side of the bar. Further, the EMG signals detected by the two electrode pairs are to be "of substantially equal magnitude and phase" so that the difference amplifier will "produce a substantially zero [EMG] signal" upon subtracting the signals from one another.

B

9   The dispute between the parties arose in the 1990's, when Biosig allegedly disclosed the patented technology to StairMaster Sports Medical Products, Inc. According to Biosig, StairMaster, without ever obtaining a license, sold exercise machines that included Biosig's patented technology, and petitioner Nautilus, Inc., continued to do so after acquiring the StairMaster brand. In 2004, based on these allegations, Biosig brought a patent infringement suit against Nautilus in the U.S. District Court for the Southern District of New York.

10   With Biosig's lawsuit launched, Nautilus asked the U.S. Patent and Trademark Office (PTO) to reexamine the '753 patent. The reexamination proceedings centered on whether the patent was anticipated or rendered obvious by prior art— principally, a patent issued in 1984 to an inventor named Fujisaki, which similarly disclosed a heart-rate monitor using two pairs of electrodes and a difference amplifier. Endeavoring to distinguish the '753 patent from prior art, Biosig submitted a declaration from Dr. Lekhtman. The declaration attested, among other things, that the '753 patent sufficiently informed a person skilled in the art how to configure the detecting electrodes so as "to produce equal EMG [signals] from the left and right hands." Although the electrodes' design variables—including spacing, shape, size, and material—cannot be standardized across all exercise machines, Dr. Lekhtman explained, a skilled artisan could undertake a "trial and error" process of equalization. This would entail experimentation with different electrode configurations in order to optimize EMG signal cancellation. In 2010, the PTO issued a determination confirming the patentability of the '753 patent's claims.

11   In 2011, the District Court conducted a hearing to determine the proper construction of the patent's claims, including the claim term "in spaced relationship with each other." According to Biosig, that "spaced relationship" referred to the distance between the live electrode and the common electrode in each electrode pair. Nautilus, seizing on Biosig's submissions to the PTO during the reexamination, maintained that the "spaced relationship" must be a distance "greater than the width

of each electrode." The District Court ultimately construed the term to mean "there is a defined relationship between the live electrode and the common electrode on one side of the cylindrical bar and the same or a different defined relationship between the live electrode and the common electrode on the other side of the cylindrical bar," without any reference to the electrodes' width.

12   Nautilus moved for summary judgment, arguing that the term "spaced relationship," as construed, was indefinite under § 112, ¶ 2. The District Court granted the motion. Those words, the District Court concluded, "did not tell [the court] or anyone what precisely the space should be," or even supply "any parameters" for determining the appropriate spacing.

13   The Federal Circuit reversed and remanded. A claim is indefinite, the majority opinion stated, "only when it is 'not amenable to construction' or 'insolubly ambiguous.'" Under that standard, the majority determined, the '753 patent survived indefiniteness review. Considering first the "intrinsic evidence"—i.e., the claim language, the specification, and the prosecution history—the majority discerned [that] these sources of meaning make plain that the distance separating the live and common electrodes on each half of the bar "cannot be greater than the width of a user's hands"; that is so "because claim 1 requires the live and common electrodes to independently detect electrical signals at two distinct points of a hand." Furthermore, the majority noted, the intrinsic evidence teaches that this distance cannot be "infinitesimally small, effectively merging the live and common electrodes into a single electrode with one detection point."

14   We granted certiorari, and now vacate and remand.

III

A

15   Although the parties here disagree on the dispositive question—does the '753 patent withstand definiteness scrutiny—they are in accord on several aspects of the § 112, ¶ 2 inquiry. First, definiteness is to be evaluated from the perspective of someone skilled in the relevant art. Second, in assessing definiteness, claims are to be read in light of the patent's specification and prosecution history. Third, definiteness is measured from the viewpoint of a person skilled in the art *at the time the patent was filed.*

16   The parties differ, however, in their articulations of just how much imprecision § 112, ¶ 2 tolerates. In Nautilus' view, a patent is invalid when a claim is "ambiguous, such that readers could reasonably interpret the claim's scope differently." Biosig and the Solicitor General would require only that the patent provide reasonable notice of the scope of the claimed invention.

17   Section 112, we have said, entails a "delicate balance." *Festo*, 535 U.S. at 731. On the one hand, the definiteness requirement must take into account the inherent

limitations of language. Some modicum of uncertainty, the Court has recognized, is the "price of ensuring the appropriate incentives for innovation." *Id.*, at 732. One must bear in mind, moreover, that patents are "not addressed to lawyers, or even to the public generally," but rather to those skilled in the relevant art. *Carnegie Steel Co. v. Cambria Iron Co.*, 185 U.S. 403, 437 (1902).

18   At the same time, a patent must be precise enough to afford clear notice of what is claimed, thereby "appris[ing] the public of what is still open to them." *Markman*, 517 U.S. at 373. Otherwise there would be "[a] zone of uncertainty which enterprise and experimentation may enter only at the risk of infringement claims." *United Carbon Co. v. Binney & Smith Co.*, 317 U.S. 228, 236 (1942). And absent a meaningful definiteness check, we are told, patent applicants face powerful incentives to inject ambiguity into their claims. *See* Federal Trade Commission, *The Evolving IP Marketplace: Aligning Patent Notice and Remedies with Competition* 85 (2011) (quoting testimony that [the] patent system fosters "an incentive to be as vague and ambiguous as you can with your claims" and "defer clarity at all costs"). Eliminating that temptation is in order, and "the patent drafter is in the best position to resolve the ambiguity in . . . patent claims." *Halliburton Energy Servs., Inc. v. M–I LLC*, 514 F.3d 1244, 1255 (Fed. Cir. 2008).

19   To determine the proper office of the definiteness command, therefore, we must reconcile concerns that tug in opposite directions. Cognizant of the competing concerns, we read § 112, ¶ 2 to require that a patent's claims, viewed in light of the specification and prosecution history, inform those skilled in the art about the scope of the invention with reasonable certainty. The definiteness requirement, so understood, mandates clarity, while recognizing that absolute precision is unattainable. The standard we adopt accords with opinions of this Court stating that "the certainty which the law requires in patents is not greater than is reasonable, having regard to their subject-matter." *Minerals Separation, Ltd. v. Hyde*, 242 U.S. 261, 270 (1916). *See also United Carbon*, 317 U.S. at 236 ("claims must be reasonably clear-cut"); *Markman*, 517 U.S. at 389 (claim construction calls for "the necessarily sophisticated analysis of the whole document," and may turn on evaluations of expert testimony).

B

20   In resolving Nautilus' definiteness challenge, the Federal Circuit asked whether the '753 patent's claims were "amenable to construction" or "insolubly ambiguous." Those formulations can breed lower court confusion, for they lack the precision § 112, ¶ 2 demands. It cannot be sufficient that a court can ascribe *some* meaning to a patent's claims; the definiteness inquiry trains on the understanding of a skilled artisan at the time of the patent application, not that of a court viewing matters *post hoc*. To tolerate imprecision just short of that rendering a claim "insolubly ambiguous" would diminish the definiteness requirement's public-notice

function and foster the innovation-discouraging "zone of uncertainty," *United Carbon*, 317 U.S. at 236, against which this Court has warned.

21   Appreciating that "terms like 'insolubly ambiguous' may not be felicitous," Biosig argues the phrase is a shorthand label for a more probing inquiry that the Federal Circuit applies in practice. But although this Court does not "micromanag[e] the Federal Circuit's particular word choice" in applying patent-law doctrines, we must ensure that the Federal Circuit's test is at least "probative of the essential inquiry." *Warner–Jenkinson Co. v. Hilton Davis Chemical Co.*, 520 U.S. 17, 40 (1997). Falling short in that regard, the expressions "insolubly ambiguous" and "amenable to construction" permeate the Federal Circuit's recent decisions concerning § 112, ¶ 2's requirement. We agree with Nautilus and its *amici* that such terminology can leave courts and the patent bar at sea without a reliable compass.[48]

IV

22   Both here and in the courts below, the parties have advanced conflicting arguments as to the definiteness of the claims in the '753 patent. Nautilus maintains that the claim term "spaced relationship" is open to multiple interpretations reflecting markedly different understandings of the patent's scope, as exemplified by the disagreement among the members of the Federal Circuit panel. Biosig responds that "spaced relationship," read in light of the specification and as illustrated in the accompanying drawings, delineates the permissible spacing with sufficient precision.

23   "[M]indful that we are a court of review, not of first view," *Cutter v. Wilkinson*, 544 U.S. 709, 718, n.7 (2005), we decline to apply the standard we have announced to the controversy between Nautilus and Biosig. As we have explained, the Federal Circuit invoked a standard more amorphous than the statutory definiteness requirement allows. We therefore follow our ordinary practice of remanding so that the Court of Appeals can reconsider, under the proper standard, whether the relevant claims in the '753 patent are sufficiently definite.

---

[48] [n.10 in opinion] The Federal Circuit suggests that a permissive definiteness standard "accord[s] respect to the statutory presumption of patent validity." 715 F.3d 891, 902 (Fed. Cir. 2013). As the parties appear to agree, however, this presumption of validity does not alter the degree of clarity that § 112, ¶ 2 demands from patent applicants; to the contrary, it incorporates that definiteness requirement by reference. *See* § 282, ¶ 2(3) (defenses to infringement actions include "[i]nvalidity of the patent or any claim in suit for failure to comply with . . . any requirement of [§ 112]").

The parties nonetheless dispute whether factual findings subsidiary to the ultimate issue of definiteness trigger the clear-and-convincing-evidence standard and, relatedly, whether deference is due to the PTO's resolution of disputed issues of fact. We leave these questions for another day. The court below treated definiteness as "a legal issue [the] court reviews without deference," 715 F.3d, at 897, and Biosig has not called our attention to any contested factual matter—or PTO determination thereof—pertinent to its infringement claims.

Discussion Questions: *Nautilus*

1. *Is "Spaced Relationship" Indefinite?* On remand, the Federal Circuit stated that "we may now steer by the bright star of 'reasonable certainty,' rather than the unreliable compass of 'insoluble ambiguity'" and concluded that the claim is not indefinite because "a skilled artisan would understand the inherent parameters of the invention as provided in the intrinsic evidence." *Biosig Instruments v. Nautilus*, 783 F.3d 1374, 1379, 1384 (Fed. Cir. 2015). Do you agree? What would have been the benefits and costs of requiring more precise language, such as stating that the electrodes must be mounted "between 0.1 and 6.0 inches apart"?

2. *Is "Reasonable Certainty" Indefinite?* The new "reasonable certainty" standard for indefiniteness can be criticized as indefinite itself, but can you think of a better legal standard? Nautilus asked the Court to hold that claims are invalid if they are "ambiguous, such that readers could reasonably interpret the claim's scope differently." During oral argument, Justice Sotomayor asked:

> Now, I have a really big problem, which is we as Justices disagree on the meaning of things all the time, and one side will say, this is perfectly clear from the text of the statute, from its history, from its context. And we do all the statutory tools, and there will be one or more of us who will come out and say, no, we think it's a different interpretation. Would we have any valid patents in the world if that's the standard that we adopt?

Nautilus's lawyer didn't have a good response; do you?

On the other hand, the Justices also gave patent owner Biosig a hard time for its argument. Biosig supported the Federal Circuit's old standard that claims are indefinite only if "insolubly ambiguous" but supported a "reasonable certainty" standard as long as it was clear that claims like theirs are reasonably certain. The Justices worried that claims would never be indefinite under such a standard. As Justice Scalia noted, "There's never more than one correct construction. . . . I mean, we always have to come up with an answer. . . . Have you ever heard of a court that says, well, you know, it could mean either one of these? It's a tie!" If you were Biosig's lawyer, how would you respond?

Although the Justices complained at oral argument that "reasonable certainty" is "not much of a test," this is the standard they settled on. Could you do better?

3. *Indefiniteness Rejections During Examination. Nautilus* was an appeal from a patent litigation suit involving a granted patent rather than an appeal from the USPTO's rejection of a patent application during examination. If an examiner rejects a claim for indefiniteness, the applicant can amend the claim to impose greater clarity. Given this, do you think the indefiniteness standard should be the same during prosecution and litigation? Before *Nautilus* was decided, Judge Dyk of the Federal

Circuit argued that "[c]onstruing ambiguous and poorly drafted claims continues to be the principal task that our court faces in patent cases" and that the USPTO should take a more active role in policing claim drafting by "reject[ing] applications when the claims are not clear." Timothy B. Dyk, *Ten Prescriptions for What Ails Patent Law*, 17 Stan. Tech. L. Rev. 345 (2014).

The USPTO previously used "a lower threshold of ambiguity" such that a claim was indefinite when "amenable to two or more plausible constructions," *Ex parte Miyazaki*, 89 U.S.P.Q.2d 1207 (B.P.A.I. 2008), or "when it contains words or phrases whose meaning is unclear," *In re Packard*, 751 F.3d 1307 (Fed. Cir. 2014). Does *Nautilus* specify the standard examiners should apply? *See* Lisa Larrimore Ouellette & Jonathan Masur, *How Will* Nautilus *Affect Indefiniteness at the PTO?*, Patently-O (June 5, 2014), https://patentlyo.com/patent/2014/06/nautilus-affect-indefiniteness.html. In 2017, the PTAB decided in a precedential opinion that it would follow the "meaning is unclear" standard in the examination context, *Ex Parte McAward*, 2017 WL 3947829 (P.T.A.B. 2017), and a 2021 memo from the USPTO Director later clarified that the PTAB "shall follow *Nautilus* in AIA post-grant proceedings." However, nonprecedential PTAB opinions in examination appeals still cite a variety of standards (including the "insolubly ambiguous" standard!), illustrating the difficulty of quality control.

If claims do not meet the legal standard for indefiniteness during examination, should examiners ask applicants to clarify the meaning of any claim terms in the prosecution record? Examiners may "require information that does not directly support a rejection," *Star Fruits v. United States*, 393 F.3d 1277 (Fed. Cir. 2005) (citing 37 C.F.R. § 1.105), although they do not generally use this authority to clarify claim terms that were not found indefinite.

4. *Inherently Ambiguous Claim Terms.* In our experience, students new to patent law tend to be quicker than examiners or the courts at identifying claims that seem insufficiently definite. Claims are routinely granted and upheld even when they contain approximations (like "about," "essentially," "substantially"), references to objects of variable size (like "so dimensioned as to be insertable" into an automobile), open-ended numerical ranges (like "less than X%"), and the very common phrase "an effective amount" (meaning an amount effective for accomplishing some stated purpose). *See* MPEP § 2173. Should the indefiniteness standard be further revised to prevent applicants from using this kind of inherently ambiguous language?

Practice Problems: Applying the *Nautilus* Indefiniteness Standard

In general, one cannot assess indefiniteness just by looking at the claim—it is also important to consider the specification, and expert testimony may be necessary to determine whether a claim provides reasonable certainty to a PHOSITA. In this sense, the definiteness determination provides a preview of the claim construction process we will consider in Chapter 8. (Indeed, definiteness is most often resolved as part of the claim construction process.) The following examples provide simplified claims and relevant context from recent Federal Circuit cases. Do you think the underlined claim terms render the claims indefinite?

1. The asserted claims are directed to light emitting diodes (LEDs) with improved heat dissipation. The claims require "a thermally conductive <u>elongated</u> core" that draws heat from the LEDs and dissipates it into the air. The accused infringer argues that "elongated" is indefinite because the specification does not use the term "elongated" or describe the core's dimensions. The patentee responds that "elongated" refers to whether a core was long enough to pull heat away from the LEDs. During prosecution, the patentee distinguished two prior art references with extended cores as not containing an "elongated" element. *GE Lighting Solutions v. Lights of America*, 663 F. App'x 938 (Fed. Cir. 2016).

2. The patent-in-suit is directed to a lawn mower with improved flow control baffles. A baffle is a metal structure under the mower deck that directs air flow and grass clippings during operation. The asserted claim requires a "flow control baffle" to have an "<u>elongated and substantially straight</u> baffle portion" between two "arcuate baffle portions," as illustrated in the side view below. The accused infringer argues that "elongated and substantially straight" provides no objective standard for whether a baffle portion is straight enough or long enough to be covered by the claim. The patentee responds that a PHOSITA would understand the term to mean the baffle portion is long enough to transition between the arcuate portions and straight relative to the other components. *Exmark Manufacturing v. Briggs & Stratton Power Products*, 879 F.3d 1332 (Fed. Cir. 2018).

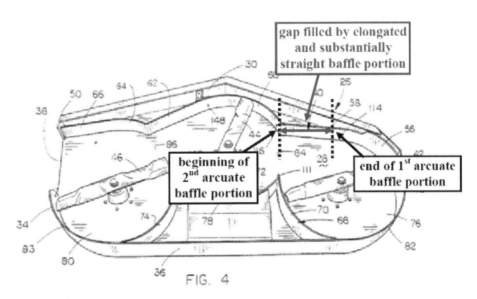

FIG. 4

3. The asserted claims cover multilayer capacitors—electrical components that store and release energy—with a "fringe-effect capacitance" between two contacts that is "<u>capable of being determined by measurement in terms of a standard unit</u>." The

specification discloses a method of measuring capacitance called insertion loss testing that was well known in the art. The accused infringer argues that the claim is indefinite because the insertion loss method had not previously been applied to measure fringe-effect capacitance, and the specification provides no guidance on how to do this. The patent owner's expert testified that a PHOSITA would be able to develop a test methodology for this purpose. *Presidio Components v. American Technical Ceramics*, 875 F.3d 1369 (Fed. Cir. 2017).

4. The claims at issue are directed to a method of manufacturing a polymer "having a <u>molecular weight</u> of about 5 to 9 kilodaltons." A kilodalton is a widely used unit of atomic mass. Both the patent owner and accused infringer agree that the claim term "molecular weight" could refer to any of three measures of a polymer's molecular weight: peak average molecular weight (M_p), number average molecular weight (M_n), and weight average molecular weight (M_w). Each measure is calculated in a different manner, and the patent provides no guidance on which to use. During prosecution of two continuation patents of the patent-in-suit, the patentee overcame indefiniteness rejections from the USPTO—in one case by defining "molecular weight" as M_w, and in the other by defining it as M_p. The response defining "molecular weight" as M_w included a scientific error. *Teva Pharmaceuticals v. Sandoz*, 789 F.3d 1335 (Fed. Cir. 2015).

5. The claimed invention addresses the problem of website visitors being lured away from a host website by clicking an advertisement. Under the system disclosed in the patent, when a visitor clicks an advertising link, they are taken to a composite website that displays the product information from the third-party advertiser, but retains the host website's "look and feel," which "gives the viewer of the page the impression that she is viewing pages served by the host" website. Here is a simplified version of the claim:

> A system serving web pages comprising:
> (a) a computer store containing data, for each of a plurality of first web pages, defining a plurality of <u>look and feel elements</u> corresponding to the plurality of first web pages, wherein each of the first web pages displays at least one active link associated with a commerce object associated with a buying opportunity of a selected one of a plurality of merchants; and
> (b) a server coupled to the computer store and programmed to:
>> (i) receive from the web browser of a computer user a signal indicating activation of one of the links displayed by one of the first web pages; and
>> (ii) automatically generate and transmit to the web browser a second web page that displays: information associated with the commerce object associated with the link that has been activated, and the plurality of <u>look and feel elements</u> corresponding to the source page.

The specification describes "look and feel elements" as "including logos, colors, page layout, navigation systems, frames, 'mouse-over' effects, or other elements that are consistent through some or all of a host's website." The patent owner's expert testified that a skilled artisan would interpret these "other elements" as elements such as headers, footers, fonts, and images. Is "look and feel elements" indefinite? *DDR Holdings, LLC v. Hotels.com, L.P.*, 773 F.3d 1245, 1260 (Fed. Cir. 2014).

6. The patents-in-suit are directed to an "attention manager for occupying the peripheral attention of a person in the vicinity of a display device." The specification has two primary embodiments: a "wallpaper" embodiment that displays images in spatial portions of the screen not occupying the user's primary attention, and a "screensaver" embodiment that displays images after detecting an idle period. The relevant claims include the following step:

> . . . providing to the content display system a set of instructions for enabling the content display system to selectively display, in an unobtrusive manner that does not distract a user of the display device or an apparatus associated with the display device from a primary interaction with the display device or apparatus, an image or images generated from a set of content data . . .

The accused infringer argues that the "unobtrusive manner" phrase is indefinite because it is highly subjective. The patentee responds that it is sufficiently defined through its relationship to the wallpaper embodiment. *Interval Licensing LLC v. AOL, Inc.*, 766 F.3d 1364 (Fed. Cir. 2014).

B. Definiteness for Means-Plus-Function Claim Elements

As noted at the end of Chapter 1, § 112(f) (known as § 112 ¶ 6 for pre-AIA claims) gives patent drafters the option to write claim elements in terms of the function they perform rather than what they are, such as a "a means for fastening" rather than "a button."

35 U.S.C. § 112(f)

> An element in a claim for a combination may be expressed as a means or step for performing a specified function without the recital of structure, material, or acts in support thereof, and such claim shall be construed to cover the corresponding structure, material, or acts described in the specification and equivalents thereof.

Claim limitations written in functional terms are known as means-plus-function elements. Writing a claim element in functional terms can be beneficial for patentees who do not want to list all the means for performing that function in their claim, but under § 112(f), this benefit comes at the cost of narrowing claim scope: means-plus-function elements cover only the corresponding structure in the specification (and equivalents). "Structure" is a term of art for whatever performs the claimed function. In some cases, like the button that is a means for fastening, the structure is something tangible. But the structure for a means-plus-function claim element need not be a physical structure; for example, the structure for a software function is the corresponding algorithm. If there is no corresponding structure, the claim is invalid for indefiniteness under § 112(b).

Importantly, it is *not* generally true that claim terms are limited to the specific examples in the application. As we will discuss in more detail in Chapter 8 on claim construction, the Federal Circuit has repeatedly emphasized that courts should "avoid importing limitations from the specification into the claims." *Phillips v. AWH Corp.*, 415 F.3d 1303, 1323 (Fed. Cir. 2005) (en banc). But means-plus-function claim elements are an exception to this general rule: when § 112(f) is triggered, importing limitations from the specification is required.

Consider a hypothetical claim directed to a novel sneaker. Rather than expressing one of the claim elements as "shoelaces," the patentee could express this element as "a means for securing the shoe around a foot." Under § 112(f), this "means for securing" element would then be construed to cover the corresponding structure in the specification. If the specification explains that "the shoe may be secured around a foot using traditional closure mechanisms such as shoelaces or velcro," then the "means for securing" element is construed to cover shoelaces, velcro, and their equivalents—and thus would not cover no-tie elastic systems or mechanical systems that allow users to adjust shoe fit by turning a knob. If the specification does *not* mention any means for securing the shoe, then the claim is invalid for indefiniteness.

Analyzing functional claims for indefiniteness thus involves two steps: (1) Is there a means-plus-function element triggering § 112(f)? (2) If so, does that means-plus-function element have corresponding structure in the specification? If not, the claim is invalid for indefiniteness under § 112(b). We consider these steps in turn.

1. Does § 112(f) Apply to a Claim Limitation?

Before 2015, the inquiry into whether a claim limitation should be construed under § 112(f) focused on whether the limitation employed the word "means." Use of "means" created a presumption that § 112(f) applied; failure to use "means" created a "strong" presumption that § 112(f) did not apply. Claim drafters responded by replacing "means" with generic terms like "module," "mechanism," "element," or "device" in an effort to achieve broader claims without the restrictions of § 112(f). In

2015, the Federal Circuit decided en banc that a "strong" presumption for elements not using "means" was unwarranted. *Williamson v. Citrix Online, LLC*, 792 F.3d 1339, 1349 (Fed. Cir. 2015). There is still a presumption that "means" triggers § 112(f) and the absence of "means" does not, but it can be overcome. A claim limitation does *not* trigger § 112(f) if "the words of the claim are understood by persons of ordinary skill in the art to have a sufficiently definite meaning as the name for structure." *Id.*

The invention at issue in *Williamson v. Citrix* was a system for a virtual classroom purporting to provide "the benefits of classroom interaction without the detrimental effects of complicated hardware or software, or the costs and inconvenience of convening in a separate place." (Little did the inventor know how valuable this field would become in 2020!) One limitation of the claims was a "*distributed learning control module* for receiving communications transmitted between the presenter and the audience member computer systems and for relaying the communications to an intended receiving computer system and for coordinating the operation of the streaming data module." The Federal Circuit held that "distributed learning control module" should be construed under § 112, ¶ 6 because "'module' is simply a generic description for software or hardware that performs a specified function" and none of the surrounding claim language "impart[s] structure into the term 'module.'" *Id.* at 1350–51.

The result in *Williamson* would have been different if "distributed learning control module" had a well understood meaning in the computer technology field. As summarized by the USPTO in MPEP § 2181:

> If persons of ordinary skill in the art reading the specification understand the term to have a sufficiently definite meaning as the name for the structure that performs the function, even when the term covers a broad class of structures or identifies the structures by their function (e.g., "filters," "brakes," "clamp," "screwdriver," and "locks"), 35 U.S.C. § 112(f) will not apply. The term is not required to denote a specific structure or a precise physical structure to avoid the application of 35 U.S.C. § 112(f). The following are examples of structural terms that have been found *not* to invoke 35 U.S.C. § 112(f) or pre-AIA § 112, ¶ 6: "circuit," "digital detector," "detent mechanism," "reciprocating member," "connector assembly," "perforation," "sealingly connected joints," and "eyeglass hanger member." It is important to remember that there are no absolutes in the determination of terms used as a substitute for "means" that serve as generic placeholders. The examiner must carefully consider the term in light of the specification and the commonly accepted meaning in the technological art. Every application will turn on its own facts.

A limitation will not invoke 35 U.S.C. § 112(f) if there is a structural modifier that further describes the term "means" or the generic placeholder. For example, although a generic placeholder like "mechanism" standing alone may invoke § 112(f) when coupled with a function, it will not invoke § 112(f) when it is preceded by a structural modifier (e.g., "detent mechanism"). *Greenberg v. Ethicon Endo-Surgery*, 91 F.3d 1580 (Fed. Cir. 1996) (holding that the term "detent mechanism" did not invoke § 112, ¶ 6 because the structural modifier "detent" denotes a type of structural device with a generally understood meaning in the mechanical arts). By contrast, a generic placeholder (e.g., "mechanism," "element," "member") coupled with a function may invoke § 112(f) when it is preceded by a non-structural modifier that does not have any generally understood structural meaning in the art (e.g., "colorant selection mechanism," "lever moving element," or "movable link member").

To determine whether a word, term, or phrase coupled with a function denotes structure, examiners may check whether: (1) the specification provides a description sufficient to inform one of ordinary skill in the art that the term denotes structure; (2) general and subject matter specific dictionaries provide evidence that the term has achieved recognition as a noun denoting structure; and/or (3) the prior art provides evidence that the term is an art-recognized structure to perform the claimed function. It is necessary to decide on an element-by-element basis whether 35 U.S.C. § 112(f) applies.

In short, what matters is whether the claim is written in such a way that a PHOSITA can tell what the claim element *is*, or if the PHOSITA could only tell what the claim element *does*. If a claim element could equally have been written in the form "a means for [performing a function]" or "a [function] means," such as "a means for fastening" or "a fastening means," this indicates that the claim element is only telling a PHOSITA what the element *does*. In such a case, it is a means-plus function element. And if it is a means-plus-function element, it is limited to the corresponding structure in the specification (or is indefinite if there is no corresponding structure).

This means that if the claim term is "a fastening thing-a-ma-bob," the relevant question is whether the term "thing-a-ma-bob" itself conveys some kind of structure to a PHOSITA, or whether it is simply a generic placeholder for "means." If it conveys some kind of structure, this is not a means-plus-function element. If it is simply a generic placeholder, it *is* a means-plus-function element.

Practice Problem: Does § 112(f) Apply?

Consider the cutlery apparatus at right, which combines a fork, spoon, and knife so that a person may eat and cut his food using one hand. The fork is on a retractable shaft, and the knife blade is on the bottom edge of the spoon. When activated, the spoon/knife combination rotates about the fork to cut the food item in which the fork is impaled. The first patent claim reads:

1. A cutlery apparatus comprising:
    (a) a cutlery handle;
    (b) a fork movably engaged with the cutlery handle; and
    (c) *a means for cutting* disposed adjacent to the fork and rotatably attached to the cutlery handle.

Does § 112(f) apply to "a means for cutting"? Would your analysis differ if "a means for cutting" in element (c) were replaced with the following language?[49]

2. "a device configured for cutting"

3. "a knife blade"

4. "a knife blade means for cutting"

2. Does a § 112(f) Limitation Have a Corresponding Structure?

If a claim limitation triggers § 112(f), it must be supported by a corresponding structure in the specification, or else it is indefinite under § 112(b). The structure "must be disclosed in the written description in such a manner that one skilled in the art will know and understand what structure corresponds to the means limitation." *Atmel Corp. v. Info. Storage Devices*, 198 F.3d 1374, 1382 (Fed. Cir. 1999). Claims with means-plus-function elements are far more likely than claims drafted in other formats to be held indefinite. See John R. Allison & Lisa Larrimore Ouellette, *How Courts Adjudicate Patent Definiteness and Disclosure*, 65 Duke L.J. 609 (2016).

Whether a means-plus-function claim element has a disclosed structure is closely related to the question of whether it is adequately described and enabled under § 112(a), but the issues are distinct: "The inquiry is whether one of skill in the art would understand the specification itself to disclose a structure, not simply whether that person would be capable of implementing a structure." *Biomedino v. Waters Techs.*, 490 F.3d 946 (Fed. Cir. 2007). For example, a disclosure that an invention "may be controlled by known differential pressure, valving and control equipment" was not a disclosure of structure corresponding to the claimed "control means for automatically operating valves," even though this may have been sufficient to enable a PHOSITA to practice the invention. *Id.*

Interpreting claim elements as triggering § 112(f) and requiring a corresponding structure has played a particularly important role in limiting broad

---

[49] See https://www.uspto.gov/sites/default/files/documents/112f_cbt_slides.pdf (slide 21 et seq.).

software patent claims that are written in functional terms. For computer-implemented inventions, the Federal Circuit has held that the specification must disclose an algorithm for performing the claimed function. A general-purpose microprocessor "can serve as structure for a computer-implemented function only where the claimed function is 'coextensive' with a microprocessor itself," such as for "receiving," "storing," and "processing" data. *EON Corp. IP Holdings v. AT&T Mobility*, 785 F.3d 616, 622 (Fed. Cir. 2015). Otherwise, an algorithm is required, which may be expressed "in any understandable terms including as a mathematical formula, in prose, in a flow chart, or in any other manner that provides sufficient structure." MPEP § 2181.

In a prominent case, *Aristocrat Technologies v. International Game Technology*, 521 F.3d 1328 (Fed. Cir. 2008), the Federal Circuit held a claim directed to an electronic slot machine to be indefinite because the "game control means" lacked corresponding structure:

> Aristocrat contends that the language of claim 1 referring to "the game control means being arranged to pay a prize when a predetermined combination of symbols is displayed in a predetermined arrangement of symbol positions selected by a player" implicitly discloses an algorithm for the microprocessor. That is, when the winning combination of symbols is displayed, the program should pay a prize. But that language simply describes the function to be performed, not the algorithm by which it is performed. Aristocrat's real point is that devising an algorithm to perform that function would be within the capability of one of skill in the art, and therefore it was not necessary for the patent to designate any particular algorithm to perform the claimed function. As we have noted above, however, that argument is contrary to this court's law. . . .

> Finally, Aristocrat contends that "the written description delineates what constitutes 'appropriate programming' through the disclosed embodiments of the invention." Again, however, the description of the embodiments is simply a description of the outcome of the claimed functions, not a description of the structure, i.e., the computer programmed to execute a particular algorithm. In making this argument, Aristocrat relies on Figure 1 and Table 1 from the patent, which provide examples of how player selections translate to possible winning combinations. The corresponding portion of the written description contains mathematical descriptions of how many winning combinations would be produced. Aristocrat refers to these examples as "algorithms." The figures, tables, and related discussion, however, are not algorithms. They are simply examples of the results of the operation of an unspecified algorithm. Like the mathematical equation set forth in claim 1, these combinations of figures and tables

are, at best, a description of the claimed function of the means-plus-function claim. Aristocrat has elected to claim using section 112 paragraph 6 and therefore must disclose corresponding structure. It has disclosed, at most, pictorial and mathematical ways of describing the claimed function of the game control means. That is not enough to transform the disclosure of a general-purpose microprocessor into the disclosure of sufficient structure.

Many software patents have been invalidated under the same logic as *Aristocrat*, but some commentators have argued for more vigorous enforcement of these requirements. Consider the argument from Mark A. Lemley, *Software Patents and the Return of Functional Claiming*, 2013 Wis. L. Rev. 905 (2013):

> It is broad functional claiming of software inventions that is arguably responsible for most of the well-recognized problems with software patents. Writing software can surely be an inventive act, and not all new programs or programming techniques are obvious to outside observers. So some software inventions surely qualify for patent protection. Even if there are too many software patents, the patent thicket and patent troll problems won't go away if we simply reduce the number of software patents somewhat. And while the lack of clear boundaries is a very real problem, the most important problem a product-making software company faces today is not suits over claims with unclear boundaries but suits over claims that purport to cover any possible way of achieving a goal. The fact that there are lots of patents with broad claims purporting to cover those goals creates a patent thicket. And while the breadth of those claims should (and does) make them easier to invalidate, the legal deck is stacked against companies who seek to invalidate overbroad patent claims.

> This is a problem primarily in software. We wouldn't permit in any other area of technology the sorts of claims that appear in thousands of different software patents. Pharmaceutical inventors don't claim "an arrangement of atoms that cures cancer," asserting their patent against any chemical, whatever its form, that achieves that purpose. Indeed, the whole idea seems ludicrous. . . . But in software, as we will see, claims of just that form are everywhere.

> While there are some arguments in favor of broad functional claims in software, they are insufficient to justify the costs they impose. As it did seventy-five years ago, the law should rein in efforts to claim to own a goal itself rather than a particular means of achieving that goal. Doing so should not require legislative action; it is enough to interpret existing Section 112(f) in light of the realities of software and modern patent practice. And so, with one fell swoop—without changing

the patent statute and without invalidating existing patents—we may be able to solve most of the software patent problem.

Do you agree with Professor Lemley that there is a software patent problem? If so, do you agree that a stricter interpretation of § 112(f) would help address it? In the next chapter, we will discuss patentable subject matter, a doctrine that has ballooned in recent years in part to deal with a perceived problem with software patents of dubious validity asserted by "patent trolls." As you learn about patentable subject matter, consider whether you think indefiniteness is a better tool to address these policy concerns.

Practice Problem: Definiteness and Functional Claims

Your firm's client, Life360, makes a smartphone application that allows users to see where their friends and family are on a private map, stay in touch with group and one-to-one messaging, and get help in an emergency. Life360 has been sued for infringement of patent 7,031,728, which has an effective filing date in 2004. As explained in the abstract, the invention allows "cellular phone users to monitor each other's location and status, to initiate cellular phone calls by touching a symbol on the display screen with a stylus or finger which can also include conferencing calling." Here is the asserted claim:

> 3. A communication system to provide a cellular phone network for a group of participants, each of the participants having an individual portable cellular phone that includes a CPU and a GPS navigational system that can accurately determine the location of each cellular phone, each of the cellular phones in the communications net of participants containing:
>
> (a) said CPU and memory;
>
> (b) a touch screen display;
>
> (c) a symbol generator in said CPU that can generate symbols that represent each of the participants' cell phones in the communication network on the touch screen display;
>
> (d) a database that stores the individual telephone numbers related to each of the symbols;
>
> (e) cellular phone call initiating software in said CPU connected to the telephone number database and the symbols on the touch screen display, whereby touching an individual symbol will automatically initiate a cellular phone telephone call to the user represented by the symbol; and

(f) said display including databases that display geographical information that includes showing the geographical location of each of the symbols representing participants in the communication network, fixed locations, and entered items of interest.

A partner at your law firm has asked you to work with another junior associate to see if there is a viable challenge to this claim's validity using 35 U.S.C. § 112(b), (f). How would you analyze this problem? Below are figure 1 from the '728 patent and the most relevant excerpts from the specification.

Referring now to the drawings and, in particular, FIG. 1, the present invention is shown generally at 10 that includes a small handheld cellular phone/ communications system in housing 12 that includes an on/off power switch 19, a microphone 38, and an LCD display 16 that is also a touch screen system. The small area 16 a is the Navigation Bar that depicts the telephone, GPS and other status data and the active software. With the touch screen system, the screen symbols are entered through GPS inputs or by the operator using a

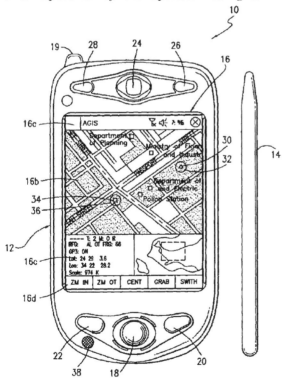

stylus or finger 14 by manipulatively directing the stylus or finger 14 to literally touch display screen 16.

Cellular phone units such as these are currently on sale and sold as a complete unit (or with an external connected GPS) that can be used for cellular telephone calls and sending cellular SMS and TCP/IP or other messages using the unit's display and computer.

The heart of the invention lies in the software applications provided in the system. Mounted inside housing 12 as part of the unit is the display function screen and the CPU. The CPU includes databases that provide for a geographical map and georeferenced entities that is shown as display portion 16 b that includes as part of the display various areas of interest in the particular local map section.

When looking at FIG. 1, permanent geographical locations and buildings are shown. For example, the police station is shown and when the symbol is touched by the stylus or finger, the latitude and longitude of the symbol's location, as shown in display section 16 c, is displayed at the bottom left of the screen. The bottom right side of display 16 c is a multifunction inset area that can contain a variety of information including: a) a list of the communication link participants; b) a list of received messages; c) a map, aerial photograph or satellite image with an indication of the zoom and off set location of the main map display, which is indicated by a square that depicts the area actually displayed in the main geographical screen 16 b; d) applicable status information; and

e) a list of the communication net participants.

Also shown on the display screen 16, specifically the geographical display 16 b, is a pair of different looking symbols 30 and 34, a small triangle and a small square, which are not labeled. These symbols 30 and 34 can represent communication net cellular phone users in the displayed geographical area that are part of the overall cellular phone communications net used in this invention wherein each of the users has a similar cellular phone to the one shown in FIG. 1. The latitude and longitude of symbol 30 is associated within a database along with a specific phone number. The screen display 16 b, which is a touch screen, provides x and y coordinates of the screen 16 b to the CPU's software. The software has an algorithm that relates the x and y coordinates to latitude and longitude and can access a communications net participant's symbol or an entity's symbol as being the one closest to that point.

In order to initiate a telephone call to the cellular phone user represented by symbol (triangle) 30 at a specific GPS provided latitude and longitude which has been sent to the cellular phone shown in FIG. 1, the operator or initiator of what we call cellular phone one in FIG. 1 can take the stylus or finger 14, touch the triangle 30 with the stylus or finger, and then touch a "call" software switch from a matrix of displayed switches that will overlay the display area 16 c and immediately the cellular phone one will initiate a cellular phone telephone call to the cellular phone user at the location shown that represents symbol 30. A second cellular phone user is represented by symbol 34 which is a small square but could be any shape or icon to represent an individual cellular phone unit in the display area. The ring 32 around symbol 30 indicates that the symbol has been touched and that a telephone call can be initiated by touching the soft switch that says "call." When this is done, the telephone call is placed. Another type of symbolic display can indicate that the call is in effect.

See Advanced Ground Info. Sys., Inc. v. Life360, Inc., 830 F.3d 1341 (Fed. Cir. 2016).

6. Patentable Subject Matter

Consider the patentability doctrines covered thus far. To be valid, a patent must claim an invention that is new and nonobvious. The invention must be useful. It must be described in the specification such that a person skilled in the art would know how to make and use it. The claims must provide reasonable certainty as to what they cover. One might imagine that would be it; so long as a patent satisfied those requirements, it would be considered valid.

Yet this has never been the law. U.S. patent law has always required that an invention also fall into one or more statutory categories. Even if an invention is new and useful, if it does not fit within one of those categories, it cannot be patented. This is called the doctrine of "patentable subject matter." Section 101 of the Patent Act provides the relevant statutory language:

35 U.S.C. § 101

Whoever invents or discovers any new and useful process, machine, manufacture, or composition of matter, or any new and useful improvement thereof, may obtain a patent therefor, subject to the conditions and requirements of this title.

As a matter of the plain text, it is hard to imagine any invention that does not fall into the broad categories of "process, machine, manufacture, or composition of matter." For starters, what physical substance is not a "composition of matter"? Even atoms, the building blocks of matter, are themselves compositions of other matter—protons, neutrons, and electrons. Protons and neutrons are themselves compositions of quarks. And when it comes to intangible inventions, what type of invention could not be described as a "process"? In addition, the statutory text indicates that patents should be available for those who merely "discover[]" something new and useful. Congress has enacted separate bars on patenting inventions "useful solely in the utilization of special nuclear material or atomic energy in an atomic weapon," 42 U.S.C. § 2181(a), and inventions "directed to or encompassing a human organism," America Invents Act, Pub. L. No. 112-29, § 33(a), 125 Stat. 284 (2011). But the Patent Act itself imposes no apparent limits.

The broad text notwithstanding, the courts have long recognized several implicit exceptions to the statutory categories of patentable subject matter. The Supreme Court has held that "laws of nature," "natural phenomena," and "abstract ideas" cannot be patented, even if they are new and useful. In recent years the boundaries of these categories have expanded, and in some areas of technology the limitations on patentable subject matter have become much more important. This shift has taken place across four recent Supreme Court cases over a five-year period: *Bilski v. Kappos*, 561 U.S. 593 (2010); *Mayo Collaborative Services v. Prometheus Laboratories*, 566 U.S. 66 (2012); *Association for Molecular Pathology v. Myriad Genetics, Inc.*, 569 U.S. 576 (2013); and *Alice Corp. v. CLS Bank*, 573 U.S. 208 (2014). We will read the last three of those cases below. Those cases have had a dramatic impact on the patentability of a range of inventions, particularly computer- and internet-related methods.

What purpose is served by these exclusions from patentable subject matter? The Supreme Court has framed the doctrine in utilitarian terms, asserting that laws of nature, natural phenomena, and abstract ideas "are the basic tools of scientific and technological work" and that patents on these tools "might tend to impede innovation more than it would tend to promote it." *Alice*, 573 U.S. at 216. There is little empirical support for these empirical judgments, and many commentators have expressed skepticism that the doctrine of patentable subject matter can accomplish patent law's utilitarian goals better than the other doctrines we have covered so far. Patentable subject matter has enabled *faster* patent invalidations, as the legal issues can often be resolved on a motion to dismiss without the need for expensive discovery, but stakeholders are divided on whether this is a good thing.

To implement the patentable subject matter exclusions, the Supreme Court has created a new two-step test, known as the "*Alice/Mayo* test" after the two cases in which it was developed. That test operates as follows:

- Step 1: Determine whether the claim in question is "directed to" a natural law, product of nature, or abstract idea. If the claim is *not* directed to one of these exemptions, the claim is patentable subject matter under § 101.

- Step 2: If the claim *is* directed to one of the exempt categories, remove the natural law, product of nature, or abstract idea from the claim and examine what remains. If the rest of the claim includes an "inventive concept" such that the claim as a whole "amounts to significantly more" than a patent on the ineligible concept, the claim is patentable under § 101.[1]

Of course, this simple statement of the two-step test raises as many questions as it answers, including what it means for a claim to be "directed to" a natural law, product of nature, or abstract idea, and what it means for a claim to include an "inventive concept." This chapter explores the law of patentable subject matter and attempts to answer those questions. It also examines the extent to which this doctrine

---

[1] In USPTO materials such as the MPEP, these two steps are referred to as "Step 2A" and "Step 2B," with "Step 1" being the initial question of whether the claim is to a process, machine, manufacture, or composition of matter. We will instead use the terminology of the courts.

constrains patenting in various technological fields. We will begin with patents on laws of nature and products of nature, and then we consider abstract ideas.

As you read these cases and materials, consider the following questions: What is the doctrine of patentable subject matter accomplishing that the doctrines of novelty, nonobviousness, utility, and sufficient disclosure are not? What additional purposes or policies is it serving, and what policies or purposes might it be hindering? If answering these questions seems challenging, you are not alone. Patentable subject matter is probably the most contentious patent law doctrine today, with many advocating for judicial or legislative revision. But the Supreme Court has repeatedly denied certiorari in other patentable subject matter cases, and a push for legislative reform died in 2019 after a failure to reach stakeholder consensus. As you read this chapter, consider whether you think patentable subject matter reform is warranted.

A. Laws of Nature, Natural Phenomena, and Products of Nature

The modern story of patentable subject matter begins with *Bilski v. Kappos*, 561 U.S. 593 (2010), in which the Supreme Court reaffirmed that abstract ideas are unpatentable. But *Bilski* did not provide a workable test for determining the limits of patentable subject matter. The Court took up that problem two years later in *Mayo Collaborative Services v. Prometheus Laboratories*, 566 U.S. 66 (2012).

Mayo concerned a patent on a medical diagnostic method, which implicates the patentable subject matter exception for "laws of nature." In this section, we take up the law governing laws of nature, beginning with *Mayo*, followed by the subcategory of "products of nature." Cases involving these types of inventions make up a small but important fraction of all of the patentable subject matter cases adjudicated by the federal courts over the past five years. (The majority involve the exception for "abstract ideas," which we take up in the next section.) But more importantly, these cases were the initial vehicle for the most important doctrinal development in patent law of the past several decades. *Mayo* is the case in which that development first picked up steam.

Mayo Collaborative Services v. Prometheus Laboratories, 566 U.S. 66 (2012)

Justice Stephen Breyer delivered the opinion of the Court.

The Court has long held that [§ 101] contains an important implicit exception. "[L]aws of nature, natural phenomena, and abstract ideas" are not patentable. *Diamond v. Diehr*, 450 U.S. 175 (1981); *see also O'Reilly v. Morse*, 15 How. 62 (1854). Thus, the Court has written that "a new mineral discovered in the earth or a new plant found in the wild is not patentable subject matter. Likewise, Einstein could not patent his celebrated law that E=mc², nor could Newton have patented the law of gravity. Such discoveries are 'manifestations of . . . nature, free to all men and reserved exclusively to none.'" *Diamond v. Chakrabarty*, 447 U.S. 303, 309 (1980).

2   "Phenomena of nature, though just discovered, mental processes, and abstract intellectual concepts are not patentable, as they are the basic tools of scientific and technological work." *Gottschalk v. Benson*, 409 U.S. 63 (1972). And monopolization of those tools through the grant of a patent might tend to impede innovation more than it would tend to promote it.

3   The Court has recognized, however, that too broad an interpretation of this exclusionary principle could eviscerate patent law. For all inventions at some level embody, use, reflect, rest upon, or apply laws of nature, natural phenomena, or abstract ideas. Thus, in *Diehr* the Court pointed out that "a process is not unpatentable simply because it contains a law of nature or a mathematical algorithm." 450 U.S. at 187. It added that "an application of a law of nature or mathematical formula to a known structure or process may well be deserving of patent protection." *Id.* at 187.

4   Still, as the Court has also made clear, to transform an unpatentable law of nature into a patent-eligible *application* of such a law, one must do more than simply state the law of nature while adding the words "apply it." *See, e.g., Benson, supra*, at 71–72.

5   The case before us lies at the intersection of these basic principles. It concerns patent claims covering processes that help doctors who use thiopurine drugs to treat patients with autoimmune diseases determine whether a given dosage level is too low or too high. The claims purport to apply natural laws describing the relationships between the concentration in the blood of certain thiopurine metabolites and the likelihood that the drug dosage will be ineffective or induce harmful side effects. We must determine whether the claimed processes have transformed these unpatentable natural laws into patent-eligible applications of those laws. We conclude that they have not done so and that therefore the processes are not patentable.

6   Our conclusion rests upon an examination of the particular claims before us in light of the Court's precedents. Those cases warn us against interpreting patent statutes in ways that make patent eligibility "depend simply on the draftsman's art" without reference to the "principles underlying the prohibition against patents for [natural laws]." *Parker v. Flook*, 437 U.S. 584, 593 (1978). They warn us against upholding patents that claim processes that too broadly pre-empt the use of a natural law. *Morse, supra*, at 112–120; *Benson, supra*, at 71–72. And they insist that a process that focuses upon the use of a natural law also contain other elements or a combination of elements, sometimes referred to as an "inventive concept," sufficient to ensure that the patent in practice amounts to significantly more than a patent upon the natural law itself. *Flook, supra*, at 594; *see also Bilski v. Kappos*, 561 U.S. 593, at

610–11 ("[T]he prohibition against patenting abstract ideas cannot be circumvented by attempting to limit the use of the formula to a particular technological environment or adding insignificant postsolution activity.").

We find that the process claims at issue here do not satisfy these conditions. In particular, the steps in the claimed processes (apart from the natural laws themselves) involve well-understood, routine, conventional activity previously engaged in by researchers in the field. At the same time, upholding the patents would risk disproportionately tying up the use of the underlying natural laws, inhibiting their use in the making of further discoveries.

I

A

The patents before us concern the use of thiopurine drugs in the treatment of autoimmune diseases, such as Crohn's disease and ulcerative colitis. When a patient ingests a thiopurine compound, his body metabolizes the drug, causing metabolites to form in his bloodstream. Because the way in which people metabolize thiopurine compounds varies, the same dose of a thiopurine drug affects different people differently, and it has been difficult for doctors to determine whether for a particular patient a given dose is too high, risking harmful side effects, or too low, and so likely ineffective.

At the time the discoveries embodied in the patents were made, scientists already understood that the levels in a patient's blood of certain metabolites, including, in particular, 6–thioguanine and its nucleotides (6–TG) and 6–methyl–mercaptopurine (6–MMP), were correlated with the likelihood that a particular dosage of a thiopurine drug could cause harm or prove ineffective. But those in the field did not know the precise correlations between metabolite levels and likely harm or ineffectiveness. The patent claims at issue here set forth processes embodying researchers' findings that identified these correlations with some precision.

More specifically, the patents—U.S. Patent No. 6,355,623 and U.S. Patent No. 6,680,302—embody findings that concentrations in a patient's blood of 6–TG or of 6–MMP metabolite beyond a certain level (400 and 7,000 picomoles (pmol) per 8×10^8 red blood cells, respectively) indicate that the dosage is likely too high for the patient, while concentrations in the blood of 6–TG metabolite lower than a certain level (about 230 pmol per 8×10^8 red blood cells) indicate that the dosage is likely too low to be effective.

The patent claims seek to embody this research in a set of processes. Like the Federal Circuit we take as typical claim 1 of the '623 patent, which describes one of the claimed processes as follows:

A method of optimizing therapeutic efficacy for treatment of an immune-mediated gastrointestinal disorder, comprising:

(a) administering a drug providing 6–thioguanine to a subject having said immune-mediated gastrointestinal disorder; and

(b) determining the level of 6–thioguanine in said subject having said immune-mediated gastrointestinal disorder,

wherein the level of 6–thioguanine less than about 230 pmol per 8×10^8 red blood cells indicates a need to increase the amount of said drug subsequently administered to said subject and

wherein the level of 6–thioguanine greater than about 400 pmol per 8×10^8 red blood cells indicates a need to decrease the amount of said drug subsequently administered to said subject.

For present purposes we may assume that the other claims in the patents do not differ significantly from claim 1.

B

12   Respondent, Prometheus Laboratories, Inc., is the sole and exclusive licensee of the '623 and '302 patents. It sells diagnostic tests that embody the processes the patents describe. For some time petitioners, Mayo Clinic Rochester and Mayo Collaborative Services (collectively Mayo), bought and used those tests. But in 2004 Mayo announced that it intended to begin using and selling its own test—a test using somewhat higher metabolite levels to determine toxicity (450 pmol per 8×10^8 for 6–TG and 5,700 pmol per 8×10^8 for 6–MMP). Prometheus then brought this action claiming patent infringement.

13   [The district court found Mayo's test infringing but granted summary judgment for Mayo on the grounds that the claims were not patent eligible. The Federal Circuit reversed, and the Supreme Court granted certiorari.]

II

14   Prometheus' patents set forth laws of nature—namely, relationships between concentrations of certain metabolites in the blood and the likelihood that a dosage of a thiopurine drug will prove ineffective or cause harm. Claim 1, for example, states that if the levels of 6–TG in the blood (of a patient who has taken a dose of a thiopurine drug) exceed about 400 pmol per 8×10^8 red blood cells, then the administered dose is likely to produce toxic side effects. While it takes a human action (the administration of a thiopurine drug) to trigger a manifestation of this relation in a particular person, the relation itself exists in principle apart from any human action. The relation is a consequence of the ways in which thiopurine compounds are metabolized by the body—entirely natural processes. And so a patent that simply describes that relation sets forth a natural law.

15   The question before us is whether the claims do significantly more than simply describe these natural relations. To put the matter more precisely, do the patent claims add *enough* to their statements of the correlations to allow the processes they describe to qualify as patent-eligible processes that *apply* natural laws? We believe that the answer to this question is no.

A

16   If a law of nature is not patentable, then neither is a process reciting a law of nature, unless that process has additional features that provide practical assurance that the process is more than a drafting effort designed to monopolize the law of nature itself. A patent, for example, could not simply recite a law of nature and then add the instruction "apply the law." Einstein, we assume, could not have patented his famous law by claiming a process consisting of simply telling linear accelerator operators to refer to the law to determine how much energy an amount of mass has produced (or vice versa). Nor could Archimedes have secured a patent for his famous principle of flotation by claiming a process consisting of simply telling boat builders to refer to that principle in order to determine whether an object will float.

17   What else is there in the claims before us? The process that each claim recites tells doctors interested in the subject about the correlations that the researchers discovered. In doing so, it recites an "administering" step, a "determining" step, and a "wherein" step. These additional steps are not themselves natural laws but neither are they sufficient to transform the nature of the claim.

18   First, the "administering" step simply refers to the relevant audience, namely, doctors who treat patients with certain diseases with thiopurine drugs. That audience is a pre-existing audience; doctors used thiopurine drugs to treat patients suffering from autoimmune disorders long before anyone asserted these claims. In any event, the "prohibition against patenting abstract ideas cannot be circumvented by attempting to limit the use of the formula to a particular technological environment." *Bilski, supra*, at 610–11.

19   Second, the "wherein" clauses simply tell a doctor about the relevant natural laws, at most adding a suggestion that he should take those laws into account when treating his patient. That is to say, these clauses tell the relevant audience about the laws while trusting them to use those laws appropriately where they are relevant to their decisionmaking (rather like Einstein telling linear accelerator operators about his basic law and then trusting them to use it where relevant).

20   Third, the "determining" step tells the doctor to determine the level of the relevant metabolites in the blood, through whatever process the doctor or the laboratory wishes to use. As the patents state, methods for determining metabolite levels were well known in the art. Indeed, scientists routinely measured metabolites as part of their investigations into the relationships between metabolite levels and efficacy and toxicity of thiopurine compounds. Thus, this step tells doctors to engage

in well-understood, routine, conventional activity previously engaged in by scientists who work in the field. Purely "conventional or obvious" "[pre]-solution activity" is normally not sufficient to transform an unpatentable law of nature into a patent-eligible application of such a law. *Flook*, 437 U.S. at 590.

21   Fourth, to consider the three steps as an ordered combination adds nothing to the laws of nature that is not already present when the steps are considered separately. Anyone who wants to make use of these laws must first administer a thiopurine drug and measure the resulting metabolite concentrations, and so the combination amounts to nothing significantly more than an instruction to doctors to apply the applicable laws when treating their patients.

22   The upshot is that the three steps simply tell doctors to gather data from which they may draw an inference in light of the correlations. To put the matter more succinctly, the claims inform a relevant audience about certain laws of nature; any additional steps consist of well-understood, routine, conventional activity already engaged in by the scientific community; and those steps, when viewed as a whole, add nothing significant beyond the sum of their parts taken separately. For these reasons we believe that the steps are not sufficient to transform unpatentable natural correlations into patentable applications of those regularities.

B

1

23   A more detailed consideration of the controlling precedents reinforces our conclusion. The cases most directly on point are *Diehr* and *Flook*, two cases in which the Court reached opposite conclusions about the patent eligibility of processes that embodied the equivalent of natural laws. The *Diehr* process (held patent eligible) set forth a method for molding raw, uncured rubber into various cured, molded products. The process used a known mathematical equation, the Arrhenius equation, to determine when (depending upon the temperature inside the mold, the time the rubber had been in the mold, and the thickness of the rubber) to open the press. It consisted in effect of the steps of: (1) continuously monitoring the temperature on the inside of the mold, (2) feeding the resulting numbers into a computer, which would use the Arrhenius equation to continuously recalculate the mold-opening time, and (3) configuring the computer so that at the appropriate moment it would signal "a device" to open the press. *Diehr*, 450 U.S. at 177–79.

24   The Court pointed out that the basic mathematical equation, like a law of nature, was not patentable. But it found the overall process patent eligible because of the way the additional steps of the process integrated the equation into the process as a whole. Those steps included "installing rubber in a press, closing the mold, constantly determining the temperature of the mold, constantly recalculating the appropriate cure time through the use of the formula and a digital computer, and automatically opening the press at the proper time." *Id.* at 187. It nowhere suggested

that all these steps, or at least the combination of those steps, were in context obvious, already in use, or purely conventional. And so the patentees did not "seek to pre-empt the use of [the] equation," but sought "only to foreclose from others the use of that equation in conjunction with all of the other steps in their claimed process." *Ibid.* These other steps apparently added to the formula something that in terms of patent law's objectives had significance—they transformed the process into an inventive application of the formula.

25   The process in *Flook* (held not patentable) provided a method for adjusting "alarm limits" in the catalytic conversion of hydrocarbons. Certain operating conditions (such as temperature, pressure, and flow rates), which are continuously monitored during the conversion process, signal inefficiency or danger when they exceed certain "alarm limits." The claimed process amounted to an improved system for updating those alarm limits through the steps of: (1) measuring the current level of the variable, e.g., the temperature; (2) using an apparently novel mathematical algorithm to calculate the current alarm limits; and (3) adjusting the system to reflect the new alarm-limit values. 437 U.S. at 585–87.

26   The Court, as in *Diehr*, pointed out that the basic mathematical equation, like a law of nature, was not patentable. But it characterized the claimed process as doing nothing other than "provid[ing] a[n unpatentable] formula for computing an updated alarm limit." *Id.* at 586. Unlike the process in *Diehr*, it did not "explain how the variables used in the formula were to be selected, nor did the [claim] contain any disclosure relating to chemical processes at work or the means of setting off an alarm or adjusting the alarm limit." *Diehr, supra*, at 192, n.14. And so the other steps in the process did not limit the claim to a particular application. Moreover, "[t]he chemical processes involved in catalytic conversion of hydrocarbons[,] . . . the practice of monitoring the chemical process variables, the use of alarm limits to trigger alarms, the notion that alarm limit values must be recomputed and readjusted, and the use of computers for 'automatic monitoring-alarming'" were all "well known," to the point where, putting the formula to the side, there was no "inventive concept" in the claimed application of the formula. *Flook, supra*, at 594. "[P]ost-solution activity" that is purely "conventional or obvious," the Court wrote, "can[not] transform an unpatentable principle into a patentable process." *Id.* at 589.

27   The claim before us presents a case for patentability that is weaker than the (patent-eligible) claim in *Diehr* and no stronger than the (unpatentable) claim in *Flook*. Beyond picking out the relevant audience, namely, those who administer doses of thiopurine drugs, the claim simply tells doctors to: (1) measure (somehow) the current level of the relevant metabolite, (2) use particular (unpatentable) laws of nature (which the claim sets forth) to calculate the current toxicity/inefficacy limits, and (3) reconsider the drug dosage in light of the law. These instructions add nothing specific to the laws of nature other than what is well-understood, routine, conventional activity, previously engaged in by those in the field. And since they are steps that must be taken in order to apply the laws in question, the effect is simply to

tell doctors to apply the law somehow when treating their patients. The process in *Diehr* was not so characterized; that in *Flook* was characterized in roughly this way.

2

Other cases offer further support for the view that simply appending conventional steps, specified at a high level of generality, to laws of nature, natural phenomena, and abstract ideas cannot make those laws, phenomena, and ideas patentable. This Court has previously discussed in detail an English case, *Neilson*, which involved a patent claim that posed a legal problem very similar to the problem now before us. The patent applicant there asserted a claim

> for the improved application of air to produce heat in fires, forges, and furnaces, where a blowing apparatus is required. [The invention] was to be applied as follows: The blast or current of air produced by the blowing apparatus was to be passed from it into an air-vessel or receptacle made sufficiently strong to endure the blast; and through or from that vessel or receptacle by means of a tube, pipe, or aperture into the fire, the receptacle be kept artificially heated to a considerable temperature by heat externally applied.

Morse, 15 How., at 114–115. The English court concluded that the claimed process did more than simply instruct users to use the principle that hot air promotes ignition better than cold air, since it explained how the principle could be implemented in an inventive way. Baron Parke wrote (for the court):

> It is very difficult to distinguish [Neilson's claim] from the specification of a patent for a principle, and this at first created in the minds of some of the court much difficulty; but after full consideration, we think that the plaintiff does not merely claim a principle, but a machine embodying a principle, and a very valuable one. We think the case must be considered as if the principle being well known, the plaintiff had first invented a mode of applying it by a mechanical apparatus to furnaces; and his invention then consists in this—by interposing a receptacle for heated air between the blowing apparatus and the furnace. In this receptacle he directs the air to be heated by the application of heat externally to the receptacle, and thus he accomplishes the object of applying the blast, which was before of cold air, in a heated state to the furnace.

Neilson v. Harford, Webster's Patent Cases, at 371. Thus, the claimed process included not only a law of nature but also several unconventional steps (such as inserting the receptacle, applying heat to the receptacle externally, and blowing the air into the furnace) that confined the claims to a particular, useful application of the principle.

29   In *Bilski* the Court considered claims covering a process for hedging risks of price changes by, for example, contracting to purchase commodities from sellers at a fixed price, reflecting the desire of sellers to hedge against a drop in prices, while selling commodities to consumers at a fixed price, reflecting the desire of consumers to hedge against a price increase. One claim described the process; another reduced the process to a mathematical formula. 561 U.S. at 599. The Court held that the described "concept of hedging" was "an unpatentable abstract idea." *Id.* at 611. The fact that some of the claims limited hedging to use in commodities and energy markets and specified that "well-known random analysis techniques [could be used] to help establish some of the inputs into the equation" did not undermine this conclusion, for "*Flook* established that limiting an abstract idea to one field of use or adding token postsolution components did not make the concept patentable." *Id.* at 612.

30   Finally, in *Benson* the Court considered the patentability of a mathematical process for converting binary-coded decimal numerals into pure binary numbers on a general purpose digital computer. The claims "purported to cover any use of the claimed method in a general-purpose digital computer of any type." 409 U.S. at 64, 65. The Court recognized that "a novel and useful structure created with the aid of knowledge of scientific truth" might be patentable. *Id.* at 67. But it held that simply implementing a mathematical principle on a physical machine, namely, a computer, was not a patentable application of that principle. For the mathematical formula had "no substantial practical application except in connection with a digital computer." *Benson*, *supra*, at 71. Hence the claim (like the claims before us) was overly broad; it did not differ significantly from a claim that just said "apply the algorithm."

3

31   The Court has repeatedly emphasized this last mentioned concern, a concern that patent law not inhibit further discovery by improperly tying up the future use of laws of nature. Thus, in *Morse* the Court set aside as unpatentable Samuel Morse's general claim for "the use of the motive power of the electric or galvanic current . . . however developed, for making or printing intelligible characters, letters, or signs, at any distances," 15 How. at 86. The Court explained:

> For aught that we now know some future inventor, in the onward march of science, may discover a mode of writing or printing at a distance by means of the electric or galvanic current, without using any part of the process or combination set forth in the plaintiff's specification. His invention may be less complicated—less liable to get out of order—less expensive in construction, and in its operation. But yet if it is covered by this patent the inventor could not use it, nor the public have the benefit of it without the permission of this patentee.

Id. at 113. Similarly, in *Benson* the Court said that the claims before it were "so abstract and sweeping as to cover both known and unknown uses of the [mathematical formula]." 409 U.S. at 67, 68. In *Bilski* the Court pointed out that to allow "petitioners to patent risk hedging would pre-empt use of this approach in all fields." 561 U.S. at 612. And in *Flook* the Court expressed concern that the claimed process was simply "a formula for computing an updated alarm limit," which might "cover a broad range of potential uses." 437 U.S. at 586.

32   These statements reflect the fact that, even though rewarding with patents those who discover new laws of nature and the like might well encourage their discovery, those laws and principles, considered generally, are "the basic tools of scientific and technological work." *Benson, supra*, at 67. And so there is a danger that the grant of patents that tie up their use will inhibit future innovation premised upon them, a danger that becomes acute when a patented process amounts to no more than an instruction to "apply the natural law," or otherwise forecloses more future invention than the underlying discovery could reasonably justify.

33   The laws of nature at issue here are narrow laws that may have limited applications, but the patent claims that embody them nonetheless implicate this concern. They tell a treating doctor to measure metabolite levels and to consider the resulting measurements in light of the statistical relationships they describe. In doing so, they tie up the doctor's subsequent treatment decision whether that treatment does, or does not, change in light of the inference he has drawn using the correlations. And they threaten to inhibit the development of more refined treatment recommendations (like that embodied in Mayo's test) that combine Prometheus' correlations with later discovered features of metabolites, human physiology or individual patient characteristics. The "determining" step too is set forth in highly general language covering all processes that make use of the correlations after measuring metabolites, including later discovered processes that measure metabolite levels in new ways.

34   We need not, and do not, now decide whether were the steps at issue here less conventional, these features of the claims would prove sufficient to invalidate them. For here, as we have said, the steps add nothing of significance to the natural laws themselves. Unlike, say, a typical patent on a new drug or a new way of using an existing drug, the patent claims do not confine their reach to particular applications of those laws. The presence here of the basic underlying concern that these patents tie up too much future use of laws of nature simply reinforces our conclusion that the processes described in the patents are not patent eligible, while eliminating any temptation to depart from case law precedent.

III

35   We have considered several further arguments in support of Prometheus' position. But they do not lead us to adopt a different conclusion. First, the Federal Circuit, in upholding the patent eligibility of the claims before us, relied on this Court's determination that "[t]ransformation and reduction of an article 'to a different state or thing' is the clue to the patentability of a process claim that does not include particular machines." *Benson, supra*, at 70–71. It reasoned that the claimed processes

are therefore patent eligible, since they involve transforming the human body by administering a thiopurine drug and transforming the blood by analyzing it to determine metabolite levels.

36   The first of these transformations, however, is irrelevant. As we have pointed out, the "administering" step simply helps to pick out the group of individuals who are likely interested in applying the law of nature. And the second step could be satisfied without transforming the blood, should science develop a totally different system for determining metabolite levels that did not involve such a transformation. Regardless, in stating that the "machine-or-transformation" test is an *important and useful clue* to patentability, we have neither said nor implied that the test trumps the "law of nature" exclusion. *Bilski*, 561 U.S. at 603. That being so, the test fails here.

37   Second, Prometheus argues that, because the particular laws of nature that its patent claims embody are narrow and specific, the patents should be upheld. Thus, it encourages us to draw distinctions among laws of nature based on whether or not they will interfere significantly with innovation in other fields now or in the future.

38   But the underlying functional concern here is a *relative* one: how much future innovation is foreclosed relative to the contribution of the inventor. A patent upon a narrow law of nature may not inhibit future research as seriously as would a patent upon Einstein's law of relativity, but the creative value of the discovery is also considerably smaller. And, as we have previously pointed out, even a narrow law of nature (such as the one before us) can inhibit future research.

39   In any event, our cases have not distinguished among different laws of nature according to whether or not the principles they embody are sufficiently narrow. And this is understandable. Courts and judges are not institutionally well suited to making the kinds of judgments needed to distinguish among different laws of nature. And so the cases have endorsed a bright-line prohibition against patenting laws of nature, mathematical formulas, and the like, which serves as a somewhat more easily administered proxy for the underlying "building-block" concern.

40   Third, the Government argues that virtually any step beyond a statement of a law of nature itself should transform an unpatentable law of nature into a potentially patentable application sufficient to satisfy § 101's demands. The Government does not necessarily believe that claims that (like the claims before us) extend just minimally beyond a law of nature should receive patents. But in its view, other statutory provisions—those that insist that a claimed process be novel, 35 U.S.C. § 102, that it not be obvious in light of prior art, § 103, and that it be "full[y], clear[ly], concise[ly], and exact[ly]" described, § 112—can perform this screening function. In particular, it argues that these claims likely fail for lack of novelty under § 102.

41   This approach, however, would make the "law of nature" exception to § 101 patentability a dead letter. The approach is therefore not consistent with prior law. The relevant cases rest their holdings upon § 101, not later sections.

42   We recognize that, in evaluating the significance of additional steps, the § 101 patent-eligibility inquiry and, say, the § 102 novelty inquiry might sometimes overlap. But that need not always be so. And to shift the patent-eligibility inquiry entirely to these later sections risks creating significantly greater legal uncertainty, while assuming that those sections can do work that they are not equipped to do.

43   What role would laws of nature, including newly discovered (and "novel") laws of nature, play in the Government's suggested "novelty" inquiry? Intuitively, one would suppose that a newly discovered law of nature is novel. The Government, however, suggests in effect that the novelty of a component law of nature may be disregarded when evaluating the novelty of the whole. But §§ 102 and 103 say nothing about treating laws of nature as if they were part of the prior art when applying those sections. And studiously ignoring all laws of nature when evaluating a patent application under §§ 102 and 103 would make all inventions unpatentable because all inventions can be reduced to underlying principles of nature which, once known, make their implementation obvious.

44   Section 112 requires only a "written description of the invention . . . in such full, clear, concise, and exact terms as to enable any person skilled in the art . . . to make and use the same." It does not focus on the possibility that a law of nature (or its equivalent) that meets these conditions will nonetheless create the kind of risk that underlies the law of nature exception, namely the risk that a patent on the law would significantly impede future innovation.

45   These considerations lead us to decline the Government's invitation to substitute §§ 102, 103, and 112 inquiries for the better established inquiry under § 101.

46   Fourth, Prometheus, supported by several amici, argues that a principle of law denying patent coverage here will interfere significantly with the ability of medical researchers to make valuable discoveries, particularly in the area of diagnostic research. That research, which includes research leading to the discovery of laws of nature, is expensive; it "ha[s] made the United States the world leader in this field"; and it requires protection.

47   Other medical experts, however, argue strongly against a legal rule that would make the present claims patent eligible, invoking policy considerations that point in the opposite direction. The American Medical Association, the American College of Medical Genetics, the American Hospital Association, the American Society of Human Genetics, the Association of American Medical Colleges, the Association for Molecular Pathology, and other medical organizations tell us that if "claims to exclusive rights over the body's natural responses to illness and medical treatment are permitted to stand, the result will be a vast thicket of exclusive rights over the use of critical scientific data that must remain widely available if physicians are to provide sound medical care."

48   We do not find this kind of difference of opinion surprising. Patent protection is, after all, a two-edged sword. On the one hand, the promise of exclusive rights provides monetary incentives that lead to creation, invention, and discovery. On the other hand, that very exclusivity can impede the flow of information that might permit, indeed spur, invention, by, for example, raising the price of using the patented ideas once created, requiring potential users to conduct costly and time-consuming searches of existing patents and pending patent applications, and requiring the negotiation of complex licensing arrangements. At the same time, patent law's general rules must govern inventive activity in many different fields of human endeavor, with the result that the practical effects of rules that reflect a general effort to balance these considerations may differ from one field to another.

49   In consequence, we must hesitate before departing from established general legal rules lest a new protective rule that seems to suit the needs of one field produce unforeseen results in another. And we must recognize the role of Congress in crafting more finely tailored rules where necessary. *Cf.* 35 U.S.C. §§ 161–164 (special rules for plant patents). We need not determine here whether, from a policy perspective, increased protection for discoveries of diagnostic laws of nature is desirable.

50   For these reasons, we conclude that the patent claims at issue here effectively claim the underlying laws of nature themselves. The claims are consequently invalid. And the Federal Circuit's judgment is reversed.

Discussion Questions: *Mayo*

1. *Two-Step Test.* Patent law—and law in general—is full of multi-part tests in which various factors are balanced against one another. For instance, the rules governing whether a particular document constitutes a printed publication are properly described as a multi-part test. It is worth noting, however, that *Mayo* sets forth what is properly understood as a multi-*step* test. The answers to Step 1 and Step 2 of the *Mayo* test are not weighed against one another to arrive at a final result. Rather, a court must proceed sequentially through the two steps of the *Mayo* test. If the claim "passes" the test at *either step*—either because it is not directed to a law of nature, product of nature, or abstract idea at Step 1, or because it contains an inventive concept at Step 2—then the claim is valid under § 101. What kinds of factors seem most relevant at each step?

2. *Pre*-Mayo *Precedents.* Prior to *Bilski* and *Mayo*, the leading precedents on patenting abstract ideas and laws of nature were *Benson, Flook,* and *Diehr*, all of which are discussed at some length in the *Mayo* opinion. If you hadn't read *Mayo* and were examining the law as it stood before 2012, what would you say was the distinction between the cases that led the Supreme Court to hold the claims invalid in *Benson* and *Flook* and valid in *Diehr*? What was it about the invention in *Diehr* that rendered the claim patentable? Is the *Mayo* Court's basis for differentiating these

cases credible? Can you think of anything else that might distinguish *Diehr* from *Benson* and *Flook*? (If you find them challenging to distinguish, you are not alone.)

3. *Searching for an Inventive Concept.* What do you think the Court means by "inventive concept?" Is that meant to be synonymous with "novel and nonobvious," or does the Court intend something else? If the Court means "novel and nonobvious," why didn't it use those words?

In many inventions such as the one in *Mayo*, the natural law or abstract idea is itself the inventive concept. That is, the natural relationship at issue in *Mayo* was completely unknown in the art until the inventors discovered it. Why should this not be enough to make the claim patentable? Why require inventors to develop *two* inventive concepts: the natural law itself, and something besides the natural law?

4. *The Draftsman's Art.* Suppose you were given a chance to redraft the claims in *Mayo* in light of what you now know of the doctrine. Is there a way to redraft the claims to make them patentable? Or is the invention simply unpatentable no matter how the claims are drawn?

5. *Do We Need Patentable Subject Matter Limits?* What is the doctrine of patentable subject matter accomplishing that the doctrines of novelty, nonobviousness, utility, etc. would not? What value is it adding? If your answer is that we should not grant patents on basic building blocks of nature (including laws of nature), why not? Is it improper to grant these types of patents, and if so, why? Would it harm the progress of innovation to grant them, and if so, why?

For instance, suppose someone were able to obtain a patent on a basic scientific law or principle. Would this inhibit the progress of science and technology? Obviously, a patent has no value if it is not exploited commercially. Wouldn't the patent owner have an incentive to license the patented technology as broadly as possible? Under what circumstances might we expect licensing efforts to fail or fall short?

Association for Molecular Pathology v. Myriad Genetics, 569 U.S. 576 (2013)

Justice Clarence Thomas delivered the opinion of the Court.

1   Respondent Myriad Genetics, Inc., discovered the precise location and sequence of two human genes, mutations of which can substantially increase the risks of breast and ovarian cancer. Myriad obtained a number of patents based upon its discovery. This case involves claims from three of them and requires us to resolve whether a naturally occurring segment of deoxyribonucleic acid (DNA) is patent eligible under 35 U.S.C. § 101 by virtue of its isolation from the rest of the human genome. We also address the patent eligibility of synthetically created DNA known as complementary DNA (cDNA), which contains the same protein-coding information found in a segment of natural DNA but omits portions within the DNA segment that

do not code for proteins. For the reasons that follow, we hold that a naturally occurring DNA segment is a product of nature and not patent eligible merely because it has been isolated, but that cDNA is patent eligible because it is not naturally occurring.

I

A

2   The human genome consists of approximately 22,000 genes packed into 23 pairs of chromosomes. Each "cross-bar" in the DNA helix consists of two chemically joined nucleotides. The possible nucleotides are adenine (A), thymine (T), cytosine (C), and guanine (G), each of which binds naturally with another nucleotide: A pairs with T; C pairs with G. Sequences of DNA nucleotides contain the information necessary to create strings of amino acids, which in turn are used in the body to build proteins. Only some DNA nucleotides, however, code for amino acids; these nucleotides are known as "exons." Nucleotides that do not code for amino acids, in contrast, are known as "introns."

3   DNA's informational sequences and the processes that create mRNA, amino acids, and proteins occur naturally within cells. Scientists can, however, extract DNA from cells using well known laboratory methods. These methods allow scientists to isolate specific segments of DNA—for instance, a particular gene or part of a gene— which can then be further studied, manipulated, or used. It is also possible to create DNA synthetically through processes similarly well known in the field of genetics. One such method begins with an mRNA molecule and uses the natural bonding properties of nucleotides to create a new, synthetic DNA molecule. The result is the inverse of the mRNA's inverse image of the original DNA, with one important distinction: Because the natural creation of mRNA involves splicing that removes introns, the synthetic DNA created from mRNA also contains only the exon sequences. This synthetic DNA created in the laboratory from mRNA is known as complementary DNA (cDNA).

B

4   This case involves patents filed by Myriad after it made one such medical breakthrough. Myriad discovered the precise location and sequence of what are now known as the BRCA1 and BRCA2 genes. Mutations in these genes can dramatically increase an individual's risk of developing breast and ovarian cancer.

5   Once it found the location and sequence of the BRCA1 and BRCA2 genes, Myriad sought and obtained a number of patents. [The following claims are representative.] The first claim [of Patent No. 5,747,282] asserts a patent on "[a]n isolated DNA coding for a BRCA1 polypeptide," which has "the amino acid sequence set forth in SEQ ID NO:2." SEQ ID NO:2 sets forth a list of 1,863 amino acids that the typical BRCA1 gene encodes. Put differently, claim 1 asserts a patent claim on the DNA code that tells a cell to produce the string of BRCA1 amino acids listed in SEQ ID NO:2.

6   Claim 2 of the '282 patent operates similarly. It claims "[t]he isolated DNA of claim 1, wherein said DNA has the nucleotide sequence set forth in SEQ ID NO:1." Like SEQ ID NO:2, SEQ ID NO:1 sets forth a long list of data, in this instance the sequence of cDNA that codes for the BRCA1 amino acids listed in claim 1. Importantly, SEQ ID NO:1 lists only the cDNA exons in the BRCA1 gene, rather than a full DNA sequence containing both exons and introns. As a result, the Federal Circuit recognized that claim 2 asserts a patent on the cDNA nucleotide sequence listed in SEQ ID NO:1, which codes for the typical BRCA1 gene.

7   Claim 5 of the '282 patent claims a subset of the data in claim 1. In particular, it claims "[a]n isolated DNA having at least 15 nucleotides of the DNA of claim 1." The practical effect of claim 5 is to assert a patent on any series of 15 nucleotides that exist in the typical BRCA1 gene. Because the BRCA1 gene is thousands of nucleotides long, even BRCA1 genes with substantial mutations are likely to contain at least one segment of 15 nucleotides that correspond to the typical BRCA1 gene.

II

A

8   We have "long held that [§ 101] contains an important implicit exception: Laws of nature, natural phenomena, and abstract ideas are not patentable." *Mayo v. Prometheus*, 566 U.S. 66, 70 (2012). As the Court has explained, without this exception, there would be considerable danger that the grant of patents would "tie up" the use of such tools and thereby "inhibit future innovation premised upon them." *Id.* at 86. The rule against patents on naturally occurring things is not without limits, however, for "all inventions at some level embody, use, reflect, rest upon, or apply laws of nature, natural phenomena, or abstract ideas," and "too broad an interpretation of this exclusionary principle could eviscerate patent law." *Id.* at 71. As we have recognized before, patent protection strikes a delicate balance between creating "incentives that lead to creation, invention, and discovery" and "impeding the flow of information that might permit, indeed spur, invention." *Id.* at 92.

B

9   It is undisputed that Myriad did not create or alter any of the genetic information encoded in the BRCA1 and BRCA2 genes. The location and order of the nucleotides existed in nature before Myriad found them. Nor did Myriad create or alter the genetic structure of DNA. Instead, Myriad's principal contribution was uncovering the precise location and genetic sequence of the BRCA1 and BRCA2 genes within chromosomes 17 and 13. The question is whether this renders the genes patentable.

10   Myriad recognizes that our decision in *Diamond v. Chakrabarty* is central to this inquiry. In *Chakrabarty,* scientists added four plasmids to a bacterium, which enabled it to break down various components of crude oil. 447 U.S. 303, 305 & n.1 (1980). The Court held that the modified bacterium was patentable. It explained that

the patent claim was "not to a hitherto unknown natural phenomenon, but to a nonnaturally occurring manufacture or composition of matter—a product of human ingenuity having a distinctive name, character [and] use." *Id.* at 309–10. The *Chakrabarty* bacterium was new "with markedly different characteristics from any found in nature" due to the additional plasmids and resultant "capacity for degrading oil." *Id.* at 305 n.1, 310. In this case, by contrast, Myriad did not create anything. To be sure, it found an important and useful gene, but separating that gene from its surrounding genetic material is not an act of invention.

11   Groundbreaking, innovative, or even brilliant discovery does not by itself satisfy the § 101 inquiry. In *Funk Brothers Seed Co. v. Kalo Inoculant Co.,* 333 U.S. 127 (1948), this Court considered a composition patent that claimed a mixture of naturally occurring strains of bacteria that helped leguminous plants take nitrogen from the air and fix it in the soil. The Court held that the composition was not patent eligible because the patent holder did not alter the bacteria in any way. His patent claim thus fell squarely within the law of nature exception. So do Myriad's. Myriad found the location of the BRCA1 and BRCA2 genes, but that discovery, by itself, does not render the BRCA genes "new . . . composition[s] of matter," § 101, that are patent eligible.

12   Indeed, Myriad's patent descriptions highlight the problem with its claims. For example, a section of the '282 patent's Detailed Description of the Invention indicates that Myriad found the location of a gene associated with increased risk of breast cancer and identified mutations of that gene that increase the risk. In subsequent language Myriad explains that the location of the gene was unknown until Myriad found it among the approximately eight million nucleotide pairs contained in a subpart of chromosome 17. Myriad seeks to import these extensive research efforts into the § 101 patent-eligibility inquiry. But extensive effort alone is insufficient to satisfy the demands of § 101.

13   Nor are Myriad's claims saved by the fact that isolating DNA from the human genome severs chemical bonds and thereby creates a nonnaturally occurring molecule. Myriad's claims are simply not expressed in terms of chemical composition, nor do they rely in any way on the chemical changes that result from the isolation of a particular section of DNA. Instead, the claims understandably focus on the genetic information encoded in the BRCA1 and BRCA2 genes. If the patents depended upon the creation of a unique molecule, then a would-be infringer could arguably avoid at least Myriad's patent claims on entire genes (such as claims 1 and 2 of the '282 patent) by isolating a DNA sequence that included both the BRCA1 or BRCA2 gene and one additional nucleotide pair. Such a molecule would not be chemically identical to the molecule "invented" by Myriad. But Myriad obviously would resist that outcome because its claim is concerned primarily with the information contained in the genetic *sequence,* not with the specific chemical composition of a particular molecule.

14   Finally, Myriad argues that the PTO's past practice of awarding gene patents is entitled to deference, citing *J.E.M. Ag Supply, Inc. v. Pioneer Hi–Bred Int'l, Inc.,* 534 U.S. 124 (2001). We disagree. Undercutting the PTO's practice, the United States argued in the Federal Circuit and in this Court that isolated DNA was *not* patent eligible under § 101 and that the PTO's practice was not "a sufficient reason to hold that isolated DNA is patent-eligible." These concessions weigh against deferring to the PTO's determination.[2]

C

15   cDNA does not present the same obstacles to patentability as naturally occurring, isolated DNA segments. As already explained, creation of a cDNA sequence from mRNA results in an exons-only molecule that is not naturally occurring.[3] Petitioners concede that cDNA differs from natural DNA in that "the non-coding regions have been removed." They nevertheless argue that cDNA is not patent eligible because "[t]he nucleotide sequence of cDNA is dictated by nature, not by the lab technician." That may be so, but the lab technician unquestionably creates something new when cDNA is made. cDNA retains the naturally occurring exons of DNA, but it is distinct from the DNA from which it was derived. As a result, cDNA is not a "product of nature" and is patent eligible under § 101, except insofar as very short series of DNA may have no intervening introns to remove when creating cDNA. In that situation, a short strand of cDNA may be indistinguishable from natural DNA.

III

16   It is important to note what is *not* implicated by this decision. First, there are no method claims before this Court. Had Myriad created an innovative method of manipulating genes while searching for the BRCA1 and BRCA2 genes, it could possibly have sought a method patent. But the processes used by Myriad to isolate DNA were well understood by geneticists at the time of Myriad's patents and are not at issue in this case.

17   Similarly, this case does not involve patents on new *applications* of knowledge about the BRCA1 and BRCA2 genes. Nor do we consider the patentability of DNA in

---

[2] [n.7 in opinion] Myriad also argues that we should uphold its patents so as not to disturb the reliance interests of patent holders like itself. Concerns about reliance interests arising from PTO determinations, insofar as they are relevant, are better directed to Congress.

[3] [n.8 in opinion] Some viruses rely on an enzyme called reverse transcriptase to reproduce by copying RNA into cDNA. In rare instances, a side effect of a viral infection of a cell can be the random incorporation of fragments of the resulting cDNA, known as a pseudogene, into the genome. Such pseudogenes serve no purpose; they are not expressed in protein creation because they lack genetic sequences to direct protein expression. Perhaps not surprisingly, given pseudogenes' apparently random origins, petitioners have failed to demonstrate that the pseudogene consists of the same sequence as the BRCA1 cDNA. The possibility that an unusual and rare phenomenon *might* randomly create a molecule similar to one created synthetically through human ingenuity does not render a composition of matter nonpatentable.

which the order of the naturally occurring nucleotides has been altered. Scientific alteration of the genetic code presents a different inquiry, and we express no opinion about the application of § 101 to such endeavors. We merely hold that genes and the information they encode are not patent eligible under § 101 simply because they have been isolated from the surrounding genetic material.

Justice Antonin Scalia, concurring in part and concurring in the judgment.

18   I join the judgment of the Court, and all of its opinion except Part I–A and some portions of the rest of the opinion going into fine details of molecular biology. I am unable to affirm those details on my own knowledge or even my own belief. It suffices for me to affirm, having studied the opinions below and the expert briefs presented here, that the portion of DNA isolated from its natural state sought to be patented is identical to that portion of the DNA in its natural state; and that complementary DNA (cDNA) is a synthetic creation not normally present in nature.

Discussion Questions: *Myriad*

1. *What Distinguishes cDNA?* Why does the Court hold that cDNA strands are patentable and isolated DNA strands are not? In what way or ways are those two products different? Do they perform different functions? Which of them, if either, is different from what appears in nature? Are they different structurally from each other, and if so, in what way?

What is the distinction between the mixture of bacteria found unpatentable in *Funk Brothers* and the cDNA found patentable in *Myriad*? Why couldn't the cDNA be characterized as a mixture or rearrangement of existing natural substances (the base pairs) and held unpatentable on those grounds?

Look back at footnote 8, which indicates that viruses can create cDNA strands in nature. In that footnote, the Court notes that it is only a "possibility" that the relevant cDNA strand was created in nature by a virus at some point. Suppose it could be proven that a virus randomly created the BRCA cDNA strand once, in a small town in Nevada, at 6:34 pm on a Friday in October. Should that affect the patentability of the invention? What if it could be shown that a virus regularly created the BRCA cDNA strand?

2. *Should Generalist Judges Decide Technical Patent Cases?* Justice Scalia's concurrence in *Myriad* involves the problems faced by generalist judges (and justices) in adjudicating patent cases. What should we make of that concurrence? Do we think the problem Justice Scalia describes will be more acute in patentable subject matter cases than in other types of patent cases? Is this a reason to rethink our approach to judging patent cases?

3. *Do Patentee Reliance Interests Matter?* One argument that Myriad made in defense of its patents was that it had relied upon the patentability of DNA molecules when constructing its business. As we noted above, DNA had been patentable for many years prior to the *Myriad* decision. Do these reliance interests constitute a good argument in favor of leaving the law as it is? Under what circumstances should reliance interests such as these play a role in judicial decision-making, if at all? *See* Jonathan S. Masur & Adam K. Mortara, *Patents, Property, and Prospectivity*, 71 Stan. L. Rev. 963 (2019).

4. *Are Products of Nature Different from Laws of Nature?* Are the doctrinal rules that the Supreme Court laid down to govern products of nature (in *Myriad*) and the rules that it laid down to govern laws of nature (in *Mayo*) the same or different? If they appear to be different, can you devise a way to unify them? In *Alice v. CLS Bank*, which we will read in the next section, the Supreme Court states that the two-step *Mayo/Alice* test is now *the* test for evaluating all patentable subject matter issues. Why do you think the Court didn't apply this test in *Myriad*?

5. Myriad*'s Impact on Innovation.* There have been few evidence-based studies before or after *Myriad* on the impact of patents on DNA-related research, largely because researchers cannot observe the counterfactual world in which patent eligibility rules were different. Even before *Myriad*, the number of gene patents granted each year was declining since a peak in 1999, including because the 1990 Human Genome Project led to the sequencing of most genes by the early 2000s. Although researchers have not been able to determine whether the prospect of gene patents (or the absence of that incentive post-*Myriad*) caused any measurable change in R&D, they have used pre-*Myriad* data to study the effect of *existing* gene patents on *follow-on* innovation on those genes, including scientific publications and the use of genes in pharmaceutical clinical trials and diagnostic tests. Using a clever empirical design to identify the causal effect of patents, Bhaven Sampat and Heidi Williams determined that "gene patents have had no quantitatively important effect on follow-on innovation." Bhaven Sampat & Heidi L. Williams, *How Do Patents Affect Follow-on Innovation? Evidence from the Human Genome*, 109 Am. Econ. Rev. 203 (2019). What does this result make you think of the Supreme Court's view that Myriad's patents "would 'tie up' the use of [genes] and thereby inhibit future innovation"?

6. *The Morality of Patenting Human Genes and Biological Samples.* Are there special concerns raised by the fact that Myriad was seeking to patent part of the human genome? Was there a risk that Myriad might sue people who had the BRCA gene in their own bodies? Is it problematic for Myriad to "own" the rights to the basic building blocks of human genetics? Do you think these concerns figured into the Supreme Court's decision, or should they have? If your answer to either of these last questions is "yes," do you think the Court's decision to allow only the cDNA patents effectively solves the problem?

Are similar concerns raised with patents derived from biological samples? *The Immortal Life of Henrietta Lacks*, a best-selling book with a film adaptation by Oprah Winfrey, tells the history of Henrietta Lacks, a Black woman whose cancer cells were cultured without her knowledge or consent in 1951, shortly before her death. The resulting HeLa cell line is still used for medical research, and although the cells themselves were not patented, there are thousands of U.S. patents involving HeLa cells. Should an invention's origins in biological samples affect its patentability? Should people who provide valuable genetic resources receive any IP rights in those resources or other forms of compensation?

Nat. Alternatives Int'l v. Creative Compounds, 918 F.3d 1338 (Fed. Cir. 2019)

Kimberly A. Moore, Circuit Judge.

BACKGROUND

Natural Alternatives owns a number of patents that relate to dietary supplements containing beta-alanine and have substantially similar specifications. Beta-alanine is an amino acid [i.e., one of 20 naturally occurring building blocks of proteins encoded by DNA]. Together with histidine, another amino acid, it can form dipeptides [two linked amino acids] that are found in muscles. The dipeptides are involved in the regulation of intra-cellular pH during muscle contraction and development of fatigue, and variations in dipeptide concentrations affect the anaerobic work capacity of individual athletes [i.e., how much intense exercise athletes can do without getting oxygen to their cells]. One of these dipeptides is carnosine, which contributes to hydronium ion buffering. During certain sustained exercise, hydronium ions and lactate can accumulate and severely reduce intracellular pH. The reduced pH interferes with the creatine-phosphorylcreatine system, a part of the process by which energy is generated in cells, particularly muscle cells. The claimed patents generally relate to the use of beta-alanine in a dietary supplement to increase the anaerobic working capacity of muscle and other tissue. [Eds: It is not necessary to understand the details of biochemistry to understand this case; the key point is simply that the inventors discovered that taking beta-alanine as a dietary supplement improves athletic performance.]

I.

Several of the asserted patents claim methods of treatment using beta-alanine ("the Method Claims"). Claim 1 of the '596 patent and claim 1 of the '865 patent have been treated as representative of the claims in those patents. Claim 1 of the '596 patent recites:

> 1. A method of regulating hydronium ion concentrations in a human tissue comprising:

providing an amount of beta-alanine to blood or blood plasma *effective to increase beta-alanylhistidine dipeptide synthesis in the human tissue*; and

exposing the tissue to the blood or blood plasma, whereby the concentration of beta-alanylhistidine is increased in the human tissue.

3   Claim 1 of the '865 patent recites:

1. A method of increasing anaerobic working capacity in a human subject, the method comprising:

a) providing to the human subject an amount of an amino acid to blood or blood plasma *effective to increase beta-alanylhistidine dipeptide synthesis* in the tissue, wherein said amino acid is at least one of:

    i) beta-alanine that is not part of a dipeptide, polypeptide or oligopeptide;

    ii) an ester of beta-alanine that is not part of a dipeptide, polypeptide or oligopeptide; or

    iii) an amide of beta-alanine that is not part of a dipeptide, polypeptide or oligopeptide; and

b) exposing the tissue to the blood or blood plasma, whereby the concentration of beta-alanylhistidine is increased in the tissue,

wherein the amino acid is provided through a *dietary supplement*.

4   Natural Alternatives' proposed construction of the "effective" limitations is to "elevates beta-alanine above natural levels to cause an increase in the synthesis of beta-alanylhistidine dipeptide in the tissue." It defines "dietary supplement" as "an addition to the human diet, which is not a natural or conventional food, which effectively increases athletic performance when administered to the human over a period of time." It also defines "increasing anaerobic working capacity" as "increasing the amount of work performed by a muscle under lactate producing conditions."

5   The district court held both claims are directed to natural laws. It held claim 1 of the '865 patent is directed to the natural law that "ingesting certain levels of beta-alanine, a natural substance, will increase the carnosine concentration in human tissue and, thereby, increase the anaerobic working capacity in a human." It held claim 1 of the '596 patent is directed to the natural law that "ingesting certain levels of beta-alanine, a natural substance, will increase the carnosine concentration in human tissue and, thereby, aid in regulating hydronium ion concentration in the tissue." We do not agree.

6   Administering certain quantities of beta-alanine to a human subject alters that subject's natural state. Specifically, homeostasis is overcome, and the subject's body will produce greater levels of creatine. This, in turn, results in specific physiological benefits for athletes engaged in certain intensive exercise. The claims not only embody this discovery, they require that an infringer actually administer the dosage form claimed in the manner claimed, altering the athlete's physiology to provide the described benefits. These are treatment claims and as such they are patent eligible.

7   As we explained in *Vanda Pharmaceuticals Inc. v. West-Ward Pharmaceuticals International Ltd.*, 887 F.3d 1117 (Fed. Cir. 2018), claims that are directed to particular methods of treatment are patent eligible. The claims in *Vanda* involved a method of treating patients with schizophrenia that first required performing a genetic test to determine if a patient was a CYPD2D6 performer. Based on the results of that test, a particular dose of iloperidone was selected and internally administered. As a result, the risk of QTc prolongation, a dangerous side effect, was decreased. We held that the claims were not directed to a natural relationship between iloperidone, CYP2D6 metabolism, and QTc prolongation. While we acknowledged that the inventors had recognized the underlying relationships, we explained that those were not what was claimed. Instead, the claims were directed to a patent-eligible method of using iloperidone to treat schizophrenia, a specific method of treatment for specific patients using a specific compound at specific doses to achieve a specific outcome.

8   Unlike the claims held ineligible in *Mayo*, which required only the observation of a natural law, the *Vanda* claims required a doctor to affirmatively administer a drug to alter a patient's condition from their natural state. In *Mayo*, the discovery underlying the claims was that when blood levels were above a certain level harmful effects were more likely and when they were below another level the drug's beneficial effects were lost. Nothing in the claim required any application of that discovery beyond the steps that must be taken in order to apply the laws in question. The claims at issue in *Mayo* involved administering a prior art drug to a subject and determining the level of drug metabolite in that subject. The claims further provided that particular levels of measured metabolite indicated a need to increase or decrease the amount of drug subsequently administered to the subject. The claims did not, however, require any actual action be taken based on the measured level of metabolite. The claim, therefore, "was not a treatment claim," because "it was not limited to instances in which the doctor actually decreases (or increases) the dosage level." *Vanda*, 887 F.3d at 1136. This was expressly recognized in *Mayo*, which distinguished the *Mayo* claim from "a typical patent on a new drug or a *new way of using an existing drug*," because the *Mayo* claim did not "confine [its] reach to particular applications" of the natural laws relied upon. 566 U.S. at 87 (emphasis added). Such claims rely on the relationship between the administration of the drug and the physiological effects in the patient. The fact that the human body responds to the treatment through biochemical processes does not convert the claim into an ineligible one.

9   The Method Claims are directed to patent eligible new ways of using an existing product, beta-alanine, [and] they are treatment claims. This falls clearly within the scope of § 101, which allows for patents on "any new and useful process," including "a new use of a known . . . composition of matter, or material." 35 U.S.C. §§ 100(b), 101. As the Supreme Court explained in *Mayo*, such patents on a new use of an existing drug are "typical." 566 U.S. at 87.

10   While the Method Claims have similarities to the claims found ineligible in *Mayo*, as they utilize an underlying natural law, this is not sufficient to establish that they are directed to that law. In *Mayo*, the Court held the claims did not do significantly more than simply describe the natural "relationships between concentrations of certain metabolites in the blood and the likelihood that a dosage of a thiopurine drug will prove ineffective or cause harm." The Method Claims similarly rely on the relationships between the administration of beta-alanine and beta-alanylhistidine dipeptide synthesis, but under Natural Alternatives' constructions, the Method Claims require specific steps be taken in order to bring about a change in a subject, altering the subject's natural state. Unlike the claims in *Mayo*, the Method Claims at issue are treatment claims.

11   Like the claims in *Vanda*, the Method Claims contain specific elements that clearly establish they are doing more than simply reciting a natural law. Like the *Vanda* claims, which specify a patient population to be treated, the Method Claims specify particular results to be obtained by practicing the method. Claim 1 of the '596 patent is directed to a "method of regulating hydronium ion concentrations in a human tissue," and claim 1 of the '865 patent is directed to a "method of increasing anaerobic working capacity in a human subject." Similarly, both the *Vanda* claims and the Method Claims specify a compound to be administered to achieve the claimed result. Claim 1 of the '596 patent achieves the result through the administration of the specific compound beta-alanine, and claim 1 of the '865 patent requires use of one of the three specified forms of beta-alanine. The claims in *Vanda* further specified the dosages of the compound to be administered. The Method Claims likewise contain a dosage limitation by virtue of the "effective" limitation. As we looked to the specification in *Vanda* to determine the significance of the dosing ranges, here, the specification provides a method for calculating dosage based on a subject's weight. This goes far beyond merely stating a law of nature, and instead sets forth a particular method of treatment.

12   Similarly, the fact that the active ingredient in the supplement is a molecule that occurs in nature and is consumed as part of the human diet also does not alter our analysis.[4] Creative Compounds argues that, if it were discovered that beta-alanine

_____

[4] [n.2 in opinion] The U.S. Patent and Trademark Office has adopted guidance on how examiners should determine whether a claim is eligible under § 101 and provided examples of eligible and ineligible claims. Under these guidelines, a claim to a practical application of a natural product to treat a particular disease is patent eligible. The parties dispute the persuasiveness of this document and the weight we should afford it under *Skidmore v. Swift*

or another natural compound can be used to treat or cure Alzheimer's or some other disease, the method for doing so would not be patent eligible. That is not the case before us. That flies in the face of the Patent Act, which expressly permits patenting a new use of an existing product. The Supreme Court has also rejected the idea that claims to methods making use of natural products are equivalent to claims to the natural products themselves. *See Ass'n for Molecular Pathology v. Myriad Genetics, Inc.*, 569 U.S. 576, 595 (2013) (distinguishing between method claims for manipulating genes and claims to the genes); *Funk Brothers Seed Co. v. Kalo Inoculant Co.*, 333 U.S. 127, 130 (1948) ("We do not have presented the question whether the methods of selecting and testing the non-inhibitive strains are patentable. We have here only product claims."). Moreover, while beta-alanine may exist in nature, Natural Alternatives has argued that the quantities being administered do not, and that the claimed consumption greatly exceeds natural levels.

13   The Method Claims at issue are treatment claims. They cover using a natural product in unnatural quantities to alter a patient's natural state, to treat a patient with specific dosages outlined in the patents. We hold, therefore, that the Method Claims are not directed to ineligible subject matter.

II.

14   The district court also considered the patent eligibility of a number of claims to dietary supplements ("the Product Claims"). The parties and the district court treated claim 6 of the '376 patent and claim 1 of the '084 patent as representative of the claims in those patents. Claim 6 of the '376 patent depends on claims 1 and 5.

15   Turning to the Product Claims before us, claim 6 of the '376 patent depends on claims 1 and 5.

1. A composition, comprising:

glycine; and

a) an amino acid selected from the group consisting of a beta-alanine, an ester of a beta-alanine, and an amide of a beta-alanine, or

b) a di-peptide selected from the group consisting of a beta-alanine di-peptide and a beta-alanylhistidine di-peptide.

5. The composition of claim 1, wherein the composition is a dietary supplement or a sports drink.

& Co., 323 U.S. 134 (1944). The issue before us is a matter of law and the result is clear, thus this is not a case in which *Skidmore* deference would affect the outcome.

6. The composition of claim 5, wherein the *dietary supplement* or sports drink is a supplement for humans.

16   Claim 1 of the '084 patent recites:

1. A human *dietary supplement*, comprising a beta-alanine in a unit dosage of between about *0.4 grams to 16 grams*, wherein the supplement provides a unit dosage of beta-alanine.

17   Although beta-alanine is a natural product, the Product Claims are not directed to beta-alanine. A claim to a manufacture or composition of matter made from a natural product is not directed to the natural product where it has different characteristics and "the potential for significant utility." *See Diamond v. Chakrabarty*, 447 U.S. 303, 310 (1980). Just as the Method Claims are directed to specific methods of treatment that employ a natural law, the Product Claims are directed to specific treatment formulations that incorporate natural products, but they have different characteristics and can be used in a manner that beta-alanine as it appears in nature cannot.

18   In the Product Claims, beta-alanine and glycine are incorporated into particular dosage forms. Claim 6 of the '376 patent is directed to a "dietary supplement or sports drink" that uses a combination of glycine and one of the specified forms of beta-alanine. Under Natural Alternatives' claim constructions, the quantity of beta-alanine must be sufficient to "effectively increase[] athletic performance," and the specification provides a method for determining such an amount. Similarly, the "dietary supplement" in claim 1 of the '084 patent uses the product beta-alanine at a dosage of "between about 0.4 grams to 16 grams" to "effectively increase[] athletic performance." In each case, the natural products have been isolated and then incorporated into a dosage form with particular characteristics. At this stage in the litigation, it has been sufficiently alleged that these characteristics provide significant utility, as the claimed dosage forms can be used to increase athletic performance in a way that naturally occurring beta-alanine cannot. Accordingly, neither claim is directed to ineligible subject matter.

19   Moreover, even though claim 6 contains a combination of glycine and beta-alanine, both of which are natural products, that is not necessarily sufficient to establish that the claimed combination is "directed to" ineligible subject matter. The Court's decision in *Funk Brothers* does not stand for the proposition that any combination of ineligible subject matter is itself ineligible. In *Funk Brothers*, the Court held that claims to a mixture of two naturally occurring bacteria were not patent eligible where each bacteria species in the claimed combination "ha[d] the same effect it always had," and the "combination of species produce[d] . . . no enlargement of the range of their utility." 333 U.S. at 131. The combination of the bacteria into the same package did "not improve in any way their natural function." Here, as Creative Compounds' counsel acknowledged at oral argument, the record indicates that the claimed combination of glycine and beta-alanine could have synergistic effects

allowing for outcomes that the individual components could not have. Given that this is the pleading stage, we would have to accept this statement as true even if it were just an allegation in the pleadings. Instead, what we have goes far beyond that, including a statement in an article attached to an expert report explaining that "one of insulin's effects is to increase amino acid (such as beta-alanine) into our cells," a statement in the specification that "[i]t may be that glycine enhances insulin sensitivity," and an expert declaration explaining that direct supplementation of a different amino acid had no effect unless "co-supplemented with glucose or other compounds increasing the concentration of insulin in circulation." All of these suggest that when combined the beta-alanine and glycine have effects that are greater than the sum of the parts. At a minimum, there are sufficient factual allegations to render judgment on the pleadings inappropriate. Accordingly, given the factual allegations, these claims would still survive a motion for judgment on the pleadings at the first step of the *Alice* test.

20   Finally, even if the Product Claims were directed to ineligible subject matter, judgment on the pleadings would still be inappropriate under step two. Like claim 1 of the '865 patent, the Product Claims contain a dietary supplement limitation, with the same proposed construction. As we explained with regard to the Method Claims, the specification does not contain language supporting the idea that this limitation was well-understood, routine, and conventional. The language in the specification does not support this proposition, and patentee's claim construction contradicts Creative Compounds' position, so such a determination may not be made on a motion for judgment on the pleadings.

Discussion Questions: *Natural Alternatives*

1. *Diagnostics Versus Treatments*. The Federal Circuit's holding on the method claims in *Natural Alternatives* rests quite heavily on the distinction the court draws between diagnostic methods (which are not patentable) and treatment methods (which are patentable). The court first drew this distinction in *Vanda Pharmaceuticals*, which is cited heavily in *Natural Alternatives*. *Vanda* is a highly complex case about a pharmaceutical drug; *Natural Alternatives*, the case we chose to include in this book, is about a sports drink. What can we say, except: you're welcome. Do you think this line between diagnostics and treatments is tenable? Is there anything in the *Mayo* opinion that would support or undermine the Federal Circuit's rule that treatments are patentable and diagnostics are not? What if the claim is to a new diagnostic followed by an old treatment, where the treatment dosage and other details aren't adjusted in light of the diagnostic?

Relatedly, do you think the *Mayo* patent was properly classified by the Federal Circuit as a diagnostic patent? The dissent in *Vanda* criticized the characterization of the *Mayo* invention as a diagnostic because the representative claim was to "[a] method of optimizing therapeutic efficacy for treatment of an immune-mediated gastrointestinal disorder" that included "administering a drug" to a patient with this disorder. The *Vanda* majority responded that the *Mayo* claim was not a treatment claim because "a doctor . . . could violate the patent even if he did not actually alter his treatment decision in the light of the test" such that the claim would "tie up the doctor's subsequent treatment decision whether that treatment does, or does not, change in light of the inference he has drawn using the correlations." The *Mayo* court also noted that "unlike, say, a typical patent on a new drug or a new way of using an existing drug, the patent claims do not confine their reach to particular applications of those laws." Which view do you find more convincing as a legal matter? As a policy matter?

2. *What About* Myriad? In *Natural Alternatives*, the Federal Circuit cites the earlier Supreme Court cases *Chakrabarty* and *Funk Brothers* but does not cite *Myriad* in its discussion of the product claims. Why do you think that is? Is that approach justified? Is the court's result consistent with *Myriad*?

Applying the Two-Step Test to "Nature" Claims: MPEP § 2106

The Supreme Court first announced the two-step test for patentable subject matter in 2012 in *Mayo*: (1) Is the claim directed to an ineligible concept? (2) If so, what else is there? Is there an inventive concept that amounts to significantly more than a patent on the ineligible concept? Needless to say, that left a great deal of prior Supreme Court caselaw on patentable subject matter that had been decided using other tests. The following table illustrates how the Supreme Court has attempted to retrofit its earlier patentable subject matter (PSM) precedents (including abstract ideas, laws of nature, and products of nature) into this new two-step test. (Please note that we are only describing how the Supreme Court has characterized these old cases, not endorsing it.)

Case	1. Ineligible concept?	2. What else?	PSM?
Neilson (Eng. 1841)	hot air promotes ignition better than cold air	unconventional steps implemented in inventive way	YES
Funk Bros. (1948)	mixture of naturally occurring bacteria	nothing; combination did not improve natural function	NO
Benson (1972)	binary-to-digital conversion	implemented on a computer, but that is only practical use	NO
Flook (1978)	new formula for alarm limits in chemical reaction	well known chemical process & use of computers	NO

Chakrabarty (1980)	NO (genetically modified bacterium is not natural)	N/A	YES
Diehr (1981)	Arrhenius equation (already known)	novel rubber curing apparatus	YES
Bilski (2010)	risk hedging	limited to a few markets	NO
Mayo (2012)	relationship between metabolite concentrations & thiopurine dose	conventional "administering" and "determining" steps	NO
Myriad (2013) isolated DNA	isolated DNA is a product of nature	nothing; claim is to natural product itself	NO
Myriad (2013) cDNA	NO (synthetic cDNA is not natural)	N/A	YES

As the Supreme Court noted in *Mayo*, "all inventions at some level embody, use, reflect, rest upon, or apply laws of nature, natural phenomena, or abstract ideas." Even a claim to a standard spring-loaded mousetrap could be characterized as directed to the abstract idea of catching mice, or the natural laws involving the physics of springs and mechanical forces. But the Court recognized that "too broad an interpretation of this exclusionary principle could eviscerate patent law." Given the malleability of the two-step test, we think patent lawyers should always at least consider whether a claim is patentable subject matter. And figuring out whether a claim is more analogous to those that have survived the *Mayo* test or those that have failed requires some creativity and good lawyering.

The difficulties of applying this complicated framework led to widespread complaints about inconsistency in USPTO examination decisions involving patentable subject matter. To help patent examiners apply this doctrine, the USPTO has issued extensive guidance to examiners. Although the Federal Circuit has not yet granted any deference to the USPTO's interpretation of substantive patent law, this guidance is a useful resource for students looking for more examples of how the USPTO explains Federal Circuit caselaw to non-lawyer patent examiners. As you read the following MPEP excerpts, consider whether they are a faithful summary of current law.

The USPTO has divided *Mayo* Step 1 into two prongs: a claim is only "directed to" an ineligible concept if it (1) "recites" an ineligible concept (as opposed to merely "involving" an exception) and (2) fails to integrate that concept into a "practical application." MPEP § 2106.04 explains the *recite* vs. *involve* distinction as follows:

An example of a claim that recites a judicial exception is "A machine comprising elements that operate in accordance with F = ma." This claim sets forth the principle that force equals mass times acceleration (F = ma) and therefore recites a law of nature exception. Because F = ma represents a mathematical formula, the claim could alternatively be considered as reciting an abstract idea. Because this claim recites a judicial exception, it requires further analysis. An example of a claim that merely involves, or is based on, an exception is a claim to "A teeter-totter comprising an elongated member pivotably attached to a base member, having seats and handles attached at opposing sides of the elongated member." This claim is based on the concept of a lever pivoting on a fulcrum, which involves the natural principles of mechanical advantage and the law of the lever. However, this claim does not recite these natural principles and therefore is not directed to a judicial exception. Thus, the claim is eligible without further analysis.

The USPTO then explains the application of this *Mayo* Step 1 test to "nature" claims:

> [N]ot every claim describing a natural ability or quality of a product, or describing a natural process, necessarily recites a law of nature or natural phenomenon. Thus, in a claimed method of treating cancer with chemotherapy, the cancer cells' inability to survive chemotherapy is not considered to be a law of nature. Similarly, in a claimed method of treating headaches with aspirin, the human body's natural response to aspirin is not considered to be a law of nature. These claims are accordingly eligible unless they recite another exception. Similarly, a method of producing a new compound is not directed to the individual components' ability to combine to form the new compound.

> Even if a claim does recite a law of nature or natural phenomenon, it may still be eligible. For example, claims reciting a naturally occurring relationship between a patient's genotype and the risk of QTc prolongation (a law of nature) were held eligible as not "directed to" that relationship because they also recited a step of treating the patient with an amount of a particular medication that was tailored to the patient's genotype. *Vanda Pharms.*, 887 F.3d at 1134-36. This particular treatment step applied the natural relationship in a manner that integrated it into a practical application.

The MPEP further emphasizes that for products of nature, the key question at *Mayo* Step 1 is whether the nature-based product limitations in the claim have "markedly different characteristics" from naturally occurring products.

If a claim is directed to an ineligible concept at Step 1, it is necessary to move to Step 2: determining whether the rest of the claim includes an "inventive concept" that adds "significantly more" to the ineligible concept. *Mayo* emphasized that it is not enough to add "well-understood, routine, conventional activity" or to merely tell someone "to apply the law." Merely applying the concept in a particular field of use is also insufficient. Although the USPTO emphasizes that "the search for an inventive concept should not be confused with a novelty or non-obviousness determination," there are overlaps: if what remains after removing the ineligible concept from the claim is nonobvious, then it likely passes Step 2.

Practice Problems: Laws of Nature and Products of Nature

Consider the following claims. Do you think these claims involve patentable subject matter? If you will need more technical information to answer the question, explain what information you will need.

1. The patented invention is a method for detecting genetic abnormalities in a fetus. Prior to the invention of this method, the only known way of obtaining a genetic sample from a fetus was to draw amniotic fluid directly from the pregnant person's uterus, in a method known as amniocentesis. This method was considered dangerous because it involved poking a long needle into the pregnant person's uterus, near the fetus. The key to this invention was the groundbreaking discovery that some of the fetus's nucleic acid circulates in the bloodstream of the pregnant person (known as cell-free fetal DNA). A doctor could thus draw blood from the pregnant person, separate out and amplify the fetus's DNA using conventional methods, and run genetic tests on the fetus's DNA. The claim reads:

> A method for detecting a paternally inherited nucleic acid of fetal origin performed on a maternal serum or plasma sample from a pregnant female, which method comprises amplifying a paternally inherited nucleic acid from the serum or plasma sample and detecting the presence of a paternally inherited nucleic acid of fetal origin in the sample.

Ariosa Diagnostics v. Sequenom, 788 F.3d 1371 (Fed Cir 2015).

2. The invention is a method of repeatedly freezing liver cells (hepatocytes) in such a manner that they can be unfrozen and then used for transplant or other medical purposes. The individual steps of freezing and thawing were known, but prior to this invention, scientists had believed that liver cells could not survive multiple freeze-thaw cycles. The claim reads:

> A method of producing a desired preparation of multi-cryopreserved hepatocytes, said hepatocytes being capable of being frozen and thawed at least two times, and in which greater than 70% of the hepatocytes of said preparation are viable after the final thaw, said method comprising:

(a) Subjecting hepatocytes that have been frozen and thawed to density gradient fractionation to separate viable hepatocytes from nonviable hepatocytes,

(b) recovering the separated viable hepatocytes, and

(c) cryopreserving the recovered viable hepatocytes . . . .

Rapid Litigation Management v. CellzDirect, 827 F.3d 1042 (Fed. Cir. 2016).

3. When an artery is damaged or inflamed, the body releases the enzyme myeloperoxidase (MPO). Methods of detecting MPO were known, but the inventors discovered that MPO is an indicator of a patient's risk of cardiovascular disease. The claim reads:

A method of assessing the risk of requiring medical intervention in a patient who is presenting with chest pain, comprising:

(a) characterizing the levels of myeloperoxidase (MPO) activity, MPO mass, or both, respectively in the bodily sample from the human patient, wherein said bodily sample is blood or a blood derivative,

(b) wherein a patient whose levels of MPO activity, MPO mass, or both is characterized as being elevated in comparison to levels of MPO activity, MPO mass or both in a comparable bodily samples obtained from individuals in a control population is at risk of requiring medical intervention to prevent the occurrence of an adverse cardiac event within the next six months.

Cleveland Clinic v. True Health Diagnostics, 859 F.3d 1352 (Fed Cir. 2017).

4. Some of you may remember the creation of Dolly, the famous cloned sheep. That was the invention: a perfect genetic clone of a living animal. The claim reads as follows:

A live-born clone of a pre-existing, non-embryonic, donor mammal, wherein the mammal is selected from cattle, sheep, pigs, and goats.

In re Roslin Institute (Edinburgh), 750 F.3d 1333 (Fed. Cir. 2014).

5. The invention is a method for taking a person's temperature by scanning across their skin (typically the forehead). The technology for reading temperature from the skin was well known, but prior to this invention, scientists thought skin temperature could not be systematically correlated with body temperature. The inventors discovered the relationship between skin temperature and internal body temperature. The patent described the newly calculated coefficient for translating skin measurements into body temperature readings. If you've had your temperature taken by scanning your forehead (perhaps during the COVID-19 pandemic), you've used the technology described in this patent. The claim reads:

> A method of detecting human body temperature comprising making at least three radiation readings per second while moving a radiation detector to scan across a region of skin over an artery to electronically determine a body temperature approximation, distinct from skin surface temperature.

Exergen v. Kaz, 725 F. App'x 959 (Fed. Cir. 2018).

6. This invention relates to the cell-free fetal DNA invention from problem 1. One of the technical hurdles in examining fetal DNA was separating it from the DNA of the pregnant individual, with which it was mixed. The inventors discovered that the fragments of fetal DNA present in the pregnant person's bloodstream were typically very small, generally less than 500 base pairs. The invention is a method of separating fetal blood from the pregnant individual's blood by discriminating among DNA fragments based on size. The claim reads:

> A method for preparing a deoxyribonucleic acid (DNA) fraction from a pregnant human female useful for analyzing a genetic locus involved in a fetal chromosomal aberration, comprising:
> (a) extracting DNA from a substantially cell-free sample of blood plasma or blood serum of a pregnant human female to obtain extracellular circulatory fetal and maternal DNA fragments;
> (b) producing a fraction of the DNA extracted in (a) by: (i) size discrimination of extracellular circulatory DNA fragments, and (ii) selectively removing the DNA fragments greater than approximately 500 base pairs, wherein the DNA fraction after (b) comprises a plurality of genetic loci of the extracellular circulatory fetal and maternal DNA; and
> (c) analyzing a genetic locus in the fraction of DNA produced in (b).

Illumina, Inc. v. Ariosa Diagnostics, Inc., 967 F.3d 1319 (Fed. Cir. 2020).

B. Abstract Ideas

In the wake of *Mayo* and *Myriad*, questions remained (at least in the minds of Federal Circuit judges) over the scope and application of the *Mayo* test. In particular, patents involving abstract ideas quickly emerged as the most important set of § 101 cases and occupied the majority of the courts' attention. This trend has continued; a study of all patentable subject matter cases decided by the federal courts in 2015–19 found that 90% were in the software and information technology industries, which largely involve abstract ideas rather than laws of nature. Mark A. Lemley & Samantha Zyontz, *Does* Alice *Target Patent Trolls?*, 18 J. Empirical Legal Stud. 47 (2021). After *Mayo*, the Federal Circuit was torn about how (or whether) to apply that case in the context of abstract ideas, and the Supreme Court's 2010 abstract ideas decision in *Bilski v. Kappos* was not entirely helpful. This culminated in the en banc Federal Circuit deadlocking six-to-six (and producing five separate opinions) in a case concerning computerized methods for managing financial settlement risk. That case was *Alice v. CLS Bank*. And when a circuit court of appeals sitting en banc deadlocks and cannot issue a controlling opinion, the Supreme Court has little choice but to take the case.

Alice Corp. v. CLS Bank Int'l, 573 U.S. 208 (2014)

Justice Thomas delivered the opinion of the Court.

1   The patents at issue in this case disclose a computer-implemented scheme for mitigating "settlement risk" (i.e., the risk that only one party to a financial transaction will pay what it owes) by using a third-party intermediary. The question presented is whether these claims are patent eligible under 35 U.S.C. § 101, or are instead drawn to a patent-ineligible abstract idea. We hold that the claims at issue are drawn to the abstract idea of intermediated settlement, and that merely requiring generic computer implementation fails to transform that abstract idea into a patent-eligible invention. We therefore affirm the judgment of the United States Court of Appeals for the Federal Circuit.

I

A

2   Petitioner Alice Corporation is the assignee of several patents that disclose schemes to manage certain forms of financial risk. The claims at issue relate to a computerized scheme for mitigating "settlement risk"—i.e., the risk that only one party to an agreed-upon financial exchange will satisfy its obligation. In particular, the claims are designed to facilitate the exchange of financial obligations between two parties by using a computer system as a third-party intermediary. The intermediary creates "shadow" credit and debit records (i.e., account ledgers) that mirror the balances in the parties' real-world accounts at "exchange institutions" (e.g., banks). The intermediary updates the shadow records in real time as transactions are entered, allowing "only those transactions for which the parties' updated shadow records indicate sufficient resources to satisfy their mutual obligations." At the end of the day, the intermediary instructs the relevant financial institutions to carry out the "permitted" transactions in accordance with the updated shadow records, thus mitigating the risk that only one party will perform the agreed-upon exchange.

3   In sum, the patents in suit claim (1) the foregoing method for exchanging obligations (the method claims), (2) a computer system configured to carry out the method for exchanging obligations (the system claims), and (3) a computer-readable medium containing program code for performing the method of exchanging obligations (the media claims). All of the claims are implemented using a computer; the system

and media claims expressly recite a computer, and the parties have stipulated that the method claims require a computer as well.

II

"We have long held that [§ 101] contains an important implicit exception: Laws of nature, natural phenomena, and abstract ideas are not patentable." *Ass'n for Molecular Pathology v. Myriad Genetics, Inc.,* 569 U.S. 576, 589 (2013) (internal quotation marks and brackets omitted). We have interpreted § 101 and its predecessors in light of this exception for more than 150 years. *Bilski v. Kappos,* 561 U.S. 593; *see also O'Reilly v. Morse,* 15 How. 62 (1854); *Le Roy v. Tatham,* 14 How. 156 (1853).

We have described the concern that drives this exclusionary principle as one of pre-emption. *See, e.g., Bilski,* at 611–12 (upholding the patent "would pre-empt use of this approach in all fields, and would effectively grant a monopoly over an abstract idea"). Laws of nature, natural phenomena, and abstract ideas are "the basic tools of scientific and technological work." *Myriad,* 569 U.S. at 589. "[M]onopolization of those tools through the grant of a patent might tend to impede innovation more than it would tend to promote it," thereby thwarting the primary object of the patent laws. *Mayo v. Prometheus,* 566 U.S. 66, 71 (2012); *see* U.S. Const. art. I, § 8, cl. 8 (Congress "shall have Power . . . To promote the Progress of Science and useful Arts"). We have "repeatedly emphasized this . . . concern that patent law not inhibit further discovery by improperly tying up the future use of" these building blocks of human ingenuity. *Mayo,* 566 U.S. at 85 (citing *Morse,* 15 How. at 113).

At the same time, we tread carefully in construing this exclusionary principle lest it swallow all of patent law. At some level, "all inventions . . . embody, use, reflect, rest upon, or apply laws of nature, natural phenomena, or abstract ideas." *Id.* at 71. Thus, an invention is not rendered ineligible for patent simply because it involves an abstract concept. "[A]pplication[s]" of such concepts "to a new and useful end," we have said, remain eligible for patent protection. *Gottschalk v. Benson,* 409 U.S. 63, 67 (1972).

Accordingly, in applying the § 101 exception, we must distinguish between patents that claim the "buildin[g] block[s]" of human ingenuity and those that integrate the building blocks into something more, *Mayo,* 566 U.S. at 89, thereby "transform[ing]" them into a patent-eligible invention, *id.* at 72. The former "would risk disproportionately tying up the use of the underlying" ideas, *id.* at 73, and are therefore ineligible for patent protection. The latter pose no comparable risk of pre-emption, and therefore remain eligible for the monopoly granted under our patent laws.

III

8   In *Mayo Collaborative Services v. Prometheus Laboratories, Inc.*, 566 U.S. 66 (2012), we set forth a framework for distinguishing patents that claim laws of nature, natural phenomena, and abstract ideas from those that claim patent-eligible applications of those concepts. First, we determine whether the claims at issue are directed to one of those patent-ineligible concepts. If so, we then ask, "[w]hat else is there in the claims before us?" To answer that question, we consider the elements of each claim both individually and "as an ordered combination" to determine whether the additional elements "transform the nature of the claim" into a patent-eligible application. We have described step two of this analysis as a search for an "inventive concept"—i.e., an element or combination of elements that is "sufficient to ensure that the patent in practice amounts to significantly more than a patent upon the [ineligible concept] itself."

A

9   We must first determine whether the claims at issue are directed to a patent-ineligible concept. We conclude that they are: These claims are drawn to the abstract idea of intermediated settlement.

10   The "abstract ideas" category embodies "the longstanding rule that '[a]n idea of itself is not patentable.'" *Benson*, 409 U.S. at 67. In *Benson*, for example, this Court rejected as ineligible patent claims involving an algorithm for converting binary-coded decimal numerals into pure binary form, holding that the claimed patent was "in practical effect . . . a patent on the algorithm itself." 409 U.S. at 71–72. And in *Parker v. Flook*, 437 U.S. 584, 594–95 (1978), we held that a mathematical formula for computing "alarm limits" in a catalytic conversion process was also a patent-ineligible abstract idea.

11   We most recently addressed the category of abstract ideas in *Bilski v. Kappos*, 561 U.S. 593 (2010). The claims at issue in *Bilski* described a method for hedging against the financial risk of price fluctuations. Claim 1 recited a series of steps for hedging risk, including: (1) initiating a series of financial transactions between providers and consumers of a commodity; (2) identifying market participants that have a counterrisk for the same commodity; and (3) initiating a series of transactions between those market participants and the commodity provider to balance the risk position of the first series of consumer transactions. Claim 4 "pu[t] the concept articulated in claim 1 into a simple mathematical formula." The remaining claims were drawn to examples of hedging in commodities and energy markets.

12   "[A]ll members of the Court agree[d]" that the patent at issue in *Bilski* claimed an "abstract idea." *Id.* at 609; *see also id.* at 619 (Stevens, J., concurring in judgment). Specifically, the claims described "the basic concept of hedging, or protecting against risk." The Court explained that "[h]edging is a fundamental economic practice long prevalent in our system of commerce and taught in any introductory finance class."

The concept of hedging as recited by the claims in suit was therefore a patent-ineligible "abstract idea, just like the algorithms at issue in *Benson* and *Flook*." *Id.* at 611.

13   It follows from our prior cases, and *Bilski* in particular, that the claims at issue here are directed to an abstract idea. Petitioner's claims involve a method of exchanging financial obligations between two parties using a third-party intermediary to mitigate settlement risk. The intermediary creates and updates "shadow" records to reflect the value of each party's actual accounts held at "exchange institutions," thereby permitting only those transactions for which the parties have sufficient resources. At the end of each day, the intermediary issues irrevocable instructions to the exchange institutions to carry out the permitted transactions.

14   On their face, the claims before us are drawn to the concept of intermediated settlement, i.e., the use of a third party to mitigate settlement risk. Like the risk hedging in *Bilski*, the concept of intermediated settlement is "a fundamental economic practice long prevalent in our system of commerce." The use of a third-party intermediary (or "clearing house") is also a building block of the modern economy. Thus, intermediated settlement, like hedging, is an "abstract idea" beyond the scope of § 101.

15   In any event, we need not labor to delimit the precise contours of the "abstract ideas" category in this case. It is enough to recognize that there is no meaningful distinction between the concept of risk hedging in *Bilski* and the concept of intermediated settlement at issue here. Both are squarely within the realm of "abstract ideas" as we have used that term.

B

16   Because the claims at issue are directed to the abstract idea of intermediated settlement, we turn to the second step in *Mayo*'s framework. We conclude that the method claims, which merely require generic computer implementation, fail to transform that abstract idea into a patent-eligible invention.

1

17   At *Mayo* step two, we must examine the elements of the claim to determine whether it contains an "inventive concept" sufficient to "transform" the claimed abstract idea into a patent-eligible application. A claim that recites an abstract idea must include "additional features" to ensure "that the [claim] is more than a drafting effort designed to monopolize the [abstract idea]." *Mayo* made clear that transformation into a patent-eligible application requires "more than simply stat[ing] the [abstract idea] while adding the words 'apply it.'"

18   The introduction of a computer into the claims does not alter the analysis at *Mayo* step two. In *Benson*, for example, we considered a patent that claimed an algorithm implemented on "a general-purpose digital computer." 409 U.S. at 64.

Because the algorithm was an abstract idea, the claim had to supply a "new and useful" application of the idea in order to be patent eligible. But the computer implementation did not supply the necessary inventive concept; the process could be "carried out in existing computers long in use." *Id.* We accordingly "held that simply implementing a mathematical principle on a physical machine, namely a computer, [i]s not a patentable application of that principle." *Mayo*, 566 U.S. at 84 (citing *Benson*, 409 U.S. at 64).

19   *Flook* is to the same effect. There, we examined a computerized method for using a mathematical formula to adjust alarm limits for certain operating conditions (e.g., temperature and pressure) that could signal inefficiency or danger in a catalytic conversion process. 437 U.S. at 585–86. Once again, the formula itself was an abstract idea, and the computer implementation was purely conventional. 437 U.S. at 594 (noting that the "use of computers for 'automatic monitoring-alarming'" was "well known"). In holding that the process was patent ineligible, we rejected the argument that "implement[ing] a principle in some specific fashion" will "automatically fal[l] within the patentable subject matter of § 101." *Id.* at 593. Thus, "*Flook* stands for the proposition that the prohibition against patenting abstract ideas cannot be circumvented by attempting to limit the use of [the idea] to a particular technological environment." *Bilski*, 561 U.S. at 610–11.

20   In *Diamond v. Diehr*, 450 U.S. 175 (1981), by contrast, we held that a computer-implemented process for curing rubber was patent eligible, but not because it involved a computer. The claim employed a "well-known" mathematical equation, but it used that equation in a process designed to solve a technological problem in "conventional industry practice." The invention in *Diehr* used a "thermocouple" to record constant temperature measurements inside the rubber mold—something "the industry ha[d] not been able to obtain." The temperature measurements were then fed into a computer, which repeatedly recalculated the remaining cure time by using the mathematical equation. These additional steps, we recently explained, "transformed the process into an inventive application of the formula." *Mayo*, 566 U.S. at 81. In other words, the claims in *Diehr* were patent eligible because they improved an existing technological process, not because they were implemented on a computer.

21   These cases demonstrate that the mere recitation of a generic computer cannot transform a patent-ineligible abstract idea into a patent-eligible invention. Stating an abstract idea "while adding the words 'apply it'" is not enough for patent eligibility. *Mayo*, 566 U.S. at 72. Nor is limiting the use of an abstract idea "to a particular technological environment." *Bilski*, 561 U.S. at 610–11. Stating an abstract idea while adding the words "apply it with a computer" simply combines those two steps, with the same deficient result. Thus, if a patent's recitation of a computer amounts to a mere instruction to "implemen[t]" an abstract idea "on . . . a computer," *Mayo*, 566 U.S. at 84, that addition cannot impart patent eligibility. This conclusion accords with the pre-emption concern that undergirds our § 101 jurisprudence. Given the ubiquity of computers, wholly generic computer implementation is not generally the sort of

"additional featur[e]" that provides any "practical assurance that the process is more than a drafting effort designed to monopolize the [abstract idea] itself."

22   The fact that a computer "necessarily exist[s] in the physical, rather than purely conceptual, realm," is beside the point. There is no dispute that a computer is a tangible system (in § 101 terms, a "machine"), or that many computer-implemented claims are formally addressed to patent-eligible subject matter. But if that were the end of the § 101 inquiry, an applicant could claim any principle of the physical or social sciences by reciting a computer system configured to implement the relevant concept. Such a result would make the determination of patent eligibility "depend simply on the draftsman's art," *Flook*, 437 U.S. at 593, thereby eviscerating the rule that "[l]aws of nature, natural phenomena, and abstract ideas are not patentable."

2

23   The representative method claim in this case recites the following steps: (1) "creating" shadow records for each counterparty to a transaction; (2) "obtaining" start-of-day balances based on the parties' real-world accounts at exchange institutions; (3) "adjusting" the shadow records as transactions are entered, allowing only those transactions for which the parties have sufficient resources; and (4) issuing irrevocable end-of-day instructions to the exchange institutions to carry out the permitted transactions. Petitioner principally contends that the claims are patent eligible because these steps "require a substantial and meaningful role for the computer." As stipulated, the claimed method requires the use of a computer to create electronic records, track multiple transactions, and issue simultaneous instructions; in other words, "[t]he computer is itself the intermediary."

24   In light of the foregoing, the relevant question is whether the claims here do more than simply instruct the practitioner to implement the abstract idea of intermediated settlement on a generic computer. They do not.

25   Taking the claim elements separately, the function performed by the computer at each step of the process is "[p]urely conventional." Using a computer to create and maintain "shadow" accounts amounts to electronic recordkeeping—one of the most basic functions of a computer. *See, e.g., Benson*, 409 U.S. at 65 (noting that a computer "operates . . . upon both new and previously stored data"). The same is true with respect to the use of a computer to obtain data, adjust account balances, and issue automated instructions; all of these computer functions are "well-understood, routine, conventional activit[ies]" previously known to the industry. In short, each step does no more than require a generic computer to perform generic computer functions.

26   Considered "as an ordered combination," the computer components of petitioner's method "ad[d] nothing . . . that is not already present when the steps are considered separately." Viewed as a whole, petitioner's method claims simply recite the concept of intermediated settlement as performed by a generic computer. The method claims do not, for example, purport to improve the functioning of the computer

itself. Nor do they effect an improvement in any other technology or technical field. Instead, the claims at issue amount to "nothing significantly more" than an instruction to apply the abstract idea of intermediated settlement using some unspecified, generic computer. Under our precedents, that is not *"enough"* to transform an abstract idea into a patent-eligible invention.

C

27   Petitioner's claims to a computer system and a computer-readable medium fail for substantially the same reasons. Petitioner conceded below that its media claims rise or fall with its method claims. As to its system claims, petitioner emphasizes that those claims recite "specific hardware" configured to perform "specific computerized functions." But what petitioner characterizes as specific hardware—a "data processing system" with a "communications controller" and "data storage unit," for example—is purely functional and generic. Nearly every computer will include a "communications controller" and "data storage unit" capable of performing the basic calculation, storage, and transmission functions required by the method claims. As a result, none of the hardware recited by the system claims "offers a meaningful limitation beyond generally linking 'the use of the [method] to a particular technological environment,' that is, implementation via computers."

28   Put another way, the system claims are no different from the method claims in substance. The method claims recite the abstract idea implemented on a generic computer; the system claims recite a handful of generic computer components configured to implement the same idea. This Court has long warned against interpreting § 101 in ways that make patent eligibility depend simply on the draftsman's art. Holding that the system claims are patent eligible would have exactly that result.

Justice Sotomayor, with whom Justice Ginsburg and Justice Breyer join, concurring.

29   I adhere to the view that any "claim that merely describes a method of doing business does not qualify as a 'process' under § 101." *Bilski v. Kappos*, 561 U.S. 593, 614 (2010) (Stevens, J., concurring in judgment); *see also In re Bilski*, 545 F.3d 943, 972 (Fed. Cir. 2008) (Dyk, J., concurring) ("There is no suggestion in any of the early [English] consideration of process patents that processes for organizing human activity were or ever had been patentable"). As in *Bilski*, however, I further believe that the method claims at issue are drawn to an abstract idea. I therefore join the opinion of the Court.

Discussion Questions: *Alice*

1. *The Alice/Mayo Test.* Do you think the test that the Supreme Court uses in *Alice* is different from or the same as the test used in *Mayo*? If it is the same, why do

you think the Supreme Court felt the need to grant certiorari in *Alice*? Was it merely the fact the Federal Circuit was deadlocked, or was there something more?

2. *Justifying Patentable Subject Matter Exceptions.* The Supreme Court reiterates that the concern underlying its implicit exceptions to the statutory categories of patent eligibility is "preemption": the idea that tying up "the basic tools of scientific and technological work . . . might tend to impede innovation more than it would tend to promote it." As we noted at the beginning of this chapter, this reads as an empirical, utilitarian judgment that such patents should be denied because they do not provide a net benefit to society. In making judgments such as these, should courts also consider the wide array of non-patent innovation incentives when setting patent policy? Or should they confine themselves to scrutinizing the effects of patent law in isolation? *See* Lisa Larrimore Ouellette, *Patentable Subject Matter and Nonpatent Innovation Incentives*, 5 U.C. Irvine L. Rev. 1115 (2015).

In addition, many of the parties arguing for robust exceptions to patent eligibility have been motivated more by noneconomic moral concerns than by utilitarian ones. For instance, the challengers to the gene patent claims in *Myriad* argued that claims on human genes commodified human life and impinged on rights of privacy. Some of the parties challenging software claims in cases like *Bilski* and *Alice* argued that the claims should be invalidated because of the expressive value of freedom in computer programming. Many aspects of software are considered "expressive" and thus protectable under copyright law. *Cf. Google v. Oracle*, 141 S. Ct. 1183 (2021) (holding that Google's copying of Oracle's Java Application Programming Interface is copyright fair use). What role should these different values play in patent law?

3. *The Draftsman's Art.* Suppose you were given a chance to redraft the claims in *Alice* in light of what you now know of the doctrine. Is there a way to redraft the claims to make them patentable? Or is the invention simply unpatentable no matter how the claims are drawn?

Enfish v. Microsoft, 822 F.3d 1327 (Fed. Cir. 2016)

Todd M. Hughes, Circuit Judge.

[1]   Enfish sued Microsoft for infringement of several patents related to a "self-referential" database. On summary judgment, the district court found all claims invalid as ineligible under § 101. Enfish appeals. We find that the claims are not directed to an abstract idea, so we reverse the summary judgment based on § 101.

I

2   Microsoft develops and sells a variety of software products, including the product ADO.NET. At least through the late 1990s and early 2000s, Enfish developed and sold software products, including a new type of database program.

3   Enfish received U.S. Patent 6,151,604 and U.S. Patent 6,163,775 in late 2000. The '604 and '775 patents are directed to an innovative logical model for a computer database. A logical model is a model of data for a computer database explaining how the various elements of information are related to one another. Contrary to conventional logical models, the patented logical model includes all data entities in a single table, with column definitions provided by rows in that same table.

4   This "self-referential" property can be best understood in contrast with the more standard "relational" model. With the relational model, each entity (i.e., each type of thing) that is modeled is provided in a separate table. For instance, a relational model for a corporate file repository might include the following tables:

document table,

person table,

company table.

The document table might contain information about documents stored on the file repository, the person table might contain information about authors of the documents, and the company table might contain information about the companies that employ the persons. Using this relational model, if a database were to store information about a document called proj.doc, a person called Scott Wlaschin, and a company called DEXIS, then the result might be:

Document Table			
ID	Title	Address	Author
1	PROJECT PLAN	C:\WORD\PROJ.DOC	1

Person Table		
ID	Label	Employed By
1	SCOTT WLASCHIN	1

Company Table		
ID	Label	Address
1	DEXIS	117 EAST COLORADO

5   To indicate that Scott Wlaschin is the author of proj.doc and that he is employed by DEXIS, the relational model uses relationships as follows:

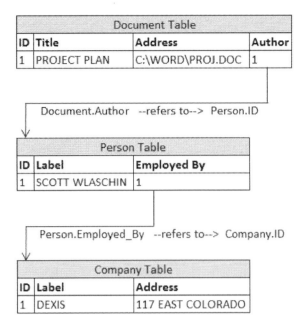

6   Here, the top-most relationship explains that the value for "Author" in the Document table refers to the "ID" column of the Person table. Because the row for proj.doc has AUTHOR = 1, the row in the Person table that has ID = 1 is the author of proj.doc. By this technique, the relational model captures information about each type of entity in a separate table, with relationships between those tables informing the relationships between rows in different tables.

7   The patented self-referential model has two features that are not found in the relational model: first the self-referential model can store all entity types in a single table, and second the self-referential model can define the table's columns by rows in that same table. For example, a self-referential model corresponding to the example relational model discussed above might look like the following:

				SELF-REFERENTIAL TABLE		
ID	Type	Title	Label	Address	Employed By (#4)	Author
#1	DOCUMENT	PROJECT PLAN		C:\WORD\PROJ.DOC		#2
#2	PERSON		SCOTT WLASCHIN		#3	
#3	COMPANY		DEXIS	117 EAST COLORADO		
#4	FIELD		EMPLOYED BY			

8   This self-referential table stores the same information that is stored by the example relational model shown above. However, all of the information about documents, persons, and companies are stored in a single table.

9   Further, an additional row is included in the self-referential table: the row beginning with ID = # 4. Such a row with TYPE = "field" is a special row, because it defines characteristics of a column in that same table. In this case, the row with ID = # 4 corresponds to the penultimate column, which is denoted by also marking that column with the ID of # 4. The row with ID = # 4 defines a single characteristic of the corresponding column, viz., its label. Because the row with ID = # 4 has LABEL =

"Employed By," we know that the corresponding column is labeled "Employed By," as seen in the penultimate column. In other situations, the row might define other characteristics of the column, such as the type of data that the column can hold, e.g., text, integer numbers, or decimal numbers. Because the patent describes a model where the table's columns are defined by rows in that same table, it is "self-referential."

10   The patents teach that multiple benefits flow from this design. First, the patents disclose an indexing technique that allows for faster searching of data than would be possible with the relational model. Second, the patents teach that the self-referential model allows for more effective storage of data other than structured text, such as images and unstructured text.

11   Finally, the patents teach that the self-referential model allows more flexibility in configuring the database. For instance, the database could be launched with no or only minimal column definitions. Then, as a new attribute of information is encountered, such as an email address, an "Email" column could be added simply by inserting a new row of TYPE = "field" and LABEL = "email."

12   In 2012, Enfish filed suit against Microsoft in district court in California, alleging that Microsoft's ADO.NET product infringes the '604 and '775 patents. ADO.NET provides an interface by which software applications can store, retrieve, and otherwise manipulate data stored in a database. [The district court found five claims, including representative claim 17 of the '604 patent, invalid under § 101.]

13   This court, as well as the Supreme Court, has long grappled with the exception [to § 101] that "[l]aws of nature, natural phenomena, and abstract ideas are not patentable." *Ass'n for Molecular Pathology v. Myriad Genetics*, 569 U.S. 576 (2013) (quoting *Mayo Collaborative Servs. v. Prometheus Labs.*, 566 U.S. 66 (2012)). Supreme Court precedent instructs us to "first determine whether the claims at issue are directed to a patent-ineligible concept." *Alice Corp. v. CLS Bank Int'l*, 573 U.S. 208 (2014). If this threshold determination is met, we move to the second step of the inquiry and "consider the elements of each claim both individually and 'as an ordered combination' to determine whether the additional elements 'transform the nature of the claim' into a patent-eligible application." *Id.*

14   The Supreme Court has not established a definitive rule to determine what constitutes an "abstract idea" sufficient to satisfy the first step of the *Mayo/Alice* inquiry. Rather, both this court and the Supreme Court have found it sufficient to compare claims at issue to those claims already found to be directed to an abstract idea in previous cases. For instance, fundamental economic and conventional business practices are often found to be abstract ideas, even if performed on a computer.

15   In setting up the two-stage *Mayo/Alice* inquiry, the Supreme Court has declared: "We must first determine whether the claims at issue are directed to a patent-ineligible concept." *Alice*, 573 U.S. at 218. That formulation plainly

contemplates that the first step of the inquiry is a meaningful one, i.e., that a substantial class of claims are *not* directed to a patent-ineligible concept. The "directed to" inquiry, therefore, cannot simply ask whether the claims *involve* a patent-ineligible concept, because essentially every routinely patent-eligible claim involving physical products and actions *involves* a law of nature and/or natural phenomenon—after all, they take place in the physical world. Rather, the "directed to" inquiry applies a stage-one filter to claims, considered in light of the specification, based on whether their character as a whole is directed to excluded subject matter.

16   The Supreme Court has suggested that claims "purport[ing] to improve the functioning of the computer itself," or "improv[ing] an existing technological process" might not succumb to the abstract idea exception. *See Alice*, 573 U.S. at 223–225. While it is true that the Court discussed improvements to computer-related technology in the second step of its analysis in *Alice*, that was because the Court did not need to discuss the first step of its analysis at any considerable length.

17   We do not read *Alice* to broadly hold that all improvements in computer-related technology are inherently abstract and, therefore, must be considered at step two. Indeed, some improvements in computer-related technology when appropriately claimed are undoubtedly not abstract, such as a chip architecture, an LED display, and the like. Nor do we think that claims directed to software, as opposed to hardware, are inherently abstract. Therefore, we find it relevant to ask whether the claims are directed to an improvement to computer functionality versus being directed to an abstract idea, even at the first step of the *Alice* analysis.

18   For that reason, the first step in the *Alice* inquiry in this case asks whether the focus of the claims is on the specific asserted improvement in computer capabilities (i.e., the self-referential table for a computer database) or, instead, on a process that qualifies as an "abstract idea" for which computers are invoked merely as a tool. In *Bilski* and *Alice* and virtually all of the computer-related § 101 cases we have issued in light of those Supreme Court decisions, it was clear that the claims were of the latter type—requiring that the analysis proceed to the second step of the *Alice* inquiry, which asks if nevertheless there is some inventive concept in the application of the abstract idea. In this case, however, the plain focus of the claims is on an improvement to computer functionality itself, not on economic or other tasks for which a computer is used in its ordinary capacity.

19   Accordingly, we find that the claims at issue in this appeal are not directed to an abstract idea within the meaning of *Alice*. Rather, they are directed to a specific improvement to the way computers operate, embodied in the self-referential table. Specifically, claim 17 of the '604 patent recites:

    A data storage and retrieval system for a computer memory, comprising:

means for configuring said memory according to a logical table, said logical table including:

a plurality of logical rows, each said logical row including an object identification number (OID) to identify each said logical row, each said logical row corresponding to a record of information;

a plurality of logical columns intersecting said plurality of logical rows to define a plurality of logical cells, each said logical column including an OID to identify each said logical column; and

means for indexing data stored in said table.

20   The district court construed the "means for configuring" language as requiring a four-step algorithm:[5]

1. Create, in a computer memory, a logical table that need not be stored contiguously in the computer memory, the logical table being comprised of rows and columns, the rows corresponding to records, the columns corresponding to fields or attributes, the logical table being capable of storing different kinds of records.

2. Assign each row and column an object identification number (OID) that, when stored as data, can act as a pointer to the associated row or column and that can be of variable length between databases.

3. For each column, store information about that column in one or more rows, rendering the table self-referential, the appending, to the logical table, of new columns that are available for immediate use being possible through the creation of new column definition records.

4. In one or more cells defined by the intersection of the rows and columns, store and access data, which can include structured data, unstructured data, or a pointer to another row.

21   The district court concluded that the claims were directed to the abstract idea of "storing, organizing, and retrieving memory in a logical table" or, more simply, "the concept of organizing information using tabular formats." Likewise, Microsoft urges the court to view the claims as being directed to "the concepts of organizing data into a logical table with identified columns and rows where one or more rows are used to

---

[5] [n.3 in opinion] Construction of a means-plus-function limitation includes two steps. First, the court must determine the claimed function. Second, the court must identify the corresponding structure in the written description of the patent that performs the function. And the corresponding structure for a function performed by a software algorithm is the algorithm itself.

store an index or information defining columns." However, describing the claims at such a high level of abstraction and untethered from the language of the claims all but ensures that the exceptions to § 101 swallow the rule. *See Alice*, 573 U.S. at 217 (noting that "we tread carefully in construing this exclusionary principle [of laws of nature, natural phenomena, and abstract ideas] lest it swallow all of patent law").

22   Here, the claims are not simply directed to *any* form of storing tabular data, but instead are specifically directed to a *self-referential* table for a computer database. For claim 17, this is reflected in step three of the "means for configuring" algorithm described above. The necessity of describing the claims in such a way is underscored by the specification's emphasis that "the present invention comprises a flexible, self-referential table that stores data." Moreover, our conclusion that the claims are directed to an improvement of an existing technology is bolstered by the specification's teachings that the claimed invention achieves other benefits over conventional databases, such as increased flexibility, faster search times, and smaller memory requirements.

23   In finding that the claims were directed simply to "the concept of organizing information using tabular formats," the district court oversimplified the self-referential component of the claims and downplayed the invention's benefits. The court determined that the patents' self-referential concept could be satisfied by creating a table with a simple header row. But that is simply not the case. For example, step three of the algorithm described above explains that the table stores information related to each column in rows of that very same table, such that new columns can be added by creating new rows in the table.

24   Moreover, we are not persuaded that the invention's ability to run on a general-purpose computer dooms the claims. Unlike the claims at issue in *Alice* or, more recently in *Versata Development Group v. SAP America, Inc.*, 793 F.3d 1306 (Fed. Cir. 2015), which Microsoft alleges to be especially similar to the present case, the claims here are directed to an improvement in the functioning of a computer. In contrast, the claims at issue in *Alice* and *Versata* can readily be understood as simply adding conventional computer components to well-known business practices. *See Alice*, 573 U.S. at 222–226; *Versata Dev. Grp.*, 793 F.3d at 1333–34 (computer performed "purely conventional" steps to carry out claims directed to the "abstract idea of determining a price using organization and product group hierarchies"); *see also Mortgage Grader, Inc. v. First Choice Loan Servs. Inc.*, 811 F.3d 1314, 1324–25 (Fed. Cir. 2016) (claims attaching generic computer components to perform "anonymous loan shopping" not patent eligible); *Ultramercial, Inc. v. Hulu, LLC*, 772 F.3d 709, 714–17 (Fed. Cir. 2014) (claims applying an exchange of advertising for copyrighted content to the Internet); *buySAFE, Inc. v. Google, Inc.*, 765 F.3d 1350, 1354–55 (Fed. Cir. 2014) (claims adding generic computer functionality to the formation of guaranteed contractual relationships). And unlike the claims here that are directed to a specific improvement to computer functionality, the patent-ineligible claims at issue in other cases recited use of an abstract mathematical formula on any general purpose computer, *see*

Gottschalk v. Benson, 409 U.S. 63 (1972), or recited a purely conventional computer implementation of a mathematical formula, *see Parker v. Flook*, 437 U.S. 584, 594 (1978), or recited generalized steps to be performed on a computer using conventional computer activity, *see Internet Patents*, 790 F.3d at 1348–49 (claims directed to abstract idea of maintaining computer state without recitation of specific activity used to generate that result).

25   Similarly, that the improvement is not defined by reference to "physical" components does not doom the claims. To hold otherwise risks resurrecting a bright-line machine-or-transformation test, *cf. Bilski v. Kappos*, 561 U.S. 593, 604 (2010) ("The machine-or-transformation test is not the sole test for deciding whether an invention is a patent-eligible 'process.'"), or creating a categorical ban on software patents, *cf. id.* at 603 ("This Court has not indicated that the existence of these well-established exceptions gives the Judiciary *carte blanche* to impose other limitations that are inconsistent with the text and the statute's purpose and design."). Much of the advancement made in computer technology consists of improvements to software that, by their very nature, may not be defined by particular physical features but rather by logical structures and processes. We do not see in *Bilski* or *Alice*, or our cases, an exclusion to patenting this large field of technological progress.

26   Because the claims are not directed to an abstract idea under step one of the *Alice* analysis, we do not need to proceed to step two of that analysis. We recognize that, in other cases involving computer-related claims, there may be close calls about how to characterize what the claims are directed to. In such cases, an analysis of whether there are arguably concrete improvements in the recited computer technology could take place under step two. Here, though, we think it is clear for the reasons stated that the claims are not directed to an abstract idea, and so we stop at step one. We conclude that the claims are patent-eligible.

ChargePoint v. SemaConnect, 920 F.3d 759 (Fed. Cir. 2019)

Sharon Prost, Chief Judge.

I

1   The technology at issue in this patent infringement case pertains to charging stations for electric vehicles. The battery in an electric vehicle is recharged by connecting the vehicle to an electrical outlet. At the time the patent application was filed, this process "typically require[d] hours and [was] often done overnight or while the electric vehicle [was] parked for a significant time." U.S. Patent No. 8,138,715 col. 1 ll. 24–26.

2   Generally, the supply of electricity available from a power grid may vary, and in some cases the grid may lack sufficient electricity to meet demand. During such periods, supply to certain customers or services may be reduced based on a preplanned

load prioritization scheme. The idea of reducing electricity consumption during periods of high demand is one form of what is referred to as "demand response." Demand response may also involve increasing demand during periods when demand is low compared to supply, by reducing the cost of electricity.

3   ChargePoint contends that its inventors created improved charging stations that address the various needs inherent in electric vehicle charging. This was accomplished by creating *networked* charging stations. According to ChargePoint, this network connectivity allows the stations to be managed from a central location, allows drivers to locate charging stations in advance, and allows all users to interact intelligently with the electricity grid.

4   ChargePoint sued SemaConnect for infringement [of four patents] in December 2017. The district court granted SemaConnect's motion to dismiss under Rule 12(b)(6) with prejudice, holding each asserted claim ineligible for patenting under § 101.

II

5   Subject matter eligibility under § 101 may be determined at the Rule 12(b)(6) stage of a case. *Aatrix Software*, 882 F.3d at 1125. Dismissal at this early stage, however, is appropriate "only when there are no factual allegations that, taken as true, prevent resolving the eligibility question as a matter of law." *Id.*

6   In analyzing whether the claims are patent eligible, we employ the two-step analysis articulated in *Mayo Collaborative Services v. Prometheus Laboratories, Inc.*, 566 U.S. 66 (2012), and further delineated in *Alice Corp. v. CLS Bank Int'l*, 573 U.S. 208 (2014). "First, we determine whether the claims at issue are directed to one of those patent-ineligible concepts." *Alice*, 573 U.S. at 217. If the claims are directed to a patent ineligible concept, we begin the "search for an 'inventive concept'—i.e., an element or combination of elements that is 'sufficient to ensure that the patent in practice amounts to significantly more than a patent upon the [ineligible concept] itself.'" *Id.* at 217–18.

A

7   Claims 1 and 2 of the '715 patent are both apparatus claims. They recite:

1. An apparatus, comprising:

a control device to turn electric supply on and off to enable and disable charge transfer for electric vehicles;

a transceiver to communicate requests for charge transfer with a remote server and receive communications from the remote server via a data control unit that is connected to the remote server through a wide area network; and a controller, coupled with the control device and the transceiver, to cause the control device to turn the electric supply on based on communication from the remote server.

2. The apparatus of claim 1, further comprising an electrical coupler to make a connection with an electric vehicle, wherein the control device is to turn electric supply on and off by switching the electric coupler on and off.

8   It is clear from the language of claim 1 that the claim *involves* an abstract idea—namely, the abstract idea of communicating requests to a remote server and receiving communications from that server, i.e., communication over a network. But at step one, "it is not enough to merely identify a patent-ineligible concept underlying the claim; we must determine whether that patent-ineligible concept is what the claim is 'directed to.'" *Thales Visionix v. United States*, 850 F.3d 1343, 1349 (Fed. Cir. 2017). We therefore continue our analysis to determine whether the focus of claim 1, as a whole, is the abstract idea. As explained below, we conclude that it is.

9   While the § 101 inquiry must focus on the language of the asserted claims themselves, the specification may nonetheless be useful in illuminating whether the claims are "directed to" the identified abstract idea. For example, in some cases the "directed to" inquiry may require claim construction, which will often involve consideration of the specification.

10   The "directed to" inquiry may also involve looking to the specification to understand "the problem facing the inventor" and, ultimately, what the patent describes as the invention. For example, in *In re TLI Communications* we held ineligible a claim to a method for recording and administering digital images using a phone. 823 F.3d 607, 610 (Fed. Cir. 2016). In our step one analysis, we explained that "the problem facing the inventor was not how to combine a camera with a cellular telephone, how to transmit images via a cellular network, or even how to append classification information to that data." *Id.* at 612. Instead, quoting the specification, we explained that "the inventor sought to 'provid[e] for recording, administration and archiving of digital images simply, fast and in such way that the information therefore may be easily tracked.'" *Id.* We also pointed to the specification to explain why the tangible components recited in the method claim were merely "conduit[s] for the abstract idea." *Id.* at 612. We reached that conclusion in part because the specification "fail[ed] to provide any technical details for the tangible components, but instead predominately describe[d] the system and methods in purely functional terms." *Id.*

11   In this case, ChargePoint has not expressed a need for claim construction, so we need not look to the specification for that purpose. We do, however, view the specification as useful in understanding "the problem facing the inventor" as well as what the patent describes as the invention. Here, the specification suggests that claim 1 is directed to the abstract idea of communication over a network to interact with a device connected to the network. The problem identified by the patentee, as stated in

the specification, was the lack of a communication network that would allow drivers, businesses, and utility companies to interact efficiently with the charging stations. For example, the specification states that "[t]here is a need for a communication network which facilitates finding the recharging facility, controlling the facility, and paying for the electricity consumed." Looking to future needs, the specification anticipates that "there will be a need for a system for collection of taxes and consumption information." From these statements, it is clear that the problem perceived by the patentee was a lack of a communication network for these charging stations, which limited the ability to efficiently operate them from a business perspective.

12   The specification also makes clear—by what it states and what it does not— that the invention of the '715 patent is the idea of *network-controlled* charging stations. Notably, the specification never suggests that the charging station itself is improved from a technical perspective, or that it would operate differently than it otherwise could. Nor does the specification suggest that the invention involved overcoming some sort of technical difficulty in adding networking capability to the charging stations.

13   In short, looking at the problem identified in the patent, as well as the way the patent describes the invention, the specification suggests that the invention of the patent is nothing more than the abstract idea of communication over a network for interacting with a device, applied to the context of electric vehicle charging stations. Although this is not necessarily dispositive of the "directed to" inquiry, it strongly suggests that the abstract idea identified in claim 1 may indeed be the focus of that claim.

14   With these indications from the specification in mind, we return to the claim language itself to consider the extent to which the claim would preempt building blocks of science and technology. *See Intellectual Ventures I LLC v. Capital One Bank (USA)*, 792 F.3d 1363, 1369 (Fed. Cir. 2015) ("At step one of the *Alice* framework, it is often useful to determine the breadth of the claims in order to determine whether the claims extend to cover a 'fundamental ... practice long prevalent in our system.'" (quoting *Alice*, 573 U.S. at 219)). We agree with SemaConnect that, based on the claim language, claim 1 would preempt the use of any networked charging stations.

15   The breadth of the claim language here illustrates why any reliance on the specification in the § 101 analysis must always yield to the claim language. Even a specification full of technical details about a physical invention may nonetheless conclude with claims that claim nothing more than the broad law or abstract idea underlying the claims, thus preempting all use of that law or idea. This was the case in *O'Reilly v. Morse*, 56 U.S. 62 (1853). In *Morse*, the Court upheld claims related to the details of Samuel Morse's invention of the electromagnetic telegraph, but invalidated a claim for the use of "electromagnetism, however developed for marking or printing intelligible characters, signs, or letters, at any distances." *Id.* at 112. The

Court expressed concern that such a broad claim would cover any application of printing at a distance via electromagnetism regardless of whether those applications used the invention in the patent.

16   A similar scenario arose in *Wyeth v. Stone*, 30 F. Cas. 723 (C.C.D. Mass. 1840). There, the patent described the inventor's machine for cutting ice in great detail. But Justice Story, riding circuit, held that one claim effectively "claim[ed] an exclusive title to the art of cutting ice by means of any power, other than human power." *Id.* at 727. He reasoned that "[s]uch a claim is utterly unmaintainable" because "[i]t is a claim for an art or principle in the abstract, and not for any particular method or machinery, by which ice is to be cut." *Id.*

17   As we explained in *Interval Licensing LLC v. AOL, Inc.*, in *Morse* and *Wyeth*, each inventor "lost a claim that encompassed all solutions for achieving a desired result" because those claims "were drafted in such a result-oriented way that they amounted to encompassing the 'principle in the abstract' no matter how implemented." 896 F.3d 1335, 1343 (Fed. Cir. 2018). In our view, this is effectively what ChargePoint has done in this case. Even if ChargePoint's specification had provided, for example, a technical explanation of how to enable communication over a network for device interaction (which, as discussed above, it did not), the claim language here would not require those details. Instead, the broad claim language would cover any mechanism for implementing network communication on a charging station, thus preempting the entire industry's ability to use networked charging stations. This confirms that claim 1 is indeed "directed to" the abstract idea of communication over a network to interact with network-attached devices.

18   We conclude our "directed to" analysis by addressing ChargePoint's argument that the claims asserted are patent eligible because the claimed invention "build[s] a better machine." We are not persuaded. Claim 1 indicates that the abstract idea is associated with a physical machine that is quite tangible—an electric vehicle charging station. Claim 2 goes further, explaining that a vehicle may be connected to the apparatus via an electrical coupler. But as the Supreme Court indicated in *Alice*, whether a device is "a tangible system (in § 101 terms, a 'machine')" is not dispositive. *See* 573 U.S. at 224. Resolving the § 101 inquiry based on such an argument "would make the determination of patent eligibility 'depend simply on the draftsman's art.'" *Id.* at 224.

19   In short, the inventors here had the good idea to add networking capabilities to existing charging stations to facilitate various business interactions. But that is where they stopped, and that is all they patented. We therefore hold that claim 1 is "directed to" an abstract idea.

20   As to dependent claim 2, the additional limitation of an "electrical coupler to make a connection with an electric vehicle" does not alter our step one analysis. The character of claim 2, as a whole, remains directed to the abstract idea of

communication over a network to interact with a device, applied in the context of charging stations.

21   [Two other asserted apparatus claims, claims 1 and 8 of Patent No. 8,432,131, are similar to the '715 claims.]

22   ChargePoint contends that claims 1 and 8 of the '131 patent teach "a charging station with improved technical features that enable it to adjust the amount of electricity delivered to cars based on demand-response communications with utilities." To the extent ChargePoint is arguing that modification itself is an improvement, nothing in the specification explains from a technical perspective how that modification occurs. And the fact that the electricity flow is modified *based on demand response principles* does nothing to make this claim directed to something other than the abstract idea. Demand response is itself an abstract concept—a familiar business choice to alter terms of dealing to help match supply and demand. As we have said before, "[a]dding one abstract idea . . . to another abstract idea . . . does not render the claim non-abstract." *RecogniCorp, LLC v. Nintendo Co.*, 855 F.3d 1322, 1327 (Fed. Cir. 2017). We therefore conclude that claims 1 and 8 are also directed to the abstract idea of communicating over a network.

B

23   At step two of the *Alice* inquiry—the search for an inventive concept—we "consider the elements of each claim both individually and 'as an ordered combination' to determine whether the additional elements 'transform the nature of the claim' into a patent-eligible application." *Id.* at 217. "[P]atentees who adequately allege their claims contain inventive concepts survive a § 101 eligibility analysis under Rule 12(b)(6)." *Aatrix Software*, 882 F.3d at 1126–27.

24   Where a claim is directed to an abstract idea, the claim must include "additional features to ensure that the [claim] is more than a drafting effort designed to monopolize the [abstract idea]." *Alice*, 573 U.S. at 221. These additional features cannot simply be "well-understood, routine, conventional activit[ies] previously known to the industry." *Id.* Indeed, adding novel or non-routine components is not necessarily enough to survive a § 101 challenge. Instead, the inventive concept must be "sufficient to ensure that the patent in practice amounts to significantly more" than a patent on the abstract idea. *See Mayo*, 566 U.S. at 72–73.

25   Whether a claim "supplies an inventive concept that renders a claim 'significantly more' than an abstract idea to which it is directed is a question of law" that may include underlying factual determinations. *BSG Tech LLC v. Buyseasons, Inc.*, 899 F.3d 1281, 1290 (Fed. Cir. 2018). For example, within the overall step two analysis, "whether a claim element or combination of elements is well-understood, routine and conventional to a skilled artisan in the relevant field is a question of fact" that "must be proven by clear and convincing evidence." *Berkheimer v. HP Inc.*, 881 F.3d 1360, 1368 (Fed. Cir. 2018).

26   Here, ChargePoint argues that it presented sufficient factual allegations to preclude dismissal at the Rule 12(b)(6) stage. Specifically, ChargePoint argues that its patents represent an unconventional solution to technological problems in the field, and thus contain an inventive concept.

27   The problems in the art identified by ChargePoint are, generally: the sparse availability of charging stations and the need for more widespread stations; the need for a communication network that facilitates finding an available charging station, controlling the station, and paying for electricity; and the need for real time communication to effectively implement demand response and vehicle-to-grid transfer.

28   ChargePoint contends that it solved these problems in an unconventional way through: (a) the ability to turn electric supply on based on communications from a remote server; (b) a "network-controlled" charging system; and (c) a charging station that receives communication from a remote server, including communications made to implement a demand response policy.

29   In essence, the alleged "inventive concept" that solves problems identified in the field is that the charging stations are network-controlled. But network control is the abstract idea itself, and "a claimed invention's use of the ineligible concept to which it is directed cannot supply the inventive concept that renders the invention 'significantly more' than that ineligible concept." *BSG Tech*, 899 F.3d at 1290.

30   Turning to claims 1 and 8 of the '131 patent, ChargePoint contends that these claims capture technical improvements related to demand response. ChargePoint disputes the district court's conclusion that "the combination of connecting generic networking equipment to a charging device to carry out a demand response plan already existed and was well-understood, routine, and conventional." But, as the district court pointed out, the "Background of the Invention" section of the specification demonstrates that demand response has been in use in other consumer services, such as with air conditioning and lighting, which may be reduced during periods of high demand. Indeed, demand response is simply a familiar business choice of terms of dealing to help match supply and demand. This cannot supply an inventive concept in this case.

31   Despite ChargePoint's reliance on *BASCOM Glob. Internet Servs., Inc. v. AT&T Mobility LLC*, 827 F.3d 1341 (Fed. Cir. 2016), the claims in this case do not improve the technology the way the claims in *BASCOM* did. There, the patent improved prior art content filtering solutions by making them more dynamic, thus using software to improve the performance of the computer system itself. *Id.* at 1351. Here, the claims do nothing to improve how charging stations function; instead, the claims merely add generic networking capabilities to those charging stations and say "apply it." *See Alice*, 573 U.S. at 223. This is simply an "abstract-idea-based solution implemented with generic technical components in a conventional way." *BASCOM*, 827 F.3d at 1351.

32   In short, we agree with SemaConnect that the only possible inventive concept in the asserted claims is the abstract idea itself. ChargePoint, of course, disagrees with this characterization, arguing that its patents claim "charging stations *enabled* to use networks, not the network connectivity itself." But the specification gives no indication that the patented invention involved how to add network connectivity to these charging stations in an unconventional way. From the claims and the specification, it is clear that network communication is the only possible inventive concept. Because this is the abstract idea itself, this cannot supply the inventive concept at step two. The claims are therefore ineligible.

33   For the foregoing reasons, we affirm the district court's determination that claims 1 and 2 of the '715 patent, claims 1 and 8 of the '131 patent [and the other asserted claims omitted from the discussion above] are ineligible under § 101.

USPTO Guidance on Abstract Ideas: MPEP § 2106

As noted above, the USPTO has issued extensive guidance to help patent examiners evaluate patentable subject matter, collected in MPEP § 2106. The Federal Circuit has not granted deference to this guidance, and the USPTO generally reads the caselaw as more favorable to patent eligibility than a neutral observer of the Federal Circuit might find it to be. Nonetheless, it is a helpful conceptual framework for approaching this complicated doctrine.

The USPTO notes that "the courts have declined to define abstract ideas," though it is clear that "software and business methods are not excluded categories." The agency has organized abstract ideas identified in the caselaw into three groups:

1. **Mathematical concepts:** e.g., the binary conversion procedure in *Benson*, the mathematical formula for calculating an alarm limit in *Flook*, the Arrhenius equation in *Diehr*, the mathematical formula for hedging in *Bilski*

2. **Certain methods of organizing human activity:**

    ○ fundamental economic principles or practices (e.g., hedging, insurance, mitigating risk, a method of price optimization, rules for a wagering game)

    ○ commercial or legal interactions (e.g., agreements in the form of contracts, legal obligations, marketing or sales activities or behaviors, business relations)

    ○ managing personal behavior or relationships or interactions between people (e.g., social activities, teaching, and following rules or instructions)

3. **Mental processes:** concepts that can practically be performed in the human mind (including an observation, evaluation, judgment, opinion)

As with laws of nature, a claim is not "directed to" an abstract idea if it merely *involves* rather than *recites* that idea. *See, e.g., Thales Visionix, Inc. v. United States*, 850 F.3d 1343 (Fed. Cir. 2017) (determining that the claims to a method of using data from inertial sensors to more accurately calculate the position of an object on a moving platform did not merely recite "the abstract idea of using mathematical equations for determining the relative position of a moving object to a moving reference frame").

Again, as with laws of nature, even if a claim recites an abstract idea, the USPTO cautions that it is not "directed to" the idea at *Alice/Mayo* Step 1 if it integrates the idea into a practical application. It is not enough, however, to merely recite the words "apply it" (or an equivalent), to add insignificant extra-solution activity, or to merely link the use of the exception to a particular technological environment. Limitations that may have integrated an idea into a practical application include improving the functioning of a computer, implementing the idea with a particular machine or manufacture that is integral to the claim, or effecting a transformation or reduction of a particular article to a different state or thing. Note that tangible implementation does not guarantee eligibility, nor does intangibility doom the claims. With the caveat that this "integrates into a practical application" gloss has not been endorsed by the Federal Circuit, MPEP § 2106.04(d) offers these examples of whether a claim integrates an idea into a practical application:

> In *Solutran, Inc. v. Elavon, Inc.*, 931 F.3d 1161 (Fed. Cir. 2019), the claims were to methods for electronically processing paper checks, all of which contained limitations setting forth receiving merchant transaction data from a merchant, crediting a merchant's account, and receiving and scanning paper checks after the merchant's account is credited.
>
> In part one of the *Alice/Mayo* test, the Federal Circuit determined that the claims were directed to the abstract idea of crediting the merchant's account before the paper check is scanned. The court first determined that the recited limitations of "crediting a merchant's account as early as possible while electronically processing a check" is a "long-standing commercial practice." The Federal Circuit then continued with its analysis under part one of the *Alice/Mayo* test finding that the claims are not directed to an improvement in the functioning of a computer or an improvement to another technology. In particular, the court determined that the claims "did not improve the technical capture of information from a check to create a digital file or the technical step of electronically crediting a bank account" nor did the claims "improve how a check is scanned." This analysis is equivalent to the Office's analysis of determining that the exception is not integrated

into a practical application [such that they are directed to an abstract idea at *Alice/Mayo* Step 1 and must be evaluated at *Alice/Mayo* Step 2 to determine if they are valid].

In *Finjan Inc. v. Blue Coat Systems, Inc.*, 879 F.3d 1299 (Fed. Cir. 2018), the claimed invention was a method of virus scanning that scans an application program, generates a security profile identifying any potentially suspicious code in the program, and links the security profile to the application program.

The Federal Circuit noted that the recited virus screening was an abstract idea, and that merely performing virus screening on a computer does not render the claim eligible. The court then continued with its analysis under part one of the *Alice/Mayo* test by reviewing the patent's specification, which described the claimed security profile as identifying both hostile and potentially hostile operations. The court noted that the security profile thus enables the invention to protect the user against both previously unknown viruses and "obfuscated code," as compared to traditional virus scanning, which only recognized the presence of previously-identified viruses. The security profile also enables more flexible virus filtering and greater user customization. The court identified these benefits as improving computer functionality, and verified that the claims recite additional elements (e.g., specific steps of using the security profile in a particular way) that reflect this improvement. Accordingly, the court held the claims eligible as not being directed to the recited abstract idea. This analysis is equivalent to the Office's analysis of determining that the additional elements integrate the judicial exception into a practical application [and that the claims are thus patent eligible].

If a claim isn't directed to an ineligible concept at Step 1, then it is patent eligible. But if it is directed to an ineligible concept, we move to Step 2: the search for an "inventive concept" that adds "significantly more" to the ineligible concept. Limitations courts have found to not add "significantly more" include adding the words "apply it," adding insignificant extra-solution activity, or linking the exception to a particular technological environment. Limitations that have qualified as "significantly more" include improving the functioning of a computer, implementing the idea with a particular machine, or transforming a particular article to a different state or thing.

But wait—aren't these Step 2 considerations the same ones the USPTO suggested considering for the "practical application" prong of Step 1? Indeed they are! Nonetheless, the USPTO is correct that the Federal Circuit uses similar considerations at both steps of the *Alice/Mayo* test, and the choice of whether to resolve a given case at Step 1 or Step 2 is often befuddling to even careful students of Federal

Circuit caselaw. All we can suggest is to strongly consider making arguments in the alternative in patentable subject matter briefs (or exam answers).

American Axle and the State of Patent Eligibility at the Federal Circuit

As the foregoing should make clear, determining whether a claim is "directed to" an ineligible concept, and separating the ineligible concept from the rest of the claim, is not a trivial exercise. All of science and technology relies at some level on abstract ideas and laws of nature. Distinguishing between claims that effectively claim those abstract ideas (and are thus unpatentable), and claims that merely draw upon them at some higher level of abstraction (and are thus patentable), is a task that frequently divides even the expert judges of the Federal Circuit.

The most recent instance of this is *American Axle v. Neapco Holdings*, 967 F.3d 1285, 1290 (Fed. Cir. 2020). The case involves a process for manufacturing driveline shafts, which are a part used in automobiles (and other motorized vehicles) to transfer power from the engine to the wheels. Driveline shafts spin very quickly and, as a result, can begin to vibrate rapidly. This may cause damage to the automobile and its drivetrain, and so one of the goals within the industry is to produce driveline shafts that will dampen any potential vibration. The patentee claimed to have invented a means of manufacturing a hollow driveline shaft with a liner inside the shaft that could be "tuned" (that is, adjusted) to dampen vibrations more effectively. Here is one claim from the patent:

> 22. A method for manufacturing a shaft assembly of a driveline system, the driveline system further including a first driveline component and a second driveline component, the shaft assembly being adapted to transmit torque between the first driveline component and the second driveline component, the method comprising:
>
> providing a hollow shaft member;
>
> tuning a mass and a stiffness of at least one liner, and
>
> inserting the at least one liner into the shaft member;
>
> wherein the at least one liner is a tuned resistive absorber for attenuating shell mode vibrations and wherein the at least one liner is a tuned reactive absorber for attenuating bending mode vibrations.

The challenging aspect of this claim is that it relies quite explicitly on a natural law: a driveline shaft with a liner that has been tuned in the proper manner will not vibrate as much when rotated. This fact derives from the physical laws of motion governing different types of materials. In practice, tuning might be more complicated than just applying these laws of physics, but the claim broadly covers any method of "tuning," by whatever steps happen to work. Indeed, the breadth of the claim is illustrated by testimony of the patentee's expert that one would infringe the claim by any method resulting in a tuned driveline shaft, even if unintentional. On the other hand, the claim is directed toward a highly tangible type of technology that has existed for decades: the manufacturing of automobile driveline shafts. It is not a software or business method patent, the types of inventions to which the Courts have most aggressively applied § 101 law. In addition, the patent does not seem to be trying to claim the law of nature writ large, but instead is only claiming its application in a particular engineering context.

The Federal Circuit panel held claim 22 invalid under *Mayo* as directed at a natural law. *Id.* at 1299. The full Federal Circuit, by a tie vote of 6-6, then elected not to rehear the case en banc, leaving the panel opinion undisturbed. 966 F.3d 1347 (Fed. Cir. 2020). This denial of rehearing en banc generated no fewer than five separate opinions from the twelve Federal Circuit judges. After the patentee filed for certiorari, the Supreme Court requested the views of the Solicitor General, who filed a brief recommending review in May 2022. By the time you read this casebook, the Supreme Court will have decided whether or not to take this opportunity to clarify the law it made in *Mayo* and *Alice*.

Practice Problems: Abstract Ideas

Consider the following claims. Do you think these claims involve patentable subject matter under *Alice*? If you will need more technical information to answer the question, explain what information you will need.

1. The invention is a method for sorting emails between various users and various mailboxes. The user could design a system of rules that would direct certain emails to certain mailboxes or folders based on the identity of the sender, the subject of the email, or other characteristics. The patent claims priority to 1997 and notes that the invention can operate on existing communications networks and that mailboxes can be connected to the network using conventional e-mail protocols. The claim reads:

> A post office for receiving and redistributing email messages on a computer network, the post office comprising:
> (a) a receipt mechanism that receives an e-mail message from a sender, the e-mail message having at least one specified recipient;
> (b) a database of business rules, each business rule specifying an action for controlling the delivery of an e-mail message as a function of an attribute of the e-mail message;
> (c) a rule engine coupled to receive an e-mail message from the receipt mechanism and coupled to the database to selectively apply the business rules to the e-mail message to determine from selected

ones of the business rules a set of actions to be applied to the e-mail
message . . . .

Intellectual Ventures v. Symantec, 838 F.3d 1307 (Fed. Cir. 2016).

2. The invention is an automated method of creating digitally animated
characters that can lip sync to music more convincingly. The invention involves a
database of "morph targets" showing how people's lips move when they are making a
variety of different sounds, which are transitioned between by selecting appropriate
"morph weighs." For instance, the face halfway between the neutral face and one
making an "oh" sound is expressed by setting the "oh" morph weight to 50%. When
the song called for a particular type of sound, the method would automatically load
the proper visual image from the database and display it for the digitally animated
character. The patent claims priority to 1997 and describes prior art processes that
required animators to manually select the appropriate morph weight for each frame
of the animation. The claim reads:

> A method for automatically animating lip synchronization and facial
> expression of three-dimensional characters comprising:
> (a) obtaining a first set of rules that define output morph weight set
>   stream as a function of phoneme sequence and time of said phoneme
>   sequence;
> (b) obtaining a timed data file of phonemes having a plurality of sub-
>   sequences;
> (c) generating an intermediate stream of output morph weight sets and
>   a plurality of transition parameters between two adjacent morph
>   weight sets by evaluating said plurality of sub-sequences against
>   said first set of rules;
> (d) generating a final stream of output morph weight sets at a desired
>   frame rate from said intermediate stream of output morph weight
>   sets and said plurality of transition parameters; and
> (e) applying said final stream of output morph weight sets to a sequence
>   of animated characters to produce lip synchronization and facial
>   expression control of said animated characters.

McRO v. Bandai Namco Games Am., 837 F.3d 1299 (Fed. Cir. 2016).

3. The invention is technology used to stream video to online users. A user
would send a video to the streaming service, which would convert the video into a
streaming format and then associate it with a picture that represented the video, so
that the picture could be embedded in a website. The patent claims priority to 2000,
when sending files over the Internet and converting video files to streaming format
were in the prior art. The patent explains that the invention improves computer
functionality by overcoming the burden of manually posting a link associated with a
video to a web page. The claim reads:

A method of streaming a video to users over a network, the method comprising the steps of:

(a) receiving, by a receiving computer via a web page, a video file sent by a user on a second computer on a network;

(b) executing, by the receiving computer, in response to receiving the video file, an automated function automatically performing each of:

> (i) converting the video file into a streaming video file comprising a streaming video format, the video file being converted independent from receiving a command to perform such conversion from the user;

> (ii) generating an identification tag comprising a video frame image representing a subject matter of the streaming video file and identifying the streaming video file; and

> (iii) embedding the identification tag comprising the video frame image into a web page for serving the streaming video file to one or more users on one or more computers on the network.

VideoShare v. Google, 2016 WL 4137524 (D. Del. Aug. 2, 2016), *aff'd*, 695 F. App'x 577 (Fed. Cir. 2016).

4. Prior art computer memory systems lacked versatility because they were designed and optimized based on the specific type of processor selected for use in that system. The invention purports to overcome these deficiencies by creating a memory system with programmable operational characteristics that can be tailored for use with multiple different processors without the accompanying reduction in performance. The patent claims priority to 1990 and includes a microfiche appendix with 263 frames of computer code, but it is unclear whether a PHOSITA would understand how this code relates to the claimed programmable operational characteristics. The claim reads:

A computer memory system connectable to a processor and having one or more programmable operational characteristics, said characteristics being defined through configuration by said computer based on the type of said processor, wherein said system is connectable to said processor by a bus, said system comprising:

(a) a main memory connected to said bus; and

(b) a cache connected to said bus;

(c) wherein a programmable operational characteristic of said system determines a type of data stored by said cache.

Visual Memory v. NVIDIA, 867 F.3d 1253 (Fed. Cir. 2017).

7. Inventorship and Double Patenting

In addition to satisfying the patentability requirements covered thus far, a patent also must correctly name the inventor or joint inventors—the individual people who contributed the ideas behind one or more of the claims. Inventorship is important for at least three reasons.

First, failure to correctly name inventors renders a patent invalid, although mistakes can be corrected if the error was made in good faith.

Second, by default, the inventors are joint owners of the patent, each of whom may independently license the patent. In most cases, inventors contract around this default by assigning patent rights to their employers; for example, an invention created in a university lab by a professor and her grad students will be owned by the university. But if a patent omits an inventor, a third party who wants to use the invention can seek correction of inventorship plus a license from the omitted inventor.

Third, inventorship matters because under both pre- and post-AIA § 102, an inventor's own earlier patent application is not prior art against her before publication the way it is against third parties. But courts have developed a separate doctrine—*double patenting*—to prevent an inventor from improperly extending the effective exclusivity period of the earlier application.

In this chapter, we first explain the law of inventorship and how finding omitted inventors can be used as a litigation strategy, and then we turn to double patenting.

A. Inventorship

The correct inventors for a patent are those individuals who contributed to the *conception* of at least one claim in the patent. As we explained in Chapter 2, invention begins with conception, or the formation of a definite and permanent idea of the complete and operative invention. Invention then concludes with reduction to practice, which is accomplished either by making the invention and ascertaining that it works for its intended purpose (actual reduction to practice) or filing an enabling patent application (constructive reduction to practice). For inventorship purposes, reduction to practice is irrelevant—a person who contributes to reduction to practice but not to conception is not an inventor.

The following statutory provisions govern inventors and joint inventors and their default ownership rights:

35 U.S.C. § 116 – Inventors

(a) Joint Inventions.— When an invention is made by two or more persons jointly, they shall apply for patent jointly and each make the required oath [unless they are deceased, incapacitated, unable to be found, or are required to assign the invention but have refused to file an inventor's oath]. Inventors may apply for a patent jointly even though (1) they did not physically work together or at the same time, (2) each did not make the same type or amount of contribution, or (3) each did not make a contribution to the subject matter of every claim of the patent.

(b) Omitted Inventor.— If a joint inventor refuses to join in an application for patent or cannot be found or reached after diligent effort, the application may be made by the other inventor on behalf of himself and the omitted inventor. The Director, on proof of the pertinent facts and after such notice to the omitted inventor as he prescribes, may grant a patent to the inventor making the application, subject to the same rights which the omitted inventor would have had if he had been joined. The omitted inventor may subsequently join in the application.

(c) Correction of Errors in Application.— Whenever through error a person is named in an application for patent as the inventor, or through error an inventor is not named in an application, the Director may permit the application to be amended accordingly, under such terms as he prescribes.

35 U.S.C. § 256 – Correction of Named Inventor

(a) Correction.— Whenever through error a person is named in an issued patent as the inventor, or through error an inventor is not named in an issued patent, the Director may, on application of all the parties and assignees, with proof of the facts and such other requirements as may be imposed, issue a certificate correcting such error.

(b) Patent Valid if Error Corrected.— The error of omitting inventors or naming persons who are not inventors shall not invalidate the patent in which such error occurred if it can be corrected as provided in this section. The court before which such matter is called in question may order correction of the patent on notice and hearing of all parties concerned and the Director shall issue a certificate accordingly.

35 U.S.C. § 262 – Joint Owners

In the absence of any agreement to the contrary, each of the joint owners of a patent may make, use, offer to sell, or sell the patented invention within the United States, or import the patented invention into the United States, without the consent of and without accounting to the other owners.

Failure to correctly identify inventors has consequences, as. noted above. It can result in the rejection of a patent application or invalidation of a granted patent if inventorship is not corrected—and if the failure was deliberate, the patent may be unenforceable for inequitable conduct (discussed in Chapter 12). More importantly, it can change ownership of the patent. By default, each inventor is a co-owner with the right to license the patent independently, so correcting a patent to add an omitted inventor also adds a new owner to the patent. Consider how generic pharmaceutical manufacturers that wanted to produce a patented HIV drug used inventorship rules in the following case.

Burroughs Wellcome v. Barr Laboratories, 40 F.3d 1223 (Fed. Cir. 1994)

Haldane Mayer, Circuit Judge.

1   Burroughs Wellcome Co. is the owner of six United States patents that cover various preparations of 3'–azidothymidine (AZT) and methods for using that drug in the treatment of persons infected with the human immunodeficiency virus (HIV). Each of these patents names the same five inventors—Janet Rideout, David Barry, Sandra Lehrman, Martha St. Clair, and Phillip Furman (Burroughs Wellcome inventors)—all of whom were employed by Burroughs Wellcome at the time the inventions were alleged to have been conceived. The defendants-appellants concede that all five are properly named as inventors on the patents.

2   In mid–1984, scientists discovered that AIDS was caused by a retrovirus known [today] as HIV. After the identification of HIV, Burroughs Wellcome began to search for a cure, screening compounds for antiretroviral activity using two murine (or mouse) retroviruses.

3   At about this time, scientists at the National Institutes of Health (NIH), led by Samuel Broder, were looking for effective AIDS therapies as well. Unlike Burroughs Wellcome, Broder and his colleagues used live HIV, and were able to develop a test that could demonstrate a compound's effectiveness against HIV in humans using a unique line of T-cell clones. The NIH scientists began to seek compounds from private pharmaceutical companies for screening in their cell line. After Burroughs Wellcome contacted Broder in the fall of 1984, he agreed to accept compounds from Burroughs Wellcome under code for testing against live HIV.

4   Burroughs Wellcome's Rideout selected AZT and a number of other compounds for testing in the murine screens on October 29, 1984. The tests, performed at Burroughs Wellcome facilities by St. Clair, showed that AZT had significant activity against both murine retroviruses at low concentrations. In light of these positive results, the Burroughs Wellcome inventors met on December 5, 1984, to discuss patenting the use of AZT in the treatment of AIDS. Burroughs Wellcome's patent committee thereafter recommended that the company prepare a patent application for future filing. By February 6, 1985, the company had prepared a draft application for filing in the United Kingdom. The draft disclosed using AZT to treat patients infected with HIV, and set out various pharmaceutical formulations of the compound in an effective dosage range to treat HIV infection.

5   Two days earlier, on February 4, 1985, Burroughs Wellcome had sent a sample of AZT, identified only as Compound S, to Broder at NIH. In an accompanying letter, Lehrman told Broder of the results of the murine retrovirus tests and asked that he screen the compound for activity against HIV in the [NIH's unique] cell line. Another NIH scientist, Hiroaka Mitsuya, performed the test in mid-February 1985, and found that Compound S was active against HIV. Broder informed Lehrman of the results by telephone on February 20, 1985. Burroughs Wellcome filed its patent application in the United Kingdom on March 16, 1985 [and subsequently filed U.S. patent applications claiming priority to this first application].

6   After Burroughs Wellcome learned that AZT was active against HIV, it began the process of obtaining Food and Drug Administration (FDA) approval for AZT as an AIDS therapy. As a part of the clinical trials leading to FDA approval, Broder and another NIH scientist, Robert Yarchoan, conducted a Phase I human patient study which showed that treatment with AZT could result in an increase in the patient's T-cell count. Broder reported this result to Lehrman on July 23, 1985. In 1987, the FDA approved AZT for marketing by Burroughs Wellcome; Burroughs Wellcome markets the drug for treatment of HIV infection under the trademark Retrovir.

7   On March 19, 1991, Barr Laboratories, Inc. (Barr) sought FDA approval to manufacture and market a generic version of AZT. As part of the process, Barr certified to the FDA that Burroughs Wellcome's patents were invalid or were not infringed by the product described in its ANDA. After Barr informed Burroughs Wellcome of its action, Burroughs Wellcome commenced this case for patent infringement against Barr on May 14, 1991, alleging technical infringement of its patents under 35 U.S.C. § 271(e)(2)(A). [After Novopharm filed its own generic application and was sued by Burroughs Wellcome, the suits were consolidated.]

8   Barr filed a counterclaim under 35 U.S.C. § 256 (1988) seeking correction of the patents to list Broder and Mitsuya as coinventors. Barr admitted that its AZT product would infringe the patents, but contended that it did not because Barr had obtained a license to manufacture and sell AZT from the government, which should

be deemed the owner of the interest of coinventors Broder and Mitsuya in the AZT patents.

9   The district court granted Burroughs Wellcome's motion for judgment as a matter of law against all of the defendants, concluding that the Burroughs Wellcome inventors had conceived of the subject matter of the inventions at some time before February 6, 1985, without the assistance of Broder, Mitsuya, or Yarchoan. The court rejected the arguments of Barr and Novopharm that they should be allowed to present evidence that the Burroughs Wellcome inventors had no reasonable belief that the inventions would actually work—that AZT was in fact active against HIV—until they were told the results of the NIH testing.

Discussion

10   The arguments of both Barr and Novopharm are directed to when the inventors conceived the invention. Burroughs Wellcome says it was before they learned the results of the NIH tests; Barr and Novopharm say that confirmation of the inventions' operability, which came from the NIH tests, was an essential part of the inventive process. If Burroughs Wellcome is right, then the patents name the proper inventors, they are not invalid, and the appellants are liable for infringement. If Barr and Novopharm are correct, then Broder, Mitsuya, and Yarchoan should have been named as joint inventors and the resolution of Burroughs Wellcome's infringement suits is premature.

11   A joint invention is the product of a collaboration between two or more persons working together to solve the problem addressed. 35 U.S.C. § 116 (1988); *Kimberly–Clark Corp. v. Procter & Gamble Distrib. Co.*, 973 F.2d 911, 917 (Fed. Cir. 1992). People may be joint inventors even though they do not physically work on the invention together or at the same time, and even though each does not make the same type or amount of contribution. 35 U.S.C. § 116. The statute does not set forth the minimum quality or quantity of contribution required for joint inventorship.

12   Conception is the touchstone of inventorship, the completion of the mental part of invention. It is "the formation in the mind of the inventor, of a definite and permanent idea of the complete and operative invention, as it is hereafter to be applied in practice." *Hybritech Inc. v. Monoclonal Antibodies, Inc.*, 802 F.2d 1367, 1376 (Fed. Cir. 1986). Conception is complete only when the idea is so clearly defined in the inventor's mind that only ordinary skill would be necessary to reduce the invention to practice, without extensive research or experimentation. Because it is a mental act, courts require corroborating evidence of a contemporaneous disclosure that would enable one skilled in the art to make the invention.

13   Thus, the test for conception is whether the inventor had an idea that was definite and permanent enough that one skilled in the art could understand the invention; the inventor must prove his conception by corroborating evidence, preferably by showing a contemporaneous disclosure. An idea is definite and

permanent when the inventor has a specific, settled idea, a particular solution to the problem at hand, not just a general goal or research plan he hopes to pursue. The conception analysis necessarily turns on the inventor's ability to describe his invention with particularity. Until he can do so, he cannot prove possession of the complete mental picture of the invention. These rules ensure that patent rights attach only when an idea is so far developed that the inventor can point to a definite, particular invention.

14   But an inventor need not know that his invention will work for conception to be complete. He need only show that he had the idea; the discovery that an invention actually works is part of its reduction to practice.

15   Barr and Novopharm suggest that the inventor's definite and permanent idea must include a reasonable expectation that the invention will work for its intended purpose. They argue that this expectation is of paramount importance when the invention deals with uncertain or experimental disciplines, where the inventor cannot reasonably believe an idea will be operable until some result supports that conclusion. Without some experimental confirmation, they suggest, the inventor has only a hope or an expectation, and has not yet conceived the invention in sufficiently definite and permanent form. But this is not the law. An inventor's belief that his invention will work or his reasons for choosing a particular approach are irrelevant to conception.

16   It is undoubtedly true that "[i]n some instances, an inventor is unable to establish a conception until he has reduced the invention to practice through a successful experiment." *Amgen v. Chugai Pharmaceutical*, 927 F.2d 1200, 1206 (Fed. Cir. 1991). But in such cases, it is not merely because the field is unpredictable; the alleged conception fails because it is incomplete. Then the event of reduction to practice in effect provides the only evidence to corroborate conception of the invention.

17   Under these circumstances, the reduction to practice can be the most definitive corroboration of conception, for where the idea is in constant flux, it is not definite and permanent. A conception is not complete if the subsequent course of experimentation, especially experimental failures, reveals uncertainty that so undermines the specificity of the inventor's idea that it is not yet a definite and permanent reflection of the complete invention as it will be used in practice. It is this factual uncertainty, not the general uncertainty surrounding experimental sciences, that bears on the problem of conception.

18   We emphasize that we do not hold that a person is precluded from being a joint inventor simply because his contribution to a collaborative effort is experimental. Instead, the qualitative contribution of each collaborator is the key—each inventor must contribute to the joint arrival at a definite and permanent idea of the invention as it will be used in practice.

19   Nor do we suggest that a bare idea is all that conception requires. The idea must be definite and permanent in the sense that it involves a specific approach to

the particular problem at hand. It must also be sufficiently precise that a skilled artisan could carry out the invention without undue experimentation. And, of course, the alleged conception must be supported by corroborating evidence.

20   [Five of the patents at issue] encompass compositions and methods of using AZT to treat AIDS. The Burroughs Wellcome inventors claim conception of these inventions prior to the NIH experiments, based on the draft British patent application. That document is not itself a conception, for conception occurs in the inventors' minds, not on paper. The draft simply corroborates the claim that they had formulated a definite and permanent idea of the inventions by the time it was prepared.

21   The Burroughs Wellcome inventors set out with the general goal of finding a method to treat AIDS, but by the time Broder confirmed that AZT was active against HIV, they had more than a general hope or expectation. They had thought of the particular antiviral agent with which they intended to address the problem, and had formulated the idea of the inventions to the point that they could express it clearly in the form of a draft patent application, which Barr and Novopharm concede would teach one skilled in the art to practice the inventions. The draft expressly discloses the intended use of AZT to treat AIDS. It sets out the compound's structure, which, along with at least one method of preparation, was already well known. The draft also discloses in detail both how to prepare a pharmaceutical formulation of AZT and how to use it to treat a patient infected with HIV. The listed dosages, dose forms, and routes of administration conform to those eventually approved by the FDA. The draft shows that the idea was clearly defined in the inventors' minds; all that remained was to reduce it to practice—to confirm its operability and bring it to market.

22   An examination of the events that followed the preparation of Burroughs Wellcome's draft confirms the soundness of the conception. Broder and Mitsuya received from Burroughs Wellcome a group of compounds, known to Broder and Mitsuya only by code names, selected for testing by the Burroughs Wellcome inventors. They then tested those compounds for activity against HIV in their patented cell line. The test results revealed for the first time that one of the compounds, later revealed to be AZT, was exceptionally active against the virus.

23   Here, though, the testing was brief, simply confirming the operability of what the draft application disclosed. True, the science surrounding HIV and AIDS was unpredictable and highly experimental at the time the Burroughs Wellcome scientists made the inventions. But what matters for conception is whether the inventors had a definite and permanent idea of the operative inventions. In this case, no prolonged period of extensive research, experiment, and modification followed the alleged conception. By all accounts, what followed was simply the normal course of clinical trials that mark the path of any drug to the marketplace.

24   That is not to say, however, that the NIH scientists merely acted as a "pair of hands" for the Burroughs Wellcome inventors. Broder and Mitsuya exercised

considerable skill in conducting the tests, using their patented cell line to model the responses of human cells infected with HIV. Lehrman did suggest initial concentrations to Broder, but she hardly controlled the conduct of the testing, which necessarily involved interpretation of results for which Broder and Mitsuya, and very few others, were uniquely qualified. But because the testing confirmed the operability of the inventions, it showed that the Burroughs Wellcome inventors had a definite and permanent idea of the inventions. It was part of the reduction to practice and inured to the benefit of Burroughs Wellcome.

25   Barr and Novopharm allege error in the district court's refusal to hear their evidence of the poor predictive value of the murine retrovirus screens for activity against HIV. Regardless of the predictive value of the murine tests, however, the record shows that soon after those tests, the inventors determined, for whatever reason, to use AZT as a treatment for AIDS, and they prepared a draft patent application that specifically set out the inventions, including an enabling disclosure. Obviously, enablement and conception are distinct issues, and one need not necessarily meet the enablement standard of 35 U.S.C. § 112 to prove conception. But the enabling disclosure does suffice in this case to confirm that the inventors had concluded the mental part of the inventive process—that they had arrived at the final, definite idea of their inventions, leaving only the task of reduction to practice to bring the inventions to fruition.

26   The question is not whether Burroughs Wellcome reasonably believed that the inventions would work for their intended purpose, the focus of the evidence offered by Barr and Novopharm, but whether the inventors had formed the idea of their use for that purpose in sufficiently final form that only the exercise of ordinary skill remained to reduce it to practice. Whether or not Burroughs Wellcome believed the inventions would in fact work based on the mouse screens is irrelevant.

27   We do not know precisely when the inventors conceived their inventions, but the record shows that they had done so by the time they prepared the draft patent application that thoroughly and particularly set out the inventions as they would later be used. The district court correctly ruled that on this record, the NIH scientists were not joint inventors of these inventions.

28   [For the sixth patent, which claimed the use of AZT to increase a patient's T-cell count, the Federal Circuit vacated the district court's judgment because the record did not support resolution as a matter of law of whether the inventors had this definite and permanent idea in mind. Judge Lourie dissented from this portion of the opinion, concluding that increasing a patient's T-cell count was an inherent result of practicing the other patents.]

Discussion Questions: Inventorship

1. *AZT and the HIV/AIDS Crisis.* The federal government was not a party to this lawsuit, but they played an important role. What was their role, and why do you think they were siding with the generic manufacturers Barr Laboratories and Novopharm? Is it relevant that this litigation occurred at the height of the HIV/AIDS epidemic and involved one of the first antiretroviral drugs that was effective at treating the disease? What role do you think patents should play in the middle of a public health crisis?

Does your answer differ for patents in other countries? As we will discuss in Chapter 20, the 1994 Agreement on Trade-Related Aspects of Intellectual Property Rights (TRIPS) requires all but the least-developed nations to protect the IP rights of all 164 TRIPS members. Most pharmaceuticals are patented around the world. In the 2013 documentary *Fire in the Blood*, which depicts barriers to access to low-cost HIV/AIDS drugs in Africa, activist Zackie Achmat noted that it took nearly 40 years for the U.S. government to put apartheid South Africa on a sanctions watch list, but it took less than three years to put democratic South Africa on a sanctions watch list for importing generic AIDS drugs in violation of patent laws.

Is patent law a good tool for improving access to medicines, in the United States or abroad? Should judges faced with a technical legal question about inventorship—as in *Burroughs Wellcome*—consider the broader policy concerns at stake? If so, how?

2. *The Different Standards of Patent Inventorship and Scientific Authorship.* As *Burroughs Wellcome* explains, a researcher who contributes only to the reduction to practice of an invention is not an inventor. But under the norms of scientific authorship, such a researcher often would be included as an author on a corresponding paper. Here is the first paper on the in vitro results using NIH's patented cell line:

Proc. Natl. Acad. Sci. USA
Vol. 82, pp. 7096–7100, October 1985
Medical Sciences

3'-Azido-3'-deoxythymidine (BW A509U): An antiviral agent that inhibits the infectivity and cytopathic effect of human T-lymphotropic virus type III/lymphadenopathy-associated virus *in vitro*

(inhibition of human T-lymphotropic virus type III/thymidine analogue/acquired immune deficiency syndrome/retrovirus)

HIROAKI MITSUYA*, KENT J. WEINHOLD[†], PHILLIP A. FURMAN[‡], MARTY H. ST. CLAIR[‡], SANDRA NUSINOFF LEHRMAN[‡], ROBERT C. GALLO[§], DANI BOLOGNESI[†], DAVID W. BARRY[‡], AND SAMUEL BRODER*

*The Clinical Oncology Program and §Laboratory of Tumor Cell Biology, National Cancer Institute, Bethesda, MD 20205; †Department of Surgery, Surgical Virology Laboratory, Duke University Medical Center, Durham, NC 27710; and ‡Wellcome Research Laboratories, Research Triangle Park, NC 27709

The first author, Hiroaki Mitsuya, is the NIH scientist who ran the tests, and the last author, Samuel Broder, is the leader of the NIH group, in keeping with common authorship norms in many scientific fields. Why do you think the standards for inventorship and authorship differ? Should they?

One study found that junior or female scientists who are named as authors on a paper are more likely to be excluded as inventors on the corresponding patent than their senior or male counterparts. Francesco Lissoni, Fabio Montobbio & Lorenzo Zirulia, *Misallocation of Scientific Credit: The Role of Hierarchy and Preferences*, 6 Indus. & Corp. Change 1471 (2020). How would you explain this result?

3. *Joint Inventorship Rules as a Penalty Default?* As explained above, by default, joint inventors are co-owners of any resulting patent. Each may independently exploit and license the patent, with no duty to obtain consent from other co-owners or to share patent-related income. In most cases, inventors contract around this default by assigning their interest to their employers. And when separate individuals or firms collaborate on a project, it is generally under a joint development agreement that specifies ownership of any resulting intellectual property. If co-inventors of a valuable patent do not contract around the default ownership rules, what would you expect to happen if each inventor seeks to maximize profits? Do you think they want to be in this default situation? If not, inventorship rules might be referred to as a "penalty default rule": a rule that most parties would find undesirable, and that thus encourages them to contract around the rule. Can you think of why this default rule might be justified from a social welfare perspective? What kind of inventors might be disadvantaged by this rule?

4. *The History of Black Inventorship in the United States.* As discussed in Chapter 1, some scholars have argued that patent law has democratized innovation throughout U.S. history, although inventors from disadvantaged groups still face barriers to successfully receiving rewards from the patent system. Shontavia Johnson recounts the history of Black inventorship in the United States, shedding light on the many legal and practical barriers Black inventors have faced, and highlighting how they have been innovating nonetheless throughout the centuries.

One quintessential example of early American ingenuity is the story of Benjamin Montgomery, who was born into slavery in Virginia in 1819 and later sold in Mississippi to Joseph Davis, the brother of Jefferson Davis. While enslaved in Mississippi, Montgomery invented a certain type of boat propeller with significant utility for those who depended on steamboats to deliver goods along the waterways. Montgomery could not receive a patent for the invention as he was a slave and not considered a citizen. Nonetheless, Montgomery found success. He operated a general store on the plantation, built relationships, and continued to innovate. He eventually earned enough money to purchase his wife's freedom. After the Civil War ended, he also purchased the plantation he worked on as a slave and became one of the wealthiest planters in Mississippi. . . .

During these early American years, free black Americans were also inventing and contributing to the country's transition into a land of innovation. Thomas Jennings, the first known black patentee, was born free and successfully patented a dry cleaning method in 1821. This proved to be lucrative for him, as the ability to exclude others from making and selling his invention led Jennings to own one of New York City's largest clothing stores. [H]e used the profits from his patented invention to free the rest of his family from slavery. . . .

Another black inventor, Norbert Rillieux, revolutionized industry both domestically and abroad. Rillieux was born free in Louisiana in 1806 and studied engineering in France. Because of his intelligence, he became the youngest person ever—at age 24—to serve as an applied mechanics instructor at L'École Centrale, a prestigious French institution. Rillieux ultimately applied for and received four U.S. patents related to sugar refining once he returned to America. His inventions transformed the industry, and he became the most celebrated engineer in Louisiana at the time.

Shontavia Jackson Johnson, *The Colorblind Patent System and Black Inventors*, 11 Landslide 16 (2019).

These entrepreneurs succeeded despite huge structural barriers. The racism of the early U.S. patent system is perhaps most prominently illustrated by an odious 1858 opinion issued by Attorney General Jeremiah Black. As recently summarized by Kara Swanson:

He needed only three sentences to explain that an invention by an enslaved inventor could not be patented. The Attorney General relied on the Supreme Court's holding the previous year in *Dred Scott v. Sandford* that African Americans were not citizens, whether free or enslaved. Without the ability to swear an oath of citizenship, enslaved persons could not apply for patents. This reasoning also placed free African Americans outside the bounds of patent law.

Kara W. Swanson, *Race and Selective Legal Memory: Reflections on* Invention of a Slave, 120 Colum. L. Rev. 1077 (2020). Swanson has also recounted how marginalized inventors used false non-inventors as a form of "passing," helping them "avoid bias and stigma in the patent office and the marketplace" but also depriving them of "the public status of inventor and also, often, the full value of their inventions." Kara W. Swanson, *Inventing While a Black Woman: Passing and the Patent Archive*, 25 Stan. Tech. L. Rev. (forthcoming).

What should be done to account for the harms perpetrated by these rules? Should the USPTO attempt to track down the Black inventors who were denied patents prior to the Thirteenth Amendment and add them as named inventors to the patents that issued based on their work? Should there be other efforts to memorialize the inventors who were denied patents? Should the U.S. government attempt to calculate the value of these inventions and pay reparations to the descendants of their true inventors? What about the broader social harms caused by underrepresentation of women and racial minorities among named inventors? Are these types of harm best addressed inside or outside of the patent system?

5. *AI Inventors?* Can a computer qualify as an inventor? In 2019, the Artificial Inventor Project filed a patent application in several jurisdictions with the inventor listed as a computer program known as DABUS (Device for the Autonomous Bootstrapping of Unified Sentience). The academic spearheading this test case argued that recognizing AI inventors will incentivize development of inventive AI systems. *See* Ryan Abbott, *The Reasonable Robot: Artificial Intelligence and the Law* (2020). The USPTO, European Patent Office, and UK Intellectual Property Office refused to recognize DABUS as an inventor. If DABUS cannot be an inventor, is there a proper inventor for this patent application? Or does the invention have no inventor, which would make it unpatentable?

Do you think inventorship doctrine should be revised to account for inventions where an entity other than a natural person contributes to conception? When the USPTO requested comments on this issue in 2019, the "vast majority" responded "no," and many questioned the premise that state-of-the-art AI could conceive an invention. *See* USPTO, *Public Views on Artificial Intelligence and Intellectual Property Policy* (2020), https://www.uspto.gov/sites/default/files/documents/USPTO_AI-Report_2020-10-07.pdf.

B. Double Patenting

Patent inventorship rules are also important for applying a final patentability doctrine: a prohibition on "double patenting." As explained in Chapter 2, patents and patent applications are generally prior art as of the date they are filed, as long as they are eventually published. For example, suppose Sofía is a researcher at IBM who invents a new semiconductor design. If IBM files a patent application on January 1, 2020, which is published in due course on July 1, 2021, the application is prior art against most applications filed after January 1, 2020 under post-AIA § 102(a)(2). But § 102(a)(2) applies only to a second patent application that "names another inventor," and there is also an exception under § 102(b)(2)(C) for a second application "owned by the same person or subject to an obligation of assignment to the same person" (where ownership includes invention under a "joint research agreement," per § 102(c)). Thus, what is to prevent Sofía and IBM from filing the exact same application on February 1, 2021?

The same problem arises pre-AIA. If IBM files the first patent application on January 1, 2010, and it is published on July 1, 2011, it is generally prior art against applications filed after January 1, 2010 under pre-AIA § 102(e). But pre-AIA § 102(e) applies only to patents and patent applications filed "by another," meaning not filed by the exact same inventors (known as the "inventive entity"). It thus would not apply to a second application filed by IBM on February 1, 2011, with Sofía as the named inventor. Again, nothing in § 102 prevents IBM from obtaining identical patents with different expiration dates.

IBM could not use this tactic to extend the patent term indefinitely—once the earlier application is published (typically at 18 months after filing), it is prior art as of the publication date under post-AIA § 102(a)(1) or pre-AIA § 102(a) and (b). But it could obtain an 18-month extension. And the problem was even more significant before 1995, when the patent term was 17 years from issuance rather than 20 years from filing, such that delaying prosecution of one of the patent applications would result in a very long effective patent term.

To address this type of concern with improper extension of exclusive rights, courts have developed the doctrine of double patenting, which comes in two flavors. "Same-invention" double patenting prohibits an inventor from receiving two patents on the same invention. "Obviousness-type" double patenting prohibits an inventor from receiving a patent on an obvious variation of her earlier patent unless she files a "terminal disclaimer" such that both patents expire at the same time. In both cases, the *later-expiring* patent is the one that is invalid. These double patenting issues can arise whenever two or more patents or patent applications have at least one common inventor or common owner, or when the owners have entered a joint research agreement. For the USPTO's double patenting flowcharts, see MPEP § 804.

For an illustration of how terminal disclaimers work, consider the cover pages of the following two patents, both from the inventorship case excerpted earlier in this chapter, *Burroughs Wellcome v. Barr Laboratories*, 40 F.3d 1223 (Fed. Cir. 1994). The '232 patent was filed before June 8, 1995, so it expired 17 years from issuance, on February 9, 2005. For the '750 patent, before you look at the answer in the footnote, try to figure out: When was the effective filing date, and when did it expire?[1]

---

[1] The '750 patent was actually filed on October 20, 1987, but it is a continuation of the '232 patent that was filed September 17, 1985, so that's the effective filing date. It issued April 4, 1989, so would normally expire April 4, 2006, but it has disclaimed patent term after February 9, 2005. Both patents expire on the same day.

United States Patent [19]

Rideout et al.

[11] **Patent Number:** **4,724,232**

[45] **Date of Patent:** **Feb. 9, 1988**

[54] **TREATMENT OF HUMAN VIRAL INFECTIONS**

[75] Inventors: **Janet L. Rideout**, Raleigh; **David W. Barry**, Chapel Hill; **Sandra N. Lehrman**, Durham; **Martha H. St. Clair**, Durham; **Phillip A. Furman**, Durham, all of N.C.

[73] Assignee: **Burroughs Wellcome Co.**, Research Triangle Park, N.C.

[21] Appl. No.: **776,899**

[22] Filed: **Sep. 17, 1985**

[30] **Foreign Application Priority Data**

Mar. 16, 1985 [GB] United Kingdom 8506869
May 9, 1985 [GB] United Kingdom 8511774

[51] Int. Cl.⁴ **A61K 31/70**; A61K 9/00; A61K 9/22

[52] U.S. Cl. **514/50**; 514/51; 424/451; 536/23

[58] Field of Search 536/28, 29; 514/50, 514/51, 885; 424/451, 464

[56] **References Cited**

FOREIGN PATENT DOCUMENTS

Ostertag et al, Proc. Nat. Acad. Sci. USA 71 (1974).
Exp. Cell. Res., 116: 31-37, 1978.
P.N.A.S. 82: 7096-7100, 1985.
J.A.M. Med. Assoc. 254: 2521, 2522, 2529, 1985.
Chem. Eng. News 64: 28-40, 1986.
FDA Drug Bull. 15: 27-32, 1985.
Proc. Am. Assoc. Con. Res. 27: 422, 1986.
Con. Res. 32: 1547-1583, 1972.
The Lancet, Apr. 25, 1987, pp. 957-958.
J. Med. Chem. 26: 1691-1696, 1983.
J. Med. Chem., 26: 891-895, 1983.
Carr. Chemother Immunother. Proc Int. Cong. Chemother, 12th, vol. 2: 1062-1064, 1982.
Nucleic Acids Res. Sym. Ser., No. 9, pp. 49-52, 1980.

Primary Examiner—J. R. Brown
Assistant Examiner—John W. Rollins
Attorney, Agent, or Firm—Donald Brown; Lawrence A. Nielsen

[57] **ABSTRACT**

Treatment of AIDS or humans carrying or infected with the AIDS virus or having antibodies to the AIDS virus is disclosed using the compound 3'-azido-3'-deoxythymidine or a pharmaceutically acceptable basic salt thereof.

United States Patent [19]

Rideout et al.

[11] **Patent Number:** **4,818,750**

[45] **Date of Patent:** *Apr. 4, 1989

[54] **TREATMENT OF HUMAN VIRAL INFECTIONS**

[75] Inventors: **Janet L. Rideout**, Raleigh; **David W. Barry**, Chapel Hill; **Sandra N. Lehrman**, Durham; **Martha H. St. Clair**, Durham; **Phillip A. Furman**, Durham, all of N.C.

[73] Assignee: **Burroughs Wellcome Co.**, Research Triangle Park, N.C.

[*] Notice: The portion of the term of this patent subsequent to Feb. 9, 2005 has been disclaimed.

[21] Appl. No.: **110,968**

[22] Filed: **Oct. 20, 1987**

Related U.S. Application Data

[63] Continuation of Ser. No. 776,899, Sep. 17, 1985, Pat. No. 4,724,232.

[56] **References Cited**

PUBLICATIONS

Osterag et al., Expt. Cell Res. 116:31-37, 1978.
Osterag et al., PNAS, 71:4980-4985, 1974.
Mitsuya et al., PNAS, 82:7096-7100, 1985.
J. A. M. Med. Assoc., 254:2521, 2522, 2529, 1985.
Robins, Chem. Eng. News, 64:28-40, 1985.
FDA Drug Bull., 15:27-32, 1985.
The Lancet, Apr. 25, 1987, pp. 957-958.
Krieg et al., Exp. Cell Res., 116:21-29, 1978.
Lin et al., J. Med. Chem., 26:1691-1696, 1983.
De Clercq et al., Bischem. Pharm., 29:1849-1851, 1980.

Primary Examiner—John W. Rollins
Attorney, Agent, or Firm—Donald Brown; Lawrence A. Nielsen

[57] **ABSTRACT**

Treatment of AIDS or humans carrying or infected with the AIDS virus or having antibodies to the AIDS virus is disclosed using the compound 3'-azido-3'-deoxythymidine or a pharmaceutically basic salt thereof.

Also disclosed is the use of the 5'-mono-, di- and triphosphate of 3'-azido-3'-deoxythymidine or a pharmaceutically acceptable basic salt thereof for the same

Same-Invention Double Patenting

Same-invention double patenting is also known as *statutory* double patenting because it is (weakly) grounded in the language of 35 U.S.C. § 101, which states that an inventor "may obtain *a* patent" (emphasis added). *See In re Longi*, 759 F.2d 887, 892 (Fed. Cir. 1985). Determining whether two claims are directed to the same invention parallels the element-by-element analysis we have performed when assessing novelty. The Federal Circuit's predecessor court has summarized the doctrine:

> 35 U.S.C. § 101 prevents two patents from issuing on the same invention. As we have said many times, "invention" here means what is defined by the claims. A good test, and probably the only objective test, for "same invention," is *whether one of the claims could be literally infringed without literally infringing the other.* If it could be, the claims do not define identically the same invention. If it is determined that the same invention is being claimed twice, 35 U.S.C. § 101 forbids the grant of the second patent, regardless of the presence or absence of a terminal disclaimer.

In re Vogel, 422 F.2d 438, 441 (C.C.P.A. 1970) (emphasis added).

Obviousness-Type Double Patenting

Obviousness-type double patenting is also known as *non-statutory* double patenting because it "is a judicially created doctrine grounded in public policy (a policy reflected in the patent statute) rather than based purely on the precise terms of the statute." *Longi*, 759 F.2d at 892. Obviousness-type double patenting prevents an inventor from obtaining a second patent that is an obvious variation on an earlier one. The test is similar to the § 103 analysis, except that it is only the *claims* of the earlier patent that are prior art:

> The doctrine of obviousness-type double patenting is intended to prevent the extension of the term of a patent by prohibiting the issuance of the claims in a second patent not patentably distinct from the claims of the first patent. A later patent claim is not patentably distinct from an earlier claim if the later claim is obvious over, or anticipated by, the earlier claim.

> As a general rule, obviousness-type double patenting determinations turn on a comparison between a patentee's earlier and later claims, with the earlier patent's written description considered only to the extent necessary to construe its claims. This is so because the nonclaim portion of the earlier patent ordinarily does not qualify as prior art against the patentee and because obviousness-type double

patenting is concerned with the improper extension of exclusive rights—rights conferred and defined by the claims. The focus of the obviousness-type double patenting doctrine thus rests on preventing a patentee from claiming an obvious variant of what it has previously *claimed*, not what it has previously *disclosed*.

Eli Lilly & Co. v. Teva Parenteral Medicines, 689 F.3d 1368, 1376, 1378–79 (Fed. Cir. 2012).

The Federal Circuit has emphasized two justifications for this doctrine. "The first is to prevent unjustified timewise extension of the right to exclude granted by a patent no matter how the extension is brought about. The second rationale is to prevent multiple infringement suits by different assignees asserting essentially the same patented invention." *In re Hubbell*, 709 F.3d 1140, 1145 (Fed. Cir. 2013).

When the two patents involved in an obviousness-type double patenting rejection or invalidation are commonly owned, the problem can be cured by filing a terminal disclaimer on the later-expiring patent, which effectively causes it to expire at the same time as the earlier patent. 35 U.S.C. § 253(b) states that "any patentee or applicant may disclaim or dedicate to the public the entire term, or any terminal part of the term, of the patent granted or to be granted." A terminal disclaimer can be filed to overcome the invalidation of a patent for obviousness-type double patenting during litigation. *Eli Lilly*, 689 F.3d at 1375. (Why does the law not allow patent owners to cure most other validity problems during litigation?)

However, the terminal disclaimer fixes the problem "only for and during such period that said patent is commonly owned with the application or patent which formed the basis for the judicially created double patenting" or, if created under a joint research agreement, "only for and during such period that said patent and the patent, or any patent granted on the application, which formed the basis for the double patenting are not separately enforced." 37 C.F.R. § 1.321(c)-(d). Terminal disclaimers can thus complicate sales of patent portfolios because if the patents are sold separately, the patent with the terminal disclaimer would become unenforceable.

Discussion Questions: Double Patenting

1. *Why Treat an Inventor's Own Earlier Patent Applications Differently?* The complicated doctrine of double patenting evolved because both pre- and post-AIA treat earlier patent applications as prior art as of their filing date (rather than as of their publication date) only if the applications were filed by other applicants. Why are prior patent filings by the same inventor or owner (including companies working under a joint research agreement) treated differently? Once an inventor has filed one patent, she can file additional patents that claim obvious improvements on the first patent until the first patent is published, but an unrelated inventor cannot. One justification may be to encourage the inventor to file the first patent early, without worrying about

whether it might prevent her from patenting later work. Do you find this convincing? For additional justifications and effects of treating an applicant's own earlier patent applications differently and suggestions for reform, see Amy R. Motomura, *Innovation and Own Prior Art*, 72 Hastings L.J. 565 (2021).

2. *Obviousness in Light of the Claims?* When judging whether an applicant is engaged in obviousness-type double patenting, why do courts look only to the claims of the prior patent and not the specification? Suppose an inventor filed for a second patent with claims that were obvious in light of the specification of the first patent. If that first patent belonged to any other party, the second patent would be invalid as obvious. But under these rules, the same inventor can obtain a second patent on the same material. Does that seem appropriate? Are there, or should there be, boundaries on this doctrine that prevent such sequential patenting?

Practice Problem: Inventorship, Double Patenting, and § 102 Review

Given the facts below, does anyone receive a patent on the widget? Unless otherwise specified, all patent applications are published in due course.

- Jan. 2005: Juting conceives of a new invention, the widget, but she isn't sure that it will work for its intended purpose or how to test it.

- Jan. 2006: Darryl conceives of the widget and reduces it to practice.

- Jan. 2007: Jamar conceives of the widget, reduces it to practice, and makes a secret commercial offer for sale.

- Mar. 2008: Daisuke conceives of the widget and submits a paper explaining why it would work to *Journal of Inventions*. It is accepted and sent to the printers in December 2008 and received by subscribers in February 2009.

- June 2008: Jamar files a patent application claiming the widget.

- Jan. 2009: Juting meets Elisa, who knows how to test the widget and confirms that it works. Elisa also shows that they can make widgets out of vibranium, which is a not insignificant but obvious improvement.

- Apr. 2009: At a party, Elisa demonstrates a widget to 30 friends, including Alex, none of whom had ever seen a widget before.

- June 2009: Alex files a patent application claiming widgets.

- Sept. 2009: Juting and Elisa file a patent application claiming widgets.

- Nov. 2009: Jamar abandons his patent application.

- Dec. 2009: Juting and Elisa file a new patent application claiming vibranium widgets.

- Mar. 2010: Darryl recalls his earlier idea and files a patent application claiming widgets.

III. Infringement

The principal right that accompanies a valid patent is the right to exclude others from making, using, selling, or importing the patented invention. If a patent owner believes that another is engaging in such activity, the owner may sue the other party for patent infringement. At its heart, the infringement allegation is simple: the alleged infringer is making, using, selling, or importing a good or process that meets all of the limitations of the patent claim. The first step of any infringement analysis, then, is to understand what the claims of the patent mean.

In fact, interpreting the patent claims is the first step to nearly all of the patentability doctrines we described in the previous chapters as well. It is impossible to determine whether a patent claim is novel, or nonobvious, or satisfies the written description or enablement requirements without first interpreting the claim and determining, as a legal matter, what it means. Even the doctrine of patentable subject matter, which is often adjudicated before the patent claims are fully interpreted, relies on understanding what the claims mean, at least in broad strokes. The process of claim interpretation, or "claim construction," is thus at the heart of nearly all of patent law. Nonetheless, we have saved it for this point in the book. The reason is that it is essential to understand what makes a patent claim valid in order to understand what is at stake in claim construction. Additionally, the Federal Circuit has "emphasized the importance of the context provided by an [infringement] analysis of the accused device when ruling on claim construction and the problems presented by construing claims in the absence of such context." *Jang v. Bos. Sci. Corp.*, 532 F.3d 1330, 1337 (Fed. Cir. 2008).

Accordingly, we discuss the law of claim construction in Chapter 8 before turning directly to patent infringement in Chapters 9–11. Infringement comes in two general flavors: "direct" and "indirect." In a case involving direct infringement, the claim is that the accused device includes all of the elements of the claim, either "literally" (meaning the element is actually present) or as an "equivalent" (meaning the accused device has a feature that is equivalent to the claim element). Indirect infringement involves the claim that one party is facilitating the infringement of another party. Thus, in a case of indirect infringement, the actual infringer may be "off screen"—meaning not a party to the lawsuit. The following table provides an overview of the statutes governing infringement that will be discussed in subsequent chapters.

As we will see, the law of infringement employs many of the same concepts and doctrinal rules as the law of validity. But there are a variety of new doctrines and additional wrinkles, which we will explore in detail. First, a discussion of rules surrounding claim construction.

Type of Infringement	Overview
9. Direct (§ 271(a))	§ 271(a) provides strict liability for any entity that "makes, uses, offers to sell, or sells any patented invention, within the United States or imports into the United States any patented invention." Direct infringement can be *literal*, requiring every claim element to be met (mirroring the anticipation analysis) or infringement under the *doctrine of equivalents*, if for every claim element, the infringing device or method has an element performing the same function in the same way for the same result.
10. Indirect (§ 271(b)-(c))	An entity can also be *indirectly* liable under § 271(b) for *inducing* another entity to directly infringe, or under § 271(c) for *contributing* to another entity's direct infringement by selling something especially adapted for use in an infringement. Indirect liability requires knowledge of (or willful blindness to) the patent.
11(A). Divided (§ 271(a), (e)-(g))	When multiple entities perform different steps of a method patent, there is direct infringement only if a single entity directs or controls the performance or where the actors form a joint enterprise. There cannot be indirect infringement without direct infringement.
11(B). Cross-Border (§ 271(f)-(g))	Although there is generally a presumption against extraterritorial application of U.S. law, entities are liable under § 271(f) for exporting "components of a patented invention" so as to induce their combination abroad, or where the components are especially adapted for use in an infringement abroad. And entities are liable under § 271(g) for importing, offering to sell, selling, or using within the United States a product made abroad by a process patented in the United States.
11(C). Government (§ 271(h), 28 U.S.C. § 1498(a))	The federal government can be sued only for patent damages under § 1498(a), with damages calculated by the Court of Federal Claims, not for an injunction. State governments can generally be sued only for an injunction, not damages.
11(D). Pharmaceutical (§ 271(e))	Under the 1984 Hatch-Waxman Act for small-molecule drugs and the 2011 Biologics Price Competition and Innovation Act for biologic drugs, a generic firm's FDA application to market a patent-protected drug allows the brand-name firm to commence patent litigation.

8. Claim Construction

As we noted above, many critical patent doctrines turn on the meaning of the patent claims. Claim language can be complex or ambiguous, which makes their interpretation essential. In the 1996 case *Markman v. Westview Instruments*, 517 U.S. 370, the Supreme Court held that claim construction is a legal question to be decided by the judge, not the jury. This followed from the fact that a patent is a legal document, issued by the government, and thus analogous to a statute. In most patent trials, the district judge will solicit briefing on contested claim construction issues relatively early in the proceeding and will typically hold a hearing—sometimes referred to as a "Markman" hearing—to decide those issues. For instance, the Northern District of California, which includes Silicon Valley and is the site of many patent trials, has a set of local rules governing patent cases.[1] Those local rules provide that the parties to a patent dispute must first notify one another of the patent claims that they believe are infringed or invalid, and then within fourteen days must notify one another and the court of any claim terms the parties believe need to be construed by the court. The court will then construe the claims before deciding any motions for summary judgment on invalidity or infringement. This means that the court's single construction of the claims will govern all parts of the case to come, including all issues related to validity (anticipation, obviousness, enablement, written description, etc.) and all issues related to infringement.

There are a variety of sources of meaning a court can draw upon when construing a patent's claims. First, of course, is the text and context of the claim language itself. A court can also look to the patent specification and the patent's prosecution history—the record of communications with the USPTO during the application process—as guides to meaning. Together, these three sources of meaning are referred to as "intrinsic evidence," because they are intrinsic to the patent itself. Courts can also turn to "extrinsic" sources of information as to the patent's meaning, including dictionaries, scientific and technical papers and treatises, and even expert testimony.[2] The relationship between these different sources of meaning, and which should take precedence when they conflict, is the subject of the case that follows. We then provide opportunities to practice these claim construction rules in the very next chapter, Chapter 9, which concerns direct patent infringement.

---

[1] The rules are available at https://www.cand.uscourts.gov/rules/patent-local-rules.

[2] Although claim interpretation is a question of law, the value and meaning of extrinsic sources will sometimes raise underlying issues of fact, as when a court must evaluate the testimony of a party's expert who has testified about the meaning of the claims. These issues of fact, like all issues of fact, are reviewed by the courts of appeal with deference to the district court's findings. *Teva Pharms. USA, Inc. v. Sandoz, Inc.*, 574 U.S. 318 (2015).

Phillips v. AWH Corp., 415 F.3d 1303 (Fed. Cir. 2005) (en banc)

William C. Bryson, Circuit Judge.

1   Edward H. Phillips invented modular, steel-shell panels that can be welded together to form vandalism-resistant walls. The panels are especially useful in building prisons because they are load-bearing and impact-resistant, while also insulating against fire and noise. Mr. Phillips obtained a patent on the invention, U.S. Patent No. 4,677,798, [and sued AWH Corp. for infringement].

2   With regard to the patent infringement issue, the district court focused on the language of claim 1, which recites "further means disposed inside the shell for increasing its load bearing capacity comprising internal steel baffles extending inwardly from the steel shell walls." [The district court held that AWH's walls did not include "baffles" because the internal panels were at a 90-degree angle to the wall face, and the '798 patent shows baffles only at other angles. The court granted summary judgment of noninfringement.]

3   [On appeal, a divided Federal Circuit panel affirmed. In the majority, Judge Alan Lourie, joined by Judge Pauline Newman, sustained the judgment of noninfringement. In dissent, Judge Timothy Dyk would have reversed on the basis that nothing in the specification limited "baffles" to less than its "plain meaning," which included baffles at 90 degrees. The Federal Circuit agreed to hear the appeal en banc.]

I

4   Claim 1 of the '798 patent is representative of the asserted claims with respect to the use of the term "baffles." It recites:

> Building modules adapted to fit together for construction of fire, sound and impact resistant security barriers and rooms for use in securing records and persons, comprising in combination, an outer shell . . . , sealant means . . . and further means disposed inside the shell for increasing its load bearing capacity comprising internal steel baffles extending inwardly from the steel shell walls.

5   As a preliminary matter, we agree with the panel that the term "baffles" is not means-plus-function language that invokes 35 U.S.C. § 112, paragraph 6. To be sure, the claim refers to "means disposed inside the shell for increasing its load bearing capacity," a formulation that would ordinarily be regarded as invoking the means-plus-function claim format. However, the claim specifically identifies "internal steel baffles" as structure that performs the recited function of increasing the shell's load-bearing capacity. In contrast to the "load bearing means" limitation, the reference to "baffles" does not use the word "means," and we have held that the absence of that term creates a rebuttable presumption that section 112, paragraph 6, does not apply.

6   Means-plus-function claiming applies only to purely functional limitations that do not provide the structure that performs the recited function. While the baffles in the '798 patent are clearly intended to perform several functions, the term "baffles" is nonetheless structural; it is not a purely functional placeholder in which structure is filled in by the specification. The claims and the specification unmistakably establish that the "steel baffles" refer to particular physical apparatus. The claim characterizes the baffles as "extend[ing] inwardly" from the steel shell walls, which plainly implies that the baffles are structures. The specification likewise makes clear that the term "steel baffles" refers to particular internal wall structures and is not simply a general description of any structure that will perform a particular function. Because the term "baffles" is not subject to section 112, paragraph 6, we agree with the panel that the district court erred by limiting the term to corresponding structures disclosed in the specification and their equivalents. Accordingly, we must determine the correct construction of the structural term "baffles," as used in the '798 patent.

II

7   The first paragraph of section 112 of the Patent Act, 35 U.S.C. § 112, states that the specification

> shall contain a written description of the invention, and of the manner and process of making and using it, in such full, clear, concise, and exact terms as to enable any person skilled in the art to which it pertains . . . to make and use the same . . .

The second paragraph of section 112 provides that the specification

> shall conclude with one or more claims particularly pointing out and distinctly claiming the subject matter which the applicant regards as his invention.

8   Those two paragraphs of section 112 frame the issue of claim interpretation for us. The second paragraph requires us to look to the language of the claims to determine what "the applicant regards as his invention." On the other hand, the first paragraph requires that the specification describe the invention set forth in the claims. The principal question that this case presents to us is the extent to which we should resort to and rely on a patent's specification in seeking to ascertain the proper scope of its claims.

A

9   It is a "bedrock principle" of patent law that "the claims of a patent define the invention to which the patentee is entitled the right to exclude." Because the patentee is required to "define precisely what his invention is," the [Supreme] Court [has] explained, it is "unjust to the public, as well as an evasion of the law, to construe it in a manner different from the plain import of its terms." *White v. Dunbar*, 119 U.S. 47, 52 (1886).

10   We have frequently stated that the words of a claim "are generally given their ordinary and customary meaning." *Vitronics v. Conceptronic*, 90 F.3d 1576, 1582 (Fed. Cir. 1996). We have made clear, moreover, that the ordinary and customary meaning of a claim term is the meaning that the term would have to a person of ordinary skill in the art in question at the time of the invention, i.e., as of the effective filing date of the patent application.

11   The inquiry into how a person of ordinary skill in the art understands a claim term provides an objective baseline from which to begin claim interpretation. That starting point is based on the well-settled understanding that inventors are typically persons skilled in the field of the invention and that patents are addressed to and intended to be read by others of skill in the pertinent art.

12   Importantly, the person of ordinary skill in the art is deemed to read the claim term not only in the context of the particular claim in which the disputed term appears, but in the context of the entire patent, including the specification.

B

13   In some cases, the ordinary meaning of claim language as understood by a person of skill in the art may be readily apparent even to lay judges, and claim construction in such cases involves little more than the application of the widely accepted meaning of commonly understood words. In such circumstances, general purpose dictionaries may be helpful. In many cases that give rise to litigation, however, determining the ordinary and customary meaning of the claim requires examination of terms that have a particular meaning in a field of art. Because the meaning of a claim term as understood by persons of skill in the art is often not immediately apparent, and because patentees frequently use terms idiosyncratically, the court looks to "those sources available to the public that show what a person of skill in the art would have understood disputed claim language to mean." *Innova*, 381 F.3d at 1116. Those sources include "the words of the claims themselves, the remainder of the specification, the prosecution history, and extrinsic evidence concerning relevant scientific principles, the meaning of technical terms, and the state of the art." *Id.*

1

14   Quite apart from the written description and the prosecution history, the claims themselves provide substantial guidance as to the meaning of particular claim terms.

15   To begin with, the context in which a term is used in the asserted claim can be highly instructive. To take a simple example, the claim in this case refers to "steel baffles," which strongly implies that the term "baffles" does not inherently mean objects made of steel.

16   Other claims of the patent in question, both asserted and unasserted, can also be valuable sources of enlightenment as to the meaning of a claim term. Because claim terms are normally used consistently throughout the patent, the usage of a term in one claim can often illuminate the meaning of the same term in other claims. Differences among claims can also be a useful guide in understanding the meaning of particular claim terms. For example, the presence of a dependent claim that adds a particular limitation gives rise to a presumption that the limitation in question is not present in the independent claim.

2

17   The claims, of course, do not stand alone. Rather, they are part of "a fully integrated written instrument," *Markman,* 52 F.3d at 978, consisting principally of a specification that concludes with the claims. For that reason, claims "must be read in view of the specification, of which they are a part." *Id.* at 979. As we stated in *Vitronics v. Conceptronic,* the specification "is always highly relevant to the claim construction analysis. Usually, it is dispositive; it is the single best guide to the meaning of a disputed term." 90 F.3d 1576, 1582 (Fed. Cir. 1996).

18   The importance of the specification in claim construction derives from its statutory role. The close kinship between the written description and the claims is enforced by the statutory requirement that the specification describe the claimed invention in "full, clear, concise, and exact terms." 35 U.S.C. § 112.

19   Consistent with that general principle, our cases recognize that the specification may reveal a special definition given to a claim term by the patentee that differs from the meaning it would otherwise possess. In such cases, the inventor's lexicography governs. In other cases, the specification may reveal an intentional disclaimer, or disavowal, of claim scope by the inventor. In that instance as well, the inventor has dictated the correct claim scope, and the inventor's intention, as expressed in the specification, is regarded as dispositive.

3

20   In addition to consulting the specification, we have held that a court "should also consider the patent's prosecution history, if it is in evidence." *Markman,* 52 F.3d at 980. The prosecution history, which we have designated as part of the "intrinsic evidence," consists of the complete record of the proceedings before the PTO and includes the prior art cited during the examination of the patent. Like the specification, the prosecution history provides evidence of how the PTO and the inventor understood the patent. Furthermore, like the specification, the prosecution history was created by the patentee in attempting to explain and obtain the patent. Yet because the prosecution history represents an ongoing negotiation between the PTO and the applicant, rather than the final product of that negotiation, it often lacks the clarity of the specification and thus is less useful for claim construction purposes. Nonetheless, the prosecution history can often inform the meaning of the claim

language by demonstrating how the inventor understood the invention and whether the inventor limited the invention in the course of prosecution, making the claim scope narrower than it would otherwise be.

C

21   Although we have emphasized the importance of intrinsic evidence in claim construction, we have also authorized district courts to rely on extrinsic evidence, which "consists of all evidence external to the patent and prosecution history, including expert and inventor testimony, dictionaries, and learned treatises." *Markman*, 52 F.3d at 980. However, while extrinsic evidence "can shed useful light on the relevant art," we have explained that it is "less significant than the intrinsic record in determining 'the legally operative meaning of claim language.'" *C.R. Bard, Inc. v. U.S. Surgical Corp.*, 388 F.3d 858, 862 (Fed. Cir. 2004).

22   Within the class of extrinsic evidence, the court has observed that dictionaries and treatises can be useful in claim construction. We have especially noted the help that technical dictionaries may provide to a court "to better understand the underlying technology" and the way in which one of skill in the art might use the claim terms. *Vitronics*, 90 F.3d at 1584 n.6. Because dictionaries, and especially technical dictionaries, endeavor to collect the accepted meanings of terms used in various fields of science and technology, those resources have been properly recognized as among the many tools that can assist the court in determining the meaning of particular terminology to those of skill in the art of the invention.

23   We have also held that extrinsic evidence in the form of expert testimony can be useful to a court for a variety of purposes, such as to provide background on the technology at issue, to explain how an invention works, to ensure that the court's understanding of the technical aspects of the patent is consistent with that of a person of skill in the art, or to establish that a particular term in the patent or the prior art has a particular meaning in the pertinent field. However, conclusory, unsupported assertions by experts as to the definition of a claim term are not useful to a court.

24   We have viewed extrinsic evidence in general as less reliable than the patent and its prosecution history in determining how to read claim terms, for several reasons. First, extrinsic evidence by definition is not part of the patent and does not have the specification's virtue of being created at the time of patent prosecution for the purpose of explaining the patent's scope and meaning. Second, while claims are construed as they would be understood by a hypothetical person of skill in the art, extrinsic publications may not be written by or for skilled artisans and therefore may not reflect the understanding of a skilled artisan in the field of the patent. Third, extrinsic evidence consisting of expert reports and testimony is generated at the time of and for the purpose of litigation and thus can suffer from bias that is not present in intrinsic evidence. Fourth, there is a virtually unbounded universe of potential extrinsic evidence of some marginal relevance that could be brought to bear on any claim construction question. In the course of litigation, each party will naturally

choose the pieces of extrinsic evidence most favorable to its cause, leaving the court with the considerable task of filtering the useful extrinsic evidence from the fluff. Finally, undue reliance on extrinsic evidence poses the risk that it will be used to change the meaning of claims in derogation of the "indisputable public records consisting of the claims, the specification and the prosecution history, thereby undermining the public notice function of patents.

III

25   Although the principles outlined above have been articulated on numerous occasions, some of this court's cases have suggested a somewhat different approach to claim construction, in which the court has given greater emphasis to dictionary definitions of claim terms and has assigned a less prominent role to the specification and the prosecution history. The leading case in this line is *Texas Digital Systems, Inc. v. Telegenix, Inc.*, 308 F.3d 1193 (Fed. Cir. 2002).

A

26   In *Texas Digital*, the court noted that "dictionaries, encyclopedias and treatises are particularly useful resources to assist the court in determining the ordinary and customary meanings of claim terms." 308 F.3d at 1202. Those texts, the court explained, are "objective resources that serve as reliable sources of information on the established meanings that would have been attributed to the terms of the claims by those of skill in the art," and they "deserve no less fealty in the context of claim construction" than in any other area of law. *Id.* at 1203. The court added that because words often have multiple dictionary meanings, the intrinsic record must be consulted to determine which of the different possible dictionary meanings is most consistent with the use of the term in question by the inventor. If more than one dictionary definition is consistent with the use of the words in the intrinsic record, the court stated, "the claim terms may be construed to encompass all such consistent meanings." *Id.*

27   The *Texas Digital* court further explained that the patent's specification and prosecution history must be consulted to determine if the patentee has used "the words [of the claim] in a manner clearly inconsistent with the ordinary meaning reflected, for example, in a dictionary definition." 308 F.3d at 1204. The court identified two circumstances in which such an inconsistency may be found. First, the court stated, "the presumption in favor of a dictionary definition will be overcome where the patentee, acting as his or her own lexicographer, has clearly set forth an explicit definition of the term different from its ordinary meaning." *Id.* Second, "the presumption also will be rebutted if the inventor has disavowed or disclaimed scope of coverage, by using words or expressions of manifest exclusion or restriction, representing a clear disavowal of claim scope." *Id.*

28   The *Texas Digital* court explained that it advanced the methodology set forth in that opinion in an effort to combat what this court has termed "one of the cardinal

sins of patent law—reading a limitation from the written description into the claims," *SciMed Life Sys.*, 242 F.3d at 1340. The court concluded that it is improper to consult "the written description and prosecution history as a threshold step in the claim construction process, before any effort is made to discern the ordinary and customary meanings attributed to the words themselves." *Texas Digital*, 308 F.3d at 1204.

B

29   Although the concern expressed by the court in *Texas Digital* was valid, the methodology it adopted placed too much reliance on extrinsic sources such as dictionaries, treatises, and encyclopedias and too little on intrinsic sources, in particular the specification and prosecution history. While the court noted that the specification must be consulted in every case, it suggested a methodology for claim interpretation in which the specification should be consulted only after a determination is made, whether based on a dictionary, treatise, or other source, as to the ordinary meaning or meanings of the claim term in dispute. Even then, recourse to the specification is limited to determining whether the specification excludes one of the meanings derived from the dictionary, whether the presumption in favor of the dictionary definition of the claim term has been overcome by "an explicit definition of the term different from its ordinary meaning," or whether the inventor "has disavowed or disclaimed scope of coverage, by using words or expressions of manifest exclusion or restriction, representing a clear disavowal of claim scope." 308 F.3d at 1204. In effect, the *Texas Digital* approach limits the role of the specification in claim construction to serving as a check on the dictionary meaning of a claim term if the specification requires the court to conclude that fewer than all the dictionary definitions apply, or if the specification contains a sufficiently specific alternative definition or disavowal. That approach, in our view, improperly restricts the role of the specification in claim construction.

30   Assigning such a limited role to the specification, and in particular requiring that any definition of claim language in the specification be express, is inconsistent with our rulings that the specification is "the single best guide to the meaning of a disputed term," and that the specification "acts as a dictionary when it expressly defines terms used in the claims or when it defines terms by implication." *Vitronics*, 90 F.3d at 1582.

31   The main problem with elevating the dictionary to such prominence is that it focuses the inquiry on the abstract meaning of words rather than on the meaning of claim terms within the context of the patent. Properly viewed, the "ordinary meaning" of a claim term is its meaning to the ordinary artisan after reading the entire patent. Yet heavy reliance on the dictionary divorced from the intrinsic evidence risks transforming the meaning of the claim term to the artisan into the meaning of the term in the abstract, out of its particular context, which is the specification. Thus, there may be a disconnect between the patentee's responsibility to describe and claim

his invention, and the dictionary editors' objective of aggregating all possible definitions for particular words.

32   The problem is that if the district court starts with the broad dictionary definition in every case and fails to fully appreciate how the specification implicitly limits that definition, the error will systematically cause the construction of the claim to be unduly expansive. The risk of systematic overbreadth is greatly reduced if the court instead focuses at the outset on how the patentee used the claim term in the claims, specification, and prosecution history, rather than starting with a broad definition and whittling it down. Thus, the use of the dictionary may extend patent protection beyond what should properly be afforded by the inventor's patent.

33   Even technical dictionaries or treatises, under certain circumstances, may suffer from some of these deficiencies. There is no guarantee that a term is used in the same way in a treatise as it would be by the patentee. In fact, discrepancies between the patent and treatises are apt to be common because the patent by its nature describes something novel.

34   Moreover, different dictionaries may contain somewhat different sets of definitions for the same words. A claim should not rise or fall based upon the preferences of a particular dictionary editor, or the court's independent decision, uninformed by the specification, to rely on one dictionary rather than another.

35   As we have noted above, however, we do not intend to preclude the appropriate use of dictionaries. Dictionaries or comparable sources are often useful to assist in understanding the commonly understood meaning of words and have been used both by our court and the Supreme Court in claim interpretation. A dictionary definition has the value of being an unbiased source "accessible to the public in advance of litigation." *Vitronics*, 90 F.3d at 1585.

36   We also acknowledge that the purpose underlying the *Texas Digital* line of cases—to avoid the danger of reading limitations from the specification into the claim—is sound. Moreover, we recognize that the distinction between using the specification to interpret the meaning of a claim and importing limitations from the specification into the claim can be a difficult one to apply in practice. However, the line between construing terms and importing limitations can be discerned with reasonable certainty and predictability if the court's focus remains on understanding how a person of ordinary skill in the art would understand the claim terms. For instance, although the specification often describes very specific embodiments of the invention, we have repeatedly warned against confining the claims to those embodiments. In particular, we have expressly rejected the contention that if a patent describes only a single embodiment, the claims of the patent must be construed as being limited to that embodiment. That is not just because section 112 of the Patent Act requires that the claims themselves set forth the limits of the patent grant, but also because persons of ordinary skill in the art rarely would confine their definitions of terms to the exact representations depicted in the embodiments.

37   To avoid importing limitations from the specification into the claims, it is important to keep in mind that the purposes of the specification are to teach and enable those of skill in the art to make and use the invention and to provide a best mode for doing so. One of the best ways to teach a person of ordinary skill in the art how to make and use the invention is to provide an example of how to practice the invention in a particular case. Much of the time, upon reading the specification in that context, it will become clear whether the patentee is setting out specific examples of the invention to accomplish those goals, or whether the patentee instead intends for the claims and the embodiments in the specification to be strictly coextensive. The manner in which the patentee uses a term within the specification and claims usually will make the distinction apparent.

38   In the end, there will still remain some cases in which it will be hard to determine whether a person of skill in the art would understand the embodiments to define the outer limits of the claim term or merely to be exemplary in nature. While that task may present difficulties in some cases, we nonetheless believe that attempting to resolve that problem in the context of the particular patent is likely to capture the scope of the actual invention more accurately than either strictly limiting the scope of the claims to the embodiments disclosed in the specification or divorcing the claim language from the specification.

IV

A

39   The critical language of claim 1 of the '798 patent—"further means disposed inside the shell for increasing its load bearing capacity comprising internal steel baffles extending inwardly from the steel shell walls"—imposes three clear requirements with respect to the baffles. First, the baffles must be made of steel. Second, they must be part of the load-bearing means for the wall section. Third, they must be pointed inward from the walls. Both parties, stipulating to a dictionary definition, also conceded that the term "baffles" refers to objects that check, impede, or obstruct the flow of something. The intrinsic evidence confirms that a person of skill in the art would understand that the term "baffles," as used in the '798 patent, would have that generic meaning.

40   The other claims of the '798 patent specify particular functions to be served by the baffles. For example, dependent claim 2 states that the baffles may be "oriented with the panel sections disposed at angles for deflecting projectiles such as bullets able to penetrate the steel plates." The inclusion of such a specific limitation on the term "baffles" in claim 2 makes it likely that the patentee did not contemplate that the term "baffles" already contained that limitation. Independent claim 17 further supports that proposition. It states that baffles are placed "projecting inwardly from the outer shell at angles tending to deflect projectiles that penetrate the outer shell." That limitation would be unnecessary if persons of skill in the art understood that the baffles inherently served such a function. Dependent claim 6 provides an additional

requirement for the baffles, stating that "the internal baffles of both outer panel sections overlap and interlock at angles providing deflector panels extending from one end of the module to the other." If the baffles recited in claim 1 were inherently placed at specific angles, or interlocked to form an intermediate barrier, claim 6 would be redundant.

41   The specification further supports the conclusion that persons of ordinary skill in the art would understand the baffles recited in the '798 patent to be load-bearing objects that serve to check, impede, or obstruct flow. At several points, the specification discusses positioning the baffles so as to deflect projectiles. The patent states that one advantage of the invention over the prior art is that "[t]here have not been effective ways of dealing with these powerful impact weapons with inexpensive housing." While that statement makes clear the invention envisions baffles that serve that function, it does not imply that in order to qualify as baffles within the meaning of the claims, the internal support structures must serve the projectile-deflecting function in all the embodiments of all the claims. The specification must teach and enable all the claims, and the section of the written description discussing the use of baffles to deflect projectiles serves that purpose for claims 2, 6, 17, and 23, which specifically claim baffles that deflect projectiles.

42   The specification discusses several other purposes served by the baffles. For example, the baffles are described as providing structural support. The patent states that one way to increase load-bearing capacity is to use "at least in part inwardly directed steel baffles 15, 16." The baffle 16 is described as a "strengthening triangular baffle." Importantly, Figures 4 and 6 do not show the baffles as part of an "intermediate interlocking, but not solid, internal barrier." In those figures, the baffle 16 simply provides structural support for one of the walls, as depicted below:

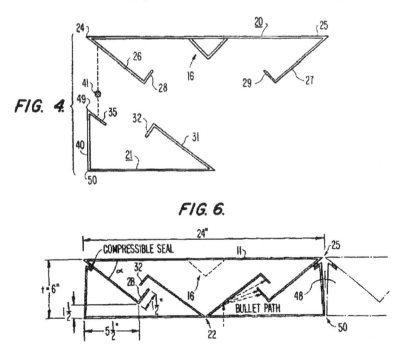

FIG. 4.

FIG. 6.

43   Other uses for the baffles are listed in the specification as well. In Figure 7, the overlapping flanges "provide for overlapping and interlocking the baffles to produce substantially an intermediate barrier wall between the opposite [wall] faces":

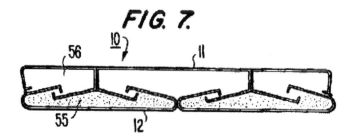

FIG. 7.

44   Those baffles thus create small compartments that can be filled with either sound and thermal insulation or rock and gravel to stop projectiles. By separating the interwall area into compartments (*see, e.g.*, compartment 55 in Figure 7), the user of the modules can choose different types of material for each compartment, so that the module can be "easily custom tailored for the specific needs of each installation." When material is placed into the wall during installation, the baffles obstruct the flow of material from one compartment to another so that this "custom tailoring" is possible.

45   The fact that the written description of the '798 patent sets forth multiple objectives to be served by the baffles recited in the claims confirms that the term "baffles" should not be read restrictively to require that the baffles in each case serve all of the recited functions. We have held that "[t]he fact that a patent asserts that an invention achieves several objectives does not require that each of the claims be construed as limited to structures that are capable of achieving all of the objectives." *Liebel–Flarsheim v. Medrad*, 358 F.3d 898, 908 (Fed. Cir. 2004). Although deflecting projectiles is one of the advantages of the baffles of the '798 patent, the patent does not require that the inward extending structures always be capable of performing that function. Accordingly, we conclude that a person of skill in the art would not interpret the disclosure and claims of the '798 patent to mean that a structure extending inward from one of the wall faces is a "baffle" if it is at an acute or obtuse angle, but is not a "baffle" if it is disposed at a right angle.

B

46   Invoking the principle that "claims should be so construed, if possible, as to sustain their validity," *Rhine v. Casio, Inc.*, 183 F.3d 1342, 1345 (Fed. Cir. 1999), AWH argues that the term "baffles" should be given a restrictive meaning because if the term is not construed restrictively, the asserted claims would be invalid.

47   While we have acknowledged the maxim that claims should be construed to preserve their validity, we have not applied that principle broadly, and we have certainly not endorsed a regime in which validity analysis is a regular component of claim construction. Instead, we have limited the maxim to cases in which "the court concludes, after applying all the available tools of claim construction, that the claim

is still ambiguous." *Liebel–Flarsheim*, 358 F.3d at 911. In such cases, we have looked to whether it is reasonable to infer that the PTO would not have issued an invalid patent, and that the ambiguity in the claim language should therefore be resolved in a manner that would preserve the patent's validity.

48   In this case, the claim term at issue is not ambiguous. Thus, it can be construed without the need to consider whether one possible construction would render the claim invalid while the other would not. The doctrine of construing claims to preserve their validity, a doctrine of limited utility in any event, therefore has no applicability here.

49   In sum, we reject AWH's arguments in favor of a restrictive definition of the term "baffles." Because we disagree with the district court's claim construction, we reverse the summary judgment of noninfringement. In light of our decision on claim construction, it is necessary to remand the infringement claims to the district court for further proceedings.

50   [Judge Lourie, joined by Judge Newman (the original panel majority), wrote separately to "fully join the portion of the court's opinion resolving the relative weights of specification and dictionaries in interpreting patent claims" but dissenting from the decision to reverse and remand for reconsideration of the infringement claims; he would have affirmed the judgment of noninfringement. Judge Mayer dissented, arguing that claim construction should not be treated as a matter of law and that the Federal Circuit should defer to the district court's construction.]

Discussion Questions: *Phillips v. AWH*

1. *Competing Lines of Precedent.* As *Phillips* explains, prior to that decision there were two competing lines of precedent describing different approaches to claim construction. One line, known as the "contextual," "holistic," or "specification-first" approach and most closely associated with *Vitronics v. Conceptronic*, 90 F.3d 1576 (Fed. Cir. 1996), emphasized intrinsic evidence, particularly the specification. The other, known as the "textual," "procedural," or "dictionary-first" approach and most closely associated with *Texas Digital Systems, Inc. v. Telegenix, Inc.*, 308 F.3d 1193 (Fed. Cir. 2002), emphasized the plain meaning of the text of the claims as interpreted using dictionaries and other sources of extrinsic evidence. *Phillips*, which was decided en banc, decided the matter in favor of the *Vitronics* approach. It is nonetheless striking that it took the Federal Circuit 23 years—from its creation in 1982 until 2005—to attempt to settle what seems like a fundamental question. Can you think of reasons why the court might have let this issue linger for so long? What, if anything, does this episode tell us about the merits of having a single, specialized court of appeals deciding all patent cases?

2. *The Relationship Between the Specification and the Claims.* The *Phillips* court emphasized that "the specification is the single best guide to the meaning of a disputed term." But it also stated that courts must "avoid importing limitations from

the specification into the claims" or "limiting the scope of the claims to the embodiments." How is a court supposed to do both of these things? Suppose, for instance, that a claim calls for making a particular element from "metal," but the specification discusses only zinc, iron, and cadmium as possible metals. How should a court decide whether to read the claim's reference to "metal" as encompassing only those three metals, or whether it should be read to capture every type of metal? How did the *Phillips* court go about making this decision?

Note in addition that there is a canon of patent claim construction that courts should construe claims so as to render them valid. Construing a claim more broadly than the specification, as in the example of a claim for "metal" above, could leave it vulnerable to a written description or enablement challenge. Should this canon of claim construction militate in favor of restricting the scope of a claim to the embodiments described in the specification? Or would that run afoul of the *Phillips* court's admonition against importing limitations from the specification into the claims?

3. *The Road Not Taken.* Suppose *Phillips* had been decided under the now-discarded *Texas Digital* framework. Do you think it would have come out differently? What sources would the court have looked to, and in what direction would they have pointed?

4. *Types of Extrinsic Evidence.* The *Phillips* court largely paints the various types of extrinsic evidence with a broad brush. But in reality, there are potentially significant differences between technical materials (treatises, papers, and the like), general dictionaries, expert testimony, and other types of extrinsic evidence that might be offered in court. Which of these sorts of evidence do you think are most reliable and should carry the greatest weight with a court? Does it depend on the type of patent claim at issue?

5. *Canons of Claim Construction.* The Federal Circuit has developed a number of guidelines for interpreting patent claims, which are analogous to the canons of statutory interpretation courts use when evaluating statutes. A sampling of these canons is provided below. What weight do you think each of these canons receives after *Phillips*? What weight *should* each canon receive?

- Claims should be construed objectively from the perspective of a PHOSITA at the time of filing.
- Claims should be construed consistently for assessing validity and infringement.
- Intrinsic evidence should be considered first, starting with the claim language, then looking at the specification, and concluding with the prosecution history.
- Claim terms should be construed based on their ordinary meaning.
- The full scope of ordinary meaning applies unless intrinsic evidence suggests a narrower definition.

- Dictionaries, particularly technical dictionaries or treatises, may be useful guides to ordinary meaning.
- When dictionaries conflict, the specification and prosecution history will be needed to determine which definition should apply.
- A patentee may be her own lexicographer, using definitions different from the ordinary meaning.
- Different claims are presumed to have different meanings.
- Different words in the same claim are presumed to have different meanings.
- No claim limitation should be rendered meaningless.
- A given claim term is presumed to have the same meaning in different claims.
- Claim terms must be construed in light of the specification.
- The specification in which the claim resides is preferred, but related applications (including provisionals, parents, and foreign counterparts) may be used.
- Material incorporated by reference may be considered as intrinsic evidence.
- The purpose of the invention may be considered when construing claims.
- Claims should not be redrafted by reading in limitations from the specification or by expanding claim scope to cover embodiments in the specification.
- If the specification lists a preferred embodiment, a claim should generally be construed so that the preferred embodiment is within the claim scope.
- If the patentee has a commercial embodiment of the invention, it should *not* be used when construing claims.
- A patentee may disclaim claim scope in the specification or prosecution history, including by disparaging aspects of prior art devices or distinguishing the claimed invention from prior art.
- Claims in an issued patent should be construed to preserve validity if possible.

6. *Did* Phillips *Change Anything?* An empirical study of every Federal Circuit claim construction decision from 1995 to 2007 concluded that *Phillips* had little effect on whether Federal Circuit panels adopted a more contextual or textual methodology. R. Polk Wagner & Lee Petherbridge, *Did* Phillips *Change Anything? Empirical Analysis of the Federal Circuit's Claim Construction Jurisprudence, in Intellectual Property and the Common Law* (Shyamkrishna Balganesh, ed. 2013). Even though *Phillips* nominally resolved the debate in favor of the contextualists, if you are representing a client that benefits from a more textualist approach, what language from *Phillips* would you quote in your brief?

In addition, why do you think *Phillips* had only a small effect on the methodology used by Federal Circuit panels? Do you think it is caused by some feature of the Federal Circuit, or is it inherent to patent cases in some fashion? Or do you think this is just typical circuit behavior, and we should expect to see it in other contexts across other courts as well?

7. *The "Broadest Reasonable Interpretation."* The methodology outlined in *Phillips* applies when a claim in a granted patent is being litigated in federal district court or in the course of an IPR or other USPTO-based review. But when a patent application that has not yet resulted in an issued patent is being examined by the USPTO, the agency—including both the examiner and the PTAB, if the examiner's decision is appealed—does not use *Phillips* to interpret the claim. Instead, the agency gives the claim what is known as its "broadest reasonable interpretation." This is just what it sounds like—the USPTO interprets the claim as broadly as reasonably possible. This means that a claim might have one meaning during examination and another during litigation. In addition, a broader claim is of course more likely to be held invalid for anticipation, obviousness, or lack of enablement or written description, and this will make the claim less likely to pass muster during examination. Do you think it makes sense for the USPTO and the federal courts to use different modes of claim interpretation? What are the advantages of doing so? The downsides?

9. Direct Infringement

With an understanding of claim construction in place, we now turn to direct infringement. As noted above, direct infringement is governed by 35 U.S.C. § 271(a), which states:

> [W]hoever without authority makes, uses, offers to sell, or sells any patented invention, within the United States or imports into the United States any patented invention during the term of the patent therefor, infringes the patent.

Direct infringement is in many respects the inverse of anticipation and obviousness. Most importantly, just as with anticipation, the "all-elements rule" applies. Just as invalidity requires an element-by-element comparison between a single piece of prior art and the patent claim, direct infringement requires an element-by-element comparison between the patent claim and the accused device. If you know how to interpret a claim, and you know how to apply the all-elements rule, then you know how to perform a direct infringement analysis.

A. Literal Infringement

The first subspecies of direct infringement is literal infringement. In a case of literal infringement, every element of the patent claim is literally present in the accused device. The symmetry between literal infringement and anticipation has given rise to the patent maxim, "that which infringes if later, anticipates if earlier." *Miller v. Eagle Mfg. Co.*, 151 U.S. 186 (1894). In other words, any literally infringing device would anticipate the patent if it predated the patent; any real-world piece of prior art that anticipates the patent would literally infringe if it postdated the patent.

Between the claim construction doctrine from the previous section and your knowledge of the all-elements rule from the doctrine of anticipation, you have all of the tools necessary to conduct a literal infringement analysis. The following exercises, based on Federal Circuit cases, offer opportunities to apply those tools. For each of them, consider the available facts. What claim construction arguments would you make on behalf of the patentee? On behalf of the accused infringer?

Exercise: *Unique Concepts, Inc. v. Brown*, 939 F.2d 1558 (Fed. Cir. 1991)

Patented invention: Plaintiff Unique Concepts is the exclusive licensee of the '260 patent, which is directed to an "assembly of border pieces" used to attach a fabric wall covering to a wall, as shown in Figure 2 from the patent. Claim 1 of the patent reads:

> An assembly of border pieces for creating a framework attachable to a wall or other flat surface for mounting a fabric sheet which is cut to dimensions at least sufficient to cover the surface, said assembly comprising linear border pieces and right angle corner border pieces which are arranged in end-to-end relation to define a framework that follows the perimeter of the area to be covered, each piece including [a number of additional elements].

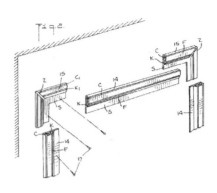

Accused devices: Unique has sued Kevin Brown, alleging that his products infringe claim 1. Brown argues that his products do not infringe because they do not have corner pieces which were preformed at a right angle, instead employing two linear pieces which are each mitered, i.e., cut at a 45-degree angle, and then placed together to form a right angle (as shown). Thus, he argues that his products do not have the required "right angle corner border pieces."

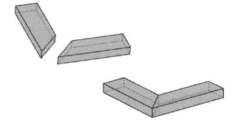

Specification: The drawings show only preformed corner pieces and no mitered pieces, and the specification repeatedly refers to the preformed pieces in the drawings as "corner pieces" or "right angle border pieces." The specification does once refer to "improvised corner pieces" as an alternative:

> Instead of using preformed right-angle corner pieces of the type previously disclosed, one may improvise corner pieces by miter-cutting the ends of a pair of short linear border pieces at right angles to each other. The advantage of such corner pieces resides in the fact that linear pieces may be mass-produced at low cost by continuous extrusion, whereas preformed corner pieces must be molded or otherwise fabricated by more expensive techniques. On the other hand, a preformed corner piece is somewhat easier for a do-it-yourselfer to work with.

Prosecution history: The examiner rejected the original claim 1, which also referred to "right angle corner border pieces," as unpatentable over references with preformed corners. In response, the applicant amended the claim and argued against the references, stating that the invention "greatly simplifies the mounting of a fabric covering" such that an "amateur" can do it because "the fabric need not be cut so precisely"—the fabric only has to be cut roughly to size, and the excess can be stuffed in the storage channel. The attorney and examiner then had an unrecorded telephone interview, following which the examiner canceled certain claims, including claim 9:

> 9. An assembly as set forth in claim 1, wherein said right-angle corner pieces are formed by a pair of short linear pieces whose ends are mitered
>
> . . .

The reason for its cancelation is unclear; Brown's expert said that it was because "it was simply not something that a do-it-yourselfer could do." The amended claim 1 was allowed.

Exercise: *Brookhill-Wilk 1 v. Intuitive Surgical*, 334 F.3d 1294 (Fed. Cir. 2003)

Patented Invention: Plaintiff Brookhill is the owner of the '003 patent, which is directed to systems and methods for performing robotic surgery. The systems and methods use robotic surgical tools and telecommunication links to permit a surgeon to operate from a "remote location beyond a range of direct manual contact." Claim 10 of the '003 patent reads:

> A surgical system, comprising: an endoscopic instrument; camera means on said endoscopic instrument for obtaining video images of internal body tissues inside a patient's body via said endoscopic instrument; transmission means operatively connected to said camera means for transmitting, over an electromagnetic signaling link to *a remote location beyond a range of direct manual contact* with said patient's body and said endoscopic instrument, a video signal encoding said video image;
>
>> receiver means for receiving actuator control signals *from said remote location* via said electromagnetic signaling link;
>>
>> a surgical instrument insertable into the patient's body and movable relative to the patient's body and said endoscopic instrument; and
>>
>> robot actuator means operatively connected to said surgical instrument and said receiver means for actuating said surgical instrument in response to the actuator control signals received by said receiver means *from said remote location.*

Accused Device: Brookhill has sued Intuitive, claiming that Intuitive's *da Vinci* robotic surgical system infringes the '003 patent. The surgeon in the *da Vinci* system is located in the same operating room as the patient. The parties have agreed that if Claim 10 is found to not cover instances where the surgeon is located in the same operating room as the patient, the court would be required to find that the patent is not infringed.

Specification: The written description in the '003 patent explains that an endoscopic instrument and a surgical instrument may each be placed within hollow tubes, inserted through a small incision in the abdominal wall of a patient, and thereby reach the surgical site. The endoscope remotely transmits to a computer that generates an image of the internal body tissues of the patient on a monitor. The specification sets forth no specific parameters as to the distance between the surgeon and patient but teaches generally that a surgeon using the disclosed assembly may operate without directly touching the patient, the surgical instruments, or the endoscope.

The specification further states that the advantage of the invention is that it allows a surgeon to operate at some distance, possibly across the world, from the operating room in which the patient is located. The description of the preferred embodiment is as follows:

> It is to be understood, of course, that surgeons and other personnel are present in the operating room at the time of surgery to oversee and supervise the proper operation of the equipment. These personnel may communicate with the remote surgeon via computers and telecommunications links and/or through other telecommunications or electromagnetic signaling linkages such as the telephone network.

The Objects of the Invention section of the specification describes the invention as "reduc[ing] surgical costs" and "facilitat[ing] the performance of operations by surgeons from all over the world."

The Background section states that in traditional settings, "the surgeon is always present in the operating room to manipulate the surgical instruments."

Dictionary Terms: The word "remote" has the following possible meanings in *Webster's Third New International Dictionary*:

1. "separated by intervals greater than usual"

2. "far apart . . . far removed; not near; far; distant"

Prosecution History: Claim 10 originally used the phrase "remote location beyond a range of direct visual contact." The patent examiner rejected this phrase as too indefinite because "the range of direct visual contact may be different for certain operators of the system and this cannot be given weight in the claims." To overcome the indefiniteness rejection, Brookhill replaced the word "visual" with the word "manual." In support of this change, Brookhill stated that the amended text "means that the remote location is beyond the arm's reach of the patient. Inasmuch as an arm's length is a well understood difference, it is believed that the remote location is sufficiently defined for purposes of the Patent Statute." Brookhill further stated that "[t]his amendment clarifies that a remote operator who is generating actuator control signals . . . is so far from the patient and the endoscopic instrument as to be unable to manipulate the instrument at the patient's side." The examiner subsequently allowed the claims and the patent issued.

Exercise: *K-2 Corp. v. Salomon S.A.*, 191 F.3d 1356 (Fed. Cir. 1999)

Patented Invention: Plaintiff K-2 Corp. is the owner of the '466 patent, which is directed to an in-line roller skate that has a soft, pliable inner "bootie" surrounded in certain areas by molded plastic or straps affixed to the base of the skate. This allows the wearer's foot to breathe and forms the skate, as shown in Figure 1 from the patent below. Claim 1 of the patent reads:

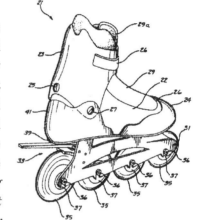

In an in-line roller skate having an upper shoe portion and a lower frame portion . . . a non-rigid shoe portion adapted to receive and substantially enclose the entire foot of the skater . . . support means positioned adjacent selected areas of said non-rigid shoe portion for providing support to aid the skater in maintaining said in-line roller skate in a substantially vertical position . . . and a base portion, . . . *said non-rigid shoe portion being permanently affixed to said base portion at least at said toe area and said heel area for substantially preventing movement therebetween at least in a horizontal plane,* wherein at least a portion of said non-rigid shoe portion extends continuously from said base portion to at least the top of said ankle support cuff.

Accused Devices: K-2 Corp. has sued Salomon S.A., alleging their products infringe upon claim 1 of the '466 patent. Salomon makes an inline skate (called the TR skate) which includes a soft inner bootie fastened to the lower, rigid plastic frame of the skate by the use of rivets and a screw in the toe area, and by a removable hex-head screw in the heel area. Salomon argues that the use of a removable screw in the heel area of the TR skate does not meet the "permanently affixed" limitation found in claim 1 of the '466 patent.

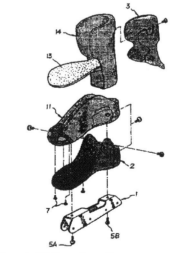

Salomon's TR Skate: Bootie/Base Attachment Detail

Specification: In the specification, a rivet is cited as a conventional fastening means to accomplish a permanent connection.

Prosecution History: There is a prior art reference, called the Johnson reference, which is a patent that discloses an in-line skate with an easily removable upper shoe portion affixed at the toe and mid-foot with a "detachable" connection. K-2 noted in its patent application that an advantage of the "permanently affixed" connection was that it avoided the "sliding heel" problem of the Johnson reference, where the shoe slid in the horizontal dimension. The examiner rejected prior K-2 claims in light of the Johnson reference, and K-2 added the "permanently affixed" language in response.

B. Infringement by Equivalents

The doctrine of literal infringement suffers from the same limitation as the doctrine of novelty: if even a single element of a claim is not present in the accused device, the device does not infringe. This raises the possibility that a potential infringer could evade liability simply by making minor, immaterial changes to her products. Consider, for instance, the baffles in *Phillips*, and suppose that the court had held that the claim did not cover right-angled baffles. Is a right-angled baffle really all that different from a baffle at 89 degrees, or 91 degrees? Does it make sense to condition the patentee's ability to win her lawsuit on whether the accused device has such a miniscule difference?

The doctrine of equivalents exists to fill this gap. The doctrine of equivalents is in many ways the analogue of the doctrine of obviousness; or, put another way, the doctrine of equivalents is to literal infringement as obviousness is to anticipation. With respect to validity, there are some inventions that are not anticipated, because there is no single piece of prior art that contains all of the necessary elements, but nonetheless add so little to the existing state of knowledge that it would do more harm than good to allow them to be patented. The law of obviousness exists to block patents in these circumstances. Similarly, there are some accused devices that do not literally infringe, because they do not possess every element of the asserted claim, but are nonetheless so similar to the asserted claim that it would seem contrary to the goals of the patent system *not* to hold that they infringe. The doctrine of equivalents exists to allow patentees to establish infringement in these circumstances.

The primary policy rationale behind the doctrine of equivalents is to prevent would-be infringers from escaping liability by making trivial changes to their inventions that evade the literal language of the claims. Without the doctrine of equivalents, patents would be substantially weaker—and competitors might spend a great deal of time and effort in the largely wasteful enterprise of making small changes to evade them. At the same time, there is a tradeoff in clarity. By broadening claims' scope beyond their literal meaning to include equivalents, the doctrine of equivalents introduces some additional uncertainty into the question of which devices will infringe and which will not. On the other hand, imagine how patent applicants would respond if the doctrine of equivalents did not exist. How might patent applicants change the ways in which they draft claims if they were not able to claim equivalents?

1. Determining Equivalency

Importantly, the all-elements rule still applies in cases involving the doctrine of equivalents. It is not enough for a court (or jury) just to eyeball the patent claim and the accused device and conclude that they're equivalent to one another. Rather, the court must consider the elements of the patent claim one-by-one, as in a case of literal infringement. For each element, the court must determine whether the element is literally present in the accused device, whether an equivalent to the element is present in the accused device, or neither. A court can "mix and match" literal infringement and infringement by the equivalents—it could find that some elements are literally present and others are present as equivalents—and this is sufficient for a finding of infringement. But of course if any claim element is *neither* literally present in the accused device *nor* present as an equivalent, then the device does not infringe the claim.

To illustrate how infringement analysis operates when the doctrine of equivalents and literal infringement are combined, consider *Sage Products, Inc. v. Devon Industries, Inc.*, 126 F.3d 1420 (Fed. Cir. 1997). The patent was on a container for disposing of medical syringes and other hazardous waste without touching waste already in the container, pictured below. Claim 1, the only independent claim in the patent, read as follows:

> 1. A disposal container comprising:
>
> (a) a hollow upstanding container body,
>
> (b) an elongated slot at the top of the container body for permitting access to the interior of the container body,
>
> (c) barrier means disposed adjacent said slot for restricting access to the interior of said container body, at least a portion of said barrier means comprising
>
> > (i) a first constriction extending over said slot, and
> >
> > (ii) a complementary second constriction extending beneath said slot, and
>
> (d) a closure disposed adjacent said slot.

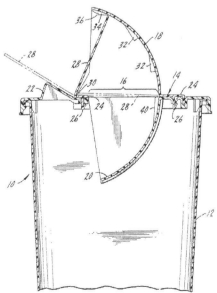

The district court held (and the Federal Circuit agreed) that the accused device did not literally include "an elongated slot at the top of the container body" (element (b)) or "a first constriction extending over said slot" (element (c)(i)), and thus the accused device did not literally infringe.

On appeal, the patent owner argued that equivalents of those two elements were present in the accused device and pointed to a variety of candidate parts that it alleged were equivalent. The Federal Circuit rejected all of these arguments. It held that all but one of the patent owner's proposed equivalents to element (b) (the elongated slot) were in the middle of the container body, rather than at the top. This could not constitute an equivalent. The final candidate put forward by the patent holder was located at the top of the container, but it was a hinged opening, which could allow full access to the container. Accordingly, it was not the equivalent of a "constriction."

What is the legal standard for determining whether part of an accused device is "equivalent" to a claim element? The primary legal standard is the "function-way-result" test, sometimes known as the "triple identity" test. As the name would indicate, this test involves considering whether the feature of the accused device in question:

1. performs substantially the same function as the claim element;
2. in substantially the same way as the claim element;
3. yielding substantially the same result as the claim element.

See, e.g., Abbott Laboratories v. Sandoz, Inc., 566 F.3d 1282, 1296 (Fed. Cir. 2009). The Federal Circuit also sometimes uses another test, called the "insubstantial differences" test. As this name should indicate, for purposes of this test the question is simply whether the differences between the claim element and the feature of the accused device are "insubstantial" or not. *Id.*

The function-way-result test is widely accepted as the better test for mechanical inventions. *Warner-Jenkinson Co., Inc. v. Hilton Davis Chem. Co.*, 520 U.S. 17, 39 (1997). Nonetheless, the Federal Circuit will occasionally use the insubstantial differences test when evaluating other types of inventions. Our view, however, is that the insubstantial differences test is question-begging: what is the standard for when a difference is substantial or insubstantial? The test adds nothing to the requirement that the device and the claim element be "equivalent." Accordingly, we recommend that practitioners focus on the function-way-result test, though it is worth being aware of the alternative.

Dawn Equip. Co. v. Kentucky Farms Inc., 140 F.3d 1009 (Fed. Cir. 1998), provides a useful illustration of the function-way-result test. The patent at suit was an improved mechanism for adjusting the height of a farming tool that might be towed behind a tractor. The patented invention involved a system of pins and springs connected to a rotatable shaft: to adjust the height of the tool, the operator would remove the pin using the rotatable shaft, compress or decompress the spring to the desired height, and then reinsert the pin. The accused device (pictured at right) instead used a system with two telescoping bars, one inserted inside of the other, each with multiple holds. The operator would extend or contract the exterior bar until reaching the desired height, then line up the holes and insert multiple pins to hold the bars in place.

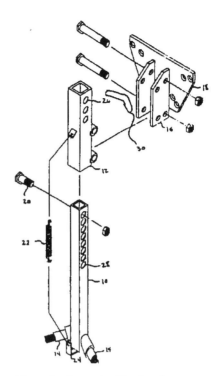

The court held that the accused device was not an equivalent:

> While the functions of the two mechanisms are the same (i.e., locking and releasing a connecting member), the way and result are not substantially the same. The mechanisms are structurally quite different, and operate quite differently. In the patented device, the pin is permanently fixed to the rotatable shaft and is locked into and released from engagement with the slot by rotating the shaft. In sharp contrast, in the accused device, the pin is not attached to anything and is inserted in and removed from the holes and by hand.

Id. at 1016. The court went on to note that the mere fact that both inventions used pins was not enough for the "way" portion of the test. The rotatable shaft and slot were important elements of the patented invention, but nothing akin to them was present in the accused device. In addition, the court noted, the accused device did not achieve the same result—reducing the time and accident risks involved in changing the height of the farming tool—as did the patented invention:

> The patent touts that the invention reduces adjustment time, prevents misadjustment and eliminates the problem of easily lost pins. The disclosed shaft, pin and slot mechanism plays a major role in achieving these results. Because the mechanism is easy and quick to operate, adjustment time is reduced, and because the mechanism only allows for two positions (lowered and raised), misadjustment is prevented. Furthermore, because the pin is fixed to the rotatable shaft, the pin cannot be lost. In sharp contrast, the accused device's loose pin and holes combination accomplishes none of these touted results. As the patent describes, a loose pin and holes mechanism is time consuming to adjust, is prone to misadjustment because of the multiple holes, and the loose pin is easily lost.

Id. at 1017. As this example illustrates, the function-way-result test will necessarily involve a highly technical and fact-specific analysis of the claim and accused device at issue. Accordingly, equivalence is a question of fact for the jury, *Sage Products, Inc. v.*

Devon Industries, Inc., 126 F.3d 1420, 1423 (Fed. Cir. 1997), which is often decided through testimony by dueling experts.

2. Prosecution History Estoppel

As you know, patent applicants often amend their claims during patent prosecution. These amendments change the scope of what the claims literally encompass, of course. In addition, these claim amendments have long been understood to restrict the scope of what a patentee can later claim as an equivalent to a claim element as well. For instance, suppose that a patent applicant starts with a claim that includes a "gear." Imagine that the patent examiner rejects this claim on the grounds that there is prior art that similarly includes a gear, made of wood. The patentee amends her claim to specify that the invention must include a "metal gear," in order to avoid the prior art. Suppose then that someone else begins selling the same invention, but with a gear made from stone. The patentee cannot later claim that a "stone gear" is an equivalent to her "metal gear." She is estopped from claiming this equivalent because she amended the claim. This is known as the doctrine of "prosecution history estoppel." *See Warner-Jenkinson Co., Inc. v. Hilton Davis Chem. Co.*, 520 U.S. 17, 29-31 (1997).

This "metal gear" example presents an easy case in two respects. First, the patentee amended the claim due to existing prior art. Amendments made because of prior art have long been thought to trigger the doctrine of prosecution history estoppel. But what about amendments made for other reasons, or for no discernable reason? Do all amendments trigger prosecution history estoppel, or only some? Second, the amendment directly implicated the equivalent that the patent owner later tried to claim. That is, the patentee amended the element to specify a particular material (metal), and then later tried to claim another type of material (stone). The amendment thus could not be more relevant to the putative equivalent, and the case for applying the doctrine of prosecution history estoppel could not be stronger. But what if the amendment is not so closely connected with the equivalent the patent owner is trying to recapture? Should amending a claim element bar a patent owner from recapturing all potential equivalents to the element, or only some elements? Those are the questions the Supreme Court took up in *Festo*.

Festo Corp. v. Shoketsu Kinzoku Kogyo Kabushiki Co., 535 U.S. 722 (2002)

Justice Anthony Kennedy delivered the opinion of the Court.

This case requires us to address once again the relation between two patent law concepts, the doctrine of equivalents and the rule of prosecution history estoppel. The Court considered the same concepts in *Warner–Jenkinson Co. v. Hilton Davis Chemical Co.*, 520 U.S. 17 (1997), and reaffirmed that a patent protects its holder against efforts of copyists to evade liability for infringement by making only insubstantial changes to a patented invention. At the same time, we appreciated that by extending protection beyond the literal terms in a patent the doctrine of equivalents can create substantial uncertainty about where the patent monopoly ends. If the range of equivalents is unclear, competitors may be unable to determine what is a permitted alternative to a patented invention and what is an infringing equivalent.

2   To reduce the uncertainty, *Warner–Jenkinson* acknowledged that competitors may rely on the prosecution history, the public record of the patent proceedings. In some cases the Patent and Trademark Office (PTO) may have rejected an earlier version of the patent application on the ground that a claim does not meet a statutory requirement for patentability. 35 U.S.C. § 132. When the patentee responds to the rejection by narrowing his claims, this prosecution history estops him from later arguing that the subject matter covered by the original, broader claim was nothing more than an equivalent. Competitors may rely on the estoppel to ensure that their own devices will not be found to infringe by equivalence.

3   In the decision now under review the Court of Appeals for the Federal Circuit held that by narrowing a claim to obtain a patent, the patentee surrenders all equivalents to the amended claim element. Petitioner asserts this holding departs from past precedent in two respects. First, it applies estoppel to every amendment made to satisfy the requirements of the Patent Act and not just to amendments made to avoid pre-emption by an earlier invention, i.e., the prior art. Second, it holds that when estoppel arises, it bars suit against every equivalent to the amended claim element.

4   We granted certiorari to consider these questions.

I

5   Petitioner Festo Corporation owns two patents for an improved magnetic rodless cylinder, a piston-driven device that relies on magnets to move objects in a conveying system. The device has many industrial uses and has been employed in machinery as diverse as sewing equipment and the Thunder Mountain ride at Disney World. Although the precise details of the cylinder's operation are not essential here, the prosecution history must be considered.

6   Petitioner's patent applications, as often occurs, were amended during the prosecution proceedings. The application for the first patent, the Stoll Patent (U.S. Patent No. 4,354,125), was amended after the patent examiner rejected the initial application because the exact method of operation was unclear and some claims were made in an impermissible way. (They were multiply dependent.) 35 U.S.C. § 112. The inventor, Dr. Stoll, submitted a new application designed to meet the examiner's objections and also added certain references to prior art. The second patent, the Carroll Patent (U.S. Patent No. 3,779,401), was also amended during a reexamination

proceeding. The prior art references were added to this amended application as well. Both amended patents added a new limitation—that the inventions contain a pair of sealing rings, each having a lip on one side, which would prevent impurities from getting on the piston assembly. The amended Stoll Patent added the further limitation that the outer shell of the device, the sleeve, be made of a magnetizable material.

7   After Festo began selling its rodless cylinder, respondents (SMC) entered the market with a device similar, but not identical, to the ones disclosed by Festo's patents. SMC's cylinder, rather than using two one-way sealing rings, employs a single sealing ring with a two-way lip. Furthermore, SMC's sleeve is made of a nonmagnetizable alloy. SMC's device does not fall within the literal claims of either patent, but petitioner contends that it is so similar that it infringes under the doctrine of equivalents.

8   SMC contends that Festo is estopped from making this argument because of the prosecution history of its patents. The sealing rings and the magnetized alloy in the Festo product were both [claimed] for the first time in the amended applications. In SMC's view, these amendments narrowed the earlier applications, surrendering alternatives that are the very points of difference in the competing devices—the sealing rings and the type of alloy used to make the sleeve. As Festo narrowed its claims in these ways in order to obtain the patents, says SMC, Festo is now estopped from saying that these features are immaterial and that SMC's device is an equivalent of its own.

9   The United States District Court for the District of Massachusetts disagreed. It held that Festo's amendments were not made to avoid prior art, and therefore the amendments were not the kind that give rise to estoppel. A panel of the Court of Appeals for the Federal Circuit affirmed. We granted certiorari, vacated, and remanded in light of our intervening decision in *Warner–Jenkinson*. The Court of Appeals ordered rehearing en banc to address questions that had divided its judges since our decision in *Warner–Jenkinson*.

10   The en banc court reversed, holding that prosecution history estoppel barred Festo from asserting that the accused device infringed its patents under the doctrine of equivalents. The court held, with only one judge dissenting, that estoppel arises from any amendment that narrows a claim to comply with the Patent Act, not only from amendments made to avoid prior art. More controversial in the Court of Appeals was its further holding [with four judges dissenting]: When estoppel applies, it stands as a complete bar against any claim of equivalence for the element that was amended. Previous decisions had held that prosecution history estoppel constituted a flexible bar, foreclosing some, but not all, claims of equivalence, depending on the purpose of the amendment and the alterations in the text. The court concluded, however, that this case-by-case approach has proved unworkable. In the court's view a complete-bar rule, under which estoppel bars all claims of equivalence to the narrowed element, would promote certainty in the determination of infringement cases.

II

11   The patent laws "promote the Progress of Science and useful Arts" by rewarding innovation with a temporary monopoly. U.S. Const., Art. I, § 8, cl. 8. The monopoly is a property right; and like any property right, its boundaries should be clear. This clarity is essential to promote progress, because it enables efficient investment in innovation. A patent holder should know what he owns, and the public should know what he does not. For this reason, the patent laws require inventors to describe their work in "full, clear, concise, and exact terms," 35 U.S.C. § 112, as part of the delicate balance the law attempts to maintain between inventors, who rely on the promise of the law to bring the invention forth, and the public, which should be encouraged to pursue innovations, creations, and new ideas beyond the inventor's exclusive rights.

12   Unfortunately, the nature of language makes it impossible to capture the essence of a thing in a patent application. The inventor who chooses to patent an invention and disclose it to the public, rather than exploit it in secret, bears the risk that others will devote their efforts toward exploiting the limits of the patent's language. The language in the patent claims may not capture every nuance of the invention or describe with complete precision the range of its novelty. If patents were always interpreted by their literal terms, their value would be greatly diminished. Unimportant and insubstantial substitutes for certain elements could defeat the patent, and its value to inventors could be destroyed by simple acts of copying. For this reason, the clearest rule of patent interpretation, literalism, may conserve judicial resources but is not necessarily the most efficient rule. The scope of a patent is not limited to its literal terms but instead embraces all equivalents to the claims described.

13   It is true that the doctrine of equivalents renders the scope of patents less certain. It may be difficult to determine what is, or is not, an equivalent to a particular element of an invention. If competitors cannot be certain about a patent's extent, they may be deterred from engaging in legitimate manufactures outside its limits, or they may invest by mistake in competing products that the patent secures. In addition the uncertainty may lead to wasteful litigation between competitors, suits that a rule of literalism might avoid. These concerns with the doctrine of equivalents, however, are not new. Each time the Court has considered the doctrine, it has acknowledged this uncertainty as the price of ensuring the appropriate incentives for innovation, and it has affirmed the doctrine over dissents that urged a more certain rule. When the Court in *Winans v. Denmead* first adopted what has become the doctrine of equivalents, it stated that "[t]he exclusive right to the thing patented is not secured, if the public are at liberty to make substantial copies of it, varying its form or proportions." 56 U.S. 330, 343 (1854). The dissent argued that the Court had sacrificed the objective of "[f]ul[l]ness, clearness, exactness, preciseness, and particularity, in the description of the invention." *Id.* at 347 (opinion of Campbell, J.).

14   The debate continued in *Graver Tank & Mfg. Co. v. Linde Air Products Co.*, 339 U.S. 605 (1950), where the Court reaffirmed the doctrine. *Graver Tank* held that patent claims must protect the inventor not only from those who produce devices falling within the literal claims of the patent but also from copyists who "make unimportant and insubstantial changes and substitutions in the patent which, though adding nothing, would be enough to take the copied matter outside the claim, and hence outside the reach of law." *Id.* at 607. Justice Black, in dissent, objected that under the doctrine of equivalents a competitor "cannot rely on what the language of a patent claims. He must be able, at the peril of heavy infringement damages, to forecast how far a court relatively unversed in a particular technological field will expand the claim's language . . . ." *Id.* at 617.

15   Most recently, in *Warner–Jenkinson,* the Court reaffirmed that equivalents remain a firmly entrenched part of the settled rights protected by the patent. A unanimous opinion concluded that if the doctrine is to be discarded, it is Congress and not the Court that should do so:

> [T]he lengthy history of the doctrine of equivalents strongly supports adherence to our refusal in *Graver Tank* to find that the Patent Act conflicts with that doctrine. Congress can legislate the doctrine of equivalents out of existence any time it chooses. The various policy arguments now made by both sides are thus best addressed to Congress, not this Court. 520 U.S. at 28.

III

16   Prosecution history estoppel requires that the claims of a patent be interpreted in light of the proceedings in the PTO during the application process. Estoppel is a "rule of patent construction" that ensures that claims are interpreted by reference to those "that have been cancelled or rejected." *Schriber–Schroth Co. v. Cleveland Trust Co.*, 311 U.S. 211, 220–21 (1940). The doctrine of equivalents allows the patentee to claim those insubstantial alterations that were not captured in drafting the original patent claim but which could be created through trivial changes. When, however, the patentee originally claimed the subject matter alleged to infringe but then narrowed the claim in response to a rejection, he may not argue that the surrendered territory comprised unforeseen subject matter that should be deemed equivalent to the literal claims of the issued patent.

17   A rejection indicates that the patent examiner does not believe the original claim could be patented. While the patentee has the right to appeal, his decision to forgo an appeal and submit an amended claim is taken as a concession that the invention as patented does not reach as far as the original claim. Were it otherwise, the inventor might avoid the PTO's gatekeeping role and seek to recapture in an infringement action the very subject matter surrendered as a condition of receiving the patent.

18   Prosecution history estoppel ensures that the doctrine of equivalents remains tied to its underlying purpose. Where the original application once embraced the purported equivalent but the patentee narrowed his claims to obtain the patent or to protect its validity, the patentee cannot assert that he lacked the words to describe the subject matter in question. The doctrine of equivalents is premised on language's inability to capture the essence of innovation, but a prior application describing the precise element at issue undercuts that premise. In that instance the prosecution history has established that the inventor turned his attention to the subject matter in question, knew the words for both the broader and narrower claim, and affirmatively chose the latter.

A

19   The first question in this case concerns the kinds of amendments that may give rise to estoppel. Petitioner argues that estoppel should arise when amendments are intended to narrow the subject matter of the patented invention, for instance, amendments to avoid prior art, but not when the amendments are made to comply with requirements concerning the form of the patent application. In *Warner–Jenkinson* we recognized that prosecution history estoppel does not arise in every instance when a patent application is amended. Our "prior cases have consistently applied prosecution history estoppel only where claims have been amended for a limited set of reasons," such as "to avoid the prior art, or otherwise to address a specific concern—such as obviousness—that arguably would have rendered the claimed subject matter unpatentable." 520 U.S. at 30–32. While we made clear that estoppel applies to amendments made for a "substantial reason related to patentability," *id.* at 33, we did not purport to define that term or to catalog every reason that might raise an estoppel. Indeed, we stated that even if the amendment's purpose were unrelated to patentability, the court might consider whether it was the kind of reason that nonetheless might require resort to the estoppel doctrine. *Id.* at 40–41.

20   Petitioner is correct that estoppel has been discussed most often in the context of amendments made to avoid the prior art. It does not follow, however, that amendments for other purposes will not give rise to estoppel. Prosecution history may rebut the inference that a thing not described was indescribable. That rationale does not cease simply because the narrowing amendment, submitted to secure a patent, was for some purpose other than avoiding prior art.

21   We agree with the Court of Appeals that a narrowing amendment made to satisfy any requirement of the Patent Act may give rise to an estoppel. As that court explained, a number of statutory requirements must be satisfied before a patent can issue. The claimed subject matter must be useful, novel, and not obvious. 35 U.S.C. §§ 101–103. In addition, the patent application must describe, enable, and set forth the best mode of carrying out the invention. § 112.

22   Petitioner contends that amendments made to comply with § 112 concern the form of the application and not the subject matter of the invention. The PTO might

require the applicant to clarify an ambiguous term, to improve the translation of a foreign word, or to rewrite a dependent claim as an independent one. In these cases, petitioner argues, the applicant has no intention of surrendering subject matter and should not be estopped from challenging equivalent devices. While this may be true in some cases, petitioner's argument conflates the patentee's reason for making the amendment with the impact the amendment has on the subject matter.

23   Estoppel arises when an amendment is made to secure the patent and the amendment narrows the patent's scope. If a § 112 amendment is truly cosmetic, then it would not narrow the patent's scope or raise an estoppel. On the other hand, if a § 112 amendment is necessary and narrows the patent's scope—even if only for the purpose of better description—estoppel may apply. A patentee who narrows a claim as a condition for obtaining a patent disavows his claim to the broader subject matter, whether the amendment was made to avoid the prior art or to comply with § 112. We must regard the patentee as having conceded an inability to claim the broader subject matter or at least as having abandoned his right to appeal a rejection. In either case estoppel may apply.

B

24   Petitioner concedes that the limitations at issue—the sealing rings and the composition of the sleeve—were made for reasons related to § 112, if not also to avoid the prior art. Our conclusion that prosecution history estoppel arises when a claim is narrowed to comply with § 112 gives rise to the second question presented: Does the estoppel bar the inventor from asserting infringement against any equivalent to the narrowed element or might some equivalents still infringe? The Court of Appeals held that prosecution history estoppel is a complete bar, and so the narrowed element must be limited to its strict literal terms. Based upon its experience the Court of Appeals decided that the flexible-bar rule is unworkable because it leads to excessive uncertainty and burdens legitimate innovation. For the reasons that follow, we disagree with the decision to adopt the complete bar.

25   Though prosecution history estoppel can bar a patentee from challenging a wide range of alleged equivalents made or distributed by competitors, its reach requires an examination of the subject matter surrendered by the narrowing amendment. The complete bar avoids this inquiry by establishing a *per se* rule; but that approach is inconsistent with the purpose of applying the estoppel in the first place—to hold the inventor to the representations made during the application process and to the inferences that may reasonably be drawn from the amendment. By amending the application, the inventor is deemed to concede that the patent does not extend as far as the original claim. It does not follow, however, that the amended claim becomes so perfect in its description that no one could devise an equivalent. After amendment, as before, language remains an imperfect fit for invention. The narrowing amendment may demonstrate what the claim is not; but it may still fail to capture precisely what the claim is. There is no reason why a narrowing amendment

should be deemed to relinquish equivalents unforeseeable at the time of the amendment and beyond a fair interpretation of what was surrendered. Nor is there any call to foreclose claims of equivalence for aspects of the invention that have only a peripheral relation to the reason the amendment was submitted. The amendment does not show that the inventor suddenly had more foresight in the drafting of claims than an inventor whose application was granted without amendments having been submitted. It shows only that he was familiar with the broader text and with the difference between the two. As a result, there is no more reason for holding the patentee to the literal terms of an amended claim than there is for abolishing the doctrine of equivalents altogether and holding every patentee to the literal terms of the patent.

26   In *Warner–Jenkinson* we struck the appropriate balance by placing the burden on the patentee to show that an amendment was not for purposes of patentability:

> Where no explanation is established, however, the court should presume that the patent application had a substantial reason related to patentability for including the limiting element added by amendment. In those circumstances, prosecution history estoppel would bar the application of the doctrine of equivalents as to that element.

Id. at 33.

27   When the patentee is unable to explain the reason for amendment, estoppel not only applies but also "bar[s] the application of the doctrine of equivalents as to that element." *Id.* These words do not mandate a complete bar; they are limited to the circumstance where "no explanation is established." They do provide, however, that when the court is unable to determine the purpose underlying a narrowing amendment—and hence a rationale for limiting the estoppel to the surrender of particular equivalents—the court should presume that the patentee surrendered all subject matter between the broader and the narrower language.

28   Just as *Warner–Jenkinson* held that the patentee bears the burden of proving that an amendment was not made for a reason that would give rise to estoppel, we hold here that the patentee should bear the burden of showing that the amendment does not surrender the particular equivalent in question. This is the approach advocated by the United States, and we regard it to be sound. The patentee, as the author of the claim language, may be expected to draft claims encompassing readily known equivalents. A patentee's decision to narrow his claims through amendment may be presumed to be a general disclaimer of the territory between the original claim and the amended claim. There are some cases, however, where the amendment cannot reasonably be viewed as surrendering a particular equivalent. The equivalent may have been unforeseeable at the time of the application; the rationale underlying the amendment may bear no more than a tangential relation to the equivalent in question; or there may be some other reason suggesting that the patentee could not reasonably be expected to have described the insubstantial substitute in question. In those cases

the patentee can overcome the presumption that prosecution history estoppel bars a finding of equivalence.

29   This presumption is not, then, just the complete bar by another name. Rather, it reflects the fact that the interpretation of the patent must begin with its literal claims, and the prosecution history is relevant to construing those claims. When the patentee has chosen to narrow a claim, courts may presume the amended text was composed with awareness of this rule and that the territory surrendered is not an equivalent of the territory claimed. In those instances, however, the patentee still might rebut the presumption that estoppel bars a claim of equivalence. The patentee must show that at the time of the amendment one skilled in the art could not reasonably be expected to have drafted a claim that would have literally encompassed the alleged equivalent.

IV

30   On the record before us, we cannot say petitioner has rebutted the presumptions that estoppel applies and that the equivalents at issue have been surrendered. Petitioner concedes that the limitations at issue—the sealing rings and the composition of the sleeve—were made in response to a rejection for reasons under § 112, if not also because of the prior art references. As the amendments were made for a reason relating to patentability, the question is not whether estoppel applies but what territory the amendments surrendered. While estoppel does not effect a complete bar, the question remains whether petitioner can demonstrate that the narrowing amendments did not surrender the particular equivalents at issue. On these questions, SMC may well prevail, for the sealing rings and the composition of the sleeve both were noted expressly in the prosecution history. These matters, however, should be determined in the first instance by further proceedings in the Court of Appeals or the District Court.

31   The judgment of the Federal Circuit is vacated, and the case is remanded for further proceedings consistent with this opinion.

Discussion Questions: *Festo*

1. *The Policy Behind the Doctrine of Equivalents.* What are the policy objectives that the law seeks to achieve using the doctrine of equivalents? What are the tradeoffs involved in this doctrine? That is, what values or policy objectives are being sacrificed by having a doctrine of equivalents?

2. *Substantial Reasons Related to Patentability.* The *Festo* Court holds that all amendments to address substantial reasons related to patentability give rise to the presumption of prosecution history estoppel. What do you think the Court means by a "substantial reason related to patentability?" What reason might a patentee have for amending a claim, or what rule might force a patentee to amend a claim, that

wouldn't fall in this category? Not giving a reason is insufficient to avoid the presumption: the Court notes that "[w]here no explanation is established [for an amendment], the court should presume that the patent application had a substantial reason related to patentability."

3. *The Flexible Bar.* The Court opts for a "flexible" bar, rather than a complete bar. This means that even if a presumption of prosecution history estoppel applies to a claim amendment, the patentee can rebut that presumption. The Court says that there are two categories of situations in which an amendment will not bar subsequent equivalents to a claim element. The first category is if the equivalent was unforeseeable—that is, the patent applicant could not have anticipated the equivalent and thus could not have drafted a claim that would encompass it at the time the claim was being amended. The second category is if the rationale underlying the amendment was "tangential" to the equivalent that the patent owner seeks to capture. Consider the following examples:

(a) Gabrielle applies for a patent on an invention that involves a "gear" with "teeth." During prosecution, the patent examiner rejects the patent on the basis of prior art involving a gear that has five teeth. Gabrielle then revises her claim element such that it reads "gear with six teeth." Marco then begins producing the same invention, but the gear in his invention has eight teeth. Can Gabrielle argue that Marco's gear is an equivalent to hers, or is she barred by the doctrine of prosecution history estoppel?

(b) Imagine the same patent with the same prosecution history as (a) above. This time, however, Marco's invention uses a gear with six "links." In a gear of this type, a link is similar (though not identical) to a tooth. Can Gabrielle argue that Marco's gear is an equivalent to hers, or is she barred by the doctrine of prosecution history estoppel?

(c) Imagine that Ellen invents a chemical reaction that operates at a "pH between 6 and 10." During prosecution, the patent examiner rejects the patent on the basis of prior art that operates at a pH of 9.5. Ellen then amends her claim element to specify that the invention must operate at a pH between "6 and 9." Michael then begins producing the same invention, except that his operates at a pH of 9.2. Can Ellen argue that Michael's invention is equivalent to hers, or is she barred by the doctrine of prosecution history estoppel?

(d) Imagine the same patent with the same prosecution history as (c) above. This time, however, Michael's invention operates at a pH of 5. Can Ellen argue that Michael's invention is equivalent to hers, or is she barred by the doctrine of prosecution history estoppel? *See Biagro W. Sales, Inc. v. Grow More, Inc.*, 423 F.3d 1296 (Fed. Cir. 2005).

(e) Imagine that Alysia obtains a patent on a "microfluidic system," which is a device that uses microscopic channels—the width of a hair—to carry fluids.

During prosecution, Alysia amends her patent claim to specify that the channels be "non-flourinated" (that is, that they contain no flourine) and thus will not react with the fluid being carried through the channels, which is flourinated. This amendment was made to distinguish the invention from prior art that used a different method to avoid having the channel react chemically with the fluid it is carrying. The accused device is a similar microfluidic system that contains 0.02% Kynar, a non-reactive resin that contains de minimis amounts of fluorine. Can Alysia argue that the accused device is equivalent to hers, or is she barred by the doctrine of prosecution history estoppel? *See Bio-Rad Laboratories, Inc. v. 10X Genomics Inc.*, 967 F.3d 1353 (Fed. Cir. 2020).

4. *The Boundaries of a Claim Element.* Recall that the doctrine of prosecution history estoppel only applies to the particular claim element that has been amended, not to the entire claim. Accordingly, determining when a claim element begins and ends can be critical to the prosecution history estoppel analysis. For instance, consider the pH element described in example (d) above. If the pH range is actually two elements—one element requiring a pH greater than 6 and one element requiring a pH less than 9—then the first element (the lower end of the range) was never amended, and prosecution history estoppel does not apply. How would a court decide in such a case whether the pH range is one element or two elements?

For that matter, suppose the claim were written to require that "the chemical reaction operate at a pH above 6, and also that the chemical reaction operate at a pH below 9." That formulation is, of course, functionally identical to requiring that it operate at a "pH above 6 and below 9." Should a court treat those two claims differently? Would it be justified in construing the first version of the claim to involve two separate pH elements and the second version of the claim to involve just one pH element? If you think that the court should construe both versions of the claim to involve just one pH element, what principles should guide a court in deciding how many elements a claim contains and what each of those elements are?

5. *The Policy Behind Prosecution History Estoppel.* Festo's patent claim calls for two sealing rings with one lip each, while the accused device (which Festo argues is equivalent) has one sealing ring with two lips. Maybe two rings with one lip are equivalent to one ring with two lips, or maybe they aren't; that is a question for the function-way-result test. But Festo was never allowed to argue that they are equivalent because (on remand) it was barred by prosecution history estoppel. *Festo Corp. v. Shoketsu Kinzoku Kogyo Kabushiki Co., Ltd.*, 344 F.3d 1359 (Fed. Cir. 2003); *Festo Corp. v. Shoketsu Kinzoku Kogyo Kabushiki Co., Ltd.*, 493 F.3d 1368 (Fed. Cir. 2007). (It only required two more Federal Circuit opinions, two additional petitions for certiorari, a few more district court opinions, and six additional years.)

Now, if there is prior art that includes a single ring with two lips, it would seem improper to allow Festo to capture that claim scope. Either two rings are the same as one ring, in which case Festo's patent should probably be invalid as obvious, or they are not, in which case Festo's patent is probably not infringed. (There is not perfect symmetry between obviousness and the doctrine of equivalents, as there is with anticipation and literal infringement, but it's relatively close.) But a court could determine the best way to interpret the patent, and whether the claim is infringed, on its own, without referring to what occurred during examination or what claim scope Festo might have surrendered. It might be that Festo surrendered claim scope (one ring with two lips) entirely unnecessarily.

In fact, prosecution history estoppel is really only relevant when the equivalent that a patentee wants to claim is *not* part of the prior art. After all, prosecution history estoppel operates to prevent a patentee from claiming an equivalent precisely when the patentee could have written a claim to literally cover that equivalent, and when that claim would have been valid and infringed. If the claim would not have been valid, there is no point to prosecution history estoppel.

In addition, keep in mind that prosecution history estoppel only operates when there has been an amendment. If Festo had originally drafted its claim to include two rings, each with one lip, the doctrine of prosecution history estoppel would not apply. In other words, Festo could have had precisely the same patent issued, but without implicating the doctrine of prosecution history estoppel, if it had written the claims to include sealing rings in the first place. Why should it matter how Festo arrived at the claim that was eventually issued? Why should otherwise identical claims be treated differently, just because one was amended during prosecution and one was not?

6. *The Doctrine of Equivalents and Claim Construction.* The key policy objective of the doctrine of equivalents—preventing infringers from evading the literal claim language by insubstantial changes—can often also be addressed through claim construction. That is, a court could simply construe claims slightly more capaciously to include minor variants, rather than construing claims narrowly and forcing the patent owner to rely on the doctrine of equivalents. Some scholars have suggested that after *Markman v. Westview*, claim construction eclipsed the doctrine of equivalents in importance. *See* John R. Allison & Mark A. Lemley, *The (Unnoticed) Demise of the Doctrine of Equivalents*, 59 Stan. L. Rev. 955 (2007); David L. Schwartz, *Explaining the Demise of the Doctrine of Equivalents*, 26 Berkeley Tech. L.J. 1157 (2011). What are the advantages and disadvantages of addressing these policy concerns through each doctrine?

Additional Limitations on Equivalents

1. *The Disclosure-Dedication Rule.* In *Johnson & Johnston Associates v. R.E. Service*, 285 F.3d 1046 (Fed. Cir. 2002), the plaintiff's claim included, as one element, a "sheet of aluminum." The specification disclosed that the invention could be made with other metals as well, including steel and nickel. The defendant produced a similar invention, except for the fact that it used a sheet of steel rather than

aluminum, and the plaintiff sued for infringement under the doctrine of equivalents. The Federal Circuit held that the patentee could not capture steel as an equivalent because, by disclosing the use of steel but not claiming it, it had placed the use of steel into the public domain:

> [W]hen a patent drafter discloses but declines to claim subject matter, as in this case, this action dedicates that unclaimed subject matter to the public. Application of the doctrine of equivalents to recapture subject matter deliberately left unclaimed would conflict with the primacy of the claims in defining the scope of the patentee's exclusive right.

Id. at 1054.

There is a certain logic to this decision, in that the claims do define the scope of the patentee's property right, and the specification does constitute a public disclosure that can operate as prior art. But if this doctrine were applied with full force, it would effectively eliminate the doctrine of equivalents. Anything disclosed in the specification and not claimed would be part of the public domain, and the patentee could not capture it as an equivalent; and if an equivalent were *not disclosed* in the specification, claiming it would create enablement and written description problems. The patentee's claims would only encompass what was disclosed in the specification *and* claimed—in other words, the patentee's only option would be literal infringement.

However, the Federal Circuit has since moved to limit the force of this doctrine. In subsequent cases, the court held that the rule

> does not mean that any generic reference in a written specification necessarily dedicates all members of that particular genus to the public. Rather, the disclosure must be of such specificity that one of ordinary skill in the art could identify the subject matter that had been disclosed and not claimed. Additionally, this court [has] further clarified that before unclaimed subject matter is deemed to have been dedicated to the public, that unclaimed subject matter must have been identified by the patentee as an alternative to a claim limitation.

SanDisk Corp. v. Kingston Tech. Co., Inc., 695 F.3d 1348, 1363–64 (Fed. Cir. 2012). Accordingly, if the patentee in *Johnson & Johnston* had simply mentioned that "other metals" could be made to work in the invention, it seems likely that the court would have permitted it to argue that steel was an equivalent. It was naming steel, specifically, that barred the patentee.

Think back to *Unique Concepts*. Could the patent owner have argued that mitered corner pieces were equivalent to preformed corner pieces, and thus that the accused device infringed under the doctrine of equivalents? Why or why not?

2. *The Ensnarement Doctrine.* Another doctrine that exists to police the reach of the doctrine of equivalents is called "ensnarement." "Ensnarement bars a patentee from asserting a scope of equivalency that would encompass, or 'ensnare,' the prior art." *DePuy Spine, Inc. v. Medtronic Sofamor Danek, Inc.*, 567 F.3d 1314, 1322 (Fed. Cir. 2009). That is, a patentee cannot claim that a claim has a particular scope via the doctrine of equivalents if a claim that had the same scope via literal infringement would be anticipated or obvious. This requirement makes a great deal of sense: if a claim drafted to cover a certain scope *literally* would be invalid, the patentee should not be allowed to capture the same scope through equivalents. One might even think that this doctrine would be an axiomatic part of the doctrine of equivalents, but patent law has bestowed upon it its own name.

For instance, *DePuy Spine* involved a claim for a medical device in which a screw was connected to a "spherically-shaped" portion of the device. The accused device connected the screw to a "conically-shaped" portion of the device instead. The patentee claimed that a device with a conically-shaped portion was an equivalent to its claim. To evaluate this argument, the Federal Circuit first formulated a hypothetical claim that covered the accused device by substituting the word "conically" for "spherically." It then determined that this hypothetical claim would not have been obvious in light of prior art. *Id.* at 1329. Accordingly, the doctrine of ensnarement did not apply, and the patentee was permitted to argue that the accused device infringed under the doctrine of equivalents.

An Infringement–Validity Flow Chart

With the addition of infringement by the equivalents, we have now introduced a significant number of moving pieces into the infringement analysis. The doctrine of prosecution history estoppel itself has two steps, and that does not include the doctrine of equivalents analysis itself, much less any other step in the process of determining validity and infringement. In order to help sort through the many steps in adjudicating a patent, we offer the following highly simplified flow chart:

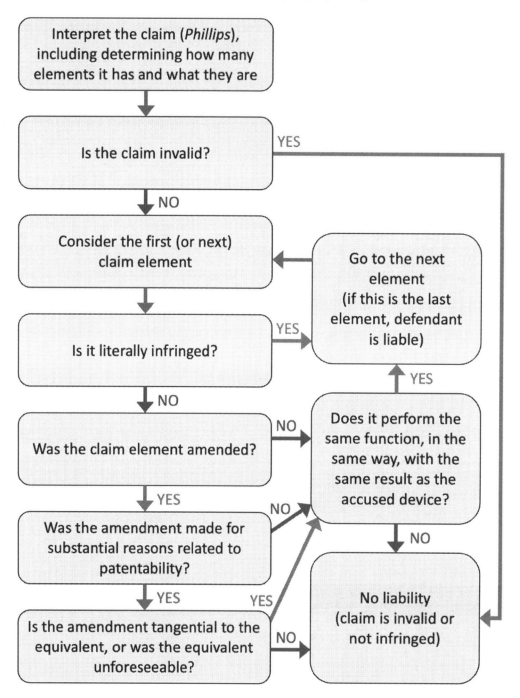

10. Indirect Infringement

Thus far, we have been discussing what is known as "direct infringement": the party sued for infringement is a party that has made, used, or sold the patented invention. But there are some cases in which the patent holder might want to sue a party that has merely facilitated the infringement, rather than the party that has directly infringed. For instance, recall the Swiffer patent from Chapter 1. Suppose a company sells standard mops, along with instructions describing how to convert those standard mops into Swiffers. The company knows full well—indeed, intends—that individuals will purchase its mops and convert them into Swiffers. Can the owner of the Swiffer patent sue this mop company, or may it only sue the individual customers who build their own Swiffers? Or, for instance, imagine that a third firm sells specially designed reservoirs of cleaning fluid that are meant to be combined with the mops when they are made into Swiffers. Can the patent owner sue this company that is making specialty parts?

This is similar to the concept of "aiding and abetting" liability from criminal law: there are instances in which another party has performed a sufficiently critical function in helping to further the infringement that there is a basis for holding that party liable as well. This is known as "indirect infringement."

Indirect infringement comes in two flavors: inducement, which is governed by 35 U.S.C. § 271(b), and contributory infringement, which is governed by 35 U.S.C. § 271(c). (Recall that ordinary direct infringement falls under 35 U.S.C. § 271(a).) Here is the relevant statutory text:

35 U.S.C. § 271

(b) Whoever actively induces infringement of a patent shall be liable as an infringer.

(c) Whoever offers to sell or sells within the United States or imports into the United States a component of a patented machine, manufacture, combination or composition, or a material or apparatus for use in practicing a patented process, constituting a material part of the invention, knowing the same to be especially made or especially adapted for use in an infringement of such patent, and not a staple article or commodity of commerce suitable for substantial noninfringing use, shall be liable as a contributory infringer.

These statutory sections raise two principal questions that the cases below will address. First, what types of actions will trigger liability? And second, what level of knowledge is required of the indirect infringer? In the hypothetical examples above, does the company that manufactures reservoirs of cleaning solution have to know that its customers will use its product to build make-shift Swiffers? Does it have to know that they will be infringing the Swiffer patent? As you consider these doctrinal questions, you should be thinking about what purpose the doctrines of inducement and contributory infringement are meant to serve, and why direct infringement is not sufficient by itself.

For ease of explication, we will take these statutory sections out of order. We begin below with a case on § 271(c) contributory infringement (*Aro II*) before turning to a case on § 271(b) inducement (*Sanofi v. Watson*). In addition to being the canonical case on contributory infringement, *Aro II* introduces a key defense to patent infringement that we will return to in Chapter 12: under the *exhaustion* doctrine, the first authorized sale of a patented product "exhausts" the patent owner's rights over that product, and the patent owner can no longer sue the user of that product for infringement. Because General Motors had a license to the convertible top patent at issue, their customers could use the convertibles without an additional license.

The General Motors customers could also purchase and install replacement fabi. for their convertible tops from Aro Manufacturing because the Supreme Court had he ¹ in the earlier *Aro I* case that fabric replacement was merely "repair" (covered by the ex austion defense) rather than "reconstruction" (which would require a new patent licer e). Repair is permitted because it perpetuates the use of an existing item (to which the M customers already had licenses); reconstruction would not have been permitted becau e it would entail construction of a new item (for which there would be no license). Bu *Ford* did not have a license, and in *Aro II*, the Court considers whether Aro Manuf turing is liable for selling convertible top replacement fabric to *Ford's* consumers.

A. Contributory Infringement

Aro Mfg. v. Convertible Top Replacement ("Aro II"), 377 U.S. 476 (1964)

Mr. Justice Brennan delivered the opinion of the Court.

1   Respondent Convertible Top Replacement Co., Inc., (CTR) acquired by assignment from the Automobile Body Research Corporation (AB) all rights for the territory of Massachusetts in United States Patent No. 2,569,724, known as the Mackie-Duluk patent. This is a combination patent covering a top-structure for automobile "convertibles." Structures embodying the patented combination were included in 1952–1954 models of convertibles manufactured by the General Motors Corporation and the Ford Motor Company. They were included in the General Motors

cars by authority of a license granted to General Motors by AB; Ford, however, had no license during the 1952–1954 period, and no authority whatever under the patent until July 21, 1955, when it entered into an agreement with AB; Ford's manufacture and sale of the automobiles in question therefore infringed the patent. Petitioner Aro Manufacturing Co., Inc. (Aro), which is not licensed under the patent, produces fabric components designed as replacements for worn out fabric portions of convertible tops; unlike the other elements of the top structure, which ordinarily are usable for the life of the car, the fabric portion normally wears out and requires replacement after about three years of use. Aro's fabrics are specially tailored for installation in particular models of convertibles, and these have included the 1952–1954 General Motors and Ford models equipped with the Mackie-Duluk top-structures.

2   CTR brought this action against Aro in 1956 to enjoin the alleged infringement and contributory infringement, and to obtain an accounting, with respect to replacement fabrics made and sold by Aro for use in both the General Motors and the Ford cars embodying the patented structures. The interlocutory judgment entered for CTR by the District Court for the District of Massachusetts and affirmed by the Court of Appeals for the First Circuit was reversed here. *Aro Mfg. Co. v. Convertible Top Replacement Co.*, 365 U.S. 336 ("*Aro I*"). Our decision dealt, however, only with the General Motors and not with the Ford cars. Like the Court of Appeals, we treated CTR's right to relief as depending wholly upon the question whether replacement of the fabric portions of the convertible tops constituted infringing "reconstruction" or permissible "repair" of the patented combination. The lower courts had held it to constitute "reconstruction," making the car owner for whom it was performed a direct infringer and Aro, which made and sold the replacement fabric, a contributory infringer; we disagreed and held that it was merely "repair." The reconstruction-repair distinction is decisive, however, only when the replacement is made in a structure whose original manufacture and sale have been licensed by the patentee, as was true only of the General Motors cars; when the structure is unlicensed, as was true of the Ford cars, the traditional rule is that even repair constitutes infringement. Thus, the District Court had based its ruling for CTR with respect to the Ford cars on the alternative ground that, even if replacement of the fabric portions constituted merely repair, the car owners were still guilty of direct infringement, and Aro of contributory infringement, as to these unlicensed and hence infringing structures. This aspect of the case was not considered or decided by our opinion in *Aro I*.

3   On remand, however, another judge in the District Court read our opinion as requiring the dismissal of CTR's complaint as to the Ford as well as the General Motors cars, and entered judgment accordingly. CTR appealed the dismissal insofar as it applied to the Ford cars, and the Court of Appeals reinstated the judgment in favor of CTR to the extent. In our view the Court of Appeals was correct in holding that its "previous decision in this case was not reversed insofar as unlicensed Ford cars are concerned." However, we granted certiorari to consider the issue that had not been decided in *Aro I*: whether Aro is liable for contributory infringement, under

35 U.S.C. § 271(c), with respect to its manufacture and sale of replacement fabrics for the Ford cars.

4   CTR contends, and the Court of Appeals held, that since Ford infringed the patent by making and selling the top-structures without authority from the patentee, persons who purchased the automobiles from Ford likewise infringed by using and repairing the structures; and hence Aro, by supplying replacement fabrics specially designed to be utilized in such infringing repair, was guilty of contributory infringement under 35 U.S.C. § 271(c). In *Aro I*, 365 U.S. at 341-42, the Court said:

> It is admitted that petitioners (Aro) know that the purchasers intend to use the fabric for replacement purposes on automobile convertible tops which are covered by the claims of respondent's combination patent, and such manufacture and sale with that knowledge might well constitute contributory infringement under § 271(c), if, but only if, such a replacement by the purchaser himself would in itself constitute a *direct* infringement under § 271(a), for it is settled that if there is no *direct* infringement of a patent there can be no *contributory* infringement. . . . It is plain that § 271(c)—a part of the Patent Code enacted in 1952—made no change in the fundamental precept that there can be no contributory infringement in the absence of a direct infringement. That section defines contributory infringement in terms of direct infringement—namely the sale of a component of a patented combination or machine for use "in an infringement of such patent." And § 271(a) of the new Patent Code, which defines "infringement," left intact the entire body of case law on direct infringement. The determinative question, therefore, comes down to whether the car owner would infringe the combination patent by replacing the worn-out fabric element of the patented convertible top on his car . . . .

Similarly here, to determine whether Aro committed contributory infringement, we must first determine whether the car owners, by replacing the worn-out fabric element of the patented top-structures, committed direct infringement. We think it clear, under § 271(a) of the Patent Code and the "entire body of case law on direct infringement" which that section "left intact," that they did.

5   Section 271(a) provides that "whoever without authority makes, uses or sells any patented invention . . . infringes the patent." It is not controverted—nor could it be—that Ford infringed by making and selling cars embodying the patented top-structures without any authority from the patentee. If Ford had had such authority, its purchasers would not have infringed by using the automobiles, for it is fundamental that sale of a patented article by the patentee or under his authority carries with it an "implied license to use." *Adams v. Burke*, 84 U.S. (17 Wall.) 453, 456 (1873). But with Ford lacking authority to make and sell, it could by its sale of the cars confer on the purchasers no implied license to use, and their use of the patented

structures was thus "without authority" and infringing under § 271(a).[1] Not only does that provision explicitly regard an unauthorized user of a patented invention as an infringer, but it has often and clearly been held that unauthorized use, without more, constitutes infringement.

6   If the owner's *use* infringed, so also did his *repair* of the top-structure, as by replacing the worn-out fabric component. Where use infringes, repair does also, for it perpetuates the infringing use. Consequently replacement of worn-out fabric components with fabrics sold by Aro, held in *Aro I* to constitute "repair" rather than "reconstruction" and thus to be permissible in the case of licensed General Motors cars, was not permissible here in the case of unlicensed Ford cars. Here, as was not the case in *Aro I*, the direct infringement by the car owners that is prerequisite to contributory infringement by Aro was unquestionably established.

7   We turn next to the question whether Aro, as supplier of replacement fabrics for use in the infringing repair by the Ford car owners, was a contributory infringer under § 271(c) of the Patent Code. We think Aro was indeed liable under this provision.

8   Such a result would plainly have obtained under the contributory-infringement case law that § 271(c) was intended to codify. Indeed, most of the law was established in cases where, as here, suit was brought to hold liable for contributory infringement a supplier of replacement parts specially designed for use in the repair of infringing articles. In *Union Tool Co. v. Wilson*, 259 U.S. 107, 113-14 (1922), the Court held that where use of the patented machines themselves was not authorized, "There was, consequently, no implied license to use the spare parts in these machines. As such use, unless licensed, clearly constituted an infringement, the sale of the spare parts to be so used violated the injunction [enjoining infringement]." As early as 1897, Circuit Judge Taft, as he then was, thought it "well settled" that "where one makes and sells one element of a combination covered by a patent with the intention and for the purpose of bringing about its use in such a combination he is guilty of contributory infringement and is equally liable to the patentee with him who in fact organizes the complete combination." *Thomson-Houston Elec. Co. v. Ohio Brass Co.*, 80 F. 712, 721 (6th Cir. 1897).

9   In enacting § 271(c), Congress clearly succeeded in its objective of codifying this case law. The language of the section fits perfectly Aro's activity of selling "a component of a patented . . . combination . . . , constituting a material part of the invention, . . . especially made or especially adapted for use in an infringement of such patent and not a staple article or commodity of commerce suitable for substantial noninfringing use." Indeed, this is the almost unique case in which the component was

---

[1] [n.5 in opinion] We have no need to consider whether the car owners, if sued for infringement by the patentee, would be entitled to indemnity from Ford on a breach of warranty theory. In fact they were not sued, and were released from liability by the agreement between Ford and AB.

hardly suitable for *any* noninfringing use.[2] On this basis both the District Court originally and the Court of Appeals in the instant case held that Aro was a contributory infringer within the precise letter of § 271(c).

10   However, the language of § 271(c) presents a question, apparently not noticed by the parties or the courts below, concerning the element of knowledge that must be brought home to Aro before liability can be imposed. It is only sale of a component of a patented combination *"knowing* the same to be especially made or especially adapted for use in an infringement of such patent" that is contributory infringement under the statute. Was Aro "knowing" within the statutory meaning because—as it admits, and as the lower courts found—it knew that its replacement fabrics were especially designed for use in the 1952–1954 Ford convertible tops and were not suitable for other use? Or does the statute require a further showing that Aro knew that the tops were patented, and knew also that Ford was not licensed under the patent so that any fabric replacement by a Ford car owner constituted infringement?

11   On this question a majority of the Court is of the view that § 271(c) does require a showing that the alleged contributory infringer knew that the combination for which his component was especially designed was both patented and infringing.[3] With respect to many of the replacement-fabric sales involved in this case, Aro clearly had such knowledge. For by letter dated January 2, 1954, AB informed Aro that it held the Mackie-Duluk patent; that it had granted a license under the patent to General Motors but to no one else; and that "It is obvious, from the foregoing and from an inspection of the convertible automobile sold by the Ford Motor Company, that anyone selling ready-made replacement fabrics for these automobiles would be guilty of contributory infringement of said patent." Thus the Court's interpretation of the knowledge requirement affords Aro no defense with respect to replacement-fabric sales made after January 2, 1954. It would appear that the overwhelming majority of the sales were in fact made after that date, since the oldest of the cars were 1952 models and since the average life of a fabric top is said to be three years. With respect to any sales that were made before that date, however, Aro cannot be held liable in the absence of a showing that at that time it had already acquired the requisite

---

[2] [n.7 in opinion] Aro's factory manager admitted that the fabric replacements in question not only were specially designed for the Ford convertibles but would not, to his knowledge, fit the top-structures of any other cars.

[3] [n.8 in opinion] This view is held by The Chief Justice and Justices Black, Douglas, Clark, and White. [Eds: The only one of these five Justices to join Justice Brennan's majority opinion is Justice White; the others join Justice Black in a dissent, which argues that consumers and repairmen should never be liable for direct infringement, and especially not here, where the patent owner has already recovered for past infringements from Ford.] Justices Harlan, Brennan, Stewart and Goldberg dissent from this interpretation of the statute. They are of the view that the knowledge Congress meant to require was simply knowledge that the component was especially designed for use in a combination and was not a staple article suitable for substantial other use, and not knowledge that the combination was either patented or infringing.

knowledge that the Ford car tops were patented and infringing. When the case is remanded, a finding of fact must be made on this question by the District Court, and, unless Aro is found to have had such prior knowledge, the judgment imposing liability must be vacated as to any sales made before January 2, 1954. As to subsequent sales, however, we hold, in agreement with the lower courts, that Aro is liable for contributory infringement within the terms of § 271(c).

12   [In omitted portions of the majority opinion, the Court held that the July 21, 1955 settlement between Ford and AB resolving their past and future patent disputes also prevented Aro from being liable for replacement fabric sales made after this agreement. Aro is thus liable only for earlier sales, although a plurality of the Court suggested that the 1955 agreement "does have the effect of limiting the amount that CTR can recover for the pre-agreement infringement, and probably of precluding recovery of anything more than nominal damages." The plurality opined that "after a patentee has collected from or on behalf of a direct infringer damages sufficient to put him in the position he would have occupied had there been no infringement, he cannot thereafter collect actual damages from a person liable only for contributing to the same infringement." A concurrence by Justice White and a dissent by Justice Black are omitted.]

Discussion Questions: Aro II

1. *Direct Infringement as a Prerequisite.* Toward the beginning of the opinion, the Court quotes a lengthy excerpt from its predecessor case (*Aro I*) in which it held that "if there is no direct infringement of a patent there can be no contributory infringement." This is a critical axiom of patent law, and one that remains in the law to the present day. But why should it be the case? Why not allow a patent owner to sue a party that is attempting to contribute to another's infringement, even if that attempt is unsuccessful?

2. *Repair vs. Reconstruction.* Why is there a difference between "repair" and "reconstruction," and why does it mean the GM cars aren't at issue? Why is it clear that Ford and its customers are directly infringing?

3. *The Lawsuit's Targets.* Given that Ford and its customers are directly infringing, why isn't CTR suing them, rather than suing Aro? Start with the customers—why can't CTR simply sue them (and only them) for their acts of infringement? If suing the customers is not a good option, why can't CTR simply sue Ford? What does it have to gain from suing Aro instead of (or in addition to) Ford?

4. *Noninfringing Uses?* What work is the provision that excludes liability for "substantial noninfringing uses" meant to do? What is the paradigm case of a substantial noninfringing use? What about the sales to owners of GM cars? Those were noninfringing uses. Could Aro have argued that it shouldn't be liable because the sales to GM owners are a "substantial noninfringing use?" Why or why not?

5. *What Knowledge?* Why is the statute's knowledge requirement ambiguous, and how does the Court resolve the ambiguity? (Don't skip footnote 8! Who is authoring this opinion, and what does he think on this point?) What are the pros and cons of the two views as a policy matter?

How do we know that Aro had the necessary knowledge, and when did it acquire that knowledge? Can Aro be held liable for any acts of infringement that occurred before it acquired the necessary knowledge?

The *Aro II* Court imposes a high knowledge requirement before a party can be liable for contributory infringement. Direct infringement (under § 271(a)) is strict liability. Even criminal law almost never requires that a party have knowledge of the legal status of one's actions, as opposed to the fact that one is taking the actions in the first place. Why do you think the Court imposes such a high knowledge standard here?

6. *Strategic Behavior in Light of the Knowledge Requirement.* What incentives does the requirement that contributory infringement be "knowing" create for parties such as Aro that might be liable as contributory infringers? Does Aro have an incentive to search for patents they might be infringing? What about the patent holder—what obligations does this impose on it?

Suppose contributory infringement were strict liability, as direct infringement is. What costs and benefits, and for which parties, would that rule create, compared with the rule requiring knowledge? Suppose that you represented a firm, such as Aro, that might be liable as a contributory infringer but is no longer protected by the requirement of knowledge. What advice would you give to the firm's managers? What options does the firm have?

B. Inducement

Sanofi v. Watson Labs. Inc., 875 F.3d 636 (Fed. Cir. 2017)

Richard Taranto, Circuit Judge.

[As explained in detail in Chapter 11, patents related to approved drugs must be listed in the FDA's "Orange Book," which allows generic manufacturers to determine which (if any) patents they might infringe if they begin selling a generic version of the drug. When a generic firm seeks to market a generic version of an FDA-approved drug, it files a "paragraph IV" certification in which it certifies that any non-expired patents listed in the Orange Book are either invalid or not infringed. Needless to say, the original developer of the drug often disagrees with the generic firm's assessment of its patents, and 35 U.S.C. § 271(e)(2)(A) allows the patent owner to initiate litigation against the generic firm to resolve these disputes before the generic firm begins selling its products.]

2   [In 2009, the pharmaceutical firm Sanofi received FDA approval for the cardiovascular drug dronedarone, which it began selling under the brand name Multaq. The generic firms Watson Laboratories and Sandoz subsequently sought to market generic dronedarone and filed paragraph IV challenges to the related patents, including Patent No. 8,410,167, which claims methods of reducing hospitalization by administering dronedarone to patients having specified characteristics. Notably, the patent covering the compound dronedarone itself was set to expire in 2019, while the '167 patent, which covered a method of treatment, was valid until 2029. Litigation over this method of treatment was thus of great importance to all of the parties involved. After a three-day bench trial, the district court ruled that Watson's and Sanofi's sale of their proposed generic drugs would induce physicians to infringe all but one of the asserted claims. Watson and Sanofi appealed this finding of inducement.]

I

3   [Five clinical trials involving dronedarone are relevant to the inducement issue. The first two trials, EURIDIS and ADONIS, primarily found that dronedarone reduced the recurrence of a heart problem known as atrial fibrillation. They also found, in a "post hoc analysis" of an issue the studies were not designed to address, that the drug reduced hospitalization and death. Two additional studies, ANDROMEDA and PALLAS, had to be terminated early due to adverse results.]

4   [The fifth study,] called ATHENA, was designed to address the potential for clinical benefits of dronedarone that the EURIDIS/ADONIS researchers had identified in their post-hoc analysis. ATHENA involved administration of dronedarone to patients who had a recent history of atrial fibrillation and/or flutter and at least one of several specified characteristics believed to be associated with cardiovascular risk. The study assessed differences in cardiovascular hospitalization or death (secondarily, in hospitalization or death regardless of cause) between patients given dronedarone and patients given a placebo. The study produced positive results for dronedarone. Those results led to the filings that resulted in the '167 patent and to the FDA's approval of Multaq®.

5   The '167 patent claims methods of reducing cardiovascular hospitalization by administering dronedarone to patients meeting conditions mirroring those stated in the ATHENA trial. Claim 1 is representative:

> A method of decreasing a risk of cardiovascular hospitalization in a patient, said method comprising administering to said patient an effective amount of dronedarone or a pharmaceutically acceptable salt thereof, twice a day with a morning and an evening meal, wherein said patient does not have severe heart failure, (i) wherein severe heart

failure is indicated by: a) NYHA Class IV heart failure or b) hospitalization for heart failure within the last month; and (ii) wherein said patient has a history of, or current, paroxysmal or persistent non-permanent atrial fibrillation or flutter; and (iii) wherein the patient has at least one cardiovascular risk factor selected from the group consisting of:

i. an age greater than or equal to 75;

ii. hypertension;

iii. diabetes;

iv. a history of cerebral stroke or of systemic embolism;

v. a left atrial diameter greater than or equal to 50 mm; and

vi. a left ventricular ejection fraction less than 40%.

'167 patent, col. 28, line 64 through col. 29, line 15.

6   The extensive information (the "label") that Sanofi includes along with its Multaq® product—which Watson and Sandoz propose to use for their generic versions without any change material to this case—relies on the key studies described above. Section 1 of the label, as revised in March 2014, is titled "Indications and Usage." It provides (emphasis and brackets in original):

> Multaq® is indicated to reduce the risk of hospitalization for atrial fibrillation in patients in sinus rhythm with a history of paroxysmal or persistent atrial fibrillation (AF) [see Clinical Studies (14)].

That sentence says that Multaq® is indicated for use in certain patients and refers to section 14 on "Clinical Studies" for identification of those patients. Section 14 primarily describes the ATHENA study (section 14.1), but also contains a short description of the EURIDIS and ADONIS studies (section 14.2). And it refers to two studies that had to be terminated early because of negative results in their patient pools: the ANDROMEDA study (section 14.3) and the PALLAS study (section 14.4).

7   Both Watson and Sandoz plan to market their generic versions of Multaq® with the same labeling, including sections 1 and 14. See AstraZeneca LP v. Apotex, Inc., 633 F.3d 1042, 1045–46 (Fed. Cir. 2010) (explaining that, in general, an applicant for an abbreviated new drug application must "show that 'the labeling proposed for the new

drug is the same as the labeling approved for the listed drug.'" (quoting 21 U.S.C. § 355(j)(2)(A)(v))).[4]

II

8   Watson and Sandoz challenge the district court's inducement finding as to the '167 patent [as well as other omitted issues].

9   Under 35 U.S.C. § 271(b), "[w]hoever actively induces infringement of a patent shall be liable as an infringer." Here, the district court found, the inducing act will be the marketing by Watson and Sandoz of their generic dronedarone drugs with the label described above. And the induced act will be the administration of dronedarone by medical providers to patients meeting the criteria set forth in the '167 patent claims.

10   "In contrast to direct infringement, liability for inducing infringement attaches only if the defendant knew of the patent and that 'the induced acts constitute patent infringement.'" *Commil USA, LLC v. Cisco Sys., Inc.*, 575 U.S. 632 (2015) (quoting *Global-Tech Appliances, Inc. v. SEB S.A.*, 563 U.S. 754, 766 (2011)). Neither of those two knowledge requirements is disputed here. If and when Watson and Sandoz receive FDA approval and market dronedarone with the label at issue, they will know of the '167 patent (they already do) and that a medical provider's administration of the drug to the claimed class of patients is an act of infringement (which Watson and Sandoz do not dispute).

11   The dispute in this case involves an aspect of the connection between the marketing and the medical providers' infringement that is different from the two knowledge requirements and is inherent in the word "induce" as it has been understood in this area. The Supreme Court stated the following in *Global-Tech*:

> The term "induce" means "[t]o lead on; to influence; to prevail on; to move by persuasion or influence." The addition of the adverb 'actively' suggests that the inducement must involve the taking of affirmative steps to bring about the desired result.

563 U.S. at 760 (quoting Webster's New International Dictionary (2d ed. 1945)). The purposeful-causation connotation of that language is reinforced by the Court's statement: "When a person actively induces another to take some action, the inducer obviously knows the action that he or she wishes to bring about." *Id.*

12   Further reinforcement is found in the Supreme Court's discussion of inducement of copyright infringement in *Metro-Goldwyn-Mayer Studios Inc. v. Grokster Ltd.*, 545 U.S. 913, 936–37 (2005), which the Court in *Global-Tech* cited in

---

[4] [Eds: Federal law requires a generic manufacturer to use the same label as originally used for the patented drug (and approved by the FDA for that use) absent unusual circumstances.]

discussing patent infringement. In *Grokster*, the Court explained that inducement is present where "'active steps . . . taken to encourage direct infringement,' such as advertising an infringing use or instructing how to engage in an infringing use, show an affirmative intent that the product be used to infringe." 545 U.S. at 936. The Court cited, for support, this court's decision in *Water Techs. Corp. v. Calco, Ltd.*, which focused on intent and noted that intent is a factual determination that may rest on circumstantial evidence. 850 F.2d 660, 668 (Fed. Cir. 1988). The Supreme Court in *Grokster* held: "one who distributes a device with the object of promoting its use to infringe copyright, as shown by clear expression or other affirmative steps taken to foster infringement, is liable for the resulting acts of infringement by third parties." 545 U.S. at 936–37.

13   This court has accordingly explained that, for a court to find induced infringement, "[i]t must be established that the defendant possessed specific intent to encourage another's infringement." *DSU Med. Corp. v. JMS Co.*, 471 F.3d 1293, 1306 (Fed. Cir. 2006) (en banc in relevant part). The court has articulated certain necessary conditions: the plaintiff must show "that the alleged infringer's actions induced infringing acts and that he knew or should have known his actions would induce actual infringements." *DSU Med.*, 471 F.3d at 1306. And the court has repeatedly explained that, for the finder of fact to find the required intent to encourage, "[w]hile proof of intent is necessary, direct evidence is not required; rather, circumstantial evidence may suffice." *Id.* When proof of intent to encourage depends on the label accompanying the marketing of a drug, "[t]he label must encourage, recommend, or promote infringement." *Takeda Pharm. USA, Inc. v. West-Ward Pharm. Corp.*, 785 F.3d 625, 631 (Fed. Cir. 2015).

14   In this case, the district court relied on those standards. And, applying those standards, the court found that Sanofi had proven intentional encouragement of infringement of the ['167] claims. We review the district court's finding of inducement based on encouragement and inferred intent for clear error. *See AstraZeneca LP v. Apotex, Inc.*, 633 F.3d 1042, 1056 (Fed. Cir. 2010). We find no such error.

15   The label itself has a short "Indications and Usage" section, one sentence long. It states what dronedarone is indicated for: it "is indicated to reduce the risk of hospitalization for atrial fibrillation." And it states which patients are covered by this indication: "patients in sinus rhythm with a history of paroxysmal or persistent atrial fibrillation (AF) *[see Clinical Studies (14)]*." The reference to the Clinical Studies section (14) of the label expressly directs the reader to that section for elaboration of the class of patients for whom the drug is indicated to achieve the stated objective, i.e., reduced hospitalization. Section 14 leads with and features a subsection on the ATHENA study, which sets forth the positive results, relating to reduced hospitalization, for patients having the risk factors written into the '167 patent. And it is only the ATHENA subsection—not any of the three other brief subsections—that identifies a class of patients as having been shown to achieve reduced hospitalization from use of dronedarone. The EURIDIS/ADONIS subsection says nothing about

reduced hospitalization; and the ANDROMEDA and PALLAS subsections are negative warnings, describing studies that had to be terminated early because of adverse results. The label thus directs medical providers to information identifying the desired benefit for only patients with the patent-claimed risk factors.

16   There was considerable testimony that this label encourages—and would be known by Watson and Sandoz to encourage—administration of the drug to those patients, thereby causing infringement. Approximately 77% of Multaq® prescriptions have actually been written for patients with the claimed risk factors. Moreover, Dr. Kim, an expert for Sanofi, testified that a person of ordinary skill in the art would read the drug label and understand that the only FDA-approved use of dronedarone came out of the ATHENA trial, and that a physician would find "clear encouragement" from the label to use dronedarone in a manner that infringes the '167 patent, especially in light of label's description of the ANDROMEDA study, which warns of the safety concerns of using dronedarone on patients other than those for whom the ATHENA trial showed reduced hospitalization. Dr. Zusman, who testified for Watson and Sandoz, agreed that persons of skill in the art "look to drug labels, in part, for information about the use of the drug in special or specific populations, and that it is important for the [person of skill] to look at the label's indications section to see if a drug is indicated for administration to patients of certain characteristics with a certain intent." On the record in this case, the district court could draw the required inducement inferences.

17   Watson and Sandoz contend that, because Multaq® has substantial noninfringing uses not forbidden by the proposed labels, the district court could not permissibly find intent to encourage an infringing use. But there is no legal or logical basis for the suggested limitation on inducement. Section 271(b), on inducement, does not contain the "substantial noninfringing use" restriction of section 271(c), on contributory infringement. And the core holding of *Grokster*, a copyright decision that drew expressly on patent and other inducement law, is precisely that a person can be liable for inducing an infringing use of a product even if the product has substantial noninfringing uses (like the peer-to-peer software product at issue there, which was capable of infringing and non-infringing uses). 545 U.S. at 934–37. There is no basis for a different inducement rule for drug labels.

18   The content of the label in this case permits the inference of specific intent to encourage the infringing use. As noted above, inducement law permits the required factual inferences about intended effects to rest on circumstantial evidence in appropriate circumstances. Moreover, in *AstraZeneca v. Apotex*, the court upheld an inducement finding without the kind of explicit limiting commands that Watson and Sandoz suggest a label must contain. 633 F.3d at 1058–60. In *Eli Lilly & Co. v. Teva Parenteral Medicines, Inc.*, the court stated that "[d]epending on the clarity of the [drug label's] instructions, the decision to continue seeking FDA approval of those instructions may be sufficient evidence of specific intent to induce infringement." 845 F.3d 1357, 1368–69 (Fed. Cir. 2017). Unlike in *Takeda*, the inference in the present

case is based on interpreting the label's express statement of indications of use and the internally referred-to elaboration of those indications. *See* 785 F.3d 625. And this case is not like *Vita-Mix Corp v. Basic Holding, Inc.*, in which the defendant, in its (non-pharmaceutical) product instructions, encouraged a noninfringing use in a way that showed an intent to discourage infringement. 581 F.3d 1317, 1328–29 (Fed. Cir. 2009). The evidence in this case supports the finding of intentional encouragement of infringing use and, therefore, of inducement.

Note on *Global-Tech Appliances, Inc. v. SEB S.A.*, 563 U.S. 754 (2011)

Sunbeam hired Global-Tech to produce a deep fryer meeting certain specifications. Global-Tech purchased a deep fryer produced by another company and, without telling its patent attorney that it was copying an existing product, asked its attorney to investigate whether there were any patents covering the invention. The attorney failed to locate the patent, Global-Tech produced the invention, and—having induced Sunbeam to sell the infringing product—was sued by the patent owner for inducement.

The problem for the patent owner was the difficulty in proving knowledge. Global-Tech was aware of the potential that the deep fryer it was copying might be covered by a patent, but it and its attorney never located the actual patent. Could Global-Tech be said to have *known* of the patent's existence?

In an 8-1 decision, the Supreme Court held that Global-Tech was liable for inducement because it had engaged in "willful blindness":

> While the Courts of Appeals articulate the doctrine of willful blindness in slightly different ways, all appear to agree on two basic requirements: (1) The defendant must subjectively believe that there is a high probability that a fact exists and (2) the defendant must take deliberate actions to avoid learning of that fact. We think these requirements give willful blindness an appropriately limited scope that surpasses recklessness and negligence. Under this formulation, a willfully blind defendant is one who takes deliberate actions to avoid confirming a high probability of wrongdoing and who can almost be said to have actually known the critical facts.

Global-Tech Appliances, Inc. v. SEB S.A., 563 U.S. 754, 769-70 (2011).

The best way to understand *Global-Tech* is as a slight expansion on the long-standing requirement that the indirect infringer have knowledge of the infringement. After *Global-Tech*, willful blindness will suffice. And though *Global-Tech* did not involve contributory infringement under § 271(c), we can be almost certain that willful blindness will suffice for contributory infringement liability as well. What do you think motivated the court's expansion of the knowledge standard? If the Court had not elected to adopt a "willful blindness" standard, would the patent holder have lost the case? If you were Global-Tech's lawyer, what would you have argued in defense of your client?

It is notable that before *Global-Tech*, the Supreme Court had never definitively decided whether willful blindness (or its close cousin, "deliberate indifference") was sufficient to satisfy a statutory requirement of knowledge, though several circuits had found it to be. *See U.S. v. Jacobs*, 475 F.2d 270 (2d Cir. 1973); *U.S. v. Giovannetti*, 919 F.2d 1223 (7th Cir. 1990); *U.S. v. Jewell*, 532 F.2d 697 (9th Cir. 1976); *U.S. v. Glick*, 710 F.2d 639 (10th Cir. 1983). In his *Global-Tech* dissent, Justice Kennedy took the Court to task for reaching a decision so critical to *criminal* law in a *civil* case, without the benefit of briefing from the criminal bar. *Glob.-Tech*, 563 U.S. at 774 (Kennedy, dissenting). This has been something of a quixotic quest on Justice Kennedy's part. Thirty-five years earlier, when he was "merely" Judge Kennedy of the Ninth Circuit, he penned a dissent in an en banc case arguing against the adoption of willful blindness as a substitute for knowledge in that circuit. *Jewell*, 532 F.2d at 705 (Kennedy, dissenting). However, Justice Kennedy was not able to convince a majority of the Ninth Circuit—or even a single additional Supreme Court justice—to side with him.

Discussion Questions: Inducement

1. *Inducement and "Skinny" Labels.* The outcome in *Sanofi* is driven by the contents of the label that Sandoz and Watson planned to place on the drug. That label directly referenced patented methods. Accordingly, it was reasonable to believe that a doctor who read the label might be induced to practice the patented method. As the opinion notes, Sandoz and Watson had little choice in the matter: under most circumstances, the FDA requires generic drug labels to mirror the label on the brand-name drug, and Sanofi's label included the reference to the patented method.

However, under certain circumstances, a generic manufacturer is permitted to use a so-called "skinny" label that describes some but not other potential uses for the drug. *See* 21 U.S.C. § 355(j)(2)(A)(viii). Generic manufacturers employ these skinny labels in order to avoid precisely the problem that confronted Sandoz and Watson: manufacturing a drug where the patent on the chemical has expired, but one method of using the drug remains patented. In *GlaxoSmithKline v. Teva Pharmaceuticals*, 7 F.4th 1320 (Fed. Cir. 2021), the Federal Circuit (over a dissent from Chief Judge Sharon Prost) held that Teva had induced infringement of a patented method despite its use of a skinny label that did not indicate the patented method. Part of the court's reasoning was that the label indicated that the generic drug was chemically and therapeutically identical to the branded drug (as it must be), and that doctors would have known to use the branded drug to practice the patented method. Does this seem like the right outcome? How direct or explicit should a manufacturer's labeling have to be before the manufacturer becomes liable for inducing infringement?

Teva's attorney is petitioning for Supreme Court review, so this may not be the last word. (We will keep you posted!)

2. *What Constitutes Inducement?* Recall that 35 U.S.C. § 271(b) requires not just inducement but "active inducement." As *Sanofi* makes clear, providing a label that references a patented method is enough to constitute active inducement. What other sorts of activities are sufficient to constitute active infringement? Consider the following problems; which of these cases should give rise to inducement liability?

(a) A firm sells a medical device used to practice a patented method and provides instructions for how to use that product in the patented manner. *See C.R. Bard, Inc. v. Adv. Cardiovascular Sys., Inc.*, 911 F.2d 670 (Fed. Cir. 1990).

(b) A firm floods the market with devices that cut vegetables into spiral curls before a patent issues on the device. Once the patent is issued, the firm stops selling the device. However, all of the customers who purchased the device are now direct infringers each time they make use of it. *See Nat'l Presto Indus., Inc. v. W. Bend Co.*, 76 F.3d 1185, 1196 (Fed. Cir. 1996).

(c) One semiconductor firm provides technical support to another semiconductor firm that is engaged in direct infringement. That technical support includes offering technical presentations to the direct infringer on how to use the infringing technology and helping to troubleshoot problems that the direct infringer has with the technology. *See MEMC Elec. Materials, Inc. v. Mitsubishi Materials Silicon Corp.*, 420 F.3d 1369, 1372 (Fed. Cir. 2005).

3. *The Targets of an Indirect Infringement Suit.* Why do you think Sanofi bothered to sue Sandoz and Watson? Why not just sue the direct infringers, the people who are using the drug in a manner that violates the '167 patent? After all, it is easier to prove direct infringement than indirect infringement because direct infringement is strict liability. More generally, why does indirect liability exist if there is always also a direct infringer—isn't it redundant?

4. *The Difference Between Contributory Infringement and Inducement.* Were Sandoz and Watson liable as contributory infringers under § 271(c)? It's not likely, because the drug they planned to sell had substantial noninfringing uses. So this case provides an example of parties who are liable for inducement without being liable as contributory infringers. Contributory infringement also requires that the infringer sell or import a component of a patented invention (or something used in practicing a patented method). Accordingly, a party could be liable for inducing infringement by providing instructions for practicing a patented method without being liable for contributory infringement if it did not sell anything.

But now consider the converse. Is it possible to be liable as a contributory infringer without also being liable as an inducer? Consider what Aro was doing: it manufactured and sold fabric pieces that could only be used in an infringing manner. So far as we know, it did not provide instructions for how to use those pieces or otherwise urge anyone to use them to infringe. But what could Aro have possibly expected the purchasers to do with the fabric other than infringe? Is manufacturing and selling the fabric enough, by itself, to constitute inducement? More generally, can a party ever be a contributory infringer under § 271(c) without inducing infringement under § 271(b)? Has contributory infringement become entirely redundant? Liability for inducement does require a showing of specific *intent* to cause infringement that isn't required for contributory infringement, but this intent can often be inferred from the kind of circumstantial evidence that gave rise to liability in *Global-Tech*.

5. *Letters from Counsel and* Commil v. Cisco. Both contributory infringement and inducement depend on the indirect infringer having knowledge of both the patent *and the fact that it is infringing the patent*. But of course the mere fact that there is a patent does not mean that infringement is taking place. The patent might be invalid, or the patent's claim terms might be best construed in such a way that the patent is not infringed. Even if a potential indirect infringer has knowledge of the existence of a patent, it would seem that a reasonably grounded good faith belief that the patent is not infringed should defeat a claim of indirect infringement.

Based on this understanding, firms at risk of indirect infringement liability have long solicited "opinion letters" from law firms stating that, in the opinion of the attorney drafting the letter, the patent is invalid or not infringed.[5] If the letter is credible, it can defeat the knowledge requirement for indirect infringement. That is, *even if the letter is wrong*, and the court holds that the patent is valid and infringed (by the direct infringer), the indirect infringer might still escape liability because it lacks the necessary knowledge. What sorts of incentives do you think this doctrine creates for the law firms hired to produce opinion letters? Is it in the client's interest for the law firm to produce the most honest, accurate letter possible? What limits a potential infringer's ability to shop for a favorable letter, or what might limit a law firm's ability to write a letter in bad faith that reaches a legal conclusion the firm does not believe?

In *Commil USA, LLC v. Cisco Systems, Inc.*, 135 S. Ct. 1920 (2015), the Supreme Court held that while a good faith belief that the patent was *not infringed* was a valid defense against a charge of indirect infringement, a good faith belief that the patent was *invalid* was not. Wrote the Court:

---

[5] An accused infringer will typically seek an opinion letter from a law firm other than the firm that will represent it at trial, in order to be able to disclose the letter to the court without appearing to waive its attorney-client privilege. A thorough opinion letter by a reputable firm can cost $10,000–$25,000, and firms often view them as a means of cultivating business with potential new clients.

The question the Court confronts today concerns whether a defendant's belief regarding patent validity is a defense to a claim of induced infringement. It is not. The scienter element for induced infringement concerns infringement; that is a different issue than validity. Section 271(b) requires that the defendant "actively induce[d] infringement." That language requires intent to "bring about the desired result," which is infringement. And because infringement and validity are separate issues under the Act, belief regarding validity cannot negate the scienter required under § 271(b).

Id. at 1928. Accordingly, for an opinion letter to be valuable, the letter must state that the patent is not infringed. A belief that the patent is invalid is unhelpful to the accused indirect infringer (unless that belief happens to be true).

Does the Court's rule make any sense? In dissent, Justice Scalia wrote: "To talk of infringing an invalid patent is to talk nonsense. . . . Because only valid patents can be infringed, anyone with a good-faith belief in a patent's *in*validity necessarily believes the patent *cannot* be infringed." *Id.* at 1931. What is the best defense you can offer for the distinction the Court draws between infringement and invalidity? What incentives will this create for the lawyers who draft opinion letters after *Commil*? How will such an attorney be inclined to interpret a patent's claims—broadly or narrowly?

Commil was decided in the shadow of a perceived problem with non-practicing entities (or, less charitably, "patent trolls") asserting weak (i.e., very likely to be invalid) patents. These patents were often drafted with implausibly broad claims, so the best defense to them was frequently to claim that they were invalid, rather than that they were not infringed. Even if the patent troll was likely to lose at trial, the troll could often settle the lawsuit for nuisance value. And given the high cost of patent lawsuits, nuisance value could be quite substantial—tens or even hundreds of thousands of dollars. Cisco and other troll defendants had relied on opinion letters asserting invalidity as a defense against trolls, an avenue that this opinion foreclosed. In its opinion, the Court went so far as to mention the problem of patent trolls explicitly. It explained that patent defendants could use other procedural tools to defend themselves against shakedowns from trolls, including requesting Rule 11 sanctions or attorneys' fees (which we will discuss in Chapter 16) in response to frivolous lawsuits. Do you think these are equally effective mechanisms?

6. *Other Indicators of Knowledge.* A letter from counsel is of course not the only means by which an accused indirect infringer can defeat the requirement of knowledge. If the accused infringer obtains a favorable preliminary ruling in a case, which seems likely to dispose of the case in the infringer's favor, that too can eliminate the knowledge necessary to be liable. At the same time, the preliminary ruling has to be plausible, and the alleged infringer has to actually believe that it is likely to win the case! In one recent case, the defendant obtained a very favorable claim construction that, if it had stood, would have essentially disposed of the case in the

defendant's favor. However, the claim construction was self-evidently flawed, and the district court later withdrew it and substituted a construction less favorable to the defendant. The Federal Circuit held that the defendant could point to the initial claim construction as a piece of evidence indicating that it lacked the necessary knowledge while that claim construction was in effect. But the plaintiff was still entitled to argue on remand that the defendant did not and could not have believed the claim construction was correct and thus might still have the necessary knowledge. As the court explained, the defendant "might have believed that the March 2011 claim-construction ruling was erroneous (though reasonable) and would likely be reversed (as it was in 2013)." *TecSec, Inc. v. Adobe Inc.*, 978 F.3d 1278, 1287 (Fed. Cir. 2020).

This result stemmed from the fact that the knowledge standard is inherently subjective, rather than objective. *Id.* at 1286-87. Even if the defendant has an objectively strong argument that the patent is not infringed, the defendant can still be held liable if it nonetheless *believes* that the patent is being infringed. And even if the defendant has an objectively weak argument that the patent is not infringed, the defendant cannot be held liable if it believes that the patent is not infringed. (For the many infringers that are corporations, the relevant state of mind is the state of mind of whomever is making decisions for the corporation.) At the same time, American courts do not administer truth serum or lie detector tests to key witnesses, and it is rare that the CEO of a corporation will Tweet that she is aware that the corporation is inducing infringement. Accordingly, it is typically necessary to rely on objective facts and circumstances—including the strength of the letter from counsel or judicial decision being relied upon—when judging even subjective states of mind. Are there other forms of evidence that might be probative of subjective knowledge? Is subjective knowledge the right standard?

11. Other Infringement Issues

The majority of patent infringement cases will fall under the ordinary rules for direct and indirect patent infringement that were discussed in Chapters 9 and 10. But in some cases, an entity will engage in conduct that seems to undermine the patent right but doesn't fall within these rules. In this chapter, we discuss the law that has evolved to cover four such situations: (A) divided infringement, where different entities carry out different steps of a method patent; (B) cross-border infringement, where some of the infringing conduct occurs overseas; (C) government infringement, where the infringing entity has sovereign immunity; and (D) pharmaceutical infringement, where specialized statutory frameworks allow resolution of patent disputes before an infringing product is on the market.

A. Divided Infringement

Imagine a widget, covered by an existing patent, that is assembled in two different locations. A firm in California builds half of the widget and then ships it to a firm in Illinois, where the remainder of the widget is assembled. Despite the fact that the widget was assembled in two different places, by two different firms, there is still a direct infringer: the Illinois firm, which completed the widget. Indeed, when an infringing *product* is created, there will always be a direct infringer: the party that put the final components in place, thus creating the full invention.

But the same is not necessarily true for a patented method. Suppose that the California firm performs some steps of a patented method, and then the Illinois firm performs the remaining steps of the patented method. All of the elements of the claim have been performed (by someone), but no single party has performed all of the steps. Thus, it would seem that there is no direct infringer. And as the Supreme Court explained in *Aro II* (in the previous chapter), without a direct infringer there can be no indirect infringer. Is it possible, then, that no one can be held liable for infringing the patent?

This is what is known as the "divided infringement problem": all the elements of the claim have been met, but not by any single party that can obviously be held responsible. This issue has taken on much greater significance in the age of internet-based firms and internet patents, because it is easier for two or more firms to coordinate to perform the steps of a patented process. In fact, most interactive apps and websites require the user to take some actions and the app's owner or operator to take some actions in order for the app to perform its stated functions. Think about posting a tweet on Twitter, checking your account balance with a banking app, or uploading a photo to Instagram—the app does not function without actions by both the user and the firm that built the app. Depending upon how a patent covering this type of invention is written, it is entirely possible that the users and the app's firm might collectively be performing all of the steps of the process, without any one entity performing all of them itself.

When this is the case, should any party be held liable for infringement? If so, what type of infringement, and on what basis? This is the question that the Federal Circuit, and then the Supreme Court, and then the Federal Circuit again, confronted in *Limelight v. Akamai*.

Limelight Networks v. Akamai Techs., 572 U.S. 915 (2014)

Justice Alito delivered the opinion of the Court.

1   This case presents the question whether a defendant may be liable for inducing infringement of a patent under 35 U.S.C. § 271(b) when no one has directly infringed the patent under § 271(a) or any other statutory provision. The statutory text and structure and our prior case law require that we answer this question in the negative. We accordingly reverse the Federal Circuit, which reached the opposite conclusion.

I

A

2   Respondent the Massachusetts Institute of Technology is the assignee of U.S. Patent No. 6,108,703 ('703 patent), which claims a method of delivering electronic data using a "content delivery network," or "CDN." Respondent Akamai Technologies, Inc., is the exclusive licensee. Proprietors of Web sites, known as "content providers," contract with Akamai to deliver their Web sites' content to individual Internet users. The '703 patent provides for the designation of certain components of a content provider's Web site (often large files, such as video or music files) to be stored on Akamai's servers and accessed from those servers by Internet users. The process of designating components to be stored on Akamai's servers is known as "tagging." By "aggregat[ing] the data demands of multiple content providers with differing peak usage patterns and serv[ing] that content from multiple servers in multiple locations," as well as by delivering content from servers located in the same geographic area as the users who are attempting to access it, Akamai is able to increase the speed with which Internet users access the content of its customers' Web sites.

3   Petitioner Limelight Networks, Inc., also operates a CDN and carries out several of the steps claimed in the '703 patent. But instead of tagging those components of its customers' Web sites that it intends to store on its servers (a step included in the '703 patent), Limelight requires its customers to do their own tagging. Respondents claim that Limelight "provides instructions and offers technical

assistance" to its customers regarding how to tag, but the record is undisputed that Limelight does not tag the components to be stored on its servers.

B

4   In 2006, respondents sued Limelight, claiming patent infringement. The case was tried to a jury, which found that Limelight had committed infringement and awarded more than $40 million in damages. [The district court granted Limelight's motion for judgment as a matter of law in light of *Muniauction, Inc. v. Thomson Corp.*, 532 F.3d 1318 (2008), which held that direct infringement requires a defendant to either perform each step of a claimed method itself, or to exercise control or direction over performance of the steps it does not itself perform. A Federal Circuit panel affirmed.]

5   The Federal Circuit granted en banc review and reversed. The en banc court found it unnecessary to revisit its § 271(a) direct infringement case law. Instead, it concluded that the "evidence could support a judgment in [respondents'] favor on a theory of induced infringement" under § 271(b). This was true, the court explained, because § 271(b) liability arises when a defendant carries out some steps constituting a method patent and encourages others to carry out the remaining steps—even if no one would be liable as a direct infringer in such circumstances, because those who performed the remaining steps did not act as agents of, or under the direction or control of, the defendant. The Court of Appeals did not dispute that "there can be no indirect infringement without direct infringement," but it explained that "[r]equiring proof that there has been direct infringement . . . is not the same as requiring proof that a single party would be liable as a direct infringer."

6   Limelight sought certiorari, which we granted.

II

7   Neither the Federal Circuit nor respondents dispute the proposition that liability for inducement must be predicated on direct infringement. One might think that this simple truth is enough to dispose of this appeal. But the Federal Circuit reasoned that a defendant can be liable for inducing infringement under § 271(b) even if no one has committed direct infringement within the terms of § 271(a) (or any other provision of the patent laws), because direct infringement can exist independently of a violation of these statutory provisions.

8   The Federal Circuit's analysis fundamentally misunderstands what it means to infringe a method patent. A method patent claims a number of steps; under this Court's case law, the patent is not infringed unless all the steps are carried out. The Federal Circuit held in *Muniauction* that a method's steps have not all been performed as claimed by the patent unless they are all attributable to the same defendant, either because the defendant actually performed those steps or because he directed or controlled others who performed them. *See* 532 F.3d at 1329–30. Assuming without

deciding that the Federal Circuit's holding in *Muniauction* is correct, there has simply been no infringement of the method in which respondents have staked out an interest, because the performance of all the patent's steps is not attributable to any one person. And, as both the Federal Circuit and respondents admit, where there has been no direct infringement, there can be no inducement of infringement under § 271(b).

9   The Federal Circuit's contrary view would deprive § 271(b) of ascertainable standards. If a defendant can be held liable under § 271(b) for inducing conduct that does not constitute infringement, then how can a court assess when a patent holder's rights have been invaded?

10   Section 271(f)(1) reinforces our reading of § 271(b). That subsection imposes liability on a party who "supplies or causes to be supplied in or from the United States all or a substantial portion of the components of a patented invention . . . in such manner as to actively induce the combination of such components outside of the United States in a manner that would infringe the patent *if such combination occurred within the United States*" (emphasis added). As this provision illustrates, when Congress wishes to impose liability for inducing activity that does not itself constitute direct infringement, it knows precisely how to do so. The courts should not create liability for inducement of non-infringing conduct where Congress has elected not to extend that concept.

11   The Federal Circuit seems to have adopted the view that Limelight induced infringement on the theory that the steps that Limelight and its customers perform would infringe the '703 patent if all the steps were performed by the same person. But we have already rejected the notion that conduct which would be infringing in altered circumstances can form the basis for contributory infringement, and we see no reason to apply a different rule for inducement. In *Deepsouth Packing Co. v. Laitram Corp.*, 406 U.S. 518 (1972), a manufacturer produced components of a patented machine and then exported those components overseas to be assembled by its foreign customers.[1] (The assembly by the foreign customers did not violate U.S. patent laws.) In both *Deepsouth* and this case, the conduct that the defendant induced or contributed to would have been infringing if committed in altered circumstances: in *Deepsouth* if the machines had been assembled in the United States, and in this case if performance of all of the claimed steps had been attributable to the same person. In *Deepsouth,* we rejected the possibility of contributory infringement because the machines had not been assembled in the United States, and direct infringement had consequently never occurred. Similarly, in this case, performance of all the claimed steps cannot be attributed to a single person, so direct infringement never occurred. Limelight cannot be liable for inducing infringement that never came to pass.

---

[1] [n.4 in opinion] Section 271(f) now prohibits the exporter's conduct at issue in *Deepsouth.*

12   Respondents, like the Federal Circuit, criticize our interpretation of § 271(b) as permitting a would-be infringer to evade liability by dividing performance of a method patent's steps with another whom the defendant neither directs nor controls. We acknowledge this concern. Any such anomaly, however, would result from the Federal Circuit's interpretation of § 271(a) in *Muniauction*. A desire to avoid *Muniauction*'s natural consequences does not justify fundamentally altering the rules of inducement liability that the text and structure of the Patent Act clearly require— an alteration that would result in its own serious and problematic consequences, namely, creating for § 271(b) purposes some free-floating concept of "infringement" both untethered to the statutory text and difficult for the lower courts to apply consistently.

III

13   Respondents ask us to review the merits of the Federal Circuit's *Muniauction* rule for direct infringement under § 271(a). We decline to do so today.

14   In the first place, the question presented is clearly focused on § 271(b), not § 271(a). We granted certiorari on the following question: "Whether the Federal Circuit erred in holding that a defendant may be held liable for inducing patent infringement under 35 U.S.C. § 271(b) even though no one has committed direct infringement under § 271(a)." The question presupposes that Limelight has not committed direct infringement under § 271(a). And since the question on which we granted certiorari did not involve § 271(a), petitioner did not address that important issue in its opening brief. Our decision on the § 271(b) question necessitates a remand to the Federal Circuit, and on remand, the Federal Circuit will have the opportunity to revisit the § 271(a) question if it so chooses.

The Aftermath of *Akamai*

On remand, the Federal Circuit did not take the hint. The Federal Circuit panel ignored the Supreme Court's rather unsubtle suggestion that it rethink the *Muniauction* doctrine, which the Supreme Court had identified as the source of the problem, and reaffirmed the *Muniauction* rule that one party was responsible for another party's actions only when there was (1) a joint enterprise or (2) direct supervisory control.

That view did not stand long, however. The Federal Circuit quickly took the case en banc and issued the following opinion:

Akamai Techs. v. Limelight Networks, 797 F.3d 1020 (Fed. Cir. 2015) (en banc)

Per Curiam.

1   This case was returned to us by the United States Supreme Court, noting "the possibility that [we] erred by too narrowly circumscribing the scope of § 271(a)" and suggesting that we "will have the opportunity to revisit the § 271(a) question." We hereby avail ourselves of that opportunity.

2   Sitting en banc, we unanimously set forth the law of divided infringement under 35 U.S.C. § 271(a). We conclude that, in this case, substantial evidence supports the jury's finding that Limelight Networks, Inc. directly infringes U.S. Patent 6,108,703 under § 271(a). We therefore reverse the district court's grant of judgment of noninfringement as a matter of law.

I. Divided Infringement

3   Direct infringement under § 271(a) occurs where all steps of a claimed method are performed by or attributable to a single entity. *See BMC Res., Inc. v. Paymentech, L.P.*, 498 F.3d 1373, 1379–81 (Fed. Cir. 2007). Where more than one actor is involved in practicing the steps, a court must determine whether the acts of one are attributable to the other such that a single entity is responsible for the infringement. We will hold an entity responsible for others' performance of method steps in two sets of circumstances: (1) where that entity directs or controls others' performance, and (2) where the actors form a joint enterprise.

4   To determine if a single entity directs or controls the acts of another, we continue to consider general principles of vicarious liability. In the past, we have held that an actor is liable for infringement under § 271(a) if it acts through an agent (applying traditional agency principles) or contracts with another to perform one or more steps of a claimed method. We conclude, on the facts of this case, that liability under § 271(a) can also be found when an alleged infringer conditions participation in an activity or receipt of a benefit upon performance of a step or steps of a patented method and establishes the manner or timing of that performance. *Cf. Metro–Goldwyn–Mayer Studios Inc. v. Grokster, Ltd.*, 545 U.S. 913, 930 (2005) (stating that an actor "infringes vicariously by profiting from direct infringement" if that actor has the right and ability to stop or limit the infringement). In those instances, the third party's actions are attributed to the alleged infringer such that the alleged infringer becomes the single actor chargeable with direct infringement. Whether a single actor directed or controlled the acts of one or more third parties is a question of fact, reviewable on appeal for substantial evidence, when tried to a jury.

5   Alternatively, where two or more actors form a joint enterprise, all can be charged with the acts of the other, rendering each liable for the steps performed by the other as if each is a single actor. A joint enterprise requires proof of four elements:

(1) an agreement, express or implied, among the members of the group;

(2) a common purpose to be carried out by the group;

(3) a community of pecuniary interest in that purpose, among the members; and

(4) an equal right to a voice in the direction of the enterprise, which gives an equal right of control.

Restatement (Second) of Torts § 491 cmt. c. As with direction or control, whether actors entered into a joint enterprise is a question of fact, reviewable on appeal for substantial evidence.

6   We believe these approaches to be most consistent with the text of § 271(a), the statutory context in which it appears, the legislative purpose behind the Patent Act, and our past case law. Section 271(a) is not limited solely to principal-agent relationships, contractual arrangements, and joint enterprise, as the vacated panel decision held. Rather, to determine direct infringement, we consider whether all method steps can be attributed to a single entity.

II. Application to the Facts of this Case

7   The facts of this case need not be repeated in detail once again, but the following constitutes the basic facts. In 2006, Akamai Technologies, Inc. filed a patent infringement action against Limelight alleging infringement of several patents, including the '703 patent. The case proceeded to trial, at which the parties agreed that Limelight's customers—not Limelight—perform the "tagging" and "serving" steps in the claimed methods. For example, as for claim 34 of the '703 patent, Limelight performs every step save the "tagging" step, in which Limelight's customers tag the content to be hosted and delivered by Limelight's content delivery network. After the close of evidence, the district judge instructed the jury that Limelight is responsible for its customers' performance of the tagging and serving method steps if Limelight directs or controls its customers' activities. The jury found that Limelight infringed claims 19, 20, 21, and 34 of the '703 patent. Following post-trial motions, the district court [granted Limelight's motion for judgment of noninfringement as a matter of law].

8   We reverse and reinstate the jury verdict. The jury heard substantial evidence from which it could find that Limelight directs or controls its customers' performance of each remaining method step, such that all steps of the method are attributable to Limelight. Specifically, Akamai presented substantial evidence demonstrating that Limelight conditions its customers' use of its content delivery network upon its customers' performance of the tagging and serving steps, and that Limelight establishes the manner or timing of its customers' performance. We review the

evidence supporting "conditioning use of the content delivery network" and "establishing the manner or timing of performance" in turn.

9   First, the jury heard evidence that Limelight requires all of its customers to sign a standard contract. The contract delineates the steps customers must perform if they use the Limelight service. These steps include tagging and serving content. As to tagging, Limelight's form contract provides: "Customer shall be responsible for identifying via the then current [Limelight] process all [URLs] of the Customer Content to enable such Customer Content to be delivered by the [Limelight network]." In addition, the contract requires that Limelight's customers "provide [Limelight] with all cooperation and information reasonably necessary for [Limelight] to implement the [Content Delivery Service]." As for the serving step, the form contract states that Limelight is not responsible for failures in its content delivery network caused by its customers' failure to serve content. If a customer's server is down, Limelight's content delivery network need not perform. Thus, if Limelight's customers wish to use Limelight's product, they must tag and serve content. Accordingly, substantial evidence indicates that Limelight conditions customers' use of its content delivery network upon its customers' performance of the tagging and serving method steps.

10   Substantial evidence also supports finding that Limelight established the manner or timing of its customers' performance. Upon completing a deal with Limelight, Limelight sends its customer a welcome letter instructing the customer how to use Limelight's service. In particular, the welcome letter tells the customer that a Technical Account Manager employed by Limelight will lead the implementation of Limelight's services. The welcome letter also contains a hostname assigned by Limelight that the customer "integrate[s] into [its] webpages." This integration process includes the tagging step. Moreover, Limelight provides step-by-step instructions to its customers telling them how to integrate Limelight's hostname into its webpages if the customer wants to act as the origin for content. If Limelight's customers do not follow these precise steps, Limelight's service will not be available. Limelight's Installation Guidelines give Limelight customers further information on tagging content. Lastly, the jury heard evidence that Limelight's engineers continuously engage with customers' activities. Initially, Limelight's engineers assist with installation and perform quality assurance testing. The engineers remain available if the customer experiences any problems. In sum, Limelight's customers do not merely take Limelight's guidance and act independently on their own. Rather, Limelight establishes the manner and timing of its customers' performance so that customers can only avail themselves of the service upon their performance of the method steps.

11   We conclude that the facts Akamai presented at trial constitute substantial evidence from which a jury could find that Limelight directed or controlled its customers' performance of each remaining method step. As such, substantial evidence

supports the jury's verdict that all steps of the claimed methods were performed by or attributable to Limelight. Therefore, Limelight is liable for direct infringement.

Discussion Questions: Divided Infringement

1. *Expansion of Liability.* Under the new Federal Circuit rule, a party is responsible for the actions of another if it "conditions participation in an activity or receipt of a benefit upon performance of a step or steps of a patented method and establishes the manner or timing of that performance." Why do you think the Federal Circuit chose this language and this rule? What sort of conduct is it attempting to reach? Which sorts of parties will be most obviously captured by the new rule?

2. *Direct or Indirect Infringement?* At the end of the day, is Limelight a direct or indirect infringer? Does it matter? How do you think firms in Limelight's position viewed the outcome of this case?

3. *Alternatives.* Suppose the Federal Circuit had declined to revisit *Muniauction.* Akamai would have lost this case, of course, but what about similarly situated parties going forward? If you were advising a company like Akamai—or, for that matter, any firm designing an app—can you think of a way of drafting your claims to circumvent the divided infringement problem? Could Akamai's claims have been drafted to hold Limelight liable, even though some of the steps essential to the invention were performed by a different party?

If your answer to the prior question is "yes," and you believe that claims could be drafted to capture Limelight's actions even under the old law, do you think the Federal Circuit's en banc decision in *Limelight* was necessary? Would the Federal Circuit have been better off leaving the law as it stood and relying on patent applicants to draft better claims?

Practice Problems: Divided Infringement

Consider the following claims and allegedly infringing conduct involving more than one party. For each claim:

(a) Is either party liable for infringement after *Akamai v. Limelight*?
(b) Would either party have been liable for infringement under *Muniauction*, before *Akamai* was decided?
(c) If your answer to (b) is "no," can you figure out a way to redraft the claim such that one party would be liable?

Claim 1: A method of treating a sprained ankle, comprising applying a weak electric current to the affected area for fifteen minutes, then waiting three hours, then soaking the affected area in warm water for two hours.

In practice, a doctor applies the weak electric current to a patient's ankle during an out-patient procedure; the patient then goes home and later soaks the ankle in warm water.

Claim 2: A method for sharing photos over the internet, comprising designating the photos to be shared, uploading those photos to a central server, designating the people with whom the photos will be shared, notifying those people, and then allowing those individuals to download the photos from the server.

In practice, a software company builds the app that allows the user to designate and upload photos, supplies the server to be used in this process, and then allows the designated individuals to download photos from the server. Individual users perform the remaining steps.

B. Cross-Border Infringement

One of the key principles of private international law is *territoriality*: the idea that a state's laws only have force within the state's boundaries. In general, there is a strong presumption against the extraterritorial application of U.S. law. Patent law is no exception. In *Brown v. Duchesne*, 60 U.S. 183 (1856), the Supreme Court stated that the Constitution's IP Clause grants a power that "is domestic in its character, and necessarily confined within the limits of the United States." The patentee's rights "cannot extend beyond the limits to which the law itself is confined." *Id.*

But the original conception of territoriality, which limited legal effects to geographic boundaries, was created when the effects of commercial behavior were largely local. Over time, the United States has adopted the "effects doctrine," under which its laws may reach foreign conduct that has substantial effects within the United States. As patentable goods have increasingly crossed national borders, this controversial expansion in the reach of U.S. law has occurred in patent law as well. In this section, we examine two recent additions to the patent infringement statute: § 271(f), which creates liability for exporting "components" of a patented invention for "combination" abroad, and § 271(g), which creates liability for importing, offering to sell, selling, or using within the United States a product made abroad by a process patented in the United States.

The direct patent infringement statute we have discussed so far, 35 U.S.C. § 271(a), is limited to "whoever without authority makes, uses, offers to sell, or sells any patented invention, *within the United States* or imports *into the United States*" (emphasis added). Performing a patented process or assembling a patented device outside the United States is not an infringement under this statute. Thus, when a manufacturer was sued under § 271(a) in 1967 for selling *parts* of a patented shrimp deveining machine for assembly and use abroad, the Supreme Court held that this was not a § 271(a) infringement. *Deepsouth Packing Co. v. Laitram Corp.*, 406 U.S. 518 (1972). The Court stated that it would require "a clear congressional indication of intent" to extend U.S. patent law "beyond the limits of the United States." *Id.* at 531.

Congress responded with such a clear indication of intent in 1984 by enacting § 271(f) to create liability for this kind of activity:

35 U.S.C. § 271(f)

(1) Whoever without authority supplies or causes to be supplied in or from the United States all or a substantial portion of the components of a patented invention, where such components are uncombined in whole or in part, in such manner as to actively induce the combination of such components outside of the United States in a manner that would infringe the patent if such combination occurred within the United States, shall be liable as an infringer.

(2) Whoever without authority supplies or causes to be supplied in or from the United States any component of a patented invention that is especially made or especially adapted for use in the invention and not a staple article or commodity of commerce suitable for substantial noninfringing use, where such component is uncombined in whole or in part, knowing that such component is so made or adapted and intending that such component will be combined outside of the United States in a manner that would infringe the patent if such combination occurred within the United States, shall be liable as an infringer.

Note the parallels between § 271(f)(1) and § 271(b) and between § 271(f)(2) and § 271(c): this new statute creates liability for exporting products that induce or contribute to foreign conduct that would have been direct infringement under § 271(a) had it occurred in the United States. As the Supreme Court stated in *Limelight v. Akamai*, 572 U.S. 915, 922 (2014), "when Congress wishes to impose liability for inducing activity that does not itself constitute direct infringement, it knows precisely how to do so."

One limitation on § 271(f) is that it doesn't apply to method claims under the Federal Circuit's en banc decision in *Cardiac Pacemakers v. St. Jude Medical*, 576

F.3d 1348 (Fed. Cir. 2009). The court noted that "a component of a tangible product, device, or apparatus is a tangible part of the product, device, or apparatus, whereas a component of a method or process is a step in that method or process," and that the component of a method cannot be "supplied" as required by the statutory language. *Id.* at 1362–64.

In 1988, Congress closed another perceived loophole in the patent infringement statute related to products made abroad by processes patented in the United States. Here, the perceived problem was that parties would use a patented process overseas to make a product and then import that product into the United States. If only the process, and not the product, were patented, this would allow the importer to evade the U.S. patent while still reaping the full benefits of infringement. Congress's response was to pass § 271(g):

35 U.S.C. § 271(g)

Whoever without authority imports into the United States or offers to sell, sells, or uses within the United States a product which is made by a process patented in the United States shall be liable as an infringer, if the importation, offer to sell, sale, or use of the product occurs during the term of such process patent.

In an action for infringement of a process patent, no remedy may be granted for infringement on account of the noncommercial use or retail sale of a product unless there is no adequate remedy under this title for infringement on account of the importation or other use, offer to sell, or sale of that product.

A product which is made by a patented process will, for purposes of this title, not be considered to be so made after— (1) it is materially changed by subsequent processes; or (2) it becomes a trivial and nonessential component of another product.

This statute involves a number of limitations. The first paragraph limits it to processes that result in a "product," which has been interpreted as limited to physics products; "the production of information is not covered." *Bayer AG v. Housey Pharms.*, 340 F.3d 1367, 1377 (Fed. Cir. 2003). Under the second paragraph, noncommercial users and retail sellers may not be sued "unless there is no adequate remedy" against importers or commercial users or sellers. And under the third paragraph, a product is not "made" by a patented process if it is then "materially changed"—such as an intermediate chemical compound that is then transformed to a new chemical form, *Eli Lilly & Co. v. Am. Cyanamid Co.*, 82 F.3d 1568 (Fed. Cir. 1996)—or if it is "a trivial and nonessential component."

The presumption against extraterritoriality still applies when interpreting § 271(f)–(g), as the Supreme Court made clear in *Microsoft v. AT&T*, 550 U.S. 437 (2007). In that case, AT&T sued Microsoft for infringement under § 271(f), alleging that Microsoft's Windows software was a "component" that, when installed on computers abroad, rendered them capable of infringing AT&T's patent for digitally compressing recorded speech. Importing those computers into the United States would be infringement under § 271(a), but AT&T wanted Microsoft held liable solely for its *export* of the Windows software for installation on computers made and sold abroad. The Supreme Court held that software can be a "component," but only if it is a particular copy of Windows (such as a copy on a CD-ROM). What Microsoft actually exported was a master disk from which further copies were made, which the Court analogized to a blueprint or a single component to be replicated.

> Any doubt that Microsoft's conduct falls outside § 271(f)'s compass would be resolved by the presumption against extraterritoriality. The presumption that United States law governs domestically but does not rule the world applies with particular force in patent law.

> As a principle of general application, moreover, we have stated that courts should "assume that legislators take account of the legitimate sovereign interests of other nations when they write American laws." *F. Hoffmann–La Roche Ltd. v. Empagran S.A.*, 542 U.S. 155 (2004). Thus, the United States accurately conveyed in this case: "Foreign conduct is generally the domain of foreign law," and in the area here involved, in particular, foreign law "may embody different policy judgments about the relative rights of inventors, competitors, and the public in patented inventions." Brief for United States as Amicus Curiae 28. Applied to this case, the presumption tugs strongly against construction of § 271(f) to encompass as a "component" not only a physical copy of software, but also software's intangible code, and to render "supplie[d] . . . from the United States" not only exported copies of software, but also duplicates made abroad.

> AT&T argues that the presumption is inapplicable because Congress enacted § 271(f) specifically to extend the reach of United States patent law to cover certain activity abroad. But as this Court has explained, "the presumption is not defeated just because a statute specifically addresses an issue of extraterritorial application," *Smith v. United States*, 507 U.S. 197 (1993); it remains instructive in determining the *extent* of the statutory exception, *see Empagran*, 542 U.S. at 161–165.

> AT&T alternately contends that the presumption holds no sway here given that § 271(f), by its terms, applies only to domestic conduct,

i.e., to the supply of a patented invention's components "from the United States." § 271(f)(1). AT&T's reading, however, "converts a single act of supply from the United States into a springboard for liability each time a copy of the software is subsequently made abroad and combined with computer hardware abroad for sale abroad." Brief for United States as Amicus Curiae 29. In short, foreign law alone, not United States law, currently governs the manufacture and sale of components of patented inventions in foreign countries. If AT&T desires to prevent copying in foreign countries, its remedy today lies in obtaining and enforcing foreign patents.

Microsoft, 550 U.S. at 454–56. AT&T also argued that denying liability would create a "loophole" for software makers, but the Court concluded that any such loophole "is properly left for Congress to consider, and to close if it finds such action warranted." *Id.* at 457. Do you agree with the Court's reasoning?

In contrast, the Federal Circuit interpreted § 271(g) broadly in *Syngenta Crop Protection v. Willowood*, 944 F.3d 1344 (Fed. Cir. 2019). In that case, it held that infringement under § 271(g) does *not* require a single entity to perform all the claim steps, unlike for § 271(a)-(c) as interpreted by the *Akamai* decisions. The court stated that "our conclusion that a single entity need not perform every step of a patented process abroad under § 271(g) does not extend patent protection to cover extraterritorial conduct that would not otherwise trigger liability within the United States." Do you agree?

The Supreme Court adopted a narrow reading of § 271(f) in *Life Technologies Corp. v. Promega Corp.*, 137 S. Ct. 734 (2017). In that case, the infringement claim was based on the export of an enzyme known as *Taq* polymerase—one out of five components of a patented toolkit for genetic testing. The enzyme has other uses, so the suit could not be based on § 271(f)(2) for export of a component "especially made or especially adapted for use in the invention and not a staple article or commodity of commerce suitable for substantial noninfringing use." Rather, the claim was for inducement under § 271(f)(1), which requires export of "all or a substantial portion of the components of a patented invention . . . in such manner as to actively induce the[ir] combination." The Court held that *one* component cannot be "all or a substantial portion of the components." Liability under § 271(f)(1) is thus narrower than its domestic counterpart, § 271(b), which does not require the infringer to sell anything.

In yet another § 271(f) case, *WesternGeco LLC v. ION Geophysical Corp.*, 138 S. Ct. 2129 (2018), the Supreme Court reaffirmed the presumption against extraterritoriality but held that the presumption had been overcome. WesternGeco owned patents related to a system for surveying the ocean floor, and it proved at trial that it had lost ten survey contracts due to ION Geophysical's infringement under § 271(f)(2) and was awarded nearly $100 million in damages for its lost profits. The infringer argued that awarding damages for lost foreign sales violated the presumption against extraterritoriality, but the Court upheld the award because "[t]he conduct that § 271(f)(2) regulates . . . is the *domestic* act of 'suppl[ying] in or from the United States.'" We will discuss lost profits damages in detail in Chapter 14.

C. Government Infringement

Infringement suits against governments raise special legal issues because of *sovereign immunity*, which generally prevents sovereigns from being sued without consent. As one of us wrote:

> This doctrine might strike nonlawyers as bizarre, and is controversial among lawyers and legal academics. Defenders of sovereign immunity argue that the principle preserves each sovereign's dignity and protects public finance by stopping lawsuits seeking damages. Numerous sovereigns enjoy immunity under U.S. law: the federal government, the 50 states (including their state universities) and the U.S. territories, foreign nations, and the [574] federally recognized Indian tribes.

Gregory Ablavsky & Lisa Larrimore Ouellette, *Selling Patents to Indian Tribes to Delay the Market Entry of Generic Drugs*, 178 JAMA Internal Med. 179 (2018).

Infringement of U.S. patents by foreign governments generally doesn't arise because patents are territorial, but the federal government, U.S. states, and Native nations have all been defendants in patent lawsuits. In this section, we briefly review how the rules of patent infringement change in each of these contexts.

1. Federal Government

Congress has enacted a limited waiver of federal sovereign immunity in 28 U.S.C. § 1498, which states that when a patented invention "is used or manufactured by or for the United States without license of the owner thereof or lawful right to use or manufacture the same, the owner's remedy shall be by action against the United States in the United States Court of Federal Claims for the recovery of his reasonable and entire compensation for such use and manufacture." In other words, if a patent owner believes that the federal government has infringed its patent, it can bring suit for damages in the Court of Federal Claims. The Court of Federal Claims is an Article I court in D.C. that hears monetary claims against the U.S. government, with appeals to the Court of Appeals for the Federal Circuit. This statute is the *only* option for patent infringement suits against the federal government. The federal government thus may not be sued for an injunction.

Although § 1498 effectively grants the federal government a compulsory license to use patented inventions, with the license fee determined by the Court of Federal Claims, the government has not made aggressive use of this provision. There is thus relatively little caselaw on how "reasonable and entire compensation" should be determined. As we will discuss in Chapters 14 and 15, normal patent damages allow recovery of "damages adequate to compensate for the infringement, but in no event less than a reasonable royalty." 35 U.S.C. § 284. Patent damages are thus based on calculation of a "reasonable royalty" unless the patentee can prove other damages such as lost profits. Similarly, in the § 1498 context, the Federal Circuit has stated that "[g]enerally, the preferred manner of reasonably and entirely compensating the patent owner is to require the government to pay a reasonable royalty for its license as well as damages for its delay in paying the royalty." *Hughes Aircraft Co. v. United States*, 86 F.3d 1566, 1572 (Fed. Cir. 1996), *vacated on other grounds*, 520 U.S. 1183 (1997). But lost profits are also available, if proven: "Since both section 284 and section 1498 speak of 'compensation,' albeit 'adequate' compensation in the former and 'reasonable and entire' in the latter, lost profits should be recoverable in at least some infringement actions against the government." *Gargoyles, Inc. v. United States*, 113 F.3d 1572, 1576 (Fed. Cir. 1997).

Section 1498 has been in the spotlight recently as a potential tool for promoting broader access to medicines:

> We propose that the federal government invoke its power under [§ 1498] to reduce excessive prices for important patent-protected medicines. Using this law would permit the government to procure generic versions of patented drugs and in exchange pay the patent-holding companies reasonable royalties to compensate them for research and development. This would allow patients in federal programs, and perhaps beyond, to be treated with inexpensive generic medicines according to clinical need—meaning that many more patients could be reached for no more, and perhaps far less, money than is currently spent. Another benefit would be a reduction in the opportunity for companies to extract monopoly profits that far exceed their risk-adjusted costs of research and development.

Amy Kapczynski & Aaron S. Kesselheim, *'Government Patent Use': A Legal Approach to Reducing Drug Spending*, 35 Health Aff. 791 (2016); *see also* Hannah Brennan, Amy Kapczynski, Christine H. Monahan & Zain Rizvi, *A Prescription for Excessive Drug Pricing: Leveraging Government Patent Use for Health*, 18 Yale J.L. & Tech. 275 (2016); Editorial Board, *How the Government Can Lower Drug Prices*, N.Y. Times (June 20, 2018), https://www.nytimes.com/2018/06/20/opinion/prescription-drug-costs-naloxone-opioids.html.

What are the advantages and disadvantages of this proposal? Do you think a patent owner's "reasonable and entire compensation" should be based on recovery of risk-adjusted R&D costs? If this rule were widely applied, pharmaceutical innovators would have the same incentive, in risk-adjusted terms, to work on *any* project, regardless of social value. Are there ways to promote access to medicines while giving firms incentives to focus on projects with the highest probability of saving lives and generating the greatest health improvements? *See* Daniel J. Hemel & Lisa Larrimore Ouellette, *Valuing Medical Innovation* (unpublished manuscript).

2. State Governments

For suits against state governments, Congress unsuccessfully attempted to abrogate state sovereign immunity with the 1992 Patent and Plant Variety Protection Remedy Clarification Act (Patent Remedy Act). This Act added § 271(h) to the patent infringement statute to specify that "any State, any instrumentality of a State, and any officer or employee of a State or instrumentality of a State acting in his official capacity" may be liable as an infringer and "shall be subject to the provisions of this title in the same manner and to the same extent as any nongovernmental entity." Congress also addressed state sovereign immunity even more directly by adding 35 U.S.C. § 296, which provides that states and state officials "shall not be immune, under the eleventh amendment of the Constitution of the United States or under any other doctrine of sovereign immunity, from suit in Federal court by any person, including any governmental or nongovernmental entity, for infringement of a patent under section 271, or for any other violation under this title."

The Supreme Court held these provisions unconstitutional in *Florida Prepaid Postsecondary Education Expense Board v. College Savings Bank*, 527 U.S. 627 (1999). The Court held that Congress may abrogate state sovereign immunity where necessary to secure protections of the Fourteenth Amendment, but in enacting the Patent Remedy Act, "Congress identified no pattern of patent infringement by the States, let alone a pattern of constitutional violations." *Id.* at 640. And even if it had identified such a pattern, "only where the State provides no remedy, or only inadequate remedies, to injured patent owners for its infringement of their patent could a deprivation of property without due process result." *Id.* at 643. The Court noted that Congress "barely considered the availability of state remedies for patent infringement," and the limited testimony it heard was focused on the point "not that state remedies were constitutionally inadequate, but rather that they were less convenient than federal remedies, and might undermine the uniformity of patent law." *Id.* at 643–44.

What state remedies for patent infringement is the Court referring to? The Federal Circuit provided some examples in *Pennington Seed v. Produce Exchange*, 457 F.3d 1334 (Fed. Cir. 2006), in which it rejected an argument that the University of Arkansas was subject to suit due to a lack of state law remedies. The Court noted that the Arkansas Claims Commission may hear claims against the state for damages up to $10,000, that the state legislature may consider monetary awards greater than

$10,000, and a judicial claim for conversion may be available. *Id.* at 1340. "While these remedies may be 'uncertain' or 'less convenient,' or may 'undermine the uniformity of patent law,' these attributes are not sufficient to show that the patentee's due process rights have been violated." *Id.* at 1340–41 (quoting *Florida Prepaid*, 527 U.S. at 644–45). Do those sound like useful or adequate remedies?

It is therefore difficult to obtain money damages for patent infringement from state patent infringers, but it is possible to sue for an injunction against future infringement. Under the doctrine established by *Ex parte Young*, 209 U.S. 123 (1908), plaintiffs may obtain injunctions against state officials acting contrary to federal law, even if the state retains sovereign immunity. *Ex parte Young* applies to state patent infringement—"continuing prospective violations of a federal patent right by state officials may be enjoined by federal courts under the *Ex parte Young* doctrine"—although there must be a causal connection between the state officials and the unlawful action in question. *Pennington Seed*, 457 F.3d at 1341. Thus, state patent infringement may be enjoined by federal courts but not remedied by normal money damages, whereas federal patent infringement may *not* be enjoined but does allow suits for money damages in the Court of Federal Claims. Does this distinction make sense?

States may use sovereign immunity as a shield when patents are asserted against them, but not as a sword when asserting their own patents. The Federal Circuit has rejected the argument that sovereign immunity protects state patent plaintiffs from transfers for improper venue: "When a State sues in federal court, it waives sovereign immunity with respect to its asserted claims, subjecting itself to the jurisdiction of the federal courts, and must accept the federal statutory provisions that govern the allocation of cases among the courts." *Board of Regents of the University of Texas System v. Boston Scientific Corp.*, 936 F.3d 1365 (Fed. Cir. 2019).

Similarly, sovereign immunity cannot protect states from challenges to the validity of their patents. As we will discuss in more detail in Chapter 17, the 2011 America Invents Act created new administrative procedures for the USPTO to review the validity of patents it had previously granted, including inter partes review (IPR). State universities argued that they enjoyed immunity from having their patents challenged in IPR proceedings, but the Federal Circuit rejected this argument in *Regents of the University of Minnesota v. LSI Corp.*, 926 F.3d 1327 (Fed. Cir. 2019)—relying on a recent case on tribal sovereign immunity that will be discussed in the following section, *Saint Regis Mohawk Tribe v. Mylan Pharmaceuticals Inc.*, 896 F.3d 1322 (Fed. Cir. 2018).

3. Native Nations

As of this writing, there are 574 federally recognized Native nations within the United States with their own sovereign immunity. Caselaw on tribal sovereign immunity is complex; for instance, Greg Ablavsky argues that "the status of Native nations within federal law has almost always been defined with reference to other sovereigns . . . ignoring the differences between the situation of tribes and other sovereigns" to serve "a particular purpose: either to cabin the scope of tribal authority or to aggrandize federal power." Gregory Ablavsky, *Sovereign Metaphors in Indian Law*, 80 Mont. L. Rev. 11, 12 (2019).

Like state governments, tribal governments are immune from suits for patent infringement, although there is limited caselaw on the subject. *See Specialty House of Creation, Inc. v. Quapaw Tribe*, 2011 WL 308903 (N.D. Okla. Jan. 27, 2011); *Home Bingo Network v. Multimedia Games, Inc.*, No. 1:05-CV-0608, 2005 WL 2098056 (N.D.N.Y. Aug. 30, 2005). Unlike state governments, however, many tribal governments have not instituted separate procedures that would allow patent owners to collect in cases of infringement. If Native nations began to engage in frequent and intentional patent infringement, how do you think Congress and the federal courts would respond?

Also like state governments, tribal governments cannot use sovereign immunity to block most challenges to patent validity. Tribes are different from states in that filing suit is not considered a waiver of sovereign immunity, so tribes can still invoke sovereign immunity against counterclaims. *See Oklahoma Tax Comm'n v. Citizen Band Potawatomi Indian Tribe of Oklahoma*, 498 U.S. 505 (1991). But a defendant sued by a patent-owning tribe can still raise invalidity as an affirmative defense,[2] and a declaratory judgment of invalidity may also be available under *Ex parte Young*.

Patents owned by a tribe can also be challenged in IPR. Tribal sovereign immunity came to a prominent intersection with federal patent law in September 2017, when the global pharmaceutical company Allergan transferred six patents for its blockbuster dry eye drug Restasis to the Saint Regis Mohawk Tribe, a federally recognized tribe of about 15,000 members in upstate New York with a $50 million annual budget. Under the deal, the Tribe received $13.75 million up front and the possibility of $15 million in annual royalties—a fraction of Restasis's $1.5 billion in annual revenues. The deal also enabled the Tribe to assert sovereign immunity in an IPR proceeding in which a generic manufacturer was challenging the patents.

In *Saint Regis Mohawk Tribe v. Mylan Pharmaceuticals Inc.*, 896 F.3d 1322, 1327 (Fed. Cir. 2018), the Federal Circuit held that tribal sovereign immunity cannot be asserted in IPR because IPR "is more like an agency enforcement action" in which immunity does not apply "than a civil suit brought by a private party" in which it does.

---

[2] Patent infringement defendants typically plead invalidity as both an affirmative defense and a counterclaim. The counterclaim provides greater strategic leverage in that it survives termination of the plaintiff's claim. Thus, it can be upheld on appeal even if the court also upholds a finding of noninfringement. *See Cardinal Chem. Co. v. Morton Int'l*, 508 U.S. 83 (1993).

And as noted in the prior section, the Federal Circuit then relied on *Saint Regis Mohawk Tribe* to reach the same result with respect to state sovereign immunity.

It is easy to understand deals such as this one from the tribe's perspective because of the limitations on tribes' economic options. As one of us has explained:

> For tribes, economic development and sovereignty are closely linked, especially because federal law substantially limits tribes' powers to tax. American Indians and Alaska Natives have the highest poverty rate of any racial group in the United States. A small fraction of tribes enjoy large gaming revenues, but most must struggle for funds to supplement chronically underfunded federal programs to provide services for their citizens. . . . Responding to the Allergan deal requires more than a stopgap narrowly focused on the use of tribal sovereign immunity in IPR proceedings challenging drug patents.

Gregory Ablavsky & Lisa Larrimore Ouellette, *Selling Patents to Indian Tribes to Delay the Market Entry of Generic Drugs*, 178 JAMA Internal Med. 179 (2018). Are there better ways to address the underlying challenges that led the Saint Regis Mohawk Tribe to pursue its deal with Allergan?

D. Pharmaceutical Infringement and the FDA

Patent scholars often distinguish the role of patents in the pharmaceutical industry from their role in other sectors. For example, in their 2009 book *The Patent Crisis and How the Courts Can Solve It*, Dan Burk and Mark Lemley write: "It is the IT industries that are the poster child for the claims of a patent crisis . . . while for most of the companies in the biomedical industry the patent system is working just fine." Patent skeptics James Bessen and Michael Meurer similarly single out pharmaceuticals, concluding that "by the late 1990s litigation costs clearly exceeded the profits from patents outside the chemical and pharmaceutical industries." *Patent Failure: How Judges, Bureaucrats, and Lawyers Put Innovators at Risk* (2008). As we discussed in Chapter 1, pharmaceutical executives drop drugs without strong patent protection from development pipelines, and drugs with shorter effective patent terms (due to long clinical trials) receive less private R&D investment. *See* Benjamin N. Roin, *Unpatentable Drugs and the Standards of Patentability*, 87 Tex. L. Rev. 503, 545 (2009); Eric Budish, Benjamin N. Roin & Heidi Williams, *Do Firms Underinvest in Long-Term Research? Evidence from Cancer Clinical Trials*, 105 Am. Econ. Rev. 2044 (2015).

It should thus be unsurprising that some of the most important patent litigation disputes involve pharmaceuticals. Pharmaceutical patent infringement follows the same basic rules as patent infringement in other industries: an accused drug infringes only if it has every element of a patent claim, or its equivalent. And as you saw from Chapter 10, the mental state for indirect infringement is the same. You have encountered many other pharmaceutical patent infringement cases in earlier chapters, including *Schering v. Geneva*, 339 F.3d 1373 (Fed. Cir. 2003) (the inherent anticipation case in Chapter 2), *In re '318 Patent Infringement Litigation*, 583 F.3d 1317 (Fed. Cir. 2009) (the utility case in Chapter 4), and *Idenix v. Gilead*, 941 F.3d 1149 (Fed. Cir. 2019) (the enablement and written description case in Chapter 4). But we discuss pharmaceutical patent infringement separately here because Congress has created special statutory frameworks to resolve patent disputes in this industry, and some familiarity with these statutes is important in patent litigation practice.

Unlike in most industries, the pharmaceutical market is strictly regulated by an administrative agency: the Food and Drug Administration (FDA). Before a new drug is allowed on the market, the FDA requires the drug's sponsor to run costly clinical trials to show that the drug is safe and effective. A second company that wants to sell an equivalent drug could receive FDA approval by running its own clinical trials, but duplicating the first company's trials would be both wasteful and ethically problematic (because it would require denying patients in the control group a drug that has already been shown to be effective). The second company can thus seek approval through an abbreviated process based on the data generated by the first company's trials.

The details of this abbreviated process depend on whether the drug is classified as a *small-molecule* drug or a *biologic*. Small-molecule drugs are ones with simple chemical structures, often around 20 to 100 atoms. They are relatively easy to reproduce through chemical synthesis. Biologics, in contrast, range in size from around 200 to 50,000 atoms, and their precise structures are often unknown and not easily characterized. Biologics regulated by the FDA include a wide range of products, including vaccines, therapeutic proteins, and gene therapy. The figure below illustrates models of the small-molecule drug aspirin compared with a subclass of the biologic antibody IgG. (An antibody is a type of protein used by the immune system to identify foreign objects.)

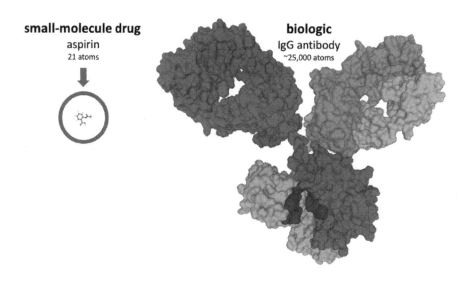

The other major class of medical technologies regulated by the FDA is medical devices, a broad category that includes a wide array of products: bandages, wheelchairs, MRI machines, diagnostic tests, pacemakers, surgical devices, etc. Medical devices do not have a special statutory framework for resolving patent issues the way small-molecule drugs and biologics do, although there is an unusual exception from patent liability for medical practitioners performing certain medical procedures in 35 U.S.C. § 287(c). This does not immunize the manufacturers of medical devices used for those procedures from indirect liability.

Both small-molecule drugs and biologics are typically protected by numerous patents. For small-molecule drugs, in addition to "primary" patents claiming the new active ingredient, chemical compounds are protected by various "secondary" patents, including *formulation* claims that claim a specific pharmaceutical preparation such as a tablet or sustained-release form, *method of use* claims that claim a method of treating a specific disease with the compound, and claims to minor chemical modifications such as polymorphs, isomers, prodrugs, esters, and salts. Secondary patents are most frequently used to extend the patent life of the most lucrative drugs, a process known as "evergreening." *See* Amy Kapczynski, Chan Park & Bhaven Sampat, *Polymorphs and Prodrugs and Salts (Oh My!): An Empirical Analysis of "Secondary" Pharmaceutical Patents*, 7 PLoS One e49470 (2012). They are also much less likely to be upheld in patent litigation. C. Scott Hemphill & Bhaven Sampat, *Drug Patents at the Supreme Court*, 339 Science 1386 (2013). What examples of evergreening have you encountered in previous chapters?

For biologics, their greater scientific complexity is reflected in a more complex patent landscape, and this landscape has also been more obscure due to the lack of any patent listing requirement before December 2020 and the small number of cases challenging these patents. As a rough comparison, best-selling small-molecule drugs from 2002 to 2004 had an average of just over five patents per drug, while the best-selling biologics in 2018 were estimated to have over seventy patents per drug.

For small-molecule drugs, the governing statute for promoting generic entry and resolving disputes over these patents is the Drug Price Competition and Patent Term Restoration Act of 1984, which is generally known as the Hatch-Waxman Act. The Hatch-Waxman Act was quite successful at increasing entry of generic drugs. Based on this success, Congress enacted a similar framework for biologics as part of the 2010 Affordable Care Act: the Biologics Price Competition and Innovation Act (BPCIA). The goal of the BPCIA was to spur entry of generic versions of biologics, which are known as *biosimilars*.

In exchange for granting an abbreviated approval process to generic and biosimilar entrants, the Hatch-Waxman Act and the BPCIA both gave a new benefit to firms that bring new drugs to market: a non-patent form of intellectual property protection known as *regulatory exclusivity*. There are two key types of regulatory exclusivity: *data exclusivity*, which prevents a generic or biosimilar firm from relying on the original firm's clinical trial data for a certain period, and *market exclusivity*, which prevents any new approval for an equivalent drug, even if the new entrant has conducted its own clinical trials. As a practical matter, both effectively prevent generic or biosimilar entry in most cases due to the cost and ethical concerns with conducting new trials.

For small-molecule drugs, a firm hoping to bring a new drug to market files a New Drug Application (NDA) with the FDA. After approval, the sponsor receives five years of data exclusivity if the drug has a new active ingredient and three years of data exclusivity for old drugs that required new clinical trials (such as to receive approval for a new indication). For biologics, the process starts with a Biologics License Application (BLA). After approval, the sponsor receives twelve years of data exclusivity, including four years before the first biosimilar application may even be filed.

Approval of an NDA or BLA also comes with a patent term extension. Under 35 U.S.C. § 156, the sponsor may extend *one* patent on the drug for half the time spent in clinical trials, up to a maximum of five years, and with total life not to exceed 14 years after FDA approval. Additionally, the sponsor may request "orphan" designation for the drug under 21 U.S.C. § 360bb(a)(2) if it treats a disease that either (A) "affects less than 200,000 persons in the United States" at the time of the request or (B) "for which there is no reasonable expectation that the cost of developing and making available in the United States a drug for such disease or condition will be recovered from sales in the United States of such drug." Orphan designation grants the sponsor a tax credit for 25% of its clinical trial expenses and a seven-year market exclusivity period. Finally, under 21 U.S.C. § 355a, if the FDA sends the sponsor a written request for pediatric clinical studies and the sponsor complies, the drug receives a six-month "pediatric exclusivity" attached to the *end* of all other regulatory exclusivity and patent periods.

To help potential generic and biosimilar manufacturers determine when they will be able to enter the market, the FDA publishes information about approved drugs and their exclusivity periods. For small-molecule drugs, the relevant database is the *Orange Book*. The *Orange Book* has included patent information for each drug since it was first published in 1985 and may be searched on the FDA's website by brand name, active ingredient, or NDA number. For biologics, the equivalent database is known as the *Purple Book*. Biologic manufacturers were not originally required to list patent information in the *Purple Book*, making it more difficult for potential biosimilar manufacturers to understand the patent landscape for each drug. But in the COVID-19 relief bill passed in December 2020, Congress amended 42 U.S.C. § 262(k) to require the FDA to include patent information.

A potential generic or biosimilar manufacturer begins the abbreviated approval process by filing an abbreviated New Drug Application (ANDA) or an abbreviated Biologics License Application (aBLA). (We don't know why "abbreviated" is capitalized differently; it just is.) The scientific standard for demonstrating that the product is sufficiently similar to rely on the original drug's clinical trial data differs between the two contexts due to the greater complexity of biologics. For small-molecule drugs, the ANDA must provide evidence of "bioequivalence," meaning that there is no "significant difference in the rate and extent to which the active ingredient . . . becomes available at the site of drug action." 21 C.F.R. § 314.3. For biologics, the aBLA must demonstrate "biosimilarity," including evidence that the product is "highly similar" to the reference product (based on characterizing structure and function to the extent possible) and "has no clinically meaningful differences" from the reference product, as demonstrated through clinical response studies (which are less burdensome than randomized controlled trials). There is also a higher standard for biologic "interchangeability," meaning the biosimilar may be substituted for the original biologic without intervention of the prescribing healthcare provider.

More relevantly for patent practitioners, filing an ANDA or aBLA can initiate patent litigation. Under the Hatch-Waxman Act, an ANDA must include certifications for each *Orange Book* patent, which are referred to by the paragraphs of 21 U.S.C. § 355(j)(2)(A)(vii): the applicant can certify under paragraph I or II that the patent information has not been filed or has expired, under paragraph III that the applicant will wait for the patent to expire, or—most importantly for us—under paragraph IV that the patent is invalid or not infringed. To provide an incentive to challenge patents, the first generic firm to file an ANDA with a paragraph IV certification receives 180 days of generic market exclusivity once their ANDA is approved, meaning that the FDA will not approve a second ANDA for the same drug.

Within 20 days of FDA receipt of the ANDA, the filer must notify the original NDA sponsor. Under 35 U.S.C. § 271(e)(2)(A), filing an ANDA constitutes an artificial act of patent infringement—in that the product is not yet on the market—and if the NDA sponsor files suit within 45 days, ANDA approval is stayed for 30 months to provide time to resolve the patent issues. If the NDA sponsor doesn't file suit within 45 days, the FDA may approve the ANDA, but many generic companies would prefer not to launch at risk of substantial patent damages. Hatch-Waxman addressed this concern by allowing the generic to sue for a declaratory judgment of invalidity or noninfringement under § 271(e)(5)).

Under the BPCIA, filing an aBLA can also initiate patent litigation, but the BLA sponsor cannot sue right away: it must wait and see whether the applicant initiates a complex back-and-forth under 42 U.S.C. § 262 known as the "patent dance." If the biosimilar applicant chooses to dance, it must send its aBLA to the original BLA sponsor within 20 days after the FDA accepts it. Then the BLA sponsor has 60 days to provide a list of patents that could be asserted, the biosimilar applicant has 60 days to respond with invalidity and noninfringement contentions, the BLA sponsor has 60 days to reply with validity and infringement contentions, and then the parties jointly negotiate a list of key patents to be adjudicated in the first litigation phase—with the goal of increasing efficiency by leaving some patents for a second, later phase.

If the biosimilar applicant chooses to dance, the BLA sponsor may file a patent infringement suit on the negotiated patents under 35 U.S.C. § 271(e)(2)(C)(i), and neither party may file a declaratory judgment action on patents not selected for the first wave of litigation. But the Supreme Court has held that the biosimilar applicant cannot be forced to dance under federal law, *Sandoz v. Amgen*, 137 S. Ct. 1664 (2017), and the Federal Circuit has held that the dance also cannot be forced under state law, *Amgen v. Sandoz*, 877 F.3d 1315, 1327 (Fed. Cir. 2017). If the biosimilar applicant elects not to dance, then the BLA sponsor may sue under 35 U.S.C. § 271(e)(2)(C)(ii) based on any patent it could have asserted through the dance.

The second wave of litigation contemplated by the BPCIA can commence after the FDA approves the product and the biosimilar applicant provides notice to the original BLA sponsor, the latter of which must occur 180 days before it intends to market the drug. (The Supreme Court has held that this 180-day notice period may begin before FDA approval. *Sandoz v. Amgen*, 137 S. Ct. at 1677.) During the second wave, the BLA sponsor can assert patents not included in the first wave and can seek a preliminary injunction to prevent marketing. Both parties may file declaratory judgment actions during this phase.

Like the Hatch-Waxman Act, the BPCIA incentivizes market entry by providing a market exclusivity period to the first "interchangeable" biosimilar applicant before subsequent biosimilars will be determined to be interchangeable. Unlike the 180-day generic exclusivity period under Hatch-Waxman, the biosimilar exclusivity varies in time, expiring on the earliest of: 1 year after marketing, 18 months after resolution of patent litigation, 42 months after approval if patent litigation is ongoing at that point, or 18 months after approval if the applicant has not been sued. 42 U.S.C. § 262(k)(6).

The complex BPCIA statutory scheme has led to numerous thorny questions of statutory interpretation, including the issues that reached the Supreme Court in *Sandoz v. Amgen*. In *Sandoz*, the Federal Circuit famously borrowed from Winston Churchill to call the BPCIA "a riddle wrapped in a mystery inside an enigma." *Amgen Inc. v. Sandoz Inc.*, 794 F.3d 1347, 1351 n.1 (Fed. Cir. 2015), *rev'd in part*, 137 S. Ct. 1664 (2017). We will not attempt to canvass all the remaining open questions here; we simply note that this is a wonderful area of practice for students interested in detailed statutory interpretation, and that the legal issues require little understanding of the science behind biologic medicines.

Has the BPCIA accomplished its goal of promoting biosimilar entrance? Yes, but slowly. Through the end of 2017—six years after the BPCIA's enactment—only three biosimilars launched in the United States. At that point, the European Union had thirty-three biosimilars on the market, largely due to an earlier regulatory framework. Biosimilar launches have picked up speed since then, with three in 2018, seven in 2019, and five in 2020, but these numbers are still tiny compared with the number of generic small-molecule drugs.

The following table summarizes the key differences between the legal frameworks for allowing new entrants based on small-molecule drugs and biologics.

	Small-Molecule Drugs	Biologics
Governing statute	Hatch-Waxman Act of 1984 (amending Food, Drug and Cosmetic Act, 21 U.S.C. § 355, and the Patent Act, 35 U.S.C.)	Biologics Price Competition and Innovation Act (BPCIA) (2010) (amending Public Health Service Act, 42 U.S.C. § 262, and the Patent Act, 35 U.S.C.)
Initial FDA application	New Drug Application (NDA)	Biologics License Application (BLA)
Data exclusivity	5 years for new active ingredient; 3 years for other drugs requiring clinical trials	12 years (including 4 years before the first biosimilar application may be filed)
Patent term extension	up to 5 years for 1 patent under 35 U.S.C. § 156	same
Orphan drug benefits	7 years market exclusivity and 25% tax credit for clinical trial expenses	same
Pediatric exclusivity	6 months added to all exclusivities (including patents) for pediatric studies	same
Patent listing	Orange Book	Purple Book (new patent listing requirement as of Dec. 2020)
Generic/ biosimilar FDA application	Abbreviated New Drug Application (ANDA) showing bioequivalence; ¶ IV certification of invalidity or noninfringement for each listed patent	Abbreviated Biologics License Application (aBLA)
Statute making abbreviated application an act of patent infringement	35 U.S.C. § 271(e)(2)(A) (if suit isn't filed within 45 days, courts have declaratory jurisdiction under § 271(e)(5))	35 U.S.C. § 271(e)(2)(C) (plus more complex declaratory jurisdiction rules)
Incentive for patent challenge	180-day market exclusivity for first generic to file ¶ IV certification and then get approved	12 to 42 months for first interchangeable biosimilar

Infringement Review Exercise

The following exercise reviews a number of concepts covered in this chapter.

Alizon is a magical wizard who works in the United States as a scientist. In 2010, she discovered a cure for the potentially fatal dragon pox disease. She named her cure banefire potion, and she made it by heating equal parts of the common ingredients blackthorn and snake bone in a caldron while stirring counterclockwise until they react.

She immediately filed a patent application at the USPTO (where there is a special division to deal with magical patents). Her patent specification described her recipe and also noted that banefire potion unfortunately dissolves human teeth, but that it can be administered to a patient by inserting it into a capsule that dissolves in the stomach after it is swallowed. She also described her successful treatment of dragon pox patients with her new potion. Her patent issued in 2014 with two claims:

1. Banefire potion, produced by heating approximately equal weights of blackthorn and snake bone and stirring counterclockwise.

2. A method for treating dragon pox comprising: producing banefire potion; and administering said potion to a dragon pox patient using a means for preventing said potion from contacting said patient's teeth.

Her treatment was a huge commercial success, selling for $50,000 a capsule.

Merlin runs a U.S. business exporting potions ingredients. After Alizon's discovery, Merlin's firm experienced a spike in demand for exports of blackthorn and snake bone. Magical doctors in other countries combined these ingredients purchased from Merlin to produce banefire potion. Jealous of Alizon's commercial success, Merlin began experimenting with his ingredients and discovered that he could produce a potion identical to banefire potion by combining two quite different ingredients—ash and goldenseal—in a chilled container for 24 hours. He kept his process secret and began selling his potion to U.S. doctors for $30,000 per dose, along with instructions stating that doctors could use it to cure dragon pox by magically having it vanish and reappear in the patient's stomach. Most magical doctors find this method of administration easier, although a few who have difficulty with spells prefer putting the potion in dissolvable capsules. Merlin quickly overtakes Alizon in sales volume.

Alizon sues Merlin and the foreign doctors for patent infringement. What result, and why? (Don't stop your analysis just because you've found one argument that seems dispositive.)

12. Defenses

In this chapter, we consider the defenses to patent infringement. Patent rights have fewer limitations than other intellectual property rights. For example, there is no patent equivalent of copyright fair use—although some scholars have argued that there should be. *See* Maureen A. O'Rourke, *Toward a Doctrine of Fair Use in Patent Law*, 100 Colum. L. Rev. 1177 (2000); Katherine J. Strandburg, *Patent Fair Use 2.0*, 1 UC Irvine L. Rev. 265 (2011). But there are still many important defenses that patent defendants can assert.

In Chapter 11, we encountered two specialized defenses: the sovereign immunity of the defendant and the exemption from direct liability for medical practitioners performing surgical procedures under 35 U.S.C. § 287(c). This chapter focuses on general defenses under substantive patent law. Defendants often also raise procedural defects such as improper venue or lack of standing, which we will discuss in Chapter 17.

A. Invalidity and Noninfringement

We have already discussed the most important and common defenses to a claim of patent infringement: noninfringement or invalidity of the asserted claims. *See* 35 U.S.C. § 282(b). The leading patent treatise, *Chisum on Patents* § 19.01, quibbles that "'noninfringement' is, precisely speaking, not a defense but, rather, a negation of the patent owner's case." But § 282(b)(1) names noninfringement as a patent "defense," and we think it is usefully considered in the list of arguments a patent infringement defendant should consider, even though the plaintiff bears the burden of proof on infringement.

Patent defendants often raise arguments of both invalidity and noninfringement, but there are practical tradeoffs between these defenses that lead many defendants to focus on one or the other. As Roger Ford summarizes, these include:

> 1. Claim construction strategy . . . In many patent cases—perhaps most patent cases—the defendant must choose between arguing for broad claim constructions that support its invalidity arguments and arguing for narrow claim constructions that support its noninfringement arguments.

> 2. Trial Narratives . . . [A] patent holder can always present a simple, plausible narrative: "We invented this great new widget, and the defendant used (or stole) our idea." A defendant can counter with its

own simple narrative of invalidity ("The plaintiff didn't invent anything") or noninfringement ("Our product is fundamentally different")—but only if it focuses on one defense. Otherwise, the response is a story that pulls in multiple directions: "Our product is fundamentally different from this thing the plaintiff invented—which, by the way, wasn't actually new but had been invented before by this other inventor, or would have been obvious to any idiot in the field."

3. Resource Constraints . . . Besides attorneys' fees, parties can spend heavily on expert fees, expenses from investigating the accused product or process, and searching for prior art. Very few of these expenses apply to both invalidity and noninfringement arguments, so the marginal cost of pursuing both defenses can be substantial.

Roger Allan Ford, *Patent Invalidity Versus Noninfringement*, 99 Cornell L. Rev. 71, 94 (2013). Ford also notes three asymmetries that tend to push the choice toward noninfringement: (1) invalidity has a higher standard of proof because of the presumption of patent validity; (2) defendants often have a comparative informational advantage on noninfringement (because they know about their own products) and a disadvantage on invalidity (because they may have less experience with the patents at issue); and (3) defendants do not internalize all the benefits of success on invalidity (such as the ability of their competitors to freely enter the market).

Do you think underinvestment in invalidity defenses is a problem? If so, do you have suggestions of how to address it? Suggestions proposed by commentators include the following, which have met with varying degrees of success:

1. *Reduce the Costs of Challenging Validity*. In Chapter 17, we will discuss post-grant proceedings at the USPTO that were created by the 2011 America Invents Act to promote invalidity challenges in a less costly forum than the courts.

2. *Reduce the Presumption of Validity*. Some commentators have argued that the standard for invalidating patents should be lowered, at least where the USPTO hasn't considered the relevant argument or prior art. The Supreme Court rejected this argument in the litigation context in *Microsoft v. i4i*, 564 U.S. 91 (2001), but stated that a jury may be instructed that "it has heard evidence that the PTO had no opportunity to evaluate before granting the patent" and may "consider that fact when determining whether an invalidity defense has been proved by clear and convincing evidence." Empirical work with mock jurors suggests that this instruction has the same effect as explicitly lowering the standard to a preponderance of the evidence standard. David L. Schwartz & Christopher B. Seaman, *Standards of Proof in Civil Litigation: An Experiment from Patent Law*, 26 Harv. J.L. & Tech. 429 (2013). In post-grant proceedings, the presumption of validity does not apply, so invalidity may be established by a preponderance of the evidence.

3. *Allow More Parties to Challenge Validity*. The Supreme Court has broadened the range of parties who may challenge a patent's validity in litigation. In *Lear, Inc. v. Adkins*, 395 U.S. 653 (1969), the Court held that patentees may not contractually prevent licensees from challenging patent validity. And in *Minerva Surgical Inc. v. Hologic Inc.* (2021), the Court limited the doctrine of *assignor estoppel*, which previously barred invalidity challenges from parties in privity with the assignors of the patent. In *Hologic*, the Court held that assignor estoppel only applies if the assignor made explicit or implicit representations that the patent was valid when assigning it. Post-grant proceedings have gone further by allowing any party challenge a patent. We discuss these doctrines further in Chapters 17–18.

4. *Increase the Rewards of Challenging Validity*. Some commentators have proposed bounties for patent invalidation. *See* Anup Malani & Jonathan S. Masur, *Raising the Stakes in Patent Cases*, 101 Geo. L.J. 637 (2013); Joseph Scott Miller, *Building a Better Bounty: Litigation-Stage Rewards for Defeating Patents*, 19 Berkeley Tech. L.J. 667 (2004). Successful invalidators could also recoup litigation costs from other firms in the industry that benefit from the effort. *See* Gideon Parchomovsky & Alex Stein, *Intellectual Property Defenses*, 113 Colum. L. Rev. 1483 (2013).

B. Licenses and Exhaustion

Another common defense to infringement is to have a license: recall that direct infringement under § 271(a), (f), or (g) requires the infringing conduct to be conducted "without authority," meaning without an express or implied license. Of course, in some cases a patent owner will explicitly grant a license by contract. But even where there is no explicit license, courts have sometimes been willing to imply the existence of a license from the patent owner's behavior. As the Federal Circuit has explained, implied licenses can be inferred from a variety of circumstances:

> In patent law, an implied license merely signifies a patentee's waiver of the statutory right to exclude others from making, using, or selling the patented invention. In the words of the Supreme Court, "No formal granting of a license is necessary in order to give it effect. Any language used by the owner of the patent, or any conduct on his part exhibited to another from which that other may properly infer that the owner consents to his use of the patent in making or using it, or selling it, upon which the other acts, constitutes a license and a defense to an action for a tort." *De Forest Radio Tel. Co. v. United States*, 273 U.S. 236, 241 (1927).

> Since *De Forest*, this court and others have attempted to identify and isolate various avenues to an implied license. As a result, courts and commentators relate that implied licenses arise by acquiescence, by conduct, by equitable estoppel, or by legal estoppel. These labels

describe not different kinds of licenses, but rather different categories of conduct which lead to the same conclusion: an implied license.

Wang Laboratories v. Mitsubishi Electronics Am., 103 F.3d 1571, 1580 (Fed. Cir. 1997). Equitable estoppel occurs when an infringer relies on misleading conduct of the patent owner that suggests they will not be sued. Legal estoppel refers to the doctrine of assignor estoppel, which as noted above, was limited by the Supreme Court in *Minerva Surgical Inc. v. Hologic Inc.* (2021).

Under the doctrine of patent exhaustion, also known as the "first sale" doctrine, the first authorized sale of a patented product—or a product that embodies a patented method—exhausts the patent owner's rights over that product. Thus, further use, sale, and repair of the product is not "without authority" under § 271. The first sale of a patented product effectively creates an implied license by operation of law. This is why Apple can't sue you for patent infringement when you sell your old iPhone—though another patent owner could sue you if your phone embodies patents of theirs that Apple failed to license.

But suppose Apple obtains a patent on a method of using the iPhone with another valuable component—say, pairing the phone with an external keyboard. If a third party sells iPhone keyboards without licensing this patent, does exhaustion prevent Apple from suing the firm for inducing infringement by consumers who practice the patented method? And can Apple avoid exhaustion of its U.S. patents by contracting around the default rule or by selling iPhone in other countries, such that consumers who buy iPhones with a "no resale" agreement or in other countries can obtain them for a lower price? The following cases consider these questions.

Keurig v. Sturm Foods, 732 F.3d 1370 (Fed. Cir. 2013)

Alan D. Lourie, Circuit Judge.

1   Keurig manufactures and sells single-serve coffee brewers and beverage cartridges for use in those brewers. Consumers insert a cartridge into the brewer, hot water is forced through the cartridge, and a beverage is dispensed. Claim 6 of U.S. Patent 6,606,938 is representative of the method claims at issue:

6. A method of brewing a beverage from a beverage medium contained in a disposable cartridge, comprising the following steps, in sequence:

(a) piercing the cartridge with a tubular outlet probe to vent the cartridge interior;

(b) piercing the cartridge with a tubular inlet probe;

(c) admitting heated liquid into the cartridge interior via the inlet probe for combination with the beverage medium to produce a beverage; and

(d) extracting the beverage from the cartridge interior via the outlet probe.

Sturm manufactures and sells cartridges for use in Keurig's brewers under the brand name "Grove Square." Sturm does not make or sell brewers. [Keurig sued Sturm for inducing infringement by customers who buy Grove Square cartridges and use them in Keurig brewers, and the district court granted summary judgment of noninfringement on the grounds that Keurig's patent rights were exhausted.]

"The longstanding doctrine of patent exhaustion provides that the initial authorized sale of a patented item terminates all patent rights to that item." *Quanta Computer v. LG Electronics,* 553 U.S. 617, 625 (2008). The rationale underlying the doctrine rests upon the theory that an unconditional sale of a patented device exhausts the patentee's right to control the purchaser's use of that item thereafter because the patentee has bargained for and received full value for the goods.

In *Quanta,* the Court held that method claims for managing and synchronizing data transfers between computer components were exhausted when the patent holder licensed a manufacturer to produce and sell unpatented microprocessors and chipsets that performed the patented methods when incorporated with memory and buses in a computer system. The Court established that method claims are exhausted by an authorized sale of an item that substantially embodies the method if the item (1) has no reasonable noninfringing use and (2) includes all inventive aspects of the claimed method. The *Quanta* opinion emphasized the unpatented nature of the products sold. Thus, the substantial embodiment test provided a framework for determining whether the sale of an unpatented component, which by itself does not practice the patented method, is still sufficient for exhaustion. The Court held that it is.

But that is not the case before us, which presents a situation in which the product sold by Keurig was patented. Keurig acknowledges that its brewers are commercial embodiments of the apparatus claims of the '938 patent. Keurig does not dispute that its rights in its brewers were exhausted with respect to the apparatus claims. Instead, Keurig alleges that purchasers of its brewers infringe its brewer patents by using Sturm cartridges to practice the claimed methods and therefore that Sturm is liable for induced infringement. However, as the Supreme Court long ago held, "Where a person has purchased a patented machine of the patentee or his assignee, this purchase carries with it the right to the use of the machine so long as it is capable of use." *Quanta,* 553 U.S. at 625 (quoting *Adams v. Burke,* 84 U.S. 453, 455 (1873)). The Court's decision in *Quanta* did not alter this principle. Keurig sold its patented brewers without conditions and its purchasers therefore obtained the unfettered right to use them in any way they chose, at least as against a challenge from Keurig. We conclude, therefore, that Keurig's rights to assert infringement of the method claims '938 patent were exhausted by its initial authorized sale of Keurig's patented brewers.

6   To rule otherwise would allow Keurig what the Supreme Court has aptly described as an "end-run around exhaustion" by claiming methods as well as the apparatus that practices them and attempting to shield the patented apparatus from exhaustion by holding downstream purchasers of its device liable for infringement of its method claims—a tactic that the Supreme Court has explicitly admonished. Here, Keurig is attempting to impermissibly restrict purchasers of Keurig brewers from using non-Keurig cartridges by invoking patent law to enforce restrictions on the post-sale use of its patented product.

7   Keurig's argument that patent exhaustion must be adjudicated on a claim-by-claim basis is unavailing. The Court's patent exhaustion jurisprudence has focused on the exhaustion of the patents at issue in their entirety, rather than the exhaustion of the claims at issue on an individual basis. Keurig's decision to have sought protection for both apparatus and method claims thus means that those claims are judged together for purposes of patent exhaustion.

8   The noninfringement judgment of the district court is affirmed.

Kathleen M. O'Malley, Circuit Judge, concurring in the result.

9   Keurig's patent rights covering normal methods of using its brewers to brew coffee would be exhausted by the sale of the Keurig brewers, regardless of which patent or patents contain the relevant apparatus and method claims. Thus, the majority's conclusion that exhaustion should not be assessed on a claim-by-claim basis is dicta. To the extent it could be characterized as anything other than dicta, I must dissent from that conclusion. There could be instances where assessing exhaustion on a claim-by-claim basis—the same way we conduct almost every analysis related to patent law—would be necessary and appropriate.

Impression Products v. Lexmark International, 137 S. Ct. 1523 (2017)

Chief Justice Roberts delivered the opinion of the Court.

1   A United States patent entitles the patent holder, for a period of 20 years, to "exclude others from making, using, offering for sale, or selling [its] invention throughout the United States or importing the invention into the United States." 35 U.S.C. § 154(a). Whoever engages in one of these acts "without authority" from the patentee may face liability for patent infringement. § 271(a).

2   When a patentee sells one of its products, however, the patentee can no longer control that item through the patent laws—its patent rights are said to "exhaust." The purchaser and all subsequent owners are free to use or resell the product just like any other item of personal property, without fear of an infringement lawsuit.

3   This case presents two questions about the scope of the patent exhaustion doctrine: First, whether a patentee that sells an item under an express restriction on

the purchaser's right to reuse or resell the product may enforce that restriction through an infringement lawsuit. And second, whether a patentee exhausts its patent rights by selling its product outside the United States, where American patent laws do not apply. We conclude that a patentee's decision to sell a product exhausts all of its patent rights in that item, regardless of any restrictions the patentee purports to impose or the location of the sale.

I

The underlying dispute in this case is about laser printers—or, more specifically, the cartridges that contain the powdery substance, known as toner, that laser printers use to make an image appear on paper. Respondent Lexmark International, Inc. designs, manufactures, and sells toner cartridges to consumers in the United States and around the globe. It owns a number of patents that cover components of those cartridges and the manner in which they are used.

When toner cartridges run out of toner they can be refilled and used again. This creates an opportunity for other companies—known as remanufacturers—to acquire empty Lexmark cartridges from purchasers in the United States and abroad, refill them with toner, and then resell them at a lower price than the new ones Lexmark puts on the shelves.

Not blind to this business problem, Lexmark structures its sales in a way that encourages customers to return spent cartridges. It gives purchasers two options: One is to buy a toner cartridge at full price, with no strings attached. The other is to buy a cartridge at roughly 20–percent off through Lexmark's "Return Program." A customer who buys through the Return Program still owns the cartridge but, in exchange for the lower price, signs a contract agreeing to use it only once and to refrain from transferring the empty cartridge to anyone but Lexmark.

In 2010, Lexmark sued a number of remanufacturers for patent infringement with respect to two groups of cartridges. One group consists of Return Program cartridges that Lexmark sold within the United States. Lexmark argued that, because it expressly prohibited reuse and resale of these cartridges, the remanufacturers infringed the Lexmark patents when they refurbished and resold them. The other group consists of all toner cartridges that Lexmark sold abroad and that remanufacturers imported into the country. Lexmark claimed that it never gave anyone authority to import these cartridges, so the remanufacturers ran afoul of its patent rights by doing just that.

Eventually, the lawsuit was whittled down to one defendant, Impression Products, and one defense: that Lexmark's sales, both in the United States and abroad, exhausted its patent rights in the cartridges, so Impression Products was free to refurbish and resell them, and to import them if acquired abroad. Impression Products filed separate motions to dismiss with respect to both groups of cartridges. The District Court granted the motion as to the domestic Return Program cartridges, but denied the motion as to the cartridges Lexmark sold abroad. Both parties appealed.

9   The Federal Circuit considered the appeals en banc and ruled for Lexmark with respect to both groups of cartridges. We granted certiorari to consider the Federal Circuit's decisions with respect to both domestic and international exhaustion, and now reverse.

II

A

10   First up are the Return Program cartridges that Lexmark sold in the United States. We conclude that Lexmark exhausted its patent rights in these cartridges the moment it sold them. The single-use/no-resale restrictions in Lexmark's contracts with customers may have been clear and enforceable under contract law, but they do not entitle Lexmark to retain patent rights in an item that it has elected to sell.

11   The Patent Act grants patentees the "right to exclude others from making, using, offering for sale, or selling [their] invention[s]." 35 U.S.C. § 154(a). For over 160 years, the doctrine of patent exhaustion has imposed a limit on that right to exclude. *See Bloomer v. McQuewan,* 14 How. 539 (1853). The limit functions automatically: When a patentee chooses to sell an item, that product "is no longer within the limits of the monopoly" and instead becomes the "private, individual property" of the purchaser, with the rights and benefits that come along with ownership. *Id.* at 549–50.

12   This well-established exhaustion rule marks the point where patent rights yield to the common law principle against restraints on alienation. The Patent Act "promote[s] the progress of science and the useful arts by granting to [inventors] a limited monopoly" that allows them to "secure the financial rewards" for their inventions. *United States v. Univis,* 316 U.S. 241, 250 (1942). But once a patentee sells an item, it has "enjoyed all the rights secured" by that limited monopoly. *Keeler v. Standard Folding Bed Co.,* 157 U.S. 659, 661 (1895). Because "the purpose of the patent law is fulfilled . . . when the patentee has received his reward for the use of his invention," that law furnishes "no basis for restraining the use and enjoyment of the thing sold." *Univis,* 316 U.S. at 251.

13   Congress enacted and has repeatedly revised the Patent Act against the backdrop of the hostility toward restraints on alienation. That enmity is reflected in the exhaustion doctrine. The patent laws do not include the right to "restrain [ ] . . . further alienation" after an initial sale. *Straus v. Victor Talking Machine Co.,* 243 U.S. 490, 501 (1917). "The inconvenience and annoyance to the public that an opposite conclusion would occasion are too obvious to require illustration." *Keeler,* 157 U.S. at 667.

14   But an illustration never hurts. Take a shop that restores and sells used cars. The business works because the shop can rest assured that, so long as those bringing in the cars own them, the shop is free to repair and resell those vehicles. That smooth flow of commerce would sputter if companies that make the thousands of parts that go into a vehicle could keep their patent rights after the first sale. Those companies might, for instance, restrict resale rights and sue the shop owner for patent infringement. And even if they refrained from imposing such restrictions, the very threat of patent liability would force the shop to invest in efforts to protect itself from hidden lawsuits. Either way, extending the patent rights beyond the first sale would clog the channels of commerce, with little benefit from the extra control that the patentees retain. And advances in technology, along with increasingly complex supply chains, magnify the problem.

15   Turning to the case at hand, we conclude that this well-settled line of precedent allows for only one answer: Lexmark cannot bring a patent infringement suit against Impression Products to enforce the single-use/no-resale provision accompanying its Return Program cartridges. Once sold, the Return Program cartridges passed outside of the patent monopoly, and whatever rights Lexmark retained are a matter of the contracts with its purchasers, not the patent law.

B

16   The Federal Circuit reached a different result largely because it got off on the wrong foot. Exhaustion reflects a default rule that a patentee's decision to sell an item "*presumptively* grant[s] 'authority' to the purchaser to use it and resell it." 816 F.3d at 742. But, the Federal Circuit explained, the patentee does not have to hand over the full "bundle of rights" every time. *Id.* at 741. If the patentee expressly withholds a stick from the bundle—perhaps by restricting the purchaser's resale rights—the buyer never acquires that withheld authority, and the patentee may continue to enforce its right to exclude that practice under the patent laws.

17   The misstep in this logic is that the exhaustion doctrine is not a presumption about the authority that comes along with a sale; it is instead a limit on "the scope of the *patentee's rights.*" *United States v. General Elec. Co.*, 272 U.S. 476, 489 (1926). The right to use, sell, or import an item exists independently of the Patent Act. What a patent adds is a limited right to prevent others from engaging in those practices. Exhaustion extinguishes that exclusionary power.

18   The Federal Circuit also expressed concern that preventing patentees from reserving patent rights when they sell goods would create an artificial distinction between such sales and sales by licensees. Patentees, the court explained, often license others to make and sell their products, and may place restrictions on those licenses. A computer developer could, for instance, license a manufacturer to make its patented devices and sell them only for non-commercial use by individuals. If a licensee breaches the license by selling a computer for commercial use, the patentee can sue the licensee for infringement. And, in the Federal Circuit's view, our decision in

General Talking Pictures Corp. v. Western Elec. Co., 304 U.S. 175, *aff'd on reh'g*, 305 U.S. 124 (1938), established that—when a patentee grants a license "under clearly stated restrictions on post-sale activities" of those who purchase products from the licensee—the patentee can *also* sue for infringement those purchasers who knowingly violate the restrictions. If patentees can employ licenses to impose post-sale restrictions on purchasers that are enforceable through infringement suits, the court concluded, it would make little sense to prevent patentees from doing so when they sell directly to consumers.

19   The Federal Circuit's concern is misplaced. A patentee can impose restrictions on licensees because a license does not implicate the same concerns about restraints on alienation as a sale. Patent exhaustion reflects the principle that, when an item passes into commerce, it should not be shaded by a legal cloud on title as it moves through the marketplace. But a license is not about passing title to a product, it is about changing the contours of the patentee's monopoly: The patentee agrees not to exclude a licensee from making or selling the patented invention, expanding the club of authorized producers and sellers. Because the patentee is exchanging rights, not goods, it is free to relinquish only a portion of its bundle of patent protections.

20   A patentee's authority to limit *licensees* does not, as the Federal Circuit thought, mean that patentees can use licenses to impose post-sale restrictions on *purchasers* that are enforceable through the patent laws. So long as a licensee complies with the license when selling an item, the patentee has, in effect, authorized the sale. That licensee's sale is treated, for purposes of patent exhaustion, as if the patentee made the sale itself. The result: The sale exhausts the patentee's rights in that item. A license may require the licensee to impose a restriction on purchasers, like the license limiting the computer manufacturer to selling for non-commercial use by individuals. But if the licensee does so—by, perhaps, having each customer sign a contract promising not to use the computers in business—the sale nonetheless exhausts all patent rights in the item sold. The purchasers might not comply with the restriction, but the only recourse for the licensee is through contract law, just as if the patentee itself sold the item with a restriction.

21   *General Talking Pictures* involved a fundamentally different situation: There, a licensee "knowingly ma[de] . . . sales . . . *outside* the scope of its license." 304 U.S. at 181–82. We treated the sale "as if no license whatsoever had been granted" by the patentee, which meant that the patentee could sue both the licensee and the purchaser—who knew about the breach—for infringement. *General Talking Pictures Corp. v. Western Elec. Co.,* 305 U.S. 124, 127 (1938). This does not mean that patentees can use licenses to impose post-sale restraints on purchasers. Quite the contrary: The licensee infringed the patentee's rights because it did *not* comply with the terms of its license, and the patentee could bring a patent suit against the purchaser only because the purchaser participated in the licensee's infringement. *General Talking Pictures,* then, stands for the modest principle that, if a patentee has not given authority for a licensee to make a sale, that sale cannot exhaust the patentee's rights.

22   In sum, patent exhaustion is uniform and automatic. Once a patentee decides to sell—whether on its own or through a licensee—that sale exhausts its patent rights, regardless of any post-sale restrictions the patentee purports to impose, either directly or through a license.

III

23   Our conclusion that Lexmark exhausted its patent rights when it sold the domestic Return Program cartridges goes only halfway to resolving this case. Lexmark also sold toner cartridges abroad and sued Impression Products for patent infringement for "importing [Lexmark's] invention into the United States." 35 U.S.C. § 154(a). Lexmark contends that it may sue for infringement with respect to all of the imported cartridges—not just those in the Return Program—because a foreign sale does not trigger patent exhaustion unless the patentee "expressly or implicitly transfer[s] or license[s]" its rights. The Federal Circuit agreed, but we do not. An authorized sale outside the United States, just as one within the United States, exhausts all rights under the Patent Act.

24   This question about international exhaustion of intellectual property rights has also arisen in the context of copyright law. Under the "first sale doctrine," which is codified at 17 U.S.C. § 109(a), when a copyright owner sells a lawfully made copy of its work, it loses the power to restrict the purchaser's freedom "to sell or otherwise dispose of . . . that copy." In *Kirtsaeng v. John Wiley & Sons, Inc.*, we held that this " 'first sale' [rule] applies to copies of a copyrighted work lawfully made [and sold] abroad." 568 U.S. at 525. What helped tip the scales for global exhaustion was the fact that the first sale doctrine originated in "the common law's refusal to permit restraints on the alienation of chattels." *Id.* at 538. That "common-law doctrine makes no geographical distinctions." *Id.* at 539.

25   Applying patent exhaustion to foreign sales is just as straightforward. Patent exhaustion, too, has its roots in the antipathy toward restraints on alienation, and nothing in the text or history of the Patent Act shows that Congress intended to confine that borderless common law principle to domestic sales. And differentiating the patent exhaustion and copyright first sale doctrines would make little theoretical or practical sense: The two share a strong similarity and identity of purpose, and many everyday products—"automobiles, microwaves, calculators, mobile phones, tablets, and personal computers"—are subject to both patent and copyright protections. The bond between the two leaves no room for a rift on the question of international exhaustion.

26   Lexmark sees the matter differently. The Patent Act, it points out, limits the patentee's "right to exclude others" from making, using, selling, or importing its products to acts that occur in the United States. 35 U.S.C. § 154(a). A domestic sale, it argues, triggers exhaustion because the sale compensates the patentee for surrendering those *U.S.* rights. A foreign sale is different: The Patent Act does not give patentees exclusionary powers abroad. Without those powers, a patentee selling

in a foreign market may not be able to sell its product for the same price that it could in the United States, and therefore is not sure to receive the reward guaranteed by U.S. patent law. Absent that reward, says Lexmark, there should be no exhaustion. In short, there is no patent exhaustion from sales abroad because there are no patent rights abroad to exhaust.

27   The territorial limit on patent rights is, however, no basis for distinguishing copyright protections; those protections do not have any extraterritorial operation either. Nor does the territorial limit support the premise of Lexmark's argument. Exhaustion is a separate limit on the patent grant, and does not depend on the patentee receiving some undefined premium for selling the right to access the American market. The patentee may not be able to command the same amount for its products abroad as it does in the United States. But the Patent Act does not guarantee a particular price, much less the price from selling to American consumers.

28   This Court has addressed international patent exhaustion in only one case, *Boesch v. Graff*, 133 U.S. 697 (1890), decided over 125 years ago. All that case illustrates is that a sale abroad does not exhaust a patentee's rights when the patentee had nothing to do with the transaction. Our decision did not, as Lexmark contends, exempt all foreign sales from patent exhaustion. Rather, it reaffirmed the basic premise that only the patentee can decide whether to make a sale that exhausts its patent rights in an item.

29   Finally, the United States, as an *amicus,* advocates what it views as a middle-ground position: that "a foreign sale authorized by the U.S. patentee exhausts U.S. patent rights unless those rights are expressly reserved." Its position is largely based on policy rather than principle. The Government thinks that an overseas "buyer's legitimate expectation" is that a "sale conveys all of the seller's interest in the patented article," so the presumption should be that a foreign sale triggers exhaustion. But, at the same time, "lower courts long ago coalesced around" the rule that "a patentee's express reservation of U.S. patent rights at the time of a foreign sale will be given effect," so that option should remain open to the patentee.

30   The theory behind the Government's express-reservation rule wrongly focuses on the likely expectations of the patentee and purchaser during a sale. Exhaustion does not arise because of the parties' expectations about how sales transfer patent rights. More is at stake when it comes to patents than simply the dealings between the parties, which can be addressed through contract law. Instead, exhaustion occurs because, in a sale, the patentee elects to give up title to an item in exchange for payment. Allowing patent rights to stick remora-like to that item as it flows through the market would violate the principle against restraints on alienation. Exhaustion does not depend on whether the patentee receives a premium for selling in the United States, or the type of rights that buyers expect to receive. As a result, restrictions and location are irrelevant; what matters is the patentee's decision to make a sale.

31   [Justice Ginsburg dissented from the Court's holding on international exhaustion, noting that she dissented in *Kirtsaeng*, but even if she "subscribed to *Kirtsaeng*'s reasoning with respect to copyright, that decision should bear little weight in the patent context," including because "[t]he Patent Act contains no analogue to 17 U.S.C. § 109(a)," and copyright law involves greater harmonization across countries.]

Discussion Questions: Exhaustion

1. *Avoiding Method Claim Exhaustion. Keurig v. Sturm Foods* left patentees wondering how to avoid exhaustion of inventive method claims. Why was it relevant in that case whether the brewer apparatus embodied "essential features" of the method claims at issue? Would the result have been different if the cartridges had been independently patentable? What if Keurig had distributed some of its brewers for free, and only charged for the cartridges? *See LifeScan Scotland v. Shasta Techs.*, 734 F.3d 1361 (Fed. Cir. 2013) (considering these questions in the context of freely distributed blood glucose monitoring systems and glucose test strips).

2. *Patents Versus Contracts and Sales Versus Licenses.* To understand what was at stake in *Impression*, it is useful to consider Lexmark's alternatives. Lexmark could certainly have prohibited its customers from reselling the toner cartridges as a matter of contract law; these contracts could have been an automatic condition of the sale. That would have permitted Lexmark to sue anyone who resold the cartridge for breach of contract. But Lexmark doesn't want to sue the people who resell the cartridges—Lexmark's own customers—for the same reason that Aro didn't want to sue the individuals who repaired their fabric convertible tops in *Aro* and Sanofi didn't want to sue the patients who took the generic version of its drug in *Sanofi* (both in Chapter 10). These individuals are dispersed and hard to find, and suing them individually might well cost more than it is worth. Plus, it's not a great business practice to sue your customers or potential customers.

Instead, Lexmark wants to sue Impression. But the problem for Lexmark is that it doesn't have a contract with Impression, only with Lexmark's customers. Lexmark could try to sue Impression for tortious inducement of contract breach (inducing Lexmark's customers to breach their contracts with Lexmark) or some such thing, but those are difficult suits to win, particularly across international lines. In addition, it is easier to obtain treble damages (which we will discuss in Chapter 16) and other enhanced remedies via patent law than via contract law. Much better, from Lexmark's perspective, if it could sue Impression for patent infringement.

Rather than relying on contract remedies, could patent owners circumvent *Impression* through creative contract *drafting*? Exhaustion applies to authorized *sales*, not *licenses*. Could Lexmark avoid exhaustion by licensing cartridges rather than selling them? Or would a court reject this tactic as a "disguised sale"? *See* Daniel Hemel & Lisa Larrimore Ouellette, *Licensing in the Shadow of* Impression Products,

Written   Description   (May   31,   2017),
https://writtendescription.blogspot.com/2017/05/licensing-in-shadow-of-impression.html.

3. *Patent Exhaustion Winners and Losers.* The parties advocating for the broad exhaustion rules adopted by the Supreme Court in *Impression v. Lexmark* argued that exhaustion increases economic efficiency by decreasing information costs: parties will no longer need to spend as much time verifying whether aspects of imported or resold goods are protected by U.S. patents. Opponents argued that exhaustion reduces economic efficiency by increasing the ability of patent owners to price discriminate, such as by charging lower prices in low-income countries. What are the *distributive* effects of the Supreme Court's ruling? Do you find it surprising that groups focused on global access to medicines advocated in *favor* of a U.S. rule of international patent exhaustion? *See* Daniel J. Hemel & Lisa Larrimore Ouellette, *Trade and Tradeoffs: The Case of International Patent Exhaustion*, 116 Colum. L. Rev. Sidebar 17 (2016) (arguing that "while the net winners and losers from a U.S. international exhaustion rule are somewhat ambiguous, it seems clear that consumers in low-income countries do not come out ahead").

4. *Repair Versus Reconstruction.* We have already encountered one important limitation on exhaustion: it permits authorized purchasers only to use, resell, or repair their patented product, not to entirely reconstruct the product. In the Supreme Court's *Aro II* decision we read in Chapter 10, the Court discussed its holding in *Aro I*: the authorized sale by GM of cars with a patented convertible top allowed purchasers to replace the fabric in the tops because this was "repair" rather than "reconstruction." What does the repair/reconstruction doctrine permit purchasers of Keurig's patented brewers to do with those brewers? What *can't* they do? Is repair vs. reconstruction a useful dichotomy for courts to manage the underlying policy concerns?

5. *Self-Replicating Technologies.* Another limitation on exhaustion involves products that generate new copies of themselves. In *Bowman v. Monsanto*, 569 U.S. 278 (2013), the Supreme Court held that exhaustion did not allow a farmer to reproduce Monsanto's patented "Roundup Ready" seeds that were genetically engineered to be herbicide resistant. "[E]xhaustion applies only to the particular item sold, and not to reproductions." *Id.* at 287. How do you think this ruling has affected the farming industry?

C. Inequitable Conduct

Recall from Chapter 1 that patent applicants are under no affirmative obligation to search for prior art relevant to their applications. Finding prior art is the USPTO examiner's responsibility. However, applicants must identify to the USPTO any relevant prior art of which they are aware. Failure to comply with this requirement can get applicants into serious trouble.

Inequitable conduct is an equitable defense to infringement rendering a patent "unenforceable" if the patentee deceived the USPTO, such as by failing to disclose devastating prior art. "Unenforceability" is listed as a defense to patent infringement in 35 U.S.C. § 282(b)(1), and it is even more valuable for defendants than invalidity because the *entire patent* is unenforceable, not just the specific claim at issue. The unenforceability penalty has thus been called the "atomic bomb" of patent law.

In response to concerns about a perceived "plague" of inequitable conduct counterclaims, the Federal Circuit cut back on this defense in *Therasense, Inc. v. Becton, Dickinson & Co.*, 649 F.3d 1276 (Fed. Cir. 2011) (en banc). The en banc court held that the party asserting the defense must establish, by clear and convincing evidence, two elements:

1. *But-for materiality.* The applicant failed to disclose material information or materially false information, and the USPTO would not have allowed the claim if it had been aware of the information.

2. *Specific intent to deceive.* The applicant knew of the information, knew it was material, and made a deliberate decision to withhold it. Intent may be inferred from circumstantial evidence, but not solely from materiality.

Successful inequitable conduct defenses have become less frequent since *Therasense*. As one measure of prevalence, the number of Federal Circuit opinions mentioning "inequitable conduct" dropped from a high of 43 in 2008 to only 4 in 2021. The following facts have not resulted in inequitable conduct:

- The patentee failed to disclose a relevant reference during prosecution, but the reference was cumulative of references the USPTO later considered in IPR proceedings upholding the patents' validity and was thus not but-for material. *California Inst. of Tech. v. Broadcom Ltd.*, 25 F.4th 976 (Fed. Cir. 2022).

- The patentee failed to disclose to the USPTO that the parent patent of the application at issue was in litigation, but it was not material because invalidity defenses had not yet been raised in the litigation, and there was no evidence on which to base an inference of deceptive intent. *Outside the Box Innovations v. Travel Caddy*, 695 F.3d 1285 (Fed. Cir. 2012).

- A search report from the European Patent Office cited the reference as relevant to the counterpart application filed in that office, suggesting that the patentee knew the reference was material, but there was no evidence of a "deliberate decision to withhold it." *1st Media v. Elec. Arts*, 694 F.3d 1367 (Fed. Cir. 2012).

But the defense remains viable. For example, the Federal Circuit has affirmed findings of inequitable conduct in the following circumstances:

- The patentee withheld information about an earlier sale that would have barred the patent, made false statements about when the invention was reduced to practice, and threatened a client with legal action if it did not corroborate the patentee's story, resulting in a straightforward case. *GS CleanTech v. Adkins Energy*, 951 F.3d 1310 (Fed. Cir. 2020).

• The patent owner's chief scientist told the FDA that the invention's claimed pH range was "old" in order to aid FDA approval of the product, but described this range as a "critical" innovation with "unexpected" results to the USPTO, serving as circumstantial evidence of deceptive intent. *Belcher Pharms., LLC v. Hospira, Inc.*, 11 F.4th 1345 (Fed. Cir. 2021).

• There was no direct evidence of specific intent to deceive the USPTO, but the district court drew an adverse inference based on similar deceptive misconduct during litigation, such as hiding material that should have been disclosed during discovery. *Regeneron Pharmaceuticals v. Merus*, 864 F.3d 1343 (Fed. Cir. 2017).

Consider the incentives this doctrine provides to patent applicants considering whether to disclose material information. Inequitable conduct will only harm an applicant if the buried information is eventually found. If that information is certain to invalidate all claims of the patent, does the defense provide any deterrence? In other words, is there any incentive to turn over information to the USPTO that would make the entire patent invalid? On the other hand, what if the applicant makes only a very small misstatement? Does it make sense to render the entire patent unenforceable based on an act of deception that concerns only one or a few claims? Is this the optimal relationship between deterrence and culpability? *See* Tun-Jen Chiang, *The Upside-Down Inequitable Conduct Defense*, 107 Nw. U. L. Rev. 1243 (2013) (arguing that "the unenforceability penalty creates too much deterrence against minor errors, but it also produces inadequate deterrence against the most serious patentee frauds").

A patentee's duty of candor arises not only from the inequitable conduct doctrine, but also from 37 C.F.R. § 1.56, which states that patent inventors, prosecutors, and anyone else "substantively involved in the preparation or prosecution of the application" has "a duty of candor and good faith in dealing with the [USPTO], which includes a duty to disclose to the Office all information known to that individual to be material to patentability as defined in this section." The remedy for violations of this rule is dismissal of the patent application (and, less commonly, discipline of the patent prosecutor).

Of course, as we have said, none of these rules impose any search obligation on patentees. Should patentees be encouraged to search for and disclose information to examiners? Would it affect your answer if it turned out that examiners rarely use applicant-submitted prior art, as one paper has argued? *See* Christopher A. Cotropia, Mark A. Lemley & Bhaven Sampat, *Do Applicant Patent Citations Matter?*, 42 Res. Pol'y 844 (2013). As discussed in Chapter 1, patent examiners do not have enough time to conduct a thorough prior art search for every patent application on their docket, and empirical evidence suggests that these time constraints cause examiners to erroneously grant many invalid patents. Are there other ways to reduce the informational challenges faced by patent examiners?

D. Patent Misuse and Antitrust Violations

Under the judge-made doctrine of patent misuse, a patent is unenforceable when the patentee has leveraged it to obtain market power beyond the scope of the patent right. But this is a relatively limited rule. As explained in Chapter 1, providing market power—even monopoly power—is the *goal* of patent law. The idea is that the prospect of being able to charge prices above marginal cost will induce patent owners to create more new products in the first place. In addition, "a patent does not necessarily confer market power upon the patentee." *Illinois Tool Works Inc. v. Independent Ink, Inc.*, 547 U.S. 28, 45 (2006). That is, the mere fact that a party owns a patent will not be treated as sufficient evidence that the party has market power, much less that it has misused the patent to obtain market power.

To emphasize the broad nature of patent rights, Congress has imposed statutory limits on patent misuse by specifying in § 271(d) of the Patent Act that certain activities such as refusal to license do not constitute misuse.

35 U.S.C. § 271(d)

No patent owner otherwise entitled to relief for infringement or contributory infringement of a patent shall be denied relief or deemed guilty of misuse or illegal extension of the patent right by reason of his having done one or more of the following:

(1) derived revenue from acts which if performed by another without his consent would constitute contributory infringement of the patent;

(2) licensed or authorized another to perform acts which if performed without his consent would constitute contributory infringement of the patent;

(3) sought to enforce his patent rights against infringement or contributory infringement;

(4) refused to license or use any rights to the patent; or

(5) conditioned the license of any rights to the patent or the sale of the patented product on the acquisition of a license to rights in another patent or purchase of a separate product, unless, in view of the circumstances, the patent owner has market power in the relevant

market for the patent or patented product on which the license or sale is conditioned.

The Federal Circuit has also emphasized "the narrow scope of the doctrine" and that "the defense of patent misuse is not available to a presumptive infringer simply because a patentee engages in some kind of wrongful commercial conduct, even conduct that may have anticompetitive effects." *Princo Corp. v. International Trade Commission*, 616 F.3d 1318, 1329 (Fed. Cir. 2010) (en banc); *see also id.* at 1342 (Dyk, J., dissenting) (arguing that the court has "emasculate[d] the doctrine so that it will not provide a meaningful obstacle to patent enforcement").

So what kind of behavior might constitute patent misuse? Acts that could trigger misuse include tying the sale of patented product to unpatented staple articles of commerce, tying patent licenses to the license of other patents, and conditioning licenses on agreements not to sell noninfringing alternatives.

One clear example of misuse is that under *Brulotte v. Thys Co.*, 379 U.S. 29 (1964), a patentee cannot charge royalties for sales that occur after the patent term expires. This rule has been criticized because it doesn't actually extend the patent monopoly beyond the patent term: after expiration, others may use the patent for free, and there's no good reason for preventing a licensee from entering a contract that requires it to pay lower royalties for longer. Nonetheless, in *Kimble v. Marvel Entertainment*, 576 U.S. 446 (2015), the Supreme Court declined to overrule *Brulotte* on stare decisis grounds, largely due to the lack of evidence of a problem. Parties can circumvent *Brulotte* by contract, such as by (1) deferring payments for pre-expiration use to the post-expiration period, (2) specifying that some royalties are for non-patent rights such as related know-how and trade secrets, or (3) licensing the IP to a separate company that produces the product and giving the licensor some stake in that company. What kind of patentees might be disadvantaged by the *Brulotte* rule?

Another consequence of the rule reaffirmed in *Kimble* is that if a patent is declared invalid, any ongoing stream of royalty payments based on that patent can no longer be collected. For instance, imagine that a firm licenses its patented touchscreen technology to Apple in exchange for 0.00000001% of Apple's revenues from iPhone sales over a ten-year period. If the patent is declared invalid halfway through the ten-year period, Apple no longer has to make the remaining payments. How do you think this rule affects the type of licensing agreements that firms will negotiate? Is there any harm from firms structuring their agreements to avoid this type of potential problem?

Behavior that does not fall within the narrow scope of patent misuse may still be an antitrust violation, and patent litigation sometimes involves antitrust counterclaims. The Supreme Court's most recent discussion of the intersection of patent and antitrust was *FTC v. Actavis*, 570 U.S. 136 (2013). *Actavis* concerned the common practice of "reverse-payment settlements" in pharmaceutical patent infringement cases, in which the patent owner pays a prospective generic manufacturer to settle the case and stay off the market. Because of a concern that such agreements may be used to shield invalid patents from review, the Court held that reverse-payment settlements may be anticompetitive and should be scrutinized under antitrust law's "rule of reason." *Id.* at 156. For a thorough exploration of the patent-antitrust intersection, see Herbert Hovenkamp et al., *IP and Antitrust: An Analysis of Antitrust Principles Applied to Intellectual Property Law* (3d ed. 2016).

E. Prior User Rights

As discussed in Chapter 9, direct patent infringement is strict liability. This means that in general, there is no independent invention defense: someone who has no knowledge of a patent and independently develops the invention is still liable. A number of scholars have questioned this policy choice. *See, e.g.*, Stephen M. Maurer & Suzanne Scotchmer, *The Independent Invention Defence in Intellectual Property*, 69 Economica 535 (2002) ("We argue that the patent rule is inferior in any industry where the cost of independently inventing a product is not too much less than the inventor's cost."); Samson Vermont, *Independent Invention as a Defense to Patent Infringement*, 105 Mich. L. Rev. 475 (2006).

Although U.S. patent law lacks a broad independent invention defense, 35 U.S.C. § 273 provides a defense to infringement based on prior commercial use in the United States. This statutory defense for prior commercial use was first created in 1999 for business method patents, and it was then extended to all patents by the 2011 America Invents Act.

35 U.S.C. § 273(a)

A person shall be entitled to a defense [to patent infringement] if—

(1) such person, acting in good faith, commercially used the subject matter in the United States, either in connection with an internal commercial use or an actual arm's length sale or other arm's length commercial transfer of a useful end result of such commercial use; and

(2) such commercial use occurred at least 1 year before the earlier of either—

> (A) the effective filing date of the claimed invention; or

> (B) the date on which the claimed invention was disclosed to the public in a manner that qualified for the exception from prior art under section 102(b).

This defense is subject to a number of limitations. For example, it is a personal defense that applies only to "the person who performed or directed the performance of the commercial use" and may not be licensed or transferred to another party or expanded to other worksites. § 273(e)(1). The defense "is not a general license under all claims of the patent"; it only allows continuation of the existing commercial use. § 273(e)(3). Thanks to effective university lobbyists, the defense also does not apply to academic patents. § 273(e)(5).

There are no reported cases in which the 1999 prior user rights defense was raised, and a 2015 study found only three reported cases in which the expanded defense was asserted, none of which were successful. Why do you think the defense hasn't been more popular? For example, if a defendant was engaged in prior commercial use, are there any other defenses she could assert that aren't subject to the limitations described above?

The statutory defense for prior commercial use is related to a common-law "shop rights" defense that gives an employer the right to use patented technologies developed by an employee in the employer's "shop." Like prior user rights, shop rights are rarely asserted, and they also seem to be subject to important limitations:

> The "shop rights" doctrine is a judicially created defense to patent infringement (sometimes described as an implied license). It applies when an employer is sued for patent infringement by an employee who created the patented invention with the employer's resources while under its employment, even though the employer otherwise has no legal rights to the resultant invention. The doctrine has its limits, however; for example, it seems an employer can only use the invention internally in its own business. And the law regarding the doctrine's scope is far from clear. It is, at least, likely (if not certain) that the doctrine does not extend to an employer's sale of the patented invention to an unrelated third-party for the latter's unfettered use, since the "shop right" belongs only to the employer.

Beriont v. GTE Labs., Inc., 535 F. App'x 919, 923 (Fed. Cir. 2013).

F. Experimental Use

In 1813, Justice Story developed a defense from patent liability for experimental use, writing that "it could never have been the intention of the legislature to punish a man, who constructed such a [patented] machine merely for philosophical experiments, or for the purpose of ascertaining the sufficiency of the machine to produce its described effects." *Whittemore v. Cutter*, 29 F. Cas. 1120, 1121 (C.C.D. Mass. 1813). But the Federal Circuit has interpreted this doctrine narrowly, limiting it to activities "for amusement, to satisfy idle curiosity, or for strictly philosophical inquiry." *Madey v. Duke Univ.*, 307 F.3d 1351, 1362 (Fed. Cir. 2002). The doctrine does not exempt university research because even when the research has "no commercial application . . . these projects unmistakably further the institution's legitimate business objectives, including educating and enlightening students and faculty . . . increas[ing] the status of the institution, and lur[ing] lucrative research grants, students and faculty." *Id.*

Many countries have a broad defense from patent liability for research activities, and some scholars have advocated for a similar rule in the United States. *See, e.g.*, Katherine J. Strandburg, *What Does the Public Get? Experimental Use and the Patent Bargain*, 2004 Wis. L. Rev. 81. Do you think expanding the experimental use defense is a good idea? If so, what additional conduct would you exempt? What is the best argument *against* an experimental use exemption? In *Madey v. Duke*, the Federal Circuit noted that Duke University, "like other major research institutions of higher learning, is not shy in pursuing an aggressive patent licensing program from which it derives a not insubstantial revenue stream." 307 F.3d at 1362-63 n.7. Should patenting activity affect whether an institution qualifies for the defense?

Even though the United States does not have a broad experimental use defense, there is a specific statutory defense for uses related to submitting information for regulatory purposes, which is distinct from the common law experimental use exemption and is refered to by names including the "statutory experimental use defense," the "safe harbor" and the "*Bolar* exemption" (named after the case *Roche v. Bolar*, 733 F.2d 858 (Fed. Cir. 1984), which inspired Congress to enact this provision).

35 U.S.C. § 271(e)(1)

It shall not be an act of infringement to make, use, offer to sell, or sell within the United States or import into the United States a patented invention (other than [new animal drugs involving gene manipulation]) solely for uses reasonably related to the development and submission of information under a Federal law which regulates the manufacture, use, or sale of drugs or veterinary biological products.

Under this provision, a generic pharmaceutical manufacturer that wishes to apply for FDA approval may perform the tests required by the FDA without fear of liability. But this safe harbor does not protect "[b]asic scientific research on a particular compound, performed without the intent to develop a particular drug." *Merck KGaA v. Integra Lifesciences I, Ltd.*, 545 U.S. 193, 205 (2005).

Caution: Both of these experimental use defenses are distinct from "experimental use" in the § 102 context. As discussed in Chapter 2, a public use sometimes does not count as prior art if it is experimental and the inventor does not yet know that it will work for its intended purpose. In the § 102 context, the issue is whether the experiment should count as prior art that bars the inventor from filing a patent more than a year later. In the infringement context, the issue is whether the experiment should subject the researcher to liability under someone else's patent.

G. Laches

Laches is an equitable defense based on delay caused by the plaintiff. Two types of laches have been recognized under U.S. patent law: (1) laches in suing for infringement and (2) prosecution laches due to patentee-caused delay during examination. Both require unreasonable delay by the patentee and prejudice to the defendant. But neither type of laches is likely to continue to be important.

Patent law already has a six-year statutory limitations period for damages: 35 U.S.C. § 286 states that "no recovery shall be had for any infringement committed more than six years prior to the filing of the complaint or counterclaim for infringement in the action." And in *SCA Hygiene Products Aktiebolag v. First Quality Baby Products*, 137 S. Ct. 954 (2017), the Supreme Court held that laches in suing for infringement can no longer be asserted as a defense against damages that occurred within this six-year period. The six-year statutory limitations period governs, full stop. (Laches can still be an effective defense to a permanent injunction under the *eBay* framework described in Chapter 13.)

Prosecution laches can render a patent unenforceable if there is an unreasonable and unexplained delay in prosecution. This doctrine was reaffirmed as a defense to patent infringement in *Symbol Technologies v. Lemelson Medical*, 277 F.3d 1361, 1364 (Fed. Cir. 2002). Prosecution laches could be important for targeting "submarine patents" that were intentionally delayed at the patent office until the relevant technology matured, but intentional delay became a much less effective strategy after the 1995 shift in patent term from 17 years from issue to 20 years from filing. Now, an applicant who has already filed has nothing to gain (and much to lose) from delaying the issuance of the patent.

Practice Problems: Defenses

You are the general counsel for a small U.S. solar panel manufacturer, SolarCo, and you just received a letter from PatentCo stating that you are infringing one of their patents. Consider each of the following sets of facts. Do they suggest particular defenses that are likely (or unlikely) to be successful?

1. PatentCo failed to search for relevant prior art when applying for the patent.

2. PatentCo searched for prior art when applying for the patent and decided to not disclose one publication because it seemed related to one of the claims, although it does not invalidate the claim.

3. PatentCo has purchased many solar panel patents, and your primary competitors have agreed to license PatentCo's portfolio for what strikes you as an excessive royalty. You request a license agreement on these terms and the firm refuses.

4. PatentCo became aware of SolarCo's infringement five years ago, but because SolarCo was not making any profits then, PatentCo decided to wait for SolarCo's sales to increase before seeking licensing revenue.

5. The asserted patent claims a solar panel design that SolarCo began using 2 years before the patent's effective filing date. Two months ago, SolarCo switched to a different panel design that is also within the scope of PatentCo's asserted patent.

6. The asserted patent claims a manufacturing process that SolarCo is using only for research purposes, with no commercial application.

7. The asserted patent claims an electronic component that you purchased from another U.S. firm, which has a license to the patent with a field-of-use restriction stating that the firm may only sell the component for use in personal computers.

8. The asserted patent claims an electronic component that you purchased from a Japanese manufacturer, which has licensed PatentCo's Japanese patent portfolio but not its U.S. patent portfolio.

IV. Remedies

The following four chapters examine the remedies for patent infringement:

Remedy	Overview
13. Injunctions (§ 283)	Patentees may receive injunctions under § 283 if they satisfy the four-part *eBay* framework. Injunctions are more likely if the parties are in a competitive relationship, if the patentee can show lost sales or loss of goodwill, or if the patentee consistently refuses to license to others. They are less likely if the patented invention is a small component of a complex product.
14. Lost Profits Damages (§ 284)	Lost profits are available under § 284 if the patentee satisfies the four-part *Panduit* test, including by showing the absence of acceptable noninfringing alternatives. The goal of patent damages is to put the patentee in the position they would have occupied but for the infringement.
15. Reasonable Royalties (§ 284)	If a patentee cannot prove lost profits, § 284 states that damages shall be "in no event less than a reasonable royalty," which is calculated based on a hypothetical arms-length negotiation before infringement began.
16. Enhanced Damages and Attorneys' Fees (§§ 284–85)	§ 284 also allows the court to "increase the damages up to three times," and § 285 permits the award of attorneys' fees "in exceptional cases." The Supreme Court recently rejected the Federal Circuit's rigid tests for limiting these awards.

As one measure of the relative frequency of different types of damages rewards: The legal analytics site Lex Machina has recorded 440 federal district court patent cases that led to a damages award during the decade from 2011 through 2020. Of these, 30% included an award of lost profits, 76% included a reasonable royalty, and 28% included enhanced damages. (These numbers exceed 100% because all three types of damages can be awarded in a single case.)

For a valuable overview of all of these remedies—including a comparison to patent remedies in other countries—see Thomas F. Cotter, *Comparative Patent Remedies* (2013).

13. Injunctions

As we noted at the beginning of the book, patents are best understood as a type of property. And as you may recall from your 1L Property class, property can be thought of as a "bundle of rights." That is, to own property is to possess some set of rights, with the type of rights depending on the particular form of property. Patent law conveys only a limited set of rights from this bundle. For instance, recall that patents do not include the right to make or use the subject matter of the patented invention. Even if you own a patent over a particular type of invention, your patent will not protect you from being sued by another patent holder whose rights you might be infringing.

The principal right contained within the patent bundle is the right to exclude. Patents exist to prevent other parties from making, using, or selling the patented invention without the permission of the patent holder. Accordingly, injunctions—the legal mechanism by which exclusion occurs—have long been available to patent holders who prove infringement. Patent injunctions are governed by 35 U.S.C. § 283:

35 U.S.C. § 283

The several courts having jurisdiction of cases under this title may grant injunctions in accordance with the principles of equity to prevent the violation of any right secured by patent, on such terms as the court deems reasonable.

Despite the "may" in this statute, injunctions were almost always granted as a matter of course to prevailing plaintiffs before 2006. Under the Federal Circuit's rules, if a patentee proved infringement at trial, a permanent injunction was essentially guaranteed. The statute's "may" was effectively treated as a bright-line "will." And then, as we have seen in so many areas of patent law, the Supreme Court stepped in to reject the Federal Circuit's formalist, bright-line rules in favor of more flexible standards.

eBay v. MercExchange, 547 U.S. 388 (2006)

Justice Thomas delivered the opinion of the Court.

Ordinarily, a federal court considering whether to award permanent injunctive relief to a prevailing plaintiff applies the four-factor test historically employed by courts of equity. Petitioner eBay Inc. argues that this traditional test applies to disputes arising under the Patent Act. We agree and, accordingly, vacate the judgment of the Court of Appeals.

I

Petitioner eBay operates a popular Internet Web site that allows private sellers to list goods they wish to sell, either through an auction or at a fixed price. Respondent MercExchange, L.L.C., holds a number of patents, including a business method patent for an electronic market designed to facilitate the sale of goods between private individuals by establishing a central authority to promote trust among participants. *See* U.S. Patent No. 5,845,265. MercExchange sought to license its patent to eBay, as it had previously done with other companies, but the parties failed to reach an agreement. MercExchange subsequently filed a patent infringement suit. A jury found that MercExchange's patent was valid, that eBay had infringed that patent, and that an award of damages was appropriate.

Following the jury verdict, the District Court denied MercExchange's motion for permanent injunctive relief. The Court of Appeals for the Federal Circuit reversed, applying its "general rule that courts will issue permanent injunctions against patent infringement absent exceptional circumstances." We granted certiorari to determine the appropriateness of this general rule.

II

According to well-established principles of equity, a plaintiff seeking a permanent injunction must satisfy a four-factor test before a court may grant such relief. A plaintiff must demonstrate: (1) that it has suffered an irreparable injury; (2) that remedies available at law, such as monetary damages, are inadequate to compensate for that injury; (3) that, considering the balance of hardships between the plaintiff and defendant, a remedy in equity is warranted; and (4) that the public interest would not be disserved by a permanent injunction. *See, e.g., Weinberger v. Romero–Barcelo*, 456 U.S. 305, 311–13 (1982); *Amoco Production Co. v. Gambell*, 480 U.S. 531, 542 (1987). The decision to grant or deny permanent injunctive relief is an act of equitable discretion by the district court, reviewable on appeal for abuse of discretion. *See, e.g., Romero–Barcelo*, 456 U.S. at 320.

These familiar principles apply with equal force to disputes arising under the Patent Act. As this Court has long recognized, "a major departure from the long tradition of equity practice should not be lightly implied." *Id.* Nothing in the Patent Act indicates that Congress intended such a departure. To the contrary, the Patent Act expressly provides that injunctions "may" issue "in accordance with the principles of equity." 35 U.S.C. § 283.

To be sure, the Patent Act also declares that "patents shall have the attributes of personal property," § 261, including "the right to exclude others from making, using, offering for sale, or selling the invention," § 154(a)(1). According to the Court of Appeals, this statutory right to exclude alone justifies its general rule in favor of permanent injunctive relief. But the creation of a right is distinct from the provision of remedies for violations of that right. Indeed, the Patent Act itself indicates that patents shall have the attributes of personal property "[s]ubject to the provisions of this title," 35 U.S.C. § 261, including, presumably, the provision that injunctive relief "may" issue only "in accordance with the principles of equity," § 283.

7   This approach is consistent with our treatment of injunctions under the Copyright Act. Like a patent owner, a copyright holder possesses "the right to exclude others from using his property." *Fox Film Corp. v. Doyal*, 286 U.S. 123, 127 (1932); *see also id.* at 127–28 ("A copyright, like a patent, is at once the equivalent given by the public for benefits bestowed by the genius and meditations and skill of individuals and the incentive to further efforts for the same important objects"). Like the Patent Act, the Copyright Act provides that courts "may" grant injunctive relief "on such terms as it may deem reasonable to prevent or restrain infringement of a copyright." 17 U.S.C. § 502(a). And as in our decision today, this Court has consistently rejected invitations to replace traditional equitable considerations with a rule that an injunction automatically follows a determination that a copyright has been infringed. *See, e.g., New York Times Co. v. Tasini*, 533 U.S. 483, 505 (2001); *Dun v. Lumbermen's Credit Assn.*, 209 U.S. 20, 23–24 (1908).

8   Neither the District Court nor the Court of Appeals below fairly applied these traditional equitable principles in deciding respondent's motion for a permanent injunction. Although the District Court recited the traditional four-factor test, it appeared to adopt certain expansive principles suggesting that injunctive relief could not issue in a broad swath of cases. Most notably, it concluded that a "plaintiff's willingness to license its patents" and "its lack of commercial activity in practicing the patents" would be sufficient to establish that the patent holder would not suffer irreparable harm if an injunction did not issue. But traditional equitable principles do not permit such broad classifications. For example, some patent holders, such as university researchers or self-made inventors, might reasonably prefer to license their patents, rather than undertake efforts to secure the financing necessary to bring their works to market themselves. Such patent holders may be able to satisfy the traditional four-factor test, and we see no basis for categorically denying them the opportunity to do so. To the extent that the District Court adopted such a categorical rule, then, its analysis cannot be squared with the principles of equity adopted by Congress. The court's categorical rule is also in tension with *Continental Paper Bag Co. v. Eastern Paper Bag Co.*, 210 U.S. 405, 422–30 (1908), which rejected the contention that a court of equity has no jurisdiction to grant injunctive relief to a patent holder who has unreasonably declined to use the patent.

9   In reversing the District Court, the Court of Appeals departed in the opposite direction from the four-factor test. The court articulated a "general rule," unique to patent disputes, "that a permanent injunction will issue once infringement and validity have been adjudged." The court further indicated that injunctions should be denied only in the "unusual" case, under "exceptional circumstances" and "in rare instances . . . to protect the public interest." Just as the District Court erred in its

categorical denial of injunctive relief, the Court of Appeals erred in its categorical grant of such relief.

10   Because we conclude that neither court below correctly applied the traditional four-factor framework that governs the award of injunctive relief, we vacate the judgment of the Court of Appeals, so that the District Court may apply that framework in the first instance. In doing so, we take no position on whether permanent injunctive relief should or should not issue in this particular case, or indeed in any number of other disputes arising under the Patent Act. We hold only that the decision whether to grant or deny injunctive relief rests within the equitable discretion of the district courts, and that such discretion must be exercised consistent with traditional principles of equity, in patent disputes no less than in other cases governed by such standards.

11   Accordingly, we vacate the judgment of the Court of Appeals and remand the case for further proceedings consistent with this opinion.

Chief Justice Roberts, with whom Justice Scalia and Justice Ginsburg join, concurring.

12   I agree with the Court's holding that "the decision whether to grant or deny injunctive relief rests within the equitable discretion of the district courts, and that such discretion must be exercised consistent with traditional principles of equity, in patent disputes no less than in other cases governed by such standards," and I join the opinion of the Court. That opinion rightly rests on the proposition that "a major departure from the long tradition of equity practice should not be lightly implied."

13   From at least the early 19th century, courts have granted injunctive relief upon a finding of infringement in the vast majority of patent cases. This "long tradition of equity practice" is not surprising, given the difficulty of protecting a right to *exclude* through monetary remedies that allow an infringer to *use* an invention against the patentee's wishes—a difficulty that often implicates the first two factors of the traditional four-factor test. This historical practice, as the Court holds, does not *entitle* a patentee to a permanent injunction or justify a *general rule* that such injunctions should issue. The Federal Circuit itself so recognized in *Roche Products, Inc. v. Bolar Pharmaceutical Co.*, 733 F.2d 858, 865–67 (1984). At the same time, there is a difference between exercising equitable discretion pursuant to the established four-factor test and writing on an entirely clean slate. "Discretion is not whim, and limiting discretion according to legal standards helps promote the basic principle of justice that like cases should be decided alike." *Martin v. Franklin Capital Corp.*, 546 U.S. 132, 139 (2005). When it comes to discerning and applying those standards, in this area as others, "a page of history is worth a volume of logic." *New York Trust Co. v. Eisner*, 256 U.S. 345, 349 (1921) (opinion for the Court by Holmes, J.).

Justice Kennedy, with whom Justice Stevens, Justice Souter, and Justice Breyer join, concurring.

14   The Court is correct, in my view, to hold that courts should apply the well-established, four-factor test—without resort to categorical rules—in deciding whether to grant injunctive relief in patent cases. The Chief Justice is also correct that history may be instructive in applying this test. (concurring opinion). The traditional practice of issuing injunctions against patent infringers, however, does not seem to rest on "the difficulty of protecting a right to *exclude* through monetary remedies that allow an infringer to *use* an invention against the patentee's wishes." (Roberts, C.J., concurring). Both the terms of the Patent Act and the traditional view of injunctive relief accept that the existence of a right to exclude does not dictate the remedy for a violation of that right. To the extent earlier cases establish a pattern of granting an injunction against patent infringers almost as a matter of course, this pattern simply illustrates the result of the four-factor test in the contexts then prevalent. The lesson of the historical practice, therefore, is most helpful and instructive when the circumstances of a case bear substantial parallels to litigation the courts have confronted before.

15   In cases now arising trial courts should bear in mind that in many instances the nature of the patent being enforced and the economic function of the patent holder present considerations quite unlike earlier cases. An industry has developed in which firms use patents not as a basis for producing and selling goods but, instead, primarily for obtaining licensing fees. *See* FTC, *To Promote Innovation: The Proper Balance of Competition and Patent Law and Policy*, ch. 3, pp. 38–39 (Oct. 2003). For these firms, an injunction, and the potentially serious sanctions arising from its violation, can be employed as a bargaining tool to charge exorbitant fees to companies that seek to buy licenses to practice the patent. When the patented invention is but a small component of the product the companies seek to produce and the threat of an injunction is employed simply for undue leverage in negotiations, legal damages may well be sufficient to compensate for the infringement and an injunction may not serve the public interest. In addition injunctive relief may have different consequences for the burgeoning number of patents over business methods, which were not of much economic and legal significance in earlier times. The potential vagueness and suspect validity of some of these patents may affect the calculus under the four-factor test.

16   The equitable discretion over injunctions, granted by the Patent Act, is well suited to allow courts to adapt to the rapid technological and legal developments in the patent system. For these reasons it should be recognized that district courts must determine whether past practice fits the circumstances of the cases before them. With these observations, I join the opinion of the Court.

Discussion Questions: Injunctions

1. *When Are Property Rules More Efficient?* In other law school classes, you have likely encountered the distinction between protecting legal entitlements with property rules (injunctions) versus liability rules (damages), perhaps with reference

to the classic article on this point: Guido Calabresi & A. Douglas Melamed, *Property Rules, Liability Rules, and Inalienability: One View of the Cathedral*, 85 Harv. L. Rev. 1089 (1972). You have also likely encountered the "Coase theorem": that if transaction costs are sufficiently low, bargaining will lead to the efficient outcome regardless of the initial entitlement. R. H. Coase, *The Problem of Social Cost*, 3 J.L. & Econ. 1 (1960). How do these ideas apply to patent law? If the patentee's entitlement is treated as a property rule with an injunction, does that mean that the infringer necessarily must cease his activities? (Why not?) When is it more efficient to choose an injunction over damages?

To answer this question, you might consider: How efficiently can the parties bargain? As transaction costs rise, liability rules become more appealing. What determines how large or small the transaction costs are? For instance, imagine two types of products: a chemical covered by a single patent, and a smartphone covered by thousands of patents (or more). Which product's manufacturer will face higher transaction costs in bargaining with all of the potential patent owners? As noted in Chapter 1, the problem of needing to clear many uncertain and overlapping patent rights is referred to as the problem of "patent thickets."

On the other side, how difficult is it for courts to assess damages? Is clearing rights through court-enforced damages easier than through private licenses? If judicial damages awards are particularly error-prone or administratively costly, property rules may be the better choice. You should keep this question in mind as you learn the doctrines governing monetary damages in the following chapters.

Over four decades after authoring his famous article with Guido Calabresi, Doug Melamed drew on this framework in the context of patent remedies in an article with IP legend Bill Lee (who also happens to be the first Asian-American to lead a major U.S. law firm). *See* William F. Lee & A. Douglas Melamed, *Breaking the Vicious Cycle of Patent Damages*, 101 Cornell L. Rev. 385 (2016). They argue that existing patent remedies were developed in an era "in which technology users are presumed to be able to discover relevant patents in advance and either design around them or negotiate patent licenses before using the patented technology"—which is quite different from the reality of many high-tech fields today. How should patent law adapt to the changing nature of technology?

2. *Factors 1 and 2: Irreparable Injury and Inadequate Remedies at Law.* The first two factors of the *eBay* test are redundant: if monetary damages are adequate to repair the patentee's injury, then the injury is not irreparable. The Federal Circuit has been more likely to hold an injury to be irreparable with money damages if the parties are in a competitive relationship, if the patentee can show lost sales or loss of goodwill, or if the patentee consistently refuses to license to other parties. To establish irreparable harm, the Federal Circuit has held that "a patentee must establish that a sufficiently strong causal nexus relates the alleged harm to the alleged infringement," which requires a showing that "the infringing feature drives consumer demand for the

accused product—in other words, that consumers bought the accused product because it was equipped with [the claimed invention]." *TEK Global., S.R.L. v. Sealant Sys. Int'l*, 920 F.3d 777, 792 (Fed. Cir. 2019).

What are the circumstances under which we should expect that monetary damages will not be adequate? Patent infringement cases do not typically involve issues of human dignity, liberty, or other such values where money can be an inadequate substitute. They are primarily about money. This is one regard in which patent law plausibly diverges from copyright law. Copyright owners sometimes argue that some aspect of their personhood is embedded in their copyrighted works, and someone else's unauthorized (and perhaps scandalous) use of that work enacts a dignitary harm to their personhood. But one does not commonly hear patent owners complain that unauthorized sales of their inventions harm their dignity. For that matter, suppose that a firm will lose goodwill from infringement. What prevents that from being valued as part of the monetary damages calculation as well?

Perhaps the best way to think of factors 1 and 2 is as directed not to the question of when monetary damages will be inadequate, but instead to when monetary damages will be hard to calculate accurately. *Cf. Apple v. Samsung Elecs.*, 809 F.3d 633, 645 (Fed. Cir. 2015) (holding that factor 2 "strongly weighs in favor" of the patentee because the monetary losses "are very difficult to quantify"). In that vein, consider the discussion of property rules and liability rules in Note 1. Does that type of analysis provide a better basis for analyzing factors 1 and 2?

3. *Factor 3: Balance of Hardships*. The third factor of the *eBay* test balances the plaintiff's irreparable harm against the harm to the defendant. The harm to the defendant is smaller if the activity is a small part of the defendant's business or if the defendant could easily switch to a noninfringing alternative. But courts do not consider the inevitable costs to the defendant of stopping infringement and losing revenue—this is a risk the infringer takes. Why should the harm to the defendant from being forced to cease infringement matter? Suppose that the infringing product is the defendant's entire business, and ceasing infringement will devastate the defendant's bottom line. Why should this affect whether the court awards an injunction? After all, this is to say that the defendant's business is built entirely on infringing behavior. Would it matter if, when the defendant designed its product to include the patented technology, the technology was claimed only by a non-public pending patent application? In some cases, injunctions have allowed continued use for short periods using "sunset provisions" that provide time to design around the patent where an immediate injunction would be likely to put the infringer out of business.

4. *Factor 4: Public Interest*. What sorts of issues should the court take into account under the heading of the "public interest"? Courts don't consider the public interest in competition and lower prices; remember that patents are *designed* to allow the patentee to exclude competitors and charge supracompetitive prices. But the public interest may be disserved by an injunction if it would completely deprive the

public of access to an essential product; for example, injunctions on medical technologies without acceptable substitutes would disrupt patient care. What other issues should the court consider? Suppose that the allegedly infringing technology involves the national defense. Should a court consider whether issuing an injunction will affect national security? Should it account for the potential harm to the employees or other stakeholders in the infringing firm?

5. *Combining the Factors.* The Supreme Court is not entirely clear on whether the four *eBay* factors should be weighed in a balancing test or whether they are mandatory elements that must be established, and different Circuits have approached this question differently. The Federal Circuit has at times described them as mandatory elements. *See Nichia v. Everlight Americas*, 855 F.3d 1328, 1344 (Fed. Cir. 2017) ("Because [the patentee] failed to establish one of the four equitable factors, the court did not abuse its discretion in denying [the patentee's] request for an injunction."). How do you think the factors should be combined? More generally, do these seem like the key considerations for determining whether an injunction should be granted? Are there other factors you would consider?

6. *Chief Justice Roberts Versus Justice Kennedy.* Every Supreme Court justice joined the majority and agreed that "[n]either the District Court nor the [Federal Circuit] fairly applied these traditional equitable principles." But the two concurrences raised very different visions of how the new *eBay* test should be applied in practice. Justice Roberts wrote that "there is a difference between exercising equitable discretion pursuant to the established four-factor test and writing on an entirely clean slate." Justice Kennedy, by contrast, wrote that "it should be recognized that district courts must determine whether past practice fits the circumstances of the cases before them." What exactly do the Justices mean by those phrases, and what do they disagree on? Which view do you find more compelling? Which concurrence do you think Lee and Melamed would side with?

7. *The Kennedy Concurrence and the Problem of Holdup.* Justice Kennedy refers to an industry "in which firms use patents not as a basis for producing and selling goods but, instead, primarily for obtaining licensing fees" and warns that in some cases "the threat of an injunction is employed simply for undue leverage in negotiations." At first blush, this concern may be difficult to understand. What does it mean to have "undue" leverage in negotiations? A patent holder has whatever leverage the patent provides. If the patented technology is essential, the patent holder might have a great deal of leverage, but this would seem appropriate. If the patent is easily engineered around, it provides much less leverage.

Part of the answer to this question lies with the fact that Justice Kennedy is referring specifically to *non-practicing entities* (NPEs) that do not make or sell a product, sometimes pejoratively termed "patent trolls." One particular concern with non-practicing entities is that (by definition) they do not make a substitute product for the one being accused of infringement. That means that if the infringing product is forced off the market due to an injunction, the public loses access to it. This was potentially at issue in *eBay*, because eBay is a practicing entity and MercExchange was not. Why would the non-practicing entity want to force the practicing entity out of the market? If it did so, no one would earn any money. The patent would become worthless. Can you envision how a service like eBay might end up being shut down by an injunction even though that would be in neither party's interest?

Another part of the explanation is the threat of *patent holdup*. Holdup occurs when a party has already made technology-specific investments that would become worthless (or much less valuable) if an injunction prevents the party from producing the technology. To understand the problem, consider the following stylized example:

Suppose that A invents a new type of widget. A estimates that building a specialized factory to produce widgets will cost $50, and actually producing a number of widgets will cost an additional $50. But A will then be able to sell these widgets for $110, thus earning a profit of $10. After A has spent $50 to build the factory, but before A has constructed any widgets, A learns that B owns a patent that covers the same technology. B sues A for patent infringement and obtains an injunction. If A were perfectly rational, how much would A be willing to pay B to lift the injunction? Hint: the answer is not $9.99, which would leave A with the minimal profit of $0.01.

The correct answer is $59.99. The reason is that after having already invested $50 in building the factory (a sunk cost), A stands to gain $60 if it is able to manufacture and sell the widgets: $110 in sales minus $50 in production cost. A should thus be willing to pay up to $59.99 to lift the injunction, which would leave it with a gain of $0.01 (compared with the current status quo). But if A pays B $59.99, that would leave A with total expenses of $159.99 and total revenues of $110, for a loss of $49.99—less than the net loss of $50 if the injunction is not lifted, but not a business plan A would have embarked on at the outset. Even if A only pays B $30, half of what it stands to gain from lifting the injunction, it will lose $20 (costs of $130, revenues of $110) on the whole transaction. If A could repurpose its factory for other ends without paying to lift the injunction, thus preserving its value, A would not be in such a pickle. But if the factory can only be used to produce widgets, B has A over a barrel and can hold up A for an exorbitant licensing fee. This problem is not limited to NPEs—B could hold up A even if B were a productive firm—but it has been particularly salient in that context.

A legal policymaker focused on efficiency should not necessarily care whether A has to pay B a lot or a little. That is just a transfer from A to B and does not represent social loss or waste. The problem is what hold-up does to A's ex ante incentives. If A thinks that it might later be held up, it may shy away from developing the widget technology in the first place. And A may be unable to assess its risk of hold-up if it cannot locate B's patent, or if B's patent is still being examined. If A refrains from inventing and producing the widget for fear of later being held up, *that* would create social loss.

One solution to the hold-up problem is simply to award monetary damages. This can be thought of as another reason to favor monetary damages over injunctions, though again there is the question of whether the court will be able to assess damages accurately. If you were a court evaluating the hypothetical situation above, what amount of damages would you award to B? Is there amount that would reward the contributions of both A and B without greatly diminishing either's incentives?

8. *Anticommons and Royalty Stacking.* Imagine a product, like a smartphone, that is covered by a large number of patents, each of which involves a technology that is essential to the creation of the smartphone. This is known as an "anticommons": many different parties (the patent owners) each have the ability to block the overall invention from being assembled. One feature of an anticommons is that it can create substantial transaction costs for the party attempting to assemble all of the individual pieces of property. This is the problem of "patent thickets" we discussed in Note 1, above. Another feature is that it can create opportunities for one or more parties to hold up the product's manufacturer; this is the problem we discussed in Note 7, above. Yet another feature is that it can give rise to "holdout" problems (not to be confused with "holdup" problems), in which each individual patent holder wants to "hold out" and be the last to strike a deal with the product's manufacturer. There is value to being last because it creates greater opportunities for holdup or, more generally, to extract a high licensing fee. When the manufacturer is negotiating with the first parties to license their patents, the amount it is willing to pay is necessarily moderated by its knowledge that it will have to pay many others in the future and the probability that striking deals with all of them will turn out to be impossible. For the last mover, these problems dissipate, and the manufacturer's willingness to pay increases. But if everyone is trying to be last, it may be difficult or impossible for the manufacturer to ever strike deals with all of the patent holders.

In addition to these concerns, there is another problem with anticommons situations: royalty stacking. Each individual patent owner will look to license its patent at whatever quasi-monopoly price will maximize its own returns. Stacking one profit-maximizing price on top of another will raise the overall price of the good beyond even the monopoly price that a single firm would charge if it controlled all of the relevant patents. *See* Mark A. Lemley & Carl Shapiro, *Patent Holdup and Royalty Stacking*, 85 Tex. L. Rev. 1991 (2007). The mathematics behind this phenomenon are complicated, but the intuition is simply that more than one firm will be looking to maximize its profits, and paying all of them is more expensive than just paying one.[1] And as the price rises, fewer people will be able to afford the invention.

Of course, this issue, like many of the others described above, looms largest when a patented product is covered by many patents, and not just one or two. There

---

[1] Depending on the structure of the industry in which it arises, this phenomenon is sometimes referred to as the "double marginalization" effect and sometimes as the "Cournot complements" effect.

are some industries, such as electronics, where most products are likely to incorporate large numbers of patents, and some industries, such as small-molecule pharmaceutical drugs, where most products involve a much smaller number of patents. Does this suggest that courts should be more inclined to grant injunctions in some industries than others? For an argument that patent law is actually quite industry-specific and should remain so, despite its nominal facial neutrality, see Dan L. Burk & Mark A. Lemley, *Policy Levers in Patent Law*, 89 Va. L. Rev. 1575, 1577 (2003).

Practice Problems: Injunctions

For each of the following examples, do you think the court should grant an injunction to the victorious patent owner? If so, should the injunction begin to run immediately, or should the court delay the injunction for a period of time, such as to allow the infringer time to design around the patent? If the patents do not cover the entire product, should the court enjoin the infringer from making or selling the entire product or just the infringing features?

1. The patent owner is a manufacturer of emergency repair kits for fixing punctured vehicle tires. The infringer did not infringe a patent covering the entire repair kit, but it infringed patents covering features that drive consumer demand for the kit. The patent owner introduced evidence at trial that it had lost customers to the infringer in the years leading up to its successful lawsuit. The repair kit is the plaintiff's only product, and the plaintiff risks being driven out of business if an infringer is permitted to continue selling the product, even if it is paid royalties. A number of customers have already placed orders for the infringer's (infringing) product, which they expect to be filled within the next nine months. If the infringer is prohibited from producing any additional products, those customers may not be able to obtain the products they have ordered. *See TEK Global v. Sealant Sys. Int'l*, 920 F.3d 777 (Fed. Cir. 2019).

2. The patent owner and infringer are competitors in the market for a controlled-release painkiller covered by the patent. At trial, the court found that the patent owner had lost market share to the infringer as a result of the infringement. This loss had forced the patent owner to cut its sales force, reduce its promotional expenses, and change its research and development strategies. The court also found that the patent owner was at risk of harm to its reputation as a result of having had to lay off much of its sales force, which could in turn make the company a less attractive place to work in the future or reduce the value of its brand name with potential consumers. *See Endo Pharm. Inc. v. Teva Pharm. USA, Inc.*, 731 F. App'x 962 (Fed. Cir. 2018).

3. The patent owner (Apple) and infringer (Samsung) are competitors in the market for smartphones. The patents cover a variety of smartphone features,

including the "slide-to-unlock" mechanism and software that detects phone numbers and hyperlinks within smartphone applications. The patent owner demonstrated that competition from the infringer had caused it to lose sales and market share. The infringing features were not the sole driver of demand for the product, but the patent owner was able to demonstrate that at least some small fraction of the demand for its product was created by the infringing features. This included evidence that the infringer had directly copied the infringing features, along with emails from engineers working for the infringer who disparaged alternative features they had considered. It also included survey evidence that consumers valued these features and were willing to pay more for a smartphone that included them.

The monetary harm to the patent owner is hard to quantify because the patent owner sells a variety of other products and services related to its smartphone. A decrease in smartphone sales will reduce sales of these related products and services, but it is difficult to determine in what amount. If the injunction is granted, some of the infringer's products would have to be removed from store shelves, where they are currently available for sale. Some of the infringer's customers would also be in violation of the injunction if they continued to use their smartphones. *See Apple v. Samsung*, 809 F.3d 633 (Fed. Cir. 2015).

14. Lost Profits Damages

Patent plaintiffs often seek monetary damages to remedy infringing conduct. As illustrated in the figure below, even if a preliminary or permanent injunction is granted, damages may be awarded to compensate for infringement that occurred before the injunction. Damages are awarded unless an injunction was granted before infringement began. And the decreased availability of injunctions after *eBay* has placed greater importance on damages calculations, including as a remedy for ongoing infringement after the lawsuit has concluded.

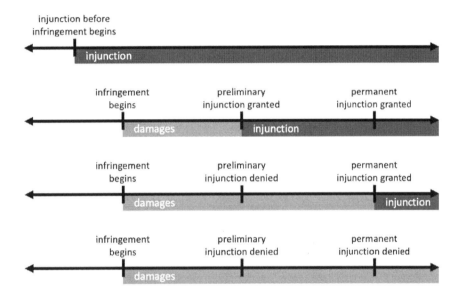

Patent damages are covered by section 284 of the Patent Act:

35 U.S.C. § 284

Upon finding for the claimant the court shall award the claimant damages adequate to compensate for the infringement, but in no event less than a reasonable royalty for the use made of the invention by the infringer, together with interest and costs as fixed by the court.

When the damages are not found by a jury, the court shall assess them. In either event the court may increase the damages up to three times the amount found or assessed. Increased damages under this paragraph shall not apply to provisional rights under section 154(d) [providing in certain cases "the right to obtain a reasonable royalty" for the period between when a patent application is published and when it is granted].

The court may receive expert testimony as an aid to the determination of damages or of what royalty would be reasonable under the circumstances.

As indicated by the first paragraph of this statute, ordinary patent damages are intended "to compensate for the infringement," meaning to put the plaintiff in the position she would have occupied but for the infringement. This compensatory goal is different from other potential remedial goals, including restitution (taking away the defendant's benefit even if it is larger than the plaintiff's loss) and punitive damages (deterring and punishing the defendant's wrongful conduct). These other goals are sometimes served by the second paragraph of § 284, which allows the court to "increase the damages up to three times." We will discuss these "enhanced" damages in Chapter 16.

Putting the plaintiff in the position she would have occupied but for the infringement is challenging because it requires the court to construct the counterfactual. What would have happened in the hypothetical world in which the infringement had not occurred? Consider some of the possibilities:

- The patentee might have made all or some of the infringer's sales—that is, the infringement may have caused the patentee to have lost profits.

- The infringer might have made all or some of the same sales by switching to a similarly priced noninfringing substitute.

- The infringer's sales might not have occurred at all; the market might have simply been smaller.

- The patentee might have granted the infringer a license to the patent in exchange for a reasonable royalty on the infringer's sales.

Can you imagine other possibilities? Patent law divides damages into two categories: *lost profits* and *reasonable royalties*. If the patentee can prove that she has lost profits, these tend to be the largest damages. If the patentee cannot prove lost profits—including because of noninfringement substitutes or the patentee's inability to exploit the demand—§ 284 guarantees that she will receive "in no event less than a reasonable royalty."

This chapter focuses on lost profits, and Chapter 15 explains how reasonable royalties are calculated. We begin this chapter with a brief overview of the economics of monopoly pricing before turning to the caselaw. But as we discuss the complex economic and doctrinal framework for each form of damages, do not lose sight of the overall goal: determining what would actually have happened in the market but for the infringement. Damages determinations often involve expert testimony and economic models, but you should not allow these models to get in the way of common sense. Just as patent litigation does not require a technical degree, it does not require an economics degree, and patent litigators need to be able to explain the underlying principles at an intuitive level to lay judges and jurors. This is an area with few hard-and-fast rules, so it is useful to be able to think of different counterfactual scenarios, and what kind of evidence might support them.

Monopoly Pricing 101

At first glance, one might think that calculating lost profits damages is easy,

in that courts could just attribute the infringer's sales and profits to the patentee. If the patentee would have had a monopoly but for the infringement, and the infringer made profits of $100 million, then the patentee lost profits of $100 million, right? Unfortunately, no. This kind of analysis has logical flaws in both directions: it can undercompensate and overcompensate the patentee.

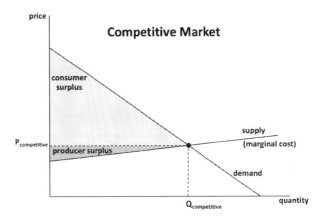

To understand these flaws, we provide a crash course on monopoly pricing. As noted in Chapter 1, few patents truly confer monopoly power, but a simple monopoly market illustrates conceptual principles that apply in many patent damages calculations. For students who have taken a course in economics or who find graphs helpful to illustrate economic principles, the simplified figures at right may be useful, but understanding the graphs isn't essential for understanding the underlying economic logic.

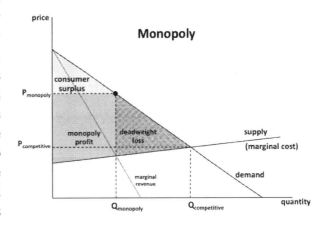

For most products, a small number of people would be willing to pay very high prices, and many more people would be willing to pay more modest amounts. For example, if pencils cost $1000 each, some pencils would be purchased by wealthy consumers who value the ability to

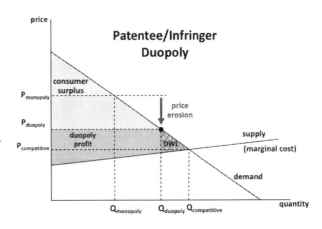

erase, but if pencils are priced at $1 each, demand would be much higher. This principle is represented by downward-sloping demand curves.

In a competitive market, if one supplier prices pencils at $1000 each, another would be able to steal the entire market by offering $900 pencils. Firms would have incentives to keep entering at lower prices until the market price equals the price of supplying another pencil (known as the marginal cost); based on current pencil prices, this appears to be under $0.10. This market benefits consumers who value pencils at more than $0.10 (a benefit known as consumer surplus) and producers who are able to supply pencils at less than $0.10 (producer surplus).

Consider what happens if we give one producer a monopoly on pencils. What price would they choose? They wouldn't raise prices as high as possible, as this would result in very few sales and few profits. But they also wouldn't sell at the competitive price. Rather, they would raise prices to the point that maximizes their profits—the blue area in the monopoly pricing graph. (In economic terms, the producer chooses the price at which their marginal revenue equals their marginal cost.)

Now suppose an infringer enters the market, so it becomes a duopoly rather than a monopoly. The infringer has an incentive to set a price lower than the monopoly price to steal market share from the patentee, and the patentee has an incentive to respond by lowering its own prices, an effect known as *price erosion*. If the patentee had chosen the profit-maximizing price, price erosion leads to a reduction in overall profits from the market. The size of the reduction is difficult to model. The two firms could compete the price down to the competitive price, but in practice, duopoly prices often fall between the competitive and monopoly prices (such as due to tacit collusion between the firms).

It should now be apparent why simply attributing the infringer's profits to the patentee can lead to *undercompensation*: if the infringer's market entrance created price erosion, then the duopoly profits will be less than the monopoly profits the patentee would have made but for the infringement. We have illustrated this point in a monopoly market for simplicity, but the price erosion that can be caused by the market entrance of an infringer generalizes to more common situations in which the patentee has market power that allows it to charge prices above marginal cost but not so much market power that it can charge the monopoly price. Of course, the extent of erosion depends on the details of the market, including how sensitive consumption is to price—an economic factor known as *elasticity of demand*—and the extent to which the infringer actually competed the price down. Furthermore, "in a credible economic analysis, the patentee cannot show entitlement to a higher price divorced from the effect of that higher price on demand for the product ... the patentee must also present evidence of the (presumably reduced) amount of product the patentee would have sold at the higher price." *Crystal Semiconductor v. TriTech Microelectronics Int'l*, 246 F.3d 1336, 1357 (Fed. Cir. 2001). These are the kinds of details each party's damages expert will debate.

Why might attributing the infringer's profits to the patentee lead to *overcompensation*? So far, we have treated the products sold in this market as fungible, such that consumers are indifferent between products sold by the patentee and the infringer. Can you think of any market in which all consumers are truly indifferent to the producer? Even for pencils, there are elementary school teachers who insist on Ticonderoga brand pencils for their classrooms. If the infringer hadn't entered the market, the infringer's customers might not have purchased from the patentee. Perhaps some would not have purchased anything. Perhaps some would have bought an alternative product that isn't infringing. Perhaps the patent holder wouldn't have had the manufacturing and marketing capacity to meet the additional demand created by the entry of the infringer. Consider how the Federal Circuit addresses these concerns in the following two cases.

Rite-Hite v. Kelley Co., 56 F.3d 1538 (Fed.Cir.1995) (en banc)

Alan Lourie, Circuit Judge.

1   Kelley Company appeals from a decision of the United States District Court for the Eastern District of Wisconsin, awarding damages for the infringement of U.S. Patent 4,373,847, owned by Rite-Hite Corporation. The district court determined, *inter alia,* that Rite-Hite was entitled to lost profits for lost sales of its devices that were in direct competition with the infringing devices, but which themselves were not covered by the patent in suit. The appeal has been taken *in banc* to determine whether such damages are legally compensable under 35 U.S.C. § 284. We affirm in part, vacate in part, and remand.

Background

2   [Rite-Hite sued Kelley for infringement of the '847 patent, which is directed to a device for securing a vehicle to a loading dock. The patent was held to be not invalid and infringed by Kelley's "Truk Stop" vehicle restraint.]

3   Rite-Hite sought damages calculated as lost profits for two types of vehicle restraints that it made and sold: the "Manual Dok–Lok" model 55 (MDL–55), which incorporated the invention covered by the '847 patent, and the "Automatic Dok–Lok" model 100 (ADL–100), which was not covered by the patent in suit. The ADL–100 was the first vehicle restraint Rite-Hite put on the market and it was covered by one or more patents other than the patent in suit. The Kelley Truk Stop restraint was designed to compete primarily with Rite-Hite's ADL–100. Both employed an electric motor and functioned automatically, and each sold for $1,000–$1,500 at the wholesale level, in contrast to the MDL–55, which sold for one-third to one-half the price of the motorized devices. Rite-Hite does not assert that Kelley's Truk Stop restraint infringed the patents covering the ADL–100.

4   Of the 3,825 infringing Truk Stop devices sold by Kelley, the district court found that, "but for" Kelley's infringement, Rite-Hite would have made 80 more sales of its MDL–55; 3,243 more sales of its ADL–100; and 1,692 more sales of dock levelers, a bridging platform sold with the restraints and used to bridge the edges of a vehicle and dock. The court awarded Rite-Hite as a manufacturer the wholesale profits that it lost on lost sales of the ADL–100 restraints, MDL–55 restraints, and restraint-leveler packages. [It also awarded a reasonable royalty on other sales.]

5   On appeal, Kelley contends that the district court erred as a matter of law in its determination of damages. Kelley does not contest the award of damages for lost sales of the MDL–55 restraints; however, Kelley argues (1) that the patent statute does not provide for damages based on Rite-Hite's lost profits on ADL–100 restraints because the ADL–100s are not covered by the patent in suit; and (2) lost profits on unpatented dock levelers are not attributable to demand for the '847 invention and, therefore, are not recoverable losses. [Other issues on appeal are omitted.]

Discussion

I. Lost Profits on the ADL–100 Restraints

6   The district court's decision to award lost profits damages pursuant to 35 U.S.C. § 284 turned primarily upon the quality of Rite-Hite's proof of actual lost profits. The court found that, "but for" Kelley's infringing Truk Stop competition, Rite-Hite would have sold 3,243 additional ADL–100 restraints and 80 additional MDL–55 restraints.

7   Kelley maintains that Rite-Hite's lost sales of the ADL–100 restraints do not constitute an injury that is legally compensable by means of lost profits. It has uniformly been the law, Kelley argues, that to recover damages in the form of lost profits a patentee must prove that, "but for" the infringement, it would have sold a product covered by the patent in suit to the customers who bought from the infringer. Under the circumstances of this case, in Kelley's view, the patent statute provides only for damages calculated as a reasonable royalty. Rite-Hite, on the other hand, argues that the only restriction on an award of actual lost profits damages for patent infringement is proof of causation-in-fact. A patentee, in its view, is entitled to all the profits it would have made on any of its products "but for" the infringement. Each party argues that a judgment in favor of the other would frustrate the purposes of the patent statute.

8   Our analysis of this question necessarily begins with the patent statute. The statute [§ 284] mandates that a claimant receive damages "adequate" to compensate for infringement. Section 284 further instructs that a damage award shall be "in no event less than a reasonable royalty"; the purpose of this alternative is not to direct the form of compensation, but to set a floor below which damage awards may not fall. Thus, the language of the statute is expansive rather than limiting. It affirmatively

states that damages must be adequate, while providing only a lower limit and no other limitation.

9   The Supreme Court spoke to the question of patent damages in *General Motors*, stating that, in enacting § 284, Congress sought to "ensure that the patent owner would in fact receive full compensation for 'any damages' [the patentee] suffered as a result of the infringement." *General Motors v. Devex*, 461 U.S. 648, 654 (1983). Thus, while the statutory text states tersely that the patentee receive "adequate" damages, the Supreme Court has interpreted this to mean that "adequate" damages should approximate those damages that will *fully compensate* the patentee for infringement.

10   In *Aro Mfg. Co. v. Convertible Top Replacement Co.*, 377 U.S. 476 (1964), the Court discussed the statutory standard for measuring patent infringement damages, explaining:

> The question to be asked in determining damages is "how much had the Patent Holder and Licensee suffered by the infringement. And that question [is] primarily: had the Infringer not infringed, what would the Patentee Holder–Licensee have made?"

377 U.S. at 507 (plurality opinion). This surely states a "but for" test. In accordance with the Court's guidance, we have held that the general rule for determining actual damages to a patentee that is itself producing the patented item is to determine the sales and profits lost to the patentee because of the infringement.

11   *Panduit Corp. v. Stahlin Bros. Fibre Works, Inc.*, 575 F.2d 1152 (6th Cir. 1978), articulated a four-factor test that has since been accepted as a useful, but non-exclusive, way for a patentee to prove entitlement to lost profits damages. The *Panduit* test requires that a patentee establish: (1) demand for the patented product; (2) absence of acceptable non-infringing substitutes; (3) manufacturing and marketing capability to exploit the demand; and (4) the amount of the profit it would have made. A showing under *Panduit* permits a court to reasonably infer that the lost profits claimed were in fact caused by the infringing sales, thus establishing a patentee's *prima facie* case with respect to "but for" causation. A patentee need not negate every possibility that the purchaser might not have purchased a product other than its own, absent the infringement. The patentee need only show that there was a reasonable probability that the sales would have been made "but for" the infringement. When the patentee establishes the reasonableness of this inference, e.g., by satisfying the *Panduit* test, it has sustained the burden of proving entitlement to lost profits due to the infringing sales. The burden then shifts to the infringer to show that the inference is unreasonable for some or all of the lost sales.

12   Applying *Panduit*, the district court found that Rite-Hite had established "but for" causation. In the court's view, this was sufficient to prove entitlement to lost profits damages on the ADL–100. Kelley does not challenge that Rite-Hite meets the *Panduit* test and therefore has proven "but for" causation; rather, Kelley argues that

damages for the ADL–100, even if in fact caused by the infringement, are not legally compensable because the ADL–100 is not covered by the patent in suit.

13   Preliminarily, we wish to affirm that the "test" for compensability of damages under § 284 is not solely a "but for" test in the sense that an infringer must compensate a patentee for any and all damages that proceed from the act of patent infringement. Notwithstanding the broad language of § 284, judicial relief cannot redress every conceivable harm that can be traced to an alleged wrongdoing. For example, remote consequences, such as a heart attack of the inventor or loss in value of shares of common stock of a patentee corporation caused indirectly by infringement are not compensable. Thus, along with establishing that a particular injury suffered by a patentee is a "but for" consequence of infringement, there may also be a background question whether the asserted injury is of the type for which the patentee may be compensated.

14   Judicial limitations on damages, either for certain classes of plaintiffs or for certain types of injuries have been imposed in terms of "proximate cause" or "foreseeability." Such labels have been judicial tools used to limit legal responsibility for the consequences of one's conduct that are too remote to justify compensation.

15   We believe that under § 284 of the patent statute, the balance between full compensation, which is the meaning that the Supreme Court has attributed to the statute, and the reasonable limits of liability encompassed by general principles of law can best be viewed in terms of reasonable, objective foreseeability. If a particular injury was or should have been reasonably foreseeable by an infringing competitor in the relevant market, broadly defined, that injury is generally compensable absent a persuasive reason to the contrary. Here, the court determined that Rite-Hite's lost sales of the ADL–100, a product that directly competed with the infringing product, were reasonably foreseeable. We agree with that conclusion. Being responsible for lost sales of a competitive product is surely foreseeable; such losses constitute the full compensation set forth by Congress, as interpreted by the Supreme Court, while staying well within the traditional meaning of proximate cause. Such lost sales should therefore clearly be compensable.

16   Recovery for lost sales of a device not covered by the patent in suit is not of course expressly provided for by the patent statute. Express language is not required, however. Statutes speak in general terms rather than specifically expressing every detail. Under the patent statute, damages should be awarded "where necessary to afford the plaintiff full compensation for the infringement." *General Motors*, 461 U.S. at 654. Thus, to refuse to award reasonably foreseeable damages necessary to make Rite-Hite whole would be inconsistent with the meaning of § 284.

17   Kelley asserts that to allow recovery for the ADL–100 would contravene the policy reason for which patents are granted: "[T]o promote the progress of . . . the useful arts." U.S. Const., art. I, § 8, cl. 8. Because an inventor is only entitled to exclusivity to the extent he or she has invented and disclosed a novel, nonobvious, and

useful device, Kelley argues, a patent may never be used to restrict competition in the sale of products not covered by the patent in suit. In support, Kelley cites antitrust case law condemning the use of a patent as a means to obtain a "monopoly" on unpatented material.

18   The present case does not involve expanding the limits of the patent grant in violation of the antitrust laws; it simply asks, once infringement of a valid patent is found, what compensable injuries result from that infringement, i.e., how may the patentee be made whole. Rite-Hite is not attempting to exclude its competitors from making, using, or selling a product not within the scope of its patent. The Truk Stop restraint was found to infringe the '847 patent, and Rite-Hite is simply seeking adequate compensation for that infringement; this is not an antitrust issue. Allowing compensation for such damage will "promote the Progress of . . . the useful Arts" by providing a stimulus to the development of new products and industries.

19   Kelley further asserts that, as a policy matter, inventors should be encouraged by the law to practice their inventions. This is not a meaningful or persuasive argument, at least in this context. A patent is granted in exchange for a patentee's disclosure of an invention, not for the patentee's use of the invention. There is no requirement in this country that a patentee make, use, or sell its patented invention. If a patentee's failure to practice a patented invention frustrates an important public need for the invention, a court need not enjoin infringement of the patent. Whether a patentee sells its patented invention is not crucial in determining lost profits damages. Normally, if the patentee is not selling a product, by definition there can be no lost profits. However, in this case, Rite-Hite did sell its own patented products, the MDL–55 and the ADL–100 restraints.

20   [T]he only *Panduit* factor that arguably was not met in the present fact situation is the second one, absence of acceptable non-infringing substitutes. Here, the only substitute for the patented device was the ADL–100, another of the patentee's devices. Such a substitute was not an "acceptable, non-infringing substitute" within the meaning of *Panduit* because, being patented by Rite-Hite, it was not available to customers except from Rite-Hite. Rite-Hite therefore would not have lost the sales to a third party. The second *Panduit* factor thus has been met. If, on the other hand, the ADL–100 had not been patented and was found to be an acceptable substitute, that would have been a different story, and Rite-Hite would have had to prove that its customers would not have obtained the ADL–100 from a third party in order to prove the second factor of *Panduit*.

21   Kelley's conclusion that the lost sales must be of the patented invention thus is not supported. Kelley's concern that lost profits must relate to the "intrinsic value of the patent" is subsumed in the "but for" analysis; if the patent infringement had nothing to do with the lost sales, "but for" causation would not have been proven. However, "but for" causation is conceded here. The motive, or motivation, for the infringement is irrelevant if it is proved that the infringement in fact caused the loss.

We see no basis for Kelley's conclusion that the lost sales must be of products covered by the infringed patent.

II. Damages on the Dock Levelers

22   The district court awarded lost profits on 1,692 dock levelers that it found Rite-Hite would have sold with the ADL–100 and MDL–55 restraints. Kelley argues that this award must be set aside. We agree.

23   When a patentee seeks damages on unpatented components sold with a patented apparatus, courts have applied a formulation known as the "entire market value rule" to determine whether such components should be included in the damage computation, whether for reasonable royalty purposes or for lost profits purposes. We have held that the entire market value rule permits recovery of damages based on the value of a patentee's entire apparatus containing several features when the patent-related feature is the "basis for customer demand."

24   The entire market value rule has typically been applied to include in the compensation base unpatented components of a device when the unpatented and patented components are physically part of the same machine. The rule has been extended to allow inclusion of physically separate unpatented components normally sold with the patented components. However, in such cases, the unpatented and patented components together were considered to be components of a single assembly or parts of a complete machine, or they together constituted a functional unit.

25   Thus, the facts of past cases clearly imply a limitation on damages, when recovery is sought on sales of unpatented components sold with patented components, to the effect that the unpatented components must function together with the patented component in some manner so as to produce a desired end product or result. All the components together must be analogous to components of a single assembly or be parts of a complete machine, or they must constitute a functional unit. Our precedent has not extended liability to include items that have essentially no functional relationship to the patented invention and that may have been sold with an infringing device only as a matter of convenience or business advantage. We are not persuaded that we should extend that liability. Damages on such items would constitute more than what is "adequate to compensate for the infringement."

26   The facts of this case do not meet this requirement. The dock levelers operated to bridge the gap between a loading dock and a truck. The patented vehicle restraint operated to secure the rear of the truck to the loading dock. Although the two devices may have been used together, they did not function together to achieve one result and each could effectively have been used independently of each other. The parties had established positions in marketing dock levelers long prior to developing the vehicle restraints. Rite-Hite and Kelley were pioneers in that industry and for many years were primary competitors. Although following Rite-Hite's introduction of its restraints onto the market, customers frequently solicited package bids for the

simultaneous installation of restraints and dock levelers, they did so because such bids facilitated contracting and construction scheduling, and because both Rite-Hite and Kelley encouraged this linkage by offering combination discounts. The dock levelers were thus sold by Kelley with the restraints only for marketing reasons, not because they essentially functioned together.

27   We distinguish our conclusion to permit damages based on lost sales of the unpatented (not covered by the patent in suit) ADL–100 devices, but not on lost sales of the unpatented dock levelers, by emphasizing that the Kelley Truk Stops were devices competitive with the ADL–100s, whereas the dock levelers were merely items sold together with the restraints for convenience and business advantage. It is a clear purpose of the patent law to redress competitive damages resulting from infringement of the patent, but there is no basis for extending that recovery to include damages for items that are neither competitive with nor function with the patented invention. These facts do not establish the functional relationship necessary to justify recovery under the entire market value rule. Therefore, the district court erred as a matter of law in including them within the compensation base. Accordingly, we vacate the court's award of damages based on the dock leveler sales.

28   [The remainder of the majority's opinion addresses separate issues and is omitted.]

Helen Nies, Circuit Judge, with whom Glenn Archer, Chief Judge, Edward Smith, Senior Circuit Judge, and Haldane Mayer, Circuit Judge join, dissenting-in-part.

29   The majority uses the provision in 35 U.S.C. § 284 for "damages" as a tool to expand the property rights granted by a patent. I dissent.

30   No one disputes that Rite-Hite is entitled to "full compensation for any damages suffered as a result of the infringement." *General Motors Corp. v. Devex Corp.*, 461 U.S. 648, 653–54 (1983). "Damages," however, is a word of art. Damages in a legal sense means the compensation which the law will award for an injury done. Thus, the question is, "What are the injuries for which full compensation must be paid?"

31   The majority divorces "actual damages" from injury to patent rights. The majority holds that a patentee is entitled to recover its lost profits caused by the infringer's competition with the patentee's business in ADL restraints, products not incorporating the invention of the patent in suit but assertedly protected by other unlitigated patents. Indeed, the majority states a broader rule for the award of lost profits on any goods of the patentee with which the infringing device competes, even products in the public domain.

32   I would hold that the diversion of ADL–100 sales is not an injury to patentee's property rights granted by the '847 patent. To constitute legal injury for which lost profits may be awarded, the infringer must interfere with the patentee's property

right to an exclusive market in goods embodying the invention of the patent in suit. The patentee's property rights do not extend to its market in other goods unprotected by the litigated patent. Rite-Hite was compensated for the lost profits for 80 sales associated with the MDL–55, the only product it sells embodying the '847 invention. That is the totality of any possible entitlement to lost profits. Under 35 U.S.C. § 284, therefore, Rite-Hite is entitled to "damages" calculated as a reasonable royalty on the remainder of Kelley's infringing restraints.

33   An examination of pre–1946 Supreme Court precedent discloses that the legal scope of actual damages for patent infringement was limited to the extent of the defendant's interference with the patentee's market in goods embodying the invention of the patent in suit. This limitation reflects the underlying public policy of the patent statute to promote commerce in new products for the public's benefit. More importantly, it protects the only property rights of a patentee which are protectable, namely those granted by the patent.

34   An inventor is entitled to a patent by meeting the statutory requirements respecting disclosure of the invention. Prior commercialization of the invention has never been a requirement in our law to *obtain* a patent. An inventor is merely required to teach others his invention in his patent application. Thus, when faced with the question of whether a patentee was entitled to enjoin an infringer despite the patentee's failure to use its invention, the Supreme Court held for the patentee. *Continental Paper Bag*, 210 U.S. 405, 424–430 (1908).

35   These clearly established principles, however, do not lead to the conclusion that the patentee's failure to commercialize plays no role in determining damages. That the *quid pro quo* for *obtaining* a patent is disclosure of the invention does not dictate the answer to the question of the legal scope of damages. The patent system was not designed merely to build up a library of information by disclosure, valuable though that is, but to get new products into the marketplace during the period of exclusivity so that the public receives full benefits from the grant.

36   Thus, a patentee may withhold from the public the benefit of use of its invention during the patent term, and the public has no way to withdraw the grant for nonuse. Like the owner of a farm, a patentee may let his property lay fallow. In doing so, "he has but suppressed his own." *E. Bement & Sons v. National Harrow*, 186 U.S. 70, 90 (1902). But it is anomalous to hold that Congress, by providing an incentive for the patentee to enter the market, intended the patentee to be rewarded the same for letting his property lay fallow during the term of the patent as for making the investment necessary to commercializing a new product or licensing others to do so, in order that the public benefits from the invention.

37   In the majority's view, the consideration of patent rights ends upon a finding of infringement. The separate question of damages under its test does not depend on patent rights but only on foreseeable competitive injury. This position cannot be squared with the premise that compensation is due only for injury to patent rights.

Thus, the majority's foreseeability standard contains a false premise, namely, that the "relevant market" can be "broadly defined" to include all competitive truck restraints made by the patentee. The *relevant* market for determining damages is confined to the market for the invention in which the patentee holds exclusive property rights. The injury, thus, must be to the protected market in goods made in accordance with the patent, not unprotected truck restraints. In sum, patent rights determine not only infringement but also damages.

38   Nothing in the statute supports the majority's "foreseeability" rule as the sole basis for patent damages. To the contrary, no-fault liability is imposed on "innocent" infringers, those who have no knowledge of the existence of a patent until suit is filed. While unknowing infringers cannot "foresee" any injury to the patentee, they are subject to liability for damages, including lost profits, for competition with the patentee's patented goods. Now they will be liable for diverting sales of the patentee's unprotected competitive products as well.

39   If damages are awardable based on lost sales of a patentee's business in established products not protected by the patent in suit, the patentee not only has an easier case as a matter of proof, but also would receive *greater* benefits in the form of lost profits on its established products than if the patentee had made the investment necessary to launch a new product. This result is not in accordance with the purpose of the patent statute. Actual damages are meant to compensate a patentee for losing the reward of the marketplace which the patentee's use of the invention would otherwise reap. Without such loss, Congress has mandated compensation in the form of a reasonable royalty.

40   It cannot be disputed that Congress intended that the patent grant provide an incentive to make investments in patented products during the patent term. If a patentee is rewarded with lost profits on its established products, the incentive is dulled if not destroyed. Why make the investment to produce and market a new drug if the patent on the new discovery not only protects the *status quo* in the market but also provides lost profits for the old?

41   For the foregoing reasons, I would hold that an injury to the patentee's marketing of products protected only by other patents—if at all—does not fall within the grant of rights protected by the '847 patent in suit and is not compensable. Thus, I would vacate the award of lost profits on 3,283 sales based on Rite-Hite's loss of business in ADL–100 restraints and remand for damages to be assessed on the basis of a reasonable royalty for those infringements.

Pauline Newman, Circuit Judge, with whom Circuit Judge Rader joins, concurring-in-part and dissenting-in-part.

42   The court today takes an important step toward preserving damages as an effective remedy for patent infringement. Patent infringement is a commercial tort, and the remedy should compensate for the actual financial injury that was caused by

the tort. Thus I concur in the majority's result with respect to entitlement to damages for lost sales of the ADL–100.

43   Yet the court draws a new bright line, adverse to patentees and the businesses built on patents, declining to make the injured claimants whole. The majority now restricts en banc the patentee's previously existing, already limited right to prove damages for lost sales of collateral items—the so-called "convoyed" sales. Such remedy is now eliminated entirely unless the convoyed item is "functionally" inseparable from the patented item. The court thus propounds a legally ambivalent and economically unsound policy, authorizing damages for the lost sales of the ADL–100 but not those dock levelers that were required to be bid and sold as a package with the MDL–55 and the ADL–100.

44   I know of no law or policy served by eliminating recovery of actual damages when patents are involved. In holding that those injured by the infringement shall not be made whole, the value of the patent property is diminished. The majority's half-a-loaf award, wherein the patentee and the other plaintiffs are denied recovery of a significant portion or all of their proven damages, is an important policy decision.

45   The basic principle of damages law is that the injured party shall be made whole. On the facts on which the district court awarded damages for certain lost sales of dock levelers, the relationships were direct, causation was proved, the scope of recovery was narrow, and the circumstances were unusual. Reversing the district court, the majority holds that if the patented and convoyed items also have a separate market, there can never be recovery for the lost sales of the convoyed items.

46   The record shows that Kelley foresaw the potential loss of dock leveler sales, and that this contributed to Kelley's infringement of Rite-Hite's truck restraint patent. The record shows Kelley and Rite-Hite both bidding on the same restraint/leveler packages. The evidence established that Rite-Hite's loss of 1,692 dock leveler sales was the direct, foreseeable, and indeed intended result of Kelley's infringement.

47   Kelley bore the risk that if it was found to infringe Rite-Hite's restraint patent, it would be liable for compensatory damages on the restraint/leveler packages. By eliminating recovery for this proven loss, this court makes a policy decision contrary to the principles of compensatory damages. Heretofore Federal Circuit precedent treated lost convoyed sales as a matter of fact and proof. I discern no clear error or discretionary abuse in the district court's award of actual damages for these specific lost sales of restraint/leveler packages.

Grain Processing v. American Maize-Products, 185 F.3d 1341 (Fed. Cir. 1999)

Randall Rader, Circuit Judge.

1   The United States District Court for the Northern District of Indiana denied Grain Processing Corporation lost profits for American Maize–Products' infringement of U.S. Patent No. 3,849,194 (the '194 patent). The district court instead awarded Grain Processing a 3% royalty on American Maize's infringing sales.

2   The district court found that American Maize proved that a noninfringing substitute was available, though not on the market or for sale, during the period of infringement. The court found further that this substitute was acceptable to all purchasers of the infringing product and concluded that American Maize rebutted the inference of "but for" causation for Grain Processing's alleged lost sales. Upholding the district court's findings and conclusions, this court affirms.

I.

3   [Claim 12 of the '194 patent, the only claim at issue, claims: "A waxy starch hydrolysate having a dextrose equivalent value between about 5 and about 25 . . ." and other elements. Starch hydrolysates are a category of chemical products used as food additives, and dextrose equivalence (D.E.) is a measure of sugar content, where higher D.E. values indicate greater sweetness and different functional properties. Maltodextrins are starch hydrolysates that have a D.E. of less than 20.]

4   Grain Processing [the assignee of the '194 patent] has manufactured and sold a line of maltodextrins under the "Maltrin" brand name since 1969. The Maltrin line includes "Maltrin M100," a 10 D.E. maltodextrin. None of the Maltrin products, including M100, fall within claim 12 because they are all made from a non-waxy starch.

5   American Maize began selling maltodextrins in 1974. It made and sold several types of maltodextrins, including "Lo–Dex 10," a 10 D.E. waxy starch maltodextrin. American Maize sold Lo–Dex 10 (called Fro–Dex 10 before 1982) during the entire time Grain Processing owned the '194 patent rights, from 1979 until the patent expired in 1991. During this time, however, American Maize used four different processes for producing Lo–Dex 10.

6   [After being sued by Grain Processing for infringement in 1981, American Maize attempted to avoid infringement by switching from Process I to Process II and then Process III, but the Federal Circuit eventually ruled in 1991 that American Maize hadn't used the correct test to measure D.E., so these processes were infringing.]

7   American Maize then adopted a fourth process (Process IV) for producing Lo–Dex 10. In Process IV, American Maize added a second enzyme, glucoamylase, to the reaction. From the time American Maize began experimenting with the glucoamylase-

alpha amylase combination, or the "dual enzyme method," it took only two weeks to perfect the reaction and begin mass producing Lo–Dex 10 using Process IV. According to the finding of the district court, this two-week development and production time is "practically instantaneous" for large-scale production. American Maize did not change any equipment, source starches, or other ingredients from Process III. Glucoamylase has been commercially available and its effect in starch hydrolysis widely known since the early 1970's, before the '194 patent issued. American Maize had not used Process IV to produce Lo–Dex earlier because the high cost of glucoamylase makes Process IV more expensive than the other processes.

8   The parties agree that Process IV yielded only noninfringing Lo–Dex 10 and that consumers discerned no difference between Process IV Lo–Dex 10 and Lo–Dex 10 made by Processes I–III. American Maize used Process IV exclusively to produce Lo–Dex 10 from April 1991 until the '194 patent expired in November 1991, and then switched back to the cheaper Process III.

9   Grain Processing claimed lost profits in the form of lost sales of Maltrin M100, price erosion, and American Maize's accelerated market entry after the patent expired. Grain Processing further claimed that, for any of American Maize's infringing sales not covered by a lost profits award, Grain Processing should receive a 28% royalty. After a three day bench trial, the district court denied lost profits and determined that a 3% reasonable royalty was adequate to compensate Grain Processing.

10   The trial court determined that Grain Processing could not establish causation for lost profits, because American Maize "could have produced" a noninfringing substitute 10 D.E. maltodextrin using Process IV. The district court also found that American Maize's production cost difference between infringing and noninfringing Lo–Dex 10 effectively capped the reasonable royalty award. American Maize showed that it cost only 2.3% more to make noninfringing Process IV products than it did to make infringing Process I–III products. The district court also found that "buyers viewed as equivalent" the Process I–III and Process IV output. The district court concluded that under these facts, American Maize, when faced with a hypothetical offer to license the '194 patent, would not have paid more than a 3% royalty rate. The court concluded that if Grain Processing had insisted on a rate greater than 3% in the hypothetical negotiations, American Maize instead would have chosen to invest in producing noninfringing Lo–Dex 10 with Process IV.

11   Grain Processing appealed the district court's denial of lost profits, alleging that American Maize cannot escape liability for lost profits on the basis of a noninfringing substitute that did not exist during, and was not developed until after, the period of infringement. This court reversed and remanded. This court noted that a product or process must be "available or on the market at the time of infringement" to qualify as an acceptable non-infringing substitute. *Grain Processing VII*, 1997 WL 71726 (Fed. Cir. 1997).

12   On remand, the district court again denied Grain Processing lost profits. The district court found that Process IV was "available" throughout the period of infringement. *Grain Processing VIII*, 979 F. Supp. at 1235.[1]

II.

13   Upon proof of infringement, Title 35, Section 284 provides that "the court shall award [the patent owner] damages adequate to compensate for the infringement but in no event less than a reasonable royalty for the use made of the invention by the infringer." 35 U.S.C. § 284. The phrase "damages adequate to compensate" means "full compensation for 'any damages' [the patent owner] suffered as a result of the infringement." *General Motors Corp. v. Devex Corp.*, 461 U.S. 648, 654 (1983). Full compensation includes any foreseeable lost profits the patent owner can prove. *See Rite-Hite v. Kelley*, 56 F.3d 1538, 1545–47 (Fed. Cir. 1995).

14   To recover lost profits, the patent owner must show "causation in fact," establishing that "but for" the infringement, he would have made additional profits. When basing the alleged lost profits on lost sales, the patent owner has an initial burden to show a reasonable probability that he would have made the asserted sales "but for" the infringement. Once the patent owner establishes a reasonable probability of "but for" causation, "the burden then shifts to the accused infringer to show that [the patent owner's 'but for' causation claim] is unreasonable for some or all of the lost sales." *Rite Hite*, 56 F.3d at 1544.

15   At trial, American Maize proved that Grain Processing's lost sales assertions were unreasonable. The district court adopted Grain Processing's initial premise that, because Grain Processing and American Maize competed head-to-head as the only significant suppliers of 10 D.E. maltodextrins, consumers logically would purchase Maltrin 100 if Lo–Dex 10 were not available. However, the district court found that American Maize proved that Process IV was available and that Process IV Lo–Dex 10 was an acceptable substitute for the claimed invention. In the face of this noninfringing substitute, Grain Processing could not prove lost profits.

---

[1] [Eds: The district court—Judge Frank Easterbrook of the Seventh Circuit, sitting by designation—seemed frustrated with the Federal Circuit for not understanding the point the first time: "I do not wish to be presumptuous, but it seems to me that my opinion did what the court of appeals believes ought to have been done. That is, I found as a matter of fact that a 'noninfringing product' was available 'no later than October 1979.' The Federal Circuit did not conclude that this finding was clearly erroneous; instead it believed that there had been a legal blunder. Yet, as the court of appeals wrote, 'to be an acceptable noninfringing substitute, the product or process must have been available *or* on the market at the time of infringement' (emphasis added). I found and reiterate (a) that noninfringing substitutes for the patented product were on the market at the time of infringement, and (b) that American Maize had 'available' at the critical time a process that would have ensured that its own product did not infringe the patent." The second time around, the Federal Circuit got it.]

16   American Maize concedes that it did not make or sell Lo–Dex 10 from Process IV until 1991, after the period of infringement. However, an alleged substitute not "on the market" or "for sale" during the infringement can figure prominently in determining whether a patentee would have made additional profits "but for" the infringement. As this court stated in *Grain Processing VII*, "to be an acceptable non-infringing substitute, the product or process must have been available *or* on the market at the time of infringement." 1997 WL 71726, at *2. This statement is an apt summary of this court's precedent, which permits available alternatives—including but not limited to products on the market—to preclude lost profits damages.

17   In *Aro Manufacturing*, the Supreme Court stated that the statutory measure of "damages" is "the difference between [the patent owner's] pecuniary condition after the infringement, and what his condition would have been if the infringement had not occurred." *Aro Mfg. Co. v. Convertible Top Replacement Co.*, 377 U.S. 476, 507 (1964) (plurality opinion). The determinative question, the Supreme Court stated, is: "had the Infringer not infringed, what would the Patent Holder–Licensee have made?" *Id.* at 507. The "but for" inquiry therefore requires a reconstruction of the market, as it would have developed absent the infringing product, to determine what the patentee "would . . . have made." *See Grain Processing VIII*, 979 F. Supp. at 1236.

18   Reconstructing the market, by definition a hypothetical enterprise, requires the patentee to project economic results that did not occur. To prevent the hypothetical from lapsing into pure speculation, this court requires sound economic proof of the nature of the market and likely outcomes with infringement factored out of the economic picture. Within this framework, trial courts, with this court's approval, consistently permit patentees to present market reconstruction theories showing all of the ways in which they would have been better off in the "but for world," and accordingly to recover lost profits in a wide variety of forms. *See, e.g., King Instruments v. Perego*, 65 F.3d 941, 953 (Fed. Cir. 1995) (upholding award for lost sales of patentee's unpatented goods that compete with the infringing goods); *Rite-Hite*, 56 F.3d at 1550 (holding that a patentee may recover lost profits on components that have a functional relationship with the patented invention); *Brooktree v. Advanced Micro Devices*, 977 F.2d 1555, 1580 (Fed. Cir. 1992) (upholding award for price erosion due to infringer's marketing activities); *Minnesota Mining & Mfg. v. Johnson & Johnson Orthopaedics*, 976 F.2d 1559, 1579 (Fed. Cir. 1992) (upholding award for price erosion due to infringing sales); *State Indus. v. Mor-Flo*, 883 F.2d 1573, 1580 (Fed. Cir. 1989) (upholding award of lost profits in proportion to patentee's market share of the relevant market including acceptable noninfringing substitutes); *Paper Converting Mach. v. Magna–Graphics*, 745 F.2d 11, 22 (Fed. Cir. 1984) (upholding award compensating the patentee for its decreasing marginal cost of producing the good, i.e., its increasing marginal profit, as its volume of production would have increased); *Lam v. Johns-Manville*, 718 F.2d 1056, 1065 (Fed. Cir. 1983) (upholding lost profits award for future lost sales, and for the patentee's increased promotional expenses); *BIC Leisure Products v. Windsurfing Int'l*, 687 F. Supp. 134, 137–38 (S.D.N.Y. 1988), *rev'd in part on other grounds*, 1 F.3d 1214 (Fed. Cir. 1993)

(permitting recovery for future depressed prices, i.e., "projected price erosion," and for accelerated market reentry by the infringer). In sum, courts have given patentees significant latitude to prove and recover lost profits for a wide variety of foreseeable economic effects of the infringement.

19   By the same token, a fair and accurate reconstruction of the "but for" market also must take into account, where relevant, alternative actions the infringer foreseeably would have undertaken had he not infringed. Without the infringing product, a rational would-be infringer is likely to offer an acceptable noninfringing alternative, if available, to compete with the patent owner rather than leave the market altogether. The competitor in the "but for" marketplace is hardly likely to surrender its complete market share when faced with a patent, if it can compete in some other lawful manner. Moreover, only by comparing the patented invention to its next-best available alternative(s)—regardless of whether the alternative(s) were actually produced and sold during the infringement—can the court discern the market value of the patent owner's exclusive right, and therefore his expected profit or reward, had the infringer's activities not prevented him from taking full economic advantage of this right. Thus, an accurate reconstruction of the hypothetical "but for" market takes into account any alternatives available to the infringer.

20   Accordingly, this court in *Slimfold Manufacturing Co. v. Kinkead Industries, Inc.* held that an available technology not on the market during the infringement can constitute a noninfringing alternative. 932 F.2d 1453 (Fed. Cir. 1991). In *Slimfold*, the patent owner (Slimfold) claimed lost profits on its bi-fold doors with a patented pivot and guide rod assembly. This court noted, however, that Slimfold did not show "that the alleged infringer [Kinkead] would not have made a substantial portion or the same number of sales *had it continued with its old hardware* or with the hardware utilized by any of the other companies." *Id.* at 1458. On the basis of this noninfringing substitute, which was not on the market at the time of infringement, this court affirmed the district court's denial of lost profits. This court determined that the record supported the district court's finding that this noninfringing "old hardware" was available to Kinkead at the time of the infringement. Furthermore, consumers considered Kinkead's noninfringing alternative an acceptable substitute for the infringing doors. Therefore, this court upheld the district court's award of a "small" royalty, rather than lost profits.

21   [The court clarifies some (misguided) dicta from an earlier case, *Zygo v. Wyko*, 79 F.3d 1356 (Fed. Cir. 1996), which had stated that "it is axiomatic that if a device is not available for purchase, a defendant cannot argue that the device is an acceptable noninfringing alternative." This is inconsistent with earlier cases like *Slimfold* and "at most reflects a finding [limited to] the record in *Zygo*."]

22   Grain Processing asserts that permitting the infringer to show substitute availability without market sales, thereby avoiding lost profits, undercompensates for infringement. Section 284, however, sets the floor for "damages adequate to

compensate for the infringement" as "a reasonable royalty." 35 U.S.C. § 284. Thus, the statute specifically envisions a reasonable royalty as a form of adequate compensation. While "damages adequate to compensate" means "full compensation," *General Motors*, 461 U.S. at 654, "full compensation" does not entitle Grain Processing to lost profits in the absence of "but for" causation. *Rite-Hite*, 56 F.3d at 1545. Moreover, although Grain Processing stresses that American Maize should not reap the benefit of its "choice" to infringe rather than use the more expensive Process IV, Grain Processing does not allege willful infringement and the record shows none. To the extent that Grain Processing feels undercompensated,[2] it must point out a reversible error in the district court's fact-finding, reasoning, or legal basis for denying lost profits or in its reasonable royalty determination.[3]

III.

23   This court next turns to the district court's findings that Process IV was in fact "available" to American Maize for producing Lo–Dex 10 no later than October, 1979, and that consumers would consider Process IV Lo–Dex 10 an acceptable substitute. This court reviews these factual findings for clear error. *See Gargoyles v. United States*, 113 F.3d 1572, 1573 (Fed. Cir. 1997); *Slimfold*, 932 F.2d at 1458.

24   The critical time period for determining availability of an alternative is the period of infringement for which the patent owner claims damages, i.e., the "accounting period." Switching to a noninfringing substitute after the accounting period does not alone show availability of the noninfringing substitute during this critical time. When an alleged alternative is not on the market during the accounting period, a trial court may reasonably infer that it was not available as a noninfringing substitute at that time. The accused infringer then has the burden to overcome this inference by showing that the substitute was available during the accounting period. Mere speculation or conclusory assertions will not suffice to overcome the inference. After all, the infringer chose to produce the infringing, rather than noninfringing, product. Thus, the trial court must proceed with caution in assessing proof of the availability of substitutes not actually sold during the period of infringement. Acceptable substitutes that the infringer proves were available during the accounting

---

[2] [n.4 in opinion] The district court's 3% royalty rate yielded damages of approximately $2.4 million; Grain Processing sought lost profits of $35 million, which with applicable interest presently implies an award approaching $100 million.

[3] [n.5 in opinion] The district court appears to have conducted a thorough royalty analysis, challenged by neither party on appeal. The court candidly stated that the 3% rate is its "best estimate," an honest observation that would apply to most reasonable royalty analyses, given the difficulty of determining a hypothetical agreement between parties which did not actually agree on anything at all. The determination is perhaps more difficult when the patentee is not selling the patented product, as is the case here. Nevertheless, the district court supported its royalty amount with sound economic data and with actual, observed behavior in the market. Though both parties maintained at trial that they would not have agreed to a license including 3% royalties at the time of infringement, the appropriateness of the rate is perhaps reflected in the decision of the parties to forego an appeal on this issue.

period can preclude or limit lost profits; substitutes only theoretically possible will not.

25   In this case, the district court did not base its finding that Process IV was available no later than October 1979 on speculation or possibilities, but rather on several specific, concrete factual findings, none of which Grain Processing challenges on appeal. The district court found that American Maize could readily obtain all of the materials needed for Process IV, including the glucoamylase enzyme, before 1979. The court also found that the effects of the enzymes in starch hydrolysis were well known in the field at that time. Furthermore, the court found that American Maize had all of the necessary equipment, know-how, and experience to use Process IV to make Lo–Dex 10, whenever it chose to do so during the time it was instead using Processes I, II or III. American Maize "did not have to 'invent around' the patent," the district court observed; "all it had to do was use a glucoamaylase enzyme in its production process."

26   The trial court also explained that "the sole reason [American Maize did not use Process IV prior to 1991] was economic: glucoamylase is more expensive than the alpha amylase enzyme American Maize had been using," and American Maize reasonably believed it had a noninfringing product. While the high cost of a necessary material can conceivably render a substitute "unavailable," the facts of this case show that glucoamylase was not prohibitively expensive to American Maize. The district court found that American Maize's "substantial profit margins" on Lo–Dex 10 were sufficient for it to absorb the 2.3% cost increase using glucoamylase.

27   Moreover, the district court's unchallenged finding that there is no "economically significant demand for a product having all of the [claimed] attributes" supports its conclusion of availability. Consumers demand "low-dextrose maltodextrins of which the patented product is just one *exemplar*." Because consumers find the "waxy" and "descriptive ratio" elements of claim 12 "irrelevant," the prospect of an available, acceptable noninfringing substitute expands because a competitor may be able to drop or replace the "irrelevant" elements from its product. *Compare Rite-Hite*, 56 F.3d 1538 (upholding lost profits award for patentee's vehicle restraint—not covered by the patent in suit—because the patentee could exclude alleged substitute products with another patent) *with King Instruments*, 65 F.3d 941 (upholding only a *partial* award of lost profits for patentee's tape rewinder—not covered by any patent—due to the availability of alternatives acceptable to some consumers); *see also Panduit*, 575 F.2d at 1156, 1160–61 (holding that consumer demand for the "unique advantages" of the patented invention, as opposed to substitutes lacking some elements, and the infringer's "inability to avoid infringement even if it had wanted to," established the lack of available, acceptable noninfringing alternatives). Grain Processing cannot exclude Process IV Lo–Dex 10 because it does not have a patent on 10 D.E. maltodextrins, "the economically significant product" as the district court stated, but rather on a particular variety of 10 D.E. maltodextrins.

28   This court therefore does not detect, and the parties do not suggest, clear error in the district court's factual findings on the availability of Process IV. These factual findings support the district court's conclusion that Process IV was available to American Maize for making noninfringing Lo–Dex 10, no later than October 1991. American Maize had the necessary chemical materials, the equipment, the know-how and experience, and the economic incentive to produce Lo–Dex 10 by Process IV throughout the entire accounting period. Whether and to what extent American Maize's alleged alternative prevents Grain Processing from showing lost sales of Maltrin 100 depends not only on whether and when the alternative was available, but also on whether and to what extent it was acceptable as a substitute in the relevant market. Consumer demand defines the relevant market and relative substitutability among products therein. Important factors shaping demand may include consumers' intended use for the patentee's product, similarity of physical and functional attributes of the patentee's product to alleged competing products, and price. Where the alleged substitute differs from the patentee's product in one or more of these respects, the patentee often must adduce economic data supporting its theory of the relevant market in order to show "but for" causation.

29   In this case, the parties vigorously dispute the precise scope of the relevant market. The district court's uncontroverted factual findings, however, render this dispute moot. In the eyes of consumers, according to the district court, Process IV Lo–Dex 10 was the same product, for the same price, from the same supplier as Lo–Dex 10 made by other processes. Process IV Lo–Dex 10 was a perfect substitute for previous versions, and therefore Grain Processing's efforts to show a distinct 10 D.E. maltodextrin market do not assist its lost profits case.

30   Market evidence in the record supports the district court's uncontroverted findings and conclusions on acceptability. First, for example, American Maize's high profit margin on Lo–Dex 10 and the consumers' sensitivity to price changes support the conclusion that American Maize would not have raised the price of Process IV Lo–Dex 10 to offset the cost of glucoamylase. Further, American Maize's sales records showed no significant changes when it introduced Process IV Lo–Dex 10 at the same price as previous versions, indicating that consumers considered its important properties to be effectively identical to previous versions. Witness testimony supported this market data. Thus, this court discerns no clear error in the district court's finding that Process IV Lo–Dex 10 was an acceptable substitute in the marketplace.

31   It follows from the district court's findings on availability and acceptability that Grain Processing's theory of "but for" causation fails. As the district court correctly noted, "[a]n [American Maize] using the dual-enzyme method between 1979 and 1991 . . . would have sold the same product, for the same price, as the actual [American Maize] did . . ." and consequently would have retained its Lo–Dex 10 sales. Grain Processing did not present any other evidence of lost profits, such as individual lost transactions as in *Rite-Hite Corp. v. Kelley Co.*, 774 F. Supp. 1514, 1525–26, 1528–

29 (E.D. Wis. 1991), *aff'd in part and vacated on other grounds*, 56 F.3d 1538. Thus, the district court properly determined that, absent infringing Lo–Dex 10, Grain Processing would have sold no more and no less Maltrin 100 than it actually did.

IV.

32   In summary, this court requires reliable economic proof of the market that establishes an accurate context to project the likely results "but for" the infringement. The availability of substitutes invariably will influence the market forces defining this "but for" marketplace, as it did in this case. Moreover, a substitute need not be openly on sale to exert this influence. Thus, with proper economic proof of availability, as American Maize provided the district court in this case, an acceptable substitute not on the market during the infringement may nonetheless become part of the lost profits calculus and therefore limit or preclude those damages.

33   This court concludes that the district court did not err in considering an alternative not on the market during the period of infringement, nor did it clearly err in determining that the alternative was available, acceptable, and precluded any lost profits. Accordingly, the district court did not abuse its discretion in denying lost profits. This court affirms the district court's decision.

Discussion Questions: Lost Profits Damages

1. Panduit *Factors*. Under the four-part *Panduit* test presented in *Rite-Hite*, one way for a patentee to prove entitlement to lost profits damages is to show (1) demand for the patented product; (2) the absence of acceptable noninfringing substitutes; (3) its own manufacturing and marketing capability to exploit the demand; *and* (4) the amount of the profit it would have made. The fourth element of the *Panduit* test is really the ultimate question rather than an independent factor. Why do the other elements make sense as a matter of economic logic? Which do you think are most likely to be contested? How does *Grain Processing* allow infringers to demonstrate acceptable noninfringing substitutes?

2. *Defining the Market*. A key issue in most lost profits cases is how to define the relevant market. The patentee wants the market defined broadly enough to include whatever she is selling, but not so broadly that it includes noninfringing substitutes. What's wrong with just defining the market as "products covered by the patent"? For a discussion of different approaches to defining markets in IP and antitrust law, see Mark A. Lemley & Mark P. McKenna, *Is Pepsi Really a Substitute for Coke? Market Definition in Antitrust and IP*, 100 Geo. L.J. 2055 (2012).

In *Rite-Hite*, the majority held that the patentee could recover lost profits because it was selling a product in the same market as the infringing product, even though the patentee's product was not covered by the patent in suit. What do Judge Nies and the judges who join her dissent think is wrong with this rule? Which view do you find more compelling? What if Rite-Hite were not selling *any* products covered by the patent-in-suit? Which rule creates a stronger incentive for industry consolidation?

How do the courts define the relevant market in each case? If you were representing the losing party in each appeal—the infringer in *Rite-Hite* or the patentee in *Grain Processing*—how would you try to define the market to obtain a different result?

What happens if the patentee is not the only firm in the market other than the infringer? In *State Industries v. Mor–Flo Industries*, 883 F.2d 1573 (Fed. Cir. 1989), the court allowed recovery under a "market-share rule," under which the patent holder can recover for lost sales proportional to its market share. In *Mor–Flo*, the patent owner had a 40% share of the relevant market (the national market for foam water heaters), and the Federal Circuit affirmed an award of lost profits on 40% of the infringing sales and a reasonable royalty on the other 60%. What economic assumptions is the market-share rule premised on? Given the assumption that the patentee would not have made the other 60% of sales, why should it receive a reasonable royalty on those sales?

Antitrust economists have developed more sophisticated tools than *Mor–Flo*'s crude approach for assessing lost market share when products are differentiated (as is the case for most products). *See, e.g.*, Carl Shapiro, *The 2010 Horizontal Merger Guidelines: From Hedgehog to Fox in Forty Years*, 77 Antitrust L.J. 49 (2010). Why do you think these tools aren't reflected in Federal Circuit doctrine on patent damages?

3. *Convoyed Sales.* In *Rite-Hite*, the court states that lost profits for unpatented components sold with patented components are available only when all the components are "analogous to components of a single assembly or be parts of a complete machine, or they must constitute a functional unit." 56 F.3d at 1550. Sale of the functionally related unpatented components is known as a "convoyed sale." Lost profits aren't available if the components don't have a functional relationship and are sold together merely because of customer demand, business convenience, or a marketing advantage. *See, e.g.*, *American Seating Co. v. USSC Group, Inc.*, 514 F.3d 1262 (Fed. Cir. 2008) (no functional relationship between patented wheelchair tie-down restraint system for buses and bus passenger seats from same supplier); *Warsaw Orthopedic, Inc. v. NuVasive, Inc.*, 778 F.3d 1365 (Fed. Cir. 2015) (no functional relationship between patented spinal implants and medical kits with unpatented screws and rods for holding the implants in place). If a patentee can prove that but for the infringement, she would have sold more of the unpatented components, why should the functional relationship matter? *See* Thomas F. Cotter, *Comparative Patent Remedies* 117–18 (2013) ("This rule is somewhat difficult to square with the overall thrust of the *Rite-Hite* opinion, with its emphasis on restoring the patentee to the position it would have occupied but for the infringement.").

4. *Apportionment.* In *Mentor Graphics v. EVE-USA*, 851 F.3d 1275 (Fed. Cir. 2017), the Federal Circuit held that where the *Panduit* test is satisfied, the patent holder is entitled to lost profits for the entire product, even if the patent covers only one component of a multicomponent product. Many commentators argued that this decision contravened the principle that damages should be based on the *value of the patented invention*, not the value of the product incorporating the invention, and that damages must be "apportioned" between those attributable to infringing versus noninfringing features. Do you think this is an important concern? For an argument that these concerns are alleviated by limiting *Mentor Graphics* to its unusual facts— only two market competitors, only one of which holds a patent on an essential feature—see Jason Reinecke, Note, *Lost Profits Damages for Multicomponent Products: Clarifying the Debate*, 71 Stan. L. Rev. 1621 (2019).

5. *Lost Profits for Foreign Sales.* As discussed in Chapter 11, in *WesternGeco LLC v. ION Geophysical Corp.*, 138 S. Ct. 2129 (2018), the Supreme Court held that lost profits are available for foreign sales in cases of infringement under 35 U.S.C. § 271(f). The patent related to a system for surveying the ocean floor, and the patentee demonstrated at trial that it had lost ten specific contracts due to infringement by a firm that manufactured components for a competing system and then shipped them to companies abroad. After *WesternGeco*, what kind of evidence would you look for if you represented an infringer arguing against lost profits for foreign sales?

Practice Problems: Lost Profits Damages

Juting exclusively licensed all substantial rights in her widget patent to Mateo. In 2019, Lizy sold 100 infringing widgets for $2 each. Mateo sued. In 2019, Mateo had the capacity to sell 1000 widgets. Each widget cost him $1 to manufacture, and he ended up selling 500 widgets at $2 each, for a total profit of $500. Lizy's manufacturing cost was $1.50 per widget, so her profits were $50. There are no noninfringing substitutes, and from the perspective of consumers, Mateo's and Lizy's widgets are identical.

1. Based solely on these facts, what damages should Mateo receive?

2. What if Mateo sold only 100 widgets rather than 500?

3. What if Mateo only had capacity to sell 500 widgets?

4. What if Lizy's manufacturing cost was only $0.50 per widget?

5. Mateo asserts that without Lizy's competition, he would have been able to charge $3 per widget. If Mateo can prove this, what would the damages be? How should Lizy respond to this argument?

6. What if Mateo proves that he would have been able to charge $3 per widget, and Lizy shows that at the $3 price, Mateo would have made only 500 sales?

7. What if Mateo shows that if he had made Lizy's 100 additional sales, his manufacturing cost for those additional widgets would have been $0.50 per widget due to economies of scale (and the cost for his first 500 widgets would still be $1 each)?

8. What if Mateo shows that Lizy's competition required him to spend $100 on advertising to maintain his market share?

9. What if Lizy shows that she could have easily switched to selling a noninfringing widget that is still identical to consumers, and which would have cost her $1.75 per widget to manufacture?

10. What if widget sales in 2019 comprised (a) 500 sales by Mateo under the patent, (b) 100 infringing sales by Lizy, and (c) 500 non-infringing sales by Kevin of a version that is identical to consumers, with all sales being made at $2 per widget?

11. What if the widget market is growing, and Mateo argues that the year of infringement damaged his brand and hurt his sales by 10% indefinitely going forward?

12. What if Mateo shows that Lizy's widget sales also caused him to lose sales of doodads needed to make a widget usable to customers, but he does not have a patent on doodads?

13. What if widgets cost Mateo $1 to manufacture regardless of the quantity, and the demand curve is as follows (and widgets can only be made in 100-unit increments)? Hint: If no one else enters the market, what quantity of widgets would Mateo choose to make?

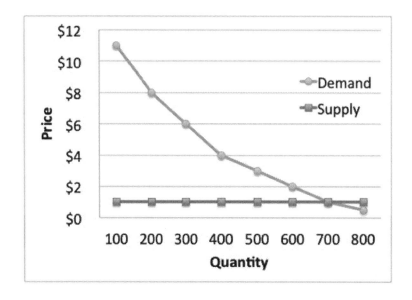

15. Reasonable Royalties

Lost profits damages might be thought of as the most straightforward means of compensating the patent owner for the infringement. But in some cases, a patent owner will be unable to prove lost profits damages. The patent owner might be a non-practicing entity (including, possibly, a research university) that does not manufacture or sell a product. It might instead be in the business of licensing its patents to firms that want to use the technology. Or it might simply have difficulty (or be uninterested) in trying to prove lost profits. As Chapter 14 should make clear, the lost profits calculation can be complex and challenging, given that it requires constructing a counterfactual world in which the infringement did not occur.

To address these circumstances, 35 U.S.C. § 284 allows successful patent plaintiffs to collect damages equal to a "reasonable royalty" for the patent(s) at issue. Just as lost profits damages are meant to compensate the patent holder by awarding it whatever profits it would have made if infringement had not occurred, reasonable royalty damages are meant to compensate the patent holder by awarding it whatever licensing fee it would have negotiated with the infringer had the infringer negotiated rather than infringing. However, just as lost profits can be difficult to calculate because they require constructing a counterfactual marketplace that never existed, so too reasonable royalty damages can be difficult to calculate because they involve constructing a hypothetical negotiation that never took place. The following case explores these issues.

LaserDynamics v. Quanta Computer, 694 F.3d 51 (Fed. Cir. 2012)

Jimmie Reyna, Circuit Judge.

1   These appeals come before us after two trials in the district court—a first trial resolving the claims of patent infringement and damages, and a second trial ordered by the district court to retry the damages issues.

I. Background

The Patented Technology and the Optical Disc Drive Industry

2   LaserDynamics, Inc. is the owner of U.S. Patent No. 5,587,981, which was issued in 1996. The patent is directed to a method of optical disc discrimination that essentially enables an optical disc drive (ODD) to automatically identify the type of optical disc—e.g., a compact disc (CD) versus a digital video disc (DVD)—that is inserted into the ODD. Claim 3, which was asserted at trial, is representative:

3. An optical disk reading method comprising the steps of:

> processing an optical signal reflected from encoded pits on an optical disk until total number of data layers and pit configuration standard of the optical disk is identified;

> collating the processed optical signal with an optical disk standard data which is stored in a memory; and

> settling modulation of servomechanism means dependent upon the optical disk standard data which corresponds with the processed optical signal;

> (c) [sic] the servomechanism means including:

> a focusing lens servo to modulate position of a focusing lens; and

> a tracking servo to modulate movement of a pickup.

3   This automated process saves the user from having to manually identify the kind of disc being inserted before the ODD can begin to read the data on the disc. The patented technology is alleged to be particularly useful in laptop computers where portability, convenience, and efficiency are essential. At least as early as 2006, a laptop computer was not commercially viable unless it included an ODD that could automatically discriminate between optical discs. [Eds: As with many technologies, this success was short-lived; Apple started eliminating ODDs from laptops in 2012, and other firms have followed suit.]

4   Yasuo Kamatani is the sole inventor of the '981 Patent. In 1998, viewing DVD technology as the next major data and video format, Mr. Kamatani founded LaserDynamics and assigned the '981 Patent to the company. Mr. Kamatani is the sole employee of LaserDynamics, which is exclusively in the business of licensing Mr. Kamatani's patents to ODD and consumer electronics manufacturers.

5   When LaserDynamics was founded, the DVD market had reached few mainstream consumers, and there was some skepticism as to the likely success of this technology compared with the established VHS format. By 2000, however, DVD sales and the ODD market were sharply rising. By 2003, most homes had DVD players and nearly every computer had an ODD. An ODD having automatic disc discrimination capability quickly became the industry standard for DVD players and computers.

LaserDynamics' Licensing History of the '981 Patent

6   According to LaserDynamics, it was initially difficult to generate interest in licensing the '981 Patent, due to the novelty of the technology and LaserDynamics' limited operating capital and bargaining power. Nevertheless, LaserDynamics entered into sixteen licensing agreements from 1998 to 2001. These licenses were granted to well known electronics and ODD manufacturers such as Sony, Philips,

NEC, LG, Toshiba, Hitachi, Yamaha, Sanyo, Sharp, Onkyo, and Pioneer. All of the licenses were nonexclusive licenses granted in exchange for one time lump sum payments ranging from \$57,000 to \$266,000. These sixteen licenses were admitted into evidence in the first trial, as explained below.

7   Several other lump sum licenses were granted by LaserDynamics between 1998 and 2003 to other ODD and electronics manufacturers via more aggressive licensing efforts involving actual or threatened litigation by LaserDynamics.

8   On February 15, 2006, LaserDynamics entered into a license agreement with BenQ Corporation to settle a two-year long litigation for a lump sum of \$6 million. This settlement agreement was executed within two weeks of the anticipated trial against BenQ. By the time of the settlement, BenQ had been repeatedly sanctioned by the district court for discovery misconduct and misrepresentation.

9   Finally, in 2009 and 2010, LaserDynamics entered into license agreements with ASUSTeK Computer and Orion Electric Co., Ltd., respectively, for lump sum payments of \$1 million or less.

10   In total, twenty-nine licenses were entered into evidence in the second damages trial. With the exception of the \$6 million BenQ license, all twenty-nine licenses were for lump sum amounts of \$1 million or less.

Quanta Computer Inc. and Quanta Storage Inc.

11   Quanta Storage, Inc. (QSI) is a manufacturer of ODDs that was incorporated in 1999. QSI is headquartered in Taiwan and is a partially-owned subsidiary of Quanta Computer, Inc. (QCI), with which it shares some common officers, directors, and facilities. QCI's corporate headquarters are also located in Taiwan, and its factories are located in China. QCI holds a minority share in QSI and does not control QSI's operations.

12   QCI assembles laptop computers for its various customers, which include name brand computer companies such as Dell, Hewlett Packard (HP), Apple, and Gateway. QCI does not manufacture ODDs, but will install ODDs into computers as instructed by its customers. QSI first sold its ODDs for integration into laptop computers in the United States in 2001. In 2002, LaserDynamics offered QSI a license under the '981 Patent, but QSI disputed whether its ODDs were within the scope of the '981 Patent and declined the offer. QCI sold its first computer in the United States using an ODD from QSI in 2003. It was not until August 2006 that LaserDynamics offered a license to QCI concurrently with the filing of this lawsuit. To date, neither QSI nor QCI has entered into a licensing agreement with LaserDynamics relating to the '981 Patent.

II. Procedural History

13   Based on [pretrial] rulings [on exhaustion and implied licenses], LaserDynamics dropped its claims against QSI and opted to pursue its active

inducement of infringement claims against QCI only at trial. QCI was first on notice of the '981 Patent in August 2006 when the complaint was filed. Between August 2006 and the conclusion of the first trial in June 2009, QCI sold approximately $2.53 billion of accused laptops into the United States. LaserDynamics sought reasonable royalty damages under 35 U.S.C. § 284. Pursuant to the analytical framework for assessing a reasonable royalty set forth in *Georgia-Pacific Corp. v. United States Plywood Corp.*, 318 F. Supp. 1116 (S.D.N.Y. 1970), the date of the "hypothetical negotiation" between the parties was deemed by the district court to be August 2006—the date that QCI first became aware of the '981 Patent and was therefore first potentially liable for active inducement of infringement.

The First Trial

14   The damages theory advanced by LaserDynamics in the first trial was presented chiefly through LaserDynamics' expert, Mr. Emmett Murtha. Mr. Murtha opined that a running royalty of 2% of the total sales of laptop computers by QCI is what the parties would have agreed to as a reasonable royalty had they engaged in a hypothetical negotiation in August 2006.

15   To arrive at his 2% per laptop computer royalty rate, Mr. Murtha began by finding that 6% would be a reasonable royalty rate to pay with respect to an ODD alone. Mr. Murtha reached his conclusion of a 6% per ODD royalty by relying on "comparable rates in two separate licensing programs involving DVDs where the rates were 3.5 in one case and 4 percent in another case." He also relied on "a very comprehensive royalty survey that was done by the Licensing Executive Society in 1997," which he viewed as "a standard textbook for people who are seeking to set reasonable royalty rates." The licensing survey "was across whatever technologies were being licensed by the people who responded," and suggested that in general, across all of those unrelated technologies, "for a minor improvement, we would charge 2 to 5 percent. For a major improvement, we would charge 4 to 8 percent. And for a major breakthrough, 6 to 15 percent . . . ."

16   Based on his discussions with LaserDynamics' other experts, Mr. Murtha concluded that the patented technology in the ODD is responsible for one-third of the value of a laptop computer containing such an ODD. Thus, he arrived at his 2% per laptop computer rate simply by taking one-third of the 6% rate for the ODD. When Mr. Murtha's proffered 2% running royalty rate was applied to QCI's total revenues from sales of laptop computers in the United States—$2.53 billion—the resulting figure presented to the jury was $52.1 million.

17   By contrast, QCI's theory of damages was that a lump sum of $500,000 would be a reasonable royalty. QCI's expert found the 16 licenses in evidence—all lump sums ranging between $50,000 and $266,000—to be highly indicative of the value of the patented technology according to LaserDynamics, and of what a reasonable accused infringer would agree to pay for a license.

The First Jury Verdict and Post–Trial Proceedings

18   The jury ultimately returned a verdict finding QCI liable for active inducement of infringement, and awarded $52 million in damages to LaserDynamics, almost the exact amount proffered by Mr. Murtha. After the verdict, QCI filed a motion for a remittitur or new trial pursuant to Federal Rule of Civil Procedure 59(a). In this motion, QCI argued that the verdict was grossly excessive and against the great weight of the evidence, and for the first time argued that Mr. Murtha's testimony should have been excluded due to his unreliable methodology in applying the "entire market value rule"—i.e., using the revenues from sales of the entire laptop computers as the royalty base—without having established that the patented feature drives the demand for the entire laptop computer. The district court granted QCI's motion, finding that LaserDynamics had indeed improperly invoked the entire market value rule.

The Second Trial

19   [Before and during the second trial on damages, QCI made various objections that are discussed in detail below.] LaserDynamics offered testimony that damages should be $10.5 million based on a running royalty of 6% of the average price of a standalone ODD. QCI's expert testified that the appropriate damages amount was a lump sum payment of $1.2 million, based in large part on the fact that none of the now twenty-nine licenses in evidence (excluding the BenQ settlement) exceeded lump sum amounts of $1 million. Based on evidence that QCI could have switched from QSI drives to other licensed ODD suppliers to avoid infringement at a cost of $600,000, QCI's expert also opined that QCI would have paid twice that amount to have the freedom to use ODDs from any supplier. The jury ultimately awarded a lump sum amount of $8.5 million in damages.

20   [Both parties appealed on multiple grounds.]

III. Discussion

21   For reasons explained in detail below, we hold: [1] that the district court properly granted a new trial on damages following the first jury verdict; . . . [2] that the district court erred by setting the hypothetical negotiation date as August 2006; [3] that the district court erred in admitting the BenQ settlement agreement into evidence; and [4] that the district court erred in permitting Mr. Murtha to offer his opinion concerning a 6% per ODD running royalty rate based on ODD average price as a proper measure of reasonable royalty damages in the second trial. We address each of these issues in turn.

The District Court Properly Granted a New Trial on Damages

22   By statute, reasonable royalty damages are deemed the minimum amount of infringement damages "adequate to compensate for the infringement." 35 U.S.C. § 284. Where small elements of multi-component products are accused of

infringement, calculating a royalty on the entire product carries a considerable risk that the patentee will be improperly compensated for non-infringing components of that product. Thus, it is generally required that royalties be based not on the entire product, but instead on the "smallest salable patent-practicing unit."

23   The entire market value rule is a narrow exception to this general rule. If it can be shown that the patented feature drives the demand for an entire multi-component product, a patentee may be awarded damages as a percentage of revenues or profits attributable to the entire product. *Rite-Hite v. Kelley Co.*, 56 F.3d 1538, 1549, 1551 (Fed. Cir. 1995) (en banc). In other words, "[t]he entire market value rule allows for the recovery of damages based on the value of an entire apparatus containing several features, when the feature patented constitutes the basis for customer demand." *Lucent Techs. v. Gateway*, 580 F.3d 1301, 1336 (Fed. Cir. 2009).

24   Importantly, the requirement to prove that the patented feature drives demand for the entire product may not be avoided by the use of a very small royalty rate. We recently rejected such a contention and clarified that "[t]he Supreme Court and this court's precedents do not allow consideration of the entire market value of accused products for minor patent improvements simply by asserting a low enough royalty rate." *Uniloc USA v. Microsoft*, 632 F.3d 1292, 1319–20 (Fed. Cir. 2011). We reaffirm that in any case involving multi-component products, patentees may not calculate damages based on sales of the entire product, as opposed to the smallest salable patent-practicing unit, without showing that the demand for the entire product is attributable to the patented feature.

25   Regardless of the chosen royalty rate, one way in which the error of an improperly admitted entire market value rule theory manifests itself is in the disclosure of the revenues earned by the accused infringer associated with a complete product rather than the patented component only. In *Uniloc,* we observed that such disclosure to the jury of the overall product revenues "cannot help but skew the damages horizon for the jury, regardless of the contribution of the patented component to this revenue." *Id.* at 1320 (noting that "the $19 billion cat was never put back into the bag," and that neither cross-examination nor a curative jury instruction could have offset the resulting unfair prejudice). Admission of such overall revenues, which have no demonstrated correlation to the value of the patented feature alone, only serve to make a patentee's proffered damages amount appear modest by comparison, and to artificially inflate the jury's damages calculation beyond that which is "adequate to compensate for the infringement." *Id.*; *see* 35 U.S.C. § 284.

26   Turning to the facts of this case, LaserDynamics and Mr. Murtha unquestionably advanced an entire market value rule theory in the first trial. Mr. Murtha opined that a 2% running royalty applied to QCI's total revenues from sales of laptop computers in the United States—$2.53 billion—was an appropriate and reasonable royalty. The resulting figure presented to the jury was $52.1 million, and the jury awarded damages in nearly that exact amount.

27   LaserDynamics' use of the entire market value rule was impermissible, however, because LaserDynamics failed to present evidence showing that the patented disc discrimination method drove demand for the laptop computers. It is not enough to merely show that the disc discrimination method is viewed as valuable, important, or even essential to the use of the laptop computer. Nor is it enough to show that a laptop computer without an ODD practicing the disc discrimination method would be commercially unviable. Were this sufficient, a plethora of features of a laptop computer could be deemed to drive demand for the entire product. To name a few, a high resolution screen, responsive keyboard, fast wireless network receiver, and extended-life battery are all in a sense important or essential features to a laptop computer; take away one of these features and consumers are unlikely to select such a laptop computer in the marketplace. But proof that consumers would not want a laptop computer without such features is not tantamount to proof that any one of those features alone drives the market for laptop computers. Put another way, if given a choice between two otherwise equivalent laptop computers, only one of which practices optical disc discrimination, proof that consumers would choose the laptop computer having the disc discrimination functionality says nothing as to whether the presence of that functionality is what motivates consumers to buy a laptop computer in the first place. It is this latter and higher degree of proof that must exist to support an entire market value rule theory.

28   Our decision in *Lucent* is illustrative. There, the patent at issue involved a helpful and convenient "date picker" feature that was being used within the grand scheme of Microsoft's Outlook email software. We held that because the patented feature was "but a tiny feature of one part of a much larger software program," a royalty could not be properly calculated based on the value of the entire Outlook program because "there was no evidence that anybody anywhere at any time ever bought Outlook . . . *because* it had [the patented] date picker." *Lucent*, 580 F.3d at 1332–33.

29   In this case, Mr. Murtha never conducted any market studies or consumer surveys to ascertain whether the demand for a laptop computer is driven by the patented technology. On the record before us, the patented method is best understood as a useful commodity-type feature that consumers expect will be present in all laptop computers.

30   Furthermore, Mr. Murtha's one-third apportionment to bring his royalty rate down from 6% per ODD to 2% per laptop computer appears to have been plucked out of thin air based on vague qualitative notions of the relative importance of the ODD technology. The district court correctly concluded that "[a]lthough [LaserDynamics] argues that the many activities that may be performed on a computer using a disk drive, such as playing movies, music and games, transferring documents, backing up files, and installing software comprise a third of the value of a computer, [Mr. Murtha] offers no credible economic analysis to support that conclusion." This complete lack of economic analysis to quantitatively support the one-third apportionment echoes the

kind of arbitrariness of the "25% Rule" [as a starting point for royalty calculations] that we recently and emphatically rejected from damages experts, and would alone justify excluding Mr. Murtha's opinions in the first trial.

31   Finally, we reject the contention that practical and economic necessity compelled LaserDynamics to base its royalty on the price of an entire laptop computer. LaserDynamics emphasizes that QCI is in the business of assembling and selling complete laptop computers, not independent ODDs, and that QCI does not track the prices, revenues, or profits associated with individual components. Likewise, LaserDynamics points out that QCI purchases ODDs for a "mask price," which the district court described as "nominal" and essentially "an accounting fiction" that offers "little evidence of the drives' actual value."

32   LaserDynamics overlooks that a per-unit running royalty is not the only form of a reasonable royalty that the parties might have agreed to in a hypothetical negotiation. An alternate form is evidenced by the many license agreements to the '981 Patent in the record for lump sum royalties that are not calculated as a percentage of *any* component or product, which immediately belies the argument that using a laptop computer as the royalty base is "necessary." LaserDynamics' necessity argument also fails to address the fundamental concern of the entire market value rule. If difficulty in precisely identifying the value of the ODDs is what justifies using complete laptop computers as the royalty base, when it comes time to then apportion a royalty rate that accounts for the ODD contribution only, the exceedingly difficult and error-prone task of discerning the ODD's value relative to all other components in the laptop remains.

*The District Court Erred by Setting the Hypothetical Negotiation Date
as August 31, 2006*

33   During both trials, QCI was bound by the district court's ruling that the hypothetical negotiation date for purposes of the *Georgia-Pacific* reasonable royalty analysis was August 2006—i.e., when the lawsuit was filed. The district court reasoned that since QCI was being accused of active inducement of infringement, which requires knowledge of the patent, and since QCI was not notified of the patent until August 2006, this date was when QCI first became liable to LaserDynamics. Based in large part on this late date, LaserDynamics' expert Mr. Murtha testified that he disregarded almost all of LaserDynamics' twenty-nine licenses in evidence that were executed earlier, reasoning that the economic landscape had since changed.

34   We have explained that "[t]he correct determination of [the hypothetical negotiation] date is essential for properly assessing damages." *Integra Lifesciences I, Ltd. v. Merck KGaA*, 331 F.3d 860, 870 (Fed. Cir. 2003). In general, the date of the hypothetical negotiation is the date that the infringement began.

35   We have also been careful to distinguish the hypothetical negotiation date from other dates that trigger infringement liability. For example, the six-year limitation on

recovery of past damages under 35 U.S.C. § 286 does not preclude the hypothetical negotiation date from taking place on the date infringement began, even if damages cannot be collected until some time later. Similarly, the failure to mark a patented product or prove actual notice of the patent pursuant to 35 U.S.C. § 287 precludes the recovery of damages prior to the marking or notice date, but the hypothetical negotiation date may nevertheless be properly set before marking or notice occurs. In sum, "[a] reasonable royalty determination for purposes of making a damages evaluation must relate to the time infringement occurred, and not be an after-the-fact assessment." *Riles v. Shell Exploration & Prod. Co.*, 298 F.3d 1302, 1313 (Fed. Cir. 2002).

36   Here, there is no dispute that while QCI first became liable for active inducement of infringement in August 2006, QCI's sales of accused laptop computers into the United States began causing the underlying direct infringement by end users in 2003. From the premise that the hypothetical negotiation must focus on the date when the infringement began, we note that active inducement of infringement is, by definition, conduct that causes and encourages infringement. Thus, we hold that in the context of active inducement of infringement, a hypothetical negotiation is deemed to take place on the date of the first direct infringement traceable to QCI's first instance of inducement conduct—in this case, 2003.

37   Our holding is consistent with the purpose of the hypothetical negotiation framework, which seeks to discern the value of the patented technology to the parties in the marketplace when infringement began. In considering the fifteen *Georgia-Pacific* factors, it is presumed that the parties had full knowledge of the facts and circumstances surrounding the infringement at that time. Indeed, the basic question posed in a hypothetical negotiation is: if, on the eve of infringement, a willing licensor and licensee had entered into an agreement instead of allowing infringement of the patent to take place, what would that agreement be? This question cannot be meaningfully answered unless we also presume knowledge of the patent and of the infringement at the time the accused inducement conduct began. Were we to permit a later notice date to serve as the hypothetical negotiation date, the damages analysis would be skewed because, as a legal construct, we seek to pin down how the prospective infringement might have been avoided via an out-of-court business solution.

The District Court Erred in Admitting the BenQ Settlement Agreement

38   Before the second trial, QCI filed a motion *in limine* seeking to exclude the 2006 LaserDynamics–BenQ settlement agreement from evidence pursuant to Federal Rule of Evidence 403. QCI's motion emphasized the unique circumstances of the BenQ settlement, which was entered into on the eve of trial after BenQ had been repeatedly sanctioned by the district court. We conclude that the district court abused its discretion in denying QCI's motion and allowing the agreement into evidence.

39   Rule 403 provides for the exclusion of otherwise relevant evidence when the probative value of that evidence is substantially outweighed by the danger of unfair prejudice, confusing the issues, or misleading the jury. Along these lines, Federal Rule of Evidence 408 specifically prohibits the admission of settlement offers and negotiations offered to prove the amount of damages owed on a claim. The notion that license fees that are tainted by the coercive environment of patent litigation are unsuitable to prove a reasonable royalty is a logical extension of *Georgia-Pacific*, the premise of which assumes a voluntary agreement will be reached between a willing licensor and a willing licensee, with validity and infringement of the patent not being disputed. *See* 318 F. Supp. at 1120.

40   Despite the longstanding disapproval of relying on settlement agreements to establish reasonable royalty damages, we recently permitted such reliance under certain limited circumstances. *See ResQNet.com v. Lansa*, 594 F.3d 860, 870–72 (Fed. Cir. 2010) (explaining that a settlement license to the patents-in-suit in a running royalty form was "the most reliable license in [the] record" when compared with other licenses that did not "even mention the patents-in-suit or show any other discernible link to the claimed technology"). We permitted consideration of the settlement license on remand, but we cautioned the district court to consider the license in its proper context within the hypothetical negotiation framework to ensure that the reasonable royalty rate reflects "the economic demand for the claimed technology." *Id.* at 872.

41   Unlike the license in *ResQNet,* the BenQ settlement agreement is far from being the "most reliable license in [the] record." 594 F.3d at 872. Indeed, the BenQ settlement agreement appears to be the least reliable license by a wide margin. The BenQ settlement agreement was executed shortly before a trial—a trial in which BenQ would have been at a severe legal and procedural disadvantage given the numerous harsh sanctions imposed on it by the district court. The $6 million lump sum license fee is six times larger than the next highest amount paid for a license to the patent-in-suit, and ostensibly reflects not the value of the claimed invention but the strong desire to avoid further litigation under the circumstances. LaserDynamics executed twenty-nine licenses for the patent-in-suit in total, the vast majority of which are not settlements of active litigation and do not involve the unique coercive circumstances of the BenQ settlement agreement, and which are therefore far more reliable indicators of what willing parties would agree to in a hypothetical negotiation. Additionally, in light of the changing technological and financial landscape in the market for ODDs, the BenQ settlement, entered into a full three years after the hypothetical negotiation date, is in many ways not relevant to the hypothetical negotiation analysis. This record stands in stark contrast to that in *ResQNet*, where a lone settlement agreement stood apart from all other licenses in the record as being uniquely relevant and reliable. This case is therefore well outside the limited scope of circumstances under which we deemed the settlement agreement in *ResQNet* admissible and probative. The probative value of the BenQ settlement agreement is dubious in that it has very little relation to demonstrated economic demand for the patented technology, and its probative value is greatly outweighed by the risk of

unfair prejudice, confusion of the issues, and misleading the jury. Fed. R. Evid. 403. Accordingly, we conclude that the district court abused its discretion by admitting the BenQ settlement agreement into evidence, and must exclude the agreement from the proceedings on remand.

The District Court Erred in Admitting Mr. Murtha's Opinions Concerning a 6% Royalty Rate Per $41 ODD

42   Because we are remanding to the district court for a new trial on damages under the proper 2003 hypothetical negotiation date, we do not reach QCI's argument that the second jury verdict of an $8.5 million lump sum lacks evidentiary support, so as to entitle QCI to a $1.2 million judgment on damages as a matter of law. However, for the purposes of remand, we do reach QCI's *Daubert* challenge[1] to Mr. Murtha's methodology in the second trial and find that the district court erred in allowing the jury to hear his testimony concerning a 6% royalty rate derived from the Sony-made $41 ODDs.

1. Mr. Murtha's Use of the Sony–Made $41 ODDs

43   QCI argues that Mr. Murtha's testimony in the second trial was unreliable for using a $41 per ODD value that was calculated based on a relatively small sample of about 9,000 non-infringing drives made by Sony, not by QSI. We disagree.

44   LaserDynamics contends that the $41 price of the Sony ODDs was more appropriate than the $28 mask price used in the first trial with respect to QSI-made ODDs. According to LaserDynamics, since QCI does not track prices and revenues of the ODDs that it buys to incorporate into laptop computers, and does not generally sell stand alone ODDs, the $41 Sony-made drives that QCI sells as replacement parts better reflect the market value for ODDs independent of the completed laptop computers. QCI counters that the $41 price was unreliable because it was based on a small sample size of licensed and therefore non-infringing drives, which is irrelevant to the price of the accused drives, and because the record shows that the $28 mask price of the accused QSI-made drives is always higher than the price to the consumer.

45   As the district court explained, "[Mr. Murtha's] approach appears to be a reasonable attempt to value [QCI's] drives based on arms-length transactions. Although the jury may ultimately determine that [Mr. Murtha's] approach is unreasonable, the approach is not subject to a *Daubert* challenge." We conclude that the district court did not abuse its discretion in declining to exclude Mr. Murtha's use of the $41 Sony-made ODDs on *Daubert* grounds.

2. Mr. Murtha's 6% Royalty Rate Per ODD

---

[1] [Eds: Under *Daubert v. Merrell Dow Pharmaceuticals, Inc.*, 509 U.S. 579 (1993), trial judges serve as gatekeepers for expert evidence, excluding testimony that is not reliable and relevant.]

46   QCI contends that Mr. Murtha's opinion that a reasonable royalty in this case would be 6% of each ODD sold within a laptop computer by QCI was unreliable under Federal Rule of Evidence 702 and should have been excluded. We agree.

47   The first of the fifteen factors in *Georgia-Pacific* is "the royalties received by the patentee for the licensing of the patent in suit, proving or tending to prove an established royalty." 318 F. Supp. at 1120. Actual licenses to the patented technology are highly probative as to what constitutes a reasonable royalty for those patent rights because such actual licenses most clearly reflect the economic value of the patented technology in the marketplace.

48   When relying on licenses to prove a reasonable royalty, alleging a loose or vague comparability between different technologies or licenses does not suffice. For example, in *Lucent,* where the patentee had relied on various licenses in the same general computer field without proving a relationship to the patented technology or the accused infringing products, we insisted that the "licenses relied upon by the patentee in proving damages [be] sufficiently comparable to the hypothetical license at issue in suit," and noted that the patentee's failure to prove comparability "weighs strongly against the jury's award" relying on the non-comparable licenses. 580 F.3d at 1325, 1332.

49   Likewise, in *ResQNet*, the patentee's expert "used licenses with no relationship to the claimed invention to drive the royalty rate up to unjustified double-digit levels," and which had no "other discernible link to the claimed technology." 594 F.3d at 870. We rejected this testimony, holding that the district court "must consider licenses that are commensurate with what the defendant has appropriated. If not, a prevailing plaintiff would be free to inflate the reasonable royalty analysis with conveniently selected licenses without an economic or other link to the technology in question." *Id.* at 872.

50   Actual licenses to the patents-in-suit are probative not only of the proper amount of a reasonable royalty, but also of the proper form of the royalty structure. In *Wordtech Systems v. Integrated Network Solutions*, the patentee relied on thirteen patent licenses that it previously granted to third parties. 609 F.3d 1308, 1319 (Fed. Cir. 2010). We rejected the patentee's reliance on eleven of the thirteen licenses for being in the form of a running royalty (whereas the patentee had sought a lump sum payment) and for including royalty rates far lower than the jury returned. *Id.* at 1320–21. The remaining two licenses, although in the form of lump sums, were also rejected for not describing how the lump sums were calculated or the type and volume of products intended to be covered by the licenses. *Id.* at 1320. We ultimately reversed the $250,000 verdict and remanded for a new trial on damages because "the verdict was clearly not supported by the evidence and based only on speculation or guesswork." *Id.* at 1319–22.

51   In this case, the district court denied QCI's *Daubert* motion and permitted Mr. Murtha to testify concerning his opinion of a 6% running royalty rate. However, the

district court insisted that LaserDynamics prove that two DVD-related patent licensing programs and the 1997 Licensing Executives Survey relied on by Mr. Murtha (to the exclusion of the many past licenses for the '981 patent) were sufficiently comparable to the hypothetically negotiated license Mr. Murtha proffered.

52   The DVD-related patent licensing programs did not involve the '981 Patent, and no evidence shows that it even involves a disc discrimination method. The 1997 licensing survey was even further removed from the patented technology, since it was not even limited to any particular industry, but "was across whatever technologies were being licensed by the people who responded." Like the licenses we rejected in *ResQNet*, this licensing evidence relied upon by Mr. Murtha "simply [has] no place in this case." 594 F.3d at 871. Relying on this irrelevant evidence to the exclusion of the many licenses expressly for the '981 Patent served no purpose other than to "to increase the reasonable royalty rate above rates more clearly linked to the economic demand for the claimed technology." *Id.* at 872–73.

53   Aside from the BenQ settlement agreement discussed above, the licenses to the patents-in-suit were all for lump sum amounts not exceeding $1 million. Mr. Murtha's 6% running royalty theory cannot be reconciled with the actual licensing evidence, which is highly probative of the patented invention's economic value in the marketplace, and of the form that a hypothetical license agreement would likely have taken. Although Mr. Murtha conceded that QCI would be aware of LaserDynamics' prior licenses in the hypothetical negotiation, he dismissed the probative value of the licenses because they were entered into between 1998 and 2003, before the August 2006 hypothetical negotiation date. Mr. Murtha reasoned that, by 2006, the DVD market was larger and more established such that the value of the patented technology was better appreciated and LaserDynamics had more bargaining power to insist on a running royalty. Thus, in his view, LaserDynamics' past licenses could not reflect an appropriate royalty for QCI in 2006.

54   This reasoning is not supported by the record, however, which undisputedly shows that by around 2000, the DVDs and ODD markets were already experiencing tremendous growth such that by 2003 those markets were highly saturated. Most of the early lump sum licenses that were summarily rejected by Mr. Murtha were thus entered into when the value of the patented technology was readily apparent and demand was already projected to greatly increase. The resetting of the hypothetical negotiation date to 2003, the date of first direct infringement induced by QCI's conduct, further undercuts Mr. Murtha's reasoning that the licenses to the '981 patent from the 1997 to 2001 time frame were too early to be probative. That the Licensing Executives Survey relied upon by Mr. Murtha—which has no meaningful ties to the patented technology—was created in 1997 highlights the inconsistency in Mr. Murtha's selective reasoning. Such strained reasoning is unreliable and cannot be used to ignore LaserDynamics' long history of licensing the '981 Patent.

55   In sum, the 6% royalty rate was untethered from the patented technology at issue and the many licenses thereto and, as such, was arbitrary and speculative. A new trial is required because the jury's verdict was based on an expert opinion that finds no support in the facts in the record. On remand, LaserDynamics may not again present its 6% running royalty damages theory.

56   As a final matter, we do not hold that LaserDynamics' past licenses create an absolute ceiling on the amount of damages to which it may be entitled, *see* 35 U.S.C. § 284, or that its history of lump sum licenses precludes LaserDynamics from obtaining damages in the form of a running royalty. Full consideration of all the *Georgia-Pacific* factors might well justify a departure from the amount or even the form of LaserDynamics' past licensing practices, given the appropriate evidence and reasoning.

Reasonable Royalties: Discussion Questions

1. *The Date of the Hypothetical Negotiation.* Reasonable royalty damages are based on imagining a hypothetical negotiation that takes place between the patent owner and the infringer "on the eve of infringement." The goal for the court is to reconstruct what would have happened if, instead of infringing, the infringer had negotiated a royalty with the patent holder. Whatever royalty the two parties would have negotiated at that moment is by definition a reasonable royalty. As an initial matter, why does the date of the negotiation matter, particularly in a case such as this one? Why are the parties fighting over a few years?

Note that Quanta is not a direct infringer. The direct infringers are the users who employ the optical disc drive technology. Quanta is liable indirectly for inducing that infringing behavior. Quanta thus did not become liable on the date that direct infringement began (2003). Rather, it only became liable somewhat later, when it acquired the necessary knowledge (2006). Given that fact, why does the court pick the earlier date (2003) as the date of the hypothetical negotiation? Should it have chosen that date, or should it have chosen the date when Quanta's liability began?

What about the questions of hold-up and technology-specific sunk costs we discussed in Chapter 13? Suppose that before a firm begins infringement, it spends $100 million to construct a factory that can only be used to manufacture the infringing technology. Should the court set the date of the hypothetical negotiation after the construction of this factory and on the eve of when infringement begins? Should it take the possibility of hold-up into consideration when determining a reasonable royalty, and increase the royalty paid to the patent owner accordingly? For an argument that reasonable royalties systematically overcompensate due to a failure to account for lock-in costs, see William F. Lee & A. Douglas Melamed, *Breaking the Vicious Cycle of Patent Damages*, 101 Cornell L. Rev. 385 (2016).

2. *Assumptions Built into the Hypothetical Negotiation.* What other types of assumptions should be built into the court's construction of the hypothetical negotiation? The court says that when constructing the hypothetical negotiation, it will "presume knowledge of the patent and of the infringement." This means that the court will imagine that LaserDynamics and Quanta agreed that the patent was infringed at the time they were engaged in the hypothetical negotiation. What about presuming validity of the patent? Should the court similarly presume that LaserDynamics and Quanta agreed that the patent was valid when it constructs the hypothetical negotiation?

Suppose that LaserDynamics and Quanta had in fact negotiated a license in 2003. Do you think both parties would have agreed that the patent was valid and infringed? If the court's goal is to award LaserDynamics the same amount of money that it would have received in an *actual* negotiation, is it appropriate to assume that the patent is valid and infringed?

On the other hand, can you think of a reason why the court might want to assume that the patent is valid and infringed for purposes of constructing the reasonable royalty, even if the parties would not have assumed this if they had negotiated? That is, is there a reason to award LaserDynamics greater damages than it would have received in an actual negotiation in 2003? Suppose that Quanta would have paid LaserDynamics a $1 million licensing fee in 2003, and then the court in 2012 awarded LaserDynamics the same $1 million in reasonable royalty damages. What sorts of incentives does this create for Quanta?

3. *The Entire Market Value Rule.* The court spends a fair amount of time discussing the entire market value rule, which prohibits basing damages on the entire market value of the product being sold unless the patented invention is "driving demand" for the full product. First of all, why would it be inappropriate to use the entire market value in this case? In 2006, it would have been very unlikely that a consumer would have wanted to purchase a computer that could not tell the difference between DVDs and CDs.

Second, more generally, why is the entire market value rule necessary? It is easy to see the attraction of the entire market value rule. A court can easily determine the price of a Quanta computer, the final product being sold; as the case explains, it is much more difficult to determine the true price of some internal component. So, suppose the court allows the reasonable royalty calculation to be based on the entire market value of the product being sold. It can just reduce the royalty rate correspondingly. If the appropriate royalty rate were 5% of some component, it could simply assign a royalty rate of less than 5% to the entire market value of the product. What would be the problem with this approach?

4. *The* Georgia-Pacific *Factors and the Determination of a Royalty Rate.* In order to calculate the appropriate royalty rate, courts look to what are known as the

"*Georgia-Pacific* factors," from *Georgia-Pacific Corp. v. United States Plywood Corp.*, 318 F. Supp. 1116, 1119–20 (S.D.N.Y. 1970). Those factors are:

(1)   Royalties patentee receives for licensing the patent in suit

(2)   Rates licensee pays for use of comparable patents

(3)   Nature and scope of license in terms of exclusivity and territory / customer restrictions

(4)   Licensor's established policy of not licensing the invention

(5)   Commercial relationship between licensor and licensee, such as whether they are competitors or inventor and promoter

(6)   Effect of selling the patented invention on sales of other items not covered by patents by the licensee and licensor

(7)   Duration of patent and term of license

(8)   Established profitability of products made under the patent

(9)   Utility and advantages of patent over old modes and devices

(10) Nature of the patented invention; the character of the commercial embodiment of it as owned and produced by the licensor; and the benefit of those who have used the invention

(11) Extent to which the infringer has made use of the invention and the value of such use

(12) Portion of profit or selling price customarily allowed for the use of the invention

(13) Portion of realizable profit attributable to the invention as distinguished from nonpatented elements

(14) Opinion testimony of qualified experts

(15) Outcome of hypothetical arm's length negotiation at the time the infringement began

Even within an area of law that enjoys multi-factor tests (remember the eight *Wands* factors?), this is a doozy. At the same time, there is nothing magical about any or all of these factors. Not all of them are always relevant, and they're also not exclusive. Other factors that have affected royalty rates include the cost savings to the infringer of adopting the patented technology, the availability of noninfringing alternatives, and the infringer's ability to design around the patent. The best way to think of the *Georgia-Pacific* factors is as ideas to guide a court's consideration of the royalty rate. They have also been subject to plenty of criticism. A recitation of all fifteen factors will not generally be useful to a litigant (or to a student writing a patent law exam response).

Here, the *LaserDynamics* court spends the most time talking about factor 1: other licenses issued for the patent-in-suit. Does that seem like the right approach? Are there reasons a patentee might offer different rates to different licensees? Are there other factors to which the court should have paid greater attention? The court did not scrutinize any other licenses granted by Quanta for other patents, which is factor 2. Assuming that such licenses existed, should it have?

5. *Relying on Prior Licenses*. In light of the previous two notes, consider the licenses the court actually relied upon in *LaserDynamics*. As its guide to the proper award in this case, the court focused on the twenty-eight licenses that LaserDynamics had issued in the past. (Recall that it excluded the infamous BenQ license.) But keep in mind (from Note 3) that, when constructing the hypothetical negotiation, the court is supposed to presume that the parties to the negotiation agree the patent is infringed. When LaserDynamics negotiated these licenses, do you think its counter-parties believed that the patent was infringed (or valid)? Is there any way to know? If the counter-parties had agreed that the LaserDynamics patent was valid and infringed, do you think that the licensing prices they would have been willing to pay would have been lower, higher, or the same as the prices they did pay?

The problem with the court's approach is that the counterparties with whom LaserDynamics negotiated licenses almost certainly had some degree of skepticism toward whether the patent was valid and infringed, and that skepticism was almost certainly reflected in a reduced price. So these licenses might not be accurate measures of what the court claims to be seeking, namely the result of a hypothetical negotiation in which both parties presume that the patent is valid and infringed.

Moreover, the problem could become recursive. Suppose that the district court eventually awards LaserDynamics reasonable royalty damages of $500,000 based on these pre-existing licenses. Now, imagine that LaserDynamics sues another firm (say, Apple) for infringing its patent. Apple can observe the damages verdict in *LaserDynamics v. Quanta*, and it will understand that if it loses to LaserDynamics at trial, it will likely be forced to pay $500,000. If Apple believes that a court is only 50% likely to find that it is infringing the patent, then its expected damages from proceeding to trial are $500,000 × 50%, or $250,000. It will only be willing to pay LaserDynamics that much for a license. And then the next time LaserDynamics goes to trial, the court will be able to observe the Apple license for $250,000. This might cause the court to award LaserDynamics less than $500,000 the next time around, reducing the value of its patent even further. The result is a potential downward spiral, driven by the court treating licenses negotiated under conditions of uncertainty as if they had been negotiated with both parties presuming the patent valid and infringed. *See* Jonathan S. Masur, *The Use and Misuse of Patent Licenses*, 110 Nw. U. L. Rev. 115 (2015).

What should the court have done differently? How can it try to address this problem, given that it cannot know exactly what the parties believed about the validity or infringement of the patent when LaserDynamics negotiated its licenses? Is there a license the court could have relied upon that would have provided a more accurate picture of the price a defendant would have been willing to pay if it knew that the patent was valid and infringed—that is, if it knew it would lose at trial?

6. *Overcompensation.* Relying on prior licenses can lead to undercompensation for the reasons described in Note 5, but it can also lead to overcompensation. For one thing, patent owners who know that their early licenses will be used to set later royalty awards in court have an incentive not to enter agreements with any low-value licensees, skewing the evidence available to courts. *See* Erik Hovenkamp & Jonathan Masur, *How Patent Damages Skew Licensing Markets*, 36 Rev. Litig. 379 (2017). For another, licenses are negotiated in the shadow of litigation, and if judicial damages awards are inflated due to a failure to account for lock-in costs as described in Note 2, then infringers will have to pay more to avoid litigation—and those inflated licenses could then feed back into future judicial calculations. *See* Lee & Melamed, *supra*, at 438.

7. *But in No Event Less Than a Reasonable Royalty.* Recall that § 284 states that the patent owner is entitled to "damages adequate to compensate for the infringement, but in no event less than a reasonable royalty." This sets reasonable royalty damages as a floor, but a patent holder can always seek lost profit damages if it thinks they will be greater than reasonable royalty damages. In essence, a patent owner who has lost profits has a one-way option: it can choose between pursuing lost profit and reasonable royalty damages, depending on which it believes will be greater. Do you think this option could distort the amount of damages patent plaintiffs receive? *See* Omri Ben-Shahar, *Damages for Unlicensed Use*, 78 U. Chi. L. Rev. 7 (2011). *But see* Thomas F. Cotter, *Comparative Patent Remedies* 71-72 (2013).

When is it reasonable for the royalty to be zero? In *Apple v. Motorola*, Judge Richard Posner (sitting as a district court judge by designation) awarded zero damages on summary judgment after excluding the majority of damages expert testimony. On appeal, the Federal Circuit reversed, holding that "a fact finder may award no damages only when the record supports a zero royalty award." 757 F.3d 1286, 1328 (Fed. Cir. 2014). What incentives does this create for patentees? *See* Tun-Jen Chiang, *The Information Forcing Dilemma in Damages Law*, 59 Wm. & Mary L. Rev. 81 (2017). The Federal Circuit has affirmed a district court's reduction of a jury's damages award to zero where the patentee presented no damages evidence. *TecSec v. Adobe*, 978 F.3d 1278 (Fed. Cir. 2020).

16. Enhanced Damages and Attorneys' Fees

The damages described in Chapters 14 & 15—lost profits and reasonable royalties—are compensatory damages, designed to place the patent owner in the position it would have been in had infringement never occurred. But the Patent Act also permits victorious patent owners in particular cases to collect both enhanced damages—up to triple the amount of compensatory damages awarded—and attorneys' fees. These can be enormously powerful remedies. The patent defendant that finds itself paying treble damages is likely to end up far worse off than if it had never infringed in the first place. And given the high cost of patent litigation, which can often run into the millions of dollars, attorneys' fees can carry a hefty price tag and often represent a sizable proportion of the total patent award. For that matter, the Patent Act also permits victorious *defendants* to collect attorneys' fees from plaintiffs who bring frivolous cases. This chapter discusses why these enhanced rewards have been made available and the standards for determining when they should be awarded.

A. Enhanced Damages

The previous two chapters centered on 35 U.S.C. § 284, the provision of the Patent Act that requires a court to award damages for infringement. We have largely focused on the first paragraph, which discusses lost profit and reasonable royalty damages. But there is also a second paragraph to the statutory section, which reads (in relevant part): "the court may increase the damages up to three times the amount found or assessed." 35 U.S.C. § 284. When we say "relevant part," we really do mean that this is the only relevant part. The statute nowhere says when damages should be awarded or what standard the courts should use. In *Aro II* (a case that keeps coming up), the Supreme Court held that enhanced damages should be applied only in cases of "willful or bad-faith infringement." But even that standard largely begged the question as to what "willful" meant in the context of patent infringement.

To fill this void, the Federal Circuit formulated an evolving series of doctrines to lend content to the notion of willfulness. The most recent stemmed from *In re Seagate Technology, LLC*, 497 F.3d 1360 (Fed. Cir. 2007) (en banc), which the Supreme Court discusses at the beginning of the following opinion. However, over the course of a decade, critics exposed flaws in the *Seagate* test and eventually persuaded the Supreme Court to again take up the issue.

Halo Electronics v. Pulse Electronics, 136 S. Ct. 1923 (2016)

Chief Justice John Roberts delivered the opinion of the Court.

1   Section 284 of the Patent Act provides that, in a case of infringement, courts "may increase the damages up to three times the amount found or assessed." 35 U.S.C. § 284. In *In re Seagate Technology, LLC*, 497 F.3d 1360 (Fed. Cir. 2007) (en banc), the United States Court of Appeals for the Federal Circuit adopted a two-part test for determining when a district court may increase damages pursuant to § 284. Under *Seagate,* a patent owner must first "show by clear and convincing evidence that the infringer acted despite an objectively high likelihood that its actions constituted infringement of a valid patent." *Id.* at 1371. Second, the patentee must demonstrate, again by clear and convincing evidence, that the risk of infringement "was either known or so obvious that it should have been known to the accused infringer." *Id.* The question before us is whether this test is consistent with § 284. We hold that it is not.

I

A

2   Enhanced damages are as old as U.S. patent law. The Patent Act of 1793 mandated treble damages in any successful infringement suit. In the Patent Act of 1836, however, Congress changed course and made enhanced damages discretionary, specifying that "it shall be in the power of the court to render judgment for any sum above the amount found by [the] verdict . . . not exceeding three times the amount thereof, according to the circumstances of the case." Patent Act of 1836, § 14, 5 Stat. 123. In construing that new provision, this Court explained that the change was prompted by the "injustice" of subjecting a "defendant who acted in ignorance or good faith" to the same treatment as the "wanton and malicious pirate." *Seymour v. McCormick,* 57 U.S. (16 How.) 480, 488 (1854). There "is no good reason," we observed, "why taking a man's property in an invention should be trebly punished, while the measure of damages as to other property is single and actual damages." *Id.* at 488–89. But "where the injury is wanton or malicious, a jury may inflict vindictive or exemplary damages, not to recompense the plaintiff, but to punish the defendant." *Id.* at 489.

3   Some early decisions did suggest that enhanced damages might serve to compensate patentees as well as to punish infringers. *See, e.g., Clark v. Wooster*, 119 U.S. 322, 326 (1886). Such statements, however, were not for the ages, in part because the merger of law and equity removed certain procedural obstacles to full compensation absent enhancement. In the main, moreover, the references to compensation concerned costs attendant to litigation. *See Clark,* 119 U.S. at 326 (identifying enhanced damages as compensation for "the expense and trouble the plaintiff has been put to"). That concern dissipated with the enactment in 1952 of 35 U.S.C. § 285, which authorized district courts to award reasonable attorney's fees to prevailing parties in "exceptional cases" under the Patent Act. *See Octane Fitness, LLC v. ICON Health & Fitness Inc.*, 572 U.S. 545, 553 (2014).

4   It is against this backdrop that Congress, in the 1952 codification of the Patent Act, enacted § 284. "The stated purpose" of the 1952 revision "was merely

reorganization in language to clarify the statement of the statutes." *Aro Mfg. Co. v. Convertible Top Replacement Co.*, 377 U.S. 476, 505, n.20 (1964). This Court accordingly described § 284—consistent with the history of enhanced damages under the Patent Act—as providing that "punitive or 'increased' damages" could be recovered "in a case of willful or bad-faith infringement." *Id.* at 508.

B

5   In 2007, the Federal Circuit decided *Seagate* and fashioned the test for enhanced damages now before us. Under *Seagate,* a plaintiff seeking enhanced damages must show that the infringement of his patent was "willful." 497 F.3d at 1368. The Federal Circuit announced a two-part test to establish such willfulness: First, "a patentee must show by clear and convincing evidence that the infringer acted despite an objectively high likelihood that its actions constituted infringement of a valid patent," without regard to "[t]he state of mind of the accused infringer." *Id.* at 1371. This objectively defined risk is to be "determined by the record developed in the infringement proceedings." *Id.* "Objective recklessness will not be found" at this first step if the accused infringer, during the infringement proceedings, "raise[s] a 'substantial question' as to the validity or noninfringement of the patent." *Bard Peripheral Vascular, Inc. v. W.L. Gore & Assoc., Inc.*, 776 F.3d 837, 844 (Fed. Cir. 2015). That categorical bar applies even if the defendant was unaware of the arguable defense when he acted.

6   Second, after establishing objective recklessness, a patentee must show—again by clear and convincing evidence—that the risk of infringement "was either known or so obvious that it should have been known to the accused infringer." *Seagate*, 497 F.3d at 1371. Only when both steps have been satisfied can the district court proceed to consider whether to exercise its discretion to award enhanced damages. *Id.*

7   Under Federal Circuit precedent, an award of enhanced damages is subject to trifurcated appellate review. The first step of *Seagate*—objective recklessness—is reviewed *de novo*; the second—subjective knowledge—for substantial evidence; and the ultimate decision—whether to award enhanced damages—for abuse of discretion.

C

8   [The Supreme Court granted certiorari in two cases addressing the *Seagate* test: *Halo v. Pulse* and *Stryker v. Zimmer*. In *Halo*, Pulse continued to sell allegedly infringing products even after Halo sent Pulse two letters offering to license the patents because a Pulse engineer concluded that Halo's patents were invalid. The district court declined to award enhanced damages because Pulse presented a defense that "was not objectively baseless, or a 'sham,'" and the Federal Circuit affirmed. In *Stryker*, the district court awarded treble damages—for a total award over $288 million—based on "the one-sidedness of the case and the flagrancy and scope of Zimmer's infringement," such as testimony that Zimmer had "all-but instructed its design team to copy Stryker's products" and "to worry about the potential legal

consequences later." The Federal Circuit vacated the treble damages award because the defendant had asserted "reasonable defenses" at trial.]

II

A

9   The pertinent text of § 284 provides simply that "the court may increase the damages up to three times the amount found or assessed." 35 U.S.C. § 284. That language contains no explicit limit or condition, and we have emphasized that the "word 'may' clearly connotes discretion." *Martin v. Franklin Capital Corp.*, 546 U.S. 132, 136 (2005).

10   At the same time, "[d]iscretion is not whim." *Martin*, 546 U.S. at 139. In a system of laws discretion is rarely without limits, even when the statute does not specify any limits upon the district courts' discretion. "[A] motion to a court's discretion is a motion, not to its inclination, but to its judgment; and its judgment is to be guided by sound legal principles." *Martin*, 546 U.S. at 139. Thus, although there is "no precise rule or formula" for awarding damages under § 284, a district court's "discretion should be exercised in light of the considerations" underlying the grant of that discretion. *Octane Fitness*, 572 U.S. at 554.

11   Awards of enhanced damages under the Patent Act over the past 180 years establish that they are not to be meted out in a typical infringement case, but are instead designed as a "punitive" or "vindictive" sanction for egregious infringement behavior. The sort of conduct warranting enhanced damages has been variously described in our cases as willful, wanton, malicious, bad-faith, deliberate, consciously wrongful, flagrant, or—indeed—characteristic of a pirate. District courts enjoy discretion in deciding whether to award enhanced damages, and in what amount. But through nearly two centuries of discretionary awards and review by appellate tribunals, "the channel of discretion ha[s] narrowed," Friendly, *Indiscretion About Discretion*, 31 Emory L.J. 747, 772 (1982), so that such damages are generally reserved for egregious cases of culpable behavior.

B

12   The *Seagate* test reflects, in many respects, a sound recognition that enhanced damages are generally appropriate under § 284 only in egregious cases. That test, however, "is unduly rigid, and it impermissibly encumbers the statutory grant of discretion to district courts." *Octane Fitness*, 572 U.S. at 553 (construing § 285 of the Patent Act). In particular, it can have the effect of insulating some of the worst patent infringers from any liability for enhanced damages.

1

13   The principal problem with *Seagate*'s two-part test is that it requires a finding of objective recklessness in every case before district courts may award enhanced

damages. Such a threshold requirement excludes from discretionary punishment many of the most culpable offenders, such as the "wanton and malicious pirate" who intentionally infringes another's patent—with no doubts about its validity or any notion of a defense—for no purpose other than to steal the patentee's business. *Seymour*, 16 How. at 488. Under *Seagate*, a district court may not even consider enhanced damages for such a pirate, unless the court first determines that his infringement was "objectively" reckless. In the context of such deliberate wrongdoing, however, it is not clear why an independent showing of objective recklessness—by clear and convincing evidence, no less—should be a prerequisite to enhanced damages.

14   Our recent decision in *Octane Fitness* arose in a different context but points in the same direction. In that case we considered § 285 of the Patent Act, which allows district courts to award attorney's fees to prevailing parties in "exceptional" cases. 35 U.S.C. § 285. The Federal Circuit had adopted a two-part test for determining when a case qualified as exceptional, requiring that the claim asserted be both objectively baseless and brought in subjective bad faith. We rejected that test on the ground that a case presenting "subjective bad faith" alone could "sufficiently set itself apart from mine-run cases to warrant a fee award." 572 U.S. at 555. So too here. The subjective willfulness of a patent infringer, intentional or knowing, may warrant enhanced damages, without regard to whether his infringement was objectively reckless.

15   The *Seagate* test aggravates the problem by making dispositive the ability of the infringer to muster a reasonable (even though unsuccessful) defense at the infringement trial. The existence of such a defense insulates the infringer from enhanced damages, even if he did not act on the basis of the defense or was even aware of it. Under that standard, someone who plunders a patent—infringing it without any reason to suppose his conduct is arguably defensible—can nevertheless escape any comeuppance under § 284 solely on the strength of his attorney's ingenuity.

16   But culpability is generally measured against the knowledge of the actor at the time of the challenged conduct. In *Safeco Ins. Co. of America v. Burr*, 551 U.S. 47 (2007), we stated that a person is reckless if he acts "*knowing* or *having reason to know*" of facts which would lead a reasonable man to realize" his actions are unreasonably risky. The Court found that the defendant had not recklessly violated the Fair Credit Reporting Act because the defendant's interpretation had "a foundation in the statutory text" and the defendant lacked "the benefit of guidance from the courts of appeals or the Federal Trade Commission" that "might have warned it away from the view it took." *Id.* at 69–70. Nothing in *Safeco* suggests that we should look to facts that the defendant neither knew nor had reason to know at the time he acted.

17   Section 284 allows district courts to punish the full range of culpable behavior. Yet none of this is to say that enhanced damages must follow a finding of egregious misconduct. As with any exercise of discretion, courts should continue to take into

account the particular circumstances of each case in deciding whether to award damages, and in what amount. Section 284 permits district courts to exercise their discretion in a manner free from the inelastic constraints of the *Seagate* test. Consistent with nearly two centuries of enhanced damages under patent law, however, such punishment should generally be reserved for egregious cases typified by willful misconduct.

2

18   The *Seagate* test is also inconsistent with § 284 because it requires clear and convincing evidence to prove recklessness. On this point *Octane Fitness* is again instructive. There too the Federal Circuit had adopted a clear and convincing standard of proof, for awards of attorney's fees under § 285 of the Patent Act. Because that provision supplied no basis for imposing such a heightened standard of proof, we rejected it. We do so here as well. Like § 285, § 284 "imposes no specific evidentiary burden, much less such a high one." 572 U.S. at 557. And the fact that Congress expressly erected a higher standard of proof elsewhere in the Patent Act, *see* 35 U.S.C. § 273(b), but not in § 284, is telling. Furthermore, nothing in historical practice supports a heightened standard. As we explained in *Octane Fitness*, "patent-infringement litigation has always been governed by a preponderance of the evidence standard." 572 U.S. at 557. Enhanced damages are no exception.

3

19   Finally, because we eschew any rigid formula for awarding enhanced damages under § 284, we likewise reject the Federal Circuit's tripartite framework for appellate review. In *Highmark Inc. v. Allcare Health Management System, Inc.*, 572 U.S. 559 (2014), we built on our *Octane Fitness* holding to reject a similar multipart standard of review. Because *Octane Fitness* confirmed district court discretion to award attorney fees, we concluded that such decisions should be reviewed for abuse of discretion. *Highmark*, 572 U.S. at 561.

20   The same conclusion follows naturally from our holding here. Section 284 gives district courts discretion in meting out enhanced damages. It "commits the determination" whether enhanced damages are appropriate "to the discretion of the district court" and "that decision is to be reviewed on appeal for abuse of discretion." *Id.* at 563.

21   That standard allows for review of district court decisions informed by "the considerations we have identified." *Octane Fitness*, 572 U.S. at 554. The appellate review framework adopted by the Federal Circuit reflects a concern that district courts may award enhanced damages too readily, and distort the balance between the protection of patent rights and the interest in technological innovation. Nearly two centuries of exercising discretion in awarding enhanced damages in patent cases, however, has given substance to the notion that there are limits to that discretion. The Federal Circuit should review such exercises of discretion in light of the

longstanding considerations we have identified as having guided both Congress and the courts.

III

22   At the end of the day, respondents' main argument for retaining the *Seagate* test comes down to a matter of policy. Respondents and their *amici* are concerned that allowing district courts unlimited discretion to award up to treble damages in infringement cases will impede innovation as companies steer well clear of any possible interference with patent rights. They also worry that the ready availability of such damages will embolden "trolls." Trolls, in the patois of the patent community, are entities that hold patents for the primary purpose of enforcing them against alleged infringers, often exacting outsized licensing fees on threat of litigation.

23   Respondents are correct that patent law reflects "a careful balance between the need to promote innovation" through patent protection, and the importance of facilitating the "imitation and refinement through imitation" that are "necessary to invention itself and the very lifeblood of a competitive economy." *Bonito Boats, Inc. v. Thunder Craft Boats, Inc.*, 489 U.S. 141, 146 (1989). That balance can indeed be disrupted if enhanced damages are awarded in garden-variety cases. As we have explained, however, they should not be. The seriousness of respondents' policy concerns cannot justify imposing an artificial construct such as the *Seagate* test on the discretion conferred under § 284.

Justice Breyer, with whom Justice Kennedy and Justice Alito join, concurring.

24   I agree with the Court that *In re Seagate Technology, LLC*, 497 F.3d 1360 (Fed. Cir. 2007) (en banc), takes too mechanical an approach to the award of enhanced damages. But, as the Court notes, the relevant statutory provision, 35 U.S.C. § 284, nonetheless imposes limits that help produce uniformity in its application and maintain its consistency with the basic objectives of patent law. I write separately to express my own understanding of several of those limits.

25   First, the Court's references to "willful misconduct" do not mean that a court may award enhanced damages simply because the evidence shows that the infringer knew about the patent *and nothing more.* Here, the Court's opinion, read as a whole and in context, explains that "enhanced damages are generally appropriate . . . *only in egregious cases.*" They amount to a "punitive" sanction for engaging in conduct that is either "deliberate" or "wanton." And while the Court explains that "intentional or knowing" infringement "may" warrant a punitive sanction, the word it uses is *may,* not *must.* It is "circumstanc[e]" that transforms simple knowledge into such egregious behavior.

26   Second, the Court writes against a statutory background specifying that the "failure of an infringer to obtain the advice of counsel . . . may not be used to prove that the accused infringer willfully infringed." § 298. The Court does not weaken this

rule through its interpretation of § 284. Nor should it. It may well be expensive to obtain an opinion of counsel. An owner of a small firm, or a scientist working there, might, without being "wanton" or "reckless," reasonably determine that its product does not infringe a particular patent, or that that patent is probably invalid. Congress has thus left it to the potential infringer to decide whether to consult counsel—without the threat of treble damages influencing that decision. That is, Congress has determined that where both "advice of counsel" and "increased damages" are at issue, insisting upon the legal game is not worth the candle. Compare § 298 with § 284.

27   Third, as the Court explains, enhanced damages may not "serve to compensate patentees" for infringement-related costs or litigation expenses. That is because § 284 provides for the former *prior* to any enhancement. And a different statutory provision, § 285, provides for the latter.

28   Patent infringement, of course, is a highly undesirable and unlawful activity. But stopping infringement is a means to patent law's ends. Through a complex system of incentive-based laws, patent law helps to encourage the development of, disseminate knowledge about, and permit others to benefit from useful inventions. Enhanced damages have a role to play in achieving those objectives, but, as described above, that role is limited.

29   Consider that the U.S. Patent and Trademark Office estimates that more than 2,500,000 patents are currently in force. Moreover, Members of the Court have noted that some "firms use patents . . . primarily to obtain licensing fees." *eBay Inc. v. MercExchange, L.L.C.*, 547 U.S. 388, 396 (2006) (Kennedy, J., concurring). *Amici* explain that some of those firms generate revenue by sending letters to "tens of thousands of people asking for a license or settlement" on a patent "that may in fact not be warranted." How is a growing business to react to the arrival of such a letter, particularly if that letter carries with it a serious risk of treble damages? Does the letter put the company "on notice" of the patent? Will a jury find that the company behaved "recklessly," simply for failing to spend considerable time, effort, and money obtaining expert views about whether some or all of the patents described in the letter apply to its activities (and whether those patents are even valid)? These investigative activities can be costly. Hence, the risk of treble damages can encourage the company to settle, or even abandon any challenged activity.

30   To say this is to point to a risk: The more that businesses, laboratories, hospitals, and individuals adopt this approach, the more often a patent will reach beyond its lawful scope to discourage lawful activity, and the more often patent-related demands will frustrate, rather than "promote," the "Progress of Science and useful Arts." U.S. Const., Art. I, § 8, cl. 8; *see, e.g., Eon–Net LP v. Flagstar Bancorp*, 653 F.3d 1314, 1327 (Fed. Cir. 2011) (patent holder "acted in bad faith by exploiting the high cost to defend [patent] litigation to extract a nuisance value settlement"); *In re MPHJ Technology Invs., LLC*, 159 F.T.C. 1004, 1007–12 (2015) (patent owner sent more than 16,000 letters demanding settlement for using "common office equipment"

under a patent it never intended to litigate). Thus, in the context of enhanced damages, there are patent-related risks on both sides of the equation. That fact argues, not for abandonment of enhanced damages, but for their careful application, to ensure that they only target cases of egregious misconduct.

Discussion Questions: Enhanced Damages

1. *The Flaws with* Seagate. What was it about the *Seagate* test that the Supreme Court did not like? What was the conduct that the *Seagate* test would not have reached—that is, would not have classified as willful—that the Supreme Court believed should be understood as willful? Do you agree with the Court that treble damages should extend to that type of conduct?

Note that the Supreme Court describes the *Seagate* test as "unduly rigid." What other rules that we have studied has the Supreme Court described as "unduly rigid?" Why do you think the Federal Circuit continues to devise rules that the Supreme Court views as unduly rigid, and why do you think the Supreme Court continues to reject those rules? Does it have something to do with the respective roles of those courts and their positions in the judicial hierarchy?

This case involves yet another unanimous reversal of the Federal Circuit. The list of other unanimous reversals of the Federal Circuit in this book includes (but is not limited to) *Alice, Nautilus, Akamai, Myriad, Mayo, KSR, eBay,* and *Festo,* all of which were decided in a 12-year period. That's a lot for one court. There are certainly aspects of the *Seagate* test that made it a target for revision. As the Supreme Court notes, it was subject to *trifurcated review*: the objective risk of infringement was reviewed *de novo*, the subjective question of whether the infringer knew of the risk was reviewed for substantial evidence, and the overall conclusion of willfulness was reviewed for abuse of discretion. Yet that alone was not the reason the Supreme Court took this case and undid Federal Circuit law. Is there something about the Federal Circuit that creates more opportunities for unanimous reversals? Should this be seen as a feature of patent law, a feature of that court, or just a statistical anomaly?

2. *The Mens Rea of Willful Infringement.* The Court does not explicitly say what sort of mens rea is required to make a party liable for willful infringement, but it appears from the opinion that willfulness should be judged on the basis of what the infringer knew or believed at the time of infringement. This is a subjective standard: the infringer's subjective knowledge is at issue.

This means, in turn, that an infringer who is completely unaware of the fact of infringement (or unaware of the existence of the patent being infringed) cannot be liable for willfulness damages. This type of subjective standard should remind you of the standard for contributory infringement and inducement. Accordingly, willfulness liability is often triggered the same way that contributory infringement and inducement liability is triggered: with a letter informing the putative infringer of the existence of the patent and the possibility of infringement. Are there circumstances under which a failure to search for relevant patents could (or should) trigger willfulness liability? On remand, the Federal Circuit in *Halo* said the jury should consider "what Pulse knew or had reason to know at the time of the infringement"; how might an infringer have "reason to know" of the infringement without actual knowledge?

The Federal Circuit seems to be hewing to the view that only knowledge of the patent—or perhaps willful blindness or the equivalent—is sufficient to create liability for willful infringement. By way of example, in *SRI International v. Cisco Systems*, 930 F.3d 1295 (Fed. Cir. 2019), the defendant's engineers had not read the patents-in-suit until just before they were set to be deposed for the case, and the patent owner argued that this failure to read relevant patents was evidence of willfulness. Absent further evidence of knowledge, the Federal Circuit held that a jury verdict finding willful infringement could not stand. However, the court held that the defendant might still be liable for willful infringement as of the date it received a letter from the plaintiff informing it of the patent. (The defendant did not seek an opinion from counsel or pursue what the court referred to as an "advice-of-counsel" defense.)

What are the likely policy implications of the fact that enhanced damages (and indirect infringement liability) are only available when a party is aware of the patent it might be infringing? Suppose you were the general counsel of a technology firm. What advice would you give to the engineers and scientists in your firm to try and minimize your firm's legal risk from patent infringement? By shifting the relevant willfulness inquiry away from the objective risk of infringement and toward the subjective perspective of the infringer, has *Halo* made this problem better or worse?

It is worth noting that despite these rules, engineers and scientists appear to continue to read and learn from patents, though it is difficult to know whether they would do so more or less under different legal rules. *See* Lisa Larrimore Ouellette, *Do Patents Disclose Useful Information?*, 25 Harv. J.L. & Tech. 545 (2012); Lisa Larrimore Ouellette, *Who Reads Patents?*, 35 Nature Biotechnology 421 (2017) (reporting that fewer than 10% of surveyed scientists said they had been instructed to not read patents because of possible adverse legal consequences).

3. *Opinion Letters and the Breyer Concurrence.* In his concurring opinion, Justice Breyer raises the issue of opinion letters and the role they play in willfulness analysis. As with indirect infringement, the subjective state of mind necessary for willfulness damages makes opinion letters from counsel an important mechanism by which infringers can defend themselves. Suppose that a firm is informed of the existence of a patent and seeks an opinion from counsel before deciding what course of action to take. A reputable law firm produces a sound, reasonable letter concluding that the patent is infringed but invalid, and thus the firm will not be held liable. At trial, however, the court holds that the patent is in fact valid and infringed, and the defendant is liable as an infringer. Will this letter that concluded that the patent was

invalid protect the defendant from willfulness damages? Recall the holding of *Commil v. Cisco* from Chapter 10: with respect to indirect infringement, only belief of noninfringement—and not belief of invalidity—will protect a defendant from indirect infringement liability.

Justice Breyer suggests that obtaining an opinion letter may be financially impossible or impractical for a small firm. He emphasizes that the failure to obtain an opinion letter should not in and of itself be grounds for finding the small firm liable for willful infringement. In such circumstances, how should we judge the state of mind of the firm? Whose views matter, and what inferences should be drawn from those views?

4. *The Problem of Patent Trolls.* In Part III of its opinion, the Court discusses the concern that non-practicing entities will too easily be able to extract treble damages from patent defendants. Here, the Court even goes so far as to call them "trolls" for the first time. The Court's answer to this concern is that treble damages will only be available in exceptional cases, not in run-of-the-mill cases. Do you think that is right? What are the barriers to patent trolls extracting treble damages after *Halo*?

5. *Policy and Purpose?* Why do enhanced damages exist, or why should they exist? It seems clear that courts view willful infringers as particularly bad actors. But this is patent law, not criminal law—this type of morality doesn't usually play much of a role in the doctrine. One way to think about treble damages is that they are akin to punitive damages in tort. Classic economic theory suggests that punitive damages should be assessed when it is difficult to detect or punish wrongdoing. For instance, if there is only a 25% chance that A will be caught or found liable if A harms B, then in the event that A is found liable for harming B, the damages assessed against A should be quadrupled in order to adequately deter A's bad actions. How well does this translate to patent law? In a case like *Halo v. Pulse*, or in another typical patent case, how likely do you think it is that infringement will go undetected or uncompensated? Are there particular factors that will make it easier or harder to detect infringers? Is being a willful infringer a good proxy for engaging in infringement that is unlikely to be detected?

What other values or policy might the availability of treble damages be serving?

6. *How Much Should a Court Enhance Damages?* Note that 35 U.S.C. § 284 allows a court to increase damages by "up to three times." It does not necessarily have to treble them. How should a court decide by how much to increase damages? Before *Halo*, courts looked to the nine factors in *Read Corp. v. Portec, Inc.*, 970 F.2d 816 (Fed. Cir. 1992), to determine whether infringement had been willful and, if so, how much to increase damages. Those factors are:

(1) whether the infringer deliberately copied the ideas of another;

(2) whether the infringer, when he knew of the other's patent protection, investigated the scope of the patent and formed a good-faith belief that it was invalid or that it was not infringed;

(3) the infringer's behavior as a party to the litigation;

(4) the defendant's size and financial condition;

(5) the closeness of the case;

(6) the duration of the defendant's misconduct;

(7) remedial action by the defendant;

(8) the defendant's motivation for harm; and

(9) whether the defendant attempted to conceal its misconduct.

As originally envisioned by the Federal Circuit in *Portec*, the first three factors speak more to whether infringement was willful in the first place, and the last six to how much damages should be increased. In theory, then, the first three factors would have been largely superseded by *Halo*. Nonetheless, since *Halo* the Federal Circuit and lower courts have continued to rely upon all nine factors, even though the Federal Circuit has acknowledged that they are not mandatory. *See, e.g., Polara Engr. Inc v. Campbell Co.*, 894 F.3d 1339 (Fed. Cir. 2018); *Georgetown Rail Equip. Co. v. Holland L.P.*, 867 F.3d 1229 (Fed. Cir. 2017).

Consider the defendants in *Halo v. Pulse* and *Stryker v. Zimmer*: Pulse continued infringing after being offered a license because its engineer (incorrectly) determined the patents were invalid, and Zimmer instructed its design team to copy Stryker's products. How would you apply the *Portec* factors in either case? How much would you increase the damages assessed against either defendant?

Practice Problems: Enhanced Damages

For all of the following problems, assume you are the CEO of a small tech startup with approximately 20 employees. You receive a letter informing you that your firm is infringing a patent. You then take the following actions, your firm is eventually sued for patent infringement, and your firm is found liable as an infringer. Do you think you will be held liable for treble damages as a willful infringer?

1. You consult your patent attorney, and she says there is "probably about a 50% chance that the patent is valid and you're infringing it."

2. You consult your general counsel, and she says: "I'm no patent expert, but I don't think this is a problem."

3. The same situation as #2, but this time you just consult your lead engineer (who says the same thing).

4. You consult a reputable outside law firm, which says your firm is definitely infringing. Accordingly, you don't hire this firm to write an opinion letter. Then you consult a slightly shadier firm, which is quite happy to write an opinion letter stating that your firm is not infringing.

    *   If your answer to this question was that your firm will be on the hook for treble damages, please explain the mechanism by which the court will learn that you consulted the first firm.

5. You consult your patent attorney, who says that there is no way on earth that the patent is valid and infringed. At trial, however, the district court concludes that the patent is valid and infringed and that this is not even a close case. The court says that the letter you received from your patent attorney could not have been more off-base.

6. In response to the letter you take no action whatsoever. You consult no lawyer; you just continue your activities. When you're eventually sued and get to court, you lose, but the district court judge concludes that it was a very close case and you had an excellent defense (that just wasn't quite excellent enough).

    *   If your answer to this question is that the conduct was willful, please specify what the firm has done that is wrong in this case. What is the argument for punishing the firm described here more than the firm described in #5?

B. Attorneys' Fees

The so-called "American rule" in civil litigation is that the parties bear their own costs: each side must pay for its own attorneys, experts, and so forth. Indeed, as the name would suggest, that is the rule that prevails in the mine run of American civil litigation. However, there are exceptions, including in patent law. 35 U.S.C. § 285 states: "The court in exceptional cases may award reasonable attorney fees to the prevailing party." (That is the entirety of the statute; it gives no hint as to the standard for an "exceptional case.") As we will discuss at the beginning of the next chapter, patent litigation is often very expensive, so fee awards can be significant. The Federal Circuit has upheld attorneys' fee awards in the millions and even tens of millions of dollars.

The evolution of the law on attorneys' fees may sound familiar—stop us if you've heard this one before. Over a period of decades, the Federal Circuit cycled through a series of doctrines, finally settling on a rule that attorneys' fees were only available if the suit was both "objectively baseless" and "brought in subjective bad faith." *Brooks Furniture Mfg., Inc. v. Dutailier Int'l, Inc.*, 393 F.3d 1378 (Fed. Cir. 2005). This standard was itself the subject of criticism for nearly a decade before the Supreme Court was persuaded to take up the issue in *Octane Fitness, LLC v. ICON Health & Fitness, Inc.*, 572 U.S. 545 (2014). There, the Court stated that the Federal Circuit's framework was "unduly rigid" and that district courts should determine whether a case is "exceptional" as a "case-by-case exercise of their discretion, considering the totality of the circumstances."

Octane Fitness was decided two years before *Halo*, and it was the Court's decision in *Octane Fitness* that put the patent community on notice that the Supreme Court was likely to change the legal standard for willfulness damages as well. However, we have elected to present the cases out of order in this book (and to provide a substantial portion of *Halo*, and not of *Octane Fitness*) because of the greater importance of willfulness damages. Even though attorneys' fees in patent cases can be substantial, treble damages can add up to quite a bit more.

The standard the Court settled on in *Octane Fitness* is not identical to the one it propounded in *Halo*. The Court held that an "exceptional" case is "one that stands out from others with respect to the substantive strength of a party's litigating position (considering both the governing law and the facts of the case) or the unreasonable manner in which the case was litigated." 572 U.S. at 554. Accordingly, "a case presenting either subjective bad faith or exceptionally meritless claims may sufficiently set itself apart from mine-run cases to warrant a fee award." *Id.* at 555. Like the law of willfulness damages, bad faith in litigation can give rise to attorneys' fees. This includes misconduct during the litigation itself, such as discovery-related abuses or presenting arguments that the party knows to be meritless. But in addition, the Court made clear that a very weak case, even if brought in good faith, could similarly give rise to an award of attorneys' fees.

Finally, under prior Federal Circuit law, prevailing parties had to prove that they were entitled to attorneys' fees by clear and convincing evidence. The Court in *Octane Fitness* reduced that burden to preponderance of the evidence. *Id.* at 557–58. All told, these two changes in the law made it much easier for prevailing parties to obtain attorneys' fees.

One important feature of 35 U.S.C. § 285 is that it is two-sided: a court can assess attorneys' fees against either the plaintiff or the defendant for "exceptional" behavior. This provides both parties with an incentive to conform their conduct to the requirements of *Octane Fitness*. What are the likely policy implications of this two-sided threat? You might consider more generally what it would mean for the patent system if the United States departed from the American rule and adopted a "loser pays" rule for civil litigation, which is common in many other countries. For an argument that attorneys' fees are only a start, and courts should assess even higher penalties against both sides for bringing losing claims, see Anup Malani & Jonathan S. Masur, *Raising the Stakes in Patent Cases*, 101 Geo. L.J. 637 (2013).

Practice Problems: Attorneys' Fees

Consider the following situations. Which cases should be viewed as "exceptional," thus warranting an award of attorneys' fees? If you view a case as exceptional, would you award the prevailing party its full costs and fees, or only partial costs and fees?

1. The plaintiff to a lawsuit improperly paid its fact witnesses for their testimony, in violation of ethical rules of conduct, and failed to prevent document spoliation over a number of years. The plaintiff itself did not destroy any documents, but it did not prevent the party from whom it was acquiring patents from destroying documents related to those patents, even when it anticipated forthcoming litigation related to those patents. In addition, the plaintiff asserted two patents that it should have known were unenforceable because their owner had failed to pay the necessary USPTO fees on time. *See In re Rembrandt Techs. LP Pat. Litig.*, 899 F.3d 1254 (Fed. Cir. 2018).

2. In the course of a deposition related to litigation, the patent's inventor testified about the patent's alleged innovation: "I realize there is nothing novel about it." The patent was later declared invalid by the USPTO in an IPR. Nonetheless, the plaintiff did not drop the lawsuit until the claims were cancelled by the USPTO. *See Stone Basket Innovations, LLC v. Cook Med. LLC*, 892 F.3d 1175 (Fed. Cir. 2018).

3. The University of Utah filed suit for correction of ownership, claiming that one of its faculty members should have been listed as a joint owner of a valuable patent. During her deposition, however, that faculty member made several admissions undermining the university's claims. When asked if she ever did "any of the experiments or generate[d] any of the data that is included in the [relevant] patents," she responded: "Not that I know of." She also stated that her lab does not study the particular scientific process at issue in the patents. After these admissions, the University of Utah declined to withdraw its claims of joint inventorship, and those claims were eventually rejected at trial. *See Univ. of Utah v. Max-Planck-Gesellschaft zur Foerderung der Wissenschaften e.V.*, 851 F.3d 1317 (Fed. Cir. 2017).

V. U.S. and International Patent Systems

17. U.S. Patent Litigation Procedure

This chapter provides an overview of some of the rules of U.S. patent litigation procedure: (A) the law of jurisdiction, standing, and venue as applied in patent cases; (B) the specialized patent local rules adopted by many federal districts to govern patent cases; (C) the procedures for post-issuance review of granted patents at the USPTO; and (D) the law governing patent litigation at the alternative forum of the International Trade Commission.

Our brief overview only scratches the surface of the complexity of patent litigation. Patent lawsuits are often lengthy and expensive—a recent survey of patent practitioners estimated the median cost of litigation through appeal at $675,000 when less than $1 million is at stake and $4 million when at least $25 million is at stake. American Intellectual Property Law Association, *Report of the Economic Survey* (2021). And patent lawsuits involve numerous specialized rules of procedure not covered here—the rules for joinder of multiple defendants, procedures for bifurcation of liability and damages, the use of neutral experts to provide technology tutorials, etc. A useful additional free resource is the Federal Judicial Center's *Patent Case Management Judicial Guide* (3d ed. 2016), https://www.fjc.gov/sites/default/files/2017/PCMJG3d_2016_final.pdf.

A. Jurisdiction, Standing, and Venue

All of the basic rules you encountered in 1L Civil Procedure also apply in patent cases. For example, like other civil cases, a patent lawsuit commences with an adequate complaint. In 2015, a rule that allowed patent complaints to state general allegations (former Fed. R. Civ. P. 84) was withdrawn, so patent complaints must now satisfy the general pleading standards set by the Supreme Court in *Bell Atlantic Corp. v. Twombly*, 550 U.S. 544 (2007), and *Ashcroft v. Iqbal*, 556 U.S. 662 (2009).

In this section, we briefly review how the foundational concepts of (1) *jurisdiction*, (2) *venue*, and (3) *standing* apply to patent litigation.

1. *Jurisdiction*. Courts have power to decide cases only when they have jurisdiction, including both *subject matter jurisdiction* over the cause of action and *personal jurisdiction* over the defendant.

As noted in Chapter 1, patent law is unusual in that the federal courts have exclusive subject matter jurisdiction under 28 U.S.C. § 1338(a). If a suit contains any claims under the Patent Act, it thus must be brought in federal court, even if the patent claims are a minor part of the lawsuit. Cases must also be removed to federal court if the defendant successfully asserts a patent counterclaim. Patent law may still be involved in state court lawsuits that do not arise under the Patent Act, and the Supreme Court has held that "state legal malpractice claims based on underlying patent matters will rarely, if ever, arise under federal patent law for purposes of § 1338(a)." *Gunn v. Minton*, 568 U.S. 251, 258 (2013); *see also Intellisoft v. Acer America*, 955 F.3d 927 (Fed. Cir. 2020) (trade secret claim did not require resolution of substantial issue of federal patent law).

A case may also be dismissed for lack of personal jurisdiction over the defendant, which can be *general* (such as based on the state where the defendant resides) or *specific* to the asserted cause of action (including activities purposefully directed at residents of the forum state). The requirement of personal jurisdiction, unlike subject matter jurisdiction, can be waived. To determine whether specific jurisdiction exists, the Federal Circuit applies a three-part test: "(1) whether the defendant purposefully directed activities at residents of the forum; (2) whether the claim arises out of or relates to those activities; and (3) whether assertion of personal jurisdiction is reasonable and fair." *Nuance Communications v. Abbyy Software House*, 626 F.3d 1222, 1231 (Fed. Cir. 2010). For example, California courts were held to have specific jurisdiction over foreign defendants who have imported allegedly infringing goods to the state. *Id.* And in a declaratory judgment action, California courts were held to have specific jurisdiction over a foreign non-practicing patent holder that had sent cease-and-desist letters to the plaintiff and traveled to the state to discuss potential licensing arrangements. *Xilinx v. Papst Licensing*, 848 F.3d 1346 (Fed. Cir. 2017).

2. *Standing*. A patent suit can also be dismissed if the plaintiff lacks standing, either because it fails to meet the *constitutional* requirements of the Case and Controversy Clause of Article III or because it fails to accord with various *prudential* requirements that the Court has developed to define the domain of the judiciary. There are three categories of plaintiffs for standing issues. First, the owner of a patent, or of "all substantial rights" in the patent (as assessed based on the totality of the agreement), meets both constitutional and prudential standing requirements. Second, exclusive licensees who don't hold "all substantial rights" have standing as a constitutional matter, but joinder of the patent owner (typically under Fed. R. Civ. P. 19) is required to satisfy prudential standing concerns. (University patent owners are often joined to lawsuits asserted by their licensees for this reason.) Third, parties without exclusionary rights lack constitutional standing, and this defect cannot be

cured by joining the patent owner. *See Morrow v. Microsoft*, 499 F.3d 1332, 1339 (Fed. Cir. 2007); *Lone Star Silicon Innovations v. Nanya Technology*, 925 F.3d 1225 (Fed. Cir. 2019).

Patent lawsuits may also be commenced as *declaratory judgment* actions, in which a potential infringer seeks a declaratory judgment that a patent is invalid or not infringed. As summarized by the Federal Circuit:

> A party has standing to bring an action under the Declaratory Judgment Act if an "actual controversy" exists, 28 U.S.C. § 2201(a), which is the same as an Article III case or controversy.
>
> In *MedImmune, Inc. v. Genentech, Inc.*, the Supreme Court rejected our prior, more stringent standard for declaratory judgment standing insofar as it required a "reasonable apprehension of imminent suit." 549 U.S. 118 (2007). Under the Court's new standard, an Article III case or controversy exists when "the facts alleged, under all the circumstances, show that there is a substantial controversy, between parties having adverse legal interests, of sufficient immediacy and reality to warrant the issuance of a declaratory judgment." *Id.* at 127.
>
> An "adverse legal interest" requires a dispute as to a legal right—for example, an underlying legal cause of action that the declaratory defendant could have brought or threatened to bring. In the absence of a controversy as to a legal right, a mere adverse *economic* interest is insufficient to create declaratory judgment jurisdiction.

Arris Group v. British Telecommunications, 639 F.3d 1368, 1373–74 (Fed. Cir. 2011).

In Chapters 10 and 16, we discussed the letters that patent owners send to putative infringers to create the knowledge necessary to trigger liability for indirect infringement and treble damages. These letters can also have the effect of triggering declaratory judgment jurisdiction if they threaten legal action. In turn, this could allow the putative defendant to file a declaratory judgment action against the putative plaintiff before the plaintiff sues for infringement. Importantly, this allows the putative defendant to choose the judicial district where the case will be litigated. If you are the CEO of Intel, and you are facing litigation against Texas Instruments, you would much rather litigate in the Northern District of California, where your company headquarters is located, than in the Northern District of Texas, where Texas Instruments' corporate headquarters is located.

As a result, these notice letters are often worded quite strangely in an effort to avoid creating declaratory judgment jurisdiction. Instead of notifying a potential defendant that a patent exists and the owner is considering suing, the letter might simply observe that "there are some patents you might want to be aware of," and "perhaps the two firms should discuss their mutual economic interests." To the untrained eye, these letters might seem to be friendly suggestions that the two firms consider a joint venture; to the trained eye, they are the opening salvo in a patent war.

3. *Venue.* Patent lawsuits must also be filed in an appropriate venue. Patent law is unusual in having its own venue statute:

28 U.S.C. § 1400(b)

Any civil action for patent infringement may be brought in the judicial district where the defendant resides, or where the defendant has committed acts of infringement and has a regular and established place of business.

Before 2017, the Federal Circuit interpreted this statute such that corporate defendants are deemed to "reside" in any district where the defendant is subject to the court's personal jurisdiction, rendering the second portion of the statute superfluous. This broad venue rule led many patent plaintiffs to shop for favorable locations in which to file suit, and even led some locations to market themselves as friendly venues for patent plaintiffs. *See* Daniel Klerman & Greg Reilly, *Forum Selling*, 89 S. Cal. L. Rev. 241 (2016). The most egregious example was the Eastern District of Texas, where the largest city is Plano, and which successfully earned a reputation as a highly favorable venue for patent plaintiffs. (Because the plaintiff picks the venue, a venue that wants to attract business only has to be favorable to plaintiffs.) The Eastern District of Texas heard so many patent cases that beleaguered repeat defendants started to invest in the community in an effort to curry favor with potential jurors. Samsung (in)famously sponsored an ice rink in the town square in Marshall, Texas (where most of the cases were tried), directly across from the federal courthouse.

Almost needless to say, this is not how things are supposed to work. In *TC Heartland v. Kraft Foods*, 137 S. Ct. 1514 (2017), the Supreme Court narrowed this rule and held that for purposes of the patent venue statute, a corporation only "resides" in its state of incorporation. Since *TC Heartland*, the Federal Circuit has provided additional guidance as to the second portion of the venue statute: "where the defendant has committed acts of infringement and has a regular and established place of business." For example, this test is not satisfied by an executive working out of his home in the district, *In re Cray Inc.*, 871 F.3d 1355 (Fed. Cir. 2017), or by the mere presence of computer servers, *In re Google LLC*, 949 F.3d 1338 (Fed. Cir. 2020). This, in turn, has led some potential patent defendants to eliminate their physical presences in plaintiff-friendly districts in order to defeat venue there. For instance, you will search in vain for an Apple Store in the Eastern District of Texas—Apple closed all of its locations there after *TC Heartland*.

TC Heartland did not address venue for foreign corporations. The Federal Circuit has since held that venue for foreign firms is governed by the general venue statute, which states that "a defendant not resident in the United States may be sued in any judicial district." 28 U.S.C. § 1391(c)(3). *See In re HTC Corp.*, 889 F.3d 1349 (Fed. Cir. 2018).

As illustrated in the following table, *TC Heartland* has led to a substantial shift in patent filings away from the Eastern District of Texas, which is often no longer an appropriate venue. The District of Delaware (where many companies are incorporated) and the Western District of Texas (which includes Austin and San Antonio, where many defendants have operations) have seen the largest gains in share of patent cases; the Northern and Central Districts of California have also seen upticks. In the first three months of 2021, the Western District of Texas continued its upward trajectory with 25% of new filings. That upward trajectory is being driven in particular by the lone judge in the Waco division (Judge Alan Albright), not by increased filings by firms with operations in Austin and San Antonio. This is raising concerns about the Western District of Texas becoming the new Eastern District of Texas.

Most Popular Districts for Patent Case Filings (from Lex Machina)

	2014–2016	2018–2020
E.D. Tex.	37%	11%
D. Del.	13%	23%
C.D. Cal.	6%	8%
D.N.J.	5%	4%
N.D. Cal.	4%	8%
N.D. Ill.	4%	4%
S.D.N.Y.	3%	3%
W.D. Tex.	1% (15th most popular)	11%

If venue is proper in more than one district, then a defendant can file a motion to transfer venue under 28 U.S.C. § 1404(a), which allows a district court to transfer a case "[f]or the convenience of parties and witnesses [and] in the interest of justice." For example, after patent-assertion entity Uniloc sued Apple for patent infringement in the Western District of Texas, Apple moved to transfer the case to the Northern District of California on the basis that it would be more convenient to litigate where the accused products were designed, developed, and tested. The district court denied the motion, but Apple successfully petitioned the Federal Circuit for a writ of mandamus directing the district court to transfer the case. *In re Apple Inc.*, 979 F.3d 1332 (Fed. Cir. 2020).

B. Patent Local Rules

Many federal district courts have "local rules," which are procedural guidelines that supplement the Federal Rules of Civil Procedure. Local rules often establish timing and style guidelines for filing motions, holding status conferences, mediating disputes, and other procedural details. In 2000, the Northern District of California became the first federal district to adopt specialized local rules for patent infringement cases in particular. Since then, over thirty districts have promulgated their own patent local rules. *See* Jean Dassie, *District Court Local Rules for Patent Infringement Cases*, Federal Circuit Damages (Dec. 27, 2019), http://www.fedcirdamages.com/district-court-local-rules-for-patent-infringement-cases. Of the jurisdictions that hear the most patent cases, only the District of Delaware and the Western District of Texas do not have district-wide patent local rules, although some individual judges in these districts have adopted standard procedures for patent cases. As an example, here is a rough overview of the schedule provided under the Northern District of California Patent Local Rules, which was used as a model by many other districts:

- *Initial Case Management Conference.* During this conferral, the parties can discuss any modifications to Patent Local Rules.

- *Disclosure of Asserted Claims and Infringement Contentions* (14 days later). The plaintiff's initial disclosure requirements include infringement claim charts showing how each "Accused Instrumentality" infringes each asserted claim, as well as documents related to issues such as patent ownership.

- *Invalidity Contentions and Defendant's Document Production* (45 days later). The defendant must provide any asserted grounds of invalidity, with §§ 102 & 103 arguments supported by invalidity claim charts showing how each asserted claim element can be found in each alleged item of prior art. Later amendments to invalidity or infringement contentions require good cause. The defendant's required document production can also be quite burdensome, including "[s]ource code, specifications, schematics, flow charts, artwork, formulas, or other documentation sufficient to show the operation of any aspects or elements of an Accused Instrumentality identified by the patent claimant."

- *Claim Construction*:
    - *Exchange of Proposed Terms for Construction* (14 days after Invalidity Contentions). The parties exchange lists of terms they would like

construed and then "jointly identify the 10 terms likely to be most significant to resolving the parties' dispute."

- o *Exchange of Preliminary Claim Constructions and Extrinsic Evidence* (21 days later). The parties exchange proposed constructions and references to supporting evidence, including proposed testimony of experts.

- o *Joint Claim Construction and Prehearing Statement* (60 days later). The parties file a joint statement with their respective constructions.

- o *Completion of Claim Construction Discovery* (30 days later). The parties finish discovery related to claim construction, including depositions.

- o *Claim Construction Briefs* (45 days later). The plaintiff files an opening claim construction brief. The defendant then has 14 days to respond, and the plaintiff has 7 days to reply.

- o *Claim Construction Hearing* (2 weeks after reply brief, subject to the court's convenience). If necessary, the court holds a hearing, including testimony of any expert witnesses.

- • *Damages Contentions* (50 days after Invalidity Contentions). The plaintiff must explain the categories of damages it is seeking and its theories of recovery. (The defendant has 30 days to explain why it disagrees.)

The predictability provided by this timeline can be particularly helpful for clients, who often want to know the expected timeline on which litigation costs will be incurred. These patent local rules also highlight the detailed information that will be needed early in a case for infringement and invalidity contentions. Patent plaintiffs will generally want to prepare infringement claim charts before filing suit if possible, and defendants will need to begin searching for invalidating prior art as early as possible.

Does it make sense to have specialized procedural rules for patent cases? If so, should there be specialized procedures for other types of civil cases? Should patent local rules be standardized across jurisdictions? What rules might parties want to change in the initial case management conference?

C. Post-Issuance Review at the USPTO

In addition to challenging the validity of patents in court, potential infringers and other parties can also bring challenges at the USPTO. This section summarizes the three USPTO administrative procedures for invalidating granted patents: ex parte reexamination, post grant review (PGR), and inter partes review (IPR). Ex parte reexamination (sometimes shortened to "ex parte reexam") was introduced in 1981; PGR and IPR were created by the 2011 America Invents Act (AIA).[1]

Ex parte reexamination allows any person—including the patent owner[2]—to request that the USPTO reexamine any patent, but only based on novelty and nonobviousness arguments involving paper prior art (patents and printed publications). As its name suggests, this procedure is largely ex parte: If the USPTO determines that the petition raises "a substantial new question of patentability," the patent owner may respond to the petition, and the third-party requester "may file and have considered in the reexamination a reply to any statement filed by the patent owner." 35 U.S.C. § 304. Otherwise, third parties have no involvement in the proceeding. Reexamination is similar to the initial examination except that it is conducted by a panel of three examiners in the USPTO's "central reexamination unit," and the patentee cannot amend the patent after the initial response to the petition. As with initial examination, the patentee may appeal a negative decision to the PTAB, and from there to the Federal Circuit.

In contrast to ex parte reexamination, the AIA's PGR and IPR proceedings allow active participation by a third-party challenger in a trial-like proceeding before the PTAB. The AIA trials are adversarial proceedings that afford the parties some discovery and an oral hearing, although both are more limited than in district court, and the timeline is much shorter. After a petition is filed, the patent owner has three months to file a preliminary response, and then the USPTO has three months to decide whether to "institute" the proceeding and begin the trial phase. By statute, the trial phase is supposed to be concluded within twelve months, with a six-month extension for good cause.

PGR and IPR petitions differ in what kinds of arguments may be raised and when they may be filed. For the first nine months after an AIA patent is issued, it is eligible for PGR, which allows validity to be challenged by any third party who has not filed a civil action challenging the patent's validity. All validity issues that are

---

[1] The AIA also created a post-grant proceeding known as covered business method (CBM) review, which applied to non-technological financial product or service patents, but CBM review sunset in September 2020. PGR and IPR replaced another type of post-grant proceeding, inter partes reexamination, which had been created in 1999.

[2] Why would anyone challenge their own patent? The most common use is to test and strengthen the validity of a patent in light of a newly discovered piece of prior art before asserting the patent in a costly infringement suit.

defenses to infringement may be asserted in a PGR petition, including issues under §§ 101, 102, 103, and 112 as well as double patenting, but not § 112's best mode requirement. The USPTO will institute a PGR proceeding if the petition shows "that it is more likely than not that at least 1 of the claims challenged in the petition is unpatentable" or of it "raises a novel or unsettled legal question." 35 U.S.C. § 324.

All patents that are not eligible for or currently subject to PGR are eligible for the third type of proceeding, IPR, which allows validity to be challenged by any third party who has not filed a civil action challenging validity or been sued for infringement of the patent more than one year earlier. The petitioner may only raise novelty and nonobviousness arguments involving paper prior art (as with ex parte reexam). The USPTO will institute an IPR proceeding if "there is a reasonable likelihood that the petitioner would prevail with respect to at least 1 of the claims challenged in the petition." 35 U.S.C. § 314. Only about half of IPR petitions are instituted; the others are denied for failure to meet this standard or are dismissed due to settlement between the challenger and the patent owner.

Of the three post-grant proceedings, IPRs are by far the most popular. In fiscal year 2021, the USPTO received about 300 petitions for ex parte reexam, 90 for PGR, and 1,300 for IPR. The growth in IPR proceedings has also reshaped the Federal Circuit docket: in 2011, the court heard fewer than 150 appeals from the USPTO and over 400 appeals from patent infringement lawsuits in district courts; in 2021, there were over 500 USPTO appeals and fewer than 300 appeals from patent infringement suits. Over this same time, patent law has grown from 42% to 51% of the court's caseload.[3] What are the advantages of challenging validity through post-grant proceedings at the USPTO rather than in federal district court, and how do parties choose among these options?

One important factor is cost. USPTO filing fees are currently $12,600 for ex parte reexam, $19,000 for IPR (plus another $22,500 if instituted), and $20,000 for PGR (plus $27,500 if instituted), with lower fees for "small" or "micro" entities. In addition, according to a survey of practitioners, the average legal cost for ex parte reexamination is about $17,000. For IPR and PGR, the median cost of attorneys' fees to file a petition is $120,000 to $250,000 (depending on field), and the median total attorneys' fees through appeal is $450,000 to $650,000. (The cost of filing an IPR petition and defending a patent in an IPR proceeding are roughly the same.) These costs can be significant for some firms, but all of these proceedings are less expensive than the millions of dollars it might cost to litigate in court, as noted at the beginning of this chapter. *See* American Intellectual Property Law Association, *Report of the Economic Survey* (2021).

---

[3] This shift has exacerbated concerns about the negative effects of judicial specialization. *See generally* Paul R. Gugliuzza, *Rethinking Federal Circuit Jurisdiction*, 100 GEO. L.J. 1437 (2012); Laura G. Pedraza-Fariña, *Understanding the Federal Circuit: An Expert Community Approach*, 30 Berkeley Tech.L.J. 89 (2015).

Another advantage of these USPTO proceedings for those challenging validity is that the presumption of validity does not apply. That is, invalidity is established by a preponderance of the evidence rather than the higher standard of clear and convincing evidence. The agency also used to use the "broadest reasonable interpretation" claim construction standard from the examination context rather than the "ordinary meaning" *Phillips* standard used in the courts, and the Supreme Court granted *Chevron* deference to this choice in *Cuozzo Speed Technologies v. Lee*, 136 S. Ct. 2131 (2016). (*Chevron* deference means that the statute is ambiguous and that the agency has discretion to choose from among reasonable interpretations.) The USPTO then decided in 2018 that it would use the *Phillips* standard for AIA trial proceedings (PGR and IPR); the "broadest reasonable interpretation" standard still applies in ex parte reexamination.

Challengers should also consider the effect of USPTO proceedings on other proceedings, including pending or future district court litigation. Ex parte reexam petitions can be filed anonymously and have no estoppel effect. IPR and PGR proceedings bar challengers from later raising invalidity questions that were "raised or reasonably could have been raised" in the IPR or PGR proceeding. 35 U.S.C. §§ 315(e), 325(e). Most IPR petitions are filed after a patent has been asserted in district court litigation, and district courts typically stay litigation pending the USPTO proceeding. That is to say, many patent defendants prefer to litigate the validity of the patent in an IPR proceeding rather than in the course of the district court litigation, largely for the reasons described above. When litigation is not stayed, non-final judgments—including large damages awards—have sometimes been vacated in light of invalidations in parallel USPTO proceedings. *See Fresenius USA v. Baxter International*, 721 F.3d 1330 (Fed. Cir. 2013); Paul R. Gugliuzza, *(In)valid Patents*, 92 Notre Dame L. Rev. 271 (2016). Patent defendants generally praise IPR proceedings as a more cost-effective way to challenge patents, whereas patent owners have argued that IPRs have undermined confidence in the U.S. patent system.

IPR critics have launched a number of legal challenges to the IPR process and the PTAB. The Supreme Court has already heard five cases involving the PTAB: the 2016 *Cuozzo* case mentioned above on claim construction standards; *SAS Institute v. Iancu*, 138 S. Ct. 1348 (2018) (rejecting the USPTO's "partial institution" practice of sometimes granting an IPR petition on only some of the challenged claims); *Oil States Energy v. Greene's Energy Group*, 138 S. Ct. 1365 (2018) (rejecting constitutional challenges to IPRs); *Thryv v. Click-To-Call Technologies*, 140 S. Ct. 1367 (2020) (holding that certain challenges to PTAB decisions are nonappealable); and *United States v. Arthrex*, 141 S. Ct. 1970 (2021) (holding that under the Appointments Clause, because PTAB judges were not appointed and confirmed by the Senate, their decisions should be reviewable by the USPTO director).

How should policymakers evaluate these different proceedings for invalidating patents? Should they be expanded, such as by allowing IPR petitions to raise invalidity issues beyond §§ 102 and 103 challenges based on paper prior art?

The following table summarizes the key differences between ex parte reexamination, PGR, and IPR.

	Ex Parte Reexamination	Post Grant Review (PGR)	Inter Partes Review (IPR)
Statute	35 U.S.C. §§ 301–07	35 U.S.C. §§ 321–29	35 U.S.C. §§ 311–19
Petitioner	anyone (including the patent owner); can be anonymous; no estoppel	anyone who is not the patent owner and has not filed a civil action challenging validity	anyone who is not the patent owner, has not filed a civil action challenging validity, and has not been sued over the patent more than one year prior
Eligible Patents	all patents in force	only AIA patents in first nine months after issuance	all patents in force, unless eligible for or currently subject to PGR
Basis for Challenge	only §§ 102 and 103 based on paper prior art (patents and printed publications)	all validity issues that are defenses to infringement	only §§ 102 and 103 based on paper prior art (patents and printed publications)
Total Cost Estimate	around $30,000	around $500,000	around $500,000
Legal Standards	no presumption of validity; claims get broadest reasonable interpretation	"reasonable likelihood" institution standard; no presumption of validity; *Phillips* claim construction	"more likely than not" institution standard; no presumption of validity; *Phillips* claim construction
Estoppel	none	issues that were raised or reasonably could have been raised	issues that were raised or reasonably could have been raised

D. Litigation at the International Trade Commission

The federal courts and the USPTO are not the only institutions that resolve U.S. patent law issues: the International Trade Commission (ITC) also has authority to resolve certain patent infringement claims. The ITC is an independent agency in DC with jurisdiction over various trade disputes. The ITC shouldn't be confused with the Court of International Trade (or "Trade Court"), an Article III court in New York that hears some appeals from the ITC and other trade disputes, and which is also under the jurisdiction of the Federal Circuit. The ITC's patent decisions don't go through the Trade Court; they are appealed directly to the Federal Circuit. Private parties may bring an action in the ITC under Section 337 of the Tariff Act of 1930, 19 U.S.C. § 1337, and about 90% of Section 337 cases are patent cases.

There are two important prerequisites for ITC jurisdiction over patent disputes:

First, the infringing goods must be *imported*. The ITC may investigate claims of "[t]he importation into the United States, the sale for importation, or the sale within the United States after importation by the owner, importer, or consignee, of articles that . . . infringe a valid and enforceable United States patent . . . or are made, produced, processed, or mined under, or by means of, a process covered by the claims of a valid and enforceable United States patent." 19 U.S.C. § 1337(a)(1)(B). This statute also covers "importation of goods that, after importation, are used by the importer to directly infringe at the inducement of the goods' seller." *Suprema v. Int'l Trade Comm'n*, 796 F.3d 1338 (Fed. Cir. 2015) (en banc). Because ITC cases are in rem proceedings, with jurisdiction over the accused imported articles, issues regarding personal jurisdiction over foreign entities are simplified.

Second, the patentee (referred to as the "complainant") must have a *domestic industry* related to the patent. The ITC has jurisdiction "only if an industry in the United States, relating to the articles protected by the patent . . . exists or is in the process of being established." § 1337(a)(2). A domestic industry exists "if there is in the United States, with respect to the articles protected by the patent . . . (A) significant investment in plant and equipment; (B) significant employment of labor or capital; or (C) substantial investment in its exploitation, including engineering, research and development, or licensing." § 1337(a)(3). Note that it is the investments, not the patent owner, that must be "in the United States." A domestic patent owner that invests in foreign plants, labor, or licensing does not satisfy the domestic industry requirement. And a foreign patent owner can satisfy the requirement if it has made one of these investments in exploiting the invention in the United States (simply importing the finished product into the United States is not enough). The patent owner doesn't need to manufacture the patented goods itself, but expenses asserting the patent in litigation are not enough to establish a domestic industry. *See John Mezzalingua Assocs. v. Int'l Trade Comm'n*, 660 F.3d 1322 (Fed.

Cir. 2011); *InterDigital Commc'ns v. Int'l Trade Comm'n*, 707 F.3d 1295 (Fed. Cir. 2013).

If the ITC finds a Section 337 violation, the only remedy is prospective injunctive relief through *exclusion orders* and *cease-and-desist orders*, both of which are subject to presidential review. An exclusion order prohibits further entry of infringing goods, enforced by Customs and Border Protection at the border, and can be limited to specific infringing products or general orders covering products from importers who were not parties to the investigation. Cease-and-desist orders are enforced by the ITC (using civil and criminal penalties) and prohibit continued distribution of products that were already imported. The ITC may not award money damages. But because of the availability of injunctions, the ITC grew in popularity as a patent litigation forum post-*eBay*, with about 50–70 complaints per year. Patent owners may file in both the ITC for an exclusion order and in district court for damages, although the district court action must be stayed pending the outcome of the ITC dispute. *See* 28 U.S.C. § 1659; *In re Princo*, 478 F.3d 1345 (Fed. Cir. 2007). About 70% of Section 337 cases have a district court counterpart. But note that ITC cases do not have preclusive effect on district court cases. If one party wins before the ITC, the district court case can continue (and that court can reach a different result).

Procedurally, litigating in the ITC is different from litigating in district court. Cases move more quickly, with the entire dispute typically resolved within 10–15 months. There are also fewer limits on discovery than in district court, which can be particularly burdensome for the accused infringer (referred to as the "respondent"). Most cases go to trial, and trials are in front of one of six Administrative Law Judges (ALJs) rather than a jury. The costs of ITC litigation are thus extremely high and rapidly incurred, typically favoring complainants who can prepare for these costs and use them to exert settlement pressure. There is also a third party to each dispute: the Commission Investigative Attorney (or "Staff") represents the public interest and has the same rights as the complainant and respondent to gather and present evidence. Convincing the staff of the merits and policy arguments in favor of your position can bring an important strategic advantage.

What are the public benefits of patent litigation at the ITC? Should anything be done to address the litigation advantages to wealthy plaintiffs that this forum creates?

E. Alternative Dispute Resolution

Although this casebook is focused on patent litigation, the vast majority of uses of patented technology do not involve the courts. Rather, parties often reach an agreement such as a patent license without formal legal proceedings through processes known as alternative dispute resolution (ADR). We provide a brief overview of the law of patent licensing and patent transactions in Chapter 18.

The most informal ADR method is *negotiation*, or unstructured discussions between the parties to determine whether they can reach a mutually beneficial outcome. Patent *mediation* involves a neutral third party to facilitate non-binding negotiations in a more structured way. Mediation is often used to encourage settlement after a lawsuit is filed, and the Federal Judicial Center has produced a comprehensive patent mediation guide.[4] Finally, *arbitration* can provide a binding dispute resolution process that is often cheaper and faster than litigation.

The United States is an outlier in allowing arbitration of patent validity claims. The Patent Act expressly recognizes that agreements "requiring arbitration of any dispute relating to patent validity or infringement . . . shall be valid, irrevocable, and enforceable, except for any grounds that exist at law or in equity for revocation of a contract." 35 U.S.C. § 294(a). The American Arbitration Association and the International Institute for Conflict Prevention and Resolution each maintain specialized exemplaroy rules for arbitration of patent disputes, which are similar to the patent local rules discussed above in setting out a structure for exchanging infringement contentions, invalidity contentions, discovery, and claim construction.

Although arbitration is private, making it easier to maintain confidentiality, § 294(d) requires notice of the arbitration and of the resulting award to be provided to the USPTO. Parties may thus choose to limit the proceedings to only infringement and damages issues to avoid any record of an invalidity finding that third parties might rely on in the future.

---

[4] https://www.fjc.gov/sites/default/files/materials/05/Patent_Mediation_Guide.pdf

Practice Problems: Patent Litigation Procedure

1. Amandeep is the general counsel for a German consumer electronics firm, ALO. Two years ago, ALO exclusively licensed U.S. patent rights for a new invention called a thingamajigger, which ALO has developed for commercial production and begun exporting to the United States. Amandeep just learned that a Japanese firm, Wonoly, is also exporting thingamajiggers to the United States. ALO's CEO has asked Amandeep what their options are for stopping Wonoly's sales in the United States. What should she recommend?

2. Although Amandeep's legal department coordinated a patent search on the thingamajigger before ALO began thingamajigger production, she recently came across a U.S. patent issued to a Delaware corporation six months ago which the new thingamajigger might infringe. Amandeep's team has studied the claims and does not think the patent is obvious in light of the earlier patent ALO licensed, but they do think the patent is likely invalid for indefiniteness. What course of action should Amandeep recommend for ALO?

3. Amandeep has recently become aware that an American electronics firm, xJigger, is selling a facsimile of the thingamajigger to American consumers. xJigger is incorporated in the state of South Dakota, where it also has its main production facilities and most of its employees. xJigger sells thingamajiggers nationwide via its website, with roughly 55% of its business flowing to the Western District of Washington, where ALO has its American headquarters. There is also a trade show ("JiggerCon") held every year in the Western District of Washington. xJigger always sends a representative, and a large proportion of its sales are generated at this trade show. In addition, xJigger operates a small facility in Rhode Island where it produces components for the thingamajigger, to be assembled at the plant in South Dakota. In which of these three judicial districts—the District of South Dakota, the Western District of Washington, and the District of Rhode Island—would venue be proper if ALO were to sue xJigger? Which district or districts should ALO prefer to sue in, and which district or districts should it try to avoid?

18. Patent Licensing and Transactions

Much of this book has focused on the legal rules governing obtaining and litigating patents. But most uses of patented technology do not involve litigation: instead, a potential infringer can license the patent. That is, the putative infringer could reach an agreement with the patent owner that permits the infringer to use the patented technology in exchange for some amount of money (or something else of value). Licensing is important both to patent owners and the potential users of patented technology. For owners, licensing can be a significant source of revenue—sometimes the only source of revenue, if the owner is a non-practicing entity. For potential users, licensing creates freedom to operate: the firm can employ the patented technology without having to be concerned about being sued for infringement. Potential licenses can also be valuable bargaining chips: if one firm is threatened with suit by a competitor in the same industry, it can sometimes defend itself by threatening to counter-sue its competitor. The eventual solution may be a cross-license, in which each firm grants the other the right to use its patented technology.

For the most part, licenses are simply contracts and evaluated under standard contract principles. That is, the question of which patented technology a licensee is permitted to use, what activities a license covers, or how much the patent owner is to be paid in exchange for granting the license are all questions of contract interpretation. The same is true for mergers & acquisitions, assignments, and other transactions in which patent rights are bought and sold. They are creatures of contract, and the transfer of patent rights is evaluated under the same contract principles that are used to evaluate the merger or acquisition itself.

However, patents can also give rise to particular issues or complexities when they are licensed or transferred. In some cases, these issues concern the uneasy interaction between patent law and antitrust law. As explained in Chapter 1, patents create an incentive for innovation by offering the possibility of a quasi-monopoly for the patent owner, allowing it to charge supra-competitive prices. But under certain circumstances, particularly when patents are aggregated, that power can become excessive and lead to antitrust concerns. In other cases, patent law has developed a series of specialized rules to govern issues that arise in licensing and other transactions. This chapter briefly canvasses some of these specialized concerns that stem from patent transactions and the rules that have evolved to address those concerns.

For those looking for more details on the law of IP transactions and licensing, Jorge Contreras has written an excellent free casebook, which is available at iptransactions.org.

A. Standards-Essential Patents, FRAND Licensing, Patent Pools, and Monopoly

A great deal of modern technology, particularly consumer electronics, runs on technical "standards." A standard is a set of technical specifications that establishes how the technology will work, how it can be operated, and how it interacts with other types of technology. DVDs, Bluetooth, Wi-Fi, 4G and 5G cellular networks—these are all technical standards. The value of a technical standard is that it allows a panoply of different companies to create a wide variety of products that will all operate and interact seamlessly. You can connect a Samsung phone, an Apple tablet, an Amazon Fire Stick, and even a GE oven to a Wi-Fi router made by Netgear, and they'll all function properly. In the modern era it is easy to take this type of technical interoperability for granted, but there is nothing inevitable about it. It's easy to imagine an alternative universe in which Apple tablets only worked with Apple wireless routers and Samsung phones only worked with Samsung wireless routers, just as only some versions of software will run on the iOS operating system that powers Apple devices. Standards are what make this type of interoperability possible.

The problem with standards is that, when coupled with patents, they create the potential for severe monopoly power and anticommons problems. Imagine that Cisco owned a patent on some essential aspect of Wi-Fi, without which a Wi-Fi network would not be operable. (This is in fact the case.) This is known as a "standards-essential patent" or "SEP," in that it is impossible to construct a device that uses the standard without infringing the patent. In a world without standards, a competing company that did not want to license Cisco's patent could simply create and sell its own wireless network—imagine Wi-Apple—to avoid infringing the patent. But if Wi-Fi has been adopted as the industry standard by every other firm in the market, Wi-Apple becomes nearly worthless. Who would buy or install a wireless network that will only connect with Apple products, rather than a Wi-Fi network that works with everything else? Once Wi-Fi has been selected as the industry standard, every firm in the market has little choice but to use Wi-Fi and make their devices interoperable with Wi-Fi. This bestows tremendous market power on Cisco and any other company whose patented technology is essential to the standard. Cisco can charge every market participant an exorbitant price for licensing its technology, and so can any other party that owns an essential patent. There is no alternative and no way to design around Cisco's patent. A firm must either pay or leave the industry.

The industries that employ standards have tried to avoid this problem through governance systems. Technical standards are typically established by international non-governmental organizations known as "standard-setting organizations." The Institute of Electrical and Electronics Engineers, known as IEEE, is one of the most famous of these standard-setting organizations, responsible for many widely used standards. Generally, the organization that selects a standard will require every party that owns a standard-essential patent to agree ahead of time to license that patent to any manufacturer of a standardized product either for free, or on "fair, reasonable, and non-discriminatory" ("FRAND") terms. In many instances, this means in practice that before a standard such as Wi-Fi is adopted by the relevant standard-setting organization, the owner of each relevant patent must sign a contract or otherwise promise that it will license the patent on FRAND terms. The patent owner is then bound to this agreement, and failure to license on those terms in the future can subject the patent owner to contractual or antitrust liability.

What are FRAND terms? The "non-discriminatory" part of FRAND means that the patent owner must license the patent on the same terms to similarly situated licensees. That means it cannot grant more favorable licensing terms to a corporate partner than to a competitor. As for the requirements that the licensing terms be "fair" and "reasonable," they have been the subject of substantial litigation and much scholarly discussion, with no definitive resolution. The general consensus seems to be that the patent owner must license at a price that allows it to recoup value but does not eliminate the licensee's profits and does not exploit its powerful bargaining position. But as one might imagine when it comes to terms like "fair" and "reasonable," there is still quite a bit of debate as to whether the licensors of standards-essential patents are fulfilling their FRAND obligations in any given case.

Of course, even with FRAND terms, negotiating a license with every firm that owns a standards-essential patent can involve significant transaction costs. There are often hundreds or thousands (or more) of such patents that are essential to a given technological standard, and striking a deal with every such firm can be time-consuming and costly. Usefully, however, standards-essential patents also open up the possibility of "patent pools." A patent pool is a collection of patents that all concern a particular technology, such as Bluetooth or Wi-Fi. The advantage of a patent pool is that a potential licensee can license all patents in the pool in one fell swoop, often for a flat price, rather than having to negotiate separately with all of their owners.

Patent pools are voluntary associations. A group of firms that own the relevant patents can agree to form a patent pool, aggregating their patents and making them collectively available. However, patent pools are generally prohibited under antitrust law when the patents involved are substitutes for one another, rather than complements. The reason is that patent pool that involves substitute patents can constitute classic horizontal agreements in restraint of trade. They force a potential licensee who wants access to one patent to purchase access to all the patents. To understand the problem, imagine that there are three methods for manufacturing an automobile engine, each protected by a patent. In theory, this is a semi-competitive marketplace: an automobile manufacturer could negotiate separately with all three patent-holders and elect to license whichever technology is being offered at the best value. But now imagine that the three patent owners reached an agreement: anyone who wanted to license the technology from one of them would have to license the technology from all of them. This would create a full-fledged monopoly and dramatically raise the price that licensees would be forced to pay. And this monopoly would be the result of a contract between the patent owners—an agreement in restraint of trade—rather than merely the result of the patents alone. This is why patent pools that include substitute patents are generally prohibited.

On the other hand, patent pools are typically permitted when the patents involved are complements—that is, when a firm that licenses one of the patents would benefit from licensing the others as well. In such cases, there is no horizontal agreement because the firm is not being deprived of a choice between options. Instead, the firm is licensing a package of patents that are more valuable together than separately. Standards-essential patents are complementary in exactly this regard. By definition, a patentee must license all the relevant patents to construct a device that operates according to the standard. (That's what it means for patents to be "standards-essential.") A patent pool thus does not restrain trade or create an artificial monopoly; the potential licensee never had any option other than to license all the patents. Accordingly, antitrust regulators have generally permitted patent pools involving standards-essential patents. This has redounded to the benefit of both patent owners and patent licensees, who no longer need negotiate separately with each patent owner.

B. *Kimble v. Marvel* and the Structure of Licenses

As we detailed in Chapter 15 (and as *LaserDynamics v. Quanta* makes clear), there are multiple ways to structure a patent license. The two most common forms are lump sum licenses and running royalty licenses. When a license is structured as a lump sum, the licensee pays one fixed amount of money for the license. When a license is structured as a running royalty, the licensee pays some percentage of its revenues (or profits, or sales) as a royalty, extending into the future.

In some cases, licensees or licensors might prefer a lump sum royalty. For the licensee, it allows them to pay one amount of money, once, and never worry about the patent owner again, no matter how successful the licensee's product or how much money they make in the future. For the licensor, it shifts the risk that the product will fail to the licensee. In other cases, licensees or licensors might prefer to negotiate running royalties. A running royalty shifts some of the risk of the product underperforming to the licensor; and at the same time, it gives the licensee some stake in the ongoing success of the product, which can be lucrative if the product performs well. More generally, if the parties do not know how much the technology will eventually be worth, or how successful the licensee's product will eventually be, a running royalty offers a compromise solution that allows the two sides to reach agreement under conditions of uncertainty. The licensee will pay much more if the technology turns out to be more valuable, and much less if it turns out to be less valuable.

However, there are other considerations at play as well. As we explained in Chapter 12, in *Kimble v. Marvel Entertainment*, 576 U.S. 446 (2015), the Supreme Court upheld the longstanding *Brulotte* rule, which prohibits patent owners from continuing to collect royalties on a patent after that patent has been declared invalid by a court or the USPTO. Suppose that Firm A agrees to license a patent to Firm B for ten years in exchange for 1% of Firm B's sales revenue in each of those ten years. In year five of this arrangement, Firm C files an IPR against Firm A and the USPTO declares the patent invalid. Firm A can no longer enforce its agreement against Firm B—it can no longer collect revenues under the license. This is the case even if the contract between Firm A and Firm B explicitly states: "Firm B is obligated to pay Firm A 1% of its sales revenue each year even if Firm A's patent is declared invalid." That is, this is a hard and fast rule of patent licensing, not a default rule of contract interpretation. It is also an extra-textual rule, created by the courts without obvious warrant in the Patent Act.

This might seem at first blush like a sensible rule—why should a patent owner be allowed to collect royalties on an invalid patent? The problem is that the parties may have explicitly wanted to allocate the risk of the patent being invalidated to the licensee, as in the example above. There might be any number of reasons why the parties would want to structure their license this way, including the possibility that the licensee is best positioned to bear the risks of an uncertain future. (For instance, the patentee might be a large company, and the patent owner a small entity or solo inventor.) The *Brulotte* rule may thus skew decision-making by firms negotiating licenses. Licensors may lean more toward lump sums than they otherwise would, because a lump sum insulates them against the risk of the patent being invalidated. Licensees might lean more than they otherwise would toward running royalties for the opposite reason. The result may be that more firms will end up compromising on the economic suitability of licenses in order to avoid the legal risk created by the *Brulotte* rule. In any event, this is an important rule for IP attorneys to keep in mind when negotiating licensing arrangements.

C. Patents in Mergers, Acquisitions, and Other Deals

In the modern technology economy, the physical assets owned by businesses—factories, machines, land—have diminished in importance, and the intangible assets owned by businesses—patents, trade secrets, technical know-how, and other intellectual property—have grown in importance. As a result, patents are often an important component of corporate mergers and acquisitions. This means that transactional attorneys who work on deals will often need to be well-versed in patent law or able to call upon attorneys who are.

The issues surrounding patents that can arise during merger and acquisition deals are a microcosm of the issues that those deals involve more generally. A target firm (the firm being acquired) will often be involved in patent law as both a "seller" and "buyer." That is, the target will frequently have a portfolio of patents that it licenses, enforces, or simply uses as a potential deterrent against competitors. The target will also frequently be a licensee of others' patents, or it will depend on being able to navigate the thicket of patent rights in a manner that leaves it with ample freedom to operate its business.

This means that transactional attorneys must be careful to assess both the quality of the patents held by a target firm and that firm's potential susceptibility to patent suits by competitors when structuring or advising on a deal (for find another attorney who can do it for them). The strength of a firm's patent portfolio, or that firm's vulnerability to suit by other patent-holding firms, can affect the firm's value quite substantially.

The situation becomes even more complex when one firm is acquiring a piece, but not the entirety, of another firm. Imagine, for instance, that Firm A is acquiring the personal computer division of Firm B but not its mainframe server division, which primarily sells to large web business. Firm A would presumably like to acquire all of the patents involved in Firm B's personal computer division. However, these patents may overlap to some degree with Firm B's server division, which could cause problems for Firm B if the patents were sold. In addition, ownership of the patents is not strictly necessary to the personal computer division's operations. After all, patents do not provide a right to manufacture anything; they offer (only) a right to exclude others. The personal computer division merely needs a license to continue using the patented technology. Thus, an acquisition of all assets necessary to operate the personal computer division will not necessarily include that division's intellectual property, which might be one of its most valuable assets.

In some cases, corporate deals of this sort can also raise antitrust concerns. For instance, it is not uncommon for large, entrenched firms to deal with new entrants by simply acquiring them, thereby eliminating the threat of competition. In a world without patents, however, one acquisition may not be enough to make competition disappear. For instance, imagine that Facebook is concerned about competition from Small Startup A. It acquires Small Startup A and folds its business into Facebook's own operations—or shuts it down completely. Even then, there is nothing to stop another entrepreneur (or even the same entrepreneur) from opening Small Startup B and pursuing precisely the same line of business as Small Startup A. The threat of serial challenges of this nature will often deter large firms from pursuing these "killer acquisitions" as a strategy in the first instance.

The calculus changes, however, when Small Startup A owns critical patents. In that case, acquiring Small Startup A allows Facebook not only to swallow that potential competitor, but then to force other competitors out of the market as well. Facebook would of course argue that it is only using its patents as they were intended. But this type of action has echoes of the sort of horizontal agreement in restraint of trade that justifies prohibiting patent pools and other horizontal arrangements in most circumstances. For this reason, acquisitions of this type often draw antitrust scrutiny, though they are rarely invalidated. Nonetheless, it is useful to think of patents as "force multipliers"—they make killer acquisitions and other types of deals much more profitable for incumbent firms and potentially much more deleterious to competition. For an empirical study suggesting that incumbent pharmaceutical firms acquire startups for the purpose of discontinuing research projects that would compete with the incumbent's existing products, see Colleen Cunningham, Florian Ederer & Song Ma, *Killer Acquisitions*, 129 J. Pol. Econ. 649 (2021).

Even simple licensing arrangements can raise significant antitrust concerns. For instance, imagine two competitors, A and B, that each produce a particular product such as a large piece of machinery. Imagine that A and B each own a series of overlapping patents, such that A may be infringing B's patents and B may be infringing A's patents. Suppose that A sues B and B counter-sues A. The two parties then settle their lawsuit, with A granting B a license covering any sales made east of the Mississippi River and B granting A a license covering any sales made west of the Mississippi River.

At first glance, this looks like a standard patent litigation settlement via cross-license: the two parties have reached an agreement that will allow both to operate without infringing. But in fact what they have done is divided the country geographically in such a way as to eliminate competition. Customers east of the Mississippi have only one option, and customers west of the Mississippi have only one option. Of course, it is possible that a customer could purchase a machine in Illinois and transport it to California, thus creating some level of competition. But this may be challenging and costly, particularly for larger products. What was once a duopoly has become a monopoly. That would be unlawful in the absence of patents, and the fact that it occurs as the result of patent litigation does not shield it from antitrust liability.

D. Assignor Estoppel

A distant cousin to the rule prohibiting royalties after a patent has been invalidated is the doctrine of "assignor estoppel." Perhaps the most common context in which this doctrine arises involves serial entrepreneurs who sell one business and then begin another. Imagine that Juanita starts a high-tech firm and successfully applies for several patents. Juanita then sells her firm—including her patents—to Motorola and begins another startup venture involving a similar type of technology. If Juanita's new venture involves technology that is too similar to the work she did previously, she might find herself as the target of a patent infringement suit, filed by Motorola, asserting her own patents. Juanita might then try to defend herself by arguing that the patents she is being accused of infringing—the patents she sold to Motorola—are invalid.

For decades, the Federal Circuit has prohibited any party who assigns (sells or gives) a patent to any other party from thereafter challenging the validity of that patent. *Diamond Scientific Co. v. Ambico, Inc.*, 848 F.2d 1220 (Fed. Cir. 1988). The court based this rule on equitable considerations: having sold a patent, it did not seem fair for the assignor to turn around and argue that the patent it sold was invalid, and thus a nullity. In the same vein, it seemed to be violating the principle that patent owners should not be receiving payment for patents that are invalid.

At the same time, there are evident downsides to such a rule. In some cases, the assignor might be the party best positioned to challenge a patent's validity. Prohibiting the assignor from bringing such a challenge, ostensibly in the name of fairness, could have the effect of forcing other parties to pay for licenses to the (invalid) patent and thus create unfairness for them. In addition, this is another rule without textual warrant in the Patent Act, created out of whole cloth by the Federal Circuit. More than 50 years ago, the Supreme Court abolished the related doctrine of licensee estoppel, which barred the licensee to a patent from challenging that patent's validity. *Lear, Inc. v. Adkins*, 395 U.S. 653 (1969). Yet the doctrine of assignor estoppel has persisted.

Litigants continue to test and probe the contours and limits of this doctrine. In *Arista Networks v. Cisco Systems*, 908 F.3d 792 (Fed. Cir. 2018) and *Hologic v. Minerva Surgical*, 957 F.3d 1256 (Fed. Cir. 2020), the Federal Circuit refused to extend the doctrine of assignor estoppel to IPR proceedings. It held first in *Arista* that the doctrine of assignor estoppel did not prevent an assignor from filing for IPR of a patent it had previously assigned. Then, in *Hologic*, it held that an assignor who prevailed in the IPR could use the patent's invalidation as a defense in litigation, even though it could not separately have asserted in litigation that the patent was invalid. The Supreme Court granted certiorari in *Hologic* and carved back on the doctrine even further in 2021. The Court held that assignor estoppel only applies if the assignor made explicit or implicit representations regarding the validity of the patent when assigning it.

These decisions are a rather formalist gloss on what was, at least in theory, an equitable doctrine based in fairness. If it is unfair for an assignor to argue that a patent it has sold is invalid during district court litigation, it does not seem any less unfair for the same assignor to argue that the same patent is invalid in an IPR, particularly if that IPR will (if successful) end the litigation in favor of the assignor. The compromise position struck by the Federal Circuit and Supreme Court may thus prove to be unstable. It would not be surprising to see either court further limit the doctrine of assignor estoppel in the coming years.

19. Other U.S. Intellectual Property Rights

This casebook has focused on U.S. utility patents, but patents are only one of a number of types of legal entitlements over knowledge goods, which are grouped under the umbrella of "intellectual property." U.S. patent lawyers should be familiar with other forms of IP, both because legal arguments from one IP field are often imported to another and because a given product can often be protected with numerous IP rights.

Consider a wrist-worn fitness tracker, like a Fitbit. By now, you should recognize that this product can be covered by thousands of utility patents, such as on the microprocessor, battery, heartrate monitor, motion sensing, GPS tracking, wireless connectivity (e.g., Wi-Fi or Bluetooth standards), novel materials in the wristband, waterproofing technology, and more. But the tracker can *also* be protected with other forms of IP in the United States:

- **Trade secret law** protects any confidential information related to the tracker, such as manufacturing techniques that are not disclosed in a patent, the source code for the tracker's software, business plans, and lists of suppliers and customers.

- **Copyright law** protects original creative expression, including not just artistic expression such as graphics on the display screen and perhaps the overall design of the tracker, but also the software source code.

- **Trademark law** protects symbols or product designs that tell consumers about the source of the tracker, which can include not just the product name and logo but also aspects of the product design like the color or shape.

- **Regulatory exclusivity** attaches to some kinds of information submitted to regulatory agencies like the FDA; for example, certain medical devices (including some fitness trackers) receive six years of data exclusivity.

- **Design patents** protect new designs, which can include not just the overall product design but also individual features like the shape of the graphics display, aspects of the wristband design, and icons displayed on the screen.

We have already described the key forms of regulatory exclusivity associated with FDA approval in Chapter 11(D). This chapter provides a brief overview of the most prominent other forms of non-patent IP (trade secrets, copyright, and trademark), as well as the two other kinds of U.S. patents (design patents and plant patents). For those interested in learning about these areas in more depth, links to other free or low-cost IP casebooks have been collected by James Grimmelmann at https://james.grimmelmann.net/files/casebooks.

A. Non-Patent IP

1. Trade Secrets

U.S. trade secret law evolved as a matter of state common law, but every state except New York has now enacted a trade secrets statute based on the Uniform Trade Secrets Act (UTSA), although the specific language and interpretation vary by state.[1] The 2016 Defend Trade Secrets Act (DTSA) also provides a federal civil cause of action modeled on the UTSA, which doesn't preempt state law. In addition, trade secret misappropriation of commercial information may be criminally punished under the federal Economic Espionage Act of 1996.

Some of the underlying justifications for trade secret law are similar to those for utility patents: trade secret protection can encourage investment in information, limit the secrecy arms race, and encourage efficient disclosure and licensing. But trade secret law is also influenced by tort-based deterrence theories grounded in industry norms and good faith.

The definition of a "trade secret" is provided by UTSA § 1(4) and by the DTSA at 18 U.S.C. § 1839(3). Under both, establishing a trade secret involves three elements:

1. The information must be *secret*, meaning "not . . . generally known to, and not . . . readily ascertainable" by other persons. (Some states, such as California, do not have the "not readily ascertainable" language.)

2. The information must have "independent economic value" due to its secrecy. This is usually easily established; why would the information have been misappropriated if it wasn't valuable?

3. The owner must have taken "reasonable" efforts to maintain its secrecy. This may be assessed through an economic cost-benefit analysis, comparing the cost of precautions to the value of the secret.

Trade secrecy protection can last forever, but it is lost once the information is disclosed, including by third parties who have independently invented or reverse engineered the secret. Thus, the choice of whether to patent an invention or protect it as a trade secret may be informed by comparing the patent term with the expected lifespan of the secret. In practice, inventors can often patent one aspect of an invention

---

[1] The UTSA is at https://www.uniformlaws.org/viewdocument/final-act-with-comments-89. North Carolina is the only state whose statute is not explicitly based on the UTSA, but it is very similar. New York's trade secret law remains heavily influenced by the 1939 *Restatement of Torts*.

while maintaining trade secrecy protection over any aspects that are not disclosed in the patent application.

Trade secrecy "misappropriation" is defined by UTSA § 1(1)–(2) and by the DTSA at 18 U.S.C. § 1839(5)–(6). It includes acquisition, disclosure, or use of a trade secret by "improper means," which "includes theft, bribery, misrepresentation, breach or inducement of a breach of a duty to maintain secrecy, or espionage through electronic or other means." A comment to the UTSA also specifies: "Improper means could include otherwise lawful conduct which is improper under the circumstances; e.g., an airplane overflight used as aerial reconnaissance to determine the competitor's plant layout during construction of the plant. *E. I. du Pont de Nemours & Co., Inc. v. Christopher*, 431 F.2d 1012 (5th Cir. 1970)." The majority of trade secret misappropriation cases involve violation of an express or implied confidential relationship, such as disclosure of trade secrets by a former employee.

Trade secret law can be a rewarding practice area because it is geographically flexible, it often involves substantial client counseling and corporate work in addition to litigation, and there are many major open questions that still need to be resolved by the courts. There is also substantial overlap with patent practice because many lawsuits involve both patent infringement and trade secret misappropriation claims.

2. Copyright

Copyright law protects a wide variety of creative expression, including not only works that might be the subjects of literature, art, and film classes, but also product designs and computer programs. Like patent law, copyright law is grounded in the IP Clause: "To promote the progress of science and useful arts, by securing for limited times to authors and inventors the exclusive right to their respective writings and discoveries." But the "limited times" for copyrights are far longer than for patents: 70 years after the death of the author, or for corporate works, 120 years after creation or 95 years after publication, whichever is shorter.

The primary source of U.S. copyright law is the federal Copyright Act at Title 17 of the U.S. Code, although there are also limited state law protections. You don't need a formal registration or a © notice to have a valid copyright, although registering a work with the U.S. Copyright Office at copyright.gov provides important benefits. For example, copyright registration is required before filing most infringement suits, can serve as prima facie evidence of validity, and is a prerequisite for statutory damages and attorneys' fees.

Under 17 U.S.C. § 102, copyright protects "original works of authorship," which courts have interpreted to require both a *modicum of creativity*—a much lower bar than patent law's nonobviousness requirement—and *independent creation*. Thus, unlike in patent law, an independent creator can receive their own copyright protection. If you take a photograph that happens to look strikingly similar to someone else's, you can copyright your photograph (because of the minimal creativity involved in arranging the photo composition) and your photo doesn't infringe the earlier photographer's copyright. A copyrighted work must also be "fixed in any tangible medium of expression," meaning that some embodiment "is sufficiently permanent or stable to permit it to be perceived, reproduced, or otherwise communicated for a period of more than transitory duration." §§ 101–102. This broad language is intended to cover future technological development: works can be fixed using canvas, paper, sculpture, records, DVDs, MP3s, and a variety of other digital or nondigital formats.

Copyright law doesn't protect ideas—only expressions of ideas. Copyright thus cannot cover useful methods (that's for utility patent law), whether a method of accounting, a cooking recipe, or a functional computer algorithm. But it can protect a particular creative expression of any of these ideas, such as the text of a book describing how to use the accounting method, a cookbook author's asides about the memories a recipe evokes, or software in which a programmer has made one of many choices in how to express an algorithm in code. Of course, the dividing line between idea and expression can be murky. *See Google v. Oracle*, 141 S. Ct. 1183 (2021) (sidestepping the issue of whether the code at issue was copyrightable).

Copyright also doesn't protect facts, such as a factual database. (Other countries offer sui generis IP protection for databases.) If after painstaking archival research you develop a new theory about how a statute should be interpreted and you write a seminar paper describing your ideas about the facts you have uncovered, copyright law would not prevent another student from copying your ideas and facts without attribution if they do not copy the creative expression you used. (However, they will have committed plagiarism and may be sanctioned for academic misconduct!) Although facts are not themselves copyrightable, you can receive copyright protection for a *compilation* of facts (or other works, as in a cookbook or poetry anthology) based on minimal creativity in the *selection* and *arrangement*.

You also generally cannot copyright a "useful article"—one with "an intrinsic utilitarian function that is not merely to portray the appearance of the article or to convey information"—unless the "design incorporates pictorial, graphic, or sculptural features that can be identified separately from, and are capable of existing independently of, the utilitarian aspects of the article." 17 U.S.C. § 101. For example, you cannot use copyright law to protect the design of a simple utilitarian shovel or T-shirt—this is the domain of utility patent law. But you can copyright a shovel with elaborate handle carvings or a T-shirt with a creative graphic design. As with the idea/expression dichotomy, the dividing line has been contentious, and recent Supreme Court intervention has done little to resolve the issue. In a recent case that upheld the copyrightability of cheerleader uniforms, the Court held that the design of a useful article is copyrightable if the feature "(1) can be perceived as a two- or three-dimensional work of art separate from the useful article and (2) would qualify as a protectable pictorial, graphic, or sculptural work—either on its own or fixed in some other tangible medium of expression—if it were imagined separately from the useful article into which it is incorporated." *Star Athletica v. Varsity Brands*, 137 S. Ct. 1002 (2017).

A valid copyright provides protection against reproduction, adaptation into a "derivative work" (like a translation, movie version, or sequel), distribution, performance, or display. This protection extends not only to exact copies, but also to substantially similar variations, such as borrowing part of a song's melody for another song. Establishing an infringement claim requires showing (1) that the infringing work was actually copied from the original rather than independently created, and (2) that the works have "substantial similarity" from the perspective of an ordinary consumer. Before the works are compared for similarity, it is important to "filter out" any unprotected elements, such as abstract ideas, facts, and public domain materials.

Copyright protection has many statutory limitations and compulsory licensing regimes, but the most prominent limitation is the doctrine of fair use under 17 U.S.C. § 107. Use of a copyrighted work is more likely to be fair use when the use is noncommercial or for critique or research, when the copyrighted work is factual, when only a small portion of the work is used, and when the use doesn't supplant potential markets for the copyrighted work. Under the Supreme Court's interpretation of the fair use statute, the most important factor has become whether the use is "transformative": whether it "adds something new, with a further purpose or different character, altering the first with new expression, meaning, or message." Most recently, the Supreme Court relied on this transformativeness inquiry in holding Google's repurposing of certain computer software owned by Oracle to be fair use. *Google v. Oracle*, 141 S. Ct. 1183 (2021).

Finally, note that just because the author of a copyrighted work has made it available for free download online doesn't mean you are free to copy, edit, or distribute it yourself. So before you copy an image from Google search into your PowerPoint presentation, check whether the author has placed the image under an open license such as those available from Creative Commons. For example, this casebook is under a CC BY-NC-ND license, allowing you to download the casebook and share it with others in the original form (including attribution to us), but not to edit the casebook or use it commercially. But as noted at the start of the book, we are likely willing to authorize many derivative uses!

3. Trademark

Unlike patent, trade secret, and copyright law, trademark law is not designed to provide incentives for innovation. Rather, trademark law is meant to improve the quality of information about the source of goods and services, which can have benefits such as reducing search costs for consumers and providing incentives for firms to invest in consistent quality. Nonetheless—for better or worse—trademark law often allows producers to charge supracompetitive prices without using patent law. Consider, for example, the higher price charged for Tylenol than for store-brand acetaminophen, even though the products are chemically identical.

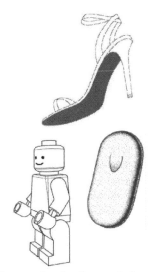

The sources of U.S. trademark law include the federal Lanham Act at 15 U.S.C. § 1051 et seq. and state common law. Like for copyright law, registration is not required for federal trademark protection; trademark rights are established through use in commerce. But registering a trademark with the USPTO provides benefits such as making it harder to argue that the mark is invalid and serving as a prerequisite for treble damages and attorneys' fees.

Trademark law can protect "any word, name, symbol, or device" used "to identify and distinguish" the source of goods or services. 15 U.S.C. § 1127. Courts have interpreted this coverage expansively to include aspects of product design, including color, shape, sound, and even fragrance (collectively referred to as "trade dress"). If consumers would immediately view a mark as signifying source, such as for coined terms like "Zappos" shoes, it is deemed "inherently distinctive" and is immediately protectable. Other marks are only protectable once they have "acquired distinctiveness," meaning that consumers have learned to view it as identifying source. For example, "American" airlines could initially be viewed as signifying a generic U.S. air carrier, but over time it has acquired distinctiveness and come to be viewed as signifying the brand American Airlines. Product design features can also gain acquired distinctiveness, as in the three chimes that signify NBC, the red shoe soles that signify Louboutin (at least among those who purchase $700 shoes), the purple color of Nexium acid reflux pills, and product shapes of everything from Lego minifigs to Pepperidge Farm Milano cookies.

Like copyright law, trademark law attempts to channel IP protection for useful product features to utility patent law by denying protection to "functional" features. The Supreme Court has defined a functional feature as one that "is essential to the use or purpose of the article" or that "affects the cost or quality of the article." *TrafFix Devices v. Marketing Displays*, 532 U.S. 23, 32 (2001). "A utility patent is strong evidence that the features therein claimed are functional." *Id.* at 29. Product features can also have "aesthetic" functionality—where a design is valued for the way it looks rather than for the source it signifies—which is unprotectable if it puts competitors at "a significant non-reputation-related disadvantage." *Id.* at 33. As with copyright's useful article doctrine, the dividing line between functional and non-functional trade dress has proven difficult to police.

A valid trademark provides protection against "likelihood of confusion" by others' use, which is evaluated by multi-factor tests that vary by federal appellate circuit. Confusion is more likely when the mark is strong, when the defendant's use is more similar to the mark, and when the defendant's goods or services are more proximate to the plaintiff's. If the mark is "famous" (think Coca-Cola or Louis Vuitton), trademark also protects against "dilution," or use of similar marks on dissimilar goods or services.

Trademark law has its own fair use doctrines, although they operate differently from copyright fair use. *Descriptive* fair use allows a third party to use a descriptive mark in good faith to describe their own goods—so even though American Airlines is a strong mark, a different airline may describe themselves as "an American air carrier." *Nominative* fair use, also known as non-trademark use, allows a third party to use a mark to refer to the mark owner's product for purposes like comparative advertising, parody, or artistic expression. The use of Mattel's "Barbie" trademark in the title and lyrics of Aqua's "Barbie Girl" song is a well-known example of permissible nominative use.

B. Design Patents

As noted in Chapter 1, in 2020, the USPTO granted 34,877 design patents in addition to 352,049 utility patents. Under 35 U.S.C. § 171, design patents are available for "any new, original and ornamental design for an article of manufacture." This broad language applies to designs of products ranging from app icons to cement mixers, and design patents can cover either surface ornamentation (like the pattern of a rug) or three-dimensional product configuration (like the shape of a chair). Many of these design features can *also* be protected using copyright and trademark law. What are the costs and benefits of IP protection for designs? Does it make sense to allow protection through overlapping IP regimes? *See* Christopher Buccafusco, Mark A. Lemley & Jonathan S. Masur, *Intelligent Design*, 68 Duke L.J. 75 (2018).

Like utility patents, design patents are examined for compliance with 35 U.S.C. §§ 102, 103, and 112, although these requirements are implemented differently and examination is far less stringent. Design patents also must be "ornamental" rather than functional. The lifespan of a design patent is 15 years from the date of grant (14 years for design patents filed before May 13, 2015). 35 U.S.C. § 173.

This section briefly reviews how the legal requirements for a design patent differ from those for a utility patent; for more in-depth coverage, see the design patent chapter of the free casebook by Sarah Burstein, Sarah Wasserman Rajec, and Andres Sawicki available at https://ssrn.com/abstract_id=3866658.

1. Claiming and Disclosing Design Patents

The disclosure requirements of 35 U.S.C. § 112(a) and the definiteness requirement of § 112(b) also apply to design patents, but unlike for utility patents, both disclosure and definiteness requirements are satisfied through drawings of the design at issue, along with a statement of the type of article of manufacture to which the design is applied. Each design patent has a single claim. Design patent drawings use solid lines to define the scope of the claim and dashed lines to provide context. Below are drawings from three different vacuum design patents owned by Dyson, where the first claims the whole vacuum design, the second focuses on the vacuum head, and the third focuses on the sphere at the bottom. Each claim consists of the statement "We claim the ornamental design for a vacuum cleaner, as shown and described" along with seven drawings showing the vacuum from different angles.

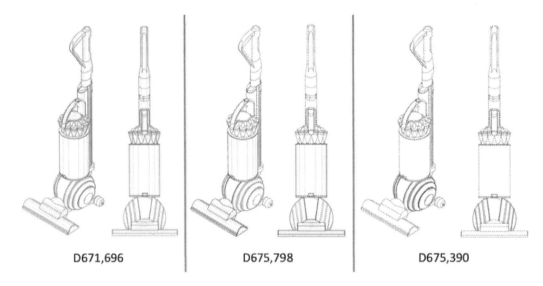

D671,696   D675,798   D675,390

As long as the configuration of the design for which protection is sought is clear (e.g., there aren't inconsistencies between drawings) and an ordinary designer could make an article having that design, the § 112 requirements are satisfied.

2. Novelty and Nonobviousness

Like utility patents, design patents must be novel and nonobvious relative to the prior art under §§ 102 and 103, but small modifications are often enough to clear these bars. The prior art is defined using § 102 with the same broad definitions of categories like "printed publication" and "public use" as in the utility patent context.

The test for whether a prior art reference anticipates a design patent is whether an "ordinary observer," considering the designs as a whole, would think that the two designs are "substantially the same." *International Seaway Trading Corp. v. Walgreens Corp.*, 589 F.3d 1233, 1239–40 (Fed. Cir. 2009).

The doctrinal framework for evaluating obviousness is more complicated. The test is from the perspective of "a designer of ordinary skill who designs articles of the type involved" rather than an "ordinary observer," and the obviousness assessment must start by identifying a "primary reference" that creates "basically the same visual impression" as the patented design as a whole. *Campbell Soup Co. v. Gamon Plus, Inc.*, 939 F.3d 1335, 1339–40 (Fed. Cir. 2019) (summarizing earlier caselaw). In most cases, no single reference meets the high standard of "basically the same," so the claimed design is nonobvious. If there is a primary reference, then the question is whether modifying that reference with related secondary references to arrive at the claimed design would have been obvious to the designer of ordinary skill. *See id.*

3. Ornamentality

Design patents have an additional validity requirement that is in some ways the opposite of the requirement that utility patents be "useful": under 35 U.S.C. § 171, the claimed design must be "ornamental," as opposed to useful or functional. As summarized by the Federal Circuit:

> A design patent cannot claim a purely functional design—a design patent is invalid if its overall appearance is "dictated by" its function. But as long as the design is not primarily functional, the design claim is not invalid, even if certain elements have functional purposes. That is because a design patent's claim protects an article of manufacture, which necessarily serves a utilitarian purpose. So a design may contain both functional and ornamental elements, even though the scope of a design patent claim must be limited to the ornamental aspects of the design. Where a design contains both functional and non-functional elements, the scope of the claim must be construed in order to identify the non-functional aspects of the design as shown in the patent.

Sport Dimension, Inc. v. Coleman Co., 820 F.3d 1316, 1320 (Fed. Cir. 2016). Factors for determining whether a design is "dictated by" function include the availability of alternative designs, whether the protected design is "the best design," and the existence of utility patents. *See id.* at 1322.

Like the useful article doctrine in copyright law and the functionality doctrine in trademark law, the ornamentality doctrine attempts to channel protection for new functional features to utility patent law. But each area of IP law defines functionality differently. For a comparison of these different channeling doctrines, see Christopher Buccafusco & Mark A. Lemley, *Functionality Screens*, 103 Va. L. Rev. 1293 (2017).

4. Design Patent Infringement

The infringement rules of 35 U.S.C. § 271 discussed in Chapters 9–11 also apply to design patents, but the test for evaluating infringement differs. Claim construction is a more flexible process that recognizes that design patents are claimed using drawings, so that in some cases, verbal descriptions are unnecessary.

As for utility patents, design patents have infringement-anticipation symmetry: any product that would infringe if it postdates the patent should anticipate if it predates the patent. The test for infringement thus mirrors the anticipation test described above: whether an "ordinary observer," considering the designs as a whole, would think that the two designs as "substantially the same." *See Seaway*, 589 F.3d at 1239–40 (quoting *Egyptian Goddess v. Swisa*, 543 F.3d 665, 676 (Fed. Cir. 2008) (en banc)). In making this comparison, the ordinary observer is "deemed to view the differences between the patented design and the accused product in the context of the prior art" because "when the claimed design is close to the prior art designs, small differences between the accused design and the claimed design are likely to be important to the eye of the hypothetical ordinary observer." *Id.* (quoting *Egyptian Goddess*). This is the only test for infringement; there is no doctrine of equivalents.

5. Design Patent Damages

In addition to all the patent remedies covered in Chapters 13–16, design patent owners who succeed in proving infringement are also entitled to disgorgement of an infringer's profits. Under 35 U.S.C. § 289, someone who makes or sells an infringing article of manufacture "shall be liable to the [design patent] owner to the extent of his total profit, but not less than $250," although the owner "shall not twice recover the profit made from the infringement."

This provision could lead to enormous profits when the patented design is a small component of a product, although the Supreme Court limited the potential scope of this remedy in *Samsung v. Apple*, 137 S. Ct. 429 (2016). In that case—a separate piece of the multinational patent war that also led to the obviousness decision you read in Chapter 3—Apple sued Samsung for infringement of numerous design patents, including on the iPhone's rounded rectangular shape and on the grid of app icons on the home screen.

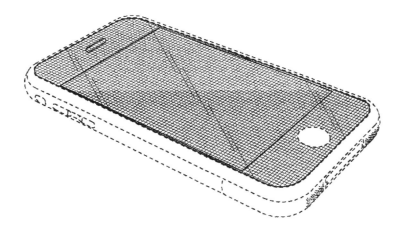

A jury found that some of Samsung's smartphones infringed Apple's design patents, and Apple was awarded $399 million in design patent damages—the entire profit Samsung made from sales of those phones. But the Supreme Court held that the "article of manufacture" for which § 289 allows total profits to be awarded can be merely a component of an article sold to consumers. Yet the Court declined to decide what the relevant "article of manufacture" was for Samsung's infringing phones. On remand, the jury was instructed to consider this issue and ended up awarding even more than the first jury: $533 million in design patent damages. The parties then settled before appealing this verdict.

Practice Problems: Designs

Consider the following design patent claims and products, which are drawn from the listed cases. If the product comes later in time, do you think it infringes? If it came earlier, do you think it anticipates the claim or renders it obvious? Should the design patent claim be invalidated for lack of ornamentality (i.e., functionality)? How would your answers differ if you were evaluating the designs for copyright or trade dress infringement?

1. *Sport Dimension, Inc. v. Coleman Co.*, 820 F.3d 1316, 1320 (Fed. Cir. 2016):

Design Patent

1. The ornamental design for a personal flotation device, as shown and described.

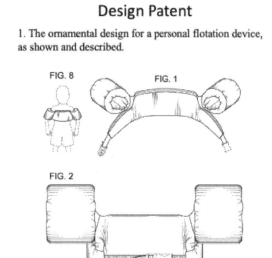

Product

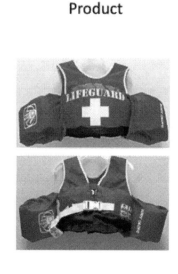

2. *Richardson v. Stanley Works Inc.*, 597 F.3d 1288 (Fed. Cir. 2010):

Design Patent

1. The ornamental design for a multi function stud climbing and carpentry tool, as shown and described.

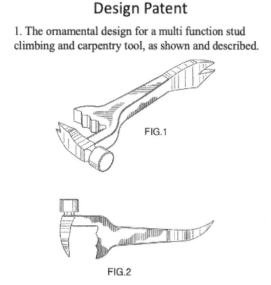

Product

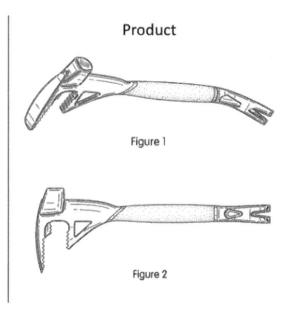

3. *Spigen Korea Co. v. Ultraproof, Inc.*, 955 F.3d 1379 (Fed. Cir. 2020):

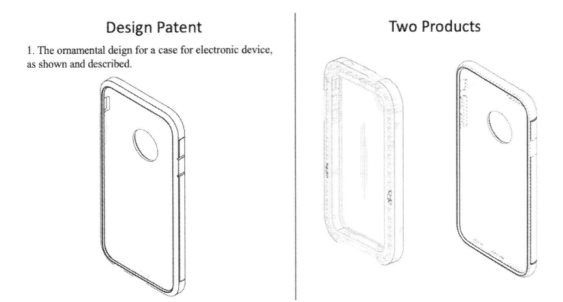

Design Patent

1. The ornamental deign for a case for electronic device, as shown and described.

Two Products

C. Plant Protection

In *J.E.M. Ag Supply, Inc. v. Pioneer Hi-Bred International, Inc.*, 534 U.S. 124 (2001), the Supreme Court held that utility patents may be issued for new plants such as hybrid varieties as long as they satisfy the patentability requirements discussed earlier in this casebook. Sometimes a biological deposit is necessary to satisfy the enablement requirement, as discussed in Chapter 4. Utility patents may also be obtained for plant-related inventions such as methods of breeding plants, chemicals made by plants, and plant seeds. New plant varieties are also often protected as trade secrets, and new variety names can be protected with trademarks.

But these are not the only forms of IP protection for plants. Plant inventors may also seek plant patents or plant variety protection certificates, and these are not mutually exclusive with utility patents. This section briefly reviews these plant-specific forms of IP; for more in-depth coverage, see Daniel J. Knauss, Erich E. Veitenheimer, and Marcelo Pomeranz, *Protecting Plant Inventions*, 11 Landslide, July–Aug. 2019.

1. Plant Patents

Under 35 U.S.C. § 161, a plant patent is available to "[w]hoever invents or discovers and asexually reproduces any distinct and new variety of plant, including cultivated sports, mutants, hybrids, and newly found seedlings, other than a tuber propagated plant or a plant found in an uncultivated state." As noted in Chapter 1, the USPTO granted 1,398 plant patents in 2020—0.4% of the number of utility patent grants. Plant patents have a term of 20 years from the date of filing.

Like design patents, plant patents contain only a single claim. The utility patent requirements of §§ 102, 103, and 112 generally apply, although § 112 is less stringent and no biological deposit is required; § 162 specifies that "[n]o plant patent shall be declared invalid for noncompliance with section 112 if the description is as complete as is reasonably possible." Drawings or photographs "must disclose all the distinctive characteristics of the plant capable of visual representation" and "must be in color if color is a distinguishing characteristic of the new variety." 37 C.F.R. §§ 1.165.

A granted plant patent "shall include the right to exclude others from asexually reproducing the plant, and from using, offering for sale, or selling the plant so reproduced, or any of its parts, throughout the United States, or from importing the plant so reproduced, or any parts thereof, into the United States." 35 U.S.C. § 163. Thus, infringement is limited to plants asexually reproduced from the patent owner's plant. An independently reproduced plant with similar characteristics does not infringe.

2. Plant Variety Protection Certificates

Plant variety protection certificates are available under the Plant Variety Protection Act, 7 U.S.C. §§ 2321–2583. Unlike plant patents, which are limited to asexually reproduced plants and exclude protection for tubers, plant variety protection certificates can be obtained by "[t]he breeder of any sexually reproduced, tuber propagated, or asexually reproduced plant variety (other than fungi or bacteria) who has so reproduced the variety." 7 U.S.C. § 2402. Plant variety protection certificates have a term of 20 years from the date of issuance, or 25 years for trees or vines.

In addition to a written description of the new variety, applications for plant variety protection certificates must include "[a] declaration that a viable sample of basic seed (including any propagating material) necessary for propagation of the variety will be deposited and replenished periodically in a public repository in accordance with regulations to be established hereunder." 7 U.S.C. § 2422.

A plant variety protection certificate is infringed by activities including sale, import, export, or reproduction of the protected variety, with exceptions for "plant breeding or other bona fide research." 7 U.S.C. §§ 2541, 2544.

20. International and Comparative Patent Law

In Chapter 11(B), we discussed *territoriality*, the international law principle that a country's laws only have force within its boundaries. Congress has extended the reach of U.S. patent law through 35 U.S.C. § 271(f)-(g), but the presumption against extraterritoriality still applies. Recall *Microsoft v. AT&T*, 550 U.S. 437 (2007), in which the Supreme Court held that § 271(f) could not reach copies of Windows software made abroad, and that "if AT&T desires to prevent copying in foreign countries, its remedy today lies in obtaining and enforcing foreign patents." Understanding the basics of obtaining and enforcing foreign patents has only become more important for U.S. patent lawyers as patentable goods and services increasingly cross national borders.

In this chapter, we provide an overview of the following issues: (A) the key treaties and international institutions that constrain and enhance domestic patent laws; (B) the procedures for acquiring multinational patent rights; (C) a comparison of how different countries define patentability requirements within international constraints ("pre-grant flexibilities"); (D) a comparison of how countries define the rights and remedies available for patent infringement ("post-grant flexibilities"); and (E) the main legal and strategic factors businesses consider when coordinating multinational patent litigation. Each of these topics could occupy a full textbook on its own, but we hope to provide an accessible overview, as well as the vocabulary and framework for conducting further research.

Although this chapter focuses on international equivalents of utility patents, many other countries have equivalents of design patents (typically called industrial designs) and plant patents (sometimes as sui generis systems for plant variety protection). Some countries also have a patent-like form of IP not available in the United States: the *utility model* or *petty patent* (not to be confused with the utility patent), which provides cheaper and narrower protection for minor inventions for terms that typically run 6–15 years.[1] The legal doctrines governing a utility model are similar to those for a patent except that the nonobviousness requirement is usually lower or absent. Utility models are typically registered rather than examined, allowing them to be obtained quickly. Countries offering utility models include Austria, China, France, Germany, Japan, Russia, Spain, and Taiwan, and many patent offices allow utility patent applications to be converted to utility model

---

[1] For more information, see https://www.wipo.int/patents/en/topics/utility_models.html.

applications. U.S. patent lawyers advising clients about possibilities for IP protection abroad should keep this option in mind.

A. International Patent Institutions and Treaties

1. WIPO, WTO, and Other Fora

The first major international agreement on intellectual property was the 1883 Paris Convention for the Protection of Industrial Property, which created a framework to allow inventors from one signatory to the Convention to obtain utility patents in other members of the Paris Union (among other things). The Paris Convention is still in force, but in 1970, its governance structure was replaced with the new Geneva-based World Intellectual Property Organization (WIPO), which then became a specialized agency of the United Nations in 1974. WIPO also administers the Patent Cooperation Treaty (PCT)—signed in 1970 and effective as of 1978—which facilitates patent filings in multiple countries and is discussed in more detail in section (B) below. WIPO treaties may be joined à la carte. As of June 2021, there were 193 members of the WIPO Convention (the agreement establishing WIPO), 175 members of the Paris Union, and 153 members of the PCT.

If a member fails to comply with its WIPO treaty obligations, there are no effective remedies, but WIPO treaties are still important for harmonizing procedures, setting norms, and creating the possibility that agreements will be imported into other treaties or into domestic law. For example, the U.S. Supreme Court still applies the *Charming Betsy* canon that domestic statutes should be construed so as not to conflict with international law. *See, e.g., F. Hoffmann-La Roche v. Empagran*, 542 U.S. 155, 164 (2004) (citing *Murray v. Schooner Charming Betsy*, 6 U.S. 64 (1804)).

WIPO receives most of its income from PCT filing fees, giving it an institutional interest in encouraging more global patent filings. It provides training, advice, and technical infrastructure to support domestic patent systems. But the agency is no longer the forum of choice for negotiating new treaties focused on strengthening or harmonizing patent law; rather, its current treaty-making activities are largely driven by developing countries and focused on non-patent areas. For example, in 2013, WIPO concluded negotiations on a treaty to facilitate access to published works for persons with visual impairments, and it is currently working on treaties related to protecting traditional knowledge and genetic resources.

The other key institution for international patent governance is the World Trade Organization (WTO), which was created in 1995 to regulate international trade. The negotiations that led to the WTO also created a comprehensive IP treaty, the Agreement on Trade-Related Aspects of Intellectual Property Rights (TRIPS). Unlike the Paris Convention, the TRIPS Agreement set a minimum patent term (20 years from filing), which is why the U.S. patent term shifted from 17 years from issuance to 20 years from filing for patents filed on or after June 8, 1995. TRIPS also states that patents must be available in "all fields of technology" based on criteria similar to the U.S. novelty, obviousness, utility, and enablement requirements, which was an important change in countries that had limited patents on inventions such as pharmaceuticals. (Least-developed countries need not offer pharmaceutical patents until 2033.) We discuss these requirements further in section (C).

TRIPS was an important change from Paris not only because it set minimum substantive standards, but also because it has teeth. WTO members may not pick and choose which WTO treaties to comply with, so TRIPS binds all WTO members—which includes almost every country.[2] And the WTO has an effective enforcement mechanism: trade sanctions. Under the WTO Dispute Settlement Understanding (DSU), disputes are heard by panels of three or five experts appointed on an ad hoc basis, with review by an Appellate Body comprised of seven experts serving four-year terms. From 1995 to 2020, WTO members initiated 598 disputes, 42 of which involved TRIPS.[3] Many disputes end with a mutually agreed-upon solution. If a member found to be in violation of TRIPS does not bring its law into conformity, the complaining member may then impose economic sanctions such as withdrawing trade concessions. This enforcement mechanism has been effective—except against the United States.[4] However, the future of WTO dispute resolution is unclear: the Trump Administration blocked appointment of new Appellate Body members, leaving the Body without a quorum and with a growing backlog of pending appeals since December 2019. As of this writing, the Biden Administration has continued this policy.

Both high- and low-income countries have become dissatisfied with WTO's consensus-based decisionmaking process. Instead, countries have looked to new fora that might serve their interests for further international negotiations, similar to "forum shopping" for a favorable court. Laurence Helfer calls this process "regime shifting":

> With negotiations in the WTO effectively stalled, both proponents and opponents of stronger intellectual property rules sought out greener pastures in other international regimes. Developing countries decamped to the World Health Organization (WHO), Food

---

[2] Only a few countries are neither members nor observers negotiating accession, such as North Korea, Monaco, and Palau. See https://www.wto.org/english/thewto_e/countries_e/org6_map_e.htm.

[3] For more details, see https://www.wto.org/english/tratop_e/dispu_e/dispustats_e.htm.

[4] The United States did not change domestic laws after losing two non-patent WTO disputes: one involving a law prohibiting registration and enforcement of Cuban trademarks (in particular, "Havana Club" rum), and one for blocking Antigua and Barbuda's online gambling industry.

and Agriculture Organization (FAO), and Convention on Biological Diversity (CBD). These organizations and negotiating venues offered these states advantages that they did not possess in the WTO and in WIPO. First, the goals of these institutions—to promote public health, plant genetic sources, and biodiversity—predisposed them to view challenges to expansive intellectual property rights sympathetically. Second, industrialized nations were either absent from these venues (the United States has never ratified the CBD, for example) or were represented by government ministries whose negotiating objectives were more sympathetic to developing country concerns. Third and finally, the WHO, FAO, and CBD, unlike the WTO, were relatively open to civil society, including NGOs that were highly critical of TRIPS and that worked with developing states to fashion strategies for challenging the treaty.

The United States and the European Communities, by contrast, shifted their efforts from the WTO and WIPO to bilateral and regional trade and investment treaties, incorporating IP protection rules into these agreements. Industrialized states could more easily leverage their economic and political clout in these intimate negotiating forums. In exchange for enhanced access to their markets, these states demanded that developing countries ratify the new WIPO treaties or adhere to intellectual property protection standards that exceeded those found in TRIPS. Opponents derisively labeled these bilateral and regional agreements as "TRIPS plus" treaties.

As compared to a single-venue regime, the existence of overlapping and parallel regimes modifies implementation politics in two distinct and opposing ways. First, the multiplicity of legal rules generated in nested, overlapping, and parallel institutions can make it more difficult to claim that states have implemented those rules in ways that violate their treaty obligations. Decision 486 of the Andean Community provides an apt illustration. Adopted by the biodiversity-rich nations of this South America sub-region in 2000, Decision 486 attempts to reconcile the intellectual property protection rules of TRIPS with the biodiversity preservation measures of the CBD. It does so by imposing various restrictions on patents derived from biological materials found in Andean Community member states. Whether these restrictions are in fact compatible with TRIPS' patent protection rules is open to debate. Yet no state has filed a WTO dispute settlement complaint challenging Decision 486 as a violation of TRIPS. To the contrary, Andean Countries have promoted the legislation as a good faith attempt to harmonize the two multilateral treaties, albeit an attempt that furthers their own interests in safeguarding the region's biological heritage.

Second, international regime complexity provides opportunities for powerful states to narrow the options available to weaker countries to implement intellectual property rules into their national legal systems. For example, TRIPS requires WTO members to protect new plant varieties. But it allows them to do so "either by patents or by an effective sui generis system or by any combination thereof." Developing countries interpreted this provision as permitting them to tailor plant variety protection laws to their domestic agricultural needs. Yet the United States and the European Union have used "TRIPS plus" treaties to restrict this discretion, pressuring several of these countries to enact legislation that favors the interests of foreign commercial plant breeders.

Laurence R. Helfer, *Regime Shifting in the International Intellectual Property System*, 7 Persp. Pol. 39, 41 (2009). For a discussion of how the World Health Organization (WHO) has regained influence in international IP law since TRIPS, see Laura G. Pedraza-Fariña, *The Intellectual Property Turn in Global Health: From a Property to a Human Rights View of Health*, 36 Osiris (2021).

As Helfer suggests, the United States has recently focused on bilateral and regional trade agreements such as the 1994 NAFTA agreement with Canada and Mexico, which are negotiated through the Office of the U.S. Trade Representative (USTR).[5] For an argument that USTR has exported a captured version of U.S. IP law, see Margot E. Kaminski, *The Capture of International Intellectual Property Law Through the U.S. Trade Regime*, 87 S. Cal. L. Rev. 977 (2014). For example, some agreements have banned rules of international exhaustion, required attorneys' fees in patent cases "*at least* in exceptional cases," or automatically blocked generic pharmaceutical entry even if the patent owner does not initiate litigation. *Id.* at 1021–26. One controversial expansion in the rights of patent owners has been to allow certain private parties to challenge countries' compliance with international obligations—although these rights have had limited impact on patent law so far. Most prominently, in 2012 Eli Lilly challenged Canada's interpretation of the utility doctrine (which had led to the revocation of its patents on two drugs) under NAFTA, but in 2017, the tribunal found against Eli Lilly and ordered them to pay most of the costs of the dispute. Three months later, the Canadian Supreme Court adopted a more forgiving utility standard. For a discussion of more positive provisions, such as on transparency and cooperation among national IP offices, see Marketa Trimble, *Unjustly Vilified TRIPS-Plus?: Intellectual Property Law in Free Trade Agreements*, 71 Am. U. L. Rev. (2022).

The USTR also exerts unilateral pressure on countries whose IP systems are viewed as non-compliant. Section 301 of the Trade Act of 1974 requires the USTR to "identify those foreign countries that deny adequate and effective protection of

---

[5] For agreement texts, see https://ustr.gov/trade-agreements.

intellectual property rights," which it does in its annual "Special 301" Report. The "Priority Foreign Countries" with inadequate IP laws may be subject to sanctions, and countries with concerning IP practices are placed on the "Watch List" or "Priority Watch List." Many countries were placed on these lists at the request of industry groups like the Pharmaceutical Research and Manufacturers of America (PhRMA).

2. Paris Convention and TRIPS: Basic Principles

Because of the prominence of the TRIPS Agreement in shaping domestic patent laws, and its explicit incorporation of most of the Paris Convention in Article 2.1, it is worth understanding the basic principles contained in these agreements. Their full texts are freely available online.[6] For a comprehensive guide on interpreting TRIPS, see Daniel Gervais, *The TRIPS Agreement: Drafting History and Analysis* (5th ed. 2021).

The principle of *national treatment* requires member countries to treat foreigners no less favorably than locals. In particular, Article 2.1 of the Paris Convention states that nationals of any Paris member state "shall, as regards the protection of industrial property, enjoy in all the other countries of the Union the advantages that their respective laws now grant, or may hereafter grant, to nationals." Articles 2.2 and 3 specify that national treatment applies to nationals of Paris members domiciled in non-Paris members and to nationals of non-Paris members who are domiciled in Paris members. The TRIPS Agreement incorporates this requirement (Article 2.1 incorporates Paris Articles 1–12 and 19) and has its own substantively equivalent national treatment rule at Article 3.1:

> Each Member shall accord to the nationals of other Members treatment no less favourable than that it accords to its own nationals with regard to the protection[7] of intellectual property, subject to the exceptions already provided in, respectively, the Paris Convention [and other treaties].

Paris Article 2.3 provides a limited exception to national treatment for laws "relating to judicial and administrative procedure," and TRIPS Article 3.2 states that such exceptions may be used only where not inconsistent with TRIPS or "a disguised restriction on trade."

---

[6] TRIPS is at https://www.wto.org/english/docs_e/legal_e/trips_e.htm and the Paris Convention is at https://wipolex.wipo.int/en/text/288514.

[7] [n.3 in original] For the purposes of Articles 3 and 4, "protection" shall include matters affecting the availability, acquisition, scope, maintenance and enforcement of intellectual property rights as well as those matters affecting the use of intellectual property rights specifically addressed in this Agreement.

TRIPS Article 4 sets forth the *most-favored-nation* principle, which requires that member countries give the same advantages to foreigners from different countries:

> With regard to the protection of intellectual property, any advantage, favour, privilege or immunity granted by a Member to the nationals of any other country shall be accorded immediately and unconditionally to the nationals of all other Members.

There is an exception for advantages "deriving from international agreements related to the protection of intellectual property which entered into force prior to the entry into force of the WTO Agreement," which includes an agreement among European Union members for common IP rules that did not necessarily benefit non-EU persons.

Paris Article 4 (incorporated by TRIPS 2.1) provides for a *right of priority*: once an inventor has filed for a patent in one Paris member, a twelve month period starts "from the date of filing of the first application" under which "any subsequent filing in any of the other countries of the Union before the expiration of [twelve months] shall not be invalidated by reason of any acts accomplished in the interval, in particular, another filing [or] the publication or exploitation of the invention . . . and such acts cannot give rise to any third-party right or any right of personal possession."

Finally, Paris Article 4*bis* (incorporated by TRIPS 2.1) provides for *independence of patents*: patents applied for in one country "shall be independent of patents obtained for the same invention in other countries."[8] In other words, one country's decision to grant or refuse a patent does not oblige any other country to do the same. In addition, Article 4*bis* discusses patent term: "Patents obtained with the benefit of priority shall, in the various countries of the Union, have a duration equal to that which they would have, had they been applied for or granted without the benefit of priority."

Practice Problems: Basic Principles of Paris and TRIPS

1. Under the national-treatment and most-favored-nation obligations, can China:

    a. Give Japanese nationals 20 years of patent protection, and Chinese nationals 30 years?

    b. Give Japanese nationals 30 years of patent protection, and Chinese nationals 20 years?

---

[8] Paris also has Articles 4*ter* and 4*quater*, with the suffixes "bis," "ter," and "quater" derived from Latin for "twice," "three times," and "four times" and indicating that these articles were inserted between Articles 4 and 5 during negotiations.

     c. Give Japanese nationals 30 years of patent protection, and U.S. nationals 20 years?

     d. Require foreigners but not domestic parties to make a security deposit for litigation costs?

2. Nitisha, a U.S. citizen, files a patent application in China on her computer-related invention, which is not patentable in the United States but is patentable in China.

     a. Do national treatment rules require the Chinese patent office (CNIPA) to grant her patent?

     b. If CNIPA grants Nitisha's application after six months, and two months later she files an application in Japan claiming priority to her Chinese application, is Japan's patent office (JPO) obligated to grant the patent?

     c. May JPO reject Nitisha's application because Zach filed a Japanese patent application for the same invention four months before Nitisha did?

     d. If the JPO grants Nitisha's application, when does it expire (assuming no patent term adjustment)?

     e. If Nitisha files a patent application in Germany ten months after her JPO application, may she claim priority to the Japanese filing?

3. Article 3.2 of the DSU says WTO agreements will be clarified "in accordance with customary rules of interpretation of public international law." This includes Article 31 of the Vienna Convention on the Law of Treaties: a treaty shall be interpreted based on the "ordinary meaning" of its terms "in their context and in light of its object and purpose." That context includes the preamble, subsequent agreements, and subsequent practices. Look at the preamble and Part I of TRIPS on the WTO website. If you were representing a developing country that was concerned about strong IP protection interfering with its technological development goals, what parts would you point to?[9]

3. Justifying International Patent Coordination

Many commentators have been skeptical of the necessity of global coordination on IP law and view TRIPS as benefiting the United States and other wealthy nations at the expense of low-income countries. For example, Susan Sell describes the role of

---

[9] For an Appellate Body decision using these sources, see *India – Patent Protection for Pharmaceutical and Agricultural Chemical Products*, WT/DS50/AB/R, 19 December 1997.

U.S. multinationals in bringing TRIPS into being, concluding: "In effect, twelve corporations made public law for the world." Susan K. Sell, *Private Power, Public Law: The Globalization of Intellectual Property Rights* 96 (2003). Amy Kapczynski similarly concludes that TRIPS reflected "a new mode of conquest and imperium" and was "an exceptionally audacious attempt to extract value from and exert control over informational domains in virtually all of the countries of the world." Amy Kapczynski, *Access to Knowledge: A Conceptual Genealogy, in Access to Knowledge in the Age of Intellectual Property* 26 (2010). For the perspective of negotiators from India, Brazil, Argentina, Malaysia, and Hong Kong, including the countervailing benefits they saw in terms of favorable trade terms from the broader WTO negotiations, see *The Making of the TRIPS Agreement: Personal Insights from the Uruguay Round Negotiations* 209–93 (Jayashree Watal & Antony Taubman eds., 2015).

Hemel and Ouellette offer the following qualified defense of international coordination on patent law and other forms of IP:

> All members of the WTO are bound by the 1994 TRIPS Agreement, which requires all but the least-developed nations to protect the IP rights of all TRIPS members at or above a basic level. For example, TRIPS members must offer twenty-year patents in "all fields of technology" to inventors in any member country, including for novel pharmaceuticals and food products that some countries had previously excluded from patentability. TRIPS is a significant step in the longer trend of IP standards gradually being revised upwards to require greater and different protection through international agreements.

> But this international framework and domestic IP policy are largely separable. Even the strongest international IP regime does not lead ineluctably to the use of IP-based innovation incentives or allocation mechanisms at the domestic level. On the incentives side, countries can still comply with TRIPS while using non-IP tools to encourage domestic innovation. For example, a country could provide incentives only though grants and prizes conditioned on relinquishing IP rights, while the national government itself retains revenues from licensing the knowledge good in other countries. Or—as is more common—countries can both subsidize the domestic production of knowledge goods through grants and tax credits and purchase domestic patent rights from the producer, while still allowing the producer to collect overseas profits (with the state potentially collecting some of those profits through a tax on the domestic producer).

> On the allocation side, countries can (and often do) choose nonprice mechanisms—closer to open access than to proprietary pricing—to distribute knowledge goods at the domestic level. For instance, a country that wants to make a patented pharmaceutical

available to its own citizens at zero or marginal cost can purchase a license from the patentee and pay for the license using funds raised through broad-based taxation. Countries with single-payer health care systems generally follow a version of this model, respecting the patentee's IP rights while avoiding domestic deadweight loss from proprietary pricing. Even countries without single-payer health care, such as the United States, often allocate access to patented pharmaceutical products through nonmarket mechanisms (e.g., the Medicaid program).

We have argued that rather than dictating domestic policy, the role of international IP law is to provide a serviceable (if imperfect) framework for cost sharing among countries that produce and consume knowledge goods. Without such a framework, certain goods for which demand transcends national boundaries would be underproduced. Absent an international cost-sharing mechanism, rational and self-interested countries will finance knowledge goods only up to the point that the marginal cost equals the marginal benefit to their own citizens, rather than the marginal benefit to all people everywhere. International IP law addresses this underinvestment problem by ensuring that when Country *A* produces a knowledge good that benefits consumers in Country *B*, Country *B* will provide at least some compensation to Country *A*. As a general matter, TRIPS prohibits Country *B* from using the Country-*A*-produced knowledge good without first reaching some sort of cost-sharing agreement with Country A (such as a license from the private producer in Country *A*, who may be separately subsidized or taxed by Country *A*'s government). In this respect, TRIPS functions as an "agreement to agree": signatory states commit to reaching an arrangement under which knowledge-good consumers share costs with knowledge-good producers. The agreement to agree operates against the background rule that absent a further arrangement, the consumer state cannot use the knowledge good for which the producer state (or one of its citizens or firms) holds a patent.

While cost-sharing through TRIPS can address the global underinvestment problem, international IP law is not the only possible cost-sharing framework. We can imagine a global prize fund or a global R&D organization, financed by mandatory national contributions, that would also provide for cost sharing among producer and consumer states. Yet international IP law has the advantage of establishing a link between the benefits to the consumer country and the size of the transfer from the consumer country to the producer country. Under international IP law, no country ever needs to pay for knowledge goods it doesn't use. No such assurance would exist with respect to a global prize fund or global R&D organization. Such an institution might channel more of its funding to "first-world problems" than to problems facing less-developed nations. (Indeed, if wealthier nations control the institutional levers of power, then this prediction seems not just plausible but likely.)

Importantly, the argument for using international IP law as a cross-border cost-sharing mechanism does not depend on whether individual countries use IP to incentivize innovation or allocate access to knowledge goods at the domestic level. International and domestic innovation policy choices are separable.

Daniel J. Hemel & Lisa Larrimore Ouellette, *Innovation Policy Pluralism*, 128 Yale L.J. 544, 588–92 (2019). For a detailed discussion of qualifications to this account, including examples of knowledge goods that are not global public goods and alternative accounts of state action, see Daniel J. Hemel & Lisa Larrimore Ouellette, *Knowledge Goods and Nation-States*, 101 Minn. L. Rev. 167 (2016).

Discussion Questions: Justifying International Patent Coordination

1. *Should India Weaken Pharmaceutical Patents?* Before TRIPS, India did not grant patents on pharmaceutical products, and it developed a robust generic drug manufacturing industry. After a transition period for developing countries, India began allowing these patents in 2005. But countries can still weaken their patent systems within the TRIPS framework, as illustrated by the many limitations on U.S. patent rights in recent decades (e.g., the increased ease of invalidating patents for lack of patentable subject matter and the decreased availability of injunctions). Sections (C) and (D) of this chapter will discuss additional "flexibilities" countries have in implementing TRIPS. Should India take advantage of these flexibilities to limit pharmaceutical patents as much as possible? *See generally* Amy Kapczynski, *Harmonization and Its Discontents: A Case Study of TRIPS Implementation in India's Pharmaceutical Sector*, 97 Cal. L. Rev. 1571 (2009).

How does this issue differ from the analysis of the U.S. patent system discussed in Chapter 1? Does your answer differ if you focus on Indian patients or Indian pharmaceutical companies rather than total Indian social welfare? Does it matter whether the patents are on treatments for hypertension (a global concern) or dengue fever (which is endemic in India but not in high-income countries)? Does it affect your analysis to know that in practice, after India's TRIPS implementation, the average price increase for patented medicines was just 3–6%, and that there was little impact on quantities sold or on the number of domestic pharmaceutical firms? *See* Mark Duggan, Craig Garthwaite & Aparajita Goyal, *The Market Impacts of Pharmaceutical Product Patents in Developing Countries: Evidence from India*, 106 Am. Econ. Rev. 99 (2016).

2. *Changing Patent Importers and Exporters.* Each year since 2008, the USPTO has granted more utility patents of foreign origin than domestic origin, and the gap continues to grow. China now has the world's largest patent office, the China National Intellectual Property Administration (CNIPA). How do these changes affect the winners and losers from TRIPS and other agreements setting minimum patent standards?

B. Acquiring Multinational Patent Rights with the PCT

As discussed above, Article 4 of the Paris Convention, which was incorporated by TRIPS, established the *right of priority*: filing a patent application in one national or regional office starts a one-year period during which applicants can file in other offices, claiming priority to the first application. If the applicant runs out this clock, they generally can't get a patent in that country later. This is a relatively short time period for applicants to decide which offices to file in, to find local patent agents to prosecute their applications, and to pay the costs for application translation, filing, and prosecution. Translation and filing costs can exceed ten thousand dollars for each patent office added, and each round of prosecution could add another ten thousand dollars per patent office. When deciding whether to file in a given office, applicants must balance these costs against the value that patent protection in that jurisdiction might add. For example, is it a large market? An important part of a competitor's supply chain? A forum in which the applicant would want to litigate or negotiate licensing fees? For inventions whose future value is uncertain, answering these questions early in the development process may be challenging.

The Patent Cooperation Treaty (PCT) provides a simpler process for obtaining patent protection in a large number of jurisdictions.[10] As illustrated on the timelines below, rather than directly filing separate patent applications in every patent office of interest within 12 months of an initial filing, applicants may initiate the PCT process by filing a single "international" application with a "receiving office" (including the USPTO or WIPO) within that 12-month period. The PCT application doesn't directly provide any patent rights; rather, it initiates a streamlined procedure for pursuing applications with individual national or regional patent offices. Perhaps most valuably, it allows applicants to delay the choice of where to pursue patent protection—and the associated costs of local patent agents, translators, and filing fees—for up to 30 months from the initial filing date (31 in some jurisdictions).

The PCT receiving office transmits the application to a patent office that serves as an International Searching Authority (ISA)—which includes the USPTO—by 13

---

[10] The PCT is available at https://www.wipo.int/pct/en/texts/articles/atoc.html, and the implementing regulations are at https://www.wipo.int/pct/en/texts/rules/rtoc1.html. The description here provides the most common time limits, but they may be different if, for example, applicants file the international application closer to the priority date.

months from the priority date. The ISA then has 3 months to produce an international search report listing relevant prior art along with a written opinion as to "whether the claimed invention appears to be novel, to involve an inventive step (to be non-obvious), and to be industrially applicable [i.e., useful]." PCT Rule 43*bis*. The application, international search report, and written opinion are published 18 months from the priority date. Within 22 months of the priority date, the applicant has the option of requesting international preliminary examination, which is the only chance to actively participate in the "international phase" of the PCT process. International preliminary examination, which must be completed by 28 months, provides an evaluation of patentability by a second ISA and gives applicants a chance to submit amendments and arguments and to interview the examiner. Finally, by 30 months from the initial priority date, applicants enter the "national phase" by directly pursuing applications with the national or regional patent offices of interest.

The national phase looks something like the patent prosecution process at the USPTO described in Chapter 1—multiplied by the number of patent offices the applicant is trying to obtain a patent from—although the procedures for each national or regional patent office differ. During the national phase it is generally necessary to translate the application into the local language and to work with a local patent attorney. Because patent laws differ by country, applicants often obtain somewhat different claims in different countries. It is also important to coordinate across offices so the applicant doesn't make inconsistent arguments. Failing to disclose something that came up in one country to an examiner at the USPTO can constitute inequitable conduct.

Paris Convention Timeline:

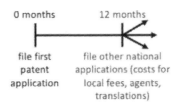

Patent Cooperation Treaty Timeline:

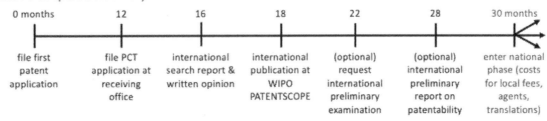

If an applicant begins with a non-provisional U.S. application, followed by a PCT application one year later, then the U.S. patent will expire 20 years from the U.S. application—one year earlier than the national or regional patents resulting from the PCT application (assuming no patent term adjustment). Applicants can avoid this disadvantage by starting with a *provisional* U.S. patent application and then filing a

PCT application one year later; as noted in Chapter 1, U.S. patents expire 20 years from the filing date of the earliest non-provisional application.

The non-U.S. patent office where U.S. applicants most commonly file—either through the PCT or direct filing—is the European Patent Office (EPO), a regional office created in 1977 by the European Patent Convention (EPC).[11] The EPC is separate from the European Union; for example, Switzerland, Iceland, Norway, and now the United Kingdom are members of the EPC but not the EU. The EPC created a unified process for prosecuting patent applications at the EPO in one of three official languages (English, French, and German), which results in a "European patent" that is effectively a bundle of individual national patents. Once a European patent is granted, it must be "validated" in designated countries for additional fees and any necessary translation costs. Under Article 2 of the EPC, a European patent "shall, in each of the Contracting States for which it is granted, have the effect of and be subject to the same conditions as a national patent granted by that State." For the first nine months after a European patent is granted, a third party may file an opposition proceeding (similar to a post-grant review proceeding at the USPTO). After that, the validity and infringement of the patent are assessed independently by national courts in designated countries, although there are ongoing efforts for a Unified Patent Court that could hear infringement and revocation cases for European patents, including "unitary patents" that could be granted by the EPO without the need for validation in individual countries.[12]

The other regional patent offices are the African Intellectual Property Organization (OAPI) (which includes mostly French-speaking African countries), the African Regional Intellectual Property Organization (ARIPO) (English-speaking African countries), the Eurasian Patent Organization (EAPO) (members of the former Soviet Union), and the Patent Office of the Cooperation Council for the Arab States of the Gulf (GCC Patent Office). National offices used frequently by U.S. applicants include the other members of the five largest patent offices—known as the "IP5"—besides the USPTO and EPO: the China National Intellectual Property Administration (CNIPA), Japan Patent Office (JPO), and Korean Intellectual Property Office (KIPO). U.S. applicants also file frequently in other high-income, English-speaking countries: the Canadian Intellectual Property Office (CIPO) and IP Australia.

---

[11]   The   EPC   text   is   at   https://www.epo.org/law-practice/legal-texts/html/epc/2016/e/ma1.html.

[12] A treaty to establish a Unified Patent Court was signed in 2013, but entry into force has been repeatedly delayed, most recently due to Brexit and constitutional challenges in Germany. It is currently on track to launch in early 2023.

Discussion Questions: Acquiring Multinational Patent Rights

1. *How Does Filing Strategy Vary by Industry?* Throughout this casebook, we have emphasized differences in how patents are used in different industries. How would your multinational patent acquisition strategy differ if you represented a biotechnology corporation versus a developer of microprocessors? For instance, how many different countries would you seek patent rights in?

2. *A Global Patent?* The PCT streamlines multinational patent acquisition, but applicants still face the substantial costs of hiring local patent agents and translators so that "applying for patents all over the world is an option feasible only to the wealthiest and most sophisticated of inventors." Marketa Trimble, *Global Patents: Limits of Transnational Enforcement* (2012). And many local patent offices still duplicate some efforts by conducting their own searches and examinations after receiving the ISA's search report and written opinion. Are there ways to improve the system? Trimble argues for a more global approach, such as a global version of the EPC that allows global enforcement and makes widespread patent protection feasible for individual inventors and small businesses. What are the benefits and costs of this approach? How would it affect patent search costs?

3. *Ending Government Patent Office Monopolies?* Michael Abramowicz and John Duffy have argued that the rise in multinational filing provides an opportunity to rethink the idea that each country's patent office should have a monopoly on deciding whether patent rights are available. The creation of the EPO caused national patent offices in Europe to become entrepreneurial; for example, the UK can deliver a low-cost examination report in four months that can help evaluate whether investing more is worthwhile, and Denmark offers opinions on patentability of either new ideas or existing patents in ten working days for an hourly charge. And with the rise of work-sharing programs among patent offices like the Patent-Prosecution Highway,[13] "applicants might have significant incentives to forum shop for better examination" such that "[a] small country like Denmark or Singapore could become the 'Delaware' of patent offices." Michael Abramowicz & John F. Duffy, *Ending the Patenting Monopoly*, 157 U. Pa. L. Rev. 1541, 1572 (2009). *But see* Jonathan S. Masur, *The PTO's Future: Reform or Abolition?*, 158 U. Pa. L. Rev. PENNumbra 1 (2009) (casting doubt on whether the Abramowicz and Duffy proposal will make much of a difference). Do you think private patent offices with appropriate incentives (e.g., fines for mistakes found in random audits) could improve global examination quality?

---

[13] The Patent-Prosecution Highway allows applications that have been allowed in participating offices to be fast-tracked. See https://www.wipo.int/pct/en/filing/pct_pph.html.

C. Pre-Grant Flexibilities: Comparative Patent Validity

At a high level, the basic requirements of patentability are largely harmonized across the globe. The TRIPS Agreement requires every WTO member to have equivalents of the U.S. requirements of novelty, nonobviousness, utility, and enablement, as specified in Articles 27 and 29:

TRIPS Article 27: Patentable Subject Matter

1. Subject to the provisions of paragraphs 2 and 3, patents shall be available for any inventions, whether products or processes, in all fields of technology, provided that they are new, involve an inventive step and are capable of industrial application.[14] Subject to [exceptions related to the TRIPS transition] and paragraph 3 of this Article, patents shall be available and patent rights enjoyable without discrimination as to the place of invention, the field of technology and whether products are imported or locally produced.

2. Members may exclude from patentability inventions, the prevention within their territory of the commercial exploitation of which is necessary to protect *ordre public* or morality, including to protect human, animal or plant life or health or to avoid serious prejudice to the environment, provided that such exclusion is not made merely because the exploitation is prohibited by their law.

3. Members may also exclude from patentability:

    (a) diagnostic, therapeutic and surgical methods for the treatment of humans or animals;

    (b) plants and animals other than micro-organisms, and essentially biological processes for the production of plants or animals other than non-biological and microbiological processes. However, Members shall provide for the protection of plant varieties either by patents or by an effective sui generis system or by any combination thereof. The provisions of this subparagraph shall be reviewed four

---

[14] [n.5 in original] For the purposes of this Article, the terms "inventive step" and "capable of industrial application" may be deemed by a Member to be synonymous with the terms "non-obvious" and "useful" respectively.

years after the date of entry into force of the WTO Agreement.

TRIPS Article 29: Conditions on Patent Applicants

1. Members shall require that an applicant for a patent shall disclose the invention in a manner sufficiently clear and complete for the invention to be carried out by a person skilled in the art and may require the applicant to indicate the best mode for carrying out the invention known to the inventor at the filing date or, where priority is claimed, at the priority date of the application.

2. Members may require an applicant for a patent to provide information concerning the applicant's corresponding foreign applications and grants.

Requiring patents in "all fields of technology" and "without discrimination as to . . . the field of technology" was an important change from prior international law. The exceptions are relatively limited. Article 27.2 allows exclusions to protect morality or "*ordre public*"—a French legal term covering important public policy exceptions. Importantly, these exceptions apply only where a country wants to *prevent* exploitation of the invention, not to *increase* exploitation by eliminating patent rights. Thus, this exception could be used to ban patents on stem cells if a country wants to avoid any stem cell research or products within its borders, but it couldn't be used to ban patents on AIDS medicines "to protect human . . . life or health" by increasing access through generic production.

Despite the harmonization provided by international patent treaties, countries still retain substantial "flexibilities," or discretion in how they implement their domestic patent laws. *See generally* Graeme Dinwoodie & Rochelle Dreyfuss, *A Neofederalist Vision of TRIPS: The Resilience of the International Intellectual Property Regime* (2012). For example, many other countries have a more limited (or nonexistent) grace period for whether pre-filing disclosures constitute prior art and do not have a separate written description requirement. India specifies that secondary pharmaceutical inventions such as new formulations are not inventions under the India Patent Act unless the inventor demonstrates "enhancement of the known efficacy" of the pharmaceutical. *See* Bhaven N. Sampat & Kenneth C. Shadlen, *Indian Pharmaceutical Patent Prosecution: The Changing Role of Section 3(d)*, 13 PloS ONE e0194714 (2018). WIPO maintains tables of information about national and regional patent laws.[15] Thomas Cotter's *Comparative Patent Remedies* (2013) provides a useful

---

[15] See https://www.wipo.int/patents/en/topics/laws.html.

overview of the law of patentability in key jurisdictions, as well as the relevant legal institutions.

As one illustration, consider how the EPO approach to assessing patentable subject matter for software differs from that in the United States. For software, Article 52 of the EPC excludes patents from "non-technical" categories including "mathematical methods" and "programs for computers," but "only to the extent to which [the patent] relates to such subject-matter or activities as such." In the 2010 decision G 3/08 (Programs for computers), the EPO Enlarged Board of Appeal[16] summarized current case law as indicating that "a claim in the area of computer programs can avoid [this exclusion] merely by explicitly mentioning the use of a computer or a computer-readable storage medium." But the Enlarged Board also found it "quite clear" that a "a claim which specifies no more than 'Program X on a computer-readable storage medium,' or 'A method of operating a computer according to program X,' will always still fail to be patentable for lack of an inventive step [i.e., obviousness]." In other words, adding "generic computer implementation" to a U.S. patent is insufficient to transform an abstract idea into patentable subject matter under *Alice v. CLS Bank*, 573 U.S. 208 (2014), but in the EPO, it does make the invention eligible—it just requires evaluation under their equivalent of the nonobviousness requirement.

Similarly, in the diagnostics context, Article 53(c) of the EPC states that European patents shall not be granted for "diagnostic methods practised on the human or animal body." In the 2005 opinion 1/04 (Diagnostic methods), the EPO Enlarged Board of Appeal specified that "diagnostic methods" must include each of four steps: (i) "collection of data" (including "interaction with" a human or animal body), (ii) "comparison of these data with standard values," (iii) "the finding of any significant deviation, i.e. a symptom, during the comparison," and (iv) "attribution of the deviation to a particular clinical picture," i.e., "diagnosis for curative purposes."[17] A method that does not claim one of these steps is patent eligible, including in vitro diagnostics and methods that include data acquisition without diagnosis, unless the omitted step is essential. Furthermore, Article 53(c) states that the exclusion "shall not apply to products, in particular substances or compositions, for use in any of these methods." Patentees can thus avoid the exclusion by claiming pharmaceutical products, medical devices, or computer systems related to the diagnostic method.

Do you think all of these rules are consistent with TRIPS's requirement that patents be available "without discrimination as to . . . the field of technology," aside from the exceptions in Article 27?

---

[16] The EPO Boards of Appeal are similar to USPTO PTAB panels, and an Enlarged Board is similar to taking a decision en banc and may involve amicus briefing. Decisions are available at https://www.epo.org/law-practice/case-law-appeals.html, and G 3/08 is at https://www.epo.org/law-practice/case-law-appeals/recent/g080003ex1.html.

[17] G 1/04: https://www.epo.org/law-practice/case-law-appeals/recent/g040001ex1.html.

Practice Problem: Patentable Subject Matter in the USPTO and EPO

Researchers at ThermCo invented forehead infrared thermometers, which can determine a person's temperature by measuring the thermal radiation emitted from their forehead. The idea that body temperature could be determined from skin temperature was novel and defied conventional wisdom: scientists previously thought that skin temperature couldn't be independently correlated with internal body temperature. The recent iterations of ThermCo's invention exploded in popularity during the COVID-19 pandemic.

ThermCo sought a number of patents on this invention at patent offices worldwide. One claim, which was successfully prosecuted through both the USPTO and the EPO, reads as follows:

A method of detecting human body temperature comprising:

(a) measuring radiation as target skin surface of the forehead is viewed, and

(b) processing the measured radiation to provide a body temperature approximation based on heat flow from an internal body temperature to ambient temperature.

A number of companies have sought to imitate ThermCo's successful product. In response to legal threats by ThermCo, the most successful competitor, GeneriCo, has filed post-grant opposition proceedings to challenge the validity of both the U.S. and European patents on patentable-subject matter grounds. What are the best arguments on behalf of each company in each jurisdiction?

D. Post-Grant Flexibilities: Rights, Exceptions, and Remedies

Countries have substantial flexibilities not only in deciding which kinds of inventions receive patents in the first place, but also in setting the exclusive rights protected by a patent, exceptions to those rights such as experimental use or compulsory licensing, and the remedies available for infringement. We refer to these as "post-grant flexibilities."

1. Rights

TRIPS Article 28 defines the exclusive rights protected by a patent: "making, using, offering for sale, selling, or importing," including for "the product obtained directly by [a patented] process." TRIPS does not require countries to provide rights against indirect infringement, but most major economies have. In Europe, infringement statutes have largely been harmonized based on the 1989 Agreement Relating to Community Patents (even though not enough countries ratified the agreement to cause it to enter into force):

> Article 25 – Right to prevent "direct use": (a) "making, offering, putting on the market or using a [patented] product . . . or importing or stocking the product for these purposes"; (b) "using a [patented] process" or "offering the process for use within . . . the Contracting States"; (c) "offering, putting on the market, using, or importing or stocking for these purposes the product obtained directly by a [patented] process."

> Article 26 – Right to prevent "indirect use": (1) "supplying or offering to supply within the territories of the Contracting States a person, other than a party entitled to exploit the patented invention, with means, relating to an essential element of that invention, for putting it into effect therein, when the third party knows, or it is obvious in the circumstances, that these means are suitable and intended for putting that invention into effect" except (2) "when the means are staple commercial products, except when the third party induces the person supplied to [infringe]."

For example, these provisions are codified by Sections 9 and 10 of the German Patent Act, and by Articles 53 and 73 of the Dutch Patent Act. The resulting scope of liability is similar to that created by 35 U.S.C. § 271(a)-(c). The current Chinese Patent Law does not have express provisions for indirect infringement, but indirect liability can be available under tort law principles.

Countries also vary in how infringement is evaluated, such as the rules for claim construction or infringement under the doctrine of equivalents, although different formal rules can lead to similar results. For example, the UK uses "purposive" construction, while German courts "focus on the objective meaning of claims" in a way that some view as distinct from the UK approach, but "in substance both U.K. and German courts today adhere to something of a middle ground." Thomas F. Cotter, *Comparative Patent Remedies* 226 (2013).

2. Exceptions

TRIPS Articles 30 and 31 allow explicit exceptions to the rights that must generally be conferred on patent owners.

TRIPS Article 30: Exceptions to Rights Conferred

Members may provide limited exceptions to the exclusive rights conferred by a patent, provided that such exceptions do not unreasonably conflict with a normal exploitation of the patent and do not unreasonably prejudice the legitimate interests of the patent owner, taking account of the legitimate interests of third parties.

A WTO panel decision from 2000 provides the clearest guidance on the meaning of terms like "limited exceptions." The panel evaluated two exceptions from liability under Canada's Patent Act: one for activities related to regulatory review (e.g., allowing generic firms to produce patented pharmaceuticals for submission to the Canadian equivalent of the FDA), and one allowing generic firms to manufacture drugs for six months prior to patent expiration so they have a stockpile ready when the patent expires. The panel held that the stockpiling provision was not a "limited exception[]," including because "there were no limits at all on the volume of production allowed, or the market destination of such production." In contrast, the regulatory review provision was "limited" because it was limited to regulatory purposes, it didn't conflict with "normal exploitation" because most patent holders don't get the benefit of exclusivity due to regulatory review, and the interest was "neither so compelling nor so widely recognized that it could be regarded as a 'legitimate interest' within the meaning of Article 30." *Canada – Patent Protection of Pharmaceutical Products* ("*Canada Generics*"), WT/DS114/R, 17 March 2000.

As discussed in Chapter 12, the United States also has an exception for activities related to regulatory review at 35 U.S.C. § 271(e)(1), but lacks a broad experimental use defense for other research. *See Madey v. Duke*, 307 F.3d 1351 (Fed. Cir. 2002). Many other countries do have a general experimental use exception, which is generally accepted as TRIPS compliant. Indeed, the *Canada Generics* panel took "as an illustration one of the most widely adopted Article 30-type exceptions in national patent laws—the exception under which use of the patented product for scientific experimentation, during the term of the patent and without consent, is not an infringement."

Article 30 is not helpful to a country that wants to issue a compulsory license for patents on a particular pharmaceutical to promote generic manufacturing. Instead, that country would have to turn to Article 31, "Other Use Without Authorization of the Right Holder." Article 31 sets out numerous conditions, including that "the proposed user has made efforts to obtain authorization from the right holder on reasonable commercial terms" (except in cases of "extreme urgency" or "public non-commercial use"), the use must be limited in "scope and duration," and the use must be terminated when no longer necessary. If a compulsory license is issued, "the right holder shall be paid adequate remuneration in the circumstances of each case, taking into account the economic value of the authorization." Originally, Article 31 was limited to use "predominately for the supply of the domestic market of the Member authorizing such use," raising concerns about its infeasibility for countries without domestic manufacturing capacity. The 2001 Doha Declaration on TRIPS and Public Health proposed amendments to permit compulsory licenses for export, which are now incorporated in Article 31*bis*.

The Doha Declaration and the ratification of Article 31*bis* were hailed as important successes by advocates for global access to medicines, but in practice, they have had little impact. The only actual use of the system was in 2007, when Rwanda notified for an HIV/AIDS drug (Apo-TriAvir), and Canada filed a generic export notification and sent two shipments, one in 2008 and one in 2009. There have been a number of compulsory licenses issued under Article 31, mostly between 2003 and 2005 over HIV/AIDS drugs, although "activity has diminished markedly since 2006." Reed Beall & Randall Kuhn, *Trends in Compulsory Licensing of Pharmaceuticals Since the Doha Declaration: A Database Analysis*, 9 PLoS Med e1001154 (2012).

3. Remedies

Part III of TRIPS covers enforcement of intellectual property rights, including remedies. These rules allow substantial flexibility in how a country implements its domestic IP enforcement system. For an excellent overview of patent remedies in jurisdictions with the most patent cases, see Thomas F. Cotter, *Comparative Patent Remedies* (2013), and his blog at https://comparativepatentremedies.blogspot.com.

For injunctions, TRIPS Article 44 specifies that judges "shall have the authority to order a party to desist from an infringement" but doesn't suggest that injunctions are mandatory or must be available in all cases. Additionally, Article 44 specifies that injunctions need not be available for "protected subject matter acquired or ordered by a person prior to knowing or having reasonable grounds to know that dealing in such subject matter would entail the infringement of an intellectual property right." In other words, countries may limit injunctions to knowing infringement rather than adopting a strict liability approach.

Injunctions are more routinely granted to successful patent litigants in most other jurisdictions than they have been in the United States after *eBay*, and they are particularly likely in Germany. *See* Cotter, *supra*. Preliminary injunctions are more variable. "Patent owners often view the Netherlands as a desirable forum in which to seek preliminary injunctions, given the availability there of a type of speedy pretrial hearing (known as the *kort geding*) and the importance of the Netherlands as a center for the distribution of products throughout Europe." *Id.* at 5. The Netherlands is also attractive for its willingness to issue cross-border preliminary injunctions throughout Europe.

TRIPS Article 45 permits similar flexibility in how countries award damages, including the ability to limit damages to cases of knowing infringement:

TRIPS Article 45: Damages

1. The judicial authorities shall have the authority to order the infringer to pay the right holder damages adequate to compensate for the injury the right holder has suffered because of an infringement of that person's intellectual property right by an infringer who knowingly, or with reasonable grounds to know, engaged in infringing activity.

2. The judicial authorities shall also have the authority to order the infringer to pay the right holder expenses, which may include appropriate attorney's fees. In appropriate cases, Members may authorize the judicial authorities to order recovery of profits and/or payment of pre-established damages even where the infringer did not knowingly, or with reasonable grounds to know, engage in infringing activity.

Average U.S. damage awards are higher than in any other jurisdiction. In other countries, damages "often can be calculated on the basis of the defendant's profits (a type of monetary award abolished in utility patent actions in the United States in 1946), or published reports of typical industry-wide royalties (as in Germany), or as in China as a fixed sum of so-called statutory damages." Cotter, *supra* at 7–8.

Discussion Questions: Post-Grant Flexibilities

1. *Local Working Requirements.* Can patentees lose any rights through failure to practice their patents? Requirements that patentees "work" their inventions locally (beyond simply importing them) are pervasive; in 1968, every industrialized country except the United States and the Soviet Union had local working requirements, and many countries still have them today, such as in Section 84 of India's Patents Act (which has resulted in India's listing in the USTR's Special 301 Report). Why would countries have such requirements? Under what theories do you think they are (or aren't) justified? *See* Jorge L. Contreras, Rohini Lakshané & Paxton M. Lewis, *Patent Working Requirements and Complex Products*, 7 NYU J. Intell. Prop. & Ent. L. 1 (2017) (empirically studying the high degree of non-compliance with working requirements in India).

In 2001, after Brazil threatened to issue compulsory licenses for patented AIDS drugs based on failure to manufacture locally, the United States filed a WTO complaint based on TRIPS Article 27.1, which proscribes "discrimination as to . . . whether products are imported or locally produced." For bargaining leverage, Brazil countered with its own request for a WTO panel, arguing that the Bayh-Dole Act, 35 U.S.C. § 204, violates TRIPS by requiring government-funded inventions that are exclusively licensed to be manufactured "substantially in the United States." The dispute settled. How do you read 27.1 in light of the compulsory licensing provisions of Articles 30 and 31, and Article 5A of the Paris Convention (incorporated by TRIPS Article 2.1), which provides that countries "shall have the right to take legislative measures providing for the grant of compulsory licenses to prevent abuses [such as] failure to work"? Were Brazil or the United States in violation? *See* Paul Champ & Amir Attaran, *Patent Rights and Local Working Under the WTO TRIPS Agreement: An Analysis of the U.S.–Brazil Patent Dispute*, 27 Yale J. Int'l L. 365 (2002).

2. *Exhaustion*. Another post-grant flexibility is the right of each country to determine its rules for patent exhaustion; TRIPS Article 6 specifies that "nothing in this Agreement shall be used to address the issue of the exhaustion of intellectual property rights." As discussed in Chapter 12, the U.S. Supreme Court changed the U.S. exhaustion rule such that sales in foreign countries now exhaust U.S. patent rights, and exhaustion cannot be contracted around. What countries would benefit from adopting similar exhaustion rules?

3. *COVID-19 IP Waiver*. In October 2020, India and South Africa asked the WTO to waive enforcement of TRIPS for all intellectual property related to the prevention, containment, and treatment of COVID-19, arguing that "[a] particular concern for countries with insufficient or no manufacturing capacity are the requirements of Article 31bis and consequently the cumbersome and lengthy process for the import and export of pharmaceutical products." The proposal was supported by many countries but opposed by others, including governments from the United States, EU, UK, Switzerland, Japan, Brazil, Canada, and Australia. In May 2021, amid a devastating wave of infections in India, the Biden Administration shifted its position to support IP waiver as applied to COVID-19 vaccines. What effect do you think removal of the TRIPS requirements would have in the vaccine context? Are there other tools for expanding global vaccine distribution?

E. Coordinating Multinational Patent Litigation

Developing a legal and business strategy for multinational patent litigation draws together many of the topics from this chapter. Although U.S. lawyers will not themselves be litigating overseas, they often help U.S. clients determine their global litigation strategy and help coordinate with local counsel. This chapter begins with practical questions to ask when choosing among potential forums before presenting two exercises: one advising a hypothetical client, and one focused on Apple's and Samsung's strategies in their global patent litigation war.

1. Choosing Among Forums

Where *Can* You File?

The first question to ask when determining where to file a patent lawsuit is: where *can* you file? Your options may be limited by many of the topics covered in 1L civil procedure:

- Where can you get *personal jurisdiction* over the defendant? It usually exists in in any state where the defendant resides or takes substantial acts to further infringement; mere ownership of IP, nationality, or physical service are typically insufficient.

- Where do courts have *subject matter jurisdiction*? This depends on where your client has relevant patents because courts are reluctant to adjudicate infringement of foreign patents (although some will do so if validity is not at issue).

- Are there *forum selection clauses* in any contracts between the parties? Selection clauses are usually enforced unless they are against public policy.

- Were there any *earlier disputes* that create collateral estoppel or res judicata issues?

  o Courts in the United States have adopted factual findings from foreign proceedings as long as the issue was identical and actually litigated and the proceedings were fundamentally fair, but they have refused to adopt conclusions as to the validity of corresponding parallel patents.

  o European courts will attach some weight to decisions in other European countries on parallel patents.

- If your client is the accused infringer, you often have the option of filing an action for a *declaratory judgment* of noninfringement or a patent invalidation request, but the rules for establishing declaratory judgment jurisdiction vary.

Where *Should* You File?

Just because your client can file a patent lawsuit somewhere doesn't mean it is a wise business move. Here are some additional questions that may inform the choice:

- What are your client's business goals? Money, market dominance, or something else?

     o   Do the available remedies in the forum serve those goals? In some cases, preliminary and permanent injunctions and border measures may be crucial; in others, clients may be interested in large damage awards. Germany is a top jurisdiction for patent plaintiffs because of the speed with which an injunction can be obtained, with parallels to the ITC in the United States. China is also increasingly popular because of the availability of injunctions against manufacturing, export, and in-country sales, but damages are very low.

     o   How important is the forum for serving those goals in terms of its market share and role in supply chains? Some countries with small markets may still be key manufacturing hubs; for example, India and Israel attract patent lawsuits because they are important generic pharmaceutical manufacturers.

- How expensive is it to litigate in the forum, and can your client afford it? Is straining your adversary's resources a goal in itself? The United States is generally the most expensive place to litigate due to expansive discovery and high legal fees. Continental Europe has lower costs, and the United Kingdom is expensive by European but not U.S. standards.[18] Japan can be moderately expensive due to many rounds of briefing without page limits. China has lower costs than any of these forums. In many other countries, attorneys' fees are routinely awarded to the prevailing party, although they are not always fully compensatory.

- Is key evidence available only in one venue, and how can that evidence be made available? The availability of discovery closely tracks litigation costs: discovery is broadly available in the United States, more difficult in Europe, and very limited in China. Note that evidence in the United States doesn't mean you need to litigate in the United States; under 28 U.S.C. § 1782, a party may ask a U.S. district court to compel production of evidence needed for a proceeding in a foreign tribunal.

- How important is timing to your client? Jurisdictions vary in how quickly litigation will proceed and whether the case will be stayed for a validity challenge; for example, trials in Germany or the Netherlands can begin less than a year after filing, but in France it might take two years to reach trial. China is also known for often resolving disputes within a year. Where slowing down litigation is a goal, it can be useful to file in a slow EU jurisdiction because other countries often grant stays for related actions. For example, actions for a declaratory judgment of noninfringement in Italy against a patentee not domiciled in Italy were known as "Italian torpedoes," although

---

[18] The average cost of patent litigation has been estimated at 50,000–200,000 € in Germany, France, and the Netherlands, and 2,000,000–4,000,000 € in the UK. Katrin Cremers et al., *Patent Litigation in Europe*, 44 Eur. J.L. & Econ. 1 (2017).

both Italian and other European courts have cabined use of this strategy. More recently, some courts have been willing to issue an "anti-suit injunction" to prevent a party from pursuing litigation in another jurisdictions—and others have responded with anti-anti-suit injunctions and anti-anti-anti-suit injunctions—making timing critical. *See* Jorge L. Contreras, *It's Anti-Suit Injunctions All the Way Down – The Strange New Realities of International Litigation Over Standards-Essential Patents*, 26 IP Litigator (2020).

- How logistically difficult is it to litigate in the forum? What language are proceedings conducted in? Can you find local counsel you trust?

- Finally, how likely to win is your client, and how predictable is the outcome? The likelihood of success may be affected by many factors beyond substantive law:

  o Is there a forum where one party will have home field advantage, or where national attitudes toward the parties or patents may favor one party?

  o Are the judges specialists or generalists? Many non-U.S. jurisdictions have specialized IP trial courts (or specialized IP chambers within a court of general jurisdiction), including the UK, Germany, France, China, and Japan. Specialists are sometimes viewed as more pro-patent, but they may also focus more on the specific requirements of patent law and less on secondary considerations like a party's reputation and commercial success.

  o Are there forum choices *within* a jurisdiction? For example, the forum shopping opportunities in Germany are similar to those that have favored E.D. Tex. and W.D. Tex. in the United States. In China, parties may litigate infringement at the patent office (which is inexpensive, but which may not award preliminary injunctions or damages), or in court, or both. Some countries offer ITC-like proceedings against imports.

  o Are validity and infringement assessed in separate ("bifurcated") proceedings? In some countries, such as Germany and China, challenges to validity must be brought in separate proceedings. Bifurcation can give rise to an "injunction gap" where infringement is found and an injunction issued before validity review is complete. A recent amendment to Germany's Patent Act is intended to reduce but may not eliminate this gap.

Is Alternative Dispute Resolution a Better Option?

Although this casebook is focused on formal legal proceedings, as we noted in Chapter 17, patent disputes may also be resolved through alternative dispute resolution (ADR), including arbitration, mediation, and negotiation. As one option, WIPO runs an Arbitration and Mediation Center, which it advertises as flexible, confidential, and capable of efficiently resolving multinational disputes in a single proceeding without the complexity of multi-jurisdictional litigation or the risk of inconsistent results.[19] Most countries do not allow arbitration of patent validity claims, but arbitration or mediation may be an attractive option for disputes involving patent ownership, license interpretation, or infringement.

2. Advising a Hypothetical Client

Your client, Drivera Inc., is an LA-based electric car startup. Drivera has developed an improved electric car battery with a faster charging time and has used the PCT to acquire numerous patent rights. The plug-in electric vehicle market is rapidly growing; in terms of vehicles sold, it is largest in China, Europe, and the United States. Drivera is currently focused only on the U.S. market, where it exceeded expectations with sales last year. Its cars are entirely manufactured in the United States have received great acclaim from reviewers, largely due to the improved battery. Drivera hopes to build on this momentum by focusing on marketing its cars to consumers who prioritize very rapid charging, but it currently has cash-flow difficulties and was recently sued for failure to pay a contractor for work on its headquarters.

Drivera's innovative battery design has been independently developed by Shenzhen-based XFA, another innovative electric car startup with its own global patent portfolio (though not on the battery design). XFA has deep cash reserves. Last year, XFA's global sales of cars with the new battery design were ten times as high as Drivera's, with most sales in China but a growing number throughout Europe. It has shipped a few cars to the United States to generate press, and it has signaled its intention to enter the U.S. market in 2019. It manufactures the key component of the battery, the flux capacitor, in China. (The flux capacitor has no current known use besides this battery.) XFA ships the flux capacitor to a factory in Germany that manufactures the battery and assembles the cars. The cars are shipped globally via Rotterdam, Netherlands (the largest port in Europe). Drivera's GC has told you that the firm views XFA as an existential threat, and that it is imperative that XFA be kept out of the U.S. market for as low a budget as possible.

You have determined that Drivera has used the PCT to acquire the following global patent rights:

- **United States:** Drivera has a U.S. patent on the flux capacitor, which it features in all its promotional materials. But in-house counsel located devastating prior art from an obscure prior use by Dr. Brown, so you think

---

[19] More information is available at https://www.wipo.int/amc/en/.

there is a 90% chance of invalidation if the patent is challenged. Drivera has a stronger U.S. patent on the process of assembling the battery components (including the flux capacitor) into a battery. You predict a 5% chance of invalidation if it is challenged in district court or the ITC and a 10% chance of invalidation in an inter partes review proceeding before the USPTO.

- **Europe:** Drivera's EPO patents (designating Germany, France, the Netherlands, and the UK) have passed the nine-month EPO opposition period. As in the United States, Drivera has a well-publicized patent on the flux capacitor. But in light of the prior use by Dr. Brown, there is a 60–80% chance of invalidation if the patent is challenged (with variation by country). Drivera also has a stronger EPO patent on the process of assembling the battery components (including the flux capacitor). You estimate a less than 5% chance of the process patent being invalidated in any given country.

- **China:** Drivera also has a Chinese patent on the flux capacitor, and under China's patent law, you think there is only a 10% chance that the patent would be invalidated if challenged. And Drivera has a Chinese patent on the process of assembling the battery components (including the flux capacitor), which you predict to have a 5% chance of invalidation. Drivera's GC has expressed uncertainty and concern about litigating in China, particularly against a Chinese firm. But you have seen studies suggesting that foreign firms have been more successful in China in recent years.[20]

What course of action do you recommend? Are there additional issues you would want to research, either about the facts or the law in different jurisdictions?

3. Case Study: *Apple v. Samsung* Smartphone Patent Wars

In Chapter 3, you read the *Apple v. Samsung* decision on the use of secondary considerations in nonobviousness, and Chapter 19 described their trip to the Supreme Court in a separate case involving design patents. But these two cases were only part of the global IP war between these companies.

When the iPhone was launched in 2007 after a top-secret three-year research project, Steve Jobs noted: "Today, Apple is going to reinvent the phone . . . . And boy, have we patented it."[21] Apple obtained utility patents in many jurisdictions on easy-

---

[20] One study reviewed all 1663 publicly available patent infringement decisions in 2014 and found that plaintiffs won in 80% of cases and received permanent injunctions in 90% of those cases, and that foreign patent holders received better results than domestic ones. The injunction rate may be misleadingly low, as the primary reasons injunctions were not granted were failure to ask and expired patents. Renjun Bian, *Patent Litigation in China: Challenging Conventional Wisdom*, 33 Berkeley Tech. L.J. 413 (2018).

[21] You can hear the applause at https://www.youtube.com/watch?v=8JZBLjxPBUU.

to-understand elements of the iPhone and iPad, including touch gestures like "pinch to zoom" and the "rubber-banding" feature in which the screen bounces back up when you pull down past the bottom. It also obtained many design patents for features including the icons, uncluttered front face, edge-to-edge glass, and rounded corners. The press lauded the phone as "revolutionary," and demand soared. By 2010, Apple had 16% of the smartphone market.

Then, in spring 2010, Samsung launched the Galaxy S, with an appearance and touch gestures that appeared to be directly copied from the iPhone. By the end of the first quarter of 2011, Samsung had over 300% growth in smartphone sales and had risen in market share from 5% to 13%. When Apple's lawyers accused Samsung of copying, Samsung's vice president denied the allegation and noted that Samsung had been developing mobile phones since 1991, including with $435 billion in R&D between 2005 and 2010 and numerous parts that it supplies to Apple for the iPhone (including memory and processors). According to Samsung, it was already developing products with the allegedly copied elements before the iPhone was announced. Like Apple, Samsung held many patents across the globe, including standard-essential patents on 3G technology that had been licensed by virtually every major mobile firm—except Apple, which argued that Samsung hadn't followed FRAND procedures.

Apple and Samsung attempted to negotiate a resolution, but in March 2011, Samsung introduced a tablet that appeared similar to the iPad. Before looking at the timeline, imagine you are outside counsel for either firm. Apple wants to leverage its multinational patent portfolio to wipe Samsung's products from the global market; Samsung wants to keep selling its very successful products and to avoid substantial damages or attorney fees. The most important markets are the United States, the European Union (including Germany, France, the UK, Italy, and the Netherlands), Australia, Japan, and South Korea. Assume that Apple and Samsung have patents similar to those described above in all these jurisdictions, but you needn't delve into the details of whether these patents are valid or infringed. Rather, focus on the differences in litigation procedures and remedies. Where should Apple file suit, and why? Should Samsung file suits proactively based on its standard-essential patents, or simply play defense? What additional information do you want to know?

After you have considered these questions, compare the actual strategies the two companies followed based on the timeline below. Why do you think they made the choices they did? Did anyone "win" the patent war?

Simplified Timeline of *Apple v. Samsung* Global Smartphone Patent War

	Apple	Samsung
2011 April	sues in US (N.D. Cal.) alleging infringement of design patents and trade dress	sues in South Korea, Japan, Germany; countersues in US